Fodor's

MAINE, VERMONT
& NEW HAMPSHIRE

Welcome to Maine, Vermont, and New Hampshire

Maine, Vermont, and New Hampshire are iconic New England, with the quaint towns, brilliant fall foliage, and picturesque landscapes the region is famous for. It's easy to enjoy the outdoors by hiking a section of the Appalachian Trail, skiing the Green Mountains, or taking a scenic drive in Acadia National Park. Smaller cities offer their own pleasures: boutiques and galleries, dockside lobster shacks, and Colonial architecture. As you plan your upcoming travels, please confirm that places are still open and let us know when we need to make updates by writing to us at this address: editors@fodors.com.

TOP REASONS TO GO

★ **Fall Foliage:** Leaf peepers gather for the country's best festival of colors.

★ **Regional Food:** Vermont maple syrup and cheese, Maine lobster and blueberries.

★ **Outdoor Fun:** Hiking, boating, biking, or simply taking in a magnificent view.

★ **Small Towns:** A perfect day includes strolling a town green and locavore dining.

★ **Fantastic Skiing:** All three states have wonderful winter retreats with superb slopes.

★ **The Coast:** Iconic lighthouses and harbors, plus whale-watching and sailing.

Contents

Fodor's Features

MAPS

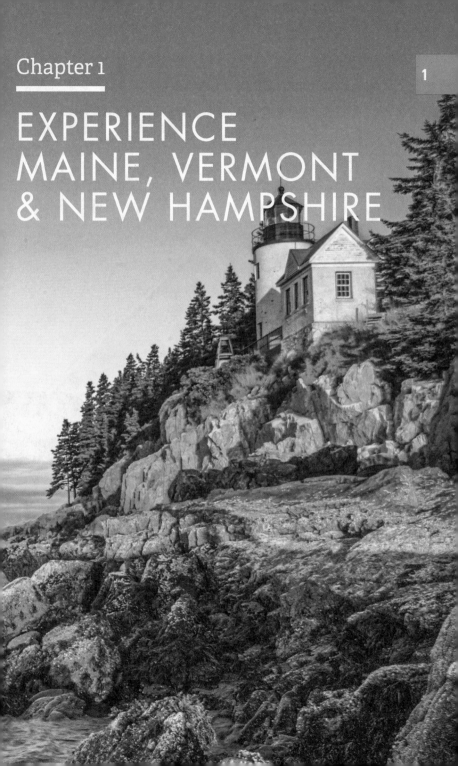

Chapter 1

EXPERIENCE MAINE, VERMONT & NEW HAMPSHIRE

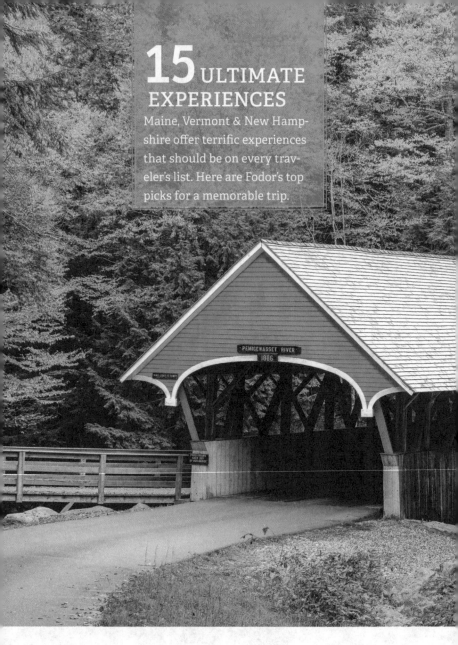

15 ULTIMATE EXPERIENCES

Maine, Vermont & New Hampshire offer terrific experiences that should be on every traveler's list. Here are Fodor's top picks for a memorable trip.

1 Count Covered Bridges

There are 54 of these iconic bridges still in use in New Hampshire. The Cornish-Windsor Bridge (1866) is New England's only covered bridge that connects two states, the country's longest wooden bridge, and the world's longest two-span covered bridge. *(Ch. 5)*

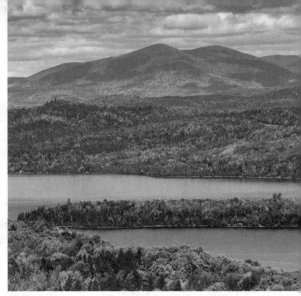

2 Get Away from it All

You won't find high-rises or neon lights in Rangeley Lakes, just peace and quiet, panoramic vistas, beautiful sunsets, and a brilliant night sky. *(Ch. 6)*

3 Boating on Lake Champlain

This lake is hugely popular for boating. You can rent vessels, take lessons, or cruise aboard *Spirit of Ethan Allen*, the lake's only "floating restaurant." *(Ch. 4)*

4 Have a Maine Lobster

A trip to Maine isn't complete without a meal featuring the official state crustacean. Whether you choose a classic lobster dinner, a bowl of lobster stew, or a lobster roll, bring your appetite. *(Ch. 7)*

5 Boating on Lake Winnipesaukee

You won't run out of space or adventures at New Hampshire's largest lake. Boat rentals are available to explore more than 250 islands, and there are numerous waterfront restaurants. *(Ch. 5)*

6 Hike Mt. Monadnock

At 3,165 feet, Mt. Monadnock looms over southwestern New Hampshire. The only way to reach the summit is by foot, and the miles of trails attract well over 120,000 hikers each year. *(Ch. 5)*

7 Visit a Working Farm

Several Vermont farmers welcome visitors for a day, overnight, or a few days. Guests can help with chores like collecting eggs, milking cows, feeding sheep, picking veggies, or baking bread. *(Ch. 4)*

8 Explore Acadia National Park

At New England's only national park, drive or bike the 27-mile Park Loop Road, climb the 1,530-foot summit of Cadillac Mountain, or explore the trails and carriage roads. *(Ch. 7)*

9 Historic and Hip Portland

The Old Port has restaurants and boutiques, while the Arts District has the Portland Museum of Art. The Eastern Prom is a 2-mile paved trail along the water. *(Ch. 7)*

10 Cruise on a Windjammer

Pretty Camden Harbor and nearby Rockland are home ports for a fleet of owner-operated schooners that take guests on voyages around Maine's rugged coast, peninsulas, and islands. *(Ch. 7)*

11 Ski Vermont

The Green Mountains form the spine of Vermont, and snuggled in and around all of the peaks are nearly two-dozen major ski resorts, including Sugarbush, Snow, Stratton, and Stowe. *(Ch. 4)*

12 Walk around Portsmouth

This port city is more than just boats. Great restaurants, galleries, and nightlife coexist with historic sites and cultural venues all within walking distance of each other. *(Ch. 5)*

13 Vermont Sugar Shacks

There are about 1,500 sugarhouses in Vermont. In 2017 those shacks produced about 2 million gallons of syrup, or about half of all maple syrup consumed in the United States. *(Ch. 4)*

14 Wend Your Way Through the White Mountains

Mt. Washington (6,288 feet) is the highest peak in New Hampshire and the northeastern U.S. There are great views, but it's cold and windy even in midsummer. *(Ch. 5)*

15 Treat Yo'self at Ben & Jerry's

At the Ben & Jerry's Factory in Waterbury, take the half-hour guided factory tour to watch ice cream being made, then mosey over to the Scoop Shop for a treat. *(Ch. 4)*

WHAT'S WHERE

1 Vermont. Vermont has farms, freshly starched towns and small cities, quiet country lanes, and bustling ski resorts. The Green Mountain state is synonymous with cheese and maple syrup, and its billboard-free back roads may be the most scenic in the region.

2 New Hampshire. Portsmouth is the star of the state's 18-mile coastline. The Lakes Region is a popular summertime escape, and the White Mountains' dramatic vistas attract photographers and adventurous hikers farther north.

3 Inland Maine. The largest New England state's rugged interior—including the Western Lakes and vast North Woods regions—attracts skiers, hikers, campers, anglers, and other outdoors enthusiasts.

4 The Maine Coast. Classic villages, rocky shorelines, and picturesque Main Streets draw scores of vacationers to Maine. Acadia National Park is where majestic mountains meet the coast; Bar Harbor is the park's gateway town.

Maine's Best Seafood Shacks

SHANNON'S UNSHELLED, BOOTHBAY HARBOR, ME

The namesake of this shack first got the idea to set up shop when her father posed the simple question: "Where can you buy a quick lobster roll in Boothbay Harbor?" Unable to answer, Shannon's Unshelled was born. The shack has been serving up grilled buns stuffed with whole lobsters ever since.

BITE INTO MAINE, CAPE ELIZABETH, ME

This spot serves high-quality lobster rolls from a cart near Portland Head Light. The traditional lobster roll is one of the best, but the contemporary twists make the trip worth it, and the LBT (Lobster, Bacon and Tomato) sandwich is sheer heaven.

MUSCONGUS BAY LOBSTER, MUSCONGUS, ME

Locals and summer people chow down on delicious seafood straight from the ocean; if you're lucky, grab a table on the deck overlooking the expansive bay. It's BYOB, so bring appropriate provisions, if soft drinks won't cut it. And, there's a kids menu.

BOB'S CLAM HUT, KITTERY, ME

With fresh, never frozen, seafood, and a cheery, old-school vibe Bob's serves up scrumptious, homemade sauces, including their famous, tangy tartar sauce, to smother over golden fried clams, alongside some of the thickest New England clam chowder around.

TWO LIGHTS LOBSTER SHACK, CAPE ELIZABETH, ME

You'd be hard-pressed to find a more stunning view than the panorama that spreads out across the ocean from this classic Maine seafood shack. Flanked by the historic twin lighthouses for which it is named, this shack has been serving up seafood since the 1920s.

FIVE ISLANDS LOBSTER, GEORGETOWN, ME
Located on a lively working wharf overlooking Sheepscot Bay, this seafood spot welcomes hungry folks with its delicious seafood and stunning views. The family-friendly atmosphere extends to the menu, which also has options for diners not entirely keen on seafood.

THE HIGHROLLER LOBSTER CO., PORTLAND, ME
Everything about this locale is spot-on, from the friendly, laid-back service to the over-the-top takes on traditional lobster rolls served on locally baked brioche rolls. There's not much that could make this classic better, but the trade-marked lobby pop—lobster tail on a stick—is worth a try.

THE SHUCK STATION, NEWCASTLE, ME
There's a lobster roll on the menu, but it's all about oysters—fried oysters, fried oyster tacos, oysters Rockefeller, oyster po'boys, BBQ oysters, and of course, raw oysters. Housed in a former gas station, this laid-back and family-friendly joint has a kids menu and numerous local beers on tap.

THE CLAM SHACK, KENNEBUNKPORT, ME
This shack is known for speedy service and great takeaway fare like its traditional boiled lobster dinners or lobster rolls on freshly baked buns. Diners can eat at one of several wooden picnic tables that overlook the Kennebunk River. There's even a lemon-ade stand to complete the experience.

RED'S EATS, WISCASSET, ME
In business since 1938, it's not uncommon to see people lining up outside Red's iconic red shack for delicious, fresh seafood. The lobster roll is a huge draw, but the menu is full of other staples like fried clams, shrimp, and scallops. Hot dogs, hamburgers, and grilled cheese round out the options.

Buy Local: Best Souvenirs

JAMS AND PRESERVES

Pick up strawberry preserves, apple butter, cranberry sauce, or blueberry jam at farmers' markets or country stores like Old Country Store & Museum (NH), East Boothbay General Store (ME), or the Vermont Country Store.

ANTIQUES AND COLLECTIBLES

Collectibles and antiques abound from cities like Portland (Old Port District) to towns like Chester, VT; Littleton, NH; and Wells, ME. In Vermont, Route 100 winds from Wilmington to Stowe past craft studios and general stores. Along the coast, Maine's Route 1 has Colonial furniture and architectural antiques shops, as well as quirky galleries.

MOCCASINS

Maine shoemakers craft some of the best moccasins, and Quoddy, known for its custom, made-to-order moccasins, deck shoes, and boots, is one of the best. Reach out when you're Down East or back home; the wait for shoes is worth it. Ditto with Wassookeag, another great Maine maker of bespoke footwear.

CANVAS BAGS

Nothing says durability like canvas; nothing says coastal New England like sailing. Portland-based Sea Bags has creative, rope-handled totes made from recycled sails. Port Canvas in Arundel, Maine, also hand-crafts sporty, custom-izable canvas totes and duffels—perfect for lugging your souvenirs home.

MAPLE SYRUP

Each spring, sugarhouses tap their maple trees and boil the resultant sap down into syrup. Although it takes about 40 gallons of sap to make 1 gallon of syrup, locally made varieties are readily available—Grades A and B and in light, medium, and dark (for baking only) shades of amber. The best known states are New Hampshire and Vermont.

TOYS

Vermont Teddy Bears are guaranteed for life; there's even a hospital for Teddy emergencies! Vermont's Real Good Toys makes finely crafted dollhouses and miniature accessories. New Hampshire's Annalee Dolls are distinctive, cute, and collectible—especially the holiday ones.

YARN AND KNITWEAR

The wares of independent spinners and knitters can be found throughout the region. Noteworthy companies include Bartlettyarns, Inc., which has been in Maine since 1821; New Hampshire's Harrisville Designs, and Maine's Swans Island Company.

FLANNEL WOOLENS

New England's textile industry declined in the 1920s and '30s, but Vermont's Johnson Woolen Mills is still going strong. The warm, soft, and often boldly checked flannel shirts, jackets, capes, wraps, scarves, and hats sold in its factory store and elsewhere are splurge-worthy classics.

CRAFT BEER AND CIDER

New England has a long brewing history, but it's the region's newer, trendier operations that are most interesting like New Hampshire's Schilling Beer Co. and Vermont's Hill Farmstead Brewery. There's a small brewery (or cidery) in almost every city and small town. Notable ciders include Maine's Urban Farm Fermentory and Vermont's family-friendly Cold Hollow.

LOBSTER

Seafood markets, lobster pounds, and even some independent lobstermen sell lobster to-go. You have 48 hours (max) from purchase to cook them, and lobsters must be kept lightly chilled but alive, with claws rubber-banded, until then. Ask about shipping or look into online retailers like Maine Lobster Now, The Lobster Guy, and Lobsters New England.

Most Picturesque Towns in Maine, Vermont, and New Hampshire

WOODSTOCK, VT
This quintessential Vermont town is ridiculously, wonderfully picturesque—classic covered bridges, local cheese makers, cider mills, working farms and orchards, sugar shacks, meandering brick streets, and a town center that is straight out of a Norman Rockwell painting.

EASTPORT, ME
Down East Maine is more than worth the hike, if only to pay a visit to Eastport, a picturesque seaside town with historic architecture situated on pristine Moose Island. A world apart, Eastport prides itself on its fishing and lobstering industries, excellent local arts scene, and vibrant indigenous community.

JACKSON, NH
With a village green reached via a covered bridge and a slew of charming country inns, farm-to-table eateries, and ruggedly scenic trails for hiking and cross-country skiing, this peaceful hamlet lies in the heart of the White Mountains.

CAMDEN, ME
With its brick architecture and Victorian mansions, Maine doesn't get any more picturesque than this village. Situated in the heart of the Mid-Coast, the charming town with its restaurants, galleries, and boutiques is surrounded by a working harbor.

KEENE, NH
Stunning brick streets, charming maple farms, quaint storefronts, classic covered bridges, and a college town vibe combine to create the quintessential New England experience. The darling of the state's southwestern Monadnock Region even has a white clapboard church with a soaring spire.

TAMWORTH, NH
The town is home to the often photographed Chocorua Lake and Mt. Chocorua. A clutch of villages—Tamworth, Chocorua, South Tamworth, Wonalancet, and Whittier—and six historic churches lie within its borders. It's also home to Barnstormers Theatre, the country's oldest repertory theatre.

WESTON, VT
A little less than 12 miles south of Okemo Mountain Resort, this little village really lives up to its much advertised charm and quaintness. The picture-perfect hamlet is home to the Weston Playhouse Theatre Company, a classic town green with Victorian bandstand, and an assortment of shops.

Camden, ME

MONHEGAN, ME
Artists have flocked to Monhegan Island since at least the mid-19th century to relish both its isolated location and staggeringly beautiful terrain. The island's dramatic cliffs overlook some of the most stunning coastal landscapes in Maine where puffin, seals, porpoises, and whales mingle among the bevy of smaller, rocky islands surrounding it.

STOWE, VT
The rolling hills and valleys beneath Mt. Mansfield, Vermont's highest peak, create the tiny village of Stowe. Here you'll find a few blocks of shops and restaurants clustered around a picture-perfect white church with a lofty steeple—not far from Stowe's fabled slopes.

DORSET, VT
Surrounded by mountains and anchored by a village green that's bordered by white clapboard homes and inns, Dorset has a solid claim to the title of Vermont's most picture-perfect town. Dorset West Road, a beautiful residential road west of the town green, and the marble Dorset Church with its two Tiffany stained-glass windows, add to the charm.

WOLFEBORO, NH
Known as the country's oldest summer resort, Wolfeboro is nestled along the shores of Lake Winnipesaukee. The downtown boasts boutiques and eateries, while the resident prep school, Brewster Academy, adds to the charm with its century-old, white clapboard buildings.

DAMARISCOTTA, ME
Just north of Wiscasset, this often overlooked village is surrounded by salt marsh preserves and oyster beds. The village's historic brick architecture and quaint but vibrant Main Street overlooks the harbor where the annual and delightfully oddball Pumpkinfest and Regatta takes place.

Maine, Vermont, and New Hampshire's Best Beaches

FOOTBRIDGE BEACH, OGUNQUIT, ME

This spot offers excellent swimming, beach combing, and bodysurfing opportunities, as well as a boat launch for kayaks, small boats, and standup paddleboards. Typically less crowded than neighboring Ogunquit Beach, it's reached by crossing a footbridge that runs over the Ogunquit River.

ROQUE BLUFFS STATE PARK, ROQUE BLUFFS, ME

Largely sandy, with some pebbly spots thrown in for good measure, this half-mile crescent beach offers bracing Atlantic Ocean swims as well as temperate dips in a sixty-acre pond that backs up to the beach.

GOOSE ROCKS BEACH, KENNEBUNKPORT, ME

A wildly popular beach in warmer months, Goose Rocks Beach is treasured for its long stretch of clean sand and close proximity to town. Parking can be tough and permits are required, but it's well worth the headache to get up early and snatch a spot.

WALLIS SANDS STATE BEACH, RYE, NH

This family-friendly swimmers' beach near Portsmouth has bright white sand, a picnic area, a store, and beautiful views of the Isles of Shoals.

SAND BAR STATE PARK, MILTON, VT

Vermont is not known for its beaches, but its plethora of lakes means that there are actually quite a few beaches worth checking out. This 2,000-foot-long beach remains shallow well out from shore, making it a perfect spot for families with young kids.

PEMAQUID BEACH, NEW HARBOR, ME

Pemaquid Beach is a draw for families and couples looking for a quintessential beach day complete with an umbrella, sand bucket, and ice cream, all of which can be rented or purchased from the kiosk near the changing facilities and community center.

MT. SUNAPEE STATE PARK, NEWBURY, NH

One of the prettiest and most relaxing of New Hampshire's many noteworthy freshwater beaches, this family-welcoming stretch of sand in the shadows of one of the state's favorite ski mountains is lovely for swimming, or renting kayaks, canoes, and stand-up paddleboards.

NORTH BEACH, BURLINGTON, VT

Located on Lake Champlain, the area's largest beach is also the

Sand Beach, Acadia, ME

only one with lifeguards during the summer. There's a grassy picnic area, a snack bar, and a playground, as well as kayak, canoe, and stand-up paddleboard rentals.

JASPER BEACH, MACHIASPORT, ME

Named after the many deep red pebbles scattered across its shore, this pocket beach tucked away in Howard Cove is definitely off the beaten path. Beach combers come to seek out the rare jasper stones among the equally red, volcanic rhyolite pebbles, while those seeking solitude find it in the salt marsh and fresh and saltwater lagoons.

SAND BEACH, ACADIA, ME

What this sandy beach lacks for in size is well compensated by its commanding view of the mountains and craggy shores that draw millions of people to Mount Desert Island each year. Several trail heads dot the beach and lead up the surrounding cliffs, where you'll be rewarded with spectacular panoramas of the shore and beach below.

MOWRY BEACH, LUBEC, ME

On the US-Canadian border, this majestic beach has dramatic tides which produce excellent clamming conditions and superb beach runs at low tide. A small boardwalk leads through a heady mess of fragrant rose bushes out to the shore from where you can spy Lubec's famous lighthouse, as well as its Canadian neighbors.

REID STATE PARK BEACH, GEORGETOWN, ME

One of the Pine Tree State's rare sandy beaches, Reid State Park is a surfer's and sunbather's paradise. Rarely crowded, even in summer, the beach stretches a mile and a half along the Atlantic, with large, undulating sand dunes and essential nesting areas for some of the state's endangered birds.

Historical Sites in Maine, Vermont, and New Hampshire

PORTLAND HEAD LIGHT, CAPE ELIZABETH, ME
Built in 1791, this 80-foot lighthouse is one of New England's most picturesque in any season. The keeper's quarters (operational 1891–1989) house a seasonally open museum; surrounding Fort William Park, site of an army fort between 1872 and 1964, is open year-round.

MAINE MARITIME MUSEUM, BATH, ME
The museum's permanent exhibits cover it all from Bath Iron Works' role in building the nation's navy to a collection of more than 100 small wooden water crafts. In warmer months, board the 1906 schooner, the *Mary E.*, for sails with docents.

STRAWBERY BANKE, PORTSMOUTH, NH
Located in colonial downtown Portsmouth, the seasonal, 10-acre living-history complex has docents in period garb portraying tavern keepers, merchants, artisans, and other everyday folk, and more than 30 structures dating from the 17th to 20th centuries.

CANTERBURY SHAKER VILLAGE, LACONIA, NH
Established in 1792, this village practiced equality of the sexes and races, common ownership, celibacy, and pacifism; the last member of the community passed away in 1992. Engaging guided tours—you can explore on your own—pass through some of the 694-acre property's more than 25 restored buildings, many of them with original furnishings, and there are daily crafts demonstrations.

BILLINGS FARM AND MUSEUM, WOODSTOCK, VT
Founded in 1871, this is one of the country's oldest operating dairy farms. In addition to watching the herds of Jersey cows, horses, and other farm animals at work and play, you can tour the restored 1890 farmhouse, and learn about 19th-century farming and domestic life. Pick up some raw-milk cheddar while you're here.

CHARLESTOWN, NH
Charlestown boasts one of New Hampshire's largest historic districts, with about 60 homes—all handsome examples of Federal, Greek Revival, and Gothic Revival architecture (and 10 built before 1800)—clustered about the town center. Several merchants on the main street distribute interesting walking tour brochures of the district.

Canterbury Shaker Village, Laconia, NH

HILDENE, MANCHESTER, VT

Built in 1905, this 24-room Georgian Revival mansion was the summer home of Abraham Lincoln's son Robert. It provides insight into the lives of the Lincoln family, as well as an introduction to the lavish Manchester life of the early 1900s. It's the centerpiece of a beautifully preserved 412-acre estate, which also contains Hildene Farm and elaborate formal gardens.

BRETTON WOODS, NH

Even if you're not staying at the dramatic Omni Mount Washington Hotel, it's worth visiting as not only is it breathtaking but it was the site of the 1944 United Nations conference that created the International Monetary Fund and the International Bank for Reconstruction and Development (and the birth of many conspiracy theories). The area is also known for one of the state's most beloved attractions, the Mount Washington Cog Railway, which was built in 1858.

MONTPELIER, VT

The country's smallest capital city has a quaint, historic downtown that's home to the Vermont History Museum; its Vermont-focused collection (everything from a catamount [the now-extinct local cougar] to Ethan Allen's shoe buckles) began in 1838. A few doors away, the country's oldest legislative chambers still in their original condition are found in the Vermont State House. Self-guided tours are available year-round, but free guided tours run from late June to October.

SHELBURNE MUSEUM, SHELBURNE, VT

Nothing says "Vermont" like a big red barn, and the museum has two that house American fine, folk, and decorative art as well as vintage toys, hats, decoys, and firearms. There's a vintage carousel, miniature circus-parade figurines in the Circus Building, and more than 200 horse-drawn vehicles.

Outdoor Activities in Maine, Vermont, and New Hampshire

SKI VERMONT AND NEW HAMPSHIRE
Not far from the U.S.-Canadian border, some of New England's best ski slopes (and top-notch resorts) can be found in Vermont's Green Mountains (Jay Peak and Stowe) and New Hampshire's White Mountains (Bretton Woods and Cannon Mountain).

CRUISING MAINE'S COAST
Experience Maine's 3,478 miles of coastline from the water. Charter a boat, big or small, in any of the state's harbors; a popular option is on a schooner ship. It can be chilly on the sea, even in summer, so you'll need to layer and bring rain gear.

MILES OF BIKE TRAILS
Many of the region's top ski resorts have become four-season destinations offering challenging mountain biking trails over the once snow-covered slopes. There's also the 110-mile Kingdom Trails in Vermont and more than 500 miles of trails in New Hampshire.

PADDLE LAKE CHAMPLAIN
Leaf peeping and Vermont are virtually synonymous, but most visitors don't think about taking in the Green Mountain State's stunning fall foliage from out on the water. Best accessed from Burlington, you can rent a stand-up paddleboard or kayak to explore the lake while surrounded by majestic mountains covered in thick forests that put on a colorful display.

HIKE THE APPALACHIAN TRAIL
Tackling the entire length of America's most notorious hiking trail is a commitment. You can always explore some of its most scenic stretches, however, many of them set along the 161-mile leg through New Hampshire. Featuring more miles above treeline than any other state, this is one of the route's most challenging and rewarding sections, with steep inclines leading to stunning alpine tundra and breathtaking views.

BOATING ON THE ALLAGASH WILDERNESS WATERWAY
The 92-mile-long series of rivers, streams, ponds, and lakes that comprises this northern Maine waterway ribbon their way through the delicate, tundralike landscape of the Northern Woods. The waterway remains fairly rustic with limited resources along the route, which seems to be one of the major reasons it attracts fans of canoeing and kayaking.

Go on a Leaf Peeping Cycle Tour along the Stowe Bike Path, VT.

LEAF PEEPING IN VERMONT

With its many nature preserves, green spaces, and hiking trails, Vermont shines in every season, but autumn may be its finest. You'd be hard-pressed to find a lovelier stroll through an autumnal Vermont landscape than in the charming village of Stowe, which is home to the Stowe Recreational Path, a paved, 5½-mile greenway that leads you to picture-perfect village and mountain views.

HIT THE LINKS IN MAINE AND NEW HAMPSHIRE

Coastal Maine and New Hampshire's mountains have some stunning, beautifully maintained golf courses that reward players with great challenges and magnificent scenery. The course at Rockport's Samoset Resort ranks among the best in coastal New England, while Crotched Mountain in the Monadnocks and Waukewan near Lake Winnipesaukee are top courses in New Hampshire.

EXPERIENCE A SCENIC BYWAY

Kancamagus Highway ("The Kanc"), a 34.5-mile scenic byway that crosses New Hampshire from Lincoln near the Vermont border to Conway near Maine, passes through the White Mountains National Forest—a beautiful ride that's truly magnificent in autumn. Stop along the way to admire the White Mountains Presidential Range or take a hike into the forest.

EXPLORE ACADIA NATIONAL PARK

Boasting around 160 miles of pristine coastal hiking trails and meandering carriage roads peppered with charming stone bridges, America's oldest national park east of the Mississippi River offers bountiful opportunities to experience Maine's raw, natural beauty.

Maine, Vermont & New Hampshire With Kids

Favorite destinations for family vacations in the region include Vermont's Lake Champlain, New Hampshire's White Mountains, and coastal Maine—but, in general, the entire region has plenty to offer families. Throughout New England, you'll have no problem finding reasonably priced, kid-friendly hotels and family-style restaurants, as well as museums, beaches, parks, planetariums, and lighthouses.

LODGING

New England has many family-oriented resorts with lively children's programs. Farms that accept guests can be great fun for children. Rental houses and apartments abound, particularly around ski areas. In the off-season, these can be especially economical, because most have kitchens—saving you the expense of restaurant dining for some or all meals.

VERMONT

ECHO Leahy Center for Lake Champlain, Burlington. Lots of activities and hands-on exhibits make learning about the geology and ecology of Lake Champlain an engaging experience.

Montshire Museum of Science, Norwich. This interactive museum uses more than 60 hands-on exhibits to explore nature and technology. The building sits amid 110 acres of nature trails and woodlands, where animals roam freely.

Shelburne Farms, Shelburne. This working dairy farm is also an educational and cultural resource center. Visitors can watch artisans make the farm's famous cheddar cheese from the milk of more than 100 purebred and registered Brown Swiss cows. A children's farmyard and walking trails round out the experience.

NEW HAMPSHIRE

Hampton Beach. This seaside diversion draws families to its almost Coney Island–like fun. Along the boardwalk, kids enjoy arcade games, parasailing, live music, and an annual children's festival. They can even learn how saltwater taffy is made.

Lake Winnipesaukee, Weirs Beach. The largest lake in the state, Lake Winnipesaukee provides plenty of family-friendly fun. Base yourself in Weirs Beach and the kids can swim, play arcade games, cruise the lake, take a scenic railroad along the shoreline, and even see a drive-in movie.

SEE Science Center, Manchester. For kids who love LEGO, the models of old Manchester and the millyard are sure to impress. There are also rotating exhibits and science demonstrations.

MAINE

Acadia National Park, Mount Desert Island. Head out on a whale- and puffin-watching trip from Bar Harbor, drive up scenic Cadillac Mountain, swim at Echo Lake Beach, hike one of the many easy trails, and don't forget to sample some wild blueberry pie.

Maine Discovery Museum, Bangor. There are three floors of fun, educational activities at the Maine Discovery Museum. Exhibits include Nature Trails; Booktown; Sounds Abound; Artscape; and Body Journey.

Maine Narrow Gauge Railroad Museum, Portland. For train fans, check out the scenic rides on these narrow-gauge trains. In the winter, they have *Polar Express*–themed trips.

Maine, Vermont & New Hampshire Today

MAINE

In recent decades, Maine's Congressional delegation has often been around 50–50—half Democrat and Republican, and half male and female, which somewhat resembles the makeup of the state. Voters legalized recreational marijuana in 2016, but regulatory snags delayed opening of retail pot shops until fall 2020. Since 2000, Somali immigration has generated both tensions and welcome cultural diversity in Lewiston and Portland. As paper mills shutter, farming is on the upswing, while the billion-dollar tourism industry struggles to find enough workers yet fuels rising real estate prices and rents in popular destinations.

VERMONT

Few states are more proud of its rugged, independent, and liberal spirit than Vermont. From Ethan Allen to Bernie Sanders, Vermonters have never been afraid to follow a different drumbeat and be outspoken about it. This is perhaps never more on display than in the state's long-standing protection of the environment that borders on obsession. It's one of only four states than ban billboards (Maine is the only other in New England), and strict regulations on land use and development makes many towns and villages appear as if pulled from Norman Rockwell paintings. During fall, the peak tourist season, the landscape literally takes your breath away with an array of fiery reds, golds, oranges, and bronze bursting from the hills and valleys. Cities are few and far between, with Burlington topping out at just 43,000 people, but a robust cultural and arts scene thrives throughout the state, thanks to the abundance of colleges, collectives, and individual artists that continually draw inspiration from the Vermont spirit and beauty. Locals and tourists do the same on the ski slopes, hiking trails, bike paths, and swimming holes, and there's plenty for all.

NEW HAMPSHIRE

With its state motto of "Live Free or Die" and a long-running political reputation as one of the nation's swingiest—albeit slightly left of center—states, New Hampshire marches to its own drummer. The fifth smallest—and 10th least populous—state in America maintains a fierce libertarian streak, collects neither sales tax or income tax, and each presidential year holds the country's first primary. Like the rest of northern New England, ruggedly mountainous New Hampshire is characterized by a mostly rural, heavily wooded topography that gives way to more densely populated small cities and suburbs only in its southeastern corner. Relatively prosperous, with the eighth-highest median household income in the country, New Hampshire has also enjoyed slow but steady growth in recent years, lagging behind only Massachusetts in population growth since 2010 among New England's six states.

What to Read and Watch

LOBSTERMAN BY DAHLOV IPCAR

Dahlov Ipcar, a native New Englander, is best remembered as a writer and illustrator of children's books, many of which took place in her home state of Maine. One such classic is *Lobsterman,* which portrays the day in the life of a lobsterman and his son as they work along the coast of Maine.

IT BY STEPHEN KING

You won't find Derry, Maine on any map, but you can visit it via a number of chilling tales courtesy of horror writer Stephen King, including his 1986 novel *It,* which follows a group of friends who try to kill a monster that terrorizes their town.

WE HAVE ALWAYS LIVED IN THE CASTLE BY SHIRLEY JACKSON

Merricat Blackwood lives in isolation on her family's Vermont estate with her sister Constance and their infirm Uncle Julian. When an estranged cousin arrives, the already uneasy state of the Blackwood home is thrown into disarray.

THE CIDER HOUSE RULES

This 1999 screen adaptation of a 1985 novel by John Irving was set in 1940s Maine and filmed in Maine, New Hampshire and Vermont (and Massachusetts, too). Featuring an all-star cast including Kathy Baker, Michael Caine, and Tobey Maguire, the film depicts the father-son-like relationship between an orphan (Maguire), and the orphanage's doctor (Caine), who takes him under his wing.

THE SECRET HISTORY BY DONNA TARTT

Richard leaves his working class, California home behind in order to attend a liberal arts college in Vermont. Once there he falls in with a privileged group of classics students. But beneath the group's veneer of charm and sophistication is a dark, violent secret.

ON GOLDEN POND

Big Squam and Little Squam lakes in central New Hampshire had starring roles in this 1981 film. So did the lakes' loons that greeted lead actors Katharine Hepburn and Henry Fonda, who played an aging (and somewhat cranky) couple returning once more to a beloved family summer retreat. It was the last role played by Fonda, whose movie daughter was played by his actual daughter, Jane Fonda.

THE IRON GIANT

This charming animated film tells the story of Hogarth, a young boy who befriends a giant robot after it crashes in Maine. When a paranoid government agent tries to destroy the giant, Hogarth enlists help to save the gentle-hearted automaton.

THE HOTEL NEW HAMPSHIRE BY JOHN IRVING

This coming of age novel, published in 1981, features a New Hampshire family whose parents met as teens while working together at a Maine summer resort. The book has a better reputation than the film adaptation that was released a few years later.

STRANGLEHOLD

This podcast series, produced by NPR, examines how New Hampshire outperforms its small stature on the nation's presidential primary stage, where it looms large in influence and attention.

WHITE CHRISTMAS

This holiday classic follows a song and dance team and a pair of performing sisters as they travel to a Vermont inn where they've been booked to perform over Christmas. The inn, owned by their old army commander, is on the verge of failure, so they stage a nationally televised yuletide extravaganza in order to save it.

Chapter 2

TRAVEL SMART MAINE, VERMONT & NEW HAMPSHIRE

Updated by
John Blodgett

★ **CAPITALS**
Augusta, ME; Concord, NH;
Montpelier, VT

♟ **POPULATION**
3,327,912

💬 **LANGUAGE**
English

$ **CURRENCY**
U.S. Dollar

☎ **AREA CODES**
ME: 207; NH: 603; VT: 802

⚠ **EMERGENCIES**
911

🚗 **DRIVING**
On the right

⚡ **ELECTRICITY**
120–240 v/60 cycles;
plugs have two or three
rectangular prongs

🕐 **TIME**
Eastern Time
(same as New York)

🌐 **WEB RESOURCES**
visitmaine.com
www.visitnh.gov
www.vermontvacation.com

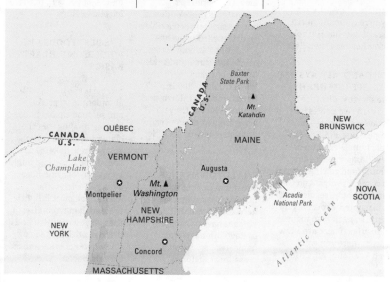

Know Before You Go

Maine, Vermont, and New Hampshire have their share of regional character, color, and flavor—not to mention a few geographical and seasonal challenges. Here are some tips that will enrich your trip and ease your travels.

IT'S WICKED GOOD TO LEARN SOME LINGO.

To avoid seeming like a chowdah-head (aka "chowder head" aka "idiot"), brush up on some basic dialect. Want a big, long sandwich? Order a grinder, not a sub or a hero, and wash it down with a frappe or a tonic, not a milk shake or soda. At the hotel, grab the clickah (clicker) to change the TV station. At the supermarket, grab a carriage to shop for picnic sundries. If people direct you to a rotary, they mean traffic circle. And, even if you're traveling north toward, say, Bar Harbor, you're headed Down East.

YOU CAN'T ALWAYS GET THEAH FROM HEAH.

The shortest distance between two points isn't always a straight—or single—line. Finding the real Maine, Vermont, or New Hampshire means driving (and getting lost on) its scenic byways. And GPS and cell-phone service will be disrupted, especially up north, so pack road maps or an atlas. There are a few places where you won't need a car, though. Cities have great public transit options to, within, and around them. You'll have to take a ferry—few take cars—to access the numerous islands off Maine's coast, but most are bike friendly so plan accordingly. In Acadia National Park, you'll have to trade your car for hiking boots, a bike, or a carriage (an actual horse and buggy, not a shopping cart).

DON'T FORGET THE DRAMAMINE.

Elevations aren't as dramatic as those out west, but car sickness is possible on drives through White Mountain National Forest, on the Kancamagus Scenic Byway, or even the North Woods' Golden Roads. Roads ribbon up, down, and around—just as they do along rugged, often-precipitous stretches of Atlantic coast.

SMALL TOWNS RULE.

You might have to dig a little deeper to sightsee here, but it's worth it. Most villages have a Colonial- or Revolutionary-era homestead or site, small museum or historical society, and time-honored tavern or country store. Photo-worthy commons (open spaces once used for grazing livestock and around which towns were built) are worth seeking out and can be found in many small towns, from Woodstock, Vermont, to Bethel, Maine.

EVEN THE BIG CITIES HERE ARE RELATIVELY SMALL.

Manchester, New Hampshire, the region's largest city, has just about 112,658 people. The next biggest, Portland, Maine, has 66,218 people, followed by Burlington, Vermont, which has just over 42,545. Despite their small size, most cities have thriving cultural scenes; several are major university towns (Burlington and Portsmouth) and/or are steeped in history (Portland). Regardless, you can allow less time for urban explorations and more time for losing yourself in the bucolic settings.

THE BEST FOODS ARE WHOLESOME, HEARTY BASICS.

Field-or-fishing-boat-totable is the norm, with abundant local produce and seafood that includes lobster; quahogs or other clams; bay or sea scallops; and pollack, hake, haddock, or cod (the latter two might appear on local menus as "scrod"). In Maine, lobster-roll meat is lightly dressed in mayonnaise; though you may also find it drizzled with melted butter. Chowder is creamy and may contain bacon.

Everywhere, though, maple syrup adorns shaved ice (or snow!) and ice cream as well as pancakes; breakfast home fries are griddled and seasoned just so; and craft beer and cider pair well with boiled dinners and Yankee pot roast. Be sure to try a Moxie, an "energizing," regionally unique tonic (aka soda).

IN THE LAND OF THE COUNTRY INN, IT'S BEST TO BOOK AHEAD.

Although there are abundant chain hotels and several large, notable Victorians—seaside and near the slopes—smaller inns, often historical and privately owned, are among the best lodgings. Loads of charm and lower room counts make booking ahead essential, especially during peak seasons, when there might also be a two-night minimum. And "peak seasons" vary. Leaf-peeping season is roughly late September to mid-October in Maine, New Hampshire, and Vermont. At the region's ski areas, the season might be November through April or even May.

THE WATER IS COLD UP HERE.

Even in late August, ocean temperatures off Maine and New Hampshire only climb to the upper 50s or lower 60s—still limb-numbingly chilly. Wet suits (and water shoes for rockier shores) are musts for surfing and stand-up paddleboarding. Obviously, the farther north you go, the shorter the beach season, with some properties reducing their hours or shuttering

entirely between Labor Day and Memorial Day or July Fourth. The lakes may be a bit warmer with water temps hovering around the 70s, but once the sun goes down it gets wicked chilly.

WHEN IT COMES TO PARKLAND, THE STATES HAVE IT.

Although much of New England is woodsy, the entire region has only one national park (Acadia) and just two national forests (Green Mountain and White Mountain). That said, there are plenty of opportunities to hike, canoe, kayak, mountain bike, camp, and otherwise embrace the outdoors in the plethora of park or recreation/wilderness areas overseen by each state.

SOME OF THE FLIES BITE.

First, it's the black flies, whose bites leave red, itchy welts. May through June is the season, which is particularly notorious in Maine. Then, in July, it's the deer flies. Summer also sees greenhead flies (aka saltmarsh greenheads) in some coastal areas. On hikes, use insect repellent and wear clothing that covers your arms and legs. And don't forget to check for ticks. The disease they're known to carry was named after a New England town: Lyme, Connecticut.

THE PEOPLE ARE WARM AND WELCOMING

The idea of the self-reliant, thrifty, and often stoic New England Yankee has taken on almost mythic proportions in American folklore,

but in some parts of New England— especially in rural Maine, New Hampshire, and Vermont— there still is some truth to this image, which shouldn't come as a surprise. You need to be independent if you farm an isolated field, live in the middle of a vast forest, or work a fishing boat miles off the coast. As in any part of the country, there are stark differences between the city mice and the country mice of New England. Both, however, are usually well educated and fiercely proud of the region, its rugged beauty, and its contributions to the nation.

SPORTS IS A RELIGION

This is Sox and Pats country. New England fans follow Massachusetts's sports teams as if they were their own. Boston is home to three of the region's four major sports teams—Red Sox baseball, Bruins hockey, and Celtics basketball. The New England Patriots (football) play in the small suburb of Foxboro, about 30 miles southwest of Downtown Boston. The city is also home to the Boston Marathon, New England's largest sporting event and the world's oldest annual marathon.

Getting Here and Around

Air

Most travelers visiting the area use a major gateway, such as Boston, Providence, Hartford, Manchester, Portland, or even Albany, and then rent a car to explore the region. Most destinations are no more than six hours apart by car, which is good because it's costly and generally impractical to fly within Maine, Vermont, and New Hampshire, unless you're going to some of the more remote parts of Inland Maine.

AIRPORTS

The main gateway to New England is Boston's Logan International Airport (BOS). New Hampshire's Manchester Boston Regional Airport (MHT), Maine's Portland International Jetport (PWM), and Vermont's Burlington International Airport (BTV) are other major airports.

Other convenient airports are Albany International Airport (ALB) in Albany, New York, near Vermont and Bangor International Airport (BGR) in Bangor, Maine.

FLIGHTS

Boston's Logan Airport has direct flights arriving from all over North America and abroad. Some sample flying times to Boston are: 2½ hours from Chicago, 6½ hours from London, and 6 hours from Los Angeles. Times from other U.S. cities are similar, if slightly shorter, to Albany and Hartford, assuming you can find direct flights.

American, Delta, JetBlue, Southwest, and United serve airports in Albany, Boston, Manchester, and Portland. Spirit flies into Boston. Cape Air, a regional carrier, serves various New England airports in Maine, New Hampshire, and Vermont.

Boat

Ferry routes provide access to islands off the Maine coast and across Lake Champlain between Vermont and upstate New York. International service between Portland and Bar Harbor in Maine and Nova Scotia is also available. With the exception of the Lake Champlain ferries—which are first come, first-served—reservations are advisable for cars.

Bus

Concord Coach buses connect Boston with Concord, New Hampshire, and Portland and Bangor, Maine; the company also operates a route between New York City and Portland. C&J buses (with Wi-Fi) serve Dover, Seabrook, and Portsmouth, New Hampshire; C&J also provides service to New York City.

Low-cost BoltBus (with Wi-Fi and electrical outlets) serves Boston, New Haven, New York, Philadelphia, and Washington, D.C. Megabus also offers low fares, and its buses (also with Wi-Fi) serve New York City and many other East Coast cities. Both use Boston's South Station; Megabus stops in Portland.

Car

As public transportation options are limited in this area, a car is almost essential. Interstate 95 enters New England at the New York border, follows the Connecticut shoreline, and then heads north to Providence, Boston, and Portland before ending at the Canadian border in Calais, Maine.

CAR RENTAL

Major airports serving the region all have on-site car-rental agencies. A few train or bus stations have one or two car-rental agencies on-site, as well.

Rates at Boston's Logan Airport begin at around $50 per day and $300 per week for an economy car with air-conditioning, automatic transmission, and unlimited mileage. The same car might go for around $60 per day and $175 per week at a smaller airport. These rates do not include state tax on car rentals, which varies depending on the airport but generally runs 12%–15%. It usually costs less to rent a car away from an airport, but be sure to consider how easy or difficult it may be to get to that off-airport location with luggage.

Most agencies won't rent to drivers under the age of 21, and several major agencies won't rent to anyone under 25 or over the age of 75. When picking up a rental car, non-U.S. residents need a voucher for any prepaid reservation made in their home country, a passport, a driver's license, and a travel policy that covers each driver. Logan Airport is spread out and usually congested; if returning a rental vehicle there, allow plenty of time to do so before heading to your flight.

GASOLINE

Gas stations are easy throughout the region, but prices vary from station to station. The majority have self-serve pumps that accept credit or debit cards.

PARKING

Finding street parking in Portland, Maine, or any resort or seaside town, can be a pain in the summer. Park in a garage or lot if it's an option. Always pay attention to signs: some streets or lots may be reserved for residents only.

ROAD CONDITIONS

Major state and U.S. routes are generally well maintained, with snowplows at the ready during the winter to salt and plow. Secondary state routes and rural roads can be a mixed bag; Route 1, for example, is well maintained; but traffic is stop-and-go and can get tied up in even the smallest coastal towns.

ROADSIDE EMERGENCIES

Call ☎ 911 for any travel emergency. For breakdowns, dial a towing service.

RULES OF THE ROAD

Throughout the region, you're permitted to make a right turn on a red light except where posted. Be alert for one-way streets and traffic circles (a.k.a rotaries). Cars entering traffic circles must yield to cars that are already in the circle.

Train

Amtrak offers frequent daily service along its Northeast Corridor route from Washington, D.C., Philadelphia, and New York to Boston, with stops in Connecticut and Rhode Island. Amtrak's high-speed Acela trains link Boston and Washington, with stops at New York, Philadelphia, and other cities along the way. The *Downeaster* connects Boston and Brunswick, Maine, with stops in coastal New Hampshire and Portland.

Other Amtrak services include the *Vermonter* between Washington, D.C., and St. Albans, Vermont and the *Ethan Allen Express* between New York and Rutland, Vermont.

Essentials

🍴 Dining

Although certain ingredients and preparations are common to the region as a whole, New England's cuisine varies greatly from place to place. Urban centers like Burlington and Portland, and upscale resort areas have stellar restaurants, many of them with culinary luminaries at the helm and a reputation for creative—and occasionally daring—menus.

Elsewhere, restaurant food tends more toward the simple, traditional, and conservative. Towns and cities have a variety of international restaurants, especially excellent Italian, French, Japanese, Indian, and Thai eateries. There are also many diners serving burgers and other comfort food—a few serve breakfast all day.

The proximity to the ocean accounts for the abundance of very fresh seafood, and the area's numerous boutique dairy, meat, and vegetable suppliers account for other choice ingredients. Menus in the more upscale and tourism-driven communities often note which Vermont dairy or Maine farm a particular goat cheese or heirloom tomato came from.

MEALS AND MEALTIMES

For an early breakfast, pick places that cater to a working clientele. City, town, and roadside establishments specializing in breakfast for early workers often open their doors at 5 or 6 am. At country inns, breakfast is seldom served before 8 am; if you need to get an earlier start, ask ahead of time. Lunch generally runs 11 am–2:30 pm; dinner is usually served 6–9 pm, with early-bird specials sometimes beginning at 5. Only in larger cities will you find dinner available much later than 9 pm. Many restaurants in New England close Monday and sometimes Sunday or Tuesday, although this is never true in resort areas during high season. However, resort-town eateries often shut down completely in the off-season.

Unless otherwise noted, the restaurants listed are open daily for lunch and dinner.

RESERVATIONS AND DRESS

It's a good idea to make a reservation if you can. We only mention them specifically when reservations are essential—there's no other way you'll ever get a table—or when they are not accepted. For popular restaurants, book as far ahead as you can, and reconfirm as soon as you arrive. Large parties should always call ahead to check the reservations policy. We mention dress only when men are required to wear a jacket or a jacket and tie.

WINE, BEER, AND SPIRITS

New England is no stranger to microbrews. Offering hearty English-style ales and special seasonal brews are breweries such as Vermont's Long Trail, Maine's Shipyard, and New Hampshire's Smuttynose Brewing Co. Green Mountain Cidery makes Woodchuck hard cider in Middlebury, Vermont.

New England is beginning to earn some respect as a wine-producing region. Cabernet Franc, Vidal, Riesling, and other grape varieties capable of withstanding the region's harsher winters and relatively shorter growing season compared to California and other leading areas have been the basis of promising enterprises. Even Vermont is getting into the act with the Snow Farm Vineyard in the Lake Champlain Islands and Boyden Valley Winery in Cambridge.

Although a patchwork of state and local regulations affect the hours and locations of places that sell alcoholic beverages,

New England licensing laws are fairly liberal. State-owned or franchised stores sell hard liquor in New Hampshire, Maine, and Vermont. Many travelers have found that New Hampshire offers the region's lowest prices due to the lack of a sales tax; look for state-run liquor "supermarkets" on interstates in the southern part of the state—but keep in mind that it's illegal to take untaxed liquor across state lines. A bottle or two isn't a problem, but undercover cops are on the lookout for anyone transporting a huge stash.

⊕ Health and Safety

Lyme disease, so named for its having been first reported in the town of Lyme, Connecticut, is a potentially debilitating disease carried by deer ticks. They thrive in dry, brush-covered areas, particularly in coastal areas. Always use insect repellent: the potential for outbreaks of Lyme disease makes it imperative that you protect yourself from ticks from early spring through summer and into fall. To prevent bites, wear light-color clothing and tuck pant legs into socks. Look for black ticks about the size of a pinhead around hairlines and the warmest parts of the body. If you have been bitten, consult a physician—especially if you see the telltale bull's-eye bite pattern. Flu-like symptoms often accompany a Lyme infection. Early treatment is imperative.

New England's most annoying insect pests are black flies and mosquitoes. The former are a phenomenon of late spring and early summer and are generally a problem only in densely wooded areas of the far north. Mosquitoes, however, are a nuisance just about everywhere. The best protection against both pests is repellent

containing DEET; if you're camping in the woods during black fly season, you'll also want to use fine mesh screening in eating and sleeping areas and even wear mesh headgear. One pest particular to coastal areas, especially salt marshes, is the greenhead fly, which has a nasty bite and is hard to kill. It is best repelled by a liberal application of Avon Skin So Soft or a similar product.

Coastal waters attract seafood lovers who enjoy harvesting their own clams, mussels, and even lobsters; permits are required, and casual harvesting of lobsters is strictly forbidden. Amateur clammers should be aware that New England shellfish beds are periodically visited by red tides, during which microorganisms can render shellfish poisonous. To keep abreast of the situation, inquire when you apply for a license (usually at town halls or police stations) and pay attention to red tide postings as you travel.

Rural New England is one of the country's safest regions. In cities—Boston, in particular—observe the usual precautions: avoid out-of-the-way or poorly lighted areas at night; clutch handbags close to your body and don't let them out of your sight; and be on your guard in subways and on buses, not only during the deserted wee hours but also during crowded rush hours, when pickpockets may be at work. Keep your valuables in the hotel or room safe. When using an ATM, choose a busy, well-lighted place such as bank lobbies.

COVID-19
COVID-19 brought all travel to a virtual standstill in 2020, and interruptions to travel have continued into 2021. Although the illness is mild in most people, some experience severe and even life-threatening complications. Once travel started up

Essentials

again, albeit slowly and cautiously, travelers were asked to be particularly careful about hygiene and to avoid any unnecessary travel, especially if they are sick.

Older adults, especially those over 65, have a greater chance of having severe complications from COVID-19. The same is true for people with weaker immune systems or those living with some types of medical conditions, including diabetes, asthma, heart disease, cancer, HIV/AIDS, kidney disease, and liver disease. Starting two weeks before a trip, anyone planning to travel should be on the lookout for some of the following symptoms: cough, fever, chills, trouble breathing, muscle pain, sore throat, new loss of smell or taste. If you experience any of these symptoms, you should not travel at all.

And to protect yourself during travel, do your best to avoid contact with people showing symptoms. Wash your hands often with soap and water. Limit your time in public places, and, when you are out and about, wear a face mask that covers your nose and mouth. Indeed, a mask may be required in some places, such as on an airplane or in a confined space like a theater, where you share the space with a lot of people. You may wish to bring extra supplies, such as disenfecting wipes, hand sanitizer (12-ounce bottles were allowed in carry-on luggage at this writing), and a first-aid kit with a thermometer.

Given how abruptly travel was curtailed at the onset of COVID-19, it is wise to consider protecting yourself by purchasing a travel insurance policy that will reimburse you for any cancellation costs related to COVID-19. Not all travel insurance policies protect against pandemic-related cancellations, so always read the fine print.

 Lodging

In New England you can bed down in a basic chain hotel or a luxurious grande dame, but unless you're staying in a city, this is really bed-and-breakfast land. Charming—and sometimes historic—inns, small hotels, and B&Bs dot the region and provide a glimpse of local life. *Hotel prices are the lowest cost of a standard double room in high season.*

HOUSE AND APARTMENT RENTALS

You are most likely to find a house, apartment, or condo rental in areas of New England where ownership of second homes is common, such as beach resorts and ski country. Home-exchange directories sometimes list rentals alongside exchanges. Another good bet is to contact real-estate agents in the area in which you are interested, or check VRBO or Airbnb.

BED-AND-BREAKFASTS

In many less touristy areas, B&Bs offer an affordable, homey alternative to chain properties. In most major towns, expect to pay about the same or more for a historic inn. Many of the region's finest restaurants are attached to country inns, so you often don't have to go far for the best meal in town. Quite a few inns serve substantial breakfasts.

HOTELS

Major hotel and motel chains are amply represented in New England. The region is also liberally supplied with small, independent motels.

Reservations are always a good idea, particularly in summer and winter resort areas; at college towns in September and at graduation time in spring; and at areas renowned for autumn foliage. Most hotels and motels will hold your reservation until 6 pm; call ahead if you plan to arrive late. All will hold a late reservation for you if you guarantee it with your credit card.

In Vermont all hotels are no-smoking by state law. All lodgings listed have private baths unless otherwise noted.

💲 Money

It costs a bit more to travel in most of New England than it does in the rest of the country, the most costly areas being Portland and coastal resort towns. You'll also find some posh inns and restaurants in parts of Vermont and New Hampshire. ATMs are plentiful, and large-denomination bills (as well as credit cards) are readily accepted in tourist destinations during the high season.

CREDIT CARDS

Major credit cards are readily accepted throughout New England, though in rural areas you may encounter difficulties or the acceptance of only MasterCard or Visa. If you'll be making an excursion into Canada, be aware that many outlets there accept Visa but not MasterCard.

Packing

The principal rule of weather in New England is that there are no rules. A cold, foggy spring morning often warms to a bright, 60°F afternoon. A summer breeze can suddenly turn chilly, and rain often appears with little warning. Thus, the best advice on how to dress is to layer your clothing; that way, you can peel off or add garments as needed for comfort. Even in summer you should bring long pants, a sweater or two, and a waterproof windbreaker, for evenings are often chilly, and sea spray can make things cool. Showers are frequent, so pack a raincoat and umbrella.

Casual sportswear—walking shoes and jeans or khakis—will take you almost everywhere, but swimsuits and bare feet will not: shirts and shoes are required attire at even the most casual venues. Dress in restaurants is generally casual, except at some of the distinguished restaurants of Boston and Maine coast towns such as Kennebunkport, and a few inns. Upscale resorts, at the very least, will require men to wear collared shirts at dinner, and jeans are often frowned upon.

In summer, bring a hat and sunscreen. You can bring or buy insect repellent. If you find yourself walking in wooded areas, near brush, or around foliage from early spring through fall, be sure to check your body for ticks, which can cause Lyme disease if not removed.

Great Itineraries

New Hampshire and Maine, 7 Days

Revel in the coastlines of two New England states—New Hampshire and Maine—on the path from the region's smallest shoreline, to its highest peak, Mt. Washington. An assortment of New England's coastal treasures are at your fingertips as you pilot the ins and outs of the jagged northeastern coastline, before ascending the heights of the White Mountains. Plenty of fascinating towns and villages will vie for your attention with charming shops, seafood restaurants and picture-perfect views.

Fly in: Manchester-Boston Regional Airport (MHT), Manchester, New Hampshire

Fly out: Manchester-Boston Regional Airport (MHT), Manchester, New Hampshire

DAY 1: NEW HAMPSHIRE COAST
Kick off your trek in the southeastern corner of the Granite State. New Hampshire fronts the Atlantic for a scant 18 miles, but its coastal landmarks range from honky-tonk **Hampton Beach** to quiet **Odiorne Point State Park** in Rye and pretty **Portsmouth,** where the cream of pre-Revolutionary society built Georgian- and Federal-style mansions—visit a few at the **Strawbery Banke Museum.** Stay the night in **Portsmouth** at the centrally located **Ale House Inn.**

DAY 2: THE YORKS
Much of the appeal of the Maine Coast lies in its geographical contrasts, from its long stretches of swimming and walking beaches in the south to the cliff-edged, rugged, rocky coasts in the north. And not unlike the physical differences of the shoreline, each town along the way reveals a slightly different character, starting with **York.**

In **York Village** take a leisurely stroll through the seven buildings of the **Museums of Old York,** getting a glimpse of 18th-century life in this gentrified town. Spend time wandering amid the shops or walking the nature trails and beaches around **York Harbor.** There are several grand lodging options here, most with views of the harbor. If you prefer a livelier pace, continue on to **York Beach,** a haven for families with plenty of entertainment venues. Stop at **Fox's Lobster House** after visiting **Nubble Light** for a seaside lunch or dinner.

Logistics: 10 miles; via I–95 N; 15 minutes, starting in Portsmouth

DAYS 3: OGUNQUIT AND THE KENNEBUNKS
For well over a century, **Ogunquit** has been a favorite vacation spot for those looking to combine the natural beauty of the ocean with a sophisticated environment. Take a morning walk along the **Marginal Way** to see the waves crashing on the rocks. In **Perkins Cove,** have lunch, stroll the shopping areas, or sign on with a lobster-boat cruise to learn about Maine's most important fishery—the state's lobster industry supplies more than 90% of the world's lobster intake. See the extraordinary collection at the **Ogunquit Museum of American Art,** take in a performance at one of the several theater venues, or just spend time on the beach.

Head north to the Kennebunks, allowing at least two hours to wander through the shops and historic homes of **Dock Square** in **Kennebunkport.** This is an ideal place to rent a bike and amble around the backstreets, head out on Ocean Avenue to view the large mansions, or ride to one of the several beaches to relax awhile. Spend your third night in Kennebunkport.

Logistics: 22 miles; via I–95 N; 30 minutes, starting in York

DAYS 4 AND 5: PORTLAND

If you have time, you can easily spend several days in Maine's largest city, exploring its historic neighborhoods, shopping and eating in the **Old Port,** or visiting one of several excellent museums. A brief side trip to **Cape Elizabeth** takes you to **Portland Head Light,** Maine's first lighthouse, which was commissioned by George Washington in 1787. The lighthouse is on the grounds of **Fort Williams Park** and is an excellent place to bring a picnic. Be sure to spend some time wandering the ample grounds. There are also excellent walking trails (and views) at nearby **Two Lights State Park.** If you want to take a boat tour while in Portland, get a ticket for Casco Bay Lines and see some of the islands that dot the bay. Spend two nights in Portland.

Logistics: 28 miles; via I–95 N; 40 minutes, staring in Kennebunkport

DAY 6: BRETTON WOODS

Wake up early and drive to Bretton Woods, where you will spend nights six and seven. The driving time from Portland to Bretton Woods is approximately three hours, due to two-lane, steep mountain roads. ■TIP→ **Be sure to drive a four-wheel-drive vehicle in winter.** Drive northwest along U.S. 302 toward **Sebago Lake,** a popular water-sports area in the summer, and continue on toward the time-honored New England towns of Naples and Bridgton. Just 15 miles from the border of New Hampshire, and nearing Crawford Notch, U.S. 302 begins to thread through New Hampshire's **White Mountains,** passing beneath brooding **Mt. Washington** before arriving in Bretton Woods.

Logistics: 98 miles; via ME 113 N and U.S. 302 W; 3 hours, starting in Portland

DAY 7: THE WHITE MOUNTAINS

In Bretton Woods, the **Mt. Washington Cog Railway** still chugs to the summit, and the **Omni Mount Washington Resort** recalls the glory days of White Mountain resorts. Beloved winter activities here include snowshoeing and skiing on the grounds of the Mount Washington Resort. You can even zipline here in winter. Afterward, defrost with a cup of steaming hot cider while checking out vintage photos of the International Monetary Conference, held here in 1944, or head to the Cave, a prohibition-era speakeasy, for a drink.

Great Itineraries

Maine's Northern Coast: Portland to Quoddy Head State Park, 6 Days

Lighthouses, beaches, lobster rolls, and water sports—Maine's northern coast has something for everyone. Quaint seaside villages and towns line the shore as U.S. 1 winds its way toward the easternmost swath of land in the United States at Quoddy Head State Park. Antiquing is a major draw, so keep an eye out for roadside shops crammed with gems. Maine's only national park, Acadia, is a highlight of the tour, drawing more than 2 million visitors per year.

Fly in: Portland International Jetport (PWM), Portland, Maine

Fly out: Bangor International Airport, (BGR), Bangor, Maine

DAY 1: PORTLAND TO BRUNSWICK
Use Maine's maritime capital as your jumping-off point to head farther up the Maine Coast, or, as Mainers call it, "Down East." Plan to spend half of your first day in Portland, then head to Brunswick for the night.

Portland shows off its restored waterfront at the **Old Port.** From there, before you depart, you can grab a bite at either of two classic Maine eateries: **Gilbert's Chowder House** or **Becky's Diner,** or check out what's new in the buzzy restaurant scene here. For a peek at the freshest catch of the day, wander over to the **Harbor Fish Market,** a Portland institution since 1968, and gaze upon Maine lobsters and other delectable seafood. Two lighthouses on nearby **Cape Elizabeth, Two Lights** and **Portland Head,** still stand vigil.

Following U.S. 1, travel northeast along the ragged, island-strewn coast of Down East Maine and make your first stop at the retail outlets of **Freeport,** home of **L.L. Bean.** Almost 3 million people visit the massive flagship store every year, where you can find everything from outerwear to camping equipment. Just 10 miles north of Freeport on U.S. 1, **Brunswick** is home to the campus of **Bowdoin College,** the superb **Bowdoin College Museum of Art,** and also features a superb coastline for kayaking. Plan for dinner and an overnight in Bath.

Logistics: 30 miles; via U.S. 1 N; 30 minutes from Portland airport.

DAY 2: BATH
In **Bath,** Maine's shipbuilding capital, tour the **Maine Maritime Museum,** stopping for lunch on the waterfront. Check out the boutiques and antiques shops, or take in the plenitude of beautiful homes. From here it's a 30-minute detour down Route 127 to Georgetown Island and Reid State Park, where you will find a quiet beach lining Sheepscot Bay—and maybe even a sand dollar or two to take home, if you arrive at low tide. For a stunning vista, make your way to Griffith Head.

Drive north and reconnect with U.S. 1. Continue through the towns of **Wiscasset** and **Damariscotta,** where you may find yourself pulling over to stop at the outdoor flea markets and intriguing antiques shops that line the road. Another hour from here is **Rockland,** where you'll spend your second night.

Logistics: 52 miles; via U.S. 1 N; 1 hour 15 minutes, starting in Brunswick.

DAY 3: ROCKLAND, CAMDEN, AND CASTINE
From Rockland, spend the day cruising on a majestic schooner or reserve a tee time at Somerset Resorts' 18-hole

championship course that overlooks the Rockland Harbor. If you're an art lover, save some time for Rockland's **Farnsworth Art Museum,** the **Wyeth Center,** and the **Maine Center for Contemporary Art.**

In **Camden** and **Castine,** exquisite inns occupy homes built from inland Maine's golden timber. Camden is an ideal place to stay overnight as you make your way closer to Acadia National Park; it is a beautiful seaside town with hundreds of boats bobbing in the harbor, immaculately kept antique homes, streets lined with boutiques and specialty stores, and restaurants serving lobster at every turn. The modest hills (by Maine standards, anyway) of nearby Mt. Battie offer good hiking and a great spot from which to picnic and view the surrounding area. It is also one of the hubs for the beloved and historic windjammer fleet—there is no better way to see the area than from the deck of one of these graceful beauties.

Logistics: 62 miles; via U.S. 1 N and Rte. 166 S; 1½ hours, starting in Rockland.

DAYS 4 AND 5: MOUNT DESERT ISLAND AND ACADIA NATIONAL PARK

On Day 4, head out early for **Bar Harbor** and plan to spend two nights here, using the bustling village as jumping-off point

for the park—Bar Harbor is less than 5 miles from the entrance to **Mount Desert Island** 's 27-mile Park Loop Road. Spend at least a day exploring **Acadia National Park,** Maine's only national park and its most popular tourist destination. Enjoy the island's natural beauty by kayaking its coast, biking the 45-mile, historic, unpaved, carriage-road system, and driving to the summit of **Cadillac Mountain** for a stunning panorama.

Logistics: 52 miles; via Rte. 166 N, U.S. 1 N and Rte. 3 E; 1¼ hours, starting in Castine.

DAY 6: BAR HARBOR TO QUODDY HEAD STATE PARK

About 100 miles farther along U.S. 1 and "Way Down East" is Quoddy Head State Park in Lubec, Maine. Here, on the easternmost tip of land in the United States, sits the **West Quoddy Head Light,** one of 60 lighthouses that dot Maine's rugged coastline. Depending on the time of year (and your willingness to get up very early), you may be lucky enough to catch the East Coast's first sunrise here.

Logistics: 103 miles; via U.S. 1 N; 2½ hours, starting in Bar Harbor. From the park, it is 119 miles (2½ hours) to the Bangor airport via Rte. 9 W.

Great Itineraries

Best of Vermont, 7 Days

Following roads that weave through the Green Mountains and charming towns, this 200-mile journey is ideal at any time of year and covers Vermont from top to bottom.

Fly in: Bradley International Airport (BDL), Hartford, Connecticut

Fly out: Burlington International Airport (BTV), Burlington, Vermont

DAY 1: BRATTLEBORO

Artsy **Brattleboro** is the perfect place to begin a tour of Vermont, and it's worth taking a day to do some shopping and exploring. Catch a movie at the art deco **Latchis Theatre,** browse in a bookstore, or simply grab a cup of joe and people-watch. For dinner, make a reservation well in advance at tiny **T.J. Buckley's,** one of the best restaurants in the state. Spend your first night in Brattleboro.

Logistics: 78 miles; via I–91 N; 1 hour and 15 minutes from Bradley airport.

DAYS 2-4: KILLINGTON

Depart Brattleboro heading west on Route 9 and link up with Route 100 in Wilmington. As you travel north along the eastern edge of **Green Mountain National Forest,** you'll pass a plethora of panoramic overlooks and delightful ski towns. Stop to snap a photo, or take a moment to peruse the selection at a funky general store, as you make your way toward gigantic Killington Peak. Spend the next three nights in **Killington,** the largest ski resort in Vermont, and an outdoor playground year-round. A tip for skiers: one of the closest places to the slopes to stay is **The Mountain Top Inn & Resort.**

Wake up early to carve the mountain's fresh powder in winter. Nonskiers can still enjoy the snow, whether at the tubing park, on a snowmobile adventure, or in snowshoes on one of several trails. In summer, long after the ground has thawed, those trails are opened to mountain bikers and hikers. For a more leisurely activity, try your hand at the 18-hole disc-golf course. The excellent Grand Spa is also a lovely way to spend the day.

Logistics: 94 miles; via Rte. 9 W, Rte. 100 N, 2½ hours, starting in Brattleboro.

DAY 5: KILLINGTON TO BURLINGTON

Continue on Route 100 north until you reach Hancock, then head west on Route 125. Welcome to the land of poet Robert Frost, who spent almost 40 years living in Vermont, summering in the nearby tiny mountain town of Ripton, where he wrote numerous poems. Plaques along the 1.2-mile **Robert Frost Interpretive Trail,** a quiet woodland walk that takes about 30 minutes, display commemorative quotes from his poems, including his classic, "The Road Not Taken." After your stroll, head north on U.S. 7 until you hit Burlington.

Burlington, Vermont's largest city and home to the **University of Vermont,** is located on the eastern shore of Lake Champlain. Bustling in the summer and fall, the **Burlington Farmers' Market** is filled with everything from organic meats and cheeses to freshly cut flowers and maple syrup. Spend the night in Burlington. In the evening, check out **Nectar's,** where the band Phish played their first bar gig, or wander into any of the many other pubs and cafés that attract local musicians.

Logistics: 84 miles; via Rte. 100 N, Rte. 125 W, and U.S. 7 N; 2½ hours, starting in Killington.

DAY 6: SHELBURNE AND LAKE CHAMPLAIN

On your second day in Burlington, you can take a day trip south to the **Magic Hat Brewing Company**; established in 1994, it was at the forefront of Vermont's micro-brewery explosion. Take a free half-hour guided or self-guided tour of the Artifac-tory (even dogs are welcome), and fill a growler from one of the 48 taps pumping out year-round, seasonal, and experimen-tal brews. A stone's throw down U.S. 7, in **Shelburne**, is family-friendly **Shelburne Farms.** Watch the process of making cheese from start to finish, or wander the gorgeous 1,400-acre estate designed by Frederick Law Olmsted, co-designer of New York's Central Park. The grounds overlook beautiful **Lake Champlain** and make the perfect setting for a picnic. In winter Shelburne Farms offers sleigh rides and other themed activities; if you're visiting in late July, don't miss the **Vermont Cheesemakers Festival,** showcas-ing more than 200 varieties of cheese crafted by 40 local purveyors. If you can't get enough, you can opt to spend the night here.

Logistics: 3.6 miles, via U.S. 7 to Magic Hat; another 3.4 miles to Shelburne Farms; 40 minutes round-trip altogether.

DAY 7: STOWE

A 30-minute drive down Interstate 89 from Burlington reunites you with Route 100 in the town of Waterbury. Head north in the direction of Stowe, and in under 2 miles you can make the obligatory pit stop at **Ben & Jerry's Ice Cream Factory.** The factory tour offers a lively behind-the-scenes look at how their ice cream is made; at the end of the tour, you get to taste limited-release creations only available at the factory before voting on your favorites.

Next, set out for the village of **Stowe.** Its proximity to Mt. Mansfield (Vermont's

highest peak at 4,395 feet) has made Stowe a popular ski destination since the 1930s. If there's snow on the ground, hit the slopes, hitch a ride on a one-horse open sleigh, or simply put your feet up by the fire and enjoy a Heady Topper (an unfiltered, hoppy, American Double IPA beloved by beer aficionados the world over). In warmer weather, pop into the cute shops and art galleries that line the town's main street and sample some of the finest cheddar cheese and maple syr-up that Vermont has to offer. Rejuvenate yourself at **Topnotch Resort,** which offers more than 100 different treatments. Spend your final night here.

Logistics: 36 miles; via I–89 S and Rte. 100 N; 45 minutes, starting in Burlington. From Stowe to the Burlington airport: 33 miles; via Rte. 100 and I–89 N; 41 minutes.

On the Calendar

January

NH Sanctioned & Jackson Invitational Snow Sculpting Competition, Jackson, NH. Started in 2000, the free event takes places at Black Mountain Ski and features more than 12 teams carving intricate snow sculptures. ⊕ *jacksonnh.com*

February

Winter Carnival, Dartmouth, NH. Started in 1911, Dartmouth's winter festival celebrates the season with races, polar bear plunges, and snow sculpture contests. ⊕ *students.dartmouth.edu*

March

Maine Maple Sunday. Participating sugarhouses, all members of the Maine Maple Producers Association, offer tours, demonstrations, activities, and free samples. ⊕ *mainemapleproducers.com*

New Hampshire Maple Weekend. Participating sugarhouses throughout the state offer tours, behind-the-scenes access, and sometimes, breakfast. ⊕ *nhmapleproducers.com/maple-month*

Winter Brewers Festival, West Dover, Vermont. At Mount Snow, more than 20 breweries pour more than 50 taps of ales, stouts, lagers, ciders, and more with live music. ⊕ *mountsnow.com*

April

Vermont Maple Festival, St. Albans, VT. This weekend is all about syrup. There's a pancake breakfast, a carnival and parade, and, of course, plenty of yummy maple treats. ⊕ *www.vtmaplefestival.org*

May

Down East Spring Birding Festival, Cobscook Bay, Maine. America's easternmost birding festival occurs during spring migration and nesting season. There are guided hikes, sightseeing boat rides, sunset cruises, and speakers. ⊕ *cobscookinstitute.org*

Wildquack Duck River Festival, Jackson, New Hampshire. This zany event features 3,500 yellow rubber ducks racing downstream. Pick the winning ducks and get rewarded with prizes that range from vacation stays to gift baskets. ⊕ *jacksonnh.com*

June

Chowder Festival, Portsmouth, New Hampshire. More than 500 gallons of chowder is served up at this annual event, which is the kickoff to the Prescott Park Arts Festival summer season. ⊕ *prescottpark.org*

Quechee Hot Air Balloon Festival, Quechee, Vermont. See 20 hot air balloons take to the skies over the Upper Valley of Vermont and New Hampshire. Admission includes live music, a kids' area, balloon glows, and access to more than 60 art and food booths. ⊕ *www.quecheeballoonfestival.com*

Strolling of the Heifers, Brattleboro, VT. An annual local food-focused showcase includes a parade of about 100 cows dressed in their Sunday best. ⊕ *www.strollingoftheheifers.com*

August

Champlain Valley Fair, Essex Junction, Vermont. The state's biggest single event has exhibits on Vermont's livestock and produce, carnival rides and games, and live entertainment. Did we mention the deep-fried cheesecake? ⊕ *www. wiltonbbf.com*

Maine Antiques Fair, Union, ME. Maine's largest antique festival takes place near Camden and Rockland. ⊕ *www.maineantiquesfestival.com*

Maine Lobster Festival, Rockland, ME. Stuff your face with lobster tails and claws during this "lobstravaganza" that puts almost 20,000 pounds of delicious crustacean at your fingertips. ⊕ *www. mainelobsterfestival.com*

Vermont Cheesemakers Festival, Shelburne, VT. Artisanal cheeses and local beer and wine highlight this daylong festival that features samples of more than 200 cheese varieties from 40 artisan cheese makers. ⊕ *www.vtcheesefest.com*

Wilton Blueberry Festival, Wilton, ME. You can pick your own wild blueberries and sample baked goods from pancakes to pies at the annual festival. ⊕ *www. wiltonbbf.com*

September

New Hampshire Highland Games & Festival, Lincoln, New Hampshire. 3-day celebration of Scottish music, food and drink, athletics, dance, and culture. ⊕ *nhscot.org*

October

Fryeburg Fair, Fryeburg, ME. Established in 1851, this festive aggie fair includes horse, ox, and tractor pulling; animal, craft, and art exhibits; sheepdog trials; cooking contests; flower shows; a farm equipment museum; and food, food, food. ⊕ *www.fryeburgfair.org*

New Hampshire Pumpkin Festival, Laconia, NH. This family-friendly gathering near Lake Winnipesaukee tries to outdo itself each October by featuring the most lighted pumpkins. ⊕ *www.nhpumpkin-festival.com*

November

Billings Farm Thanksgiving Weekend, Woodstock, Vermont. Experience Thanksgiving— preparations, menu, and entertainment— as it was celebrated in the 1890s. There are holiday food activities, events in the house, and horse-drawn wagon rides. ⊕ *billingsfarm.org*

Christmas Prelude, Kennebunkport, Maine. Take part in the hat parade, shop at the crafts fair, see the fireworks, or watch for Santa arriving on a lobster boat— these are just a few of the activities at the annual event. ⊕ *www.christmasprelude. com*

Lighting of the Nubble, York, Maine. The famous coastal Maine lighthouse gets all dressed up for the holidays in late November, and stays light through New Years Day.

December

Inn to Inn Holiday Cookie Tour, White Mountains, NH. This self-guided tour includes sweet treats, copious Christmas decorations, and charming winter scenes. ⊕ *www.countryinnsinthewhite-mountains.com*

Winter Wassail Weekend, Woodstock, VT. The annual fete features a parade with holiday-costume clad horses and riders, live music, house tours, kids' activities, and a Wassail Feast. ⊕ *www.wood-stockvt.com*

Contacts

✈ Air

AIRPORT INFORMATION Bangor International Airport. ☎ *207/992–4600*⊕ *www. flybangor.com.* **Burlington International Airport.** ☎ *802/863–2874*⊕ *www. btv.aero.* **Logan International Airport.** ☎ *800/235–6426* ⊕ *www.massport.com* Ⓜ *Blue, Silver.* **Manchester-Boston Regional Airport.** ☎ *603/624–6539*⊕ *www. flymanchester.com.* **Portland International Jetport.** ☎ *207/774–7301* ⊕ *www. portlandjetport.org.*

🚌 Bus

INFORMATION C&J. ☎ *603/430–1100*⊕ *www. ridecj.com.* **Concord Coach Lines.** ☎ *800/639–3317* ⊕ *www.concordcoach-lines.com.*

🚆 Train

INFORMATION Amtrak. ☎ *800/872–7245*⊕ *www. amtrak.com.*

🛏 Lodging

CONTACTS New England Inns & Resorts Association. ☎ *603/964–6689*⊕ *www. newenglandinnsandresorts.com.*

🧭 Tours

BIKING P.O.M.G. Bike Tours of Vermont. ☎ *802/434–2270, 888/635–2453* ⊕ *www.pomgbike.com.* **VBT Bicycling and Walking Vacations.** ☎ *800/245–3868*⊕ *www.vbt.com.*

CULINARY Maine Food for Thought. ☎ *207/619–2075* ⊕ *www.mainefood-forthought.com.*

GENERAL INTEREST New England Vacation Tours. ☎ *800/742–7669*⊕ *www. newenglandvacationtours. com.* **Northeast Unlimited Tours.** ☎ *800/759–6820* ⊕ *www.newenglandtours. com.* **Wolfe Tours & Adventures.** ☎ *888/449–6533* ⊕ *wolfetours.com.*

MOOSE TOURS Pemi Valley Moose Tours. ✉ *136 Main St., Lincoln*☎ *603/745–2744*⊕ *www.moose-toursnh.com.*

SKIING Inn to Inn. ✉ *52 Park St., Brandon* ☎ *802/247–3300*⊕ *www. inntoinn.com.*

📍 Visitor Information

CONTACTS Maine Office of Tourism. ☎ *888/624–6345* ⊕ *www.visitmaine.com.* **New Hampshire Division of Travel and Tourism Development.** ☎ *800/386–4664* ⊕ *www.visitnh.gov.* **Vermont Department of Tourism and Marketing.** ☎ *800/837–6668*⊕ *www. vermontvacation.com.*

ONLINE RESOURCES Visit New England. ⊕ *www.visitnewengland.com.* **New England Today.** ⊕ *www. newengland.com.*

Chapter 3

BEST FALL FOLIAGE DRIVES AND ROAD TRIPS

3

A CELEBRATION

Picture this: one scarlet maple offset by the stark white spire of a country church, a whole hillside of brilliant foliage foregrounded by a vintage barn, or perhaps a covered bridge straddling a cobalt river. Such iconic scenes have launched a thousand Instagram posts and turned New England into the ultimate fall destination for leaf peepers.

OF COLOR

By Susan
MacCallum-Whitcomb

Above, Vermont's Green Mountains are multicolored in the fall (and often white in winter).

Mother Nature, of course, puts on an annual autumn performance elsewhere, but this one is a showstopper. Like the landscape, the mix of deciduous (leaf-shedding) trees is remarkably varied here and creates a broader than usual palette. New England's abundant evergreens lend contrast, making the display even more vivid. Every September and October, leaf peepers arrive to cruise along country lanes, join outdoor adventures, or simply stroll on town greens.

Did you know the brilliant shades actually lurk in the leaves all year long? Leaves contain three pigments. The green chlorophyll, so dominant in summer that it obscures the red anthocyanins and orangey-yellow carotenoids, decreases in fall and reveals a crayon box of color.

PREDICTING THE PEAK

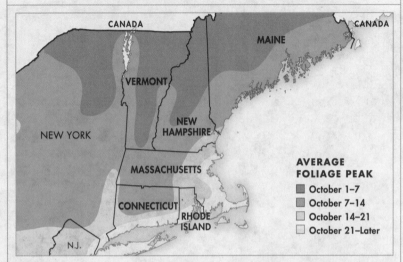

AVERAGE FOLIAGE PEAK
- ■ October 1–7
- ■ October 7–14
- □ October 14–21
- □ October 21–Later

LOCATION

Pinning down precisely when colors will appear remains an inexact science, although location plays a major role. Typically, the transformation begins in the highest and northernmost parts of New England in mid-September, then moves steadily into lower altitudes and southern sectors throughout October.

For trip planning, think in terms of regions rather than states. In Maine (a huge state that runs north–south) leaf color can peak anytime from the fourth week of September to the third week of October, depending on the locale.

WEATHER

Early September weather is another deciding factor. From the foliage aficionado's perspective, the ideal scenario is calm, temperate days capped by nights that are cool but still above freezing. If the weather is too warm, it delays the onset of the season. If it's too dry or windy, the leaves shrivel up or blow off.

COLOR CHECK RESOURCES

Curious about current conditions? In season, most states maintain websites reporting on foliage conditions. Weather Channel has peak viewing maps and Foliage Network uses a network of spotters to chart changes.

- Connecticut: ☎ 800/282–6863
- ⊕ www.ct.gov/dep
- Foliage Network:
- ⊕ www.foliagenetwork.com
- Maine: ☎ 888/624–6345
- ⊕ www.mainefoliage.com
- Massachusetts: ☎ 800/227–6277
- ⊕ www.massvacation.com

- New Hampshire: ☎ 800/258–3608
- ⊕ www.visitnh.gov
- Rhode Island: ☎ 800/556–2484
- ⊕ www.visitrhodeisland.com
- Vermont: ☎ 800/837–6668
- ⊕ www.vermontvacation.com
- Weather Channel: ⊕ www.weather.com

TOP TREES FOR COLOR

A AMERICAN BEECH. This tree's smooth, steel-gray trunk is crowned with gold, copper, and bronze-tinted leaves in autumn, giving it a metallic sheen. Though the elliptical leaves sometimes hang on all winter, its "fruit" goes fast because beechnuts are a popular snack for birds, squirrels, and even bears.

B NORTHERN RED OAK. The upside of oaks is that they retain their fall shading until late in the season—the downside is that, for most species, that color is a boring brown. Happily, the northern red isn't like other members of the oak family. Its elongated, flame-shaped leaves turn fiery crimson and incandescent orange.

C QUAKING ASPEN. Eyes and ears both prove useful when identifying this aspen. Look for small, ovate leaves that usually become almost flaxen. Or listen for the leaves' quake: a sound, audible in even a gentle breeze, which the U.S. Forest Service likens to that made by "thousands of fluttering butterfly wings."

D SUGAR MAPLE. The leaf of the largest North American maple species is so lovely that Canada put it on its national flag. Each generally has five multi-pointed lobes—plus enough anthocyanin to produce a deep red color. The tree itself produces plentiful sap and is the cornerstone of New England's syrup industry.

E WHITE ASH. This tall tree typically grows to between 65 to 100 feet. Baseball enthusiasts admire the wood (which is used to craft bats); while foliage fans admire the compound leaves, each consisting of five to nine slightly serrated, tapering leaflets. They range in hue from burgundy and purple to amber.

F WHITE BIRCH. A papery, light, bright bark makes this slender hardwood easily recognizable. Centuries ago, Native Americans used birch wood to make everything from canoes to medicinal teas. Today's photographers know the bark also makes great pictures since it provides a sharp contrast to the tree's vibrant yellow leaves.

FANTASTIC FALL ITINERARY

The Berkshires

Fall is the perfect time to visit New England—country roads wind through dense forests exploding into reds, oranges, yellows, and purples. For inspiration, here is an itinerary for the truly ambitious that links the most stunning foliage areas; choose a section to explore more closely. Like autumn itself, this route works its way south from northern Vermont into Connecticut, with one or two days in each area.

VERMONT

NORTHWEST VERMONT

In Burlington, the elms will be turning colors on the University of Vermont campus. You can ride the ferry across Lake Champlain for great views of Vermont's Green Mountains and New York's Adirondacks. After visiting the resort town of Stowe, detour off Route 100 beneath the cliffs of Smugglers' Notch. The north country's palette unfolds in Newport, where the blue waters of Lake Memphremagog reflect the foliage.

NORTHEAST KINGDOM

After a side trip along Lake Willoughby, explore St. Johnsbury, where the Fairbanks Museum and St. Johnsbury Athenaeum reveal Victorian tastes in art and natural-history collecting. In Peacham, stock up for a picnic at the Peacham Store.

NEW HAMPSHIRE

WHITE MOUNTAINS AND LAKES REGION

In New Hampshire, Interstate 93 narrows as it winds through craggy Franconia Notch. Get off the interstate for the sinuous Kancamagus Highway portion of Route 112 that passes through the mountains to Conway. In Center Harbor, in the Lakes Region, you can ride the *MS Mount Washington* for views of the Lake Winnipesaukee shoreline, or ascend to Moultonborough's Castle in the Clouds for a falcon's-eye look at the colors.

MT. MONADNOCK

In Concord, stop at the Museum of New Hampshire History and the State House. Several trails climb Mt. Monadnock, near Jaffrey Center, and colorful vistas extend as far as Boston.

⇨ **For local drives perfect for an afternoon, also see our Fall Foliage Drive Spotlights on Western Massachusetts, Connecticut, Rhode Island, Vermont, New Hampshire, and Inland Maine.**

THE MOOSE IS LOOSE!

Take "Moose Crossing" signs seriously because things won't end well if you hit an animal that stands six feet tall and weighs 1,200 pounds. Some 40,000 reside in northern New England. To search out these ungainly creatures in the wild, consider an organized moose safari in northern New Hampshire or Maine.

MASSACHUSETTS

THE MOHAWK TRAIL

In Shelburne Falls, Massachusetts, the Bridge of Flowers displays the last of autumn's blossoms. Follow the Mohawk Trail section of Route 2 as it ascends into the Berkshire Hills—and stop to take in the view at the hairpin turn just east of North Adams (or drive up Mt. Greylock, the tallest peak in New England, for more stunning vistas). In Williamstown, the Clark Art Institute houses a collection of impressionist works.

THE BERKSHIRES

The scenery around Lenox, Stockbridge, and Great Barrington has long attracted the talented and the wealthy. Near U.S. 7, you can visit the homes of novelist Edith Wharton (the Mount, in Lenox), sculptor Daniel Chester French (Chesterwood, in Stockbridge), and diplomat Joseph Choate (Naumkeag, in Stockbridge).

CONNECTICUT

THE LITCHFIELD HILLS

This area of Connecticut combines the feel of upcountry New England with exclusive urban polish. The wooded shores of Lake Waramaug are home to country inns and wineries in pretty towns. Litchfield has a perfect village green—an idealized New England town center.

LEAF PEEPER PLANNER

Hot-air balloons and ski-lift rides give a different perspective on fall's color.

Enjoying fall doesn't necessarily require a multistate road trip. If you are short on time (or energy), a simple autumnal stroll might be just the ticket: many state parks even offer free short ranger-led rambles.

HIKE AND BIKE ON A TOUR

You can sign on for foliage-focused hiking holidays with **Country Walkers** (☎ 800/234–6900 ⊕ www.country-walkers.com) and **Boundless Journeys** (☎ 800/941–8010 ⊕ www.boundless-journeys.com); or cycling ones with **Discovery Bike Tours** (☎ 800/257–2226 ⊕ www.discoverybiketours.com) and **VBT Bicycling Vacations** (☎ 800/245–3868 ⊕ www.vbt.com). Individual state tourism boards list similar operators elsewhere.

SOAR ABOVE THE CROWDS

New Hampshire's Cannon Mountain (☎ 603/823–8800 ⊕ www.cannonmt.com) is only one of several New England ski resorts that provides gondola or aerial tram rides during foliage season. Area hot-air balloon operators, like **Balloons of Vermont, LLC** (☎ 802/369–0213 ⊕ www.balloonsofvermont.com), help you take it in from the top.

ROOM AT THE INN?

Accommodations fill quickly in autumn. Vermont's top lodgings sell out months in advance for the first two weeks in October. So book early and expect a two-night minimum stay requirement. If you can't find a quaint inn, try basing yourself at a B&B or off-season ski resort. Also, be prepared for some sticker shock; if you can travel midweek, you'll often save quite a bit.

RIDE THE RAILS OR THE CURRENT

Board the **Essex Steam Train** for a ride through the Connecticut countryside (☎ 800/377–3987 ⊕ www.essexsteam-train.com) or float through northern Rhode Island on the **Blackstone Valley Explorer** riverboat (☎ 401/724–2200 ⊕ www.rivertourblackstone.com).

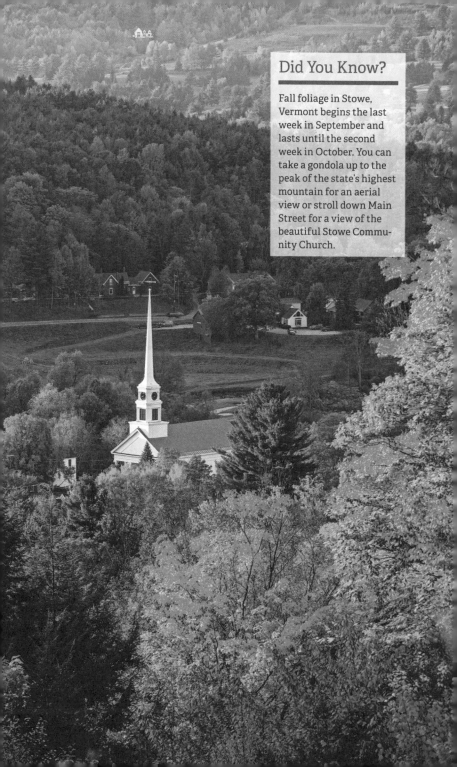

VERMONT FALL FOLIAGE DRIVE

Nearly 80% of Vermont is forested, with cities few and far between. The state's interior is a rural playground for leaf peepers, and it's widely considered to exhibit the most intense range of colors anywhere on the continent. Its tiny towns and hamlets—the few distractions from the dark reds, yellows, oranges, and russets—are as pristine as nature itself.

Begin this drive in Manchester Village, along the old-fashioned, well-to-do homes lining Main Street, and continue south to Arlington, North Bennington, and Old Bennington. Stop just a mile south along Route 7A at **Hildene.** The 412 acres of explorable grounds at the estate of Abraham Lincoln's son are ablaze with color, and the views over the Battenkill Valley are as good as any you can find. Drive south another mile along 7A to the **Equinox Valley Nursery,** where you can sample delicious apple cider and doughnuts amid views of the arresting countryside. A few more miles south along 7A is the small town of Arlington.

BEST TIME TO GO

Late September and early October are the times to go, with the southern area peaking about a week later than the north. Remember to book hotels in advance. The state has a Fall Foliage Hotline and an online interactive map (☎ 802/828–3239 ⊕ www.foliage-vermont.com).

PLANNING YOUR TIME

The drive from Manchester to Bennington outlined here takes just 30 minutes, but a relaxed pace is best suited to taking in all the sights.

From Route 7A in Arlington you can take two adventurous and stunning detours. One is pure foliage: follow Route 313 west a few miles to the New York State border for more beautiful views. Or head east 1 mile to East Arlington, where there's a delightful chocolate emporium. (You can continue even farther east from this spot to Kelly Stand Road leading into the Green Mountains—a little-known route that can't be beat.) Back on 7A South in Arlington, stop at the delightful **Arlington Dairy Bar** for a Vermont creemee.

Farther south in Shaftsbury is **Clear Brook Farm,** a brilliant place for fresh produce and pumpkins. Robert Frost spent much of his life in South Shaftsbury, and you can learn about his life at his former home, the **Stone House.** From South Shaftsbury take Route 67 through North Bennington and continue on to Route 67A in Old Bennington. Ride the elevator up the 306-foot-high **Bennington Battle Monument** to survey the season's progress across four states. Back down from the clouds, walk a few serene blocks to the cemetery of the **Old First Church,** where Robert Frost is buried, and contemplate his autumnal poem, "Nothing Gold Can Stay."

NEED A BREAK?

Arlington Dairy Bar. Along 7A waits a big red dairy barn surrounded on all sides by Vermont's color-changing landscape. There are few greater ways to enjoy fall foliage than leaning on the hood of your car with a double scoop of local pumpkin and maple walnut ice cream, or a chocolate-dipped Vermont creemee. ✉ *3158 Rte. 7A, Arlington* ☎ *802/375–2546* ⊕ *www.facebook.com/ ArlingtonDairyBar.*

Clear Brook Farm. This 25-acre certified organic farm sells its own produce, in addition to plants, baked goods, and other seasonal treats. ✉ *47 Hidden Valley Rd., Manchester* ☎ *802/442–4273* ⊕ *www.clearbrookfarm.com.*

Equinox Valley Nursery. This nursery carries fresh produce, seasonal snacks, and cider doughnuts. There's family-friendly fall activities—a corn maze, hayrides, and pumpkin carving—as well as the property's 300-odd scarecrows. ✉ *1158 Main St., Manchester* ☎ *802/362–2610* ⊕ *www. equinoxvalleynursery. com* ✍ *Free.*

NEW HAMPSHIRE FALL FOLIAGE DRIVE

Quaint villages graced with green commons, white town halls, and covered bridges: southwestern New Hampshire is dominated by the imposing rocky summit of Mt. Monadnock and the brilliant colors of autumn. Kancamagus Highway is another classic foliage route, but for more solitude and less traffic, try this more accessible route that peaks a few weeks later than the state's far north.

The Granite State is the second-most-forested state in the nation; by mid-October the colors of the leaves of its maple, birch, elm, oak, beech, and ash trees range from green to gold, purple to red, and orange to auburn. Routes 12, 101, 124, and U.S. 202 form a loop around **Mt. Monadnock.** Start on the picturesque Main Street in Keene with a stop for coffee at Prime Roast Café; for New Hampshire–made products, take a walk on Main Street or detour west on Route 9 to reach **Stonewall Farm** for something more pastoral.

BEST TIME TO GO

The best time to view foliage in southern New Hampshire is generally early October, but it can vary by up to four weeks. For updates about leaf changes, visit the Foliage Tracker page on the website of **Visit New Hampshire** (☎ 800/386–4664 ⊕ www.visitnh.gov).

PLANNING YOUR TIME

Expect to travel about 55 miles. The journey can take up to a full day if you stop to explore along the way.

From Keene, travel east on Route 101 through Dublin. In **Peterborough,** browse the local stores like the Peterborough Basket Company—the country's oldest continuously operating basket manufacturer—whose attitudes and selections mirror the state's independent spirit. If you need a bite to eat before continuing on your journey or later for dinner, stop by **Harlow's Pub,** a convivial spot in Peterborough's scenic downtown.

Then turn south on U.S. 202 toward Jaffrey Village. Just west on Route 124, in historic Jaffrey Center, be sure to visit the **Meeting House Cemetery,** where author Willa Cather is buried. One side trip, 4 miles south on U.S. 202, leads to the majestic **Cathedral of the Pines** in Rindge, one of the best places in the region for foliage viewing because evergreens offset the brilliant shades of red.

Heading west on Route 124, you can take Dublin Road to the main entrance of **Monadnock State Park** or continue along to the Old Toll Road parking area for one of the most popular routes up the mountain, the **Old Halfway House Trail.** All the hiking trails have great views, including the area's many lakes. Continuing on U.S. 124, head southwest on Fitzwilliam Road to Fitzwilliam. If you have time, pop into **Bloomin' Antiques** to browse their selection of fine art and unusual antiques.

NEED A BREAK?

Bloomin' Antiques. Fine art and unusual antiques. ⌧ 3 Templeton Tpke., Fitzwilliam ☎ 800/386–4664 ⊕ www. bloominantiquesnh.com.

Harlow's Pub. Open for lunch, dinner, and Sunday brunch, this friendly tavern with a patio overlooking Peterborough's scenic village center serves creative comfort fare and local craft beer. ⌧ 3 School St., Peterborough ☎ 603/924–6365 ⊕ www. harlowspub.com.

Stonewall Farm. A working dairy farm with a dramatic setting amid fields and forests, Stonewall is open daily and presents an active schedule of events, including maple sugaring and seasonal horse-drawn hayrides. Walking and snowshoeing trails lace the property, and a farm shop sells organic produce, gourmet snacks, and the farm's own luscious Frisky Cow Gelato. Young children love the discovery room, and the interactive greenhouse is geared for all ages. ⌧ 242 Chesterfield Rd., Keene ☎ 603/357–7278 ⊕ www.stonewallfarm. org.

INLAND MAINE FALL FOLIAGE DRIVE

Swaths of pine, spruce, and fir trees offset the red, orange, and yellow of maples and birches along this popular foliage drive through western Maine's mountains.

Wending its way to the four-season resort town of Rangeley, near its northern terminus, the route passes stunning overlooks, forest-lined lakes, waterfalls, hiking trails, and a state park. Mountain vistas are reflected in the many (often connected) lakes, ponds, rivers, and streams.

Route 17 heads north past old homesteads and fields along the Swift River Valley before making a mountainous switchback ascent to **Height of Land,** the drive's literal pinnacle. The must-stop overlook here has off-road parking, interpretive panels, stone seating, and a short path to the **Appalachian Trail.** On a clear day, you can look west to mountains on the New Hampshire border. **Mooselookmeguntic Lake** and **Upper Richardson Lake** seem to float amid the forestland below. A few miles north of here is an overlook for Rangeley Lake, also with interpretive panels.

BEST TIME TO GO

Fall color usually peaks in the first or second week of October. Get fall foliage updates at ⊕ *www.mainefoliage. com*.

PLANNING YOUR TIME

The Rangeley Lakes National Scenic Byway and a state byway (⊕ *www. exploremaine.org/ byways*) make up most of this 58-mile drive (1½ hours without stops), but plan for a relaxed, full day of exploring.

In tiny, welcoming Oquossoc, where Routes 17 and 4 meet, stop at the **Gingerbread House Restaurant** for breakfast or lunch, or for just baked goods or an ice cream. The hamlet is also home to the **Outdoor Heritage Museum**, where you can learn why visitors have come here to fish, hunt, and enjoy the outdoors since the mid-1800s. The trailhead for **Bald Mountain**, a popular hike, is just outside the village.

Rangeley, 7 miles east on Route 4, has restaurants, inns, a waterfront park, and outdoorsy shops. The countryside sweeps into view along public hiking trails at the 175-acre **Wilhelm Reich Museum**. There's also hiking at Rangeley Lakes Trail Center on Saddleback Mountain.

The road to **Rangeley Lake State Park** is accessible from both Routes 4 and 17, as is the **Appalachian Trail**. Overhanging foliage frames waterfalls at the scenic rest areas at each end of the drive: at Coos Canyon on Route 17 en route to Height of Land, and at Smalls Falls on Route 4 near Madrid, the terminus. Both spots have swimming holes, several falls, and paths with views of their drops. Coos Canyon is along the Swift River, a destination for recreational gold panning. You can rent or buy panning equipment at **Coos Canyon Rock and Gift**, across from its namesake. It also sells sandwiches, ice cream, and snacks.

NEED A BREAK?

Coos Canyon Rock and Gift. The gift shop offers jewelry, souvenirs, T-shirts, prospecting equipment, books, and more. ✉ *472 Swift River Rd. (Rte. 17), Byron* ☎ *207/364–4900* ⊕ *www.cooscanyonrock-andgift.com.*

Rangeley Lakes Heritage Trust. The trust protects 14,000 acres of land in the Rangeley Lakes area. Both online and at its Rangeley office, the trust has maps and descriptions of its 35 miles of recreational trails and access roads, along with information about fishing, hunting, snowmobiling, picnicking, and other outdoor activities. ✉ *2424 Main St., Rangeley* ☎ *207/864–7311* ⊕ *www.rlht.org.*

Wilhelm Reich Museum. This seasonal museum showcases the life and work of controversial physician-scientist Wilhelm Reich (1897–1957). There are magnificent views from the observatory and great trails throughout the 175-acre property, which is open year-round. ✉ *19 Orgonon Circle, off Rte. 4, Rangeley* ☎ *207/864–3443* ⊕ *www. wilhelmreichmuseum. org* ⌑ *Museum $8, grounds free.*

3

Best Fall Foliage Drives and Road Trips INLAND MAINE FALL FOLIAGE DRIVE

Gingerbread House Restaurant ◆
Wilhelm Reich Museum
16 Oquossoc 4 16 Rangeley
Outdoor Heritage Museum ◆
Rangeley Lake
Saddleback Maine
Bald Mountain 16
17 ◆ Rangeley Lake State Park
Mooselookmeguntic Lake
4 Madrid
Height of Land
Upper Richardson Lake
Small Falls
Phillips
South Arm
Umbagog Lake
Coos Canyon Rock and Gift
MOUNT BLUE STATE PARK
Bryon
Upton
26
Appalachian Trail
17
Weld
Andover
Frye
142
BALDPATE MTN.
Mexico
Rumford
Dixfield
0   5 mi
0   5 km
Bethel
2
Hanover
5 26

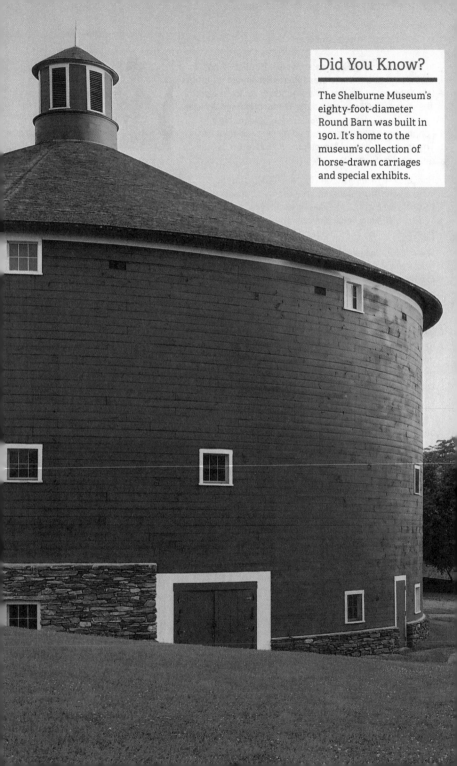

Chapter 4

VERMONT

Updated by
Julia Clancy

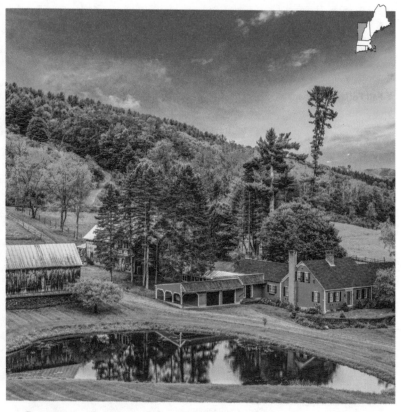

⊙ Sights	🍴 Restaurants	🛏 Hotels	🛍 Shopping	🍸 Nightlife
★★★★★	★★★★☆	★★★★☆	★★★☆☆	★★☆☆☆

WELCOME TO VERMONT

TOP REASONS TO GO

★ **Small-Town Charm:** Vermont rolls out a seemingly never-ending supply of tiny towns replete with white-steepled churches, town greens, red barns, general stores, and bed-and-breakfasts.

★ **Ski Resorts:** The East's best skiing can be found in well-managed, modern facilities with great views and lots and lots of powdery, fresh snow.

★ **Fall Foliage:** Perhaps the most vivid colors in North America wave from the trees in September and October.

★ **Gorgeous Landscapes:** This sparsely populated, heavily forested state is an ideal place to find peace and quiet amid the mountains, valleys, and lakes.

★ **Vibrant Local Eats:** The rich soil, and an emphasis on the state's maker-artisan culture, has led to great dairies, orchards, vineyards, specialty stores, and farm-to-table restaurants. Even the world-famous beer scene is known to highlight state-grown hops and locally made malt.

1 Brattleboro. A hippie enclave with an artistic and activist disposition.

2 Wilmington. The hub of Mt. Snow Valley.

3 Bennington. The economic center of southwest Vermont.

4 Arlington. Once the home of painter Norman Rockwell.

5 Manchester. Sophisticated with upscale shopping.

6 Dorset. Home to two of the state's best and oldest general stores.

7 Stratton. It's all about Stratton Mountain Resort.

8 Weston. Home to the Vermont Country Store.

9 Ludlow. Okemo Mountain Resort's home.

10 Grafton. Both a town and a museum.

11 Norwich. One of the most picturesque towns.

12 Quechee. Restaurants and shops in old mills.

13 Woodstock. Upscale shops and the venerable Woodstock Inn.

14 Killington. East Coast's largest ski resort.

15 Rutland. Slowly gaining traction as a foodie town.

16 Brandon. Artists Guild and the Basin Bluegrass Festival.

17 Middlebury. Restaurants, shops, and Middlebury College.

18 Waitsfield and Warren. The ski meccas of Mad River Glen and Sugarbush.

19 Montpelier. The state's capital.

20 Stowe. Quintessential eastern ski town.

21 Jeffersonville. The four-season Smugglers' Notch Resort.

22 Burlington. Vermont's most populous city with a lively food scene.

23 Shelburne. Shelburne Farms and Shelburne Museum.

24 Lake Champlain Islands. Numerous islands including Isle La Motte, North Hero, Grand Isle, and South Hero.

25 Montgomery and Jay. Small village near the Jay Peak ski resort and the Canadian border.

26 Lake Willoughby. Home to the world-renowned Bread and Puppet Theater museum.

27 Greensboro. Home to one of the world's best breweries.

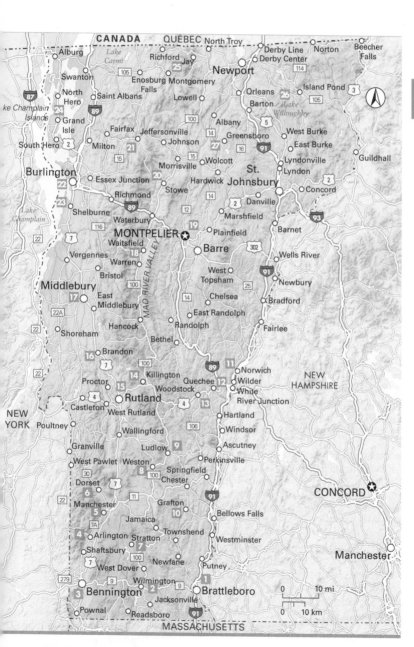

Vermont's a land of hidden treasures and unspoiled scenery. Wander anywhere in the state—nearly 80% is forest—and you'll find pristine countryside dotted with farms and framed by mountains. Tiny towns with picturesque church steeples, village greens, and covered bridges are perfect for exploring.

Sprawl has no place here. Highways are devoid of billboards by law, and on some roads cows still stop traffic twice a day en route to and from pasture. In spring, sap boils in sugarhouses, some built generations ago, while up the road a chef trained at the New England Culinary Institute in Montpelier might use the syrup to glaze a pork tenderloin.

It's the landscape, for the most part, that attracts people to Vermont. Rolling hills belie rugged terrain underneath the green canopy of forest growth. In summer, clear lakes and streams provide ample opportunities for swimming, boating, and fishing; hills attract hikers and mountain bikers. The more than 14,000 miles of roads, many of them only intermittently traveled by cars, are great for biking. In fall the leaves have their last hurrah, painting the mountainsides in vibrant yellow, gold, red, and orange. Vermont has the best ski resorts in the eastern United States, centered on the spine of the Green Mountains running north to south; and the traditional heart of skiing here is the town of Stowe. Almost anywhere you go, no matter what time of year, the Vermont countryside will make you reach for your camera.

Although Vermont may seem locked in time, technological sophistication appears where you least expect it: wireless Internet access in a 19th-century farmhouse-turned-inn and cell phone coverage from the state's highest peaks. Like an old farmhouse under renovation, though, the state's historic exterior is still the main attraction.

MAJOR REGIONS

Vermont can be divided into three regions: **Southern Vermont, Central Vermont,** and **Northern Vermont.**

Most people's introduction to the state is **Southern Vermont,** a relatively short drive from New York and Boston. As elsewhere across the state, you'll find unspoiled towns, romantic B&Bs, lush farms, and pristine forests. The area is flanked by **Bennington** on the west and **Brattleboro** on the east. There are charming towns like **Wilmington, Arlington, Manchester, Dorset, Weston, Grafton,** and **Townshend,** as well as ski destinations like **Stratton** and **Ludlow** (home to Okemo Resort).

Central Vermont is characterized by the rugged Green Mountains, which run north–south through the center of the state, and the gently rolling dairy lands east of Lake Champlain. It's home to the state's capital, **Montpelier,** the former mill towns of **Quechee** and **Middlebury,** artist enclaves like **Brandon,** and beautiful towns like **Norwich** and **Woodstock,** and plucky **Rutland.** Ski buffs flock to **Killington** and **Waitsfield** and **Warren** (for Mad River Glen and Sugarbush).

Northern Vermont is a place of contrasts. It's where you'll find the area known as the Northeast Kingdom, a refuge for nature lovers and those who love getting away from it all, as well as the state's largest city, **Burlington,** which has dramatic views of Lake Champlain and the Adirondacks, and it's neighboring **Winooski.** There's plenty of skiing in **Stowe, Jeffersonville** (Smugglers' Notch Resort), and **Jay** (Jay Peak) as well as outdoor adventures in **Lake Willoughby** and **East Burke.** And postcard-perfect scenery oozes in **Shelburne, Charlotte, Montgomery,** and the **Lake Champlain Islands.**

Planning

There are many ways to take advantage of Vermont's beauty: skiing or hiking its mountains, biking or driving its back roads, fishing or sailing its waters, shopping for local products, visiting museums and sights, or simply finding the perfect inn and never leaving the front porch.

Getting Here and Around

Distances are relatively short, yet the mountains and back roads will slow a traveler's pace. You can see a representative north–south cross section of Vermont in a few days; if you have up to a week, you can really hit the highlights.

AIR
American, Delta, JetBlue, Porter, and United fly into Burlington International Airport. Rutland State Airport has daily service to and from Boston on Cape Air.

BOAT
Lake Champlain Ferries
This company operates ferries on three routes between Vermont and New York: from Grand Isle to Plattsburgh, New York; Burlington to Port Kent; and Charlotte to Essex. ☎ 802/864–9804 ⊕ www.ferries.com ☉ No Burlington–Port Kent service late Sept.–mid-June.

CAR
Vermont is divided by a mountainous north–south middle, with a main highway on either side: scenic U.S. 7 on the western side and Interstate 91 (which begins in New Haven, Connecticut, and runs through Hartford, central Massachusetts, and along the Connecticut River in Vermont to the Canadian border) on the east. Interstate 89 runs from New Hampshire across central Vermont from White River Junction to Burlington and up to the Canadian border. For current road conditions, check ⊕ www.511vt.com or call ☎ 511 in Vermont and ☎ 800/429–7623 from other states.

TRAIN
Amtrak
Amtrak has daytime service on the *Vermonter,* linking Washington, D.C., and New York City with Brattleboro, Bellows Falls, Windsor, White River Junction, Randolph, Montpelier, Waterbury, Essex Junction, and St. Albans. Amtrak's *Ethan Allen Express* connects New York City with Castleton and Rutland. ☎ 800/872–7245 ⊕ www.amtrak.com.

Hotels

Vermont's relatively rare large chain hotels are mostly found in Burlington, Manchester, and Rutland; elsewhere it's primarily inns, B&Bs, and small motels. The inns and B&Bs, some of them quite luxurious, provide what many visitors consider the quintessential Vermont lodging experience. Most areas have traditional ski-base condos; at these you sacrifice charm for ski-and-stay deals and proximity to the lifts. Lodging rates are highest during foliage season, late September–mid-October, and lowest in late spring and November, although many properties close during these times. Winter is high season at ski resorts. *Hotel reviews have been shortened. For full reviews visit Fodors.com.*

Restaurants

Everything that makes Vermont good and wholesome is distilled in its restaurants. Many of them belong to the **Vermont Fresh Network** (⊕ *www.vermontfresh. net*), a partnership that encourages chefs to create menus emphasizing Vermont's wonderful bounty; especially in summer and early fall, the produce and meats are impeccable.

Great chefs come to Vermont for the quality of life, and the Montpelier-based New England Culinary Institute is a recruiting ground for new talent. Seasonal menus use local fresh herbs and vegetables along with native game. Look for imaginative approaches to New England foods like maple syrup (Vermont is the largest U.S. producer); dairy products (cheese in particular); native fruits and berries; heritage apples (explore the ever-growing cider scene); and regional game like venison, quail, and pheasant. Small-batch goods, from salsa to caramels, are made with Vermont ingredients. Beer has become yet another claim to fame in Vermont, thanks to more breweries per capita than any other state and recognition far and wide. Indeed, craft brewers as far away as Poland are now producing "Vermont-style" IPAs, and Hill Farmstead in Greensboro has been dubbed the best brewery in the world seven times by RateBeer, a brew-review website, since opening doors in 2010.

Your chances of finding a table for dinner vary with the season: lengthy waits are common in tourist centers at peak times—a reservation is always advisable.

Creemee vs. Soft-Serve

A creemee is Vermont's answer to soft-serve ice cream. It often has a higher fat content than typical soft-serve—thanks in part to state specialties like local dairy and maple syrup—making it especially rich, silky and, well, creamy. (Hence the name.)

Restaurant reviews have been shortened. For full reviews visit Fodors.com.

What it Costs in U.S. Dollars			
$	$$	$$$	$$$$
RESTAURANTS			
under $18	$18–$24	$25–$35	over $35
HOTELS			
under $200	$200–$299	$300–$399	over $399

Tours

Inn to Inn
TOUR—SPORTS | This company arranges guided and self-guided hiking, skiing, snowshoeing, and biking trips from inn to inn in Vermont. ✉ *52 Park St., Brandon* ☎ *802/247–3300* ⊕ *www.inntoinn.com* 🎫 *From $645.*

P.O.M.G. Bike Tours of Vermont
TOUR—SPORTS | The initials in this outfitter's name are short for "Peace Of Mind Guaranteed." The company leads weekend and multiday bike tours around the state. ☎ *802/434–2270, 888/635–2453* ⊕ *www.pomgbike.com* 🎫 *From $1995.*

VBT Bicycling and Walking Vacations
TOUR—SPORTS | This global guide company leads bike tours in Vermont and Maine.

☎ 800/245–3868 ⊕ www.vbt.com
✉ From $1795.

Visitor Information

CONTACTS Ski Vermont/Vermont Ski Areas Association. ☎ 802/223–2439 ⊕ www.skivermont.com. **Vermont Department of Tourism and Marketing.** ☎ 802/828–3237, 800/837–6668 ⊕ www.vermontvacation.com. **Vermont Foliage Hotline.** ☎ 802/828–3239 for foliage information. **Vermont's Northeast Kingdom.** ☎ 802/626–8511 ⊕ getnekedvt.com.

When to Go

In summer Vermont is lush and green, and in winter the hills and towns are blanketed white with snow, inspiring skiers to challenge the peaks at Stowe and elsewhere. Fall, however, is always the most amazing time to come. If you have never seen the state's kaleidoscope of autumn colors, it's well worth braving the slow-moving traffic and shelling out a few extra bucks for lodging. The only time things really slow down is during "stick season" in November, when the leaves have fallen but there's no snow yet, and "mud season" in late spring, when even innkeepers counsel guests to come another time. Activities in the Champlain Islands essentially come to a halt in the winter, except for ice fishing and snowmobiling, and two of the biggest attractions, Shelburne Farms and the Shelburne Museum, are closed mid-October–April. Otherwise, Vermont is open for business year-round.

Brattleboro

60 miles south of White River Junction.

Brattleboro has drawn political activists and earnest counterculturists since the 1960s. The arts-oriented town and environs (population 12,000) remains politically and culturally active; after Burlington, this is Vermont's most offbeat locale.

GETTING HERE AND AROUND
Brattleboro is near the intersection of Route 9, the principal east–west highway also known as the Molly Stark Byway, and Interstate 91. For downtown, take Exit 2 from Interstate 91.

ESSENTIALS
VISITOR INFORMATION Brattleboro Area Chamber of Commerce. ☎ 802/254–4565, 877/254–4565 ⊕ www.brattleborochamber.org.

Sights

Brattleboro Museum and Art Center
MUSEUM | Downtown is the hub of Brattleboro's art scene, at the forefront of which is this museum in historic Union Station. It presents changing exhibitions of works by local, national, and international artists, and hosts lectures, readings, and musical performances. ✉ 10 Vernon St. ☎ 802/257–0124 ⊕ www.brattleboromuseum.org ✉ $8 ☉ Closed Tues.

Putney
TOWN | Nine miles upriver, this town of fewer than 3,000 residents—the country cousin of bustling Brattleboro—is a haven for writers and fine-craft artists. There are many pottery studios to visit, the requisite general store, and a few orchards. Each November during the Putney Craft Tour, dozens of artisans open their studios and homes for live demonstrations and plenty of fun. ✉ Putney ⊕ www.discoverputney.com.

Restaurants

Cai's Dim Sum Catering
$ | **CHINESE** | The sourcing and gathering of local ingredients at the heart of chef-owner Cai Xi Silver's cooking is inspired by the food memories of her childhood in Chongqin, China. Her

Southern Vermont

family's Sichuan and Shanghai influences come to life in a to-go menu that includes delicate steamed buns, perfect dumplings, and abundance boxes highlighting regional home cooking backed by Vermont ingredients. **Known for:** steamed buns; assorted seasonal dumplings; abundance boxes with local vegetables, rice, chicken, or tofu. $ *Average main: $15* ⊠ *814 Western Ave.* ☎ *802/257-7898* ⊕ *dimsumvt.com..*

★ Peter Havens

$$$ | AMERICAN | A longtime Brattleboro favorite helmed since 2012 by chef Zachary Corbin, this chic little bistro is known for impeccably presented cuisine that draws heavily on local sources. One room is painted a warm red, another in sage, and a changing lineup of contemporary paintings adorns the walls of both rooms. **Known for:** pan-roasted duck breast; cocktail and wine list; vanilla bean crème brûlée. $ *Average main: $30* ⊠ *32 Elliot St.* ☎ *802/257-3333* ⊕ *www.peterhavens.com* ⊙ *Closed Mon. and Tues. No lunch Sun., Wed., and Thurs. Nov.–May.*

Three Stones Mexican Mayan Cocina

$ | MEXICAN | FAMILY | This cozy, family-owned restaurant is inspired by centuries of passed-down recipes from the ancient Maya, where three stones were traditionally laid to build the hearth. Dishes are infused with the culture of the Mexican state Yucutàn, and fresh tortillas are made daily alongside tamales, empanadas, and vibrant platters of rice, beans, and vegetables. **Known for:** tamales wrapped in banana leaves with achiote sauce and chicken; daily-made fresh tortillas in three authentic preparations; pumpkin seed specialty/Onzicil (toasted ground pumpkin seeds served with

salad, rice and beans). $ *Average main:*
$15 ✉ *105 Canal St.* ☎ *802/246–1035*
⊕ *threestonesrestaurant.com* ☾ *Closed*
Sun.–Tues.

Top of the Hill Grill

$ | **BARBECUE** | **FAMILY** | Don't let the dimin-
utive size of this roadside smokehouse
deceive you. The place produces big
flavors locals line up for: hickory-smoked
ribs, apple-smoked turkey, beef brisket,
and pulled pork, to name a few. **Known
for:** "burnt ends" (brisket burnt ends);
excellent view of West River; outdoor
deck. $ *Average main: $15* ✉ *632 Putney*
Rd. ☎ *802/258–9178* ⊕ *www.topofthehill-*
grill.com ☾ *Closed Nov.–Mar.*

Whetstone Station Restaurant and Brewery

$ | **INTERNATIONAL** | One of Brattleboro's
most happening hangouts is this
nano-brewery and restaurant perched
over the Connecticut River. The beer
and classic American comfort food are
good, but it's the view of the river and its
forested banks that drops jaws. **Known
for:** rooftop beer garden; "Big 'Stoner"
imperial IPA; poutine and steak tips.
$ *Average main: $16* ✉ *36 Bridge St.*
☎ *802/490–2354* ⊕ *www.whetstonesta-*
tion.com.

Coffee and Quick Bites

★ Chelsea Royal Diner

$ | **DINER** | **FAMILY** | Built into a vintage
1938 Worcester diner, one of the few
remaining in the country, the Chelsea
Royal Diner serves all-day breakfast and
Blue Plate specials from produce (eggs
included) sourced from their backyard
farm. Save room for homemade ice
cream made with local milk and cream
from the St. Albans Co-op Creamery—flavors range from VT Maple Cream to Blueberry, Pumpkin, and Mocha Malted Milk
Ball. **Known for:** homemade ice cream and
soft serve; all-Day Breakfast; Blue Plate
Specials, like Friday Fish Fry and Sunday
Yankee Pot Roast. $ *Average main: $13*

✉ *487 Marlboro Rd.* ☎ *802/254–8399*
⊕ *www.chelsearoyaldiner.com.*

Mocha Joe's Cafe

$ | **CAFÉ** | The team at this spot for coffee
and conversation takes great pride in
sourcing direct-trade beans from places
like Kenya, Ethiopia, and Guatemala,
and pairs them with an assortment
of cookies, cakes, and muffins. This is
ground zero for Brattleboro's bohemian
contingent and fellow travelers. **Known
for:** socially conscious coffee; maple latte;
trendy clientele. $ *Average main: $5*
✉ *82 Main St., at Elliot St.* ☎ *802/257–*
7794 ⊕ *www.mochajoes.com.*

Hotels

Hickory Ridge House

$$ | **B&B/INN** | The historic redbrick 1808
Federal-style mansion strikes a sturdy
pose on a wide meadow of a former
sheep farmhouse. **Pros:** surrounded by
hundreds of acres of preserved land;
historic property; great for hiking and
cross-country skiing. **Cons:** not with-
in walking distance of town; lots of
flowered upholstery, rugs, and curtains;
two-night minimum during peak periods.
$ *Rooms from: $255* ✉ *53 Hickory Ridge*
Rd., Putney ✛ *11 miles north of Brattle-*
boro ☎ *802/387–5709, 800/380–9218*
⊕ *www.hickoryridgehouse.com* ⇄ *8*
rooms ⦿ *Free breakfast.*

★ The Inn on Putney Road

$$ | **B&B/INN** | Thoughtful and comforting
details abound in this 1931 French-style
manse such as the mini-refrigerator and
basket stocked with complimentary
soda, water, granola bars, and snacks,
as well as gas fireplaces in several guest
rooms. **Pros:** lovely breakfast room; nice
blend of traditional and modern design;
pottery by artist Steven Procter scattered
throughout. **Cons:** tight parking; outside
downtown; rooms in front sometimes
suffer traffic noise. $ *Rooms from: $239*
✉ *192 Putney Rd.* ☎ *802/536–4780*

⊕ *www.vermontbandbinn.com* ⇌ *6 rooms* |◎| *Free breakfast.*

Latchis Hotel
$ | **HOTEL** | Though not lavish, the guest rooms in this 1938 art deco building have the original sinks and tiling in the bathrooms, and many overlook Main Street, with New Hampshire's mountains in the background. **Pros:** heart-of-town location; lots of personality; reasonable rates. **Cons:** limited breakfast; sound-masking machines sometimes required; few parking spots. ⑤ *Rooms from: $130* ⊠ *50 Main St.* ☎ *802/254–6300, 800/798–6301* ⊕ *www.latchishotel.com* ⇌ *33 rooms* |◎| *Free breakfast.*

Performing Arts

Latchis Theatre
THEMED ENTERTAINMENT | This movie theater's architecture represents a singular blending of art deco and Greek Revival style, complete with statues, columns, and 1938 murals by Louis Jambor (1884–1955), a noted artist and children's book illustrator. The Latchis hosts art exhibits, streams live events, and has four screening rooms. For a sense of the theater's original grandeur, buy a ticket for whatever is showing on the big screen. Though the space may not be a state-of-the-art cinema, watching a film here is far more memorable than at any multiplex. ⊠ *50 Main St.* ☎ *802/254–6300, 800/798–6301* ⊕ *www.latchis.com.*

Activities

BIKING
Brattleboro Bicycle Shop
BICYCLING | This shop rents hybrid bikes (call ahead to reserve one), does repair work, and sells maps and equipment. ⊠ *165 Main St.* ☎ *802/254–8644, 800/272–8245* ⊕ *www.bratbike.com.*

CANOEING AND KAYAKING
Vermont Canoe Touring Center
CANOEING/ROWING/SKULLING | Canoes and kayaks are available for rent here. Payment is by cash or check only. ⊠ *451 Putney Rd.* ☎ *802/257–5008* ⊕ *www. vermontcanoetouringcenter.com.*

HIKING
Fort Dummer State Park
PARK—SPORTS-OUTDOORS | You can hike and camp within the 217 acres of forest at this state park, the location of the first permanent European settlement in Vermont. That site is now submerged beneath the Connecticut River, but it is viewable from the northernmost scenic vista on Sunrise Trail. ⊠ *517 Old Guilford Rd.* ☎ *802/254–2610* ⊕ *www. vtstateparks.com/fortdummer.html* ⑤ *$4* ⊙ *Facilities closed early Sept.–late May.*

MULTISPORT OUTFITTERS
Burrows Specialized Sports
BICYCLING | This full-service sporting goods store rents and sells bicycles, snowboards, skis, and snowshoes, and has a repair shop. ⊠ *105 Main St.* ☎ *802/254–9430* ⊕ *www.burrowssports. com.*

Sam's Outdoor Outfitters
LOCAL SPORTS | At this labyrinthine two-story sports emporium you can find outerwear, shoes, and gear for all seasons and activities. Grab a bag of free popcorn while you're shopping. ⊠ *74 Main St.* ☎ *802/254–2933* ⊕ *www. samsoutfitters.com.*

Wilmington

18 miles west of Brattleboro.

The village of Wilmington, with its classic Main Street lined with 18th- and 19th-century buildings, anchors the Mt. Snow Valley. Most of the valley's lodging and dining establishments, however, can be found along Route 100, which travels 5 miles north to West Dover and

Mt. Snow, where skiers flock on winter weekends. The area abounds with cultural activity from concerts to art exhibits year-round.

GETTING HERE AND AROUND
Wilmington is at the junction of Route 9 and Route 100. West Dover and Mt. Snow are a few miles to the north along Route 100.

ESSENTIALS
VISITOR INFORMATION Southern Vermont Deerfield Valley Chamber of Commerce.
☎ *802/464–8092, 877/887–6884 ⊕ www. visitvermont.com.*

Sights

Molly Stark State Park
NATIONAL/STATE PARK | FAMILY | The park is known for its great camping (there are two loops) and popular snowshoe trails, and there's a picnic pavilion. The Molly Stark Heritage Trail runs through this area, known as a scenic bypass. There is a 1.7-mile loop hike to the fire tower atop Mt. Olga that culminates in a 360-degree view of southern Vermont and northern Massachusetts. ⊠ *705 Rte. 9 E* ☎ *802/464–5460 ⊕ www.vtstateparks. com/mollystark.html.*

Coffee and Quick Bites

Butter Mountain Bakery
$ | BAKERY | Chewy homemade bagels, craggy loaves of sourdough, and brown butter maple cookies are just a handful of the offerings waiting at this tucked away hidden gem. Keep an eye out for seasonal specials like fresh fruit galettes and walnut-studded chocolate brownies—the menu is always changing. **Known for:** crusty loaves of sourdough; seasonal galettes, like strawberry-basil; snickerdoodle cookies. ⑤ *Average main: $5* ⊠ *1 School St.* ☎ *802/780–0232.*

Who Was Molly Stark?

In the heart of Wilmington beside the Crafts Inn stands a sculpture in honor of Molly Stark, the wife of the Revolutionary War general John Stark. The general was said to have roused his troops in the Battle of Bennington, vowing victory over the British: "They are ours, or this night Molly Stark sleeps a widow!" He lived, and hence the victory path across Vermont (now Route 9) is called the Molly Stark Trail (or Byway).

Hotels

Deerhill Inn
$ | B&B/INN | The restaurant at this quintessential New England inn is among the best in town. **Pros:** complimentary house-baked cookies; some rooms have whirlpool tubs; toiletries by L'Occitane. **Cons:** must drive to Mt. Snow and town; traditional flowered wallpaper and upholstery in spots; two-night minimum required for weekends. ⑤ *Rooms from: $165* ⊠ *14 Valley View Rd., West Dover* ☎ *802/464–3100, 800/993–3379 ⊕ www. deerhillinn.com* ⌁ *13 rooms* ⊚ *Free breakfast.*

Grand Summit Hotel
$$$ | RESORT | FAMILY | Mt. Snow's comfortable main hotel is an easy choice for skiers whose main priority is getting on the slopes as quickly as possible. **Pros:** easy ski access; lots of children's activities; fitness center. **Cons:** somewhat bland decor; can be busy and crowded; resort fee. ⑤ *Rooms from: $380* ⊠ *39 Mt. Snow Rd., West Dover* ☎ *800/451–4211 ⊕ www.mountsnow.com* ⌁ *196 rooms* ⊚ *No meals.*

🏃 Activities

Molly Stark State Park is home to some of the state's most popular snowshoe trails. Mount Olga Trail is a relatively easy 1.7-mile loop culminating in a 360-degree view of southern Vermont and northern Massachusetts.

SKIING

Mount Snow

SKIING/SNOWBOARDING | The closest major ski area to all of the Northeast's big cities, Mt. Snow prides itself on its hundreds of snowmaking fan guns—more than any other resort in North America. There are four major downhill areas. The main mountain comprises mostly intermediate runs, while the north face has the majority of expert runs. The south face, Sunbrook, has wide, sunny trails. It connects to Carinthia, which is dedicated to terrain parks and glade skiing. In summer, the 600-acre resort has an 18-hole golf course, 11.3 miles of lift-serviced mountain-bike trails, and an extensive network of hiking trails. In 2018, the resort debuted a brand-new, $22 million, 42,000-square-foot Carinthia Base Lodge, five times the size of the previous lodge. **Facilities:** 86 trails; 600 acres; 1,700-foot vertical drop; 20 lifts. ⊠ *39 Mt. Snow Rd., West Dover* ☎ *802/464–3333, 802/464–2151 for snow conditions, 800/245–7669* ⊕ *www.mountsnow.com* ⛷ *Lift ticket: $110.*

Timber Creek

SKIING/SNOWBOARDING | North of Mt. Snow, this appealingly small cross-country skiing and snowshoeing center has 4½ miles of groomed loops. You can rent equipment and take lessons here. ⊠ *13 Tanglewood Rd., at Rte. 100, West Dover* ☎ *802/464–0999* ⊕ *www.timbercreekxc.com* ⛷ *$20.*

Bennington

21 miles west of Wilmington.

Bennington is the commercial focus of Vermont's southwest corner and home to Bennington College. It's really three towns in one: Downtown Bennington, Old Bennington, and North Bennington. Downtown has retained much of the industrial character it developed in the 19th century, when paper mills, gristmills, and potteries formed the city's economic base. The outskirts of town are commercial and not worth a stop, so make your way right into Downtown and Old Bennington to appreciate the area's true charm.

GETTING HERE AND AROUND

The heart of modern Bennington is the intersection of U.S. 7 and Route 9. Old Bennington is a couple of miles west on Route 9, at Monument Avenue. North Bennington is a few miles north on Route 67A.

ESSENTIALS

VISITOR INFORMATION Bennington Area Chamber of Commerce. ☎ *802/447–3311* ⊕ *www.bennington.com.*

⊙ Sights

Bennington Battle Monument

MEMORIAL | FAMILY | This 306-foot stone obelisk with an elevator to the top commemorates General John Stark's Revolutionary War victory over the British, who attempted to capture Bennington's stockpile of supplies. Inside the monument you can learn all about the battle, which took place near Walloomsac Heights in New York State on August 16, 1777, and helped bring about the surrender of British commander "Gentleman Johnny" Burgoyne two months later. The top of the tower affords commanding views of the Massachusetts Berkshires, the New York Adirondacks, and the Vermont Green

The poet Robert Frost is buried in Bennington at the Old First Church.

Mountains. ✉ *15 Monument Circle, Old Bennington* ☎ *802/447–0550* ⊕ *www.benningtonbattlemonument.com* ✉ *$5* ⊗ *Closed Nov.–Apr.*

Bennington College

COLLEGE | Contemporary stone sculpture and white-frame neo-Colonial dorms surrounded by acres of cornfields punctuate the green meadows of the placid campus of Bennington College. ✉ *1 College Dr., off U.S. 7, North Bennington* ☎ *802/442–5401* ⊕ *www.bennington.edu.*

★ Bennington Museum

MUSEUM | The rich collections here feature military artifacts, early tools, dolls, and the Bennington Flag, one of the oldest of the Stars and Stripes in existence. Other areas of interest include early Bennington pottery, the Gilded Age in Vermont, mid-20th-century modernist painters who worked in or near Bennington, glass and metalwork by Lewis Comfort Tiffany, and photography, watercolors, and other works on paper. The highlight for many visitors, though, is the largest public collection of works by Grandma Moses (1860–1961), the popular self-taught artist who lived and painted in the area. ✉ *75 Main St., Old Bennington* ☎ *802/447–1571* ⊕ *www.benningtonmuseum.org* ✉ *$10* ⊗ *Closed Jan.; Wed. Feb.–May.*

Lake Shaftsbury State Park

NATIONAL/STATE PARK | **FAMILY** | You'll find a swimming beach, nature trails, boat and canoe rentals, and a snack bar at this pretty park. ✉ *262 Shaftsbury State Park Rd., 10½ miles north of Bennington* ☎ *802/375–9978* ⊕ *www.vtstateparks.com/shaftsbury.html* ⊗ *Facilities closed early Sept.–mid-May.*

Old Bennington

HISTORIC SITE | West of downtown, this National Register Historic District is well endowed with stately Colonial and Victorian mansions. The site of the Catamount Tavern, where Ethan Allen organized the Green Mountain Boys to capture Ft. Ticonderoga in 1775, is marked by a bronze statue of Vermont's indigenous mountain lion, now extinct. ✉ *Monument Ave., Old Bennington.*

The Old First Church

CEMETERY | In the graveyard of this church, the tombstone of the poet Robert Frost proclaims, "I had a lover's quarrel with the world." ⊠ *1 Monument Circle, at Monument Ave., Old Bennington* ☎ *802/447–1223* ⊕ *www. oldfirstchurchbenn.org* ⊠ *Free.*

Park-McCullough House

HOUSE | The architecturally significant Park-McCullough House is a 35-room classic French Empire–style mansion, built in 1865 and furnished with period pieces. Several restored flower gardens grace the landscaped grounds, and a barn holds some antique carriages. Guided tours happen on the hour while the house is open. The grounds are open daily year-round. ⊠ *1 Park St., at West St., North Bennington* ☎ *802/442–5441* ⊕ *www.parkmccullough.org* ⊠ *$15* ⊙ *Closed Oct.–May; Mon.–Thurs. June–Sept.*

Robert Frost Stone House Museum

HOUSE | Robert Frost came to Shaftsbury in 1920, he wrote, "to plant a new Garden of Eden with a thousand apple trees of some unforbidden variety." The museum, now part of Bennington College, tells the story of the poet's life and highlights the nine years (1920–29) he spent living in the house with his wife and four children. It was here that he penned "Stopping by Woods on a Snowy Evening" and published two books of poetry. You can wander 7 of the Frost family's original 80 acres. Among the apple boughs you just might find inspiration of your own. ⊠ *121 Historic Rte. 7A, Shaftsbury* ☎ *802/447–6200* ⊕ *www. bennington.edu* ⊠ *$10* ⊙ *Closed Mon., Tues., and Nov.–Apr. also Sun. in May.*

Woodford State Park

PARK—SPORTS-OUTDOORS | **FAMILY** | At 2,400 feet, this has the highest state campground in Vermont. Adams Reservoir is the dominant feature and focus of activities, with swimming, fishing, and boating, including canoes, kayaks, and paddleboards for rent. A nature trail also circles the reservoir. ⊠ *142 State Park Rd.* ✛ *10 miles east of Bennington* ☎ *802/447-7169* ⊕ *www.vtstateparks. com/woodford.html* ⊙ *Facilities closed mid-Oct.–mid-May.*

Restaurants

Harvest Brewing

$ | **MEXICAN FUSION** | This nanobrewery in the heart of downtown Bennington is a haven of rich IPAs glowing with New England-style haze and inventive brews like chai-spiced stout. All of these beers become the perfect palate cleansers for good pub fare like loaded nachos and stuffed enchiladas. **Known for:** hazy IPAs; hearty Mexican-inspired pub fare; seasonal brews from smooth stouts to crisp lagers. ⑤ *Average main: $8* ⊠ *201 South St.* ☎ *802/430–9915.*

Madison Brewing Company

$$ | **BURGER** | Since opening in the 1990s as the area's first brewpub, this enclave of exposed brick and bubbling brewing tanks has become a watering hole for fresh IPAs and stacked burgers. A full bar and myriad pub fare offer plenty of reasons to elbow up to the wraparound bar. **Known for:** craft beer on draft; classic New England–style pub fare; gourmet burgers. ⑤ *Average main: $21* ⊠ *428 Main St.* ☎ *802/442–7397.*

Pangaea/Lounge

$$$ | **AMERICAN** | This rustic-chic restaurant comes with two faces: the classy, casual "Lounge" on one side that turns out tuned-up, locally sourced versions of bistro classics; and a full-blown, fine-dining experience on the "Pangaea" side. The latter is the more memorable, with gussied-up and coiffed waiters guiding you through a three-course meal of French-influenced American cuisine. **Known for:** extensive wine list; roasted Long Island duck; Vermont boar and Brie Wellington. ⑤ *Average main: $31* ⊠ *1 Prospect St., 3 miles* north of Bennington, North Bennington ☎ 802/442–7171 ⊕ www.vermontfinedining.com ⊗ No lunch.

Coffee and Quick Bites

Bakkerij Krijnen

$ | DUTCH | Some of the flakiest and most delectable pastries in Vermont can be ordered at this Dutch bakery helmed by husband-and-wife team Hans and Jennifer Krijne. Everything is made from scratch and uses local, organic, and all-natural ingredients—and tastes that way. **Known for:** artisanal breads; Douwe Egberts Dutch coffee; homemade stroopwafels. ⑤ *Average main: $10* ⊠ *1001 Main St.* ☎ *802/ 442–1001.*

🛏 Hotels

The Eddington House Inn

$ | B&B/INN | In the heart of North Bennington, just around the corner from three covered bridges and Bennington College, this impeccably maintained, 18th-century three-bedroom house is a great value. **Pros:** budget prices for a great B&B; "endless desserts" in dining room 24 hours a day; summer guest passes to Lake Paran. **Cons:** slightly off usual tourist track; only three rooms so it fills up fast; no front desk or after-hours reception. ⑤ *Rooms from: $159* ⊠ *21 Main St., North Bennington* ☎ *802/442–1511* ⊕ *www.eddingtonhouseinn.com* ⤳ *3 suites* ⭑⭕⭒ *Free breakfast.*

⭐ Four Chimneys Inn

$ | B&B/INN | This exquisite, three-story, neo-Georgian (circa 1915) looks out over a substantial lawn and a wonderful old stone wall. **Pros:** walking distance to several Bennington sights; a complimentary full country breakfast; extremely well kept. **Cons:** dinner only offered for special events; no coffee or tea in rooms; a bit stuffy. ⑤ *Rooms from: $189* ⊠ *21 West Rd., Old Bennington* ☎ *802/447–3500* ⊕ *www.fourchimneys.com* ⤳ *11 rooms* ⭕⭒ *Free breakfast.*

Billboardless Vermont

Did you know that there are no billboards in Vermont? The state banned them in 1967 (similar laws exist in Maine, Alaska, and Hawaii), and the last one came down in 1975, so when you look out your window, you see trees and other scenery—not advertisements.

The Hardwood Hill

$ | HOTEL | Built in 1937, this fully renovated roadside motel has been given a distinct artsy, boutique upgrade by a foursome of new owners, three of whom are working artists, which translates into a sculpture garden out front, regular workshops by a resident artist, and performances on the red stage on the vast, hammock-dappled back lawn. **Pros:** excellent restaurant right next door; good value for cost; "arts package" includes tickets and discounts at local sights. **Cons:** must drive to town; rooms somewhat small; no restaurant or dining area. ⑤ *Rooms from: $99* ⊠ *864 Harwood Hill Rd.* ☎ *802/442–6278* ⊕ *www.harwoodhillmotel.com* ⤳ *17 rooms* ⭕⭒ *Free breakfast.*

🎭 Performing Arts

Basement Music Series

MUSIC | The Vermont Arts Exchange sponsors this fun and funky contemporary music series at the downtown Masonic Lodge. Some performances sell out, so it's wise to purchase tickets in advance. ⊠ *504 Main St.* ☎ *800/838–3006 for ticket hotline* ⊕ *www.vtartxchange.org/music.*

Oldcastle Theatre Company

MUSIC | This fine regional theater company focuses on American classics and crowd-pleasing musicals. The group's

Vermont Maple Syrup

Vermont is the country's largest producer of maple syrup. A visit to a maple farm is a great way to learn all about sugaring, the process of extracting maple tree sap and making syrup. Sap is stored in a sugar maple tree's roots in the winter, and in the spring when conditions are just right, the sap runs up and can be tapped. Sugaring season runs March to April, which is when all maple syrup in the state is produced.

One of the best parts of visiting a maple farm is getting to taste and compare the four grades of syrup. As the sugaring season goes on and days become warmer, the sap becomes progressively darker and stronger in flavor. Grades are defined by color, clarity, density, and flavor. Is one grade better than another? Nope, it's just a question of taste. Sap drawn early in the season produces the lightest color,

and has the most delicate flavor: this is called golden. Amber has a mellow flavor. Dark is much more robust, and Very Dark is the most flavorful, making it often the favorite of first-time tasters.

When visiting a maple farm, make sure they make their own syrup, as opposed to just bottling or selling someone else's. You'll learn more about the entire process that way. **Vermont Maple Syrup** (☎ 802/858–9444 ⊕ www.vermontmaple.org), a great resource, has a map of maple farms that host tours, a directory of producers open year-round, and a list of places from which you can order maple syrup by mail. You can also get the lowdown on events such as the annual Maple Open House Weekend, when sugarhouses throughout the state open their doors to visitors.

venue also hosts occasional concerts. ✉ *331 Main St.* ☎ *802/447–0564* ⊕ *www.oldcastletheatre.org* ⊗ *Closed Dec.–Mar.*

 ## Activities

HIKING
Long Trail

HIKING/WALKING | Four miles east of Bennington, the Long Trail crosses Route 9 and runs south to the top of Harmon Hill. Allot two or three hours for this steep hike. ✉ *Bennington.*

Arlington

15 miles north of Bennington.

Smaller than Bennington and more down-to-earth than upper-crust Manchester to the north, Arlington exudes

a certain Rockwellian folksiness, and it should: the illustrator Norman Rockwell lived here from 1939 to 1953, and many neighbors served as models for his portraits of small-town life.

GETTING HERE AND AROUND
Arlington is at the intersection of Route 313 and Route 7A. Take Route 313 West to reach West Arlington.

 ## Sights

West Arlington

TOWN | Norman Rockwell once lived in this place with a quaint town green. If you follow Route 313 west from Arlington, you'll pass by the Wayside Country Store, a slightly rickety charmer where you can pick up sandwiches and chat with locals. The store carries everything from ammo and sporting goods to toys, teas, and maple syrup. Continue on, and cross West Arlington's red covered bridge, which leads to the town green. To loop back to Route 7A, take River Road along the south side of the Battenkill River, a scenic drive. ⊠ *West Arlington.*

☕ Coffee and Quick Bites

Arlington Dairy Bar
$ | **AMERICAN** | **FAMILY** | The big red barn with a sprawling lawn and walk-up ice cream window is a quintessential summer snack shack. It's where paper boats holding cheeseburgers, loaded hot dogs, and lobster rolls make way for soft serve sundaes, stacked ice cream cones, and root beer floats. **Known for:** nostalgic snack bar atmosphere; ice-cream cones and sundaes; cheeseburgers and hot dogs. ⑤ *Average main: $5* ⊠ *3158 VT Rte 7A* ☎ *802/375–2546.*

Wayside Country Store
$ | **AMERICAN** | **FAMILY** | The motto of Arlington's one-stop-shop says it all: "If we don't have it, you don't need it!" This charming country store is known for carrying anything from toilet paper to boxed cocoa mix and boasts a popular deli complete with build-your-own sandwiches, prepared foods, and house-made specials like freshly baked biscuits. **Known for:** locally made goods; deli wraps and sandwiches; specialty prepared foods, from stuffed peppers to roasted chicken legs. ⑤ *Average main: $7* ⊠ *3307 VT Rte. 313 W* ☎ *802/375–2792.*

🛏 Hotels

The Arlington Inn
$ | **B&B/INN** | The Greek Revival columns of this 1847 home lend it an imposing presence in the middle of town, but the atmosphere within is friendly and old-fashioned. **Pros:** heart-of-town location; friendly atmosphere; rigorously eco-friendly. **Cons:** expensive dining; elegant but old-fashioned decor; no tea or coffee in rooms. ⑤ *Rooms from:*

$199 ⊠ *3904 Rte. 7A* ☎ *802/375–6532* ⊕ *www.arlingtoninn.com* ⌨ *17 rooms* ⦿ *Free breakfast.*

★ Hill Farm Inn
$$ | **B&B/INN** | **FAMILY** | Few hotels or inns in Vermont can match the sumptuous views of Mt. Equinox and surrounding hillscape of this former dairy farm built in 1830, whether seen from the large wraparound porch, the fire pit (where you can roast s'mores), or the outdoor hot tub. **Pros:** outdoor pool and hot tub; perfect Vermont wedding setting; Vermont Castings stoves in many rooms. **Cons:** books up on weekends with weddings; bringing alcohol not allowed; can be buggy in summer, like all Vermont. ⑤ *Rooms from: $235* ⊠ *458 Hill Farm Rd., off Rte. 7A, Sunderland* ☎ *802/375–2269* ⊕ *www. hillfarminn.com* ⌨ *12 rooms* ⦿ *Free breakfast.*

West Mountain Inn
$$ | **B&B/INN** | **FAMILY** | This 1810 farmhouse sits on 150 mountainside acres with hiking trails and easy access to the Battenkill River, where you can canoe or go tubing; in winter, guests can sled down a former ski slope or borrow snowshoes or cross-country skis. **Pros:** atmospheric Colonial dining room; lots of activities; wood-panel dining room with fireplace. **Cons:** dining room not ideal for kids; dirt road to property uneven and pitted; tiny bathrooms in some rooms. ⑤ *Rooms from: $205* ⊠ *144 W. Mountain Inn Rd., at Rte. 313* ☎ *802/375–6516* ⊕ *www.westmountaininn.com* ⌨ *20 rooms* ⦿ *Free breakfast.*

🛍 Shopping

Village Peddler
GIFTS/SOUVENIRS | **FAMILY** | This shop has a "chocolatorium," where you can learn all about cocoa. It sells fudge and other candies and stocks a large collection of teddy bears, one of whom is giant and made of chocolate. ⊠ *261 Old Mill Rd.,*

The formal gardens and mansion at Robert Todd Lincoln's Hildene are a far cry from his father's log cabin.

East Arlington ☎ 802/375–6037 ⊕ www. villagepeddlervt.com.

Manchester

9 miles northeast of Arlington.

Well-to-do Manchester has been a popular summer retreat since the mid-19th century, when city dwellers traveled north to take in the cool, clean air at the base of 3,840-foot Mt. Equinox. Manchester Village's tree-shaded marble sidewalks and stately old homes—Main Street here could hardly be more picture-perfect—reflect the luxurious resort lifestyle of more than a century ago. A mile north on Route 7A, Manchester Center is the commercial twin to Colonial Manchester Village; it's also where you'll find the town's famed upscale factory outlets doing business in attractive faux-Colonial shops.

Manchester Village houses the world headquarters of Orvis, the outdoor-goods brand that was founded here in the 19th

century and has greatly influenced the town ever since. The complex includes a fly-fishing school featuring lessons given in its casting ponds and the Battenkill River.

GETTING HERE AND AROUND
Manchester is the main town for the ski resorts of Stratton (a half-hour drive on Route 30) and Bromley (15 minutes to the northeast on Route 11). It's 15 minutes north of Arlington along scenic Route 7A.

ESSENTIALS
VISITOR INFORMATION Green Mountain National Forest Visitor Center. ⊠ *2538 Depot St.* ☎ *802/362–2307* ⊕ *www. fs.usda.gov/main/gmfl.* **Manchester Visitor Center.** ⊠ *4826 Main St.* ☎ ⊕ *www.manchestervermont.com.*

 Sights

American Museum of Fly Fishing
MUSEUM | This museum houses the world's largest collection of angling art and angling-related objects—more than

1,500 rods, 800 reels, 30,000 flies, including the tackle of Winslow Homer, Babe Ruth, Jimmy Carter, and other notables. Every August, vendors sell antique equipment at the museum's fly-fishing festival. You can also practice your casting out back. ☒ *4070 Main St.* ☎ *802/362–3300* ⊕ *www.amff.org* ✉ *$5* ⊘ *Closed Mon.; also Sun. Nov.–May.*

★ Hildene

GARDEN | FAMILY | A twofold treat, the summer home of Abraham Lincoln's son Robert provides insight into the lives of the Lincoln family, as well as an introduction to the lavish Manchester life of the early 1900s. In 1905, Robert built a 24-room Georgian Revival mansion where he and his descendants lived until 1975. It's the centerpiece of a beautifully preserved 412-acre estate and holds many of the family's prized possessions, including one of three surviving stovepipe hats owned by Abraham and a Lincoln Bible. When the 1,000-pipe Aeolian organ is played, the music reverberates as though from the mansion's very bones.

Rising from a 10-acre meadow, Hildene Farm is magnificent. The agriculture center is built in a traditional style—post-and-beam construction of timber felled and milled on the estate, and you can watch goat cheese being made.

The highlight, though, may be the elaborate formal gardens, where a thousand peonies bloom every June. There is also a teaching greenhouse, restored 1903 Pullman car, a 600-foot floating boardwalk across the Battenkill wetlands, and more than 12 miles of walking trails. When conditions permit, you can cross-country ski and snowshoe on the property. ☒ *1005 Hildene Rd., at Rte. 7A* ☎ *802/362–1788, 800/578–1788* ⊕ *www. hildene.org* ✉ *$23.*

★ Southern Vermont Arts Center

ARTS VENUE | At the end of a long, winding driveway, this center has a permanent collection of more than 800 19th- and 20th-century American artworks and presents temporary exhibitions. The original building, a Georgian mansion set on 100 acres, contains 12 galleries with works by more than 600 artists, many from Vermont. The center also hosts concerts, performances, and film screenings. In summer and fall, the views from the café at lunchtime are magnificent. ☒ *930 SVAC Dr., West Rd.* ☎ *802/362–1405* ⊕ *www.svac.org* ✉ *Free* ⊘ *Closed Mon. Nov.–May.*

🍴 Restaurants

Chantecleer

$$$$ | EUROPEAN | There is something wonderful about eating by candlelight in an old barn; and with the rooster art above their rough-hewn wooden beams, Chantecleer's dining rooms are especially romantic. The international menu runs the gamut from veal schnitzel to New York strip to Dover sole. **Known for:** great fieldstone fireplace; duck Grand Marnier; Thursday burger night at the bar. ⑤ *Average main: $38* ☒ *8 Reed Farm La., 3½ miles north of Manchester, East Dorset* ☎ *802/362–1616* ⊕ *www.chantecleer-restaurant.com* ⊘ *Closed Mon., Tues., mid-Nov., and mid-Apr. No lunch.*

Chop House

$$$$ | STEAKHOUSE | The marble above the fireplace is chiseled "L.L. ORVIS 1832," and way before that he claimed the spot, the Green Mountain Boys gathered here to plan their Revolutionary War–era resistance. **Known for:** New York strip; craft cocktails; tuna tartare. ⑤ *Average main: $47* ☒ *3567 Main St.* ☎ *802/362–4700* ⊕ *www.equinoxresort.com* ⊘ *No lunch.*

The Crooked Ram

$ | WINE BAR | Originally a tiny bottle shop when it opened doors in 2017, the Crooked Ram has since transformed into a cozy beer-and-wine bar with an expertly sourced market. It's now a destination for hyperlocal drafts, seasonal small plates, and brimming Vermont cheese boards, plus a thoughtful stock of unique ciders and natural wines to-go. **Known for:** drafts of local craft beer in stemmed beer glasses; award-winning Vermont cheeses and charcuterie; seasonal patio seating. $ *Average main: $15* ✉ *4026 Main St.* ☎ *802/231–1315* ⊕ *thecrookeddramvt.com* ⊗ *Closed Mon. and Tues.*

Mistral's at Toll Gate

$$$$ | **FRENCH** | This classic French restaurant is tucked in a grotto on the climb to Bromley Mountain. The two dining rooms are perched over the Bromley Brook, and at night a small waterfall is magically illuminated—ask for a window table. **Known for:** chateaubriand béarnaise; crispy sweetbreads Dijonnaise; wine list. $ *Average main: $36* ✉ *10 Toll Gate Rd., off Rte. 11/30* ☎ *802/362–1779* ⊕ *www.mistralsattollgate.com* ⊗ *Closed Tues. and Wed. No lunch.*

★ Moonwink

$ | **BURMESE** | May and Wes Stannard opened this counter-service spot in 2018, spotlighting May's native Burmese cooking in Wes's childhood hometown. In one of the best stops for Burmese fare on the East Coast, you'll find vibrant noodle bowls like *Nan Gyi Thoke* (thick round rice noodles with chicken curry), fermented tea leaf salad, and "Burma Bowls" with sprouted peas and chicken curry. **Known for:** oh no kuo swel (creamy coconut broth with vegetables or chicken served over egg noodles); la phat thok (Moonwink's take on the Burmese fermented tea leaf salad); mo hinga (a special fish stew with noodles served on Friday and Saturday only). $ *Average main: $13* ✉ *4479 Main St.* ☎ *802/768–8671* ⊗ *Closed Mon. and Tues.*

★ Mystic Cafe & Wine Bar

$$ | **ECLECTIC** | This spacious, brand-new, Euro-chic restaurant is earning plenty of local praise for its gussied-up takes on international cuisines with a Vermont-farmhouse accent. That means plenty of kale, butternut squash, sweet potato, and cheddar in the salads, sandwiches, and tapas-style shared plates. **Known for:** paella with Israeli couscous; French toast; wine list. $ *Average main: $20* ✉ *4928 Main St., Manchester Center* ☎ *802/768–8086* ⊕ *www.mystic-cafeandwinebar.com* ⊗ *Closed Mon. and Tues.*

Ponce Bistro

$$$ | **INTERNATIONAL** | The Spanish influence adds much to the charm of this small, atmospheric restaurant, as does a fireplace in the front room. No alcohol is served, but glasses are happily provided for any who bring their own beer and wine, and no corkage fee, to boot. **Known for:** Spanish meat loaf; sweet and savory crepes; homemade salad dressings. $ *Average main: $28* ✉ *4659 Main St., Mendon* ☎ *802/768–8095* ⊕ *www.ponce-bistro.com* ⊗ *No dinner Sun.–Wed.*

The Reluctant Panther Inn & Restaurant

$$$$ | **AMERICAN** | The dining room at this luxurious inn is a large, modern space where rich woods and high ceilings meld into a kind of "nouveau Vermont" aesthetic. The contemporary American cuisine emphasizes farm-to-table ingredients and has earned the restaurant "Gold Barn" honors from the Vermont Fresh Network. **Known for:** wine list; chef of the year award by the Vermont Chamber of Commerce; lobster-and-Brie fondue. $ *Average main: $37* ✉ *39 West Rd.* ☎ *800/822–2331, 802/362–2568* ⊕ *www.reluctantpanther.com* ⊗ *Closed Sun. No lunch.*

★ The Silver Fork at the Old Library

$$$ | **ECLECTIC** | This intimate, elegant bistro is owned by husband-and-wife team Mark and Melody French, who spent years in Puerto Rico absorbing the flavors of the island that are reflected in the eclectic international menu. After nine years in their original space on Main Street, in 2020 the couple moved their restaurant into the newly renovated, 123-year-old Skinner Library, fashioning a bartop from the 1897 wooden shelving. **Known for:** shrimp mofongo (with mashed

plantains); wine and cocktail list; special occasions. $ *Average main: $30* ✉ *48 West Rd.* ☎ *802/768–8444* ⊕ *www.thesil- verforkvt.com* ⊘ *Closed Sun. No lunch.*

Ye Olde Tavern

$$$ | AMERICAN | This circa-1790 Colonial inn dishes up Yankee favorites along with plenty of New England charm, made all the more intimate by the candlelight. To learn more about the colorful history of the building, simply ask the manager, who makes a regular appearance at tables. **Known for:** cheddar-and-ale onion soup; traditional pot roast; 1790 Taproom Ale (custom brew by Long Trail). $ *Average main: $26* ✉ *5183 Main St.* ☎ *802/362–0611* ⊕ *www.yeoldetavern. net.*

Coffee and Quick Bites

★ Mrs. Murphy's Donuts

$ | BAKERY | FAMILY | This locally beloved doughnut shop turns out fresh doughnuts daily from their small, white-clapboard storefront. Old-fashioned doughnuts come hot from the fryer in the wee hours of the morning, so arrive early for the best selection of flavors like cinnamon, maple cream, and cakey cider doughnuts loaded with warming spices. **Known for:** cinnamon raised; cider cake; sugar-dusted crullers. $ *Average main: $3* ✉ *374 Depot St.* ☎ *802/362–1874.*

Hotels

Equinox

$$$ | RESORT | In Manchester Village, nearly all life revolves around the historic Equinox Inn, whose fame and service have carved it into the Mt. Rushmore of accommodation in Vermont. **Pros:** fitness center and pool; excellent steak house on-site; extensive network of walking trails. **Cons:** somewhat corporate feel; lines at reception can make checking in and out take long; lots of weddings can sometimes overcrowd. $ *Rooms from: $391* ✉ *3567 Main St.* ☎ *802/362–4700,*

866/837–4219 ⊕ *www.equinoxresort. com* ⊷ *147 rooms* ⦿ *No meals.*

Taconic Hotel

$$$ | HOTEL | Vermont's only Kimpton, which opened in 2015, attempts to walk the fine line between its corporate boutique design and a Vermont flavor—the latter of which is distilled, quite literally, in The Copper Grouse, the hotel's on-site enclave of seasonal plates and craft cocktails. **Pros:** locally handmade walking sticks from Manchester Woodcraft in rooms; no additional fee for pets; the house restaurant, the Copper Grouse, does a good turn on American bistro cuisine, cocktails included. **Cons:** not very Vermonty experience; only chain's rewards members get free high-speed Internet/Wi-Fi; tiny pool. $ *Rooms from: $339* ✉ *3835 Main St.* ☎ *802/362–0147* ⊕ *www.taconichotel.com* ⊷ *87 rooms* ⦿ *No meals.*

★ Wilburton Inn

$$ | B&B/INN | Stepping into this hilltop 1902 Tudor-style mansion, you might think you've stumbled on a lavish film set: there's a palpably cinematic quality to the richly paneled guest rooms and the common rooms, which make an ideal setting for "murder-mystery weekends," "Innkeeper's Daughter Cabaret," and more quirky events. **Pros:** unique activities and adornments; easy access to Manchester; views of surrounding landscape. **Cons:** limited indoor facilities; lots of floral wallpaper and traditional frills; two-night minimum stay is required on most weekends. $ *Rooms from: $205* ✉ *257 Wilburton Dr.* ☎ *802/362–2500* ⊕ *www.wilburtoninn.com* ⊷ *40 rooms* ⦿ *Free breakfast.*

Nightlife

Falcon Bar

MUSIC CLUBS | This sophisticated bar has live music on weekends. In summer, don't miss the wonderful outdoor deck. In winter, the place to be is around the giant Vermont slate firepit. ⊠ *Equinox Resort, 3567 Main St.* ☎ *800/362–4747* ⊕ *www.equinoxresort.com.*

Union Underground

BARS/PUBS | One of Manchester's newest hot spots, this part underground, part aboveground pub and restaurant offers lots of space, a sleek green-marble bar, craft beer, a pool table, and tasty classics with all the fixings. ⊠ *4928 Main St., Manchester Center* ☎ *802/367–3951.*

 # Shopping

ART AND ANTIQUES

Long Ago & Far Away

ANTIQUES/COLLECTIBLES | This store specializes in fine indigenous artwork, including Inuit stone sculpture. ⊠ *Green Mountain Village Shops, 4963 Main St.* ☎ *802/362–3435* ⊕ *www.longagoandfaraway.com.*

Manchester Woodcraft

CRAFTS | The millions of trees in the Green Mountains make Vermont a wood-carver's dreamscape. The saws, planes, and scrapers of the woodshop here turn out a range of handsome household goods, plus a wide selection of pieces and parts for DIY fans. ⊠ *175 Depot St., Manchester Center* ☎ *802/362–5770* ⊕ *www.manchesterwoodcraft.com.*

Tilting at Windmills Gallery

ANTIQUES/COLLECTIBLES | This large gallery displays the paintings and sculptures of nationally known artists. ⊠ *24 Highland Ave., Manchester Center* ☎ *802/362–3022* ⊕ *www.tilting.com.*

BOOKS

Northshire Bookstore

BOOKS/STATIONERY | **FAMILY** | The heart of Manchester Center, this bookstore is adored by visitors and residents alike for its ambience, selection, and service. Up the iron staircase is a second floor dedicated to children's books, toys, and clothes. ⊠ *4869 Main St.* ☎ *802/362–2200, 800/437–3700* ⊕ *www.northshire.com.*

CLOTHING

Manchester Designer Outlets

CLOTHING | This is the most upscale collection of stores in northern New England—and every store is a discount outlet. The architecture reflects the surrounding homes, so the place looks a bit like a Colonial village. The long list of famous-brand clothiers here includes Kate Spade, Yves Delorme, Michael Kors, Ann Taylor, Tumi, BCBG, Armani, Coach, Polo Ralph Lauren, Brooks Brothers, and Theory. ⊠ *97 Depot St.* ☎ *802/362–3736, 800/955–7467* ⊕ *www.manchesterdesigneroutlets.com.*

Orvis Flagship Store

CLOTHING | The lodgelike Orvis store carries the company's latest clothing, fly-fishing gear, and pet supplies—there's even a trout pond. At this required shopping destination for many visitors—the Orvis name is pure Manchester—there are demonstrations of how fly rods are constructed and tested. You can attend fly-fishing school across the street. ⊠ *4180 Main St.* ☎ *802/362–3750* ⊕ *www.orvis.com.*

 # Activities

BIKING

Battenkill Bicycles

BICYCLING | This shop rents, sells, and repairs bikes and provides maps and route suggestions. ⊠ *99 Bonnet St.* ☎ *802/362–2734* ⊕ *battenkillbicycles.com.*

FISHING

Battenkill Anglers

FISHING | Teaching the art and science of fly-fishing, Battenkill Anglers offers both private and group lessons. ⊠ *6204 Main St.* ☎ *802/379–1444* ⊕ *www.battenkillangler.com.*

HIKING

There are bountiful hiking trails in the Green Mountain National Forest. Shorter hikes begin at the Equinox Resort, which owns about 1,000 acres of forest and has a great trail system open to the public.

Equinox Preserve

HIKING/WALKING | A multitude of well-groomed walking trails for all abilities thread the 914 acres on the slopes of Mt. Equinox, including a trail to the summit. ✉ *Multiple trailheads, End of West Union St.* ☎ *802/366–1400 Equinox Preservation Trust* ⊕ *www.equinoxpreservationtrust.org.*

Long Trail

HIKING/WALKING | One of the most popular segments of Vermont's Long Trail leads to the top of Bromley Mountain. The strenuous 5.4-mile round-trip takes about four hours. ✉ *Rte. 11/30* ⊕ *www.greenmountainclub.org.*

Lye Brook Falls

HIKING/WALKING | This 4.6-mile hike starts off Glen Road and ends at Vermont's most impressive cataract, Lye Brook Falls. The moderately strenuous journey takes four hours. ✉ *Off Glen Rd., south from E. Manchester Rd. just east of U.S. 7* ⊕ *www.greenmountainclub.org.*

Mountain Goat

HIKING/WALKING | Stop here for hiking, cross-country-skiing, and snowshoeing equipment (some of which is available to rent), as well as a good selection of warm clothing. ✉ *4886 Main St.* ☎ *802/362–5159* ⊕ *www.mountaingoat.com.*

SPAS

★ Spa at Equinox

SPA/BEAUTY | Some of Vermont's best spa treatments are found behind the mahogany doors and beadboard wainscoting of the Equinox Spa and are well worth the splurge. At one end are an indoor pool and outdoor hot tub; at the other end are the treatment rooms. The signature 100-minute Spirit of Vermont combines Reiki, reflexology, and massage, and will leave you feeling like a whole, complete person. The locker rooms feature steam rooms and saunas. Day passes are

available for all ages. ✉ *Equinox Resort, 3567 Rte. 7A* ☎ *802/362–4700, 800/362–4747* ⊕ *www.equinoxresort.com.*

Dorset

7 miles north of Manchester.

Lying at the foot of many mountains and with a village green surrounded by white clapboard homes and inns, Dorset has a solid claim to the title of Vermont's most picture-perfect town. Dorset has just 2,000 residents, but two of the state's best and oldest general stores.

The country's first commercial marble quarry opened here in 1785. Dozens more opened, providing the marble for the main research branch of the New York Public Library and many 5th Avenue mansions, among other notable landmarks, as well as the sidewalks here and in Manchester. A remarkable private home made entirely of marble can be seen on Dorset West Road, a beautiful residential road west of the town green. The marble Dorset Church on the green has two Tiffany stained-glass windows.

Sights

★ Dorset Quarry

BODY OF WATER | **FAMILY** | On hot summer days the sight of dozens of families jumping, swimming, and basking in the sun around this massive 60-foot-deep swimming hole makes it one of the most wholesome and picturesque recreational spots in the region. First mined in 1785, the stone from the country's oldest commercial marble quarry was used to build the main branch of the New York Public Library and the Montreal Museum of Fine Arts. ✉ *Rte. 30* ☎ *Free.*

Emerald Lake State Park

PARK—SPORTS-OUTDOORS | This park has a well-marked nature trail, a small beach, boat rentals, and a snack bar. ✉ *65 Emerald Lake La., East Dorset*

☎ *802/362–1655* ⊕ *www.vtstateparks. com/emerald.html* 🎟 *$4* ⊗ *Facilities closed mid-Oct.–mid-May.*

Merck Forest & Farmland Center
FARM/RANCH | FAMILY | This 3,162-acre educational center has 30 miles of nature trails for hiking, cross-country skiing, snowshoeing, horseback riding, and rustic camping. You can visit the 62-acre farm, which grows organic fruit and vege-tables (sold at the visitor center), and check out the horses, sheep, pigs, and chickens while you're there—you're even welcome to help out with the chores. ✉ *3270 Rte. 315, Rupert* ☎ *802/394– 7836* ⊕ *www.merckforest.org* 🎟 *Free.*

Restaurants

The Dorset Inn
$$$ | AMERICAN | Built in 1796, this inn has been continuously operating ever since, and the comfortable tavern and formal dining room serve a Colonial-influenced bistro menu. A member of the Vermont Fresh Network, the restaurant benefits greatly from its strong connections with local farmers. **Known for:** wine list; brunch in sunny garden room; whiskey and bour-bon menu. ⑤ *Average main: $27* ✉ *Dor-set Green, 8 Church St.* ☎ *802/867–5500* ⊕ *www.dorsetinn.com* ⊗ *No lunch.*

Inn at West View Farm
$$$ | ECLECTIC | Chef-owner Raymond Chen was the lead line cook at New York City's Mercer Kitchen before opening this restaurant inside a traditional inn. Chen skillfully applies French techniques to Asian dishes crafted from fresh Vermont ingredients for a nice break from the usual regional cuisine. **Known for:** big picture windows with view; dim sum; roasted and confit duck. ⑤ *Average main: $30* ✉ *2928 Rte. 30* ☎ *802/867–5715, 800/769–4903* ⊕ *www.innatwestview-farm.com* ⊗ *Closed Tues. and Wed. No lunch.*

Hotels

Barrows House
$$ | HOTEL | This renovated 19th-century manse, once the residence of the town's pastor, incorporates a modern boutique aesthetic into the traditional-style inn, especially in the attached gastropub, which features a long, polished metal bar and backlighted marble. **Pros:** good bar and restaurant; chintz-free decor; large gardens. **Cons:** rooms can become drafty in cold weather; robes only in luxury suites; no coffee or tea in rooms. ⑤ *Rooms from: $275* ✉ *3156 Rte. 30* ☎ *802/867–4455* ⊕ *www.barrowshouse. com* 🛏 *27 rooms* ⊙ *Free breakfast.*

Squire House Bed & Breakfast
$$ | B&B/INN | On a wonderfully quiet road, this inn, built in 1918, has guest rooms that combine modern comforts and antique fixtures. **Pros:** big estate feels like your own; wood-burning fireplace in two rooms; crème brûlée French toast at breakfast. **Cons:** basic bathrooms; two-night minimum required for peak periods; one-night reservation costs additional $60 fee in some periods. ⑤ *Rooms from: $210* ✉ *3395 Dorset West Rd.* ☎ *802/867–0281* ⊕ *www.squirehouse. com* 🛏 *4 rooms* ⊙ *Free breakfast.*

Performing Arts

Dorset Players
THEATER | The prestigious summer theater troupe presents the annual Dorset Theater Festival. Plays are staged in a wonderful converted pre-Revolutionary War barn. ✉ *Dorset Playhouse, 104 Cheney Rd.* ☎ *802/867–5570* ⊕ *www. dorsetplayers.org.*

⬤ Shopping

Dorset Union Store
CONVENIENCE/GENERAL STORES | Dating to 1816, this 200-year-old general store is the oldest continuously operating country store in Vermont. Under the

reigns of co-owners Cindy Laudenslager and Gretchen Schmidt, it has great prepared dinners, a full deli, delicious homemade baked goods, and a big wine selection. It also sells interesting gifts, and houses its own soft-serve ice cream machine. ⊠ *Dorset Green, 31 Church St.* ☎ *802/867–4400* ⊕ *www.dorsetunion-store.com.*

Stratton

26 miles southeast of Dorset.

Stratton is really Stratton Mountain Resort, a mountaintop ski resort with a self-contained "town center" of shops, restaurants, and lodgings clustered at the base of the slopes. When the snow melts, golf, tennis, and a host of other summer activities are big attractions, but the ski village remains quiet.

GETTING HERE AND AROUND
From Manchester or U.S. 7, follow Route 11/30 east until they split. Route 11 continues past Bromley ski mountain, and Route 30 turns south 10 minutes toward Bondville, the town at the base of the mountain. At the junction of Routes 30 and 100 is the village of Jamaica, with its own cluster of inns and restaurants on the eastern side of the mountain.

Restaurants

J.J. Hapgood General Store and Eatery
$ | **AMERICAN | FAMILY |** You won't find a better meal at any other general store in the state. This is really more of a classic American restaurant, serving farm-to-table breakfast, lunch, and dinner, than a place to pick up the essentials, but like any good general store, it's a friendly and relaxed gathering spot for locals. **Known for:** buttermilk biscuits; outdoor patio; wood-fired pizzas. ⑤ *Average main: $12* ⊠ *305 Main St., Peru* ☎ *802/824–4800* ⊕ *www.jjhapgood.com* ⊙ *No dinner Mon. and Tues.*

The Red Fox Inn
$$$ | **AMERICAN |** This converted bi-level barn has the best nightlife in town, including Grammy-award-winning acts, and a fun dining room. The restaurant, serving elk chops, shepherd's pie, coq au vin, and the like is on the upper level, where you'll see wagon wheels and a carriage suspended from the A-frame ceiling. **Known for:** apple pie was served at the inauguration of President Obama; huge fireplace; Irish music with half-price Guinness, and fish-and-chips on Wednesday. ⑤ *Average main: $26* ⊠ *103 Winhall Hollow Rd., Bondville* ☎ *802/297–2488* ⊕ *www.redfoxinn.com* ⊙ *Closed mid-Apr.–mid-May; Sun. and Mon. late May–July. No lunch.*

☕ Coffee and Quick Bites

Coyote Coffee Cafe
$ | **CAFÉ |** This espresso and dessert bar offers maple lattes, baked goods, and myriad local products from the Stratton area. Another bonus: it's a close walk from the bottom of the Stratton Mountain ski trails. **Known for:** maple lattes; homemade baked goods; local grocery products, from eggs and bread to coffee and CBD. ⑤ *Average main: $5* ⊠ *8c Stratton Village Way* ☎ *802/999–4245* ⊕ *www.stratton.com/things-to-do/dining/coyote.*

Hotels

Long Trail House
$$ | **RENTAL |** Directly across the street from the ski village, this condo complex is one of the closest to the slopes. **Pros:** across the street from ski lift; views of the mountain; outdoor heated pool and hot tub. **Cons:** 4:30 check-in later than most in Vermont; two-night stay required on weekends; busy tourist center in season. ⑤ *Rooms from: $230* ⊠ *759–787 Stratton Mountain Access Rd.* ☎ *802/297–4000, 800/787–2886* ⊕ *www.stratton.com* ⬢ *145 rooms* ⦿| *No meals.*

★ Three Mountain Inn

$$ | B&B/INN | A 1780s tavern, this romantic inn in downtown Jamaica feels authentically Colonial, from the wide-plank paneling to the low ceilings. **Pros:** romantic setting; well-kept rooms; enchanting dinners alongside wood-burning fireplaces. **Cons:** 15-minute drive to skiing; two-night reservations requested for weekends and peak foliage; deposit equal to 50% of the reserved stay required. **⑤** *Rooms from: $234* ✉ *30 Depot St., Jamaica* ✛ *10 miles northeast of Stratton* ☎ *802/874–4140* ⊕ *www. threemountaininn.com* ⤳ *10 rooms* ¶⊙¶ *Free breakfast.*

⏳ Nightlife

Mulligans

BARS/PUBS | Popular Mulligans hosts bands and DJs in the downstairs Green Door Pub on weekends. Upstairs, cozy up beside the fireplace with ribs, steak, and traditional fish-and-chips, or opt for tempura plates and sushi bowls from Mulligans' newest in-house offshoot, Snowfish Sushi. ✉ *Village Sq., Stratton Mountain* ☎ *802/297–9293* ⊕ *www. mulligansstratton.com.*

🏃 Activities

SKIING

Bromley Mountain Resort

SKIING/SNOWBOARDING | FAMILY | About 20 minutes from Stratton, Bromley is a favorite with families thanks to a child-care center for kids ages six weeks–six years and programs for ages 2½–17. The trails are evenly split among beginner, intermediate, and advanced, with nothing too challenging. Beginning skiers and snowboarders have expanded access to terrain-based training in the dedicated Learning Zone, and everyone can unwind in the base lodge and "village." An added bonus: trails face south, making for glorious spring skiing and warm winter days. **Facilities:** 47 trails; 300 acres; 1,334-foot

vertical drop; 9 lifts. ✉ *3984 Rte. 11, Peru* ☎ *802/824–5522, 866/856–2201 for snow conditions* ⊕ *www.bromley.com* ✉ *Lift ticket: $80.*

Stratton Mountain

SKIING/SNOWBOARDING | About 25 minutes from Manchester, and featuring an entire faux Swiss village at its base, Stratton Mountain draws families and young professionals. Beginners will find more than 40% of the mountain accessible to them, but that doesn't mean there aren't some great steeps for the experts. The resort prides itself on its immaculate grooming and excellent cruising on all trails. An on-site day-care center takes children ages six weeks–five years for indoor activities and outdoor excursions. Children also love careening down one of four groomed lift-serviced lanes at the resort's Coca Cola Tube Park. Stratton has 11 miles of cross-country skiing, and in summer there are 15 outdoor clay tennis courts, 27 holes of golf, and hiking trails accessed by a gondola. The sports complex (open year-round) has a 75-foot indoor saltwater pool, sauna, indoor tennis courts, and a fitness center. **Facilities:** 97 trails; 670 acres; 2,003-foot vertical drop; 11 lifts. ✉ *5 Village Lodge Rd., Bondville* ☎ *802/297–4211 for snow conditions, 800/787–2886* ⊕ *www.stratton.com* ✉ *Lift ticket: $115.*

Weston

17 miles north of Stratton.

Best known as the home of the Vermont Country Store, Weston was one of the first Vermont towns to discover its own intrinsic loveliness—and marketability. With its summer theater, classic town green with Victorian bandstand, and an assortment of shops, the little village really lives up to its vaunted image.

Hotels

The Inn at Weston

$$ | B&B/INN | A short walk from the town green and a stone's throw from four ski areas, this 1848 inn is run by Bob and Linda Aldrich, whose love of plants is evident from their immaculate gardens. **Pros:** afternoon refreshments in library; terrific town location; outdoor and gazebo dining. **Cons:** high-end rooms are expensive; lots of flower wallpaper, upholstery, and bedding; on busy main road. ⑤ *Rooms from: $239 ⊠ 630 Main St.* ☎ *802/824–6789* ⊕ *www.innweston. com* ⊃ *13 rooms* ⦿ *Free breakfast.*

 Performing Arts

Weston Playhouse

THEATER | The oldest professional theater in Vermont produces plays, musicals, and other works. The season runs mid-June–late October. ⊠ *703 Main St., off Rte. 100* ☎ *802/824–5288* ⊕ *www.westonplay-house.org.*

 Shopping

The Vermont Country Store

CONVENIENCE/GENERAL STORES | This store opened in 1946 and is still run by the Orton family, though it has become something of an empire, with a large catalog and online business. One room is set aside for Vermont Common Crackers and bins of fudge and copious candy. In others you'll find nearly forgotten items such as Lilac Vegetol aftershave, as well as practical items like sturdy outdoor clothing. Nostalgia-evoking implements dangle from the rafters. The associated Bryant House restaurant next door serves three country meals a day and, if you can't get enough, there's a second store on Route 103 in Rockingham. ⊠ *657 Main St.* ☎ *802/824–3184* ⊕ *www. vermontcountrystore.com.*

Ludlow

9 miles northeast of Weston.

Ludlow, once a largely nondescript industrial town, is a budding hub of inns, restaurants, and cafés beside Okemo, one of Vermont's largest and most popular ski resorts.

GETTING HERE AND AROUND

Routes 100 and 103 join in northern Ludlow, separating about 2 miles south in the small downtown, where Route 103 becomes Main Street.

 Restaurants

★ The Downtown Grocery

$$$ | BISTRO | There's a cozy romance to this oasis of seasonal and local cooking, with its corner seats, tea lights, intimate bar, and chalkboard menu. It was the area's first farm-to-table restaurant when co-owners Abby and Rogan Lechthaler opened doors in 2010, and it has continued to be a mainstay thanks to excellent hospitality, warm-spirited creativity, and nightly-changing specials. **Known for:** seasonal cocktails; small-producer-focused wine list; nightly changing chalkboard specials. ⑤ *Average main: $30 ⊠ 41 Depot St.* ☎ *802/228–7566* ⊕ *thedowntowngrocery.com* ⦿ *Closed Tues. and Wed.*

Goodman's American Pie

$ | PIZZA | FAMILY | This place has the best wood-fired pizza in town. It also has character to spare: sit in chairs from old ski lifts and step up to the counter fashioned from a vintage VW bus to design your pie from 29 ingredients. **Known for:** arcade games and pool table in the back; pizza by the slice; outdoor deck. ⑤ *Average main: $17 ⊠ 5 Lamere Sq.* ☎ *802/228–4271* ⊕ *www.goodmansamericanpie. com* ⦿ *Closed Mon. and Tues.*

Vermont Artisanal Cheese

Vermont is the artisanal cheese capital of the country, with several dozen creameries open to the public churning out hundreds of different cheeses. Many creameries are "farmstead" operations, meaning that the animals whose milk is made into cheese are kept on-site. If you eat enough cheese during your time in the state, you may be able to differentiate between the many types of milk (cow, goat, sheep, or even water buffalo) and make associations between the geography and climate of where you are and the taste of the local cheeses.

This is one of the reasons that taking a walk around a dairy is a great idea: you can see the process in action,

from grazing to aging to eating. The **Vermont Cheese Trail map,** which you can view or download on the website of the Vermont Cheese Council (☎ 866/261–8595 ⊕ www. vtcheese.com), has a comprehensive list of dairies, many of which you can visit. Though hours are given for some, it's generally recommended that you still call ahead.

At the **Vermont Cheesemakers Festival** (☎ 802/261–8595 ⊕ www.vtcheesefest.com), which takes place in July or August in Shelburne, cheese makers gather to sell their various cheeses. Beer and wine are served to wash it all down.

★ The Hidden Kitchen at The Inn at Weathersfield
$$$ | **FRENCH FUSION** | So many Vermont restaurants claim the farm-to-table, local-sourcing, organic approach to cooking, but the chef at the Inn at Weathersfield is more passionate and rigorous than most, with more than 75% of ingredients coming from within a 25-mile radius in season. Enjoy the exquisite French-influenced regional dishes inside the inn itself, on its back patio, or in the separate "Hidden Kitchen" at the back of the property, where monthly cooking workshops and tastings take place. **Known for:** wine list; charcuterie and cheese boards; atmospheric inside and out. $ *Average main: $28* ⊠ *1342 Rte. 106, Perkinsville* ✛ *15 miles east of Ludlow* ☎ *802/263–9217* ⊕ *www.weathersfieldinn.com* ◎ *Closed Mon., Tues., and mid-Apr. and early Nov. No lunch.*

Mojo Cafe
$ | **FUSION** | In 2014, Jodi and John Seward opened this funky, casual watering hole fusing Mexican and Cajun cooking. Tacos,

burritos, bowls, and po' boys frequently feature Vermont meats and produce, while craft beers and specialty cocktails continue to highlight the state's bounty in local beer and spirits. **Known for:** blackened redfish taco with pineapple pico; alligator and andouille gumbo; funky burritos like the "Betty," with tequila-citrus tofu and avocado sauce. $ *Average main: $10* ⊠ *106 Main St.* ☎ *802/228–6656.*

☕ Coffee and Quick Bites

★ Green Mountain Sugar House
$ | **BAKERY** | **FAMILY** | This red-roofed sugarhouse on the edge of Lake Rescue has one of the best maple creemees in the state of Vermont. Locals Ann and Doug Rose have owned the sugaring house since 1985, and almost four decades later continue to uphold their destination-worthy reputation for award-winning maple syrup. **Known for:** Vermont maple creemees; award-winning maple syrup; maple brittle and fudge. $ *Average main: $5* ⊠ *820 Rte. 100 N* ☎ *800/643–9338* ⊕ *www.gmsh.com.*

Hotels

Homestyle Hostel

$ | **HOTEL** | Vermont natives Eliza Greene and Justin Hyjek opened their updated inn and restaurant in 2014, renovating a 19th-century home on Main Street to offer the kind of food and housing they grew to love while working on a hostel-meets-farmstead in the hills of Colombia. **Pros:** farm-fresh restaurant on-site; memory-foam mattresses and Egyptian cotton sheets; central location and wraparound porch. **Cons:** the restaurant and bar have limited seating; only some rooms have en suite bathrooms; the rest are private, though down the hall; 8 rooms are limited, though offer a variety of options. ⑤ *Rooms from: $140* ✉ *119 Main St.* ☎ *802/975–0030* ⊕ *homestyle-hotel.com* ➥ *8 rooms* ⑩ *No meals.*

Inn at Water's Edge

$ | **B&B/INN** | Former Long Islanders Bruce and Tina Verdrager converted their old ski house and barns into this comfortably refined haven, perfect for those who want to ski but not stay in town. **Pros:** bucolic setting on a lakefront, with swimming access; two canoes for guest use; golf and spa packages are available. **Cons:** ordinary rooms; lots of flowered wallpaper and upholstery; no sights within walking distance. ⑤ *Rooms from: $175* ✉ *45 Kingdom Rd.* ✦ *5 miles north of Ludlow* ☎ *802/228–8143, 888/706–9736* ⊕ *www.innatwatersedge.com* ➥ *11 rooms* ⑩ *Free breakfast.*

★ Inn at Weathersfield

$$ | **B&B/INN** | Set far back from the road, this 1792 home built by a Revolutionary War veteran is a world unto itself, and an Eden-esque one at that, with flowering gardens, croaking frog pond, and extensive forest on its 21 acres. **Pros:** dynamite restaurant and tavern; ideal for weddings; monthly cooking classes. **Cons:** 15-mile drive from the Okemo slopes; no sights within walking distance; no coffee or tea in rooms. ⑤ *Rooms from: $219* ✉ *1342 Rte. 106, Perkinsville* ☎ *802/263–9217* ⊕ *www.weathersfieldinn.com* ⊘ *Closed 1st 2 wks in Nov.* ➥ *12 rooms* ⑩ *Free breakfast.*

Activities

SKIING

Okemo Mountain Resort

SKIING/SNOWBOARDING | **FAMILY** | Family fun is the focus of southern Vermont's highest vertical ski resort, which has dozens of beginner trails, some wide intermediate runs, terrain parks throughout, a tubing facility, a nursery, an ice rink, indoor basketball and tennis courts, and a children's pool with slides. There's even a Kids' Night Out child-care program on Saturday evening during the regular season, so parents can have date nights. The Okemo Valley Nordic Center has miles of cross-country and snowshoeing trails. Summer diversions include golfing, mountain biking, and activities and rides in the Adventure Zone. The newer Jackson Gore base features the latest (and fanciest) venues the resort has to offer. **Facilities:** 121 trails; 667 acres; 2,200-foot vertical drop; 20 lifts. ✉ *77 Okemo Ridge Rd.* ☎ *802/228–1600 resort services, 802/228–5222 for snow conditions, 800/786–5366* ⊕ *www.okemo.com* 🎟 *Lift ticket: $92.*

Grafton

20 miles south of Ludlow.

Out-of-the-way Grafton is as much a historical museum as a town. During its heyday, citizens grazed 10,000 sheep and spun their wool into sturdy yarn for locally woven fabric. As the wool market declined, so did Grafton. In 1963 the Windham Foundation—Vermont's second-largest private foundation—commenced the town's rehabilitation. The Old Tavern (now called the Grafton Inn) was preserved, along with many other commercial and residential structures.

GETTING HERE AND AROUND

Routes 11, 35, and 103 intersect in Grafton.

 Sights

Historical Society Museum

MUSEUM | This endearingly cluttered museum documents the town's history with photographs, soapstone displays, quilts, musical instruments, furniture, tools, and other artifacts. ⊠ *147 Main St.* ☎ *802/843–2584* ⊕ *www.graftonhistori-calsociety.com* ≤ *$5* ⊘ *Closed Tues. and Wed. Memorial Day–Columbus Day, and Tues., Wed., and weekends Columbus Day–Memorial Day.*

ⓘ Restaurants

Phelps Barn Pub at The Grafton Village Inn

$$ | **BURGER** | This wood-clad restaurant with a second-floor loft, hanging tea lights, and Vermont-inspired pub fare was originally a carriage house for the guests' horses at The Grafton Village Inn. Today, it's a beautiful and rustic spot for eating local, from crispy skinned local duck breast to seasonal vegetable risotto to a Vermont beef burger capped with Grafton cheddar cheese. **Known for:** rustic interiors with a sense of history; the Phelps burger with local beef and Grafton cheddar; local ingredients as a member of the Vermont Fresh Network. ⑤ *Average main: $24* ⊠ *92 Main St.* ☎ *802/843–2248* ⊕ *www.graftoninnver-mont.com* ⊘ *Closed Sun. and Mon.*

☕ Coffee and Quick Bites

MKT: Grafton

$ | **CAFÉ** | **FAMILY** | When the 19th-century Grafton Village Store shuttered 174 years after opening, locals June Lupiani and Alexandra Hartman decided to revive the abandoned building and give it new life. Their modern, newly renovated general store opened doors in 2015, and quickly became a meeting spot for locals and travelers seeking groceries, deli sandwiches, prepared foods, and home-made pastries. **Known for:** scratch-made pastries; local groceries; deli sandwiches and salads. ⑤ *Average main: $10* ⊠ *162 Main St.* ☎ *802/843–2255.*

 Hotels

The Grafton Inn

$ | **B&B/INN** | This 1801 classic encourages you to linger on its wraparound porches, in its authentically Colonial common rooms, or with a book by the fire in its old-fashioned library, but those who want to get outside can access the nearby Grafton Ponds Outdoor Center and its 2,000 acres of trails, forests, and fields. **Pros:** handsome historic building; seasonal swim pond; game room with pool table and Ping-Pong; two dining options—the Old Tavern and Phelps Barn Pub—serve American fare. **Cons:** lots of flowered upholstery and wallpaper; resort fee; no tea or coffee in rooms. ⑤ *Rooms from: $189* ⊠ *92 Main St.* ☎ *802/234–8718, 800/843–1801* ⊕ *www. graftoninnvermont.com* ⇆ *45 rooms* ⦿ *Free breakfast.*

Norwich

6 miles north of White River Junction.

On the bank of the Connecticut River, Norwich is graced with beautifully maintained 18th- and 19th-century homes set about a handsome green. Norwich is the Vermont sister town to sophisticated Hanover, New Hampshire (home of Dartmouth College), across the river.

GETTING HERE AND AROUND

Most attractions are off Interstate 91; the town sits a mile to the west.

Central
Vermont

Sights

★ Montshire Museum of Science

MUSEUM | FAMILY | Numerous hands-on exhibits at this 100-acre science museum explore nature and technology. Kids can make giant bubbles, watch marine life swim in aquariums, construct working hot air balloons, and explore a maze of outdoor trails by the river. Adults will happily join the fun. An ideal destination for a rainy day, this is one of the finest museums in New England. ⊠ *1 Montshire Rd.* ☏ *802/649–2200* ⊕ *www.montshire.org* ⊡ *$17 mid-June–early Sept., $15 early Sept.–mid-June.*

Coffee and Quick Bites

Blue Sparrow Cafe

$ | CAFÉ | FAMILY | Locally sourced food and big smiles are touted at this small,

neighborly café on Main Street. Stop in early for organic muesli and a local egg sandwich with house-made salsa, or peruse the lengthy sandwich menu come lunchtime. **Known for:** breakfast sandwiches and burritos; coffee and pastries; creative deli sandwiches. ⑤ *Average main: $8* ⊠ *289 Main St.* ☏ *802/649–7003* ⊕ *bluesparrowkitchen. com* ⊘ *Closed Sun.*

King Arthur Flour Baker's Store

$ | BAKERY | The café at King Arthur Flour is a fine spot for both the pit-stop sandwich and the leisurely pastry and latte. The adjacent shop and market area is a must-see for those who love bread; the shelves are stocked with all the ingredients and tools in the company's Baker's Catalogue, including flours, mixes, and local jams, and syrups. **Known for:** croissants, cookies, and brownies; freshly baked loaves of bread; goods to-go, such as local butter, housemade granola, and cheesy crackers. ⑤ *Average main: $12* ✉ *105 U.S. 5 S* ☎ *802/649–3361* ⊕ *www. kingarthurflour.com.*

Activities

Lake Morey Ice Skating Trail

ICE SKATING | For the most fun you can have on skates, head to America's longest ice-skating trail. From January to March, the frozen lake is groomed for ice-skating, providing a magical 4½-mile route amid forested hillsides. Bring your own skates or rent them at the Lake Morey Resort, which maintains the trail. ✉ *1 Clubhouse Rd., Fairlee* ☎ *800/423–1211* ⊕ *www.lakemoreyresort.com.*

Quechee

11 miles southwest of Norwich, 6 miles west of White River Junction.

A historic mill town, Quechee sits just upriver from its namesake gorge, an impressive 165-foot-deep canyon cut by the Ottauquechee River. Most people view the gorge from U.S. 4. To escape the crowds, hike along the gorge or scramble down one of several trails to the river.

Sights

★ Simon Pearce

ARTS VENUE | FAMILY | A restored woolen mill by a waterfall holds Quechee's main attraction: this marvelous glassblowing factory, store, and restaurant. Water power still drives the factory's furnace. Take a free self-guided tour of the downstairs factory floor, and see the amazing glassblowers at work. The store sells beautifully crafted contemporary glass and ceramic tableware. An excellent, sophisticated restaurant with outstanding views of the falls uses Simon Pearce glassware and is justifiably popular. ✉ *The Mill,*

1760 Quechee Main St. ☎ *802/295–2711* ⊕ *www.simonpearce.com.*

Vermont Institute of Natural Science Nature Center

COLLEGE | FAMILY | Next to Quechee Gorge, this science center has 17 raptor exhibits, including bald eagles, peregrine falcons, and owls. All caged birds were found injured and are unable to survive in the wild. In summer, experience "Raptors Up Close," a 30-minute live bird program that happens three times a day. ✉ *149 Natures Way* ☎ *802/359–5000* ⊕ *www.vinsweb.org* ⚄ *$16.*

Restaurants

★ The Mill at Simon Pearce

$$$ | AMERICAN | Sparkling glassware from the studio downstairs, exposed brick, flickering candles, and large windows overlooking the falls of the roaring Ottauquechee River create an ideal setting for contemporary American cuisine—the food alone is worth the pilgrimage. The wine cellar holds several hundred labels. **Known for:** romantic atmosphere; Simon Pearce glassware and pottery; complimentary house-made potato chips. ⑤ *Average main: $28* ✉ *1760 Main St.* ☎ *802/295–1470* ⊕ *www.simonpearce. com.*

Hotels

Quechee Inn at Marshland Farm

$$ | B&B/INN | Each room in this handsomely restored 1793 country home has Queen Anne–style furnishings and period antiques and guests have privileges at the Quechee Club—a private golf, tennis, and ski club—and Wilderness Trails operates from the property. **Pros:** home of Colonel Joseph Marsh, Vermont's first lieutenant governor; spacious grounds; fresh baked cookies every afternoon. **Cons:** some bathrooms are dated; fills up with weddings; lots of flowered upholstery and wallpaper. ⑤ *Rooms from: $287* ✉ *1119 Main St.* ☎ *802/295–3133,*

Simon Pearce is a glassblowing factory, store, and restaurant; the factory's furnace is still powered by hydroelectricity from Quechee Falls.

800/235–3133 ⊕ *www.quecheeinn.com* 🛏 *25 rooms* ❙⊙❙ *Free breakfast.*

Activities

Wilderness Trails and Vermont Fly Fishing School

FISHING | In summer, Wilderness Trails leads fly-fishing workshops; rents bikes, canoes, kayaks, and paddleboards; and arranges guided canoe, kayaking, and hiking trips. In winter, the company conducts cross-country skiing and snow-shoeing treks. ⊠ *1119 Quechee Main St.* ☎ *802/295–7620.*

Woodstock

4 miles west of Quechee.

Woodstock is a Currier & Ives print come to life. Well-maintained Federal-style houses surround the tree-lined village green, across the street from a covered bridge. The town owes much of its pristine appearance to the Rockefeller

family's interest in historic preservation and land conservation and to native George Perkins Marsh, a congressman, diplomat, and conservationist who wrote the pioneering book *Man and Nature* (1864) about humanity's use and abuse of the land. Only busy U.S. 4 mars the tableau.

ESSENTIALS

VISITOR INFORMATION Woodstock Vermont Area Chamber of Commerce.
☎ *802/457–3555, 888/496–6378* ⊕ *www. woodstockvt.com.*

Sights

Billings Farm and Museum

FARM/RANCH | FAMILY | Founded by Frederick H. Billings in 1871, this is one of the oldest operating dairy farms in the country. In addition to watching the herds of Jersey cows, horses, and other farm animals at work and play, you can tour the restored 1890 farmhouse, and in the adjacent barns learn about 19th-century farming and domestic life. The biggest takeaway, however, is a renewed belief in sustainable agriculture and stewardship of the land. Pick up some raw-milk cheddar while you're here. ⊠ *69 Old River Rd. ⊹ ½ mile north of Woodstock* ☎ *802/457–2355* ⊕ *www.billingsfarm.org* ⊴ *$16* ⊙ *Closed Mar. and Apr.; weekdays Nov.–Feb.*

Marsh-Billings-Rockefeller National Historical Park

HOUSE | Vermont's only national park is the nation's first to focus on conserving natural resources. The pristine 555-acre spread includes the mansion, gardens, and carriage roads of Frederick H. Billings (1823–90), a financier and the president of the Northern Pacific Railway. The entire property was the gift of Laurance S. Rockefeller (1910–2004), who lived here with his wife, Mary (Billings's granddaughter). You can learn more at the visitor center, tour the residential complex with a guide every hour on the hour, and explore the 20 miles of trails and old carriage roads that climb Mt. Tom. ⊠ *54 Elm St.* ☎ *802/457–3368* ⊕ *www.nps. gov/mabi* ⊴ *Tour $8.*

Silver Lake

NATIONAL/STATE PARK | Vermont lakes don't get more picturesque than this gem across the street from the Barnard General Store. Plus, it's open for swimming, boating, fishing, and camping. ⊠ *20 State Park Beach Rd., Barnard* ☎ *802/234–9451* ⊕ *www.vtstateparks.com/silver.html.*

🍴 Restaurants

Angkor Wat Restaurant

$$ | CAMBODIAN | Chef Chy Tuckerman was raised in Cambodia, Thailand, Oregon, and New Hampshire until moving to Woodstock in 1997 to continue learning the art of baking at local Mountain Creamery. A decade later, he opened his sunny, BYOB restaurant just off Route 4, where he fuses the Cambodian and Thai cooking of his heritage into mouthwatering dishes like ginger chicken stir fry,

Khmer curry soup, and traditional luk lok made with beef from nearby Cloudland Farm. **Known for:** cozy atmosphere and BYOB dining; house-made desserts; dishes fusing traditional Khmer and Thai cooking. ⑤ *Average main: $18* ⊠ *61 Pleasant St.* ☎ *802/457–9029* ⊕ *www. angkorwatvt.com* ⊙ *Closed Mon.*

Barnard Inn Restaurant and Max's Tavern

$$$$ | AMERICAN | The dining room in this 1796 brick farmhouse exudes 18th-century charm, but the food is decidedly 21st century. Former San Francisco restaurant chef-owner Will Dodson creates inventive three- and four-course prix-fixe menus with international flavors, or more casual versions at Max's Tavern, also on-site. **Known for:** device-free restaurant; popular for weddings; pond and perennial gardens. ⑤ *Average main: $60* ⊠ *5518 Rte. 12, 8 miles north of Woodstock, Barnard* ☎ *802/234–9961* ⊕ *www.barnardinn.com* ⊙ *Closed Sun. and Mon. No lunch.*

Cloudland Farm

$$$$ | AMERICAN | With the table literally on the farm, this restaurant delivers a unique farm-to-table experience that makes it worth the short drive from Woodstock. All ingredients for the seasonal prix-fixe menus come fresh from the farm or local growers, especially Cloudland's own pork, beef, chicken, and turkey. **Known for:** large fireplace in dining room; homemade carrot cake with red wine caramel and carrot jam; bring your own wine or beer. ⑤ *Average main: $45* ⊠ *1101 Cloudland Rd., North Pomfret* ☎ *802/457–2599* ⊕ *www.cloudlandfarm. com* ⊙ *No lunch. Closed Sun.–Wed.*

★ Mountain Creamery

$ | AMERICAN | FAMILY | This locally beloved diner in the town center sources most of its ingredients from their own farm in Killington. "Mile High Apple Pie," ice cream made with local dairy, and daily blue plate specials are only a handful of reasons Mountain Creamery is a Woodstock mainstay. **Known for:** homemade ice cream made with local dairy;

farm-sourced diner fare; blue plate specials. $ *Average main: $12* ⊠ *33 Central St.* ☎ *802/457–1715* ⊕ *www.mountaincreameryvt.com.*

The Prince and the Pauper

$$ | FRENCH | Modern French and American fare with a Vermont accent is the focus of this candlelit Colonial restaurant off the town green. Three-course prix-fixe meals cost $53, but a less expensive bistro menu is available in the lounge. **Known for:** artwork for sale; complimentary cinema tickets; wine list. $ *Average main: $24* ⊠ *24 Elm St.* ☎ *802/457–1818* ⊕ *www.princeandpauper.com* ⊗ *No lunch.*

Ransom Tavern

$$$ | ITALIAN | Arrive early for a seat at the wraparound bar and a perfectly made negroni. The wood-fired, Neopolitan-style pizzas are excellent, as is the inventive cocktail list and the plentiful supply of local beers on draft. **Known for:** wood-fired pizza; craft cocktail and local drafts; farm-fresh ingredients. $ *Average main: $30* ⊠ *4778 South Rd., South Woodstock* ☎ *802/457–1473* ⊕ *www.kedronvalleyinn.com* ⊗ *No lunch. Closed Mon.–Wed.*

★ Worthy Kitchen

$ | AMERICAN | FAMILY | One of Woodstock's liveliest and most popular places to eat, this upscale pub and bistro remains buzzing through most evenings. The chalkboard on the wall lists the hearty menu of American comfort classics given farm-to-table twists, and the craft beer selection is excellent. **Known for:** beer list; social hot spot; burgers with Wagyu beef patties. $ *Average main: $14* ⊠ *442 Woodstock Rd.* ☎ *802/457–7281* ⊕ *www.worthyvermont.com* ⊗ *No lunch weekdays.*

☕ Coffee and Quick Bites

Mont Vert Cafe

$ | CAFÉ | This charming two-story café in the center of Woodstock sources most of its ingredients in state. It's the perfect stop for a Vermont maple latte with local dairy, produce-laden salads, and wraps or egg sandwiches worthy of a long line. **Known for:** espresso drinks; breakfast sandwiches; seasonal specials. $ *Average main: $12* ⊠ *28 Central St.* ☎ *802/457–7143* ⊕ *www.monvertcafe.com* ⊗ *Closed Thurs.*

Hotels

★ The Fan House Bed and Breakfast

$$ | B&B/INN | This charming inn dating to 1840 is as authentic as it gets in Vermont. **Pros:** 300-plus-thread-count linens and down comforters; walking distance to Silver Lake and general store; library nook. **Cons:** no major sights in walking distance; on busy main road; set back and difficult to see from road. $ *Rooms from: $200* ⊠ *6297 Rte. 12 N* ☎ *802/234–6704* ⊕ *www.thefanhouse.com* 🗖 *No credit cards* ⊗ *Closed Apr.* ➹ *3 rooms* ⊙ *Free breakfast.*

506 On the River

$ | HOTEL | FAMILY | Behind a somewhat bland prefab exterior lies an eclectic boutique experience, thanks in large part to the virtual curiosity cabinet of exotic (or faux exotic) knickknacks stuffed throughout the premises, brought by the Africa-based owners. **Pros:** impressive cocktail menu in bar; patio dining with view of river; lots of activities and space for families. **Cons:** 5 miles west of Woodstock; child-friendly means lots of children; a bit buggy. $ *Rooms from: $199* ⊠ *1653 W. Woodstock Rd., Burlington* ☎ *802/457–5000* ⊕ *www.ontheriverwoodstock.com* ➹ *45 rooms* ⊙ *Free breakfast.*

Kedron Valley Inn

$ | B&B/INN | You're likely to fall in love at first sight with the main 1828 three-story brick building here, the centerpiece of this 15-acre retreat, but wait until you see the spring-fed pond, which has a white sand beach with toys for kids. **Pros:** on-site restaurant with a great wine list;

The upscale Woodstock area is known as Vermont's horse country.

historic facade with modern interiors and amenities; next door to South Woodstock Country Store. **Cons:** 5 miles south of Woodstock; limited cell service; no sights within walking distance. $ *Rooms from: $199* ⊠ *4778 South Rd., South Woodstock* ☎ *802/457–1473, 800/836–1193* ⊕ *www.kedronvalleyinn.com* ⊘ *Closed Apr.* ⇄ *16 rooms* ❍ *Free breakfast.*

The Shire Riverview Motel

$ | **HOTEL** | Many rooms in this immaculate motel have decks, and most have fabulous views of Ottauquechee River, which runs right along the building. **Pros:** within walking distance of Woodstock's green and shops; sweeping river views; discounted access to Woodstock Recreation Center pool and fitness center. **Cons:** basic rooms; unexciting exterior; not all rooms have river views. $ *Rooms from: $198* ⊠ *46 Pleasant St.* ☎ *802/457–2211* ⊕ *shirewoodstock.com* ⇄ *42 rooms* ❍ *No meals.*

★ Twin Farms

$$$$ | **RESORT** | Let's just get it out there: Twin Farms is the best lodging in Vermont, and the most expensive, but it's worth it. **Pros:** luxury fit for A-list Hollywood stars, including Oprah Winfrey and Tom Cruise; Japanese furo in woods; on-site spa. **Cons:** steep prices; no children allowed; minimum stays during peak periods and many weekends. $ *Rooms from: $1900* ⊠ *452 Royalton Tpke., Barnard* ☎ *802/234–9999* ⊕ *www.twinfarms.com* ⇄ *20 rooms* ❍ *All-inclusive.*

★ The Woodstock Inn and Resort

$$$ | **RESORT** | **FAMILY** | A night at the Woodstock Inn, one of Vermont's premier accommodations, is an experience in itself, with a location on Woodstock's gorgeous green that's hard to beat. **Pros:** historic property; perfect central location; one of the best spas in Vermont. **Cons:** posh ambience not for everyone; slightly slick and corporate; very expensive for Vermont. $ *Rooms from: $339* ⊠ *14 The Green* ☎ *802/332–6853, 888/338–2745* ⊕ *www.woodstockinn.com* ⇄ *142 rooms* ❍ *No meals.*

🏃 Activities

GOLF

Woodstock Inn and Resort Golf Club

GOLF | Robert Trent Jones Sr. designed the resort's challenging course. ⊠ *76 South St.* ☎ *802/457–6674, 888/338–2745* ⊕ *www.woodstockinn.com/golf-club* ⊠ *$75 for 9 holes, $95 for 18 holes, weekdays; $95 for 9 holes, $135 for 18 holes, weekends* ⚑ *18 holes, 6001 yards, par 70.*

SKIING

Tubbs Snowshoes & Fischer Nordic Adventure Center

SKIING/SNOWBOARDING | The Woodstock Inn's Nordic complex has nearly 25 miles of picturesque groomed cross-country ski trails around Mt. Tom and Mt. Peg. Equipment and lessons are available. ⊠ *76 South St.* ☎ *802/457–6674* ⊕ *www. woodstockinn.com* ⊠ *Trail pass: $25.*

SPAS

The Bridge House Spa at Twin Farms

SPA/BEAUTY | A visit to Twin Farms is a trip to another world, and a spa treatment here completes the getaway. The spa at the luxury lodging expounds a philosophy of wellness that goes beyond the realm of massages and skin treatments. Employing an organic product line by Vermont-based Tata Harper and Lunaroma, the spa offers facials, polishes, aromatherapy, massages, and mud wraps that administer a heavenly reboot to your skin and muscles. ⊠ *Twin Farms, 452 Royalton Tpke., Barnard* ☎ *802/234–9999* ⊕ *www.twinfarms.com.*

Spa at the Woodstock Inn and Resort

SPA/BEAUTY | A mesmerizing, 10,000-square-foot, nature-inspired facility, this LEED-certified spa is a world unto itself, with 10 treatment rooms, ultratranquil relaxation area, eucalyptus steam room, and a sophisticated shop stocked with designer bath products. Elegant, minimalist design accentuates the beautiful setting: natural light pours into sparkling dressing rooms and the firelit Great Room, and an outdoor meditation courtyard has a hot tub and a Scandinavian-style sauna. The mood is serene, the treatments varied: start with the 80-minute Himalayan Salt Stone Massage. ⊠ *Woodstock Inn and Resort, 14 The Green* ☎ *802/457–6697, 888/338–2745* ⊕ *www.woodstockinn.com/spa.*

Killington

20 miles northwest of Woodstock.

With only a gas station, a post office, a motel, and a few shops at the intersection of U.S. 4 and Route 100, it doesn't quite feel like the East's largest ski resort is nearby. The village of Killington has suffered from unfortunate strip development along the access road to the ski resort, but the 360-degree views atop Killington Peak, accessible via the resort's gondola, make it worth the drive.

☕ Coffee and Quick Bites

Liquid Art Coffeehouse & Eatery

$ | CAFÉ | This cerulean blue A-frame is a mountainside gem for morning baked goods, award-winning chilli, and specialty drinks like the Mounds latte (espresso, steamed milk, coconut, and chocolate syrup). It also doubles as a local art gallery, so you can peruse Vermont artists over a pick-me-up. **Known for:** specialty lattes; cozy corner tables and free Wi-Fi; award-winning vegetarian chilli. ⑤ *Average main: $6* ⊠ *37 Miller Brook Rd.* ☎ *802/422–2787* ⊕ *www.liquidartvt.com* ⊘ *Closed Wed. and Thurs.*

🛏 Hotels

Birch Ridge Inn

$ | B&B/INN | A slate-covered carriageway about a mile from the Killington ski resort leads to this popular off-mountain stay, a former executive retreat in two renovated A-frames. **Pros:** variety of quirky designs; five-minute drive to the slopes;

near Killington nightlife. **Cons:** restaurant closed Sunday and Monday; outdated and tired style; no coffee or tea in rooms. ⑤ *Rooms from: $139* ✉ *37 Butler Rd.* ☎ *802/422–4293, 800/435–8566* ⊕ *www.birchridge.com* ⊗ *Closed May* ⤴ *10 rooms* ⦿ *Free breakfast.*

The Mountain Top Inn & Resort

$$$ | **RESORT** | **FAMILY** | This four-season resort hosts everything from cross-country skiing and snowshoeing on 37 miles of trails in the winter to horseback riding, tennis, and swimming and boating in the 740-acre lake throughout the rest of the year. **Pros:** family-friendly vibe; three suites have fireplaces; views of mountains and lake from some rooms. **Cons:** fees for activities can add up; tea/coffeemakers only in suites; limited to no cell service. ⑤ *Rooms from: $325* ✉ *195 Mountain Top Rd., Chittenden* ☎ *802/483–2311* ⊕ *www.mountaintopinn.com* ⤴ *59 rooms* ⦿ *No meals.*

Nightlife

McGrath's Irish Pub

BARS/PUBS | On Friday and Saturday, listen to live Irish music and sip Guinness draft at the Inn at Long Trail's pub. ✉ *709 U.S. 4* ☎ *802/755–7181* ⊕ *www.innatlongtrail.com.*

Pickle Barrel Night Club

DANCE CLUBS | During ski season, this club has live music on Friday and Saturday. After 8, the crowd moves downstairs for dancing, sometimes to big-name bands. ✉ *1741 Killington Rd.* ☎ *802/422–3035* ⊕ *www.picklebarrelnightclub.com.*

Activities

BIKING

True Wheels Bike Shop

BICYCLING | Part of the Basin Sports complex, this shop rents bicycles and has information about local routes. ✉ *2886 Killington Rd.* ☎ *802/422–3234,*

877/487–9972 ⊕ *www.basinski.com/true-wheels-bike-shop.*

FISHING

Gifford Woods State Park

FISHING | This state park's Kent Pond is a terrific fishing spot. ✉ *34 Gifford Woods Rd., ½ mile north of U.S. 4* ☎ *802/775–5354* ⊕ *www.vtstateparks.com/gifford.html* ⊗ *Facilities closed late Oct.–mid-May.*

GOLF

Killington Golf Course

GOLF | At its namesake resort, the course has a challenging layout. ✉ *4763 Killington Rd.* ☎ *802/422–6700* ⊕ *www.killington.com/summer/golf_course* ⤴ *$30 for 9 holes and $50 for 18 holes, weekdays; $45 for 9 holes and $65 for 18 holes, weekends* ⋔ *18 holes, 6186 yards, par 72* ⊗ *Closed mid-Oct.–mid-May.*

HIKING

Deer Leap Trail

HIKING/WALKING | This 3-mile round-trip hike begins near the Inn at Long Trail and leads to a great view overlooking Sherburne Gap and Pico Peak. ✉ *Trailhead off U.S. 4, just east of Inn at Long Trail, Rutland.*

SKIING

★ Killington

SKIING/SNOWBOARDING | **FAMILY** | "Megamountain" aptly describes Killington. Thanks to its extensive snowmaking capacity, the resort typically opens in early November, and the lifts often run into late April or early May. Skiing includes everything from Outer Limits, the East's steepest and longest mogul trail, to the 6½-mile Great Eastern. The 18-foot Superpipe is one of the best rated in the East. There are also acres of glades. Après-ski activities are plentiful, and Killington ticket holders can also ski Pico Mountain—a shuttle connects the two areas. Summer activities at Killington–Pico include mountain biking, hiking, and golf. **Facilities:** 155 trails; 1,509 acres; 3,050-foot vertical drop; 21 lifts.

■TIP→ **Park at the base of the Skyeship Gondola to avoid the more crowded access road.** ⊠ *4763 Killington Rd.* ☎ *802/422–3261 for snow conditions, 800/734–9435* ⊕ *www.killington.com* ⊠ *Lift ticket: $115.*

Pico

SKIING/SNOWBOARDING | When weekend hordes descend upon Killington, locals head to Pico. One of Killington's "seven peaks," Pico is physically separated from its parent resort. Trails range from elevator-shaft steep to challenging intermediate runs near the summit. Easier terrain can be found near the bottom of the mountain's nearly 2,000-foot vertical drop, and the learning slope is separated from the upper mountain, so hotshots won't bomb through it. The lower express quad can get crowded, but the upper one rarely has a line. **Facilities:** 57 trails; 468 acres; 1,967-foot vertical drop; 7 lifts. ⊠ *73 Alpine Dr., Mendon* ☎ *802/422–1330, 802/422–1200 for snow conditions* ⊕ *www.picomountain.com* ⊠ *Lift ticket: $79.*

SNOWMOBILE TOURS

Snowmobile Vermont

SNOW SPORTS | Blazing down forest trails on a snowmobile is one way Vermonters embrace the winter landscapes. Rentals are available through Snowmobile Vermont at several locations, including Killington and Okemo. Both have hour-long guided tours across groomed ski trails ($99). If you're feeling more adventurous, take the two-hour backcountry tour through 25 miles of Calvin Coolidge State Forest ($159). ⊠ *170 Rte. 100, Bridgewater Corners* ☎ *802/422–2121* ⊕ *www.snowmobilevermont.com.*

Rutland

15 miles southwest of Killington, 32 miles south of Middlebury.

The strip malls and seemingly endless row of traffic lights on and around U.S. 7 in Rutland are very un-Vermont. Two blocks west, however, stand the mansions of marble magnates. In Rutland you can grab a bite and see some interesting marble, and Depot Park hosts the county farmers' market Saturday 9–2. This isn't a place to spend too much time sightseeing, though.

ESSENTIALS

VISITOR INFORMATION Rutland Region Chamber of Commerce. ☎ *802/773–2747, 800/756–8880* ⊕ *www.rutlandvermont.com.*

 Restaurants

Little Harry's

$$ | ECLECTIC | Laminated photos of regular customers adorn the tabletops of this restaurant, which locals have packed since 1997, when chef-owners Trip Pearce and Jack Mangan brought Vermont-cheddar ravioli and lamb lo mein to downtown Rutland. The place is "little" compared to the bigger Harry's, near Ludlow. **Known for:** pad Thai; a wide variety of customers; entire menu can be packed to go. $ *Average main: $22* ⊠ *121 West St.* ☎ *802/747–4848* ⊕ *littleharrys.com* ☾ *No lunch.*

Roots

$$ | MODERN AMERICAN | Since opening in 2011, chef-owner Donald Billings has created a locavore restaurant driven by ingredients made within miles of the dining room. Humanely raised livestock and Vermont-grown produce is the inspiration behind menu favorites like laden cheeseboards, braised pork belly, and homemade Parker House rolls served warm with Vermont butter. **Known for:** Vermont beers and spirits; frequently changing locavore menu; special Prime Rib Thursday. $ *Average main: $24* ⊠ *55 Washington St.* ☎ *802/747–7414* ⊕ *www.rootsrutland.com* ☾ *Closed Sun. and Mon.*

☕ Coffee and Quick Bites

★ Jones' Donuts

$ | BAKERY | Since 1923, Jones' has been a destination for doughnuts and baked goods made fresh each day in the earliest hours of the morning. Fill a box with cinnamon rolls, pie squares, apple turnovers, and some of the best doughnuts in the state. **Known for:** maple glazed doughnuts; crullers; sticky buns. $ *Average main: $2* ✉ *23 West St.* ☎ *802/773–7810* ⊙ *Closed Mon. and Tues.*

Brandon

15 miles northwest of Rutland.

Thanks to an active group of artists, tiny Brandon is making a name for itself. In 2003 the Brandon Artists Guild, led by American folk artist Warren Kimble, auctioned off 40 life-size fiberglass pigs painted by local artists. The "Really Really Pig Show" raised money for the guild, and has since brought small-town fame to this community through its annual shows. Brandon is also home to the Basin Bluegrass Festival, held in July.

ESSENTIALS

VISITOR INFORMATION Brandon Visitor Center. ✉ *4 Grove St.* ☎ *802/247–6401* ⊕ *www.brandon.org.*

Sights

Brandon Artists Guild

MUSEUM | The guild exhibits and sells affordable paintings, sculpture, and pottery by more than 30 local member artists. ✉ *7 Center St.* ☎ *802/247–4956* ⊕ *brandonartistsguild.org* ☒ *Free* ⊙ *Closed Mon. Dec.–Apr.*

Brandon Museum at the Stephen A. Douglas Birthplace

MUSEUM | The famous statesman was born in this house in 1813. He left 20 years later to establish himself as a lawyer, becoming a three-time U.S. senator and arguing more cases before the U.S. Supreme Court than anyone else. This museum recounts the early Douglas years, early town history, and the antislavery movement in Vermont, the first state to abolish slavery. ✉ *4 Grove St., at U.S. 7* ☎ *802/247–6401* ⊕ *www.brandon.org* ☒ *Free* ⊙ *Closed Sun. and mid-Oct.–mid-May.*

Foley Brothers Brewery

WINERY/DISTILLERY | Though this is a bare bones tasting room—no food, no tours, just glass pours and growlers—we argue that it has great charm, unique Vermont personality, and some of the best beer in the state. There is space to sit outside in the summer months in a nearby field with beautiful views, and the brewery's golden retriever is locally beloved. ✉ *79 Stone Mill Dam Rd.* ☎ *802/465–8413* ⊕ *foleybrothersbrewing.com* ⊙ *Closed Mon. and Tues., and Sun. Jan.–May.*

Moosalamoo National Recreation Area

NATIONAL/STATE PARK | Covering nearly 16,000 acres of the Green Mountain National Forest, this area northeast of Brandon attracts hikers, mountain bikers, and cross-country skiers who enjoy the 70-plus miles of trails through wondrous terrain. If there is anywhere to stop and smell the flowers in Vermont, this is it. ✉ *Off Rtes. 53 and 73* ⊕ *www.moosalamoo.org.*

Mt. Independence State Historic Site

ARCHAEOLOGICAL SITE | Mt. Independence is one of the nation's most revered Revolutionary War sites, documenting the efforts to defend New York, New England, and the battle for American liberty. This key defensive position gained its name between 1776 and 1777, when the barely dried ink of the Declaration of Independence was read to United States soldiers assembled on the rugged peninsula east of Lake Champlain. Annual events include guided nature and history hikes on the site's 6 miles of hiking trails; historical lectures; archaeological investigations; a "Soldiers Atop the Mount" living history weekend; and a yearly reading of the Declaration of Independence. ✉ *497 Mt. Independence Rd., Orwell* ☎ *802/948–2000* ⊕ *historicsites.vermont. gov/mount-independence.*

Red Clover Ale

WINERY/DISTILLERY | Red Clover Ale opened in Brandon's tiny town center under the reigns of two brothers and a brother-and-law. The family trio focuses on creative ales alongside skilled representations of the classics, like their pitch-perfect pilsners and stouts. Their ongoing IPA series is as special as the birds they're named after, like American Redstart and Yellow Warbler. Excellent pop-up food vendors are occasionally found on-site—otherwise, a corkboard near the entrance is covered in local takeout menus for perusing to one's liking. ✉ *43 Center St.* ☎ *802/465–8412* ⊕ *www.redcloverale.com* ⊗ *Closed Mon.–Wed.*

Restaurants

Café Provence

$$ | CAFÉ | Robert Barral, the former executive chef of the New England Culinary Institute, graces Brandon with this informal eatery one story above the main street. Flowered seat cushions, dried-flower window valences, and other hints of Barral's Provençal birthplace abound, as do his eclectic, farm-fresh dishes. **Known for:** Sunday brunch; thin tomato pie; seafood stew. ⑤ *Average main: $23* ✉ *11 Center St.* ☎ *802/247–9997* ⊕ *www.cafeprovencevt.com* ⊗ *Closed Mon. in winter.*

Coffee and Quick Bites

Gourmet Provence Bakery

$ | BAKERY | Next door to Café Provence, this French bakery offers coffee, pastries (yes, there are croissants and eclairs), prepared food, and specialty goods during the day. There's also a modest wine shop featuring plenty of old-world bottles. **Known for:** coffee and espresso drinks; homemade pastries; wine shop and artisanal goods. ⑤ *Average main: $8* ✉ *37 Center St.* ☎ *802/247–3002* ⊕ *cafe-provencevt.com* ⊗ *Closed Mon.*

Hotels

★ Blueberry Hill Inn

$$ | B&B/INN | In the Green Mountain National Forest, 5½ miles off a mountain pass on a dirt road, you'll find this secluded inn with lush gardens and a pond with a wood-fired sauna on its bank; there's lots to do if you're into nature: biking, hiking, and cross-country skiing on 43 miles of trails. **Pros:** skis and snowshoes to rent in winter; the restaurant prepares a Vermont-infused, four-course prix-fixe menu most nights; homemade cookies. **Cons:** fills up with wedding parties; no cell phone service; no coffee or tea in rooms. ⑤ *Rooms from: $269* ✉ *1245 Goshen–Ripton Rd., Goshen* ☎ *802/247–6735* ⊕ *www.blueberryhillinn.com* ⇌ *12 rooms* ⦿ *Free breakfast.*

The Lilac Inn

$ | B&B/INN | The best B&B in town has cheery, comfortable guest rooms in a central setting half a block from the heart of Brandon. **Pros:** many rooms have king beds; within walking distance of town; garden gazebo for relaxation. **Cons:** busy in summer with weddings; quaint but tepid traditional design; no coffee or tea in rooms. ⑤ *Rooms from: $169* ✉ *53 Park St.* ☎ *802/247–5463, 800/221–0720* ⊕ *www.lilacinn.com* ⇌ *9 rooms* ⦿ *Free breakfast.*

Activities

GOLF

Neshobe Golf Club

GOLF | This bent-grass course has terrific views of the Green Mountains. Several local inns offer golfing packages. ✉ *224 Town Farm Rd.* ☎ *802/247–3611* ⊕ *neshobe.com* ⤳ *$22 for 9 holes, $42 for 18 holes* ⚑ *18 holes, 6341 yards, par 72.*

HIKING

Branbury State Park

HIKING/WALKING | A large turnout on Route 53 marks the trailhead for a moderate hike to the Falls of Lana, a highlight of this park on the shores of Lake Dunmore near the Moosalamoo National Recreation Area. ⊠ *3570 Lake Dunmore Rd.* ⊕ *www.vtstateparks.com/branbury.html* ⊡ *$4* ⊙ *Facilities closed late Oct.–late May.*

Mt. Horrid

HIKING/WALKING | For great views from a vertigo-inducing cliff, hike up the Long Trail to Mt. Horrid. The steep, hour-long hike starts at the top of Brandon Gap. ⊠ *Trailhead at Brandon Gap Rte. 73 parking lot, about 8 miles east of Brandon* ⊕ *www.fs.usda.gov/main/gmfl.*

Trails at Mt. Independence State Historic Site

HIKING/WALKING | West of Brandon, four trails—two short ones of less than a mile each and two longer ones—lead to some abandoned Revolutionary War fortifications. ⊠ *497 Mt. Independence Rd., just west of Orwell, Orwell* ✥ *Parking lot is at top of hill* ☎ *802/948–2000* ⊕ *historicsites.vermont.gov/mount-independence* ⊡ *$5* ⊙ *Closed mid-Oct.–late May.*

Middlebury

17 miles north of Brandon, 34 miles south of Burlington.

In the late 1800s Middlebury was the largest Vermont community west of the Green Mountains, an industrial center of river-powered wool and grain mills. This is Robert Frost country: Vermont's late poet laureate spent 23 summers at a farm east of Middlebury. Still a cultural and economic hub amid the Champlain Valley's serene pastoral patchwork—and the home of top-notch Middlebury College—the town and rolling countryside invite a day of exploration.

Middlebury Tasting Trail

Among Vermont's craft beer, cider, spirits, and wine explosion, the Middlebury area stands out, with a large cluster of producers with welcoming tasting rooms. Seven, all within a 10-mile radius of the city, have banded together to create the Middlebury Tasting Trail. Find full details at ⊕ *www.middtastingtrail.com.*

◉ Sights

Edgewater Gallery

MUSEUM | This gallery sits alongside picturesque Otter Creek, and the paintings, jewelry, ceramics, and pieces of furniture inside are just as arresting. Exhibitions in the bright, airy space change regularly, demonstrating the owner's ambition to be more gallery than shop, though all pieces are for sale. A second gallery is across the creek in the Battell Building. ⊠ *1 Mill St.* ☎ *802/458–0098* ⊕ *edgewatergallery.co* ⊡ *Free.*

Fort Ticonderoga Ferry

TRANSPORTATION SITE (AIRPORT/BUS/FERRY/TRAIN) | Established in 1759, the Fort Ti cable ferry crosses Lake Champlain between Shoreham and Fort Ticonderoga, New York, at one of the oldest ferry crossings in North America. The trip takes seven minutes. ⊠ *4831 Rte. 74 W, Shoreham* ☎ *802/897–7999* ⊕ *www.forttiferry.com* ⊡ *Cars $12, bicycles $2, pedestrians $1* ⊙ *Closed Nov.–Apr.*

Lincoln Peak Vineyard

WINERY/DISTILLERY | Named "Winery of the Year" at the International Cold Climate Wine Competition in 2016, this vineyard is enjoying the fruits of its labor, with an increase in traffic to its tasting room and shop. Enjoy the Frontenac, La

Crescent, and Marquette varieties on the postcard-pretty porch overlooking a small pond. ⊠ *142 River Rd.* ☎ *802/388–7368* ⊕ *www.lincolnpeakvineyard.com* ⊙ *Closed Mon. and Tues. late Oct.–Dec.; Mon.–Thurs. Jan.–late May.*

Middlebury College

COLLEGE | Founded in 1800, this college was conceived as a more godly alternative to the worldly University of Vermont, though it has no religious affiliation today. The postmodern architecture of the **Mahaney Center for the Arts,** which offers music, theater, and dance performances throughout the year, stands in provocative contrast to the early-19th-century stone buildings in the middle of town. ⊠ *131 College St.* ☎ *802/443–5000* ⊕ *www.middlebury.edu.*

Otter Creek Brewery

WINERY/DISTILLERY | One of Vermont's oldest breweries still knows how to compete with the new generation of start-ups, adopting a fun, summery, colorful tone that invites beer fans to "hop on the bus!" (get it?) at its spacious and chic tasting room. Next to the outdoor patio is a space for lawn games, and a concert series brings live music in the warm weather. ⊠ *793 Exchange St.* ☎ *802/388–0727* ⊕ *www.ottercreekbrewing.com.*

Robert Frost Interpretive Trail

TRAIL | Plaques along this easy 1.2-mile wooded trail bear quotations from Frost's poems. A picnic area is across the road from the trailhead. ⊠ *Trailhead on Rte. 125, 10 miles east of downtown* ⊕ *www. fs.usda.gov/main/gmfl.*

University of Vermont Morgan Horse Farm

FARM/RANCH | FAMILY | The Morgan horse, Vermont's official state animal, has an even temper, high stamina, and slightly truncated legs in proportion to its body. This farm, about 2½ miles west of Middlebury, is a breeding and training center where in summer you can tour the stables and paddocks. ⊠ *74 Battell Dr., off Morgan Horse Farm Rd., Weybridge* ☎ *802/388–2011* ⊕ *www.uvm.edu/morgan* ⊠ *$5* ⊙ *Closed late Oct.–Apr.*

Vermont Folklife Center

MUSEUM | The redbrick center's exhibits include photography, antiques, folk paintings, manuscripts, and other artifacts and contemporary works that examine various facets of Vermont life. ⊠ *88 Main St.* ☎ *802/388–4964* ⊕ *www.vermont-folklifecenter.org* ⊠ *Donations accepted* ⊙ *Closed Sun. and Mon.*

Woodchuck Cider House

WINERY/DISTILLERY | This cidery has come a long way since its beginnings in a two-car garage in Proctorsville in 1991, transforming into this $34 million complex that divides its space between a pub, gift shop, and factory. A self-guided tour, with informational signs, includes a look through large windows onto the production floor. ⊠ *1321 Exchange St.* ☎ *802/385–3656* ⊕ *www.woodchuck. com* ⊙ *Closed Mon. and Tues.*

🍴 Restaurants

American Flatbread Middlebury Hearth

$$ | PIZZA | If you love pizza, you're in for a treat. Wood-fired clay domes create masterful thin crusts for innovative, delicious pizzas with a distinct Vermont attitude and an array of locally sourced ingredients. **Known for:** former marble works; fireside dining with earthen oven; local beer and wine. ⑤ *Average main: $18* ⊠ *137 Maple St.* ☎ *802/388–3300* ⊕ *www.americanflatbread.com* ⊙ *Closed Sun. and Mon. No lunch.*

★ The Arcadian

$$$ | ITALIAN | Chef-owner Matt Corrente cut his teeth at awarded restaurants in Boston and New York City before opening his own place on the quiet banks of Otter Creek. Corrente's knowledge of handmade pasta and regional Italian cuisine comes to life with hyperlocal ingredients; dishes like spicy squid ink orrechiette, chewy bucatini all'Amatriciana, and a nightly special of wine-braised pork cheeks are both transporting and entirely of the Green Mountain State. **Known for:** drink menu with expert cocktails and small-producer winemakers; regional handmade pasta; mini Parmesan Haymakers, a nod to the restaurant's daytime bakery. ⑤ *Average main: $26* ✉ *7 Bakery La.* ☎ *802/989–7026* ⊕ *www.thearcadian-vt.com* ⊙ *Closed Sun. and Mon.*

★ Mary's at Baldwin Creek

$$ | AMERICAN | People drive from the far reaches of Vermont to dine at this family-owned, farm-to-table restaurant just beyond Bristol, 13 miles northeast of Middlebury. Allow a little extra time to visit the sprawling gardens around the beautiful property; they represent the slow approach to cooking that earned this restaurant its stellar reputation. **Known for:** cream of garlic soup; hand-churned, small-batch ice cream; cooking classes. ⑤ *Average main: $23* ✉ *1868 N. Rte. 116, Bristol* ☎ *802/453–2432* ⊕ *www.innatbaldwincreek.com* ⊙ *Closed Mon. and Tues.*

☕ Coffee and Quick Bites

★ Haymaker Bun Co

$ | BAKERY | This sunlit café and bakery overlooking Otter Creek houses some of the best coffee and pastries in the state thanks to chef-owner Caroline Corrente, who honed her skills at pastry school in France before zeroing in on a love for brioche dough. Corrente's specialty sweet and savory buns change daily based on what is available locally—many ingredients are found within a few miles of Haymaker's doors. **Known for:** sweet and savory brioche buns; locally roasted Brio coffee and espresso; patio seating and riverside views. ⑤ *Average main: $6* ✉ *7 Bakery La.* ☎ *802/989–7026* ⊕ *www.haymakerbuns.com* ⊙ *Closed Sun. and Mon.*

Royal Oak Coffee

$ | CAFÉ | After a decade of fine-tuning their skills and tastebuds in the coffee industry, Royal Oak co-owners Alessandra and Matthew Delia-Lobo opened their own café on Seymour Street, an easy pit stop along the Middlebury Tasting Trail. The menu, featuring Vermont-based beans from Vivid Coffee Roasters, is known for shaken ice maple lattes in the summer and frothy cardamom-vanilla lattes in the winter (a seasonal special that, say the Delia-Lobos, now never leaves the menu due to popularity). **Known for:** specialty lattes using scratch-made syrups; cold brew; Gibralters, hot and iced. ⑤ *Average main: $5* ✉ *30 Seymour St.* ☎ *802/349–1609* ⊕ *www.royaloakcoffee.com.*

Stone Leaf Teahouse

$ | CAFÉ | Partially hidden in Middlebury's historic Marble Works district, this oasis of tea is known for made-to-order spiced chai, house-roasted oolong, and loose leaf teas imported from small farmers in China, India, Nepal, Japan, and Taiwan. **Known for:** specialty teaware sold on-site; oolong roasted in-house; seasonal herbal tea blends. ⑤ *Average main: $5* ✉ *Marble Works, 111 Maple St.* ☎ *802/458–0460* ⊕ *www.stoneleaftea.com.*

Hotels

Inn on the Green

$ | B&B/INN | Listed on the National Register of Historic Places, this 1803 inn and its carriage house sit in the center of bucolic Middlebury near the college campus; the inn offers a delicious breakfast, bicycles you are free to use, and Adirondack chairs that are perfect for enjoying the grounds and views. **Pros:** ideal, central location; complimentary continental "breakfast-in-bed"; Aveda hair and skin-care products. **Cons:** some rooms small and close together; typical country-inn design; no coffee or tea in rooms. ⑤ *Rooms from: $169* ✉ *71 S. Pleasant St.* ☎ *802/388–7512, 888/244–7512* ⊕ *www.innonthegreen.com* ⇥ *11 rooms* ⏹ *Free breakfast.*

★ Swift House Inn

$ | B&B/INN | The 1814 Georgian mansion channels a classic New England style into three buildings on 4 acres of lawns and gardens. **Pros:** attractive, spacious, well-kept rooms; complimentary day pass to Middlebury Fitness Club; some rooms have private decks; on-site restaurant, Jessica's, is one of the best fine-dining options in town. **Cons:** not quite in the heart of town; weak Wi-Fi in some areas; somewhat typical country-inn design. ⑤ *Rooms from: $165* ⊠ *25 Stewart La.* ☎ *866/388–9925* ⊕ *www.swifthouseinn. com* ⤳ *20 rooms* ❍l *Free breakfast.*

ⓨ Nightlife

Two Brothers Tavern

BARS/PUBS | Head to this watering hole for pub food a cut above the usual, plus local microbrews on tap in the sports-friendly bar. Look closely at the dollar bills pasted to the ceiling. There's even a marriage proposal up there, along with the answer. Food is served until at least midnight. ⊠ *86 Main St.* ☎ *802/388–0002* ⊕ *www. twobrotherstavern.com.*

Waitsfield and Warren

32 miles northeast (Waitsfield) and 25 miles east (Warren) of Middlebury.

Skiers first discovered the high peaks overlooking the pastoral Mad River Valley in the 1940s. Today, this valley and its two towns, Waitsfield and Warren, attract the hip, the adventurous, and the low-key. Warren in particular is tiny and adorable, with a general store popular with tour buses. The gently carved ridges cradling the valley and the swell of pastures and fields lining the river seem to keep notions of ski-resort sprawl at bay. With a map from the Sugarbush Chamber of Commerce you can investigate back roads off Route 100 that have exhilarating valley views.

ESSENTIALS

VISITOR INFORMATION Visitor Information Center. ⊠ *44 Bridge St., Waitsfield* ☎ *802/496–3409* ⊕ *www.madrivervalley. com.*

Restaurants

★ American Flatbread Waitsfield

$$ | PIZZA | The organically grown flour and vegetables—and the wood-fired clay ovens that unite them—take the pizza here to another level. In summer, you can dine outside around fire pits in the beautiful valley. **Known for:** maple–fennel sausage pie; homemade fruit crisp with Mountain Creamery ice cream; Big Red Barn art gallery on-site. ⑤ *Average main: $18* ⊠ *46 Lareau Rd., off Rte. 100, Waitsfield* ☎ *802/496–8856* ⊕ *www. americanflatbread.com* ☉ *Closed Mon.– Wed. No lunch.*

The Mad Taco

$ | MEXICAN | Mexican cuisine rooted in Vermont ingredients makes this a go-to stop for locals and travelers alike—particularly those who just ascended the rugged incline of nearby Camel's Hump, one of the state's highest peaks. Chef-owner Joey Nagy and Georgia Von Trapp, his partner, source much of their local haul from their own Marble Hill Farm, fueling delicious cooking from carnitas and al pastor to fresh house-made salsa and slow-roasted yams in the outside smoker. **Known for:** tacos with local All Souls tortillas; Cubano sandwich with smoked Vermont meat; house-made margaritas and local craft beer. ⑤ *Average main: $12* ⊠ *5101 Main St., Waitsfield* ☎ *802/496–3832* ⊕ *www. themadtaco.com.*

★ Peasant

$$$ | EUROPEAN | The menu may be short in this small, rustic-chic space serving French- and Italian-influenced country fare, but the tastiness is immense, with some of the best pasta dishes in the state. Additional warmth is added by its "peasant family" operation, too, with dad in the kitchen, mom decorating the scene, and daughter running the front of house. **Known for:** unique "Peasant's Prunes" dessert; Vermont pork Bolognese with penne and Asiago; craft cocktail and wine list. [$] *Average main: $26* ⊠ *40 Bridge St., Waitsfield* ☎ *802/496–6856* ⊕ *www.peasantvt.com* ⊗ *Closed Tues. and Wed. No lunch.*

Pitcher Inn Dining Room and Tracks
$$$ | **AMERICAN** | Claiming two aesthetics and one menu, this dining experience offers a posh and pretty upstairs dining room with classic white tablecloths or a stony, subterranean "Tracks," with billiards and shuffleboard on the side. Dishes cover upscale versions of regional classics, with a few international flavors, too. **Known for:** cocktail list with Vermont spirits; duck breast; artisanal cheese board with onion chutney. [$] *Average main: $30* ⊠ *275 Main St., Warren* ☎ *802/496–6350* ⊕ *www.pitcherinn.com* ⊗ *Closed Mon. and Tues.*

☕ Coffee and Quick Bites

Canteen Creemee Company
$ | **AMERICAN | FAMILY** | Stop by the takeout window of this new-wave snack shack for fried chicken, griddled burgers, and kimchi-stuffed grilled cheese. Stay for the homemade creemees, Vermont's answer to soft-serve ice cream; state classics like maple are always on offer, as are seasonal specials like ginger, cinnamon, lemon, and fresh blueberry. **Known for:** creemees and sundaes; fried chicken; griddled burgers and hot dogs. [$] *Average main: $8* ⊠ *5123 Main St., Waitsfield* ☎ *802/496–6003* ⊕ *www.canteen-creemee.com* ⊗ *Closed Mon.–Thurs.*

🛏 Hotels

★ The Inn at Round Barn Farm
$$ | **B&B/INN** | A Shaker-style round barn—one of only five in Vermont—is the centerpiece of this eminently charming

B&B set among the hills of the Mad River Valley with resident ducks, squirrels, chipmunks, and songbirds that make it feel like a Disney movie. **Pros:** miles of walking and snowshoe trails; game room with billiard table and board games; gorgeous gardens with lily ponds. **Cons:** no a/c in common areas; fills up for wedding parties; no sights within walking distance. [$] *Rooms from: $219* ⊠ *1661 E. Warren Rd., Waitsfield* ☎ *802/496–2276* ⊕ *www.theroundbarn.com* ⟵ *12 rooms* ⦿⧮ *Free breakfast.*

Mad River Barn
$ | **B&B/INN** | This supposed former bunk house for the Civilian Conservation Corps in the 1930s is now one of the Mad River Valley's chicest accommodations, thanks to extensive renovations in 2013 that transformed it into a rustic farmhouse with an edge of industrial. **Pros:** multiple sized rooms, sleeping up to six people; game room includes shuffleboard, air hockey, foosball, and more; several family suites, with bunkbeds. **Cons:** first-floor rooms can suffer noise; lots of weddings in summer can keep it busy and booked; no TVs in rooms. [$] *Rooms from: $145* ⊠ *2849 Mill Brook Rd., Waitsfield* ☎ *802/496–3310, 800/631–0466* ⊕ *www.madriverbarn.com* ⟵ *18 rooms* ⦿⧮ *Free breakfast.*

★ The Pitcher Inn
$$$$ | **B&B/INN** | One of Vermont's three Relais & Châteaux properties, the unique Pitcher Inn has it all including a supremely romantic restaurant and bubbling brook running alongside. **Pros:** exceptional and fun design; across from Warren General Store; complimentary hybrid bikes and access to the Sugarbush Health and Racquet Club. **Cons:** two-night minimum stay on many weekends in peak period; limited to no cell phone service; restaurant closed on Tuesday. [$] *Rooms from: $500* ⊠ *275 Main St., Warren* ☎ *802/496–6350* ⊕ *www.pitcherinn.com* ⟵ *11 rooms* ⦿⧮ *Free breakfast.*

🛍 Shopping

All Things Bright and Beautiful

ANTIQUES/COLLECTIBLES | This eccentric Victorian house is filled to the rafters with stuffed animals of all shapes, sizes, and colors, as well as folk art, European glass, and Christmas ornaments. ✉ *27 Bridge St., Waitsfield* ☎ *802/496–3997.*

The Warren Store

FOOD/CANDY | This general store has everything you'd hope to find in tiny but sophisticated Vermont: a nice selection of local beer and wine, cheeses, baked goods, strong coffee, and delicious sandwiches and prepared foods. In summer, grab a quick lunch on the small deck by the water; in winter, warm up at the wood stove. Warm, woolly clothing and accessories can be found upstairs. ✉ *284 Main St., Warren* ☎ *802/496–3864* ⊕ *www.warrenstore.com.*

Activities

GOLF

Sugarbush Resort Golf Club

GOLF | Great views and challenging play are the hallmarks of this mountain course designed by Robert Trent Jones Sr. ✉ *Sugarbush, 1840 Sugarbush Access Rd., Warren* ☎ *802/583–6725* ⊕ *www. sugarbush.com* ⛳ *$105 for 18 holes, weekdays; $120 for 18 holes, weekends* 🏌 *18 holes, 6464 yards, par 70.*

MULTISPORT OUTFITTER

Clearwater Sports

TOUR—SPORTS | **FAMILY** | This outfitter rents canoes and kayaks, and leads guided river trips in warmer months. When the weather turns cold, it offers snowshoeing and backcountry skiing tours. ✉ *4147 Main St., Waitsfield* ☎ *802/496–2708* ⊕ *www.clearwatersports.com.*

SKIING

Blueberry Lake Cross Country and Snowshoeing Center

SKIING/SNOWBOARDING | This ski area has 18 miles of trails through thickly wooded glades. ✉ *424 Plunkton Rd., East Warren* ☎ *802/496–6687* ⊕ *www.blueberrylakeskivt.com* ⛳ *Trail pass: $14.*

Mad River Glen

SKIING/SNOWBOARDING | A pristine alpine experience, Mad River attracts rugged individualists looking for less polished terrain. The area was developed in the late 1940s and has changed relatively little since then. It remains one of only three resorts in the country that ban snowboarding, and it's one of only two in North America that still has a single-chair lift. Mad River is steep, with slopes that follow the mountain's fall lines. The terrain changes constantly on the interconnected trails of mostly natural snow (expert trails are never groomed). Telemark skiing and snowshoeing are also popular. **Facilities:** 53 trails; 115 acres; 2,037-foot vertical drop; 5 lifts. ✉ *62 Mad River Resort Rd., off Rte. 17, Waitsfield* ☎ *802/496–3551* ⊕ *www.madriverglen. com* ⛳ *Lift ticket: $89.*

Sugarbush

SKIING/SNOWBOARDING | **FAMILY** | A true skier's mountain, Sugarbush has plenty of steep, natural snow glades and fall-line drops. Not as rough around the edges as Mad River Glen, the resort has an extensive computer-controlled system for snowmaking and many groomed trails between its two mountain complexes. This is a great choice for intermediate skiers, who will find top-to-bottom runs all over the resort; there are fewer options for beginners. Programs for kids include the enjoyable Sugarbear Forest, a terrain garden full of fun bumps and jumps. At the base of the mountain are condominiums, restaurants, shops, bars, and a health-and-racquet club. **Facilities:** 111 trails; 484 acres; 2,600-foot vertical drop; 16 lifts. ✉ *102 Forest Dr., Warren* ✛ *From Rte. 17, take German Flats Rd. south; from Rte. 100, take Sugarbush Access Rd. west* ☎ *802/583–6300, 800/537–8427* ⊕ *www.sugarbush.com* ⛳ *Lift ticket: $119.*

Did You Know?

Vermont actually means "Green Mountains" (*monts verts* in French). The Long Trail, the Appalachian Trail, and many other hiking routes crisscross the namesake peaks, which are part of the Appalachian Mountain chain.

Montpelier

38 miles southeast of Burlington, 115 miles north of Brattleboro.

With only about 8,000 residents, little Montpelier is the country's smallest capital city, but it has a youthful energy and a quirky spirit that's earned it the local nickname "Montpeculiar." The quaint, historic downtown area bustles by day with thousands of state and city workers walking to meetings and business lunches. The nightlife can't match Burlington's, but several bars, theaters, and cinemas provide ample entertainment. The city is also a springboard for exploring the great outdoors of Central Vermont.

Vermont's capital city is easily accessible from Interstate 89, taking about 45 minutes from Burlington by car through the heart of the Green Mountains. It's also on the main Boston–Montreal bus route. Downtown is flat and easily walkable, but exploring the surrounding hills requires a modest level of fitness as well as a solid pair of shoes or boots, especially during the winter.

Sights

★ Hope Cemetery

CEMETERY | Montpelier's regional rival, Barre, the "Granite Capital of the World," may lack the polish and pedigree of the state capital, but it's home to this gorgeous cemetery filled with superbly crafted tombstones by master stonecutters. A few embrace the avant-garde, while others take defined shapes like a race car, a biplane, and a soccer ball. ⊠ *201 Maple Ave., Barre* ☎ *802/476–6245.*

Hubbard Park

HIKING/WALKING | Rising behind the Vermont State House and stretching 196 acres, this heavily forested park offers locals (and their happy, leash-free dogs) miles of pretty trails and wildlife to enjoy. On its highest peak is a romantic stone tower that looks out to 360-degree views of the surrounding mountains. ⊠ *400 Parkway St.* ☎ *802/ 223–7335 Montpelier Parks department* ⊕ *www.montpelier-vt. org* ⊠ *Free.*

★ Morse Farm Maple Sugarworks

FACTORY | FAMILY | With eight generations of sugaring, the Morses may be the oldest maple family in existence, so you're sure to find an authentic experience at their farm. Burr Morse—a local legend—heads up the operation now, along with his son Tom. More than 5,000 trees produce the sap used for syrup (you can sample all the grades), candy, cream, and sugar—all sold in the gift shop. Grab a maple creemee (soft-serve ice cream), take a seat on a swing, and stay awhile. Surrounding trails offer pleasant strolls in summer and prime cross-country skiing in winter. ⊠ *1168 County Rd.* ☎ *800/242–2740* ⊕ *www.morsefarm.com* ⊠ *Free.*

Rock of Ages Granite Quarry

NATURE SITE | Attractions here range from the awe-inspiring (the quarry resembles the Grand Canyon in miniature) to the mildly ghoulish (you can consult a directory of tombstone dealers throughout the country) to the whimsical (an outdoor granite bowling alley). At the crafts center, skilled artisans sculpt monuments and blast stone, while at the quarries themselves, workers who clearly earn their pay cut 25-ton blocks of stone from the sheer 475-foot walls. (You may recognize these walls from a chase scene in the 2009 *Star Trek* movie.) ⊠ *558 Granite-ville Rd., off I–89, Graniteville* ☎ *802/476–3119, 866/748–6877* ⊕ *www.rockofages. com* ⊠ *Guided tours $5* ☉ *Closed Sun. and mid-Oct.–mid-May.*

Vermont History Museum

MUSEUM | The collection here, begun in 1838, focuses on all things Vermont—from a catamount (the now-extinct local cougar) to Ethan Allen's shoe buckles. The museum store stocks fine books, prints, and gifts. A second location in Barre, the Vermont History Center, has rotating exhibits with notable photographs and artifacts. ✉ *109 State St.* ☎ *802/828–2291* ⊕ *www.vermonthistory. org* 🎫 *$7* 🕒 *Closed Sun. and Mon.*

Vermont State House

GOVERNMENT BUILDING | The regal capitol building surrounded by forest is emblematic of this proudly rural state. With a gleaming dome and columns of Barre granite measuring 6 feet in diameter, the State House is home to the country's oldest legislative chambers still in their original condition. Interior paintings and exhibits depict much of Vermont's sterling Civil War record. A self-guided tour, available year-round, takes you through the governor's office and the house and senate chambers. Free guided tours run from late June to October. ✉ *115 State St.* ☎ *802/828–2228* ⊕ *statehouse. vermont.gov* 🎫 *Donations accepted* 🕒 *Closed Sun.; also Sat. Nov.–June.*

🍽 Restaurants

Kismet

$$$ | **ECLECTIC** | One of Montpelier's more upscale restaurants, Kismet embraces the farm-to-table philosophy and gives it a shiny gloss and an international flavor. Tranquilly humming in the evening, particularly after State House employees get off work, Kismet buzzes most during its popular weekend brunches. **Known for:** multiple eggs Benedict versions; wine and cocktail list; expensive for Vermont. ⑤ *Average main: $34* ✉ *52 State St.* ☎ *802/223–8646* ⊕ *www.kismetkitchens. com* 🕒 *Closed Mon. and Tues. No dinner Sun. No lunch.*

Sarducci's

$$ | **ITALIAN** | **FAMILY** | Montpelier's most popular restaurant draws its crowd less for the classic American Italian dishes than the conviviality, charm, and sizeable portions, not to mention the picturesque Winooski River flowing directly alongside the windows. The pizza comes fresh from wood-fired ovens, while the rest of the menu features your favorite pennes, Alfredos, and raviolis, with pleasing tweaks on the old formulas. **Known for:** date night; large gluten-free menu; local favorite. ⑤ *Average main: $18* ✉ *3 Main St.* ☎ *802/223–0229* ⊕ *www.sarduccis. com* 🕒 *No lunch Sun.*

The Skinny Pancake

$ | **CAFÉ** | This dine-in creperie makes a great stop for breakfast, lunch, or an easy dinner. The signature crepes go sweet and savory and are filled with fruit, vegetables, and meat from more than a dozen Vermont farms. **Known for:** inventive hot chocolate recipes; Localvore's Dream crepe with chicken, cran-apple chutney, spinach, and blue cheese; Pooh Bear crepe with cinnamon sugar and local honey. ⑤ *Average main: $9* ✉ *89 Main St.* ☎ *802/262–2253* ⊕ *www.skinnypancake. com.*

★ Three Penny Taproom

$ | **ECLECTIC** | This celebrated taproom remains one of the state's best, thanks in large part to its ability to acquire beers few others in the region can. The vibe feels straight out of an artsy neighborhood in Brussels, but with the earthiness of Vermont. **Known for:** darn good burger; top happy-hour hangout in town; premier Vermont and hard-to-get brews. ⑤ *Average main: $15* ✉ *108 Main St.* ☎ *802/223–8277* ⊕ *www.threepennytaproom.com.*

★ Wilaiwan's Kitchen

$ | **THAI** | In 2012, co-owners Wilaiwan Phonjan-Azarian and Timothy Azarian traded their locally adored street cart for a brick-and-mortar location offering some of the best Thai food in the state, if not on the East Coast. Most of the menu reflects the Laotian influence of Phonjan-Azarian's upbringing in northeast Thailand, and Vermont ingredients from eggs to chiles inspire dishes that change weekly. **Known for:** weekly changing menus featuring local ingredients; noodle specials, like khao soy and gwit diow, with homemade chili pastes;

sunny interiors covered with artwork. $ Average main: $10 ⊠ 34 State St. ☎ 802/613–3587 ⊕ wilaiwanskitchen.com ⊗ Closed Sun.

Coffee and Quick Bites

Bohemian Bakery

$ | **BAKERY** | The original Bohemian Bakery began in 2010 as a Sunday-only pop-up in the home of co-owners Annie Bakst and Robert Hunt; it quickly became a weekly haunt for expertly made French pastries. The couple opened a small storefront six years later, where they now roast coffee beans in small batches and fill daily orders of rotating favorites, like buttery kougin-amman and croissants, custard-filled Danishes, and tall slices of cornmeal cake. **Known for:** seasonal tarts with fresh fruit and pastry cream; croissants of all kinds; coffee roasted in-house. $ Average main: $8 ⊠ 78 Barre St. ☎ 802/461–8119 ⊕ www.bohemian-bakeryvt.com ⊗ Closed Mon. and Tues.

★ Red Hen Baking Co.

$ | **CAFÉ** | If you're a devotee of artisanal bakeries, it'd be a mistake not to trek the 7-plus miles from Montpelier (15 from Stowe) to have lunch, pick up freshly baked bread, or sample a sweet treat at what many consider Vermont's best bakery. Red Hen supplies bread to some of the state's premier restaurants, including Hen of the Wood, and has varied offerings every day. **Known for:** breads and pastries; local hangout; soups and sandwiches. $ Average main: $8 ⊠ 961 U.S. 2, Suite B, Middlesex ☎ 802/223–5200 ⊕ www.redhenbaking.com ⊗ No dinner.

Hotels

Capitol Plaza Hotel

$ | **HOTEL** | Montpelier's only major hotel benefits much from the State House across the street, hosting many of its visiting politicians, lobbyists, and business makers, not to mention tourists seeking a certain quality of accommodation. **Pros:**

easy walking distance to all local sights, including bike path; small fitness center; the resident steak house, J. Morgans, serves probably the best cuts in town. **Cons:** somewhat bland design; slight corporate feel; street-facing room may suffer street and bell-tower noise. $ Rooms from: $192 ⊠ 100 State St. ☎ 802/223–5252, 800/274–5252 ⊕ www.capitolplaza.com ⊅ 65 rooms ⊠ No meals.

Inn at Montpelier

$$ | **B&B/INN** | The capital's most charming lodging option, this lovingly tended inn dating to 1830 has rooms filled with antique four-poster beds and Windsor chairs—all have private (if small) baths. **Pros:** beautiful home; relaxed central setting means you can walk everywhere in town; amazing porch. **Cons:** some rooms are small; somewhat bland, traditional design; no tea or coffee in rooms. $ Rooms from: $200 ⊠ 147 Main St. ☎ 802/223–2727 ⊕ www.innatmontpelier.com ⊅ 19 rooms ⊠ Free breakfast.

Shopping

Vermont Creamery

FOOD/CANDY | A leader in the artisanal cheese movement, this creamery invites aficionados to visit its 4,000-square-foot production facility, where goat cheeses such as Bonne Bouche—a perfectly balanced, cloudlike cheese—are made on weekdays. The creamery is in Websterville, southwest of Montpelier. ⊠ 20 Pitman Rd., Websterville ☎ 802/479–9371, 800/884–6287 ⊕ www.vermontcreamery.com.

Stowe

22 miles northwest of Montpelier, 36 miles east of Burlington.

Long before skiing came to Stowe in the 1930s, the rolling hills and valleys beneath Vermont's highest peak, 4,395-foot Mt. Mansfield, attracted summer tourists looking for a reprieve from city heat. Most stayed at one of two inns in the village of Stowe. When skiing made the town a winter destination, visitors outnumbered hotel beds, so locals took them in. This spirit of hospitality continues, and many of these homes are now country inns. The village itself is tiny—just a few blocks of shops and restaurants clustered around a picture-perfect white church with a lofty steeple—but it serves as the anchor for Mountain Road, which leads north past restaurants, lodges, and shops on its way to Stowe's fabled slopes. The road to Stowe also passes through Waterbury, which is rapidly regenerating thanks to a thriving arts and dining scene.

ESSENTIALS

VISITOR INFORMATION Stowe Area Association. ☎ 802/253–7321, 877/467–8693 ⊕ www.gostowe.com.

◉ Sights

★ Ben & Jerry's Factory

LOCAL INTEREST | FAMILY | The closest thing you'll get to a Willy Wonka experience in Vermont, the 30-minute tours at the famous brand's factory are unabashedly corny and only skim the surface of the behind-the-scenes goings-on, but this flaw is almost forgiven when the samples are dished out. To see the machines at work, visit on a weekday (but call ahead to confirm if they will indeed be in operation). Another highlight is the "Flavor Graveyard," where flavors of yore are given tribute with tombstones inscribed with humorous poetry. Free, family-friendly outdoor movies also play through summer on Friday. ⊠ 1281 Waterbury-Stowe Rd., Waterbury ☎ 802/882–2047 ⊕ www.benjerry.com 🎫 Tours $4.

Vermont Ski and Snowboard Museum

MUSEUM | The state's skiing and snowboarding history is documented here. Exhibits cover subjects such as the 10th Mountain Division of World War II, the national ski patrol, Winter Olympians, and the evolution of equipment. An early World Cup trophy is on loan, and one of the most memorable mobiles you'll ever see, made from a gondola and ski-lift chairs, hangs from the ceiling. One recent exhibit, Slope Style, focused on ski fashion from 1930 to 2014. ⊠ 1 S. Main St. ☎ 802/253–9911 ⊕ www.vtssm.com 🎫 $5 ⊙ Closed Sun.–Thurs.

Restaurants

Bierhall

$$ | AUSTRIAN | In 2016, the Von Trapp family finally realized its long-held dream of opening a brewery making Austrian-style lagers on the grounds, and what a brewery it is. Built of thick, massive Vermont wood beams, the cavernous chalet-style space houses a rustic-chic restaurant and bar alongside the beer-making facilities serving Germanic classics, with plenty of beer to wash it down. **Known for:** Bavarian pretzels with beer-cheese dip; chicken schnitzel; Sachertorte and apple strudel. ⑤ Average main: $20 ⊠ 1333 Luce Hill Rd. ☎ 802/253–5750 ⊕ www.vontrapp-pbrewing.com.

Cork

$$ | INTERNATIONAL | Pursuing a mission that "the best wines are grown, not made," this natural wine bar meticulously curates an inventory of organic, biodynamic, no-additive, unfiltered, and wild-fermented vintages, either for sale in the small retail section in the front, or complementing upscale bistro dishes and boards in the classy dining room. **Known for:** mostly old-world wines, with some local labels; lots of charcuterie and shareable appetizers; in the heart of Stowe village. ⑤ Average main: $23 ⊠ 35 School St. ☎ 802/760–6143 ⊕ www.corkvt.com ⊙ Closed Tues.

Doc Ponds

$$ | AMERICAN | A gastropub from the folks behind the Hen of the Wood

restaurant, this place has one of the best beer lists in the state. The food is excellent and the ski-lodge vibe is perfect for lunch or dinner, families or romantic two-top or solo bar seats. **Known for:** lengthy local beer list; pub fare with Vermont ingredients; log cabin atmosphere with apres-ski coziness. ⑤ *Average main: $22 ⊠ 294 Mountain Rd. ☎ 802/760–6066 ⊕ www.docponds.com.*

Harrison's Restaurant

$$ | AMERICAN | A lively locals' scene, booths by the fireplace, and creative American cuisine paired with well-chosen wines and regional brews make this place perfect for couples and families alike. The inviting bar is a good spot to dine alone or to chat with a regular. **Known for:** peanut-butter pie; wine and cocktail list; wood fireplace. ⑤ *Average main: $23 ⊠ 25 Main St. ☎ 802/253–7773 ⊕ www.harrisonsstowe.com ⊗ No lunch.*

★ Hen of the Wood

$$$ | ECLECTIC | Ask Vermont's great chefs where they go for a tremendous meal, and Hen of the Wood inevitably tops the list, thanks to its sophisticated, almost artful, dishes that showcase an abundance of local produce, meat, and cheese. The utterly romantic candlelit setting is riveting: a converted 1835 gristmill beside a waterfall. **Known for:** special occasions and dates; outstanding cooking; wine and cocktail list. ⑤ *Average main: $28 ⊠ 92 Stowe St., Waterbury ☎ 802/244–7300 ⊕ www.henofthewood. com ⊗ Closed Sun. and Mon. No lunch.*

Idletyme Brewing Company

$$$ | AMERICAN | In prime position on the mountain road and the Stowe Recreation Path, this brewpub benefits from the culinary chops of owner Michael Kloeti, of Michael's on the Hill. Add to that a range of Bavarian-style lagers and Vermont IPAs brewed on-site, a large outdoor patio, vegetable garden, and a rich, rustic, chic design, and it's easy to understand what makes it so popular. **Known for:**

"brew-ski" beer flights; ample space for large groups; outdoor Biergarten. ⑤ *Average main: $26 ⊠ 1859 Mountain Rd. ☎ 802/253–4765 ⊕ www.idletyme-brewing.com.*

Michael's on the Hill

$$$ | EUROPEAN | Swiss-born chef Michael Kloeti trained in Europe and New York City before opening this establishment in a 19th-century farmhouse outside Stowe. The seasonal three-course prix-fixe menus ($45 and $67) blend European cuisine with farm-to-table earthiness, exemplified by dishes such as spice-roasted duck breast and venison *navarin* (ragout). **Known for:** homemade potato gnocchi; wine list; views of Green Mountains and sunsets. ⑤ *Average main: $34 ⊠ 4182 Stowe-Waterbury Rd., 6 miles south of Stowe, Waterbury Center ☎ 802/244–7476 ⊕ www.michaelsonthehill.com ⊗ Closed Tues. No lunch.*

★ Prohibition Pig

$ | AMERICAN | This restaurant and brewery in downtown Waterbury is always packed for a reason: fabulous craft beers, sandwiches, salads, and North Carolina–style barbecue served in an airy and friendly bar and dining room. If you just want a quick bite and a draft, belly up to the tasting-room bar at the brewery in the back, or pop across the street to the Craft Beer Cellar, one of the state's best beer stores. **Known for:** duck-fat fries; "craft" mac and cheese; one of the state's best draft lists. ⑤ *Average main: $15 ⊠ 23 S. Main St., Waterbury ☎ 802/244–4120 ⊕ www.prohibitionpig. com ⊗ No lunch Tues.–Thurs.*

Zen Barn

$$ | ECLECTIC | What's more Vermont than the name "Zen Barn," especially when it includes its own yoga studio in a former hayloft? Add to that an expansive, rustic-chic interior with local art and a stage for live music, an outdoor patio looking out to green fields and mountains, and a

Continued on page 126

LET IT SNOW

WINTER ACTIVITIES IN VERMONT

by Elise Coroneos

SKIING AND SNOWBOARDING IN VERMONT

Less than 5 miles from the Canadian border, Jay Peak is Vermont's northernmost ski resort.

Ever since America's first ski tow opened in a farmer's pasture near Woodstock in January 1934, skiers have headed en masse to Vermont in winter. Today, 19 alpine and 30 nordic ski areas range in size and are spread across the state, from Mount Snow in the south to Jay Peak near the Canadian border. The snow-making equipment has also become more comprehensive over the years, with more than 80% of the trails in the state using man-made snow. Here are some of the best ski areas by various categories:

GREAT FOR KIDS Smugglers' Notch, Okemo, and **Bromley Mountain** all offer terrific kids' programs, with classes organized by age categories and by skill level. Kids as young as 3 (4 at some ski areas) can start learning. Child care, with activities like stories, singing, and arts and crafts, are available for those too young to ski; some ski areas, like Smuggler's Notch, offer babysitting with no minimum age daytime and evening.

BEST FOR BEGINNERS Beginner terrain makes up nearly half of the mountain at **Stratton,** where options include private and group lessons for first-timers. Also good are small but family-friendly **Bolton Valley** and **Bromley Mountains,** which both designate a third of their slopes for beginners.

EXPERT TERRAIN The slopes at **Jay Peak** and massive **Killington** are most notable for their steepness and pockets of glades. About 40% of the runs at these two resorts are advanced or expert. Due to its far north location, Jay Peak tends to get the most snow, making it ideal for powder days. Another favorite with advanced skiers is Central Vermont's **Mad River Glen,** where many slopes are ungroomed (natural) and the motto is "Ski it if you can." In addition, **Sugarbush, Stowe,** and **Smugglers' Notch** are all revered for their challenging untamed side country.

Mount Mansfield is better known as Stowe.   Stratton Mountain clocktower

NIGHT SKIING Come late afternoon, **Bolton Valley** is hopping. That's because it's the only location in Vermont for night skiing. Ski and ride under the lights from 4 until 8 Wednesday through Saturday, followed by a later après-ski scene.

APRÈS-SKI The social scenes at **Killington, Sugarbush,** and **Stowe** are the most noteworthy (and crowded). Book a seat on the Snowcat that takes intrepid partiers to the Motor Room Bar in Killington, or stop by Stowe's Doc Ponds for one of the best beer lists around. For live music, try Castlerock Pub in Sugarbush or the Matterhorn Bar in Stowe.

SNOWBOARDING Boarders (and some skiers) will love the latest features for freestyle tricks in Vermont. **Stratton** has four terrain parks for all abilities, one of which features a boarder cross course. **Mount Snow's** Carinthia Peak is an all-terrain park–dedicated mountain, the only of its kind in New England. Head to **Killington** for Burton Stash, another beautiful all-natural features terrain park. **Okemo** has a superpipe and eight terrain parks and a gladed park with all-natural features. Note that snowboarding is not allowed at skiing cooperative **Mad River Glen.**

CROSS-COUNTRY To experience the best of cross-country skiing in the state, simply follow the Catamount Trail, a 300-mile nordic route from southern Vermont to Canada. **The Trapp Family Lodge** in Stowe has 37 miles of groomed cross-country trails and 62 miles of back-country trails. Another top option is **The Mountain Top Inn & Resort,** just outside of Killington. Its Nordic Ski and Snowshoe Center provides instruction for newcomers, along with hot drinks and lunches when it is time to take a break and warm up.

TELEMARK Ungroomed snow and tree skiing are a natural fit with free-heel skiing at **Mad River Glen. Bromley** and **Jay Peak** also have telemark rentals and instruction.

MOUNTAIN-RESORT TRIP PLANNER

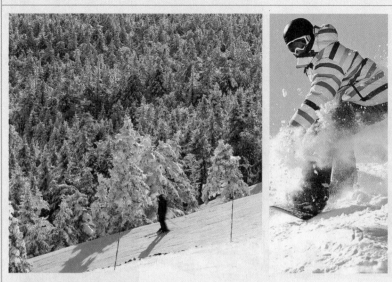

TIMING

Snow Season. Winter sports time is typically from Thanksgiving through April, weather permitting. Holidays are the most crowded.

March Madness. Most of the season's snow tends to come in March, so that's the time to go if you want to ski on fresh, nature-made powder. To increase your odds, choose a ski area in the northern part of the state.

Summer Scene. During summertime, many ski resorts reinvent themselves as prime destinations for golfers, zipline and canopy tours, mountain bikers, and weddings. Other summer visitors come to the mountains to enjoy hiking trails, climbing walls, aquatic centers, chairlift and horseback rides, or a variety of festivals.

Avoid Long Lift Lines. Try to hit the slopes early—many lifts start at 8 or 9 am, with ticket windows opening a half-hour earlier. Then take a mid-morning break as lines start to get longer and head out again when others come in for lunch.

SAVINGS TIPS

Choose a Condo. Especially if you're planning to stay for a week, save money on food by opting for a condominum unit with a kitchen. You can shop at the supermarket and cook breakfast and dinner.

Rent Smart. Consider ski rental options in the villages rather than those at the mountain. Renting right at the ski area may be more convenient, but it may also cost more.

Discount Lift Tickets. Online tickets are often the least expensive; multi-day discounts and and ski-and-stay packages will also lower your costs. Good for those who can plan ahead, early-bird tickets often go on sale before the ski season even starts.

Hit the Peaks Off-peak. In order to secure the best deals at the most competitive rates, avoid booking during school holidays. President's Week in February is the busiest, because that's when Northeastern schools have their spring break.

Top left, Killington's six mountains make up the largest ski area in Vermont. Top right, Stratton has a Snowboard-cross course.

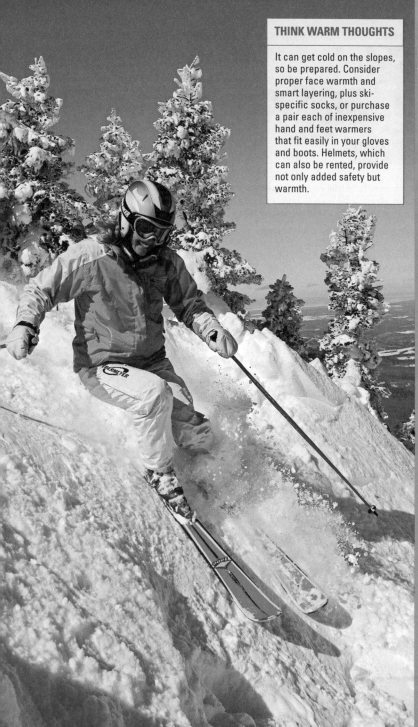

THINK WARM THOUGHTS

It can get cold on the slopes, so be prepared. Consider proper face warmth and smart layering, plus ski-specific socks, or purchase a pair each of inexpensive hand and feet warmers that fit easily in your gloves and boots. Helmets, which can also be rented, provide not only added safety but warmth.

VERMONT SKI AREAS BY THE NUMBERS

Okemo's wide slopes attract snowbirds to Ludlow in Central Vermont.

Numbers are a helpful way to compare mountains, but remember that each resort has a distinct personality. This list is composed of ski areas in Vermont with at least 100 skiable acres. For more information, see individual resort listings.

SKI AREA	Vertical Drop	Skiable Acres	# of Trails & Lifts	Terrain Type ●	■	◆/◆◆	Snowboarding Options
Bolton Valley	1704	300	70/6	36%	37%	27%	Terrain Park
Bromley Mountain	1334	178	47/9	30%	36%	34%	Terrain Park
Burke Mountain	2011	270	50/6	10%	44%	46%	Terrain Park
Jay Peak Resort	2153	385	78/22	22%	39%	41%	Terrain Park
Killington Resort	3050	1509	155/21	17%	40%	43%	Terrain Park, Halfpipe
Mad River Glen	2037	115	52/5	30%	30%	40%	Snowboarding Not Allowed
Magic Mountain	1500	205	50/6	26%	30%	44%	Terrain Park
Mount Snow Resort	1700	588	80/20	14%	73%	13%	Terrain Park, Halfpipe
Okemo	2200	655	120/19	31%	38%	31%	Terrain Park, Superpipe, TerrainCross Park
Pico Mountain	1967	468	58/7	18%	46%	36%	Triple Slope, Terrain Park
Smugglers' Notch Resort	2610	311	78/8	19%	50%	31%	Terrain Park
Stowe Mountain Resort	2160	485	116/13	16%	59%	25%	Terrain Park
Stratton Mountain Resort	2003	670	99/11	40%	30%	25%	Terrain Park, Halfpipe, SnowboardCross Course
Sugarbush Resort	2600	578	111/16	20%	45%	30%	Terrain Park
Suicide Six	650	100	24/3	30%	40%	30%	Terrain Park

CONTACT THE EXPERTS

Ski Vermont (☎ 802/223-2439 ⊕ www. skivermont.com), a non-profit association in Montpelier, Vermont, and **Vermont Department of Tourism** (⊕ www.vermontvacation. com) are great resources for travelers planning a wintertime trip to Vermont.

KNOW YOUR SIGNS

On trail maps and the mountains, trails are rated and marked:

● Beginner   ◆ Advanced

■ Intermediate   ◆◆ Expert

QUÉBEC
Alburg
Swanton
North Hero
Grand Isle
South Hero
Burlington
Vergennes
Bristol
Middlebury
East Middlebury
Shoreham
Brandon
Proctor
West Rutland
Poultney
Granville
West Pawlet
Dorset
Manchester
Arlington
Shaftsbury
Bennington
Pownal

Lake Carmi
Richford
North Troy
Derby Line
Derby Center
Norton
Newport
Enosburg Falls
Lowell
Orleans
Island Pond
Saint Albans
Barton
Albany
West Burke
Fairfax
Jeffersonville
Johnson
Milton
Morrisville
Wolcott
Lyndonville
Lyndon
Saint Johnsbury
Essex Junction
Stowe
Concord
Richmond
Danville
Shelburne
Marshfield
Littleton
Waterbury
Plainfield
Barnet
MONTPELIER
Barre
Wells River
Northfield
Newbury
West Topsham
Chelsea
Bradford
Fairlee
Randolph
East Randolph
Hancock
Bethel
Plymouth
White River Junction
Hanover
Lebanon
Rutland
Woodstock
Hartland
Windsor
Wallingford
Ascutney
Claremont
Newport
Ludlow
Springfield
Chester
Franklin
Bromley
Grafton
Jamaica
Bellows Falls
NEW HAMPSHIRE
Hillsborough
Stratton
Westminster
Newfane
Putney
Keene
West Dover
Wilmington
Brattleboro
Jacksonville
Readsboro

Jay Peak
Smugglers' Notch Resort
Stowe Resort
Q Burke Mountain
Bolton Valley Resort
Mad River Glen
Sugarbush
Pico Ski Resort
Killington
Okemo Mountain Resort
Mount Snow

NEW YORK
ORK

10 mi
10 km

Vermont Ski Areas

menu of eclectic, farm-to-table fare, and the local experience is complete. **Known for:** CBD cocktails; ramen soup; live performances. $ *Average main: $18 ⊠ 179 Guptil Rd., Waterbury* ☎ 802/244–8134 ⊕ www.zenbarnvt.com ☾ *Closed Sun. and Mon.*

Coffee and Quick Bites

PK Coffee

$ | **CAFÉ** | The inviting atmosphere of this neighborhood joint, with locations in Stowe and Waterbury, is increased by the beans they use—North Carolina–based roasters Counter Culture Coffee, known for its coffee education and sustainable sourcing. Milk comes from Sweet Rowen Farmstead, and rotating breakfast sandwiches and baked goods, like buttermilk banana bread, are made in house. **Known for:** maple lattes; expertly made espresso and drip coffee; baked goods and breakfast sandwiches. $ *Average main: $5 ⊠ 1880 Mountain Rd.* ☎ 802/760–6151 ⊕ pkcoffee.com.

🛏 Hotels

Field Guide

$ | **HOTEL** | This boutique enterprise just north of Stowe village is a whimsically stylish alternative to the town's staid resorts and cadre of inns stuck in ski-chalet mold. **Pros:** waffle kimono robes; seasonal heated pool and hot tub; Trail Suite, with a loft bedroom and view of Stowe's iconic white church. **Cons:** unique style not for everyone; no elevator; no coffee/tea in rooms. $ *Rooms from: $110 ⊠ 433 Mountain Rd.* ☎ 802/253–8088 ⊕ www.fieldguidestowe.com ➾ *30 rooms* ⦿ *Free breakfast.*

Green Mountain Inn

$ | **B&B/INN** | Smack-dab in the center of Stowe Village, this classic redbrick inn has been welcoming guests since 1833; rooms in the main building and the annex feel like a country inn, while the newer buildings refine with added luxury and space. **Pros:** easy walking distance to entire village and main sights; luxury rooms include large Jacuzzis; 300-thread-count Egyptian cotton bedding and Frette bathrobes. **Cons:** farther from skiing than other area hotels; road noise in front of building; no tea in rooms. $ *Rooms from: $169 ⊠ 18 Main St.* ☎ 802/253–7301, 800/253–7302 ⊕ www.greenmountain-inn.com ➾ *104 rooms* ⦿ *No meals.*

Stone Hill Inn

$$$ | **B&B/INN** | A contemporary, romance-inducing bed-and-breakfast where classical music plays in the hallways, Stone Hill has guest rooms with two-sink vanities and two-person whirlpools in front of double-sided fireplaces. **Pros:** perennial gardens with stream; complimentary toboggan and snowshoes; Gilchrist & Soames bathroom amenities. **Cons:** possibly depressing for single people; two-night minimum on weekends and in peak period; no children allowed. $ *Rooms from: $309 ⊠ 89 Houston Farm Rd.* ☎ 802/253–6282 ⊕ www.stonehillinn.com ➾ *9 rooms* ⦿ *Free breakfast.*

Stowe Motel & Snowdrift

$ | **HOTEL** | **FAMILY** | The accommodations at this family-owned motel on 14 acres range from studios with small kitchenettes and modern two-bedroom suites warmed by their own fireplaces to rental houses that can sleep 10 or more people. **Pros:** good value for cost; complimentary bikes; 16 acres of landscaped grounds next to river. **Cons:** basic motel-style accommodations; design and furnishings could use an update; occasional road noise. $ *Rooms from: $149 ⊠ 2043 Mountain Rd.* ☎ 802/253–7629, 800/829–7629 ⊕ www.stowemotel.com ➾ *62 rooms* ⦿ *Free breakfast.*

★ Spruce Peak

$$ | **RESORT** | At the base of the ski slopes, this lodge would be king of the hill for its location alone, but a stay here also affords many perks including the rustic-meets-contemporary

accommodations that run the gamut from studio to three-bedroom units, many with outdoor terraces. **Pros:** mountain views; lots of children's activities; many shops supply all needs. **Cons:** somewhat sterile feel; no separate kids' pool; expensive breakfast. $ Rooms from: $269 ✉ 7412 Mountain Rd. ☏ 802/253–3560, 888/478–6938 reservations ⊕ www.sprucepeak.com 🛏 300 rooms ⧈ No meals.

Stoweflake Mountain Resort and Spa
$ | RESORT | With one of the largest spas in the area, Stoweflake lets you enjoy an herb-and-flower labyrinth, a fitness center reached via a covered bridge, and a hydrotherapy waterfall that cascades into a hot tub. **Pros:** walking distances to many restaurants; wide range of rooms; across the street from the recreation path. **Cons:** mazelike layout can make rooms a bit hard to find; uninspired room design; no tea in rooms. $ Rooms from: $198 ✉ 1746 Mountain Rd. ☏ 800/253–2232 ⊕ www.stoweflake.com 🛏 180 rooms ⧈ No meals.

Sun & Ski Inn and Suites
$ | HOTEL | Not many hotels can boast having a bowling alley, but this part-new, part-renovated inn can top even that, adding an 18-hole minigolf course, an indoor pool, and small fitness center. **Pros:** close to the slopes; the family-friendly restaurant is open daily for lunch and dinner; tea/coffeemakers in rooms. **Cons:** not very Vermonty; family friendly can mean lots of children; often two-night minimum stay. $ Rooms from: $189 ✉ 1613 Mountain Rd. ☏ 802/253–7159, 800/448–5223 ⊕ www.sunandskiinn.com 🛏 39 rooms ⧈ Free breakfast.

★ Topnotch Resort
$$$ | RESORT | FAMILY | On 120 acres overlooking Mt. Mansfield, this posh property has a contemporary look, excellent dining options, and one of the best spas in Vermont, which combine to create a world unto itself. **Pros:** ski shuttle will take you directly to the slopes; complimentary tea and cookies every afternoon; American bistro cuisine at the intimate Flannel or tuned-up bar bites at the Roost, the lively lobby bar. **Cons:** boutique style may not be for everyone; no tea in rooms; room rates fluctuate wildly. $ Rooms from: $350 ✉ 4000 Mountain Rd. ☏ 800/451–8686, 802/253–8585 ⊕ www.topnotchresort.com 🛏 91 rooms ⧈ No meals.

★ Trapp Family Lodge
$$ | RESORT | FAMILY | Built by the Von Trapp family (of *The Sound of Music* fame), this Tyrolean lodge is surrounded by some of the best mountain views in Vermont and abundant romantic ambience, making it a favorite for weddings. **Pros:** alive with the sound of music; excellent beer brewed on-site; concert series and festivals in warm weather. **Cons:** some sections appear tired and in need of updating; overrun by tourists, especially on weekends; if not an active person, you'll miss half the amenities. $ Rooms from: $225 ✉ 700 Trapp Hill Rd. ☏ 802/253–8511, 800/826–7000 ⊕ www.trappfamily.com 🛏 214 rooms ⧈ No meals.

Performing Arts

Helen Day Art Center
ART GALLERIES—ARTS | Above the local library, Stowe's premier art center hosts impressive rotating exhibitions of contemporary and local art throughout the year, as well as film screenings. It also provides art education to adults and children alike through workshops, lectures, events, and courses. ✉ 90 Pond St. ☏ 802/253–8358 ⊕ www.helenday.com.

Spruce Peak Performing Arts Center
CONCERTS | Part of the Spruce Peak complex, this state-of-the-art space hosts theater, music, and dance performances. ✉ 122 Hourglass Dr. ☏ 802/760–4634 ⊕ www.sprucepeakarts.org.

Shopping

CRAFTS

Jeremy Ayers Pottery

CERAMICS/GLASSWARE | One of Vermont's most skilled and distinctive potters welcomes visitors to his shop and studio in downtown Waterbury. Keep an eye out for his Waterbury Breakfast Club, which adds food trucks and artists every other Sunday, June–September. A few apartments are also available to rent in the guesthouse; the on-site venue space, 18 Elm, is open for dinner parties and special occasion events. ⊠ *18 Elm St., Waterbury* ☎ *802/363–3592* ⊕ *www. jeremyayerspottery.com.*

FOOD AND DRINK

★ Alchemist Brewery and Visitors Center

FOOD/CANDY | The brewery that launched a beer revolution in Vermont with its "Heady Topper" now welcomes guests to its brand-new shop and tasting room. Intense demand still keeps stocks of beer for sale limited. ⊠ *100 Cottage Club Rd.* ☎ *802/882–8165* ⊕ *www.alchemist-beer.com.*

Cabot Cheese Annex Store

FOOD/CANDY | In addition to shelves of Vermont-made jams, mustards, crackers, and maple products, the store features a long central table with samples of a dozen Cabot cheeses. ⊠ *2657 Waterbury–Stowe Rd., 2½ miles north of I-89* ☎ *802/244–6334* ⊕ *www.cabotcheese. coop.*

★ Cold Hollow Cider Mill

FOOD/CANDY | FAMILY | You can watch apples pressed into possibly the world's best cider at this working mill and sample it right from the tank. Its store sells all the apple butter, jams and jellies, and Vermont-made handicrafts you could want, plus the legendary 75¢ cider doughnuts. Kids love watching the "doughnut robot" in action. ⊠ *3600 Waterbury–Stowe Rd., Waterbury Center* ✛ *3 miles north of I-89* ☎ *800/327–7537* ⊕ *www.coldhollow.com.*

Activities

CANOEING AND KAYAKING

Umiak Outdoor Outfitters

CANOEING/ROWING/SKULLING | This full-service outfitter rents canoes and kayaks, organizes tours, and sells equipment. It has seasonal outposts at the Waterbury Reservoir and at North Beach in Burlington. ⊠ *849 S. Main St.* ☎ *802/253–2317* ⊕ *www.umiak.com.*

FISHING

The Fly Rod Shop

FISHING | This shop provides a guide service, offers introductory classes, and rents tackle and other equipment. ⊠ *2703 Waterbury Rd., 1½ miles south of Stowe* ☎ *802/253–7346* ⊕ *www. flyrodshop.com.*

HIKING

Moss Glen Falls

HIKING/WALKING | Four miles outside of town, this short hike leads to a stupendous 125-foot waterfall that makes a great way to cool down in summer. ⊠ *615 Moss Glen Falls Rd.* ☎ *888/409–7579 Vermont State Parks* ⊕ *www. vtstateparks.com.*

Mt. Mansfield

HIKING/WALKING | Ascending Mt. Mansfield, Vermont's highest mountain, makes for a challenging day hike. Trails lead from Mountain Road to the summit, where they meet the north–south Long Trail. Views encompass New Hampshire's White Mountains, New York's Adirondacks, and southern Québec. The Green Mountain Club publishes a trail guide. ⊠ *Trailheads along Mountain Rd.* ☎ *802/244–7037* ⊕ *www.greenmountainclub.org.*

★ Stowe Recreation Path

HIKING/WALKING | An immaculately maintained, paved recreation path begins behind the Community Church in town and meanders about 5 miles along the river valley, with many entry points along the way. Whether you're on foot, skis, bike, or in-line skates, it's a tranquil spot to enjoy the outdoors. In autumn, there's a corn maze, and at least four shops along the path rent bikes. ⊠ *Stowe* ⊕ *www.stowerec.org.*

SKIING

Stowe Mountain Resort

SKIING/SNOWBOARDING | The name of the village is Stowe, and the name of the mountain is Mt. Mansfield—but to generations of skiers, it's all just plain "Stowe." The area's mystique attracts as many serious skiers as social ones. Stowe is a giant among Eastern ski mountains with intimidating expert runs, but its symmetrical shape allows skiers of all abilities to enjoy long, satisfying runs from the summit. Improved snowmaking capacity, new lifts, and free shuttle buses that gather skiers along Mountain Road have made it all much more convenient. Yet the traditions remain, like the Winter Carnival in January and the Sugar Slalom in April, to name two. Spruce Peak, where you'll find the Adventure Center and the Mountain Lodge, is separate from the main mountain; the peak has a teaching hill and offers a pleasant experience for intermediates and beginners. In the summer, there's a TreeTop Adventure course and an awe-inspiring zipline that extends from the top of the gondola to the bottom in three breathtaking runs. **Facilities:** 116 trails; 485 acres; 2,160-foot vertical drop; 13 lifts. ⊠ *5781 Mountain Rd.* ☎ *802/253–3000, 802/253–3600 for snow conditions* ⊕ *www.stowe.com* ☎ *Lift ticket: $99.*

SLEDDING

Peace Pups Dog Sledding

LOCAL SPORTS | **FAMILY** | This one-man (and multiple-dog) company offers two-hour tours with a team of eight Siberian huskies. You can ride inside a padded toboggan or learn how to mush and drive on your own. If you prefer to walk the trails yourself, snowshoe rentals are also available. In summer, the trails are open to hiking. Lake Elmore is a roughly 20-minute drive from Stowe. ⊠ *239 Cross Rd., Lake Elmore* ☎ *802/888–7733* ⊕ *www.peacepupsdogsledding.com* ☎ *$318 for dog sledding tours.*

SPAS

Spa and Wellness Center at Spruce Peak

SPA/BEAUTY | This 21,000-square-foot facility has 18 private treatment rooms, a fitness center, and a year-round outdoor pool and hot tub. In addition to the usual array of facials, scrubs, and massages for adults, the spa offers a separate program for kids. ⊠ *Spruce Peak, 7412 Mountain Rd.* ☎ *802/760–4782* ⊕ *www.spruce-peak.com.*

Spa at Stoweflake

SPA/BEAUTY | One of the largest spas in New England, the Spa at Stoweflake features a massaging hydrotherapeutic waterfall, a Hungarian mineral pool, 30 treatment rooms, and more than 150 treatments like the Bingham Falls Renewal, named after a local waterfall. This treatment begins with a body scrub and a Vichy shower, followed by an aromatherapy oil massage. The spacious men's and women's sanctuaries have saunas, steam rooms, and whirlpool tubs. ⊠ *Stoweflake Mountain Resort and Spa, 1746 Mountain Rd.* ☎ *802/760–1083* ⊕ *www.stoweflake.com.*

Spa at Topnotch

SPA/BEAUTY | Calm pervades the Spa at Topnotch, with its birchwood doors, natural light, and cool colors. Signature treatments include the Mt. Mansfield Saucha, a three-stage herbal body treatment, and the Little River Stone Massage, which uses the resort's own wood-spice oil. There's even Rover Reiki (really) for your canine friend. Locker areas are spacious, with saunas, steam rooms, and whirlpool tubs. The indoor pool has lots of natural light. Daily classes in tai chi, yoga, and Pilates are offered in the nearby fitness center. ⊠ *Topnotch Resort and Spa, 4000 Mountain Rd.* ☎ *802/253–6463* ⊕ *www.topnotchresort.com.*

Jeffersonville

18 miles north of Stowe.

Jeffersonville is just over Smugglers' Notch from Stowe but miles away in feeling and attitude. In summer, you can drive over the notch road as it curves precipitously around boulders that have fallen from the cliffs above, then pass open meadows and old farmhouses and sugar shacks on the way down to town. Below the notch, Smugglers' Notch Ski Resort is the hub of activity year-round. Downtown Jeffersonville, once home to an artists' colony, is quiet but has excellent dining and nice art galleries.

Like most places in Vermont, a car is essential to exploring this area. From Burlington, it's about a 45-minute drive along Route 15. Or you can cruise north on Route 108 from Stowe for 30 minutes; however, the road is closed for much of the winter.

Sights

Boyden Valley Winery & Spirits

WINERY/DISTILLERY | On a beautiful stretch of farmland west of Jeffersonville, this winery conducts tours and tastings and showcases an excellent selection of Vermont specialty products and local handicrafts. The winery's Big Barn Red is full-bodied, but the real fun may be in the ice wines, maple crème liqueur, and hard ice cider. ⊠ *64 Rte. 104, Cambridge* ☎ *802/644–8151* ⊕ *www.boydenvalley. com* ☕ *Tasting $10.*

Restaurants

158 Main Restaurant and Bakery

$ | **AMERICAN** | One of the most popular restaurants in Jeffersonville easily earns its accolades with big portions and small prices. The menu features all the classic egg, pancake, and corn-beef-hash dishes a person could wish for at breakfast, and a surprisingly wide-ranging international menu for dinner. **Known for:** $5 Two Egg Basic; Sunday brunch; homemade bread. ⑤ *Average main: $13* ⊠ *158 Main St.* ☎ *802/644–8100* ⊕ *www.158Main.com* ☉ *Closed Mon. No dinner Sun.*

Coffee and Quick Bites

Burger Barn

$ | **AMERICAN** | **FAMILY** | Local grass-fed burgers and handcut fries are the name of the game at this bright-green food truck. Try one of Burger Barn's more inventive offshoots, like the Nutty Goat: goat cheese, maple crushed walnuts, caramelized onions, bacon and mayo. **Known for:** grass-fed burgers; food truck atmosphere and outside dining; cash only. ⑤ *Average main: $8* ⊠ *4968 VT-15* ☎ *802/730–3441* ▬ *No credit cards.*

🛏 Hotels

★ Smugglers' Notch Resort

$$$ | **RESORT** | **FAMILY** | With five giant water parks for summer fun and just about every winter activity imaginable, including the new 26,000-square-foot indoor "FunZone 2.0," this resort is ideal for families; nightly rates include lift tickets, lessons, and all resort amenities. **Pros:** great place for families to learn to ski; views of several mountains; shuttles to the slopes. **Cons:** not a romantic getaway for couples; extra cost for daily cleaning; very busy during peak season. ⑤ *Rooms from: $322* ⊠ *4323 Rte. 108 S* ☎ *802/332–6841, 800/419–4615* ⊕ *www. smuggs.com* ⇥ *600 condominiums* ⑩ *No meals.*

🛍 Shopping

ANTIQUES

Route 15 between Jeffersonville and Johnson is dubbed the "antiques highway."

Buggy Man

ANTIQUES/COLLECTIBLES | This store sells all sorts of collectibles, including horse-drawn vehicles. ✉ *853 Rte. 15, 7 miles east of Jeffersonville, Johnson* ☎ *802/635–2110.*

CLOTHING
★ Johnson Woolen Mills
CLOTHING | This factory store has great deals on woolen blankets, household goods, and the famous Johnson outerwear. ✉ *51 Lower Main St. E, 9 miles east of Jeffersonville, Johnson* ☎ *802/635–2271* ⊕ *www.johnsonwoolenmills.com.*

Activities

KAYAKING
Vermont Canoe and Kayak
KAYAKING | This outfitter rents canoes and kayaks for use on the Lamoille River, and leads guided canoe trips to Boyden Valley Winery. ✉ *4805 Rte. 15, behind the Family Table* ☎ *802/644–8336* ⊕ *vtcanoeandkayak.com* ⊗ *Closed mid-Sept.–late May.*

LLAMA RIDES
Northern Vermont Llama Co.
LOCAL SPORTS | These llamas carry everything, including snacks and lunches, for half-day treks along the trails of Smugglers' Notch. Reservations are essential. ✉ *766 Lapland Rd., Waterville* ☎ *802/644–2257* ⊕ *www.northernvermontllamaco.com* ✇ *$60* ⊗ *Closed early Sept.–late May.*

SKIING
Smugglers' Notch
SKIING/SNOWBOARDING | **FAMILY** | The "granddaddy of all family resorts," Smugglers' Notch (or "Smuggs") receives consistent praise for its family programs. Its children's ski school is one of the best in the country—possibly *the* best—and there are challenges for skiers of all levels, spread over three separate areas. There's ice-skating, tubing, seven terrain parks, Nordic skiing, snowshoe trails, and a snowboarding area for kids ages 2½–6. Summer brings waterslides, treetop courses, ziplines, and crafts

workshops—in other words, something for everyone. **Facilities:** 78 trails; 300 acres; 2,610-foot vertical drop; 8 lifts. ✉ *4323 Rte. 108 S* ☎ *802/332–6854, 800/419–4615* ⊕ *www.smuggs.com* ✇ *Lift ticket: $79.*

Burlington

31 miles southwest of Jeffersonville, 76 miles south of Montréal, 349 miles north of New York City, 223 miles northwest of Boston.

As you drive along Main Street toward downtown Burlington, it's easy to see why this three-college city is often called one of the most livable small cities in the United States. Downtown Burlington is filled with hip restaurants and bars, art galleries, and vinyl-record shops. At the heart is the Church Street Marketplace, a bustling pedestrian mall with trendy shops, crafts vendors, street performers, and sidewalk cafés. To the west, Lake Champlain shimmers beneath the towering Adirondacks on the New York shore and provides the best sunsets in the state. The revitalized Burlington waterfront teems with outdoors enthusiasts who bike or stroll along its recreation path, picnic on the grass, and ply the waters in sailboats and motor craft in summer.

To the north, the eclectic enclave of Winooski, a newly refurbished ex New England mill town, houses its own cadre of interesting bars, cafés, shops, and eateries.

Sights

★ Burlington Farmers' Market
MARKET | Burlington's Saturday farmers' market is an absolute must-see when visiting in summer or fall. Set up in City Hall Park and spilling onto an adjacent street, the market is jam-packed with local farmers selling a colorful array of

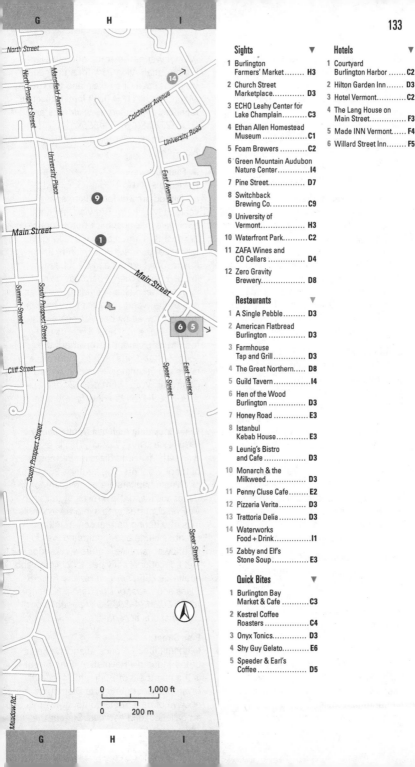

Sights ▼

1 Burlington
  Farmers' Market........ **H3**
2 Church Street
  Marketplace............. **D3**
3 ECHO Leahy Center for
  Lake Champlain.......... **C3**
4 Ethan Allen Homestead
  Museum **C1**
5 Foam Brewers **C2**
6 Green Mountain Audubon
  Nature Center............. **I4**
7 Pine Street............. **D7**
8 Switchback
  Brewing Co. **C9**
9 University of
  Vermont.................. **H3**
10 Waterfront Park.......... **C2**
11 ZAFA Wines and
   CO Cellars **D4**
12 Zero Gravity
   Brewery.................. **D8**

Restaurants ▼

1 A Single Pebble......... **D3**
2 American Flatbread
  Burlington **D3**
3 Farmhouse
  Tap and Grill **D3**
4 The Great Northern..... **D8**
5 Guild Tavern **I4**
6 Hen of the Wood
  Burlington **D3**
7 Honey Road **E3**
8 Istanbul
  Kebab House............. **E3**
9 Leunig's Bistro
  and Cafe **D3**
10 Monarch & the
   Milkweed **D3**
11 Penny Cluse Cafe........ **E2**
12 Pizzeria Verita **D3**
13 Trattoria Delia **D3**
14 Waterworks
   Food + Drink.............. **I1**
15 Zabby and Elf's
   Stone Soup **E3**

Quick Bites ▼

1 Burlington Bay
  Market & Cafe **C3**
2 Kestrel Coffee
  Roasters **C4**
3 Onyx Tonics............. **D3**
4 Shy Guy Gelato.......... **E6**
5 Speeder & Earl's
  Coffee **D5**

Hotels ▼

1 Courtyard
  Burlington Harbor **C2**
2 Hilton Garden Inn....... **D3**
3 Hotel Vermont............ **C2**
4 The Lang House on
  Main Street.............. **F3**
5 Made INN Vermont...... **F4**
6 Willard Street Inn....... **F5**

organic produce, flowers, baked goods, maple syrup, meats, cheeses, and prepared foods. Local artisans also sell their wares, and there's live music on the green. From November to April, the market is held every other Saturday at the University of Vermont's Dudley H. Davis Center. ⊠ *City Hall Park, College and St. Paul Sts.* ☎ *802/310–5172* ⊕ *www. burlingtonfarmersmarket.org* ✉ *Free.*

★ **Church Street Marketplace**
MARKET | **FAMILY** | For nearly 40 years, this pedestrian-only thoroughfare has served as Burlington's center of commerce, dining, and entertainment, with boutiques, cafés, restaurants, and street vendors the focus by day, and a lively bar and music scene at night. On sunny days, there are few better places to be in Burlington. ⊠ *2 Church St.* ☎ *802/863–1648* ⊕ *www.churchstmarketplace.com.*

ECHO Leahy Center for Lake Champlain
ZOO | **FAMILY** | Kids and adults can explore the geology and ecology of the Lake Champlain region through the center's more than 100 interactive exhibits, including the newest additions at the Action Lab. The lab's 3D Water Projection Sandbox manages to make learning about watersheds exciting. You can also get an up-close look at 70 species of indigenous animals, or immerse digitally in the natural world at the 3D theater, which presents science and nature films every day. ⊠ *1 College St.* ☎ *802/864–1848* ⊕ *www.echovermont.org* ✉ *$15.*

Ethan Allen Homestead Museum
HISTORIC SITE | When Vermont hero Ethan Allen retired from his Revolutionary activities, he purchased 350 acres along the Winooski River and built this modest cabin in 1787. The original structure is a real slice of 18th-century life, including such frontier hallmarks as saw-cut boards and an open hearth for cooking. The kitchen garden resembles the one the Allens would have had. There's also a visitor center and miles of biking and hiking trails. In warmer months, climb Ethan

Allen Tower at the south end of neighboring Ethan Allen Park for stupendous views of Lake Champlain and the Green Mountains. ■ **TIP**→ **Don't forget mosquito repellent.** ⊠ *1 Ethan Allen Homestead, off Rte. 127* ☎ *802/865–4556* ⊕ *www.ethanallenhomestead.org* ✉ *$10* ⊗ *Closed Nov.–Apr.*

★ **Foam Brewers**
WINERY/DISTILLERY | Co-founder and acclaimed brewer Todd Haire spent 13 years at Magic Hat Brewing and another two years at Switchback before opening his own Burlington operation alongside fellow co-founders Bobby Grim, Sam Keane, Jon Farmer, and Dani Casey in 2016. Since then, Foam has gained international praise, including a spot as one of the world's 10 best new breweries—bestowed by BeerAdvocate—the year they opened. Snack boards and food truck pit-stops compliment their sought-after drafts, and an outdoor patio faces the stunning views of the Lake Champlain Waterfront. ⊠ *112 Lake St.* ☎ *802/399–2511* ⊕ *www.foambrewers. com.*

Green Mountain Audubon Nature Center
NATURE PRESERVE | **FAMILY** | This is a wonderful place to discover Vermont's outdoor wonders. The center's 255 acres of diverse habitats are a sanctuary for all things wild, and the 5 miles of trails provide an opportunity to explore the workings of differing natural communities. Events include bird-monitoring walks, wildflower rambles, nature workshops, and educational activities for children and adults. ⊠ *255 Sherman Hollow Rd., 18 miles southeast of Burlington, Huntington* ☎ *802/434–3068* ⊕ *vt.audubon.org* ✉ *Donations accepted.*

Pine Street
NEIGHBORHOOD | A once-abandoned relic of the Industrial Revolution, Pine Street is the heartbeat of Burlington's recently revamped South End Arts District, an enclave of bars, restaurants, breweries, art galleries, and eateries. Start at the

intersection of Pine and Maple Street and begin walking south to find a treasure trove of all things art, music, food, and drink. Dedalus Wine Market & Bar has one of the most expansive selections of natural wine on the East Coast. Myers Bagels has been turning out wood-fired, Montréal-style bagels for over twenty years. The S.P.A.C.E Gallery and Conant Metal & Light attract artists from within state borders and far beyond, and the popular restaurant and performance venue ArtsRiot hosts weekly food truck celebrations in the warmer months. Make sure to stop by The Soda Plant, a small business incubator with over thirty local artisans, artists and makers inside a newly refurbished 19th century industrial soda factory. Brio Coffee, ZAFA Wines, CO Cellars, and Shacksbury Cider are a few of the nationally acclaimed businesses inside. ⊠ *Pine St., between Maple and Flynn.*

Switchback Brewing Co.

WINERY/DISTILLERY | Switchback may not get as much press as other more famous craft Vermont beers, but it's a solid, respected brew that's well worth exploring at the brewery and taproom in Burlington's buzzing South End. In addition to superfresh beer right from the tap and a short but savory menu of bar bites, the space hosts regular events and live music throughout the year. ⊠ *160 Flynn Ave.* ☎ *802/651–4114* ⊕ *www.switchbackvt.com.*

University of Vermont

COLLEGE | Crowning the hilltop above Burlington is the University of Vermont, known as UVM for the abbreviation of its Latin name, Universitas Viridis Montis, meaning the University of the Green Mountains. With nearly 12,000 students, this is the state's principal institution of higher learning. The most architecturally impressive buildings face the main campus green and have gorgeous lake views, as does the statue of founder Ira

Allen, Ethan's brother. ⊠ *85 S. Prospect St.* ☎ *802/656–3131* ⊕ *www.uvm.edu.*

★ Waterfront Park

CITY PARK | This formerly derelict industrial district and railroad depot underwent a remarkable transformation in the late '80s and early '90s into a gorgeous stretch of green, with a boardwalk lapped by the lake. It's also a linchpin for a number of sights and facilities, with the Echo Center on the south end, a bodacious skate park on the north, and the Burlington Bike Path running through it all. Sunsets are particularly popular. ⊠ *10 College St.* ☎ *802/864–0123 City of Burlington Parks, Recreation & Waterfront* ⊕ *www.enjoyburlington.com* ⊠ *Free.*

ZAFA Wines and CO Cellars

WINERY/DISTILLERY | Winemaker and farmer Krista Scruggs has gained national praise for her nuanced, idiosyncratic natural wines made without chemical intervention from grape-growing to fermentation that are available through a limited release annually (subscribe to the newsletter to stay in the loop). ZAFA Wines also has CO Cellars, a collaboration with local cidermakers Shacksbury Cider that can be found inside The Soda Plant on Pine Street. As a working winery for ZAFA and a innovation incubator for Shacksbury, the tasting room at CO is an exciting stop for genre-bending wines, co-ferments, and more. Electric Mayhem, for instance, merges grapes from ZAFA's Vermont vineyards with foraged wild apples for a citrusy, floral, and effervescent wine-cider hybrid that has been barrel aged for 18 months with wild yeast strains. Better yet, it's extraordinarily delicious. ⊠ *The Soda Plant, 266 Pine St., Suite 122* ⊕ *zafawines.com* ☉ *Closed Sun.–Thurs.*

Zero Gravity Brewery

WINERY/DISTILLERY | What started as a single bar tap in a pizza restaurant has turned into one of Burlington's most successful and hippest beers, thanks to frothy gems like Conehead and Green

State Lager. Its shiny new brewery in the South End Arts District is always buzzing. Tasty complements include bratwurst, Italian sausage, and crispy cheddar curds. ✉ *716 Pine St.* ☎ *802/497–0054* ⊕ *www.zerogravitybeer.com.*

Beaches

North Beach

BEACH—SIGHT | **FAMILY** | Along Burlington's "new" North End a long line of beaches stretches to the Winooski River delta, beginning with North Beach, which has a grassy picnic area, a snack bar, and boat rentals. Neighboring Leddy Park offers a more secluded beach. **Amenities:** food and drink; lifeguards; parking (fee); showers; toilets. **Best for:** partiers; swimming; walking; windsurfing. ✉ *North Beach Park, 52 Institute Rd., off North Ave.* ☎ *802/865–7247* ⊕ *www.enjoyburlington.com/venue/north-beach* 🅿 *Parking $8 (May–Oct.).*

Restaurants

American Flatbread Burlington

$$ | **PIZZA** | Seating is first-come, first-served at this popular pizza spot, and the wood-fired clay dome ovens pump out delicious and amusingly named pies like "Dancing Heart" (garlic oil, Italian grana padano cheese, toasted sesame seeds) and "Power to the People" (chicken, buffalo sauce, carrots, mozzarella, and blue cheese dressing) in full view of the tables. Fresh salads topped with locally made cheese are also popular. **Known for:** bar run by Zero Gravity Brewery; spacious outdoor seating area; many ingredients sourced from farm 2 miles away. ⑤ *Average main: $18* ✉ *115 St. Paul St.* ☎ *802/861–2999* ⊕ *www.americanflatbread.com.*

A Single Pebble

$$ | **CHINESE** | "Gather, discover, and connect" is the slogan and theme at this intimate Chinese restaurant on the first floor of a residential row house.

Traditional Cantonese- and Sichuan-style dishes are served family style, and the "mock eel" was given two chopsticks up on the Food Network's *The Best Thing I Ever Ate.* **Known for:** many vegetarian options; fire-blistered green beans wok-tossed with flecks of pork; dim sum on Sunday. ⑤ *Average main: $22* ✉ *133 Bank St.* ☎ *802/865–5200* ⊕ *www.asinglepebble.com.*

Farmhouse Tap and Grill

$$ | **AMERICAN** | The line out the door on a typical weekend night should tell you a lot about the local esteem for this farm-to-table restaurant. Serving only local beef, cheese, and produce in a classy but laid-back style, Farmhouse Tap and Grill provides one of the finest meals in the area. **Known for:** local cheese and charcuterie plates; downstairs taproom or the outdoor beer garden; raw bar. ⑤ *Average main: $20* ✉ *160 Bank St.* ☎ *802/859–0888* ⊕ *www.farmhousetg.com.*

The Great Northern

$$ | **MODERN AMERICAN** | This woody, industrial space benefits not only from being neighbors to Zero Gravity Brewery, but also its location at the heart of Burlington's hippest district, the South End. The menu follows the neighborhood zeitgeist, with foodie-friendly bistro bites for lunch and dinner, a raw bar, and a superpopular brunch on weekends. **Known for:** trendy interior design; artisanal cocktail list; hangout of the young and hip. ⑤ *Average main: $20* ✉ *716 Pine St.* ☎ *802/489–5102* ⊕ *www.thegreatnorthernvt.com* ⊗ *No dinner Sun.*

Guild Tavern

$$$ | **STEAKHOUSE** | Some of Vermont's best steak—all meat is sourced from local farms, dry-aged a minimum of 21 days, and cooked to absolute perfection—can be found roasting over hardwood coals in this tavern's open kitchens. The space itself is also a treat, with antique chicken feeders serving as light fixtures and a soapstone-topped bar in the center. **Known for:** steak for two combo; poutine with hand-cut fries; extensive cocktail list. $ *Average main: $25* ✉ *1633 Williston Rd.* ☎ *802/497–1207* ⊕ *www.guildtavern.com* ⊗ *No lunch.*

★ Hen of the Wood Burlington

$$$ | **MODERN AMERICAN** | The Burlington branch of Hen of the Wood offers a slicker, more urban vibe than its original Waterbury location but serves the same inventive yet down-to-earth cuisine that sets diners' hearts aflutter and tongues wagging. Indeed, many consider this the best restaurant in Vermont, so drop your finger anywhere on the menu and you won't go wrong. **Known for:** mushroom toast; dollar oysters every night 4–5 pm; perfect date night spot. $ *Average main: $30* ✉ *55 Cherry St.* ☎ *802/540–0534* ⊕ *www.henofthewood.com* ⊗ *No lunch.*

★ Honey Road

$$$$ | **MEDITERRANEAN** | This Church Street restaurant has garnered multiple James Beard Foundation nominations, launching it into a golden age under the helm of co-owners Allison Gibson and chef Cara Chigazola-Tobin. Serving arguably the best dinner in Burlington, high expectations are satisfied thanks to creative takes on eastern Mediterranean cuisine, including a selection of sensational mezes. **Known for:** daily Honey Time happy hour with $1 chicken wings; muhammara (hot pepper) dip with house-made pita; the cutting edge of local cuisine. $ *Average main: $45* ✉ *156 Church St.* ☎ *802/497–2145* ⊕ *www.honeyroadrestaurant.com* ⊗ *No lunch.*

Istanbul Kebab House

$$ | **TURKISH** | **FAMILY** | The classics of Turkish cuisine are served with surprising authenticity and maximum deliciousness thanks to the culinary talents of its Istanbul-raised owners, plus locally sourced produce and meats. The open terrace upstairs offers the only rooftop dining in Burlington. **Known for:** Turkish casseroles (güveç) baked in earthenware bowls; best kebabs in Burlington, if not Vermont; lavash bread made to order. $ *Average main: $19* ✉ *175 Church St.* ☎ *802/857–5091* ⊕ *www.istanbulkebabhousevt.com* ⊗ *Closed Sun.*

Leunig's Bistro and Cafe

$$$ | **CAFÉ** | This popular café delivers alfresco bistro cuisine with a distinct French flavor, plus a friendly European-style bar and live jazz. Favorite entrées include salade niçoise, *soupe au pistou* (vegetable and white bean soup with Asiago and pesto), and beef bourguignonne. **Known for:** crème brûlée; Sunday brunch; outdoor seating on Church Street. $ *Average main: $28* ✉ *115 Church St.* ☎ *802/863–3759* ⊕ *www.leunigsbistro.com.*

Monarch & the Milkweed

$ | **AMERICAN** | A trendy vibe mixes with exquisite pastries at this café and cocktail bar on the west side of City Hall Park. Buzzing nearly all day, the petite space serves elegant breakfasts by morning, "creative" coffee by day, and artisanal cocktails well into the night, particularly on weekends. **Known for:** CBD sweets; grilled-cheese sandwich; biscuits and gravy. $ *Average main: $13* ✉ *111 St. Paul St.* ☎ *802/310–7828* ⊕ *www.monarchandthemilkweed.com* ⊗ *No dinner Sun.*

Penny Cluse Cafe

$ | **AMERICAN** | **FAMILY** | The lines can be long on weekends to enter this popular breakfast and brunch spot, but it's for a reason. The bright, warm ambience makes a perfect setting for breakfast, brunch, or lunch, with inventive versions of the classic dishes, like fritatta-stuffed breakfast burritos layered with local cheddar and avocado crema; slabs of griddled homemade banana bread with maple-walnut cream cheese; and hearty rice bowls with escabeche-style vegetables. **Known for:** gingerbread-blueberry pancakes; "zydeco" breakfast with andouille sausage and corn muffins; photo ops for local and visiting politicians. $ *Average main: $13* ✉ *169 Cherry St.*

☎ 802/651–8834 ⊕ www.pennycluse.
com ⊘ No dinner.

Pizzeria Verita

$$$ | ITALIAN | "The truth is in the dough"
is the long-standing motto of Burlington's
destination for expert Neopolitan pies.
The bubbled, chewy crusts are flame-
kissed by live fire, and Italian-inspired
ingredients are sourced mostly from local
farmers like the house-made mozzarella
that graces classic pies like the beautifully simple Margherita. **Known for:** excellent
cocktails, especially the house negroni;
wood-fired Neopolitan pizza; farm-
sourced ingredients. $ Average main:
$30 ⊠ 156 St. Paul St. ☎ 802/489–5644
⊕ www.pizzeriaverita.com.

Trattoria Delia

$$$ | ITALIAN | If you didn't make that trip
to Umbria this year, the next best thing
is this Italian country eatery around the
corner from City Hall Park. The secret
to the ambience goes well beyond the
high-quality, handmade pasta dishes
to the supercozy woody interior, a
transplanted sugarhouse from New
Hampshire. **Known for:** excellent wine
list; wood-grilled prosciutto-wrapped
Vermont rabbit; primo Italian desserts.
$ Average main: $27 ⊠ 152 St. Paul St.
☎ 802/864–5253 ⊕ www.trattoriadelia.
com ⊘ No lunch.

Waterworks Food + Drink

$$$ | AMERICAN | In an old textile mill on
the banks of the Winooski River, this
restaurant comes with great views from
nearly every table thanks to a glass wall.
The expansive bar and dining room adds
to the scene with lofty wood-beam
ceilings, exposed brick, and a range of
American bistro-style dishes. **Known for:**
window seats overlooking river; cocktails;
classy, upscale ambience. $ Average
main: $25 ⊠ 20 Winooski Falls Way,
Winooski ☎ 802/497–3525 ⊕ www.
waterworksvt.com.

Zabby and Elf's Stone Soup

$ | AMERICAN | The open front, woody inte-
rior, and community spirit make Stone
Soup a downtown favorite for lunch,
especially on warm days. The small but
robust salad bar is the centerpiece, with
excellent hot and cold dishes—a perfect
complement to the wonderful soups and
fresh sandwiches. **Known for:** vegetarian
dishes; gluten-free baked goods; New
York Jewish-style cooking. $ Average
main: $13 ⊠ 211 College St. ☎ 802/862–
7616 ⊕ www.stonesoupvt.com ⊘ Closed
Sun.

☕ Coffee and Quick Bites

Burlington Bay Market & Cafe

$ | AMERICAN | This may be a local hub for
grabbing a quick sandwich or a case of
beer, but its true fame stands with its
seasonal creemee window. During the
warmer months, lines snake around the
corner for the café's beloved soft serve,
particularly the house specialty: twisted
black raspberry and maple ice cream in
a cone, extra sprinkles. **Known for:** maple
and black raspberry creemees; grocery
staples and necessities; sandwiches,
burgers, and hot dogs. $ Average main:
$5 ⊠ 125 Battery St. ☎ 802/864–0110
⊕ www.burlingtonbaycafe.com.

Kestrel Coffee Roasters

$ | CAFÉ | Two alumni of Blue Hill at Stone
Barns, one of the country's most lauded
restaurants, moved to Burlington in
2017 to realize their dreams of opening
a coffee shop together. The duo focus
on meticulously sourced beans roasted
fresh in-house, scratch-made baked
goods, and a frequently changing menu
of farm-sourced sandwiches. **Known
for:** small-batch roasted coffee beans;
homemade baked goods; maple lattes.
$ Average main: $5 ⊠ 47 Maple St.
☎ 802/391–0081 ⊕ www.kestrelcoffees.
com ⊘ Closed Mon.

Onyx Tonics

$ | CAFÉ | This coffee-tasting bar would satisfy the staunchest coffee aficionado, with its rotating menu of specialty drinks designed to highlight the texture and flavor profile of distinct beans and roasters; so it's not surprising that co-founder Jason Gonzales won a top 10 spot in the 2013 World Cup Tasting Championship (the coffee Olympics). If a coffee education is what you want with your morning cup, Onyx Tonics offers it—thankfully with a friendly and inviting atmosphere—as baristas have been known to warn against adding milk to a certain drip coffee, because it would raise the acidity of the brew and alter its delicate flavor. **Known for:** coffee-tasting bar; the VT Big Easy, coffee and chicory mixed with milk and maple syrup; featured espresso and drip coffee beans. Ⓢ *Average main: $6* ✉ *126 College St.* ☎ *802/777–2583* ⊕ *onyxtonics.com.*

Shy Guy Gelato

$ | ITALIAN | Some of the best gelato outside of Italy is found on a quiet corner of St. Paul Street. Co-owner Paul Sansone was inspired by his Italian heritage to work abroad as an apprentice to some of Southern Italy's most notable gelato masters; he returned to Vermont years later to open his own scoop shop alongside one of Burlington's longtime farm-to-table restaurant owners, Tim Elliot. **Known for:** small-batch gelato and sorbet made with local ingredients; fior di latte (fresh mozzarella) gelato; vegan-friendly sorbets. Ⓢ *Average main: $5* ✉ *457 St. Paul St.* ☎ *802/355–2320* ⊕ *shyguygelato.com* ⊘ *Closed Mon.–Wed.*

Speeder & Earl's Coffee

$ | CAFÉ | This family-owned coffee roaster has been turning out small-batch beans and blends since 1993, making it a well-loved local watering-hole for almost three decades. This quirky, funky café is a prime old-school spot to pick up a bag of beans or mull over the morning paper with a cup of Maple French Roast.

Known for: small-batch coffee blends; house-roasted beans; quirky vibes in a sunny café space. Ⓢ *Average main: $4* ✉ *412 Pine St.* ☎ *802/658–6016* ⊕ *speederandearls.com.*

Hotels

Courtyard Burlington Harbor

$$$ | HOTEL | A block from the lake and a five-minute walk from the heart of town, this attractive chain hotel has a pretty bar and lobby area with couches around a fireplace. **Pros:** right in downtown; some of the best lake views in town; across the street from park and lake. **Cons:** lacks local charm; a bit corporate in ambience; fee for self-parking. Ⓢ *Rooms from: $329* ✉ *25 Cherry St.* ☎ *802/864–4700* ⊕ *www.marriott.com* ⇆ *161 rooms* ⦿ *No meals.*

Hilton Garden Inn

$$$ | HOTEL | One of Burlington's newest hotels, this more playful edition of the Hilton family sits on an ideal location halfway between downtown and the lakefront, putting both in easy walking reach. **Pros:** some rooms have views of the lake; Vermont Comedy Club in the same building; well above average restaurant. **Cons:** uninspired design in rooms; surrounded by busy streets with traffic; small pool. Ⓢ *Rooms from: $309* ✉ *101 Main St.* ☎ *802/951–0099* ⊕ *www.hiltongardeninn3.hilton.com* ⇆ *139 rooms* ⦿ *No meals.*

★ Hotel Vermont

$$$ | HOTEL | Since opening in 2013, the Hotel Vermont has held the hospitality crown for style and cool, which is showcased in the almost magically spacious lobby, with its crackling wood fire, walls of smoky black Vermont granite, reclaimed oak floors, and local artwork. **Pros:** Juniper restaurant serves excellent cocktails; gorgeous rooms; unbelievable service. **Cons:** luxury doesn't come cheap; view of the lake often blocked by other buildings; additional fee for breakfast and

Burlington's Church Street is an open-air mall with restaurants, shops, festivals, and street performers.

self-parking. $ Rooms from: $309 ✉ 41 Cherry St. ☎ 802/651–0080 ⊕ www. hotelvt.com ⮌ 125 rooms ⦿ No meals.

The Lang House on Main Street

$$ | B&B/INN | Within walking distance of downtown in the historic hill section of town, this grand 1881 Victorian home charms completely with its period furnishings, fine woodwork, plaster detailing, stained-glass windows, and sunlit dining area. **Pros:** family-friendly vibe; interesting location; fantastic breakfast. **Cons:** no elevator; on a busy street; old-fashioned design not for everyone. $ Rooms from: $219 ✉ 360 Main St. ☎ 802/652–2500, 877/919–9799 ⊕ www. langhouse.com ⮌ 11 rooms ⦿ Free breakfast.

★ Made INN Vermont

$$ | B&B/INN | Few accommodations in Vermont find a dynamic balance between the traditional inn and trendy boutique spirit, but this eminently charming and quirky 1881 house topped with a cute cupola has done it. **Pros:** excellent location between the University of Vermont and Champlain College; vivacious and involved innkeeper; hot tub out back. **Cons:** bathrooms are private, but not en suite; rooms are modest in size; higher cost than most other inns in town. $ Rooms from: $259 ✉ 204 S. Willard St. ☎ 802/399–2788 ⊕ www.madeinnver-mont.com ⮌ 4 rooms ⦿ Free breakfast.

Willard Street Inn

$ | B&B/INN | High in the historic hill section of Burlington, this ivy-covered house with an exterior marble staircase and English gardens incorporates elements of Queen Anne and Georgian Revival styles including the stately foyer, with cherry paneling, and the flower-decked solarium that overlooks the back garden. **Pros:** innkeepers passionate about their job; lots of friendly attention; complimentary chef-plated breakfast. **Cons:** a tad old-fashioned; walk to downtown can be a drag in winter; no elevator. $ Rooms from: $175 ✉ 349 S. Willard St. ☎ 802/651–8710, 800/577–8712 ⊕ www. willardstreetinn.com ⮌ 14 rooms ⦿ Free breakfast.

Nightlife

ArtsRiot

MUSIC CLUBS | This unofficial headquarters of the South End Arts District has grown in recent years to include a full-service restaurant serving bistro bites and a concert stage that hosts local and national acts. Every Friday evening in summer, food trucks set up shop in the back parking lot. ⊠ *400 Pine St.* ☎ *802/540-0406* ⊕ *www.artsriot.com.*

Citizen Cider

BARS/PUBS | The tiny parking lot out front gets jammed after 5 pm, as the spacious "tasting room" of this hard-cider maker fills with exuberant young, hip professionals and students. Sample cider straight or in a dozen or so cocktails. There's a full bistro menu, too. ⊠ *316 Pine St., Suite 114* ☎ *802/497-1987* ⊕ *www.citizencider. com.*

Higher Ground

MUSIC CLUBS | When you feel like shaking it up to live music, come to Higher Ground—it gets the lion's share of local and national musicians. ⊠ *1214 Williston Rd., South Burlington* ☎ *802/652-0777* ⊕ *www.highergroundmusic.com.*

Mule Bar

BARS/PUBS | This Winooski watering hole pours some of the best craft brews from around the state and is a must for aficionados. Outdoor seating and above-average bar bites seal the deal for its young and hip clientele. ⊠ *38 Main St., Winooski* ☎ *802/399-2020* ⊕ *www. mulebarvt.com.*

Nectar's

BARS/PUBS | Jam band Phish got its start at Nectar's, which is always jumping to the sounds of local bands, stand-up comics, and live-band karaoke and never charges a cover. Don't leave without a helping of the bar's famous fries and gravy. ⊠ *188 Main St.* ☎ *802/658-4771* ⊕ *www.liveatnectars.com.*

Radio Bean

BARS/PUBS | For some true local flavor, head to this funky place for nightly live music, an artsy vibe, and a cocktail. Performances happen every day, but Tuesday night is arguably the most fun, as the Honkey Tonk band blazes through covers of Gram Parsons, Wilco, and the like. ⊠ *8 N. Winooski Ave.* ☎ *802/660-9346* ⊕ *www.radiobean.com.*

Performing Arts

★ Flynn Center for the Performing Arts

CONCERTS | It's a pleasure to see any show inside this grandiose art deco gem. In addition to being home to Vermont's largest musical theater company, it hosts the Vermont Symphony Orchestra, as well as big-name acts like Neko Case and Elvis Costello. The adjacent Flynn Space is a coveted spot for more offbeat, experimental performances. ⊠ *153 Main St.* ☎ *802/863-5966* ⊕ *www.flynncenter.org.*

Shopping

With each passing year, Burlington's industrial South End attracts ever greater numbers of artists and craftspeople, who set up studios, shops, and galleries in former factories and warehouses along Pine Street. The district's annual "Art Hop" in September is the city's largest arts celebration—and a roaring good time.

CLOTHING

April Cornell

CLOTHING | The Vermont designer's flagship store stocks her distinctive floral-print dresses and linens. ⊠ *131 Battery St.* ☎ *802/863-0060* ⊕ *www. aprilcornell.com.*

CRAFTS

Bennington Potters North

CERAMICS/GLASSWARE | Along with the popular pottery line, this store stocks interesting kitchen items. ⊠ *127 College St.* ☎ *802/863-2221* ⊕ *www.benningtonpotters.com.*

★ Frog Hollow

CERAMICS/GLASSWARE | This nonprofit collective and gallery sells contemporary and traditional crafts, paintings, and photographs by more than 200 Vermont artists and artisans. ⊠ *85 Church St.* ☎ *802/863–6458* ⊕ *www.froghollow.org.*

FOOD

Lake Champlain Chocolates

FOOD/CANDY | This chocolatier makes sensational truffles, caramels, candies, fudge, and hot chocolate. The chocolates are all-natural, made in Vermont, and make a great edible souvenir. Factory tours are available. A retail branch is also on Church Street. ⊠ *750 Pine St.* ☎ *802/864–1807 Pine St., 802/862–5185 Church St., 800/465–5909* ⊕ *www.lakechamplainchocolates.com.*

NU Chocolat

FOOD/CANDY | This European-style chocolate boutique combines Swiss-trained chocolatier, premier Belgian equipment, a minimalist's eye for detail, and a family-owned mentality. Owners Laura and Kevin Toohey and their children, co-founders Rowan and Virginia Toohey, spotlight their chocolate craftsmanship with delights like cocoa-dusted almonds, chocolate-covered candied orange peel, and uniquely beautiful seasonal truffles. ⊠ *180 Battery St.* ☎ *802/540–8378* ⊕ *www.nuchocolat.com.*

SPORTING GOODS

Burton

SPORTING GOODS | The folks who helped start snowboarding—a quintessential Vermont company—sell equipment and clothing at their flagship store. A second retail branch is in downtown Burlington, on 162 College Street. ⊠ *80 Industrial Pkwy.* ☎ *802/660–3200, 802/333–0400 College St.* ⊕ *www.burton.com.*

Activities

BIKING

★ Burlington Bike Path

BICYCLING | **FAMILY** | Anyone who's put the rubber to the road on the 7½-mile Burlington Bike Path and its almost equally long northern extension on the Island Line Trail sings its praises. Along the way there are endless postcard views of Lake Champlain and the Adirondack Mountains. The northern end of the trail is slightly more rugged and windswept, so dress accordingly. ⊠ *Burlington* ☎ *802/864–0123* ⊕ *enjoyburlington.com/place/burlington-greenway.*

North Star Sports

BICYCLING | In addition to stocking an extensive supply of sports apparel and accessories, this family-owned shop rents bikes and provides cycling maps. ⊠ *100 Main St.* ☎ *802/863–3832* ⊕ *www.northstarsportsvt.com.*

Ski Rack

BICYCLING | Burlington's one-stop shop for winter sports equipment, the Ski Rack also rents bikes and sells running gear throughout the year. ⊠ *85 Main St.* ☎ *802/658–3313, 800/882–4530* ⊕ *www.skirack.com.*

BOATING

Burlington Community Boathouse

BOATING | This boathouse administers the city's marina as well as a summertime watering hole called Splash, one of the best places to watch the sun set over the lake. ⊠ *Burlington Harbor, College St.* ☎ *802/865–3377* ⊕ *enjoyburlington.com.*

Community Sailing Center

BOATING | **FAMILY** | Burlington's shiny new 22,000-square-foot Community Sailing Center has 150 watercraft to rent including kayaks, sailboats, and standup paddleboards for as little as $15 an hour. Private instruction and family lessons are available, as are floating yoga classes. ⊠ *505 Lake St.* ☎ *802/864–2499*

⊕ *www.communitysailingcenter.org*
◷ *Closed mid-Oct.–mid-May.*

Lake Champlain Shoreline Cruises
BOATING | FAMILY | The trilevel *Spirit of Ethan Allen III,* a 363-passenger vessel, offers narrated cruises, theme dinners, and sunset sails with breathtaking Adirondacks and Green Mountains views. The standard 1½-hour cruise runs four times a day; sunset cruises leave at 6:30 pm on Friday and Saturday. ⊠ *Burlington Boat House, 1 College St.* ☎ *802/862–8300* ⊕ *www.soea.com* 🕙 *From $23.*

True North Kayak Tours
CANOEING/ROWING/SKULLING | This company conducts two- and five-hour guided kayak tours of Lake Champlain that include talks about the region's natural history and customized lessons. ⊠ *25 Nash Pl.* ☎ *802/238–7695* ⊕ *www. vermontkayak.com.*

SKIING
Bolton Valley Resort
SKIING/SNOWBOARDING | FAMILY | The closest ski resort to Burlington, about 25 miles away, Bolton Valley is a family favorite. In addition to downhill trails—more than half rated for intermediate and beginner skiers—Bolton offers 62 miles of cross-country and snowshoe trails, night skiing, and a sports center. **Facilities:** 71 trails; 300 acres; 1,704-foot vertical drop; 5 lifts. ⊠ *4302 Bolton Valley Access Rd., north off U.S. 2, Bolton* ☎ *802/434–3444, 877/926–5866* ⊕ *www. boltonvalley.com* 🕙 *Lift ticket: $74.*

Shelburne

5 miles south of Burlington.

A few miles south of Burlington, the Champlain Valley gives way to fertile farmland, affording views of the rugged Adirondacks across the lake. In the middle of this farmland is the village of Shelburne, chartered in the mid-18th century and partly a bedroom community

for Burlington. Shelburne Farms and the Shelburne Museum are worth at least a few hours of exploring, as are Shelburne Orchards in fall, when you can pick your own apples and drink fresh cider while admiring breathtaking views of the lake and mountains beyond.

Just south of Shelburne is beautiful, rural town of Charlotte. Expect to find open farmstands, rolling pastures and grazing cows along these serpentine roads, many of which offer hidden gems like u-pick berries and seasonal barbecues on the farm.

GETTING HERE AND AROUND
Shelburne is south of Burlington after the town of South Burlington, which is notable for its very un-Vermont traffic congestion and a commercial and fast food–laden stretch of U.S. 7. It's easy to confuse Shelburne Farms (2 miles west of town on the lake) with Shelburne Museum, which is right on U.S. 7 just south of town, but you'll want to make time for both.

Sights

★ Clemmons Family Farm
ARTS VENUE | Founded in 1962 by Jackson and Lydia Clemmons, this 148-acre farm is one of a handful of Black-owned arts and culture nonprofit organizations in the state, and one of the 22 landmarks on Vermont's African-American Heritage Trail. Along with acres of lush farmland, forest, meadows and ponds, six historic buildings offer space for artist residencies, art exhibits, creative studios, retreats, small performances, and community events celebrating the African diaspora. The Storytelling Room in the Barn House is a community hub for arts, sciences and culture programs, including featured exhibits and speakers' series. ⊠ *2213–2122 Greenbush Rd., Charlotte* ☎ *765/560–5445* ⊕ *www.clemmonsfami-lyfarm.org.*

Vermont's African American Heritage Trail

The Vermont African American Heritage Trail (⊕ *vtafricanamericanheritage.net*) helps share the link between Vermont, the first state constitution to outlaw slavery, and African American residents who have lived here since the Revolutionary War. There are 22 sights throughout the state, including seven museums: Ferrisburgh's **Rokeby Museum & the Underground Railroad**; Middlebury's **Vermont Folklife Center**; the **Brandon Museum**; Manchester's **Hildene, The Lincoln Family Home**; the **Grafton History Museum**; Windsor's **Old Constitution House State Historic Site**; and Browningston's **Old Stone House Museum and Brownington Village.** The 148-acre **Clemmons Family Farm** in Charlotte, another stop along the heritage trail, celebrates the history, culture, arts and sciences of the African American diaspora via programs like on-site artist residencies, theater performances, literary events, and guided tours through the verdant property and its six historic buildings.

Fiddlehead Brewing Company
WINERY/DISTILLERY | There isn't much to the tasting room here, but there doesn't need to be: Fiddlehead only occasionally cans its celebrated beer, making this the best place outside of a restaurant to sample it on tap (and for free). Decide which one you like best and buy a growler to go—or, better yet, take it to Folino's Pizza next door, where the pies are mighty fine. ⊠ *6305 Shelburne Rd.* ☎ *802/399–2994* ⊕ *www.fiddleheadbrewing.com* ⊡ *Free.*

Mount Philo State Park
NATIONAL/STATE PARK | FAMILY | For many Vermont kids, this is their first hike, thanks to the relatively easy, gently rising, paved road that snakes around the sides to the top, where fabulous views of the lake and landscape await. If less inclined to walk, feel free to drive. ⊠ *5425 Mt. Philo Rd., Charlotte* ☎ *802/425–2390* ⊕ *www.vtstateparks.com/philo.html* ⊡ *$4.*

★ Shelburne Farms
COLLEGE | FAMILY | Founded in the 1880s as a private estate for two very rich New Yorkers, this 1,400-acre farm is much more than an exquisite landscape: it's an educational and cultural resource center with a working dairy farm, an award-winning cheese producer, an organic market garden, and a bakery whose aroma of fresh bread and pastries is an olfactory treat. It's a brilliant place for parents to expose their kids to the dignity of farmwork and the joys of compassionate animal husbandry—indeed, children and adults alike will get a kick out of hunting for eggs in the oversize coop, milking a cow, and watching the chicken parade. There are several activities and tours daily, and a lunch cart serves up fresh-from-the-farm soups, salads, and sandwiches. Frederick Law Olmsted, the co-creator of New York City's Central Park, designed the magnificent grounds overlooking Lake Champlain; walk to Lone Tree Hill for a splendid view. If you fall in love with the scenery, arrange a romantic dinner at the lakefront mansion, or spend the night. ⊠ *1611 Harbor Rd., west of U.S. 7* ☎ *802/985–8686* ⊕ *www.shelburnefarms.org* ⊡ *$8.*

★ Shelburne Museum
MUSEUM | FAMILY | You can trace much of New England's history simply by wandering through the 45 acres and 39 buildings of this museum. Some 25 buildings were

relocated here, including an old-fashioned jail, an 1871 lighthouse, and a 220-foot steamboat, the *Ticonderoga*. The outstanding 150,000-object collection of art, design, and Americana consists of antique furniture, fine and folk art, quilts, trade signs, and weather vanes; there are also more than 200 carriages and sleighs. The Pizzagalli Center for Art and Education is open year-round with changing exhibitions and programs for kids and adults. ⊠ *6000 Shelburne Rd.* ☎ *802/985–3346* ⊕ *www.shelburnemuseum.org* 🖭 *$25* ⊗ *Call for hrs, which vary by season and museum.*

Shelburne Vineyard

WINERY/DISTILLERY | From U.S. 7, you'll see rows and rows of organically grown vines. Visit the attractive tasting room and learn how wine is made. Also available on-site is a Shelburne Vineyard collaboration called Iaepetus, a natural wine label from notable biodynamic winemaker Ethan Joseph. ⊠ *6308 Shelburne Rd.* ☎ *802/985–8222* ⊕ *www.shelburnevineyard.com* 🖭 *Tasting $7, tour free.*

Vermont Teddy Bear Company

FACTORY | **FAMILY** | On the 30-minute tour of this fun-filled factory you'll hear more puns than you ever thought possible, while learning how a few homemade bears sold from a cart on Church Street turned into a multimillion-dollar business. Patrons and children can relax, eat, and play under a large canvas tent in summer, or wander the beautiful 57-acre property. ⊠ *6655 Shelburne Rd.* ☎ *802/985–3001* ⊕ *www.vermontteddybear.com* 🖭 *Tour $4.*

🍴 Restaurants

The Bearded Frog

$$ | **ECLECTIC** | This restaurant is perfect for a casual dinner at the bar or a more sophisticated experience in the attractive dining room. At the bar, try the soups, burgers, and terrific cocktails; the dining room serves fresh salads, seared seafood, roasted poultry, grilled steaks, and decadent desserts. **Known for:** $1 pints of Fiddlehead on Friday; entire menu available to go; many gluten-free, vegetarian, and vegan choices. 🖭 *Average main: $23* ⊠ *5247 Shelburne Rd.* ☎ *802/985–9877* ⊕ *www.thebeardedfrog.com* ⊗ *No lunch.*

★ The Dining Room at the Inn at Shelburne Farms

$$$ | **AMERICAN** | Dinner here will make you dream of F. Scott Fitzgerald, as piano music wafts in from the library of this 1880s mansion on the shores of Lake Champlain. **Known for:** possibly best Sunday brunch in area; beautiful gardens; farmhouse cheddar. 🖭 *Average main: $33* ⊠ *Inn at Shelburne Farms, 1611 Harbor Rd.* ☎ *802/985–8498* ⊕ *www.shelburnefarms.org* ⊗ *Closed mid-Oct.–mid-May.*

Rustic Roots

$$ | **AMERICAN** | Scuffed wood floors and chunky country tables bring the "rustic" at this converted farmhouse—but not too much. An intimate bar and maroon walls adorned with woodcrafts and art add a touch of elegance, and the French-inspired food is carefully prepared. **Known for:** coffee-maple sausage; pastrami on rye; Bloody Marys. 🖭 *Average main: $21* ⊠ *195 Falls Rd.* ☎ *802/985–9511* ⊕ *www.rusticrootsvt.com* ⊗ *Closed Mon. and Tues. No dinner Wed., Thurs., and Sun.*

☕ Coffee and Quick Bites

Philo Ridge Farm & Market

$ | **AMERICAN** | This 400-acre diversified farm is a leader in regenerative agriculture, and its on-site market and café show the depth of the land's bounty. Two hundred of those acres are dedicated to organic vegetable, flower, herb, and fruit production, which is then channeled into the sandwiches, salads, prepared foods, and pantry goods in the on-site market. **Known for:** locally roasted coffee with Vermont milk and cream; housemade pastries; sandwiches, salads, and

At the Shelburne Museum, the restored 220-foot *Ticonderoga* steamboat is the last existing walking beam side-wheel passenger steamer.

lunch specials made with farm ingredients. ⑤ *Average main: $14* ✉ *2766 Mt. Philo Rd., Charlotte* ☎ *802/539–2912* ⊕ *philoridgefarm.com.*

Vermont Cookie Love

$ | **BAKERY** | The "Love Shack" on the side of VT Route 7 is known to have one of the best maple creemees in the state due to its use of Vermont maple syrup and high-butterfat dairy from Kingdom Creamery of Vermont. There are also coffee, vanilla, and chocolate creemees on offer, along with local Wilcox hard ice cream and house-made cookies made daily on-site. **Known for:** homemade cookies; maple and coffee soft serve; crushed cookie crumbles for topping cones and sundaes. ⑤ *Average main: $4* ✉ *6915 Rte. 7, Ferrisburgh* ☎ *802/425–8181* ⊕ *www.vermontcookielove.com* ⊗ *Creemee window closed Nov.–Mar.*

 Hotels

Heart of the Village Inn

$ | **B&B/INN** | Each of the elegantly furnished rooms at this B&B in an 1886 Queen Anne Victorian provides coziness and tastefully integrated modern conveniences. **Pros:** easy walk to shops and restaurants; elegant historical building; hypoallergenic bedding and memory foam mattresses. **Cons:** near to but not within Shelburne Farms; no room service; no children under 12. ⑤ *Rooms from: $189* ✉ *5347 Shelburne Rd.* ☎ *802/985–9060* ⊕ *www.heartofthe-village.com* ⮡ *9 rooms* ❏ *Free breakfast.*

★ The Inn at Shelburne Farms

$ | **B&B/INN** | It's hard not to feel like an aristocrat at this exquisite turn-of-the-20th-century Tudor-style inn, perched at the edge of Lake Champlain—even Teddy Roosevelt stayed here. **Pros:** stately lakefront setting in a historic mansion; endless activities; proposal-worthy restaurant. **Cons:** lowest-priced rooms have shared

baths; closed in winter; no air-conditioning.
[$] *Rooms from: $170 ⊠ 1611 Harbor Rd.*
☎ *802/985–8498 ⊕ www.shelburne-farms.org ⊗ Closed mid-Oct.–mid-May*
⇥ *28 rooms* ⊙| *No meals.*

★ **Mt. Philo Inn**

$$$ | **B&B/INN** | Practically on the slopes of Mt. Philo State Park in Charlotte, the 1896 inn offers gorgeous views of Lake Champlain from its outdoor porches and an ideal blend of historical and contemporary boutique decor. **Pros:** walking trail goes directly to Mt. Philo State Park; lots of local stonework incorporated; complimentary breakfast basket includes all the fixings. **Cons:** not walking distance to any sights; rooms too big for just one guest; you cook breakfast yourself. [$] *Rooms from: $320 ⊠ 27 Inn Rd., Charlotte* ☎ *802/425–3335 ⊕ www.mtphiloinn.com* ⇥ *4 suites* ⊙| *No meals.*

Lake Champlain Islands

Lake Champlain stretches more than 100 miles south from the Canadian border and forms the northern part of the boundary between New York and Vermont. Within it is an elongated archipelago comprising several islands—Isle La Motte, North Hero, Grand Isle, and South Hero—and the Alburg Peninsula. Enjoying a temperate climate, the islands hold several apple orchards and are a center of water recreation in summer and ice fishing in winter. A scenic drive through the islands on U.S. 2 begins at Interstate 89 and travels north to Alburg Center; Route 78 takes you back to the mainland.

ESSENTIALS

VISITOR INFORMATION Lake Champlain Islands Chamber of Commerce. ☎ *802/372–8400, 800/262–5226 ⊕ www.champlainislands.com.* **Lake Champlain Regional Chamber of Commerce.** ☎ *802/863–3489, 877/686–5253 ⊕ www.vermont.org.*

⊙ Sights

Alburgh Dunes State Park

PARK—SPORTS-OUTDOORS | This park has one of the longest sandy beaches on Lake Champlain and some fine examples of rare flora and fauna along the hiking trails. The wetlands are also an important area for wildlife refuge, providing a safe habitat for breeding, feeding, and nesting for surrounding animals like deer and wild turkey. ⊠ *151 Coon Point Rd., off U.S. 2, Alburg* ☎ *802/796–4170 ⊕ www.vtstateparks.com/alburgh.html* ⌷ *$4.*

★ Allenholm Farm

FARM/RANCH | The pick-your-own apples at this farm are amazingly tasty—if you're here at harvest time, don't miss out. The farm also has a petting area with donkeys, miniature horses, sheep, goats, and other animals. At the store, you can buy cheeses, dried fruit, homemade pies, and maple creemees. ⊠ *111 South St., South Hero* ☎ *802/372–5566 ⊕ www.allenholm.com* ⌷ *Free.*

Grand Isle State Park

PARK—SPORTS-OUTDOORS | You'll find hiking trails, boat rentals, and shore fishing at Grand Isle. ⊠ *36 E. Shore S, off U.S. 2, Grand Isle* ☎ *802/372–4300 ⊕ www.vtstateparks.com/grandisle.html* ⌷ *$4.*

Hyde Log Cabin

BUILDING | Built in 1783, this log cabin on South Hero is often cited as the country's oldest surviving specimen. It's now home to the Grand Isle Historical Society. ⊠ *228 U.S. 2, Grand Isle* ☎ *802/828–3051* ⌷ *$3 ⊗ Closed weekdays mid-Oct.–May.*

Missisquoi National Wildlife Refuge

HIKING/WALKING | On the mainland east of the Alburg Peninsula, the refuge consists of 6,729 acres of federally protected wetlands, meadows, and woods. It's a beautiful area for bird-watching, canoeing, and walking nature trails. ⊠ *29 Tabor Rd., 36 miles north of Burlington, Swanton* ☎ *802/868–4781 ⊕ www.fws.gov/refuge/missisquoi.*

Snow Farm Vineyard and Winery

WINERY/DISTILLERY | Vermont's first vineyard was started here in 1996; today, the winery specializes in nontraditional botanical hybrid grapes designed to take advantage of the island's microclimate, similar to that of Burgundy, France. Take a self-guided tour and sip some samples in the tasting room—dessert wines are the strong suit. On Thursday evening, late May–September, you can picnic and enjoy the free concerts on the lawn. ⊠ *190 W. Shore Rd., South Hero* ☎ *802/372–9463* ⊕ *www.snowfarm.com* ⊠ *Free* ۞ *Closed late Dec.–Apr.*

St. Anne's Shrine

RELIGIOUS SITE | This spot marks the site where, in 1665, French soldiers and Jesuits put ashore and built a fort, creating Vermont's first European settlement. Vermont's first Roman Catholic Mass was celebrated here on July 26, 1666. ⊠ *92 St. Anne's Rd., Isle La Motte* ☎ *802/928–3362* ⊕ *www.saintannesshrine.org* ⊠ *Free.*

Restaurants

Blue Paddle Bistro

$$ | AMERICAN | Co-owner Mandy Hotchkiss and chef-owner Phoebe R. Bright share a decades-spanning friendship; today, their ongoing collaboration manifests in the bistro's seasonal menu and hand-written, daily changing nightly specials inspired by farm-sourced ingredients. **Known for:** farm-to-table nightly specials; local beef burgers; plenty of Vermont-grown vegetables. ⑤ *Average main: $24* ⊠ *316 U.S. Rte. 2, South Hero* ☎ *802/372–4814* ⊕ *www.bluepaddlebistro.com.*

Hotels

North Hero House Inn and Restaurant

$ | B&B/INN | FAMILY | This inn has four buildings right on Lake Champlain, among them the 1891 Colonial Revival main house with a restaurant, pub, and library. **Pros:** resort really gets away from it all; superb lakefront setting; many rooms have screened-in porches. **Cons:** much less to do in winter; two-night minimum on weekends and holidays; relatively bland design. ⑤ *Rooms from: $140* ⊠ *3643 U.S. 2, North Hero* ☎ *802/372–4732, 888/525–3644* ⊕ *www.northherohouse.com* ۞ *Closed mid-Oct.–Dec.* ➟ *26 rooms* ۞ *Free breakfast.*

Ruthcliffe Lodge & Restaurant

$ | HOTEL | If you're looking for an inexpensive summer destination—to take in the scenery, canoe the lake, or go biking—this will do quite nicely as the lodge is on the rarely visited Isle La Motte. **Pros:** inexpensive rates; high-quality restaurant; laid-back vibe. **Cons:** two-night minimum stays on weekends and holiday periods; quite remote; simple, bland design. ⑤ *Rooms from: $142* ⊠ *1002 Quarry Rd., Isle La Motte* ☎ *802/928–3200* ⊕ *www.ruthcliffe.com* ۞ *Closed mid-Oct.–mid-May* ➟ *7 rooms* ۞ *Free breakfast.*

Activities

Apple Island Resort

BOATING | The resort's marina rents pontoon boats, rowboats, canoes, kayaks, and pedal boats. ⊠ *71 U.S. 2, South Hero* ☎ *802/372–3922* ⊕ *www.appleislandresort.com.*

Hero's Welcome

BOATING | This general store rents bikes, canoes, kayaks, and paddleboards; come winter, they switch to ice skates, cross-country skis, and snowshoes. ⊠ *3537 U.S. 2, North Hero* ☎ *802/372–4161* ⊕ *www.heroswelcome.com.*

North Hero State Park

PARK—SPORTS-OUTDOORS | The 399-acre North Hero has a swimming beach and nature trails. It's open to rowboats, kayaks, and canoes. ⊠ *3803 Lakeview Dr., North Hero* ☎ *802/372–8727* ⊕ *www.vtstateparks.com/northhero.html* ⊠ *$4.*

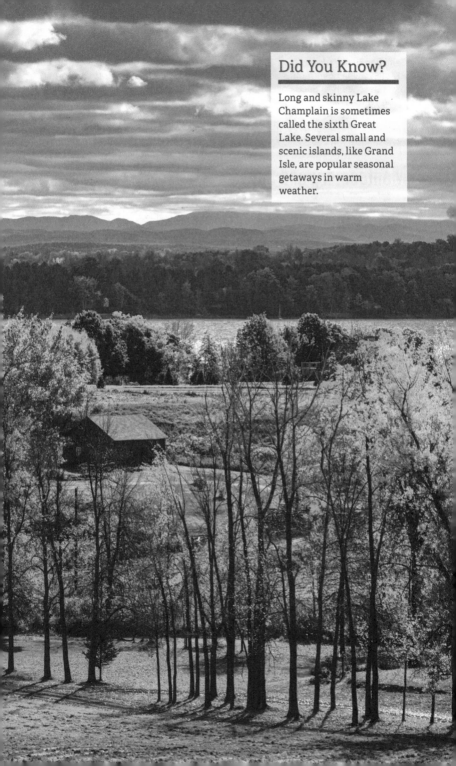

Sand Bar State Park

BEACHES | One of Vermont's best swimming beaches is at Sand Bar State Park, along with a snack bar, a changing room, and boat rentals. ⊠ *1215 U.S. 2, South Hero* ☎ *802/893–2825* ⊕ *vtstateparks. com/sandbar.html* 🎟 *$4.*

Montgomery and Jay

51 miles northeast of Burlington.

Montgomery is a small village near the Jay Peak ski resort and the Canadian border. Amid the surrounding countryside are seven covered bridges.

GETTING HERE AND AROUND
Montgomery lies at the junction of Routes 58, 118, and 242. From Burlington, take Interstate 89 north to Routes 105 and 118 east. Route 242 connects Montgomery and, to the northeast, the Jay Peak Resort.

Sights

Lake Memphremagog

BODY OF WATER | Vermont's second-largest body of water, Lake Memphremagog extends 33 miles north from Newport into Canada. Prouty Beach in Newport has tennis courts, boat rentals, and a 9-hole disc-golf course. Watch the sunset from the deck of the East Side Restaurant, which serves excellent burgers and prime rib. ⊠ *242 Prouty Beach Rd., Newport* ☎ *802/334–6345* ⊕ *www.newportrecreation.org.*

Coffee and Quick Bites

Miso Hungry

$ | JAPANESE | At the base of mammoth Jay Peak sits a wood-shingled food truck cooking arguably the best ramen in the state. Owners Momoko and Jordan Antonucci met as rafting guides in Japan, and spent three winters in Hokkaido gravitating towards the steaming bowls of noodles made at après-ski ramen trucks parked mountainside. **Known for:** spicy miso ramen; seasonal onigiri; authentic Japanese cooking made with Vermont-sourced ingredients. ⑤ *Average main: $13* ⊠ *830 Jay Peak Rd., Jay* ☎ *518/605–4474* ⊕ *www.misohungryramen.com.*

Hotels

★ The INN

$ | B&B/INN | This smart chalet-style lodge comes with tons of character. **Pros:** Trout River views from back rooms; within walking distance of shops and supplies; smart, individually designed rooms. **Cons:** noise from bar can seep into nearby rooms; two-night minimum stay; outside food and alcohol not allowed. ⑤ *Rooms from: $169* ⊠ *241 Main St.* ☎ *802/326–4391* ⊕ *www.theinn.us* 🛏 *11 rooms* ❚◎❚ *Free breakfast.*

Jay Peak Resort

$$ | HOTEL | FAMILY | Accommodations at Jay Peak include standard hotel rooms, suites, condominiums, town houses, and cottage and clubhouse suites. **Pros:** slopes never far away; 60,000-square-foot indoor water park; kids 14 and under stay and eat free and complimentary childcare is provided. **Cons:** can get noisy; not very intimate; service can be lackluster. ⑤ *Rooms from: $239* ⊠ *830 Jay Peak Rd.* ☎ *802/988–2611* ⊕ *www. jaypeakresort.com* 🛏 *515 units* ❚◎❚ *Free breakfast.*

Phineas Swann Bed & Breakfast Inn

$ | B&B/INN | The top-hatted bulldog on the sign of this 1880 farmhouse isn't just a mascot: it reflects the hotel's welcoming attitude to pet owners. **Pros:** walking distance from shops and supplies; lots of dogs; each room has different design. **Cons:** decor is a tad old-fashioned; dog theme (and actual dogs) not for everyone; no outside alcohol allowed.

$ Rooms from: $199 ✉ 195 Main St. ☎ 802/326–4306 ⊕ www.phineasswann. com ⇝ 9 rooms ⎮○⎮ Free breakfast.

Activities

ICE-SKATING
Ice Haus Arena
HOCKEY | FAMILY | The sprawling arena contains a professional-size hockey rink and seating for 400 spectators. You can practice your stick handling, and the rink is open to the public for skating several times a week. There are tournaments throughout the year. ✉ 830 Jay Peak Rd., Jay ☎ 802/988–2727 ⊕ www.jay-peakresort.com ⎆ $6.

SKIING
Hazen's Notch Association
SKIING/SNOWBOARDING | Delightfully remote at any time of the year, this center has 40 miles of marked and groomed trails and rents equipment and snowshoes. ✉ 1423 Hazen's Notch Rd. ☎ 802/326–4799 ⊕ www.hazensnotch. org ⎆ Trail pass: $12.

Jay Peak
SKIING/SNOWBOARDING | Sticking up out of the flat farmland, Jay Peak averages 349 inches of snow per year—more than any other Vermont ski area—and it's renowned for its glade skiing and powder. There are two interconnected mountains, the highest reaching nearly 4,000 feet. The smaller mountain has straight-fall-line, expert terrain that eases mid-mountain into an intermediate pitch. Beginners should stay near the bottom on trails off the Metro quad lift. There are also five terrain parks, snowshoeing, telemark skiing, and a state-of-the art ice arena for hockey, figure skating, and curling. The Pump House, an indoor water park with pools and slides, is open year-round. **Facilities:** 78 trails; 385 acres; 2,153-foot vertical drop; 9 lifts. ✉ 830 Jay Peak Rd., Jay ☎ 802/988–2611 ⊕ www. jaypeakresort.com ⎆ Lift ticket: $84.

Lake Willoughby

30 miles southeast of Montgomery (summer route; 50 miles by winter route), 28 miles north of St. Johnsbury.

The jewel of the Northeast Kingdom is clear, deep, and chilly Lake Willoughby, edged by sheer cliffs and surrounded by state forest. The only town on its shores is tiny Westmore, which has a beach and a few shops that cater to campers and seasonal residents.

Sights

Bread and Puppet Museum
MUSEUM | FAMILY | This ramshackle barn houses a surrealistic collection of props used by the world-renowned Bread and Puppet Theater. The troupe has been performing social and political commentary with the towering (they're supported by people on stilts) and eerily expressive puppets for more than 50 years. In July and August, there are performances on Saturday night and Sunday afternoon, with museum tours before Sunday shows. ✉ 753 Heights Rd., 1 mile east of Rte. 16, Glover ☎ 802/525–3031 ⊕ www. breadandpuppet.org ⎆ Donations accepted ⊙ Closed Nov.–May.

Lake Willoughby
BODY OF WATER | The cliffs of Mt. Pisgah and Mt. Hor drop to the edge of Lake Willoughby on opposite shores, giving this beautiful, deep, glacially carved lake a striking resemblance to a Norwegian fjord. The trails to the top of Mt. Pisgah reward hikers with glorious views. Take note: the beach on the southern end is Vermont's most famous nude beach. ✉ Westmore.

Greensboro

30 miles northwest of St. Johnsbury.

Tucked along the southern shore of Caspian Lake, Greensboro has been a summer resort for literati, academics, and old-money types for more than a century. Yet it exudes an unpretentious, genteel character—most of the people running about on errands seem to know each other. The town beach is right off the main street.

Sights

★ Hill Farmstead Brewery

WINERY/DISTILLERY | It is difficult to quantify owner and master brewer Shaun Hill's contribution to the international explosion of craft beer. Hill Farmstead has won Best Brewery in the World six times in the past decade, and it's a key player in Vermont tourism, where beer contributes as much to the state economy as skiing and hiking. Since opening in 2010, Hill's eighth generation family farmstead off a rural mountain pass, miles from cell service, has drawn millions of local and international travelers pilgrimaging for a coveted pint and a growler to-go. A beautiful bar is surrounded by acres of woods and lawnspace, and a small lake sits at the bottom of a sloping field—a nice spot for pondering over a pint. ⊠ *403 Hill Rd.* ☎ *802/533–7450* ⊕ *hillfarmstead.com.*

Shopping

The Willey's Store

CONVENIENCE/GENERAL STORES | This is a classic general store of the "if-we-don't-have-it-you-don't-need-it" kind. It's also the spot where locals in the know can snag hard-to-find Vermont gems like Jasper Hill Farm cheeses and bottles of Hill Farmstead beer. ⊠ *7 Breezy Ave.* ☎ *802/533–2621.*

Chapter 5

NEW HAMPSHIRE

Updated by
Andrew Collins

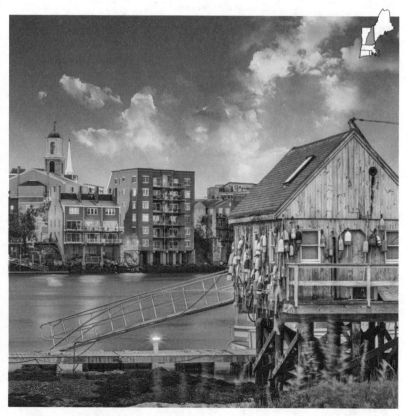

👁 Sights	🍴 Restaurants	🛏 Hotels	🛍 Shopping	🍸 Nightlife
★★★★★	★★★☆☆	★★★★☆	★★★★☆	★★★☆☆

WELCOME TO
NEW HAMPSHIRE

TOP REASONS TO GO

★ **The White Mountains:** Offering spectacular hiking and skiing, these dramatic peaks and notches are unforgettable.

★ **Lake Winnipesaukee:** Beaches, arcades, boat cruises, and classic summer camps fuel a whole season of family fun.

★ **Fall Foliage:** Head to the Kancamagus Highway in autumn for one of America's best drives, or seek out a less-trafficked route that's equally stunning.

★ **Portsmouth:** Less than an hour's drive from Boston, this small, upbeat American city abounds with colorful Colonial architecture, cosmopolitan dining, and easy access to New Hampshire's only stretch of the Atlantic coastline.

★ **Pristine Towns:** Peterborough, Walpole, Tamworth, Center Sandwich, Bethlehem, and Jackson are among the most charming tiny villages in New England.

1 Portsmouth. Colonial homes meet hip dining.

2 Rye. Sweeping beaches and lavish oceanfront homes.

3 Exeter. Café culture and a famous prep school.

4 Durham. Home of the University of NH.

5 Wolfeboro. The U.S.'s oldest summer resort.

6 Laconia and Weirs Beach. Lake Winnipesaukee's hub of family fun.

7 Meredith. A bustling marina and mills converted to hotels.

8 Plymouth. A lively college town and gateway to the White Mountains.

9 Holderness. Base camp for Squam and Little Squam lakes.

10 Center Sandwich. Lake Winnipesaukee's quiet, scenic side.

11 Tamworth. Tranquility and Mt. Chocorua views.

12 North Conway. Outlet shops and family-friendly amusements.

13 Jackson. A storybook White Mountains town.

14 Mt. Washington. Highest peak in the northeastern United States.

15 Bartlett. A scenic ski and hiking hub.

16 Bretton Woods. The cog railway and a grande dame resort.

17 Bethlehem. An artsy alpine hamlet.

18 Littleton. A scenic river town with a lively Main Street.

19 Franconia. One of the White Mountains' favorite recreation hubs.

20 Lincoln and North Woodstock. Ski resorts and kitschy family spots.

21 Waterville Valley. A four-season resort and recreation village.

22 New London. Charming gateway to Lake Sunapee.

23 Newbury. Skiing, boating, and the nation's oldest crafts fair.

24 Hanover. Home to Dartmouth College.

25 Cornish. Covered bridges and the Saint-Gaudens estate.

26 Walpole. A pretty village green and Connecticut River views.

27 Keene. A classic Main Street and views of Mt. Monadnock.

28 Peterborough. The inspiration for Thornton Wilder's *Our Town.*

29 Manchester. The Granite State's largest city.

30 Concord. The small but lively state capital.

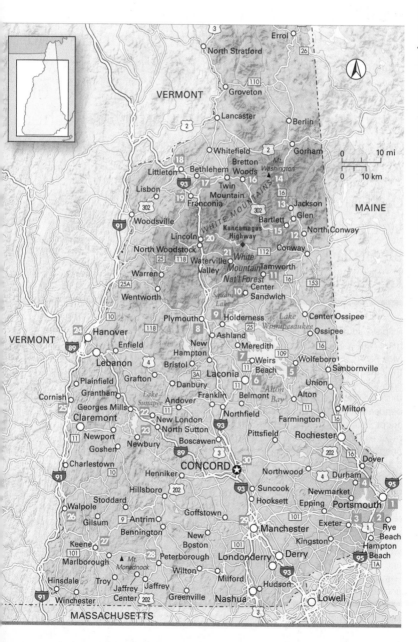

New Hampshire's precipitous terrain, clear air, and sparkling lakes attract trailblazers, artists, and countless tourists. A varied geography and myriad outdoor activities are part of the draw, but visitors also appreciate this place of beauty, history, and hospitality. Whether you're seeking adventure or just want to laze on the porch swing of a century-old inn, you'll find ample ways to engage with this rugged, diverse state that stretches from the sea to the Northeast's highest mountain peaks.

Ralph Waldo Emerson, Henry David Thoreau, Nathaniel Hawthorne, and Louisa May Alcott all visited and wrote about the state, sparking a fervent literary tradition. It also has a strong political history: this was the first colony to declare independence from Great Britain, the first to adopt a state constitution, and the first to require its constitution be referred to the people for approval. Politically, it remains a fiercely independent swing state that holds some of the earliest election primaries in the country and that's known for both its libertarian and progressive tendencies.

The state's varied terrain makes it popular with everyone from hard-core climbers and skiers to young families looking for easy access to nature. You can hike, ski, snowboard, snowshoe, and fish, as well as explore on snowmobiles, sailboats, kayaks, and mountain bikes. New

Hampshirites have no objection to others enjoying the beauty here as long as they leave a few dollars behind: it's the only state in the union with neither sales nor income taxes, so tourism brings in much-needed revenue (and tourists can enjoy tax-free shopping).

With a few communities consistently rated among the most livable in the nation, New Hampshire has grown a bit faster than most other northeastern states since 1990. The state is gradually developing two distinct personalities: one characterized by rapid urbanization in the southeast and the other by quiet village life in the west and north. Although newcomers have brought change, the free-spirited sensibility of the Granite State remains intact, as does its natural splendor.

MAJOR REGIONS

The **Seacoast,** New Hampshire's 18-mile stretch of coastline, packs in plenty of gorgeous scenery and lively diversions. The northern portion of the shoreline, from the charmingly historic regional hub, **Portsmouth,** south through the affluent town of **Rye,** is especially pristine and free from the honky-tonk excess of the southern section (around Hampton Beach and Seabrook). From Rye, you can branch inland to the prep-school town of **Exeter,** and then cut north through **Durham** (home to the University of New Hampshire). From here it's a short drive to the Lakes Region.

Throughout central New Hampshire, you'll encounter lakes and more lakes in the aptly named **Lakes Region.** The largest, Lake Winnipesaukee, has 180 miles of coastline and attracts all sorts of water-sports enthusiasts to the towns of **Wolfeboro, Laconia (with its bustling Weirs Beach section),** and **Meredith.** You'll find smaller and more secluded lakes with enchanting bed-and-breakfasts in **Holderness,** which adjoins famously scenic Squam Lake. **Plymouth, Center Sandwich,** and **Tamworth** are great bases to explore the surrounding lakes and as well as the southern reaches of the White Mountains.

Skiing, snowshoeing, and snowboarding in the winter; hiking, biking, and riding scenic railways in the summer: the Whites, as locals call **The White Mountains,** have plenty of natural wonders. **Mt. Washington,** the tallest mountain in the Northeast, can be conquered by trail, train, or car; other towns with strong railroad ties include up-and-coming **Littleton** and touristy **North Conway. Lincoln and North Woodstock** and **Waterville Valley** are lively resort areas, and **Bethlehem, Jackson,** and **Franconia** are stunning alpine jewels. **Bretton Woods** and **Bartlett** are great ski towns.

Quiet villages proliferate in the **Lake Sunapee** region; the lake itself is a wonderful place to swim, fish, or enjoy a cruise. **Hanover,** home to Dartmouth College (founded 1769), retains that true New England college-town feel, with ivy-draped buildings and cobblestone walkways. **New London** is one of the area's main hubs, while **Newbury,** on the edge of Mt. Sunapee State Park, is one of the region's outdoor recreation centers. **Cornish,** once the haunt of J. D. Salinger, is where you'll find Cornish-Windsor Bridge, the country's second-longest covered bridge.

New and old coexist in **the Monadnocks and Merrimack Valley,** the state's southwestern and south-central regions, respectively. Here high-tech firms have helped reshape the cities of **Manchester** and **Concord** while small towns in the hills surrounding Mt. Monadnock, southern New Hampshire's largest peak, like **Keene** and **Peterborough,** celebrate tradition and history. **Walpole** has one of the state's loveliest town greens.

Planning

Getting Here and Around

Some people come to New Hampshire to hike or ski the mountains, fish and sail the lakes, or cycle along backcountry roads. Others prefer to drive through scenic towns, stopping at museums and general stores or crafts shops along the way. Although New Hampshire is a small state, roads curve around lakes and mountains, making distances sometimes much longer than they appear on a map. You can get a taste of the coast, lake, and mountain areas in three to five days; eight days will give you time to make a more complete loop.

AIR

Manchester-Boston Regional Airport, the state's largest, has nonstop service from more than a dozen U.S. cities. The drive from Boston's Logan Airport to most places in New Hampshire takes one to three hours; the same is true for Bradley International Airport, near Hartford, Connecticut.

CAR

New Hampshire is an easy drive north from Boston. Many key destinations are near major highways, and local public transit is very limited, so getting around by car is the best way to explore. Interstate 93 stretches from Boston to Littleton and on into neighboring Vermont. Interstate 89 will get you from Concord to Hanover and eventually to Burlington, Vermont. To the east, Interstate 95 (a toll road) passes through southern New Hampshire's coastal area between Massachusetts and Maine. Throughout the state, quiet backcountry lanes and winding roads can take a little longer but often reward travelers with gorgeous scenery.

The speed limit on interstate and limited-access highways is usually 65 to 70 mph. On state and U.S. routes, speed limits vary considerably, from 25 mph to 55 mph, so watch signs carefully. The website of the **New Hampshire Department of Transportation** (⊕ hb.511nh.com) has up-to-the-minute information about traffic and road conditions.

TRAIN

Amtrak's *Downeaster* passenger train operates between Boston and Portland, Maine, with New Hampshire stops in Exeter, Durham, and Dover.

Hotels

In the mid-19th century, wealthy Bostonians retreated to imposing New Hampshire country homes in the summer. Grand hotels were built across the state, especially in the White Mountains, which at that time competed with Saratoga Springs, Newport, and Bar Harbor to draw the nation's elite vacationers. A

handful of these hotel-resorts survive. And many of those country houses have since been converted into inns. The smallest have only a few rooms and are typically done in period style; the largest contain 30 or more rooms and suites and often have in-room fireplaces and even hot tubs. You'll also find a great many well-kept motor lodges and cottage compounds, particularly in the White Mountains and Lakes regions. In ski areas, expect the usual ski condos and lodges, but most slopes are also within a short drive of a country inn or two. In the Merrimack River valley, as well as along major highways, chain hotels and motels predominate. The state is rife with campgrounds, especially in the White Mountains. *Hotel reviews have been shortened. For full information, visit Fodors.com.*

Restaurants

New Hampshire prides itself on its seafood: not only lobster, but also breaded haddock, steamed mussels, fried clams, and fish-and-chips. Across the state you'll find country taverns with both old-school and increasingly diverse modern American menus, many of them emphasizing regional ingredients—in smaller hamlets, the best restaurant in town is often inside the historic inn. As in the rest of New England, the state has no shortage of greasy-spoon diners, pizzerias, and pubs that serve hearty comfort fare, but a growing number of contemporary, locavore-driven bistros, third-wave coffee roasters, mixology-minded cocktail bars, and artisanal craft breweries have cropped up in recent years—along with a growing selection of Asian and other ethnic restaurants—especially in Portsmouth, Manchester, and Concord, but also in some surprisingly little towns, such as Keene, Walpole, Bethlehem, and Walpole. No matter where you go, reservations are seldom required, and dress is casual. *Restaurant reviews have been shortened. For full information, visit Fodors.com.*

What It Costs in U.S. Dollars

	$	$$	$$$	$$$$
RESTAURANTS				
	under $18	$18–$24	$25–$35	over $35
HOTELS				
	under $150	$150–$225	$226–$300	over $300

Visitor Information

CONTACTS Lakes Region Tourism Association. ☎ *603/286–8008* ⊕ *www.lakesregion.org.* **Lake Sunapee Region Chamber of Commerce.** ☎ *603/526–6575* ⊕ *www.lakesunapeeregionchamber.com.* **Ski New Hampshire.** ☎ *603/745–9396* ⊕ *www.skinh.com.* **Visit New Hampshire.** ☎ *603/271–2665, 800/386–4664* ⊕ *www.visitnh.gov.* **White Mountains Visitors Center.** ☎ *603/745–8720* ⊕ *www.visit-whitemountains.com.*

When to Go

Summer and fall are the best, but also the most popular and expensive, times to visit most of New Hampshire. Winter is a great time to travel to the White Mountains, but most other tourist sights in the state, including museums in Portsmouth and many attractions in the Lakes Region, close from late fall until May or June. In summer people flock to beaches, mountain trails, and lakeside boat launches; in the cities, festivals showcase food and beer, music, theater, and crafts. Fall brings leaf peepers, especially to the White Mountains and the Monadnocks. Skiers and snowboarders take to the slopes in winter, when Christmas lights and carnivals brighten the long, dark nights. Spring's unpredictable weather—along with April's mud and late May's black flies—tends to deter visitors. Still, the season has its joys, not the least of which is the appearance, mid-May–early June, of the state flower, the purple lilac, soon followed by the blooming of colorful rhododendrons and fields of lupine.

Portsmouth

47 miles east of Concord, 50 miles south of Portland, Maine, 56 miles north of Boston.

A small but lively Colonial port across the river from Kittery, Maine, upscale Portsmouth buzzes with trendy restaurants, swank cocktails bars, contemporary art galleries and boutiques, and acclaimed cultural venues that host nationally recognized speakers and performers—the action is focused largely around downtown's Market Square. Settled in 1623 as Strawbery Banke, Portsmouth grew into a prosperous port before the Revolutionary War, during which it harbored many Tory sympathizers. These days, this city of 22,000 has many grand residences from the 18th to the early 20th century, some of them preserved within or—such as the Wentworth-Coolidge Mansion and Governor John Langdon House—on the blocks near the fascinating Strawbery Banke Museum, and others are close by, such as the Wentworth-Gardner House. For a scenic drive or bike ride, follow Rte. 1B east from downtown across the Piscataqua River, following it around leafy New Castle Island—where you'll pass Fort Constitution and the grand, historic Wentworth by the Sea Hotel.

GETTING HERE AND AROUND

Both Interstate 95 and U.S. 1 connect Portsmouth with the rest of coastal New England, while U.S. 4 and Route 101 are the easiest ways to get here from inland New Hampshire. Downtown Portsmouth is walkable, though you'll need a car for attractions farther afield.

BOAT TOURS
Gundalow Company
BOAT TOURS | FAMILY | Sail the Piscataqua River in a flat-bottom gundalow (a type of barge) built at Strawbery Banke. Help the crew set sail, steer the vessel, and trawl for plankton while learning about the region's history from an onboard educator. Passengers are welcome to bring food and beverages. ⊠ *60 Marcy St.* ☎ *603/433–9505* ⊕ *www.gundalow. org* ⌂ *From $30* ☉ *Closed early Oct.–late May.*

Portsmouth Harbor Cruises
BOAT TOURS | Tours of Portsmouth Harbor and the Isles of Shoals, inland-river foliage trips, and sunset and wine cruises are all in this company's repertoire. ⊠ *64 Ceres St.* ☎ *603/436–8084, 800/776–0915* ⊕ *www.portsmouthharbor.com* ⌂ *From $18* ☉ *Closed Nov.–early May.*

WALKING TOURS
★ Discover Portsmouth
WALKING TOURS | FAMILY | The Portsmouth Historical Society operates this combination visitor center–museum, where you can pick up maps, get the scoop on what's happening while you're in town, and view cultural and historical exhibits. Here you can also learn about self-guided historical tours and sign up for guided ones. ⊠ *10 Middle St.* ☎ *603/436–8433* ⊕ *www.portsmouthhistory.org* ⌂ *Tours from $15.*

★ Portsmouth Black Heritage Trail
WALKING TOURS | FAMILY | Important local sites in African American history can be seen on the 75-minute guided Sankofa Tour. Included are the African Burying Ground and historic homes of local slave traders and abolitionists. Tours, which begin at the Old Meeting House, are conducted on Saturday afternoon throughout the summer. ⊠ *280 Marcy St.* ☎ *603/570–8469* ⊕ *www.blackheritagetrailnh.org* ⌂ *$20.*

VISITOR INFORMATION
The Portsmouth tourism office (Chamber Collaborative of Greater Portsmouth) is the official government source of visitor info for the entire Seacoast region.

Chamber Collaborative of Greater Portsmouth
⊠ *Portsmouth* ☎ *603/610–5510* ⊕ *www. portsmouthchamber.org.*

Sights

Albacore Park
MILITARY SITE | Built in Portsmouth in 1953, the USS *Albacore* is the centerpiece of Albacore Park. You can board this prototype submarine, which served as a floating laboratory to test an innovative hull design, dive brakes, and sonar systems for the Navy. The visitor center exhibits *Albacore* artifacts, and the nearby Memorial Garden is dedicated to those who have lost their lives in submarine service. ⊠ *600 Market St.* ☎ *603/436–3680* ⊕ *www.ussalbacore.org* ⌂ *$9* ☉ *Closed Mon. and Tues.*

Great Bay Estuarine National Research Reserve
INFO CENTER | FAMILY | Just inland from Portsmouth is one of southeastern New Hampshire's most precious assets. In this 10,235 acres of open and tidal waters, you can spot blue herons, ospreys, and snowy egrets, particularly during the spring and fall migrations. The Great Bay Discovery Center has indoor and outdoor exhibits, a library and bookshop, and a 1,700-foot boardwalk, as well as other trails, which wind through mudflats and upland forest. ⊠ *89 Depot Rd., Greenland* ☎ *603/778–0015* ⊕ *www. greatbay.org* ⌂ *Free* ☉ *Discovery Center closed Mon. and Tues., weekdays in Oct., and Nov.–Apr.*

Isles of Shoals
ISLAND | FAMILY | Four of the nine small, rocky Isles of Shoals belong to New Hampshire (the other five belong to Maine), many of them still known by the

earthy names—Hog and Smuttynose, to cite but two—17th-century fishermen bestowed on them. A history of piracy, murder, and ghosts suffuses the archipelago, long populated by an independent lot who, according to one writer, hadn't the sense to winter on the mainland. Celia Thaxter, a native islander, romanticized these islands with her poetry in *Among the Isles of Shoals* (1873). In the late 19th century, **Appledore Island** became an offshore retreat for Thaxter's coterie of writers, musicians, and artists. **Star Island** contains a small museum, the Rutledge Marine Lab, with interactive family exhibits. From May to late October you can take a narrated history cruise of the Isles of Shoals and walking tours of Star Island with Isles of Shoals Steamship Company. ✉ *Barker Wharf, 315 Market St.* ☎ *800/441–4620, 603/431–5500* ⊕ *www.islesofshoals.com* 🚢 *Cruises from $28.*

John Paul Jones House
BUILDING | FAMILY | Revolutionary War hero John Paul Jones lived at this boardinghouse while he supervised construction of the USS *America* for the Continental Navy. The 1758 hip-roof building displays furniture, costumes, glass, guns, portraits, and documents from the late 18th century. The collection's specialty is textiles, among them some extraordinary early-19th-century embroidery samplers. ✉ *43 Middle St.* ☎ *603/436–8420* ⊕ *www.portsmouthhistory.org* 🚢 *$7* 🕙 *Closed mid-Oct.–late May.*

★ Moffatt-Ladd House and Garden
GARDEN | The period interior of this striking 1763 mansion tells the story of Portsmouth's merchant class through portraits, letters, and furnishings. The Colonial Revival garden includes a horse chestnut tree planted by General William Whipple when he returned home after signing the Declaration of Independence in 1776. ✉ *154 Market St.* ☎ *603/436–8221* ⊕ *www.moffattladd.org* 🚢 *$8; garden only $5* 🕙 *Closed mid-Oct.–May.*

Prescott Park
ARTS VENUE | FAMILY | Picnicking is popular at this 3½-acre waterfront park near Strawbery Banke, whose large formal garden with fountains is perfect for whiling away an afternoon. The park contains Point of Graves, Portsmouth's oldest burial ground, and two 17th-century warehouses. The summerlong Prescott Park Arts Festival features concerts, outdoor movies, and food-related events. ✉ *105 Marcy St.* ☎ *603/436–2848* ⊕ *www.prescottpark.org.*

★ Strawbery Banke Museum
GARDEN | FAMILY | The first English settlers named what's now Portsmouth for the wild strawberries along the shores of the Piscataqua River. The name survives in this 10-acre outdoor history museum, which comprises 37 homes and other structures dating from 1695 to 1820, some restored and furnished to a particular period, others with historical exhibits. Half of the interior of the Shapley-Drisco House depicts its use as a Colonial dry-goods store, but its living room and kitchen are decorated as they were in the 1950s, showing how buildings were adapted over time. The Shapiro House has been restored to reflect the life of the Russian-Jewish immigrant family who lived there in the early 1900s. Done in decadent Victorian style, the 1860 Goodwin Mansion is one of the more opulent buildings. Although the houses are closed in winter, the grounds are open year-round, and an outdoor skating rink operates December–February. ✉ *14 Hancock St.* ☎ *603/433–1100* ⊕ *www.strawberybanke.org* 🚢 *$20* 🕙 *Homes closed Nov.–Apr. except for guided tours on Nov. weekends.*

Warner House
HOUSE | The highlight of this circa 1716 gem is the curious folk-art murals lining the hall staircase, which may be the oldest-known murals in the United States still gracing their original structure. The house, a notable example of brick

Portsmouth

Strawbery Banke Museum includes period gardens and 37 homes and other structures.

Georgian architecture, contains original art, furnishings, and extraordinary examples of area craftsmanship. The west-wall lightning rod is believed to have been installed in 1762 under the supervision of Benjamin Franklin. ⌧ *150 Daniel St.* ☎ *603/436–5909* ⊕ *www.warnerhouse. org* 🎫 *$8* ◷ *Closed Nov.–May and Tues.*

🍴 Restaurants

Black Trumpet Bistro
$$$ | **CONTEMPORARY** | This romantic harbor-view restaurant brings the bold flavors of Latin America and the Mediterranean to bear on such eclectic fare as smoked corn–and–brandade–crusted halibut, lobster and grits, and roast chicken with couscous, olive harissa, and preserved lemon. The chef belongs to the Heirloom Harvest Project and brings unusual vegetables—sometimes in surprising colors—to the table. **Known for:** creative vegetarian options; a lively upstairs wine bar; flourless dark-chocolate torte. ⑤ *Average main: $28* ⌧ *29 Ceres St.* ☎ *603/431–0887* ⊕ *www. blacktrumpetbistro.com* ◷ *No lunch.*

★ Cava
$$$ | **TAPAS** | Having a meal at this sophisticated little wine and tapas bar down a tiny alley near the downtown riverfront can feel like going on a secret mission, or being ushered into a special dinner party. It has a small exhibition kitchen and bar, and just a handful of tables and chairs, where guests can enjoy stellar food that includes an extensive selection of bocadillos, tapas, and pintxos—from Medjool dates with Serrano and manchego to char-grilled baby octopus—plus a few larger plates, such as paella. **Known for:** a superb, interesting wine list; authentic Spanish tapas; churros with hot chocolate. ⑤ *Average main: $26* ⌧ *10 Commercial Alley* ☎ *603/319–1575* ⊕ *www. cavatapasandwinebar.com* ◷ *No lunch.*

★ Cure
$$$ | **MODERN AMERICAN** | As its name hints, this buzzy neighborhood bistro in a lively dining room with redbrick walls, beam ceilings, and hardwood floors

specializes in cured, brined, and slow-cooked meats, which you can sample through beautifully presented charcuterie boards, smoked ribs, and slow-roasted Moroccan lamb shank. But take heart if you're less disposed toward red meat—you'll find plenty of creative seafood and veggie dishes on the menu, including gooey lobster mac and cheese. **Known for:** locally sourced ingredients; well-chosen wine list; lively but romantic dining room. ⑤ *Average main: $26* ⊠ *189 State St.* ☎ *603/427–8258* ⊕ *www.curerestaurantportsmouth.com* ⊘ *No lunch.*

Lexie's Joint

$ | **BURGER** | **FAMILY** | What began as a humble downtown burger joint has blossomed into a regional mini empire, thanks to the high-quality ingredients, upbeat service, and groovy "peace, love, and burgers"–themed decor. The burgers are reasonably priced and topped with all sorts of goodies, but there are also hot dogs and a few sandwiches, plus plenty of addictive sides. **Known for:** milk shakes with Shain's of Maine homemade ice cream; fried pickles with chipotle aioli; more great locations in Dover, Exeter,, and Newburyport. ⑤ *Average main: $7* ⊠ *212 Islington St.* ☎ *603/815–4181* ⊕ *www.peaceloveburgers.com.*

Mombo

$$$ | **INTERNATIONAL** | A short stroll from Strawbery Banke Museum and the pretty gardens of Prescott Park, this romantic restaurant is set in a Colonial red saltbox house with high timber-beam ceilings and wrought-iron chandeliers. In contrast to the historic setting, the food is artfully contemporary and worldly—specialties include jerk-spiced slow-braised oxtail, and pad Thai with sesame-crusted yellowfin tuna and spicy peanuts. **Known for:** elaborate cheese-and-charcuterie plate; international flair; peaceful setting in historic neighborhood. ⑤ *Average main: $28* ⊠ *66 Marcy St.* ☎ *603/433–2340* ⊕ *www.momborestaurant.com* ⊘ *Closed Mon. No lunch.*

Row 34

$$$ | **SEAFOOD** | Set in a gleaming, industrial-chic dining room with tall windows, exposed air ducts, and metal tables and chairs, this contemporary and slightly fancy take on a classic seafood house is the sort of place that's equally appropriate for special celebrations and casual beer-and-oysters happy hours with friends. From tuna tartare to scallop ceviche, you can't go wrong with anything from the raw bar, but also check out the extensive variety of steamed and grilled fare, such as roasted monkfish and grilled salmon collar. **Known for:** fantastic beer selection; $1 raw oysters at happy hour; Sunday brunch. ⑤ *Average main: $27* ⊠ *5 Portwalk Pl.* ☎ *603/319–5011* ⊕ *www.row34nh.com.*

Surf Restaurant

$$$ | **SEAFOOD** | Whether you eat inside the conversation-filled, high-ceilinged dining room or out on the breezy deck, you'll be treated to expansive views of Old Harbour and the Piscataqua River—an apt setting for consistently fresh and tasty seafood. The menu branches into several directions, including lobster rolls, shrimp-pork ramen, sushi, and Tuscan-style spaghetti with seafood, but manages everything well, and there's a well-curated wine and cocktail selection to complement your choice. **Known for:** raw-bar specialties; water views; creative sushi rolls. ⑤ *Average main: $27* ⊠ *99 Bow St.* ☎ *603/334–9855* ⊕ *www.surf-seafood.com* ⊘ *Closed Mon. No lunch Tues. and Wed.*

Vida Cantina

$ | **MODERN MEXICAN** | In a state sorely lacking notable Latin restaurants, this airy contemporary space south of downtown stands out for the ambitious modern Mexican cuisine of chef-owner and James Beard award–nominated chef David Vargas. Several kinds of street-food-style tacos are offered, including barbacoa and pork belly, along with a tangy goat cheese version of queso fundido and sous vide short rib with charred-rhubarb salsa. **Known for:** confit pig's head carnitas platter (not for the faint of heart); interesting sides, like blue cornbread and shishito peppers; boozy weekend brunches. $ *Average main: $17* ✉ *2456 Lafayette Rd.* ☎ *603/501–0648* ⊕ *www.vidacantinanh.com.*

Coffee and Quick Bites

Annabelle's Natural Ice Cream
$ | **CAFÉ** | **FAMILY** | On sunny days, a stroll around historic downtown Portsmouth isn't complete without a dish or cone of the thick and luscious ice cream doled out at this long-running parlor. Try a dish of maple-walnut, cinnamon spice, or rich French vanilla—the latter is made with golden egg yolks. **Known for:** seasonal flavors like pumpkin pie and peachy peach; fruit sorbets; all-natural ingredients. $ *Average main: $6* ✉ *49 Ceres St.* ☎ *603/436–3400* ⊕ *www.annabellesicecream.com.*

Hotels

AC Hotel Portsmouth
$$ | **HOTEL** | One of a few hotels that have opened recently in downtown Portsmouth's fast-growing, formerly industrial North End, this sleek midrise boutique hotel offers contemporary rooms with plenty of techy gadgets and creature comforts, plus a spacious lobby-bar with a fireplace, a popular rooftop restaurant, and a well-outfitted gym. **Pros:** smartly designed rooms; hip rooftop bar and restaurant; steps from dining and museums. **Cons:** lacking good views; some may find the modern, urban aesthetic a bit cold; expensive parking. $ *Rooms from: $195* ✉ *299 Vaughan St.* ☎ *603/427–0152* ⊕ *www.marriott.com* ⇨ *156 rooms* ⦿ *No meals.*

Ale House Inn
$$$ | **HOTEL** | Each of the stylish rooms in this urbane inn occupying a converted Victorian redbrick brewery on the historic riverfront has plenty of fun amenities, such as iPads filled with local information, iPod docks, and plush robes, and the modern bathrooms have handsome Italian tilework. **Pros:** welcome beers from local breweries upon arrival; free parking; bicycles for local jaunts. **Cons:** no breakfast; several steps to enter hotel; rooms are a bit compact. $ *Rooms from: $235* ✉ *121 Bow St.* ☎ *603/431–7760* ⊕ *www.alehouseinn.com* ⇨ *10 rooms* ⦿ *No meals.*

Hotel Portsmouth
$$$ | **HOTEL** | This downtown Victorian mansion built in 1881 by a sea captain is now a 32-room boutique hotel with elegantly updated furnishings, plush bed linens, and such modern conveniences as iPads preloaded with local information and flat-screen TVs. **Pros:** close to Market Square; free parking; lounge serving wine, beer, and small bites. **Cons:** thin walls result in occasional noise; some rooms have bland views; two-night minimum during busy times. $ *Rooms from: $235* ✉ *40 Court St.* ☎ *603/433–1200* ⊕ *www.thehotelportsmouth.com* ⇨ *32 rooms* ⦿ *Free breakfast.*

Martin Hill Inn
$$ | **B&B/INN** | The quiet rooms in this yellow 1815 house surrounded by flower-filled gardens are furnished with antiques and decorated with fine period antiques; a generous full breakfast is served each morning, featuring lemon-ricotta pancakes and other delectable treats. **Pros:** refrigerators in rooms; excellent breakfast; off-street parking. **Cons:** a little outside the downtown core on busy street; breakfast is served at a communal table; no children under 12. $ *Rooms from: $210* ✉ *404 Islington St.* ☎ *603/436–2287* ⊕ *www.martinhillinn.com* ⇨ *7 rooms* ⦿ *Free breakfast.*

★ Wentworth by the Sea
$$$$ | **RESORT** | Nearly demolished in the 1980s, one of coastal New England's most elegant Victorian grand resorts—where the likes of Harry Truman and Gloria Swanson once vacationed—has

Four of the nine rocky Isles of Shoals belong to New Hampshire; the other five belong to Maine.

been meticulously restored and now ranks among the cushiest golf, boating, and spa getaways in New Hampshire. **Pros:** amenities include an expansive full-service spa, heated indoor pool, and an outstanding golf course; marina with charters for harbor cruises and deep-sea fishing; excellent food in main restaurant and casual waterfront bistro. **Cons:** 10- to 15-minute drive from downtown Portsmouth; steep rates in summer; large property lacks intimacy. $ *Rooms from: $389* ⊠ *588 Wentworth Rd., New Castle* ☎ *603/422–7322, 866/384–0709* ⊕ *www.wentworth.com* 🛏 *161 rooms* ❌ *No meals.*

Nightlife

BARS AND BREWPUBS
★ Earth Eagle Brewings
BREWPUBS/BEER GARDENS | This bustling gastropub produces unusual, boldly flavorful ales in the Belgian style, some using distinctive botanicals—lemongrass, ginger root—rather than hops. The food is terrific, there's an airy outdoor beer

garden, and musicians perform many evenings. ⊠ *175 High St.* ☎ *603/502–2244* ⊕ *www.eartheaglebrewings.com.*

Portsmouth Book & Bar
BARS/PUBS | Combine an old-school indie bookstore with a funky café–cocktail bar, set it inside a restored 1817 custom-house, and you've got this endearing hangout that's popular with everyone from college students to artists to tourists. Live music and readings are offered, too. ⊠ *40 Pleasant St.* ☎ *603/427–9197* ⊕ *www.bookandbar.com.*

Performing Arts

ARTS VENUES
★ Music Hall
CONCERTS | Beloved for its acoustics, the 895-seat hall built in 1878 presents top-drawer music concerts, from pop to classical, along with dance and theater. The more intimate Music Hall Loft, around the corner, screens art films and hosts lectures. ⊠ *28 Chestnut St.* ☎ *603/436–2400* ⊕ *www.themusichall.org.*

Seacoast Repertory Theatre

THEATER | Here you'll find a year-round schedule of musicals, classic dramas, and works by up-and-coming playwrights, as well as everything from a youth theater to drag cabaret nights. ⊠ *125 Bow St.* ☎ *603/433–4472* ⊕ *www.seacoastrep. org.*

Shopping

The historic city center, especially around Market Square, abounds with gift and clothing boutiques, book and gourmet food shops, and crafts stores and art galleries.

Byrne & Carlson

FOOD/CANDY | Watch elegant cream truffles and luscious chocolates being made in the European tradition at this small artisanal shop. ⊠ *121 State St.* ☎ *207/439–0096* ⊕ *www.byrneandcarlson.com.*

Nahcotta

ART GALLERIES | This contemporary design boutique specializes in the stylish ceramics, jewelry, glassware, and art of dozens of regional talents. ⊠ *110 Congress St.* ☎ *603/433–1705* ⊕ *www.nahcotta.com.*

Off Piste

GIFTS/SOUVENIRS | Look to this quirky emporium for offbeat gifts and household goods—everything from painted buoy birdhouses to irreverent books, games, and mugs. ⊠ *37 Congress St.* ☎ *603/319–6910.*

Piscataqua Fine Arts

ART GALLERIES | This gallery mainly shows works by master woodcutter Don Gorvett, who creates spellbinding scenes of New England's coast, particularly the Portsmouth area. There are also works by some of New England's finest printmakers, including Sidney Hurwitz, Alex deConstant, and Sean Hurley. ⊠ *123 Market St.* ☎ *603/436–7278* ⊕ *www. dongorvettgallery.com.*

Portsmouth Farmers' Market

MARKET | **FAMILY** | One of the best and longest-running farmers' markets in the state showcases seasonal produce along with regional treats such as maple syrup and artisanal cheeses. There's live music, too. It's held Saturday morning, May–early November. ⊠ *Little Harbour School, 50 Clough Dr.* ⊕ *www.seacoastgrowers.org.*

Rye

8 miles south of Portsmouth.

In 1623 the English established a settlement at Odiorne Point in what is now the largely undeveloped and picturesque town of Rye, making it the birthplace of New Hampshire. Today, the area's main draws include a lovely state park, beaches, and the views from Route 1A, which is prettiest if you follow it south, passing the group of late-19th- and early-20th-century mansions known as **Millionaires' Row.** Strict town laws prohibit commercial development in Rye, creating a dramatic contrast with its frenetic neighbor, Hampton Beach.

GETTING HERE AND AROUND
Interstate 95 and U.S. 1, both west of town, provide easy access, but Rye shows its best face from coastal Route 1A.

Sights

★ Fuller Gardens

GARDEN | Arthur Shurtleff, a noted landscape architect from Boston, designed this late-1920s estate garden in the Colonial Revival style. In a gracious seaside residential neighborhood a couple of miles south of Jenness Beach, this peaceful little botanical gem encompasses 1,700 rosebushes, hosta and Japanese gardens, and a tropical conservatory. ⊠ *10 Willow Ave., North Hampton* ☎ *603/964–5414* ⊕ *www.fullergardens. org* 🎟 *$9* ⊙ *Closed Nov.–mid-May.*

★ Odiorne Point State Park

NATURE PRESERVE | FAMILY | These 135 acres of protected seaside land are where David Thompson established New Hampshire's first permanent English settlement. Several signed nature trails provide vistas of the nearby Isles of Shoals and interpret the park's military history. The rocky shore's tidal pools shelter crabs, periwinkles, and sea anemones. The park's **Seacoast Science Center** hosts exhibits on the area's natural history. Its tidal-pool touch tank and 1,000-gallon Gulf of Maine deepwater aquarium are popular with kids. ⊠ *570 Ocean Blvd.* ☎ *603/436–8043* ⊕ *www. seacoastsciencecenter.org* 🎟 *Park $4, Science Center $10.*

 Beaches

Jenness State Beach

BEACH—SIGHT | FAMILY | Good for swimming and sunbathing, this long, sandy beach is a favorite among locals who enjoy its light crowds and nice waves for bodysurfing. Wide and shallow, Jenness Beach is a great place for kids to run and build sand castles. **Amenities:** lifeguards; parking (fee); showers; toilets. **Best for:** surfing; swimming; walking. ⊠ *2280 Ocean Blvd.* ☎ *603/227–8722* ⊕ *www. nhstateparks.org* 🎟 *Parking $2/hr May–Sept., $1/hr Apr. and Oct.*

★ Wallis Sands State Beach

BEACH—SIGHT | FAMILY | This family-friendly swimmers' beach has bright white sand, a picnic area, a store, and beautiful views of the Isles of Shoals. **Amenities:** food and drink; lifeguards; parking (fee); showers; toilets. **Best for:** swimming; walking. ⊠ *1050 Ocean Blvd.* ☎ *603/436–9404* ⊕ *www.nhstateparks.org* 🎟 *$15 per car (late May–early Sept.).*

 Restaurants

The Carriage House

$$$ | SEAFOOD | Across from Jenness Beach, this elegant cottage serves innovative dishes with an emphasis on local seafood, from raw bar specialties like scallop crudo and littleneck clams on the half shell to roasted cod and tarragon lobster salad. A first-rate hanger steak and lamb stew with eggplant and fry bread round out the menu. **Known for:** classic daily blue-plate specials; breezy, refreshing cocktails; cozy upstairs tavern with ocean views. ⑤ *Average main: $28* ⊠ *2263 Ocean Blvd.* ☎ *603/964–8251* ⊕ *www.carriagehouserye.com* ☉ *No lunch.*

 Hotels

Atlantic Breeze Suites

$$ | HOTEL | FAMILY | The spacious rooms in this contemporary all-suites boutique hotel look either south over the ocean and down along the Hampton Beach shoreline or north over pristine Hampton Salt Marsh Conservation Area, and all have good-size balconies from which to soak up the views. **Pros:** free off-street parking; across the street from the beach; private balconies. **Cons:** books up way in advance in high season; on the north end of the beachfront, a bit of a walk from many restaurants; 15-minute drive from the quieter Rye beaches. ⑤ *Rooms from: $220* ⊠ *429 Ocean Blvd., Hampton Beach* ☎ *603/967–4781* ⊕ *www.atlanticbreezesuites.com* ⇨ *11 rooms* ❏ *No meals.*

☆ Activities

WHALE-WATCHING

Granite State Whale Watch

WHALE-WATCHING | FAMILY | This respected outfitter conducts naturalist-led whale-watching tours aboard the 100-passenger *Granite State*, along with excursions around the Isles of Shoals and to Star Island. ⊠ *Rye Harbor State Marina, 1870 Ocean Blvd.* ☎ *603/964–5545, 800/964–5545* ⊕ *www.granitestatewhalewatch.com* 🎟 *$40* ☉ *Closed mid-Oct.–mid-May.*

New Hampshire
Coast

Exeter

11 miles west of Rye.

During the Revolutionary War, Exeter
was the state capital, and it was here
amid intense patriotic fervor that the first
state constitution and the first Colonial
Declaration of Independence from Great
Britain were put to paper. These days
Exeter shares more in appearance and
personality with Boston's blue-blooded
satellite communities than the rest of
New Hampshire. Cheerful cafés, coffee-
houses, and shops with artisanal wares
fill the bustling town center.

GETTING HERE AND AROUND

Amtrak's *Downeaster* stops here
between Boston and Portland, Maine. By
car, Route 101 provides access from the
east or west to this walkable river town.

ESSENTIALS

**VISITOR INFORMATION Exeter Area
Chamber of Commerce.** ☎ *603/772–2411*
⊕ *www.exeterarea.org.*

Sights

American Independence Museum

HISTORIC SITE | Guided tours of this
museum that celebrates the nation's
birth focus on the family who lived here
during the Revolutionary War. Among
3,000 artifacts, see drafts of the U.S.
Constitution and the first Purple Heart, as
well as letters and documents written by
George Washington and the household
furnishings of John Taylor Gilman, one
of New Hampshire's early governors. In
July, the museum hosts the two-week
American Independence Festival, and
occasional architectural tours are offered,
too. ✉ *Ladd-Gilman House, 1 Governor's*

La. ☎ 603/772–2622 ⊕ www.independ-encemuseum.org ✉ $8 ⊙ Closed Sun. and Mon. and Dec.–Apr.

Applecrest Farm Orchards

FARM/RANCH | FAMILY | At this 250-acre farm, pick apples and berries or buy freshly baked fruit pies and cookies and outstanding homemade ice cream. A bistro serves quite good farm-to-table fare. Fall brings cider pressing, hayrides, pumpkins, and music on weekends. Author John Irving's experiences working here as a teen inspired *The Cider House Rules.* ✉ 133 Exeter Rd., Hampton Falls ☎ 603/926–3721 ⊕ www.applecrest. com.

Phillips Exeter Academy

BUILDING | The grounds of this elite 1,100-student prep school, open to the public, resemble an Ivy League university campus. The school's library is one of the masterworks of modernist architect Louis I. Kahn. The Lamont Gallery, in the Frederick R. Mayer Art Center, mounts free contemporary art exhibitions. ✉ 20 Main St. ☎ 603/772–4311 ⊕ www.exeter. edu.

🍴 Restaurants

Blue Moon Evolution

$ | MODERN AMERICAN | In this barnlike building on the edge of downtown, the menu shifts according to whatever the locavore-minded kitchen wizards have procured—maybe fresh summer peaches (grilled with feta, blueberries, and basil pesto) or sea scallops (pan-seared with sweet-and-sour kale, corn, and cherry tomatoes). Shareable apps, artisan-bread sandwiches, and creative seafood and veggies plates round out the menu. **Known for:** sustainable ingredients; cocktails infused with local berries and herbs; organic blueberry-lemon cashew tarts. $ *Average main: $16* ✉ 8 Clifford St. ☎ 603/778–6850 ⊕ www.bluemoon-evolution.com ⊙ Closed Sun.–Tues.

★ Otis

$$ | MODERN AMERICAN | Given the caliber of cuisine and the exceptional beverage program of this romantic, urbane restaurant set inside the early-19th-century Inn by the Bandstand, it's remarkable that most main dishes cost under $25—it's a terrific value. The farm-to-table menu here changes often to reflect what's in season, but has featured roasted duck breast with wild mushrooms and a signature dessert of sticky-toffee pudding, with everything always plated beautifully. **Known for:** emphasis on market-fresh, seasonal ingredients; views of charming village center; well-executed craft cocktails. $ *Average main: $24* ✉ *Inn by the Bandstand, 4 Front St.* ☎ 603/580–1705 ⊕ www.otisrestaurant.com ⊙ Closed Sun. and Mon. No lunch.

☕ Coffee and Quick Bites

Laney & Lu

$ | CAFÉ | FAMILY | This snug counter service café is a handy option for organic coffees, blended tea elixirs, and creative smoothies and bowls—the blueberry-basil with banana, avocado, spinach, and almond milk is a standout. Or tuck into a salad of locally sourced fruit, veggies, and greens, or try one of the hearty but healthy salads made on locally baked sourdough. **Known for:** artisan toasts with different toppings; fresh smoothies; a great kids' menu. $ *Average main: $9* ✉ 26 Water St., #6 ☎ 603/580–4952 ⊕ www.laneyandlu.com ⊙ No dinner.

🛏 Hotels

★ Inn by the Bandstand

$$$ | B&B/INN | This gorgeously appointed, luxury B&B in the heart of downtown Exeter exudes character and comfort, with individually themed rooms furnished with fine antiques, Oriental rugs, and cushy bedding. **Pros:** attractive downtown location; exceptional dining in Otis restaurant; fabulous breakfasts. **Cons:**

minimum stay on busy weekends; in a busy part of downtown; rates are a bit steep. $ *Rooms from: $259* ⊠ *6 Front St.* ☎ *603/772–6352* ⊕ *www.innbytheband- stand.com* ⇆ *8 rooms* ⦿ *Free breakfast.*

Shopping

★ Exeter Fine Crafts
CRAFTS | This acclaimed nonprofit cooper- ative formed in 1966 features creations by more than 300 of Northern New England's top pottery, painting, jewelry, textile, glassware, and other artisans. ⊠ *61 Water St.* ☎ *603/778–8282* ⊕ *www. exeterfinecrafts.com.*

Durham

12 miles north of Exeter, 11 miles west of Portsmouth.

A lively college town settled in 1635, and later the home of Revolutionary War hero and three-time New Hampshire governor John Sullivan, Durham became a maritime hub in the 19th century thanks to its easy access to Great Bay via the Oyster River. With the University of New Hampshire anchoring its town center, it's a good hub for exploring two other nearby riverfront communities with thriving historic downtowns, Dover and Newmarket.

GETTING HERE AND AROUND
You can reach Durham on Route 108 from the north or south and on U.S. 4 from Portsmouth or Concord. The *Downeaster* Amtrak train stops here.

Sights

★ Woodman Museum
HOUSE | FAMILY | This campus of four impressive, historic museums consists of the 1675 Damm Garrison House, the 1813 Hale House (home to abolitionist Senator John P. Hale from 1840 to 1873), the 1818 Woodman House, and the

1825 Keefe House, which contains the excellent Thom Hindle Gallery. Exhib- its focus on Early American cooking utensils, clothing, furniture, and Indian artifacts, as well as natural history and New Hampshire's involvement in the Civil War. ⊠ *182 Central Ave., Dover* ☎ *603/742–1038* ⊕ *www.woodmanmuse- um.org* ⊠ *$13* ⊗ *Closed Mon. and Tues. and mid-Dec.–Mar.*

Restaurants

Hop + Grind
$ | **BURGER** | Students and faculty from UNH, whose campus is just a few blocks away, congregate over mammoth burg- ers with flavorful, original sides (kimchi, fries topped with cilantro-pickled peppers or black-garlic-truffle aioli) and other creative takes on gastropub fare. This is a hot spot for craft-beer aficionados, who appreciate the long list of options, includ- ing a rotating cache of rare and seasonal selections. **Known for:** impressive local beer selection; fun and lively student crowd; malted milk shakes in unusual flavors. $ *Average main: $10* ⊠ *Madbury Commons, 17 Madbury Rd.* ☎ *603/397– 5564* ⊕ *www.hopandgrind.com.*

★ Stages at One Washington
$$$$ | **MODERN AMERICAN** | Offering stun- ning, reservation-only prix-fixe dinners featuring 8 to 10 small courses, this intimate open-kitchen space occupies the third floor of a converted redbrick mill building in Dover. The daily menu is based on what the talented culinary team here has sourced from farms and fishing boats—perhaps grilled lamb with apples, truffles, and miso, or lobster mushrooms with coffee, razor clams, and hazelnuts. **Known for:** artfully presented food; lavish multicourse dinners; optional wine pairings. $ *Average main: $120* ⊠ *1 Washington St., Dover* ☎ *603/842–4077* ⊕ *www.stages-dining.com* ⊗ *Closed Sun.–Tues. No lunch.*

📖 Hotels

Three Chimneys Inn

$ | **B&B/INN** | Since 1649, this stately yellow house has graced a hill overlooking the Oyster River; it now offers attractive rooms filled with period antiques and reproductions in the main house and a 1795 barn. **Pros:** charming, historic ambience; delicious breakfast included; very reasonable rates. **Cons:** a long walk (or short drive) into town; restaurant is uneven in quality; books up on fall and spring weekends. $ *Rooms from: $144* ✉ *17 Newmarket Rd.* ☎ *603/868–7800, 888/399–9777* ⊕ *www.threechimneysinn. com* ⇱ *23 rooms* ❍❘ *Free breakfast.*

🍸 Nightlife

★ **Stone Church**

MUSIC CLUBS | This cool music club and pub in beautifully restored 1835 former Methodist church on a hilly bluff in historic Newmarket presents first-rate rock, reggae, folk, jazz, and blues. ✉ *5 Granite St., Newmarket* ☎ *603/659–7700* ⊕ *www.stonechurchrocks.com.*

🛍 Shopping

★ **Emery Farm**

FOOD/CANDY | **FAMILY** | In the same family since the 1660s, Emery Farm sells berries and produce in summer, pumpkins in fall, and Christmas trees in winter. The farm shop carries breads, pies, and local crafts, and a café serves sandwiches, ice cream, cider doughnuts, and other light fare. Enjoy pumpkin-patch hayrides in autumn and visit the petting barn May–October. ✉ *147 Piscataqua Rd.* ☎ *603/742–8495* ⊕ *www.emeryfarm. com.*

🏃 Activities

Wagon Hill Farm

HIKING/WALKING | **FAMILY** | At this 139-acre property across from Emery Farm, you can stroll along scenic trails from the farmhouse to the old farm wagon and through the woods to the picnic area overlooking the Oyster River. There's sledding and cross-country skiing in winter. ✉ *U.S. 4* ⊕ *www.ci.durham.nh.us.*

Wolfeboro

40 miles northwest of Durham, 40 miles northeast of Concord.

Quietly upscale and decidedly preppy Wolfeboro has been a vacation getaway since Royal Governor John Wentworth built a home on the shore of Lake Winnipesaukee in 1768—hence its reputation as the country's oldest summer resort. Its waterfront downtown bursts with tony boutiques and eateries, while smaller Lake Wentworth—a few miles east—offers a quieter vibe. The century-old, white clapboard buildings of Brewster Academy prep school bracket the town's southern end.

GETTING HERE AND AROUND
Route 28 connects Wolfeboro with the rest of Lake Winnipesaukee. Be prepared for lots of traffic in the summer.

ESSENTIALS
VISITOR INFORMATION Wolfeboro Area Chamber of Commerce. ☎ *603/569–2200* ⊕ *www.wolfeborochamber.com.*

👁 Sights

Alton Bay

BODY OF WATER | **FAMILY** | Two mountain ridges frame picturesque Alton Bay, which is the name of both a narrow 4-mile inlet and village at the southern tip of Lake Winnipesaukee, near Wolfeboro. Cruise boats dock here, and small float planes buzz just over the bay, sometimes flying in formation. There's a boardwalk, mini golf, a public beach, and a Victorian-style bandstand, and a few basic but fun short-order eateries near the waterfront, such as Pop's Clam Shell and

New Hampshire Lakes Region

Stillwells Ice Cream. ⊠ *Rte. 11 at Rte. 28A, Alton Bay.*

★ New Hampshire Boat Museum

MUSEUM | FAMILY | Set in a 1950s quonset hut–style former dance hall near Lake Wentworth, this small but fascinating museum and boat-building center celebrates New Hampshire's maritime legacy with displays of vintage wooden boats, models, antique engines, racing photography, trophies, and vintage marina signs. You can also attend workshops on boat building and restoration, take sailing lessons, and go on 45-minute narrated rides on Lake Winnipesaukee in a reproduction 1928 triple-cockpit HackerCraft. ⊠ *399 Center St.* ☎ *603/569–4554* ⊕ *www.nhbm.org* 🎫 *$9, boat tours $25* ⊙ *Closed mid-Oct.–late May.*

Wright Museum

MILITARY SITE | Uniforms, vehicles, and other artifacts at this museum illustrate the contributions of those on the home front to the U.S. World War II effort. ⊠ *77 Center St.* ☎ *603/569–1212* ⊕ *www. wrightmuseum.org* 🎫 *$12* ⊙ *Closed Nov.–Apr.*

Beaches

Wentworth State Park

BEACH—SIGHT | FAMILY | Away from the hustle and bustle of Wolfeboro on pretty little Lake Wentworth, this simple park features a quiet beach with good fishing, picnic tables and grills, and ball fields. **Amenities:** parking (no fee); showers; toilets. **Best for:** swimming; walking. ⊠ *297 Governor Wentworth Hwy.* ☎ *603/569–3699* ⊕ *www.nhstateparks.org* 🎫 *$4.*

Restaurants

East of Suez

$$ | MODERN ASIAN | In a countrified lodge on the south side of town, this friendly restaurant serves creative Asian cuisine, with an emphasis on Philippine fare, such as *lumpia* (pork-and-shrimp spring rolls with a sweet-and-sour fruit sauce) and *pancit canton* (panfried egg noodles with sautéed shrimp and pork and Asian vegetables with a sweet oyster sauce). You can also sample Thai red curries, Japanese tempura, and Korean-style flank steak. **Known for:** BYOB policy; banana tempura with coconut ice cream; plenty of vegan options. $ *Average main: $22 ⊠ 775 S. Main St.* ☎ *603/569–1648* ⊕ *www.eastofsuez.com* ⊗ *Closed Mon. and early Sept.–late May. No lunch.*

Pavilion

$$$ | MODERN AMERICAN | Customers at the Pickering House hotel had become so enamored of the inn's occasional dinners and other food events that the owners decided in 2020 to open a full-time restaurant in the Victorian house next door. Serving creative American fare sourced locally and seasonally as much as possible, the kitchen serves an oft-changing menu that might feature herb-roasted pork tenderloin with garden pepper vinaigrette, followed by sheep's milk yogurt panna cotta with preserved Italian prune plums and brown-butter almond crumble. **Known for:** elegant early 19th-century building; exceptional wine list; creative seasonal fruit desserts. $ *Average main: $29 ⊠ 126 S. Main St.* ☎ *603/569–6948* ⊕ *www.pavilionwolfeboro.com* ⊗ *No lunch.*

Hotels

Lake Wentworth Inn

$ | HOTEL | New owners completely renovated this old motorlodge a five-minute walk from Lake Wentworth and Albee Beach, brightening up the pet-friendly rooms with an inviting midcentury cottage look and adding such family-friendly features as a game room and guest library. **Pros:** pool, game rooms, and library; short walk to beach; clean and very affordable. **Cons:** no breakfast; not directly on the water; a short drive from downtown. $ *Rooms from: $144 ⊠ 427 Center St.* ☎ *603/569–1700* ⊕ *www.lakewentworthinn.com* ⇌ *43 rooms* ⊚ *No meals.*

★ Pickering House

$$$$ | B&B/INN | Following an extensive two-year renovation by amiable innkeepers Peter and Patty Cook, this striking yellow 1813 Federal mansion now ranks among New Hampshire's most luxurious small inns. **Pros:** ultracushy rooms; the adjacent restaurant, Pavilion, is superb; in-town location. **Cons:** on busy street; among the highest rates in the region; not suitable for children. $ *Rooms from: $430 ⊠ 116 S. Main St.* ☎ *603/569–6948* ⊕ *www.pickeringhousewolfeboro.com* ⇌ *10 rooms* ⊚ *Free breakfast.*

Nightlife

Lone Wolfe Brewing

BREWPUBS/BEER GARDENS | Sample raspberry sours and the heady Dipp'ah Double IPA in the cheerful taproom of this downtown brewhouse that also serves tasty pub fare and presents live music many weekends inside or in the outdoor beer garden. ⊠ *36 Mill St.* ☎ *603/515–1099* ⊕ *www.thelonewolfe.com.*

🛍 Shopping

Black's Paper Store

GIFTS/SOUVENIRS | Browse regionally made soaps, chocolates, maple products, pottery, candles, lotions, potions, yarns, toys, and gifts at this vast old-fashioned emporium that dates back to the 1860s. ⊠ *8 S. Main St.* ☎ *603/569–4444* ⊕ *www.blacksgiftsnh.com.*

With 240 miles of shoreline, Lake Winnipesaukee has something for everyone.

The Country Bookseller

BOOKS/STATIONERY | FAMILY | You'll find an excellent regional-history section and plenty of children's titles at this independent bookstore, where you can do a little reading in the small café. ✉ *23A N. Main St.* ☎ *603/569–6030* ⊕ *www.thecountrybookseller.com.*

Yum Yum Shop

FOOD/CANDY | Picking up freshly baked breads, pastries, cookies, ice cream, and other sweets here has been a tradition since 1948. ✉ *16 N. Main St.* ☎ *603/569–1919* ⊕ *www.myyumyumshop.com.*

Activities

HIKING

Abenaki Tower

HIKING/WALKING | FAMILY | A quarter-mile hike to this 100-foot post-and-beam tower north of town, followed by a climb to the top, rewards you with views of Lake Winnipesaukee and the Ossipee mountain range. It's particularly photogenic at sunset. ✉ *Rte. 109, Tuftonboro.*

Blue Job Mountain

HIKING/WALKING | A wildflower-strewn 3.3-mile loop trail reaches the summit of Blue Job Mountain, 25 miles south of Wolfeboro, where a 1913 fire tower provides a panoramic view of the Atlantic Ocean, White Mountains, and even Boston on a clear day. ✉ *First Crown Point Rd., Strafford.*

★ Mt. Major

HIKING/WALKING | About 5 miles north of Alton Bay, a rugged 3-mile trail up a series of granite cliffs leads to this dramatic summit. At the top you'll find a four-sided stone shelter built in 1925, but the real reward is the spectacular view of Lake Winnipesaukee. ✉ *Rte. 11, Alton Bay.*

WATER SPORTS

Dive Winnipesaukee Corp

WATER SPORTS | This operation runs charters out to wrecks—including *The Lady*, a 125-foot-long cruise ship that sank in 30 feet of water in 1895—and also rents boats and gear. ✉ *Wolfeboro Bay, 4 N. Main St.* ☎ *603/569–8080* ⊕ *www.divewinnipesaukee.com.*

Laconia and Weirs Beach

25 miles west of Wolfeboro, 27 miles north of Concord.

The arrival of the railroad in 1848 turned the sleepy hamlet of Laconia into the Lakes Region's chief manufacturing hub—downtown's 1823 Belknap Mill still stands as a monument to this legacy. At the north end of town, Weirs Beach is a hub of summertime arcade activity, with souvenir shops, fireworks, the Bank of NH outdoor concert pavilion, and hordes of kids. Cruise boats also depart from here, and the refurbished Winnipesaukee Pier has family-oriented restaurants and other amusements. In June, bikers from around the world arrive for Laconia Motorcycle Week.

GETTING HERE AND AROUND

Laconia offers easy access from Interstate 93 in Tilton, where you'll find a clutch of outlet shops, to both Winnisquam and Winnipesaukee lakes, via U.S. 3 or Route 11.

 ## Sights

★ Canterbury Shaker Village

FARM/RANCH | FAMILY | Established in 1792, this village 15 miles south of Laconia flourished in the 1800s and practiced equality of the sexes and races, common ownership, celibacy, and pacifism. The last member of the religious community passed away in 1992. Shakers invented such household items as the clothespin and the flat broom and were known for the simplicity and integrity of their designs. Engaging guided tours—you can also explore on your own—pass through some of the 694-acre property's more than 25 restored buildings, many of them with original furnishings. Crafts demonstrations take place daily. The café offers light lunch fare and sells seasonal vegetables and maple syrup. An excellent shop sells handcrafted wares. ✉ 288 Shaker Rd., Canterbury ☎ 603/783–9511 ⊕ www.shakers.org ☑ $20 ✆ Closed weekdays in Nov. and in early Dec.–early May.

Funspot

AMUSEMENT PARK/WATER PARK | FAMILY | The mothership of Lake Winnipesaukee's family-oriented amusement parks, Funspot's more than 500 video games make it the world's largest arcade—there's even an arcade museum. You can also work your way through an indoor minigolf course and 20 lanes of bowling. Rates vary depending on the activity. ✉ 579 Endicott St. N, Weirs Beach ☎ 603/366–4377 ⊕ www.funspotnh.com.

★ M/S *Mount Washington*

BODY OF WATER | FAMILY | The 230-foot M/S *Mount Washington* offers 2½-hour scenic cruises of Lake Winnipesaukee, departing Weirs Beach with stops at Wolfeboro, Alton Bay, Center Harbor, and Meredith depending on the day. Sunset cruises include live music and a buffet dinner. The same company operates the *Sophie C.* ($32), which has been the area's floating post office for more than a century. The boat departs from Weirs Beach with mail and passengers, passing through parts of the lake not accessible to larger ships. The M/V *Doris E.* ($22) has one-hour scenic cruises into Meredith Bay and nearby islands throughout the summer. ✉ 211 Lakeside Ave., Weirs Beach ☎ 603/366–5531 ⊕ www.cruisenh.com ☑ From $35 ✆ Closed mid-Oct.–mid-May.

Winnipesaukee Scenic Railroad

LOCAL INTEREST | FAMILY | You can board this scenic railroad's restored cars at Weirs Beach or Meredith for one- or two-hour rides along the shoreline. Special excursions include fall foliage and the Santa train. ✉ 211 Lakeside Ave., Weirs Beach ☎ 603/745–2135 ⊕ www.hoborr.com ☑ From $20.

View simple yet functional furniture, architecture, and crafts at Canterbury Shaker Village.

Beaches

Ellacoya State Park

BEACH—SIGHT | FAMILY | Families enjoy this secluded 600-foot sandy beach and park on the southwestern shore of Lake Winnipesaukee. Ellacoya, with views of the Sandwich and Ossipee mountains, has a shallow beach that's safe for small children, sheltered picnic tables, and a small campground. **Amenities:** parking (fee); toilets. **Best for:** solitude; swimming. ⊠ *266 Scenic Rd., Gilford* ☎ *603/293–7821* ⊕ *www.nhstateparks. org* 🏷 *$5 weekends late May–early Sept.*

Restaurants

Local Eatery

$$$ | MODERN AMERICAN | Proof that impressive dining in the Lakes Region isn't always near the water, this elegant restaurant is set beneath the soaring ceiling of downtown Laconia's historic train depot. Favoring local ingredients, the kitchen turns out inventive renditions of classic American dishes, like scallops and grits with a sweet corn butter sauce, and coffee-rubbed pork tenderloin. **Known for:** Maryland-style crab cakes with remoulade; attractive patio; warm and "gooey" chocolate cobbler. ⑤ *Average main: $27* ⊠ *21 Veterans Sq.* ☎ *603/527–8007* ⊕ *www.laconialocaleatery.com* ⊘ *Closed Mon. No lunch.*

Hotels

★ Lake House at Ferry Point

$$$ | B&B/INN | This gracious red Victorian farmhouse, built as a summer getaway for the Pillsbury family of baking fame, has a peaceful setting on Lake Winnisquam. **Pros:** hearty full breakfast included; free use of kayaks; private dock and a small beach. **Cons:** not within walking distance of dining or shopping; may be a little quiet for some families; two-night minimum many weekends. ⑤ *Rooms from: $210* ⊠ *100 Lower Bay Rd., Sanbornton* ☎ *603/637–1758* ⊕ *newhampshire-inn.com* ⇆ *9 rooms* ⦿ *Free breakfast.*

Lake Opechee Inn & Spa

$$$ | HOTEL | Slightly removed from, but within a short drive of, the crowds of Weirs Beach, this boutique spa hotel set in a converted mill is a great place to chill out, enjoy a shiatsu massage or cranberry facial, and savor dinner and cocktails on a patio overlooking the lake. **Pros:** views of Lake Opechee; appealing spa and restaurant; many rooms have balconies, gas fireplaces, and jetted tubs. **Cons:** indoor pool is small; in a busy part of Laconia; 10-minute drive to Winnipesaukee. ⓢ *Rooms from: $205* ✉ *62 Doris Day Ct.* ☎ *603/524–0111* ⊕ *www.opecheeinn.com* ⮒ *34 rooms* ⦿ *Free breakfast.*

Activities

SKIING

Gunstock Mountain Resort

BICYCLING | FAMILY | This ski resort with a 2,267-foot summit and ample snow-making capacity offers plenty of beginner terrain along with snow-tubing and a 22-acre terrain park. Nearly half of the trails offer night skiing, and you'll find 13 miles of cross-country and snowshoeing runs. In summer the Adventure Park offers a fantastic zipline system—the longest run at 3,981 feet—an aerial obstacle course, a 4,100-foot mountain-side roller coaster (also open in winter), and scenic chairlift rides that access great hiking (the Ridge Trail is especially scenic). There's also mountain biking, a wetlands boardwalk, e-bike tours, kayak rentals, and a stocked fishing pond. **Facilities:** 53 trails; 227 acres; 1,340-foot vertical drop; 6 lifts. ✉ *719 Cherry Valley Rd., Gilford* ☎ *603/293–4341* ⊕ *www. gunstock.com* ⛷ *Lift ticket: $96.*

Meredith

11 miles north of Laconia.

For many years a workaday mill town with relatively little tourism appeal, Meredith has become a popular summer getaway thanks largely to the transformation in recent years of several historic downtown buildings into Mill Falls, now a cluster of hotels, restaurants, and shops overlooking Lake Winnipesaukee. Take a stroll down Main Street, which is dotted with intimate cafés, boutiques, and antiques stores, and along the lakefront, where you'll find a bustling marina, sculpture walk, and some lively dockside restaurants.

GETTING HERE AND AROUND

You can reach Meredith from Interstate 93 via Route 104, or from points south on U.S. 3 (beware the heavy weekend traffic). In town, it's easy to get around on foot.

ESSENTIALS

VISITOR INFORMATION Meredith Area Chamber of Commerce. ☎ *877/279–6121, 603/279–6121* ⊕ *www.meredithareachamber.com.*

Sights

Hermit Woods Winery

WINERY/DISTILLERY | Stop by this contemporary downtown winery to sample the light and fruity wines and hard ciders, made with local blueberries, apples, cranberries, and honeys as well as imported grapes. Tours, which include a barrel tasting, are available, and you can order cheese, charcuterie, and other treats from the deli to enjoy while sipping outside on the deck. ✉ *72 Main St.* ☎ *603/253–7968* ⊕ *www.hermitwoods. com.*

Meredith Sculpture Walk

PUBLIC ART | FAMILY | Throughout town, especially in parks beside the lake and at the gardens at Mill Falls Marketplace, you'll see colorful contemporary artworks. They're part of the Annual Meredith Sculpture walk, a year-round juried event featuring 32 distinctive pieces by renowned sculptors. Each June, a new collection of sculptures is installed. For a detailed look, take a free guided

What's your vessel of choice for exploring New Hampshire's Lakes Region: kayak, canoe, powerboat, or sailboat?

tour, offered at 10 am on Wednesday and Saturday, July and August. ⊠ *Meredith* ⊕ *www.meredithsculpturewalk.org.*

Restaurants

Canoe

$$ | **MODERN AMERICAN** | Just up the road in Center Harbor, this boathouse-inspired bistro sits high above Lake Winnipesaukee and has seating in both a quieter dining room and a convivial bar with an open kitchen. It's known for seafood, including wood-fired, bacon-wrapped scallops and a creamy, entrée-size haddock chowder topped with herbs and crushed Ritz Crackers. **Known for:** fun people-watching at the bar; great wine and beer selection; salted-caramel brownie sundaes. ⑤ *Average main: $24* ⊠ *232 Whittier Hwy., Center Harbor* ☎ *603/253–4762* ⊕ *www. magicfoodsrestaurantgroup.com* ⊙ *No lunch Mon.–Thurs.*

Lakehouse Grille

$$$ | **AMERICAN** | With big windows overlooking the lake and timber posts and ceiling beams, this popular restaurant inside the Church Landing at Mill Falls hotel captures the rustic ambience of an old-fashioned camp dining room. Feast on classic American favorites with interesting twists, such as eggs Benedict topped with Maine lobster in the morning, and char-grilled steaks, chops, and seafood in the evening. **Known for:** blueberry pie with lemon ice cream; water views; Sunday jazz brunch. ⑤ *Average main: $27* ⊠ *Church Landing, 281 Daniel Webster Hwy.* ☎ *603/279–5221* ⊕ *www. thecman.com.*

Hotels

Mill Falls at the Lake

$$$ | **HOTEL** | Choose from four lodgings at this rambling resort: relaxing Church Landing and Bay Point are both on the shore of Lake Winnipesaukee; convivial Mill Falls—with a pool—and Chase House are across the street, next to a 19th-century mill that houses shops and restaurants. **Pros:** activity center with boat rentals and lake cruises;

many dining options; spa with heated indoor-outdoor pool. **Cons:** rooms with water views are expensive; some properties aren't directly on the lake; somewhat impersonal, corporate feel. ⑤ *Rooms from: $234* ✉ *312 Daniel Webster Hwy.* ☎ *603/279–7006, 844/745–2931* ⊕ *www. millfalls.com* ⇱ *188 rooms* ⦿ *No meals.*

Nightlife

Twin Barns Brewing
BREWPUBS/BEER GARDENS | Serving a roster of well-crafted ales along with tasty comfort food (flatbread pizzas, wings), this beer-centric compound occupies a handsome 1850s restored barn with a large tented beer garden. ✉ *194 Daniel Webster Hwy.* ☎ *603/279–0876* ⊕ *www. twinbarnsbrewing.com.*

🎭 Performing Arts

Interlakes Summer Theatre
THEATER | During its 10-week season of summer stock, this striking 420-seat theater presents classic Broadway musicals like *42nd Street, Evita,* and *West Side Story.* ✉ *1 Laker La.* ☎ *603/707–6035* ⊕ *www.interlakestheatre.com.*

★ Winnipesaukee Playhouse
THEATER | Since this critically lauded theater opened in a rustic yet state-of-the-art red-barn-style venue in 2013, it's become one of the top performing arts centers in the region, presenting well-known Broadway shows and original dramas and comedies year-round. ✉ *33 Footlight Circle* ☎ *603/279–0333* ⊕ *www. winnipesaukeeplayhouse.org.*

🛍 Shopping

Annalee Dolls
TOYS | FAMILY | Everyone from young kids to ardent collectors makes the pilgrimage to the showroom of this internationally renowned shop that's been hand-crafting whimsical dolls since 1934. Annalee's expressive mice are a top draw, but holiday figurines are also highly popular. ✉ *339 Daniel Webster Hwy.* ☎ *800/433–6557* ⊕ *www.annalee.com.*

Home Comfort
HOUSEHOLD ITEMS/FURNITURE | This huge showroom is filled with designer furnishings, antiques, and accessories with lake-house flair. ✉ *38 Plymouth St., Center Harbor* ☎ *603/253–6660* ⊕ *www. homecomfortnh.com.*

★ League of New Hampshire Craftsmen
CRAFTS | This eclectic gallery offers wares by more than 250 artisans working in everything from stained glass and ceramics to wrought iron and mixed media. Prices are surprisingly reasonable for many items, and there are additional branches in Center Sandwich, Concord, Littleton, North Conway, and a few other towns. ✉ *279 Daniel Webster Hwy.* ☎ *603/279–7920* ⊕ *www.meredith. nhcrafts.org.*

🏃 Activities

BOATING
Home to a popular marina, Meredith is also near the quaint village of Center Harbor, another boating hub that's in the middle of three bays at the north end of Lake Winnipesaukee.

★ EKAL
BOATING | At the lakefront activity center at Mill Falls, you can rent standup paddleboards, kayaks, canoes, aqua cycles, and bicycles, and book excursions on a restored 1931 Chris Craft runabout. ✉ *281 Daniel Webster Hwy. (U.S. 3)* ☎ *603/677–8646* ⊕ *www.ekalactivitycenter.com.*

GOLF
Waukewan Golf Club
GOLF | This beautiful, well-groomed course with undulating fairways and several challenging blind shots has been a local favorite since the late '50s. ✉ *166 Waukewan Rd., Center Harbor* ☎ *603/279–6661*

⊕ www.waukewangolfclub.com ⬛ $30
🏌 18 holes, 5828 yards, par 71.

Plymouth

*7 miles northwest of Holderness, 22
miles south of North Woodstock.*

Home to Plymouth State College, whose
small but attractive campus clings to
a steep hill looming over an attractive,
bustling downtown, Plymouth acts as a
bridge between White Mountains and the
Lakes Region; it's especially convenient
for visiting 4,000-acre Newfound Lake,
one of the state's deepest and purest
bodies of water, as well as Squam Lake.
From town you can also reach some
great hiking to the west, including 3,121-
foot Mt. Cardigan, in nearby Alexandria,
and Big and Little Sugarloaf peaks, the
trailhead for which is reached along West
Shore Road, near the entrance to Welling-
ton State Park.

GETTING HERE AND AROUND
Plymouth is just off Interstate 93.

Sights

Polar Caves Park
CAVE | FAMILY | From the attractive log
cabin–style main lodge, an easy trail
leads to nine granite caves that formed
some 50,000 years ago, during the last
ice age. This family-friendly attraction
begun in 1922 also contains a small
petting zoo with a herd of adorable fallow
deer. ✉ 705 Rte. 25, Rumney ☎ 603/536–
1888 ⊕ www.polarcaves.com ⬛ $25
⊗ Closed mid-Oct.–mid-May.

Restaurants

★ **Benton's Sugar Shack**
$ | AMERICAN | FAMILY | A legit contender
in New Hampshire's fierce battle for the
best pancake house, this rustic tim-
ber-frame roadhouse between Plymouth and North Woodstock is run by a

family who've been producing maple
syrup for five generations. Open only
on weekends, Benton's serves stacks
of pancakes in several flavors, including
strawberry shortcake, Mounds Bar,
and Grandma's apple cinnamon. **Known
for:** sides of maple kielbasa and baked
beans; "design your own" pancakes with
custom fillings; raspberry-stuffed French
toast. ⑤ *Average main: $9* ✉ 2010 Rte.
175, Thornton ☎ 603/726–3867 ⊕ www.
bentonssugarshack.com ⊗ Closed weekdays. No dinner.

★ **Little Red Schoolhouse**
$$ | AMERICAN | FAMILY | Lobster roll
aficionados flock to this funky convert-
ed schoolhouse with screened-in and
outdoor seating high on a bluff above the
Pemigewasset River. Start with a cup of
lobster bisque or clam chowder before
digging into a traditional (lightly dressed,
with mayo) or hot-buttered lobster roll—
both come on a warm, buttered brioche
roll, best enjoyed with a side of garlic
fries. **Known for:** pretty river and forest
views; good craft beer selection; home-
made ice-cream sandwiches. ⑤ *Average
main: $18* ✉ 1994 Daniel Webster Hwy.,
Campton ☎ 603/726–6142 ⊕ www.
littleredschoolhousenh.com ⊗ Closed
mid-Oct.–mid-May.

Six Burner Bistro
$$ | MODERN AMERICAN | In this charming red Victorian house on Plymouth's
bustling Main Street, with some seats
on the front veranda and others set in
a warren of cozy rooms with art on the
walls, this casually elegant spot offers
tasty American and international fare.
Consider panfried pork dumplings with
sesame-ginger sauce, and the blackened
grilled chicken with honeydew-melon
salsa and tzatziki sauce. **Known for:** sourcing from local farms; well-selected wine
and beer list; creative salad options with
myriad protein add-ons. ⑤ *Average main:
$23* ✉ 13 S. Main St. ☎ 603/536–9099
⊕ www.sixburnerbistro.com ⊗ Closed
Sun. and Mon.

Hotels

Common Man Inn & Spa

$ | **HOTEL** | This contemporary hotel with country lodge–inspired furnishings, just off I–93 a little north of downtown, contains warmly appointed rooms in a variety of configurations; some have whirlpool tubs and fireplaces, and a few have cozy sleeping lofts. **Pros:** pets are welcome; relaxing spa; convenient to White Mountains and Lakes Region. **Cons:** often booked up with weddings; small pool; 15-minute walk from downtown. ⑤ *Rooms from: $139* ✉ *231 Main St.* ☎ *603/536–2200, 866/843–2626* ⊕ *www.thecmaninnplymouth.com* ⮐ *38 rooms* ❑❘ *Free breakfast.*

Henry Whipple House

$ | **B&B/INN** | About 2 miles south of Newfound Lake in the quiet mill town of Bristol, this magnificent turreted Queen Anne house with such original details as bronze fireplaces, chandeliers, and stained-glass windows has five antiques-filled rooms, two with wood-burning fireplaces. **Pros:** elegantly furnished; great value; great breakfasts. **Cons:** books up quickly; two-night minimum in peak periods; not within walking distance of lake. ⑤ *Rooms from: $145* ✉ *75 Summer St., Bristol* ☎ *603/744–6157* ⊕ *www.the-whipplehouse.com* ⮐ *8 rooms* ❑❘ *Free breakfast.*

Performing Arts

★ Flying Monkey

CONCERTS | Set in downtown Plymouth's brightly restored 1920s movie house, this cinema and performing arts center presents dinner theater and other live comedy and music shows, plus retro movies. A balcony bar serves wine and beer. ✉ *39 Main St.* ☎ *603/536–2551* ⊕ *www.flyingmonkeynh.com.*

Activities

★ Effortless Adventure

CAMPING—SPORTS-OUTDOORS | This trusty outfitter is a one-stop for planning camping or backpacking adventures in the White Mountains—they provide everything you need, including full one- to six-person tent and gear rental packages, and all the instruction you need, even if you're a novice camper, along with guidance on hikes, fly-fishing, yoga, and other activities. The staff can even book your campsite. ✉ *231 Main St.* ☎ *603/726–1702* ⊕ *www.effortlessadventure.com.*

★ Wellington State Park

BEACHES | **FAMILY** | At this picturesque 204-acre park on the west shore of glorious Newfound Lake, about 12 miles from Plymouth, you'll find the largest freshwater beach in the state park system. Enjoy the picnic and fishing areas, numerous hiking trails, and boat launch. **Amenities:** food and drink; parking (fee); toilets. **Best for:** swimming; walking. ✉ *617 W. Shore Rd., Bristol* ☎ *603/744–2197* ⊕ *www.nhstateparks.org* ✑ *$5 mid-May–mid-Sept.*

Holderness

8 miles northwest of Meredith.

This peaceful village straddles two of the state's most scenic lakes, Squam and Little Squam, both of which have been spared from excessive development but do offer some memorable inns that are perfect for a tranquil getaway. *On Golden Pond,* starring Katharine Hepburn and Henry Fonda, was filmed on Squam, whose beauty attracts nature lovers.

GETTING HERE AND AROUND

Holderness is easy to reach from Interstate 93 and U.S. 3.

👁 Sights

★ Squam Lakes Natural Science Center

BODY OF WATER | FAMILY | This 230-acre property includes a ¾-mile nature trail that passes by trailside exhibits of black bears, bobcats, otters, fishers, mountain lions, red foxes, and raptors. A pontoon boat cruise offers the best way to tour the waterfront—naturalists talk about native fauna, from bald eagles to loons; dinner and sunset options are available. Kids' programs teach about insects and wilderness survival skills. The center also operates nearby 1-acre Kirkwood Gardens and maintains three short hiking trails, all of which you can access for free. ⊠ *23 Science Center Rd.* ☎ *603/968–7194* ⊕ *www.nhnature.org* 🎫 *Trail $15, lake cruise $27* ⊙ *Live-animal exhibits closed Nov.–Apr.*

🍴 Restaurants

Walter's Basin

$$ | AMERICAN | A former bowling alley in the heart of Holderness makes an unlikely but charming setting for meals overlooking Little Squam Lake—local boaters dock right beneath the dining room. Among the specialties on the seafood-intensive menu are shellfish paella, and sea scallops with a creamy bacon-corn-poblano succotash, while sandwiches and salads are among the lighter options. **Known for:** dockside setting; live music some summer evenings; fried whole-belly clams. ⑤ *Average main: $22* ⊠ *859 U.S. 3* ☎ *603/968–4412* ⊕ *www. waltersbasin.com.*

🛏 Hotels

Cottage Place on Squam

$ | RENTAL | This sweet, old-fashioned compound of cottages and suites on Little Squam Lake is a terrific find—and value—for families, as nearly all units have partial or full kitchens, and many can comfortably sleep up to five guests (there's also a six-bedroom lodge that groups can rent entirely). **Pros:** reasonably priced; lots of on-site activities, from kayaking to shuffleboard; well-curated shop has fun one-of-a-kind gifts. **Cons:** the retro ambience isn't at all fancy; family popularity might be a turnoff if seeking peace and quiet; no restaurant. ⑤ *Rooms from: $139* ⊠ *1132 U.S. 3* ☎ *603/968–7116* ⊕ *www.cottageplaceonsquam.com* 🛏 *15 rooms* ⦿ *No meals.*

Glynn House

$ | B&B/INN | Squam Lake is just a short drive from this romantic inn that comprises a beautifully restored 1890s Queen Anne–style Victorian and, next door, a handsome 1920s carriage house. **Pros:** posh decor and room amenities; complimentary afternoon hors d'oeuvres; impressive multicourse breakfasts. **Cons:** not on the water; two-night minimum during some weekends; in a small, sleepy town. ⑤ *Rooms from: $159* ⊠ *59 Highland St., Ashland* ☎ *603/968–3775* ⊕ *www.glynnhouse.com* 🛏 *12 rooms* ⦿ *Free breakfast.*

★ Inn on Golden Pond

$$$ | B&B/INN | The hospitable innkeepers at this comfortable and informal B&B a short distance from Squam Lake make every possible effort to accommodate their guests—many of whom are repeat clients—from providing them with hiking trail maps to using rhubarb grown on property to make the jam served during the delicious country breakfasts. **Pros:** 50-acre property with woodland and lake views; comfortable indoor and outdoor common spaces; generous full breakfast. **Cons:** not directly on the lake; not especially fancy; can't accommodate pets. ⑤ *Rooms from: $235* ⊠ *1080 U.S. 3* ☎ *603/968–7269* ⊕ *www.innongoldenpond.com* 🛏 *8 rooms* ⦿ *Free breakfast.*

Manor on Golden Pond

$$$ | B&B/INN | A name like this is a lot to live up to, but the Manor generally succeeds: it's one of the region's most atmospheric inns, situated on a slight rise overlooking Squam Lake, with 15 acres of lawns, towering pines, and hardwood trees, and a grand restaurant serving lavish modern European fare, and a small but well-outfitted spa. **Pros:** fireplaces and Jacuzzis in many rooms; gracious common spaces; afternoon high tea is served in the library. **Cons:** the top-tier suites are quite expensive; furnishings could stand a little refreshing; not suitable for younger kids. ⑤ *Rooms from: $234* ⌧ *31 Manor Rd., off Shepard Hill Rd.* ☎ *603/968–3348, 800/545–2141* ⊕ *www.manorongoldenpond.com* ➩ *24 suites* ⎟◎⎟ *Free breakfast.*

Squam Lake Inn

$$$ | **B&B/INN** | Graceful Victorian furnishings fill this peaceful farmhouse inn a short stroll from Squam Lake, each of its 10 rooms richly outfitted with comfortable beds, organic toiletries, and soft bathrobes. **Pros:** secluded and serene; superb restaurant; sumptuous gourmet breakfasts. **Cons:** short walk from lake; open only seasonally; minimum-night stays during busy times. ⑤ *Rooms from: $249* ⌧ *28 Shepard Hill Rd.* ☎ *603/968–4417, 800/839–6205* ⊕ *www.squamlakeinn.com* ⊙ *Closed late Oct.–May* ➩ *10 rooms* ⎟◎⎟ *Free breakfast.*

 Activities

⭐ **Squam Lakes Association**

BOATING | **FAMILY** | You can rent kayaks, canoes, and standup paddleboards, reserve campsites, enroll kids in education programs, and learn about local wildlife watching, fishing, and hiking opportunities at this nonprofit organization that's been focused on lake conservation since it formed in 1904. ⌧ *534 U.S. 3* ☎ *603/968–7336* ⊕ *www.squamlakes.org.*

West Rattlesnake Mountain

HIKING/WALKING | The nearly 500-foot elevation gain of this moderately strenuous but fairly short 2.3-mile loop trail to the top of West Rattlesnake Mountain

will get your heart pounding, but the panoramic views over Squam Lake are a satisfying reward. ⌧ *Rte. 113.*

Center Sandwich

19 miles northeast of Plymouth, by way of Holderness.

With Squam Lake to the west, Lake Winnipesaukee to the south, and the Sandwich Mountains to the north, Center Sandwich offers one of the prettiest settings in the Lakes Region. So appealing are the town and its views that John Greenleaf Whittier used the Bearcamp River as the inspiration for his poem "Sunset on the Bearcamp." The town attracts artisans—crafts shops abound among its clutch of charming 18th- and 19th-century buildings.

GETTING HERE AND AROUND
You reach this rural town from Holderness via Route 113 and Meredith—by way of Center Harbor and Moultonborough—by Routes 25 and 109.

 Sights

⭐ **Castle in the Clouds**

CASTLE/PALACE | Looking like a fairy-tale castle, this grand 1914 mountaintop estate is anchored by an elaborate mansion with 16 rooms, 8 bathrooms, and doors made of lead. Owner Thomas Gustave Plant spent $7 million—the bulk of his fortune—on this project and died penniless in 1941. Tours include the mansion and the Castle Springs water facility on this high Ossipee Mountain Range property overlooking Lake Winnipesaukee. Hiking (and cross-country skiing in winter) and pony and horse rides are also offered, along with lakeview terrace jazz dinners many summer evenings at the Carriage House restaurant, which is also open for lunch when mansion tours are offered. ⌧ *455 Old Mountain Rd., Moultonborough* ☎ *603/476–5900*

⊕ *www.castleintheclouds.org* ⌷ *$18*
⊘ *Closed late Oct.–mid-May.*

Loon Center
BODY OF WATER | FAMILY | Recognizable for its eerie calls and striking black-and-white coloring, the loon resides on many New Hampshire lakes but is threatened by the gradual loss of its habitat. Two trails wind through the 200-acre Loon Center, which has made great progress in helping to restore the state's loon population; vantage points on the Loon Nest Trail overlook the spot resident loons sometimes occupy in late spring and summer. ⊠ *183 Lee's Mills Rd., Moultonborough* ☎ *603/476–5666* ⊕ *www.loon.org* ⌷ *Free* ⊘ *Closed Sun.–Wed. in winter.*

Restaurants

Corner House Inn
$$ | AMERICAN | In a converted barn adorned with paintings by local artists, this rustic tavern in an 1840s building in charming Center Sandwich village dishes up classic American fare. Salads made with local greens and a maple vinaigrette are a house specialty, but don't overlook the mac and cheese with house-made sauce and steak tips–and–lobster surf and turf. **Known for:** inviting art-filled dining room; tender steaks and prime rib; good list of reasonably priced wines. ⑤ *Average main: $22* ⊠ *22 Main St.* ☎ *603/476–3060* ⊕ *www.cornerhous-erestaurantandbar.com* ⊘ *Closed Tues. No lunch.*

☕ Coffee and Quick Bites

Sandwich Creamery
$ | CAFÉ | FAMILY | Part of the fun of visiting this rural artisan dairy in the foothills of the White Mountains, with a self-serve shop that dispenses farmstead-made cheddar cheese and ice cream, is the scenic drive up from Center Sandwich or Tamworth. You'll find ice cream and ice-cream sandwiches in about two-dozen flavors, many using local berries and produce, plus goods from other nearby purveyors, such as delicious breads from Sunnyfield Brick Oven Bakery. **Known for:** PB&J ice cream sandwiches; artisan cheddar cheeses; serene picnic area with views of the farm. ⑤ *Average main: $4* ⊠ *130 Hannah Rd.* ☎ *603/284–6675.*

🛍 Shopping

Old Country Store and Museum
LOCAL SPECIALTIES | A quirky spot to pick up maple syrup, aged cheeses, jams, molasses, penny candy, and other treats, this rambling shop dates to 1781 and also contains antique farm and forging equipment and other artifacts. ⊠ *1011 Whittier Hwy., Moultonborough* ☎ *603/476–5750* ⊕ *www.nhcountrystore.com.*

🏃 Activities

BOATING
Wild Meadow Canoes & Kayaks
BOATING | Canoes and kayaks at this shop at the north tip of Lake Winnipesaukee, near the Center Harbor town line. ⊠ *6 Whittier Hwy., Moultonborough* ☎ *603/253–7536* ⊕ *www.wildmeadowca-noes.com.*

HIKING
Red Hill
HIKING/WALKING | FAMILY | This 2,030-foot mountain really does turn red in autumn. At the top of the moderately steep 1.7-mile Fire Tower Trail, you can climb a fire tower for 360-degree views of Lake Winnipesaukee and Squam Lake, as well as the White Mountains beyond. To make a loop, return via the Cabin Trail. At the parking area, a small snack bar (open mostly on weekends) dispenses organic coffee, ice cream, and other treats. ⊠ *Red Hill Rd., 2 miles west of Rte. 25, Moultonborough.*

Tamworth

13 miles east of Center Sandwich.

President Grover Cleveland summered in what remains a place of almost unreal quaintness: Tamworth is equally photogenic in verdant summer, during the fall foliage season, or under a blanket of winter snow. Cleveland's son, Francis, returned and founded the acclaimed Barnstormers Theatre in 1931. One of America's first summer theaters, it continues to this day. Tamworth has a clutch of villages within its borders, and six historic churches. In the hamlet of Chocorua, the view through the birches of Chocorua Lake has been so often photographed that you may experience déjà vu. Rising above the lake is Mt. Chocorua (3,490 feet), which has many good hiking trails.

GETTING HERE AND AROUND

Tamworth's main village, at the junction of Routes 113 and 113A, is tiny and can be strolled.

◎ Sights

Remick Country Doctor Museum and Farm

FARM/RANCH | FAMILY | For 99 years (1894–1993) Dr. Edwin Crafts Remick and his father provided medical services to the Tamworth area and operated a family farm. These two houses now comprise a farm museum, with the second floor of the house kept as it was when Remick passed away, providing a glimpse into the life of a country doctor. The still-working farm features special activities, such as maple-syrup making, and has hiking trails and picnicking areas. ⊠ *58 Cleveland Hill Rd.* ☎ *603/323–7591* ⊕ *www.remickmuseum.org* 🖘 *Pay as you wish* ☉ *Closed Sun. and early Dec.– early May.*

★ Tamworth Distilling & Mercantile

WINERY/DISTILLERY | Using a 250-gallon copper still constructed in Kentucky, this artisanal distillery set in a stately barn just a short stroll from famed Barnstormers Theatre produces exceptional craft spirits, including Chocorua Straight Rye, Von Humboldt's Turmeric Cordial, Tamworth Garden Spruce Gin, and several flavorful cordials. If you're lucky, your stop will include a chance to sample Eau de Musc, a limited-release whiskey infused with an oil extracted from the castor glands of beavers. ⊠ *15 Cleveland Hill Rd.* ☎ *603/323–7196* ⊕ *www.tamworthdistilling.com* ☉ *Closed Mon.–Wed.*

Restaurants

★ Art in the Age Cafe

$ | CAFÉ | With its timber-beam ceiling and hardwood floors, this folksy-looking 1826 mercantile–cum–café run by nearby Tamworth Distilling stocks carefully curated artisanal foods, craft beers, and hip gifts and accessories. The menu offers delicious quinoa bowls, cage-free-egg–and–cheddar breakfast croissants, and roast pork loin sandwiches with sesame kraut and white miso mayo. **Known for:** gourmet specialty foods; a convivial mix of locals and tourists; impressive beer, wine, coffee, and tea selection. ⑤ *Average main: $9* ⊠ *85 Main St.* ☎ *603/323–5120* ⊕ *www.tamworthlyceum.com* ☉ *No dinner.*

Jake's Seafood and Grill

$$ | SEAFOOD | Oars and other nautical trappings adorn the wood-panel walls at this classic New England seafood restaurant about 8 miles southeast of Tamworth. The kitchen serves fresh fish and shellfish, notably lobster pie, fried clams, and seafood casserole, but you'll also find steak, ribs, and chicken dishes. **Known for:** Thursday-night fish fries; nostalgic, old-school decor; lobster bakes to go. ⑤ *Average main: $19* ⊠ *2055 White Mountain Hwy., West Ossipee* ☎ *603/539–2805* ⊕ *www.jakesseafood-co.com.*

Performing Arts

★ **Barnstormers Theatre**
THEATER | Founded in 1931, this highly respected theater company presents dramas and comedies June–August. ⊠ *104 Main St.* ☎ *603/323–8500* ⊕ *www. barnstormerstheatre.org.*

 Activities

White Lake State Park
PARK—SPORTS-OUTDOORS | The 72-acre stand of native pitch pine here is a National Natural Landmark. The park has a picnic area and a sandy beach, trails you can hike, trout you can fish for, and canoes you can rent. ⊠ *94 State Park Rd.* ☎ *603/323–7350* ⊕ *www.nhstateparks. org* ⊠ *$5 mid-May–early Sept.*

North Conway

20 miles north of Tamworth, 42 miles east North Woodstock, 62 miles north-west of Portland, Maine.

Before the arrival of the popular Settlers Green outlet stores, this town drew visitors for its inspiring scenery, ski resorts, and access to White Mountain National Forest. Today, however, the feeling of natural splendor is gone. Shopping is the big sport, and businesses line Route 16 for several miles. You'll get a close look at them as traffic often slows to a crawl. It's a bit of a food desert, too, with plenty of options but few of them notable.

GETTING HERE AND AROUND
Route 16 bisects town but can be clogged with traffic. Take the scenic West Side Road from Conway to Intervale, or even on Bartlett if you're headed farther north, to circumvent the traffic and take in splendid views.

ESSENTIALS
VISITOR INFORMATION Mt. Washington Valley Chamber of Commerce. ☎ *603/356–5701* ⊕ *www.mtwashingtonvalley.org.*

◉ Sights

Conway Scenic Railroad
SCENIC DRIVE | FAMILY | Departing from historic North Conway Station, the railroad operates various trips aboard vintage trains. The Notch Train to Crawford Depot or to Fabyan Station travels through rugged territory yielding wonderful views. Seating options include lunch or a seat in the Upper Dome car, which affords the most spectacular views. The Valley Train overlooks Mt. Washington during a 55-minute round-trip journey to Conway or a 1¾-hour excursion to Bartlett. The 1874 station displays lanterns, old tickets and timetables, and other artifacts. Reserve early during foliage season. ⊠ *38 Norcross Cir.* ☎ *603/356–5251, 800/232–5251* ⊕ *www.conwayscenic.com* ⊠ *From $19* ⊙ *Closed Dec.–Mar.*

Echo Lake State Park
NATIONAL/STATE PARK | FAMILY | You don't have to be a rock climber to enjoy the views from the 700-foot White Horse and Cathedral ledges, which you can reach via a 1.7-mile road. From the top, you'll see the entire valley, including Echo Lake, which offers fishing, swimming, boating, and, on quiet days, an excellent opportunity to shout for echoes. ⊠ *68 Echo Lake Rd., Conway* ☎ *603/356–2672* ⊕ *www.nhstateparks.org* ⊠ *$4 mid-May–mid-Oct.*

Weather Discovery Center
INFO CENTER | FAMILY | Ever wonder what it's like to be in a cabin at the summit of Mt. Washington while 200 mph winds shake the rafters? Find out at this fun, interactive museum, where you can experience simulations of different weather conditions and learn about how weather affects our lives. There's a twice-daily video link (one late morning and one early afternoon) with scientists atop Mt. Washington Observatory. ⊠ *2779 Main St.* ☎ *603/356–2137* ⊕ *www.mountwashington.org* ⊠ *$2.*

🍴 Restaurants

Muddy Moose

$ | **AMERICAN** | **FAMILY** | This playfully themed lodge-style restaurant buzzes with the sound of happy kids, but everyone seems to enjoy the rustic trappings, which include a huge stone fireplace, moose-antler chandeliers, and mounted animals. The comfort food here is reliably good, from barbecue rack of ribs to peppercorn-mushroom burgers, and there's a good selection of local beers. **Known for:** half-pound burgers with plenty of toppings; extensive kids offerings; Paradise four-layer chocolate cake. ⑤ *Average main: $17* ✉ *2344 White Mountain Hwy.* ☎ *603/356–7696* ⊕ *www.muddymoose. com.*

Table + Tonic Farm Bistro

$$ | **MODERN AMERICAN** | The green-thumb-savvy proprietors of the popular and adjacent Local Grocer natural foods market and café operate this hip farm-to-table bistro and bar. It features seasonal fare produced with organic produce and baked goods and boldly flavored cocktails fashioned from house-made shrubs, bitters, syrups, and cordials. **Known for:** healthy breakfast and lunch items in adjacent café and market; creative craft cocktails; attractive side patio overlooking a leafy garden. ⑤ *Average main: $22* ✉ *3358 White Mountain Hwy.* ☎ *603/356–6068* ⊕ *www.tableandtonic. com* ⊙ *Closed Tues. and Wed. No lunch.*

🛏 Hotels

The Buttonwood Inn

$$ | **B&B/INN** | A tranquil oasis in a busy resort area, the Buttonwood sits on Mt. Surprise, 2 miles northeast of North Conway village—close enough to access area dining and shopping, but far away from noise and crowds of downtown. **Pros:** comfy bedding; year-round outdoor hot tub and fire pit; 6 acres of peaceful grounds. **Cons:** too secluded for some; swimming pool is seasonal;

some rooms have private baths down the hall. ⑤ *Rooms from: $199* ✉ *64 Mt. Surprise Rd.* ☎ *603/356–2625* ⊕ *www. buttonwoodinn.com* ⊃ *10 rooms* ⑩ *Free breakfast.*

Darby Field Inn

$$ | **B&B/INN** | Most rooms in this unpretentious 1826 farmhouse near the boundary of White Mountain National Forest—just off the eastern end of the famously picturesque Kancamagus Highway—have stunning views, and several also have fireplaces. **Pros:** romantic setting; away-from-it-all feel; memorable full country breakfast included. **Cons:** not suitable for kids; a drive to the nearest town; sometimes booked with weddings. ⑤ *Rooms from: $165* ✉ *185 Chase Hill, Albany* ☎ *603/447–2181* ⊕ *www.darbyfield.com* ⊃ *13 rooms* ⑩ *Free breakfast.*

Inn at Crystal Lake

$$ | **B&B/INN** | In the quaint village of Eaton Center, about 10 miles south of North Conway, this stately 1884 Greek Revival inn contains finely appointed rooms with dramatic themes, each filled with a mix of curious and whimsical art and collectibles from the innkeepers' travels. **Pros:** short walk to the lake; convivial pub with good food; good base for White Mountains, Lakes Region, and Maine's Stone Mountain Arts Center. **Cons:** secluded area; few dining options nearby; old-fashioned decor may not suit all tastes. ⑤ *Rooms from: $169* ✉ *2356 Eaton Rd., Eaton Center* ☎ *603/447–2120* ⊕ *www.innatcrystallake.com* ⊃ *11 rooms* ⑩ *Free breakfast.*

★ Snowvillage Inn

$$ | **B&B/INN** | The finest room in this pastoral inn's main gambrel-roof house (built in 1916) has 12 windows that look out over the Presidential Range, and many guest rooms—some in a carriage house and a new outbuilding—have fireplaces. **Pros:** spectacular views; use of snowshoes and 10 acres of trails; delicious full breakfasts. **Cons:** off the beaten path; no TVs in rooms; not many

dining options nearby. ⑤ *Rooms from: $199 ⊠ 136 Stewart Rd., Eaton Center* ☎ *603/447–2818 ⊕ www.snowvillageinn. com ⇨ 17 rooms* ⦿ *Free breakfast.*

Nightlife

Delaney's Hole in the Wall

BARS/PUBS | This legendary après-ski tavern has a real fondness for ski history, displaying early photos of local ski areas, old signs and placards, and odd bits of lift equipment. Guests enjoy watching games on TV in the sports-bar area, and the kitchen turns out decent pub fare. ⊠ *2966 White Mountain Hwy.* ☎ *603/356–7776 ⊕ www.delaneys.com.*

★ Tuckerman Brewing Co.

BREWPUBS/BEER GARDENS | Offering live music on weekends, seating inside as well as—during the warmer months—in a huge tented beer garden, light snacks, and some of the freshest and tastiest beer in the state, this venerable craft brewery is on the edge of downtown Conway is a fun place to relax after a hike or mingle with friends. ⊠ *66 Hobbs St., Conway* ☎ *603/447–5400 ⊕ www. tuckermanbrewing.com.*

Shopping

CRAFTS
Handcrafters Barn

CRAFTS | The work of 150 area artists and artisans are sold in this attractive red-clapboard building. ⊠ *2473 White Mountain Hwy.* ☎ *603/356–8996 ⊕ www. handcraftersbarn.com.*

Activities

FISHING
North Country Angler

FISHING | One of the best tackle shops in the state, North Country offers casting clinics and guided fly-fishing trips throughout the region. ⊠ *2988 White Mountain Hwy.* ☎ *603/356–6000 ⊕ www.northcountryangler.com.*

SKIING
Cranmore Mountain Resort

SKIING/SNOWBOARDING | **FAMILY** | This fun-to-ski area has been a favorite with families since it opened in 1938. Most runs are naturally formed intermediates that weave in and out of glades. Beginners have several slopes and routes from the summit; experts must be content with a few short, steep pitches. Snowboarders. can explore five different terrain parks. A mountain coaster, a tubing park, a giant swing, and a zipline provide additional entertainment. Night skiing is offered on Saturday and holidays. **Facilities:** 56 trails; 170 acres; 1,200-foot vertical drop; 9 lifts. ⊠ *1 Skimobile Rd.* ☎ *800/786–6754 ⊕ www.cranmore.com* ⊠ *Lift ticket: $89.*

Mt. Washington Valley Ski Touring and Snowshoe Foundation

SKIING/SNOWBOARDING | Nearly 30 miles of groomed cross-country trails weave through the North Conway countryside, maintained by this foundation. Membership to the Mt. Washington Valley Ski Touring Club, available by the day or year, is required. Equipment rentals are available. ⊠ *279 Rte. 16/U.S. 302, Intervale* ☎ *603/356–9920 ⊕ www.mwvskitouring. org.*

Jackson

9 miles north of North Conway.

Just off Route 16 via a red covered bridge, photogenic Jackson retains its storybook New England character. Art and antiques shopping, tennis, golf, fishing, and hiking to waterfalls are among the draws, as well as a high concentration of upscale country inns. When the snow falls, Jackson becomes the state's cross-country skiing capital, and there are also four downhill ski areas nearby—hotels and inns provide ski shuttles.

ESSENTIALS
GETTING HERE AND AROUND
Jackson is on Route 16, just north of the junction with U.S. 302.

VISITOR INFORMATION Jackson Area Chamber of Commerce. ☎ 603/383–9356 ⊕ www.jacksonnh.com.

Sights

Story Land
AMUSEMENT PARK/WATER PARK | FAMILY | This theme park with life-size storybook and nursery-rhyme characters is geared to kids (ages 2–12). The 23 rides include a flumer, a river raft, and the Roar-O-Saurus and Polar Coaster roller coasters. Play areas and magic shows provide additional entertainment. The Living Shores Aquarium was added to the complex in 2020, offering 32,000-square-feet of mostly interactive, touch-friendly pools and exhibits. ⊠ 850 Rte. 16, Glen ☎ 603/383–4186 ⊕ www.storylandnh.com ⛵ $33, aquarium $25.

Restaurants

⭐ **Thompson House Eatery**
$$$ | MODERN AMERICAN | The domain of celebrated chef-owner Jeff Fournier, who's cooked at some of Boston's most celebrated restaurants, this exceptional eatery is set inside a chicly restored farmhouse in the village of Jackson. Ethereal highlights from the oft-changing menu include braised beef ragu shell-shaped lumache pasta and a Merlot broth, and a superb cheese board with blueberry and yuzu jams, nuts, and local honey. **Known for:** elegant and historic farmhouse setting; on-site shop with gourmet goods to go; seasonally flavored house-made ice creams. ⑤ Average main: $28 ⊠ 193 Main St. ☎ 603/383–9341 ⊕ www.thethompsonhouseeatery.com ⊗ Closed Mon. and Tues. No lunch.

Hotels

Inn at Ellis River
$$ | B&B/INN | Most of the rooms—which are all outfitted with armchairs and ottomans and floral-print duvet covers and featherbeds—in this unabashedly romantic 1893 inn on the Ellis River have fireplaces, and some also have balconies with Adirondack chairs and whirlpool tubs. **Pros:** pretty riverside location; abundantly charming; multicourse breakfasts and afternoon refreshments included. **Cons:** some rooms up steep stairs; not suitable for kids under 12; the least expensive rooms are a bit compact. ⑤ Rooms from: $179 ⊠ 17 Harriman Rd. ☎ 603/383–9339, 800/233–8309 ⊕ www.innatellisriver.com ⤍ 21 rooms ⍥ Free breakfast.

Inn at Jackson
$ | B&B/INN | This homey yet distinctive B&B—designed in 1902 by famed architect Stanford White for the Baldwin family of piano fame—is reasonably priced, charmingly furnished, and in the heart of the village. **Pros:** great value considering its many charms; peaceful setting; wonderful breakfasts. **Cons:** top-floor rooms lack fireplaces; bathrooms need updating; a bit frilly for some tastes. ⑤ Rooms from: $139 ⊠ Thorn Hill Rd. and Main St. ☎ 603/383–4321, 800/289–8600 ⊕ www.innatjackson.com ⤍ 14 rooms ⍥ Free breakfast.

⭐ **The Inn at Thorn Hill & Spa**
$$ | B&B/INN | With a large reception room and sweeping staircase, a deck overlooking the rolling hills around the village, and a common area with a wet bar and a cozy fireplace, this lovely inn—modeled after an 1891 Victorian designed by Stanford White—is breathtaking throughout. **Pros:** superb restaurant; soothing full spa; exceptional full breakfasts. **Cons:** rigid peak-season cancellation policy; not suitable for kids; carriage house and cottages are less sumptuous. ⑤ Rooms from: $229 ⊠ 42 Thorn Hill Rd.

☎ 603/383–4242 ⊕ www.innatthornhill.
com ⌗ 22 rooms ⦿ No meals.

Wentworth
$$ | B&B/INN | FAMILY | Thoughtful renovations have given new life and elegance to the guest rooms at this baronial 1869 Victorian, whose amenities include a full spa, a first-rate restaurant, and access to a terrific golf course and cross-country ski trails. **Pros:** discounts at neighboring Wentworth Golf Club; interesting architecture; very good farm-to-table restaurant. **Cons:** some rooms up steep stairs; two-night minimum many weekends; at a somewhat busy intersection. ⑤ Rooms from: $189 ✉ 1 Carter Notch Rd. ☎ 603/383–9700, 800/637–0013 ⊕ www.thewentworth.com ⌗ 61 rooms ⦿ Free breakfast.

 Activities

CROSS-COUNTRY SKIING

★ **Jackson Ski Touring Foundation**
SKIING/SNOWBOARDING | FAMILY | This acclaimed cross-country ski operation has an attentive staff and 80 miles of groomed trails for skiing, skate skiing, and snowshoeing. The varied terrain offers something for all abilities—lessons and rentals are offered, too. Trails wind through covered bridges and into the picturesque village of Jackson, where you can warm up in cozy trailside restaurants. ✉ 153 Main St. ☎ 603/383–9355 ⊕ www.jacksonxc.org.

ICE-SKATING

Nestlenook Farm
ICE SKATING | FAMILY | This picturesque farm maintains an outdoor ice-skating rink with rentals, music, and a bonfire as well as offering snowshoeing and sleigh rides. ✉ 66 Dinsmore Rd. ☎ 603/383–7101 ⊕ www.nestlenookfarmsleighrides.com.

Mt. Washington

12 miles north of Jackson, 39 miles east of Bretton Woods.

At 6,288 feet, Mt. Washington is the tallest peak in the northeastern United States. The world's highest winds, 231 mph, were recorded here in 1934. You can take a guided van tour, a drive, or a hike to the summit. A number of trails circle the mountain and access the other peaks in the Presidential Range, but all of them are fairly strenuous and best attempted only if you're somewhat experienced and quite fit. It gets cold up here: even in the summer, you'll want a jacket.

GETTING HERE AND AROUND
Mt. Washington Auto Road heads west from Route 16, about 2 miles north of Wildcat Mountain ski resort and 8 miles south of Gorham.

 Sights

★ **Mt. Washington Auto Road**
MOUNTAIN—SIGHT | FAMILY | The drive to the top of this imposing summit is truly memorable. Your route: the narrow, curving Mt. Washington Auto Road, which climbs 4,600 feet in about 7 miles. Drivers can download an app with a narrated tour and receive a bumper sticker that reads, "This car climbed Mt. Washington." The narration is fascinating, and the views are breathtaking. Once at the top, check out **Extreme Mount Washington,** an interactive museum dedicated to science and weather. If you're nervous about heights or the condition of your car, book a guided van tour or a ride up the cog railway in Bretton Woods. ✉ 1 Mt. Washington Auto Rd., Gorham ☎ 603/466–3988 ⊕ www.mt-washington.com ✉ Car and driver $35; guided bus tour $39; museum $2 (free with auto tour) ⦿ Closed late Oct.–early May.

Restaurants

Nonna's Kitchen

$$ | **ITALIAN** | **FAMILY** | Set in a vintage barber shop in downtown Gorham—8 miles north of the Mt. Washington Auto Road—and looking very old-school, this homey restaurant was opened in 2017 as a tribute to the owners' Italian grand-mothers. Indeed, the menu reads like a roll call of favorites from the best restaurants in Boston's or New Haven's Little Italy neighborhoods—classic antipasto, feathery gnocchi with pesto, eggplant parmigiana, veal piccata, and linguine with clams and red sauce. **Known for:** friendly service; cod puttanesca; fresh handmade pastas, cooked to order. ⑤ *Average main: $19* ✉ *19 Exchange St., Gorham* ☎ *603/915–9203* ⊕ *www. nonnasgorham.com* ⊘ *Closed Mon. and Tues. No lunch.*

Hotels

★ Glen House Hotel

$$ | **HOTEL** | The latest of four Glen House hotels that have stood on this site at the base of the Mt. Washington Auto Road since 1852, this upscale three-story retreat opened in 2018 in a Shaker-in-spired building whose soaring windows, a yellow clapboard exterior, and simple lines hark back to its predecessors. **Pros:** easy access to Mt. Washington activities; beautifully designed; excellent on-site restaurant. **Cons:** remote area; may be a bit shiny and new for some tastes; limit-ed dining options in the area. ⑤ *Rooms from: $169* ✉ *979 Rte. 16, Gorham* ☎ *603/466–3420* ⊕ *www.theglenhouse. com* ⇌ *68 rooms* ❢⃝❢ *Free breakfast.*

Activities

All trails to Mt. Washington's peak are demanding and require a considerable investment of time and effort. Perhaps the most famous is the **Tuckerman Ravine Trail,** the path used by extreme skiers

who risk life and limb to fly down the face of the steep ravine. The hike to the top can easily take six–nine hours round-trip. However you get to the top, because the weather here is so erratic, it's critical to check weather conditions, to be prepared, and to keep in mind that Mt. Washington's summit is much colder than its base.

CROSS-COUNTRY SKIING

★ Great Glen Trails Outdoor Center

SKIING/SNOWBOARDING | **FAMILY** | Featur-ing a dramatic 28-mile network of both mild and wild cross-country ski and mountain-biking trails at the foot of Mt. Washington, Great Glen provides access to more than 1,100 acres of backcoun-try. You can also book to the summit via SnowCoach, a nine-passenger van refitted with triangular snowmobile-like treads. You have the option of skiing or snowshoeing down or just enjoying the magnificent winter view. There's also a huge ski and sports shop, a food court, and a climbing wall. In summer you can also rent kayaks and book excellent paddling, rafting, and float trips along the Androscoggin River. ✉ *1 Mt. Washington Auto Rd., at Rte. 16, Gorham* ☎ *603/466–3988* ⊕ *www.greatglentrails. com* ✏ *SnowCoach tours $55.*

HIKING

Pinkham Notch

HIKING/WALKING | On Mt. Washington's eastern slopes, scenic Pinkham Notch encompasses several ravines, including famous Tuckerman. The Appalachian Mountain Club operates a visitor center that provides trail information. Guided hikes leave from here, and outdoor skills workshops are offered. On-site are an outdoors shop, a lodge with basic over-night accommodations, and a dining hall. Not all the trails ascend Mt. Washington or are necessarily strenuous. Good bets for shorter, moderate hikes include Glen Ellis Falls and Crystal Cascade, which both lead to scenic waterfalls. ✉ *AMC Pinkham Notch Visitor Center, 361 Rte.*

The highest peak in New England, Mt. Washington rewards those who drive or hike to the top with spectacular views.

16, Gorham ☎ *603/466–2721* ⊕ *www. outdoors.org.*

SKIING
Wildcat Mountain
SKIING/SNOWBOARDING | Glade skiers love Wildcat's 80 acres of tree skiing. Runs include some stunning double–black diamond trails; experts can really zip down the Lynx. Beginners, as long as they can hold a wedge, should check out the 2½-mile-long Polecat, which offers excellent views of the Presidential Range. The trails are classic New England—narrow and winding—and the vistas are stunning. For an adrenaline rush, there's a terrain park. In summer you can dart to the top on the four-passenger gondola, hike the many trails, and fish in the crystal clear streams. **Facilities:** 48 trails; 225 acres; 2,112-foot vertical drop; 5 lifts. ⊠ *Rte. 16, Gorham* ☎ *603/466–3326, 888/754–9453 for snow conditions* ⊕ *www.skiwildcat.com* 🎫 *$92.*

Bartlett

19 miles south of Mt. Washington, 9 miles northwest of North Conway.

With Bear Mountain to its south, Mt. Parker to its north, Mt. Cardigan to its west, and the Saco River to its east, Bartlett—incorporated in 1790—has an unforgettable setting. Lovely Bear Notch Road (closed in winter) has the only midpoint access to the Kancamagus Highway. There isn't much town to speak of: the dining options listed are actually nearby in Glen. It's best known for the Attitash Ski Resort.

GETTING HERE AND AROUND
U.S. 302 passes through Bartlett from Bretton Woods and west from Glen.

Restaurants

White Mountain Cider Co.
$$$ | **MODERN AMERICAN** | Set in a historic cider mill near the Saco River, this rustic yet elegant bistro and adjacent gourmet

market and deli presses fresh cider in the fall—it's served with traditional homemade cider doughnuts. But it's also a terrific farm-to-table restaurant, featuring a seasonal menu of eclectic, contemporary dishes. **Known for:** flavorful sandwiches and soups in the adjacent market; creative cocktails; friendly, knowledgeable service. $ *Average main: $25* ⊠ *207 U.S. 302, Glen* ☎ *603/383–9061* ⊕ *www.ciderconh.com* ⊘ *Closed Tues. No lunch in restaurant.*

Hotels

★ Bernerhof Inn

$$ | B&B/INN | Skiers, hikers, and adventurers who favor a luxurious, intimate lodging over a bustling condo resort adore this grand Victorian inn operated with eco-friendly practices and furnished with a mix of fine antiques and period reproductions. **Pros:** excellent on-site cooking school; exudes old-world charm; small but wonderfully relaxing spa. **Cons:** no on-site restaurant; some rooms receive little road noise; not good for kids. $ *Rooms from: $189* ⊠ *342 U.S. 302, Glen* ☎ *603/383–4200, 877/389–4852* ⊕ *www.bernerhofinn.com* ⇋ *12 rooms* ⦿❘ *Free breakfast.*

Grand Summit Hotel at Attitash

$ | HOTEL | FAMILY | All of the pleasantly furnished rooms at this ski-in, ski-out condo-style resort at the base of Bear Peak have kitchenettes, and many have private balconies with splendid views. **Pros:** appealing slope-side setting; ski-package deals; kitchenettes in rooms. **Cons:** generally bland decor; could use some sprucing up; restaurants are a bit meh. $ *Rooms from: $129* ⊠ *104 Grand Summit Rd.* ☎ *603/374–1900* ⊕ *www.grandsummitattitash.com* ⇋ *143 rooms* ⦿❘ *No meals.*

Nightlife

Red Parka Pub

BARS/PUBS | This homey pub decorated with license plates and ski memorabilia has been an institution, especially during winter ski season, since the early 1970s, providing a fun and festive venue for après-ski or-hike socializing. Beer is served in Mason jars, the kitchen serves up juicy steaks and comfort fare, and there's live music many evenings. ⊠ *3 Station St., Glen* ☎ *603/383–4344* ⊕ *www.redparkapub.com.*

Activities

SKIING

Attitash Ski Resort

SKIING/SNOWBOARDING | FAMILY | With one of New Hampshire's higher vertical drops, Attitash Mountain has dozens of trails to explore, and there are more on the adjacent Attitash Bear Peak. You'll find traditional New England ski runs and challenging terrain alongside wide-open cruisers that suit all skill levels. There are acres of glades, plus a progressive freestyle terrain park. The Attitash Adventure Center offers rentals, lessons, and children's programs. **Facilities:** 68 trails; 311 acres; 1,750-foot vertical drop; 10 lifts. ⊠ *775 U.S. 302* ☎ *800/223–7669* ⊕ *www.attitash.com* ⛷ *Lift ticket: $92.*

Bretton Woods

21 miles northwest of Bartlett.

In the early 1900s private railcars brought the elite from New York and Philadelphia to the Mount Washington Hotel, the jewel of the White Mountains. A visit to this property, which was the site of the 1944 United Nations conference that created the International Monetary Fund and the International Bank for Reconstruction and Development (and the birth of many conspiracy theories), is not to be missed. The area is also known for its cog railway to the summit of Mt. Washington, Bretton Woods ski resort, and unparalleled hiking.

GETTING HERE AND AROUND

Bretton Woods is in the heart of the White Mountains on U.S. 302. A free shuttle makes it easy to get around the resort's various facilities.

 Sights

★ Crawford Notch State Park

BODY OF WATER | FAMILY | Scenic U.S. 302 winds southeast of Bretton Woods through the steep, wooded mountains on either side of spectacular Crawford Notch. Now a state park, you can picnic and hike to Arethusa Falls, the longest drop in New England, or to the Silver and Flume cascades—they're among more than a dozen outstanding trails. The 5,775-acre park has a number of roadside photo ops, plus an Adirondack-style visitor center, gift shop, snack bar, and fishing pond. ⊠ *1464 U.S. 302, Hart's Location* ☎ *603/374–2272* ⊕ *www. nhstateparks.org.*

★ Mount Washington Cog Railway

MOUNTAIN—SIGHT | FAMILY | In 1858, Sylvester Marsh petitioned the state legislature for permission to build a steam railway up Mt. Washington. One politico retorted that Marsh would have better luck building a railroad to the moon, but 11 years later the Mount Washington Cog Railway chugged its way up to the summit along a 3-mile track on the mountain's west side. Today it's a beloved attraction—a thrill in either direction. A small museum has exhibits about the cog rail, and a casual restaurant offers great views of the trains beginning their ascent. The full trip takes three hours including an hour at the summit. ⊠ *3168 Base Station Rd.* ☎ *603/278–5404, 800/922–8825* ⊕ *www.thecog.com* 🎫 *From $72* 🕐 *Closed Dec.–Apr.*

 Hotels

★ The Notchland Inn

$$$ | B&B/INN | Built in 1862 by Sam Bemis, America's grandfather of landscape photography, the gracious granite manor house exudes mountain charm and is popular with Crawford Notch hikers who favor luxury. **Pros:** set amid soaring mountains; marvelous house and common rooms; outstanding breakfasts and dinners. **Cons:** very isolated; fills up well in advance on summer and fall weekends; not ideal for young kids. 🟊 *Rooms from: $275* ⊠ *2 Morey Rd., Hart's Location* ☎ *603/374–6131, 800/866–6131* ⊕ *www.notchland.com* 🛏 *15 rooms* 🍽 *Free breakfast.*

★ Omni Mount Washington Hotel

$$$ | RESORT | FAMILY | The two most memorable sights in the White Mountains might just be Mt. Washington and this dramatic 1902 resort with a 900-foot veranda, glimmering public rooms, astonishing views of the Presidential Range, and dozens of recreational activities like tubing, sleigh rides, horseback riding, and fly-fishing. **Pros:** incomparable setting and ambience; loads of amenities and dining options; free shuttle to skiing and activities. **Cons:** lots of kids running around the hotel; a drive from nearest decent-size town; rates soar on summer–fall weekends. 🟊 *Rooms from: $279* ⊠ *310 Mt. Washington Hotel Rd., off U.S. 302* ☎ *603/278–1000, 888/444–6664* ⊕ *www.mountwashingtonresort.com* 🛏 *200 rooms* 🍽 *No meals.*

🏃 **Activities**

SKIING

★ Bretton Woods

SKIING/SNOWBOARDING | FAMILY | New Hampshire's largest ski area is also one of the country's best family ski resorts. The views of Mt. Washington alone are worth the visit, and the scenery is especially beautiful from the two-story restaurant atop 3,000-foot-elevation

Mt. Rosebrook, reached via an all-glass eight-passenger Skyway Gondola that opened in 2019.

The resort has something for everyone, from extensive kids' programs and lessons to some seriously steep pitches near the top of the 1,500-foot vertical. And the 35 glades will keep experts busy, while snowboarders enjoy the three terrain parks. The Nordic trail system has 62 miles of cross-country ski trails. Both night skiing and snowboarding are available on weekends and holidays.

There's also the year-round Canopy Tour, with nine ziplines, two sky bridges, and three rappelling stations. **Facilities:** 102 trails; 464 acres, 1,500-foot vertical drop; 10 lifts. ⊠ *99 Ski Area Rd.* ☎ *603/278–3320, 603/278–1000 for conditions* ⊕ *www.brettonwoods.com* ⊠ *Lift ticket: $104.*

Bethlehem

14 miles west of Bretton Woods.

In the days before antihistamines, hay-fever sufferers came by the trainload to this enchanting village whose crisp air has a blissfully low pollen count. Today this progressive, artsy hamlet with fewer than 1,000 residents is notable for its art deco Colonial Theatre (which presents indie films and concerts), distinctive galleries and cafés, and stately Victorian and Colonial homes, many of which line the village's immensely picturesque Main Street, a highly enjoyable locale for a stroll.

GETTING HERE AND AROUND
U.S. 302 and Route 142 intersect in the heart of this small village center that's easy to explore on foot.

Sights

The Rocks Estate

FARM/RANCH | FAMILY | The estate of John Jacob Glessner (1843–1936), one of the founders of International Harvester, now serves as a 1,400-acre conservation and education center. The property is named for the many surface boulders on the estate when Glessner bought it—some were used to erect the rambling rock walls that flanks the estate's striking shingle-style restored buildings. The Rocks presents natural-history programs and has self-guided tours and hiking trails with excellent views of the Presidential Range. Come winter, cross-country ski trails and a select-your-own-Christmas-tree farm open up. In early spring, you can watch how maple syrup is made. ⊠ *4 Christmas La., Bethlehem* ☎ *603/444–6228* ⊕ *www.therocks.org.*

Restaurants

★ Cold Mountain Cafe

$$ | ECLECTIC | Adjacent to the Marketplace at WREN, this homey art-filled storefront eatery and wine bar is one of the area's social focal points, with a welcoming staff and a thoughtful, international menu. Pork tacos, Indian lamb stew, and heirloom tomato caprese salads are a few of the best dishes, but save room for the flourless chocolate torte with strawberry-balsamic coulis. **Known for:** friendly, upbeat crowd and staff; bounteous salads; intriguing cocktail list. ⑤ *Average main: $22* ⊠ *2015 Main St., Bethlehem* ☎ *603/869–2500* ⊕ *www.coldmountaincafe.com* ⊗ *Closed Sun.*

☕ Coffee and Quick Bites

Maia Papaya

$ | CAFÉ | Pause during your stroll through inviting Bethlehem for breakfast, lunch, smoothies, lattes, or homemade chai tea at this quirky organic café that specializes in vegetarian fare and made-from-scratch baked goods (try not to pass up one of the justly renowned scones). On cool mornings, warm up with the rich and delicious bread pudding French toast; terrific lunchtime options include the artichoke melt panini or the bountiful green salad. **Known for:** plenty of gluten-free and vegetarian options; fruit-filled oat bars; organic oatmeal with local maple syrup. ⑤ *Average main: $7* ✉ *2161 Main St., Bethlehem* ☎ *603/869–9900* ⊕ *www. themaiapapaya.com* ☾ *No dinner.*

Hotels

★ Adair Country Inn and Restaurant

$$$ | B&B/INN | An air of yesteryear refinement suffuses Adair, a three-story Georgian Revival home that attorney Frank Hogan built as a wedding present for his daughter in 1927—her hats adorn the place, as do books and old photos from the era. **Pros:** a superb, romantic restaurant; rates include a memorable breakfast and afternoon tea; cross-country skiing and hiking trails. **Cons:** not within walking distance of town; sometimes books up with weddings; closed for a month each fall and spring. ⑤ *Rooms from: $279* ✉ *80 Guider La., Bethlehem* ☎ *603/444–2600, 888/444–2600* ⊕ *www. adairinn.com* ☾ *Closed mid-Nov. and Apr.* ⇥ *11 rooms* ⎟⊚⎟ *Free breakfast.*

★ Bear Mountain Lodge

$$$ | B&B/INN | This striking log cabin–style inn on 26 secluded acres with arresting views of the Presidential Range looks like something you'd expect to find out West, and indeed, its owners based the design on lodges they visited in Alaska. **Pros:** gorgeous decor and architecture; utterly tranquil setting; exquisite full breakfasts. **Cons:** Western log cabin style isn't to everyone's taste; not within walking distance of town; minimum-night stays during busy times. ⑤ *Rooms from: $245* ✉ *3249 Main St., Bethlehem* ☎ *603/869–2189* ⊕ *www.bearmountainlodge.net* ⇥ *10 rooms* ⎟⊚⎟ *Free breakfast.*

Nightlife

★ Rek-Lis Brewing Company

BREWPUBS/BEER GARDENS | After a day of hiking or skiing, grab a seat inside this cozy tavern or out on one of the expansive decks and savor the outstanding house-made beers along with guest taps from other notable breweries. There's great pub food, too, and a popular Sunday brunch. ✉ *2085 Main St., Bethlehem* ☎ *603/991–2357* ⊕ *www.reklisbrewing. com.*

🛍 Shopping

★ Marketplace at WREN

ART GALLERIES | WREN (the Women's Rural Entrepreneurial Network) has been a vital force in little Bethlehem's steady growth into a center of artists, craftspersons, and other business owners. At WREN's headquarters, there's an outstanding gallery that presents monthly juried exhibits and a retail gift boutique, Local Works, featuring crafts, foods, and other products. ✉ *2011 Main St., Bethlehem* ☎ *603/869–9736* ⊕ *www.wrenworks.org.*

Littleton

5 miles west of Bethlehem.

One of northern New Hampshire's largest towns (this isn't saying much, mind you) sits on a granite shelf along the Ammonoosuc River, whose swift current and drop of 235 feet enabled the community to flourish as a mill center in its early days. The railroad came through later, and Littleton grew into the region's commercial hub. Long merely a place to stock up than a real destination, it's reinvented itself in recent decades, and its lively Main Street now abounds with intriguing shops and eateries set inside tidy 19th- and early-20th-century buildings you might expect to see in an old Jimmy Stewart movie.

GETTING HERE AND AROUND

Littleton sits just off Interstate 93, and its downtown is easily explored on foot.

ESSENTIALS

VISITOR INFORMATION Littleton Area Chamber of Commerce. ☎ *603/444–6561* ⊕ *www.littletonareachamber.com.*

Sights

The Great North Woods

INFO CENTER | The collective name for New Hampshire's northern panhandle, which is reached from Littleton via Route 116 to U.S. 3, the Great North Woods covers about 1,800 square miles, an area slightly larger than Rhode Island. Sparsely populated and with few roads, this expanse of dense woodland and mountains is hugely popular with fishing, hunting, hiking, and other backcountry recreation enthusiasts, but it's also appealing for a picturesque country drive, especially for moose viewing (drive carefully) and admiring fall foliage from mid-September through early October. The Canadian border is about 85 miles from Whitefield and takes two hours each way without stops, but passes through interesting little towns—like Lancaster, Colebrook, and Pittsburg—and snakes along the shores of the upper Connecticut River and the three pristine Connecticut Lakes. From Colebrook, you can also detour east along a dramatic stretch of Route 26 to Dixville Notch, site of the famous but currently closed Balsams Grand Resort Hotel and one of the first election districts in the nation to vote in presidential general elections. The area has a handful of popular businesses, like Le Rendez Vous pastry shop in Colebrook, Rainbow Grille in Pittsburg, and the Cabins at Lopstick and Glen at Bear Tree lodgings, both in Pittsburg. ⊠ *North County Chamber of Commerce, Colebrook* ☎ *603/237–8939* ⊕ *www. chamberofthenorthcountry.com.*

Weeks State Park

HOUSE | A few miles north of Whitefield's famous Mountain View Grand Resort, this 446-acre park occupies the early 20th-century estate of conservationist and U.S. Senator John W. Weeks, whose 1911 Weeks Act enabled the acquisition of some 19 million acres of wilderness, including White Mountain National Forest. An auto road winds to the 2,037-foot summit of Prospect Mountain, where a stone tower offers astounding views of Vermont and New Hampshire. One-hour tours of the Weeks mansion are available, and a 3.4-mile loop hiking trail traverses the property. ⊠ *200 Week's State Park Rd., Lancaster* ☎ *603/788–4004* ⊕ *www. nhstateparks.org* ⬛ *$4.*

Restaurants

★ Schilling Beer Taproom

$ | **AMERICAN** | With a storybook setting in a converted 18th-century mill on the Ammonoosuc River, this craft brewpub offers tasty wood-fired pizzas, bratwurst sandwiches, house-baked soft pretzels, and other fare that pairs well with its distinctive European ales. The pie topped with prosciutto, pears, chèvre, mozzarella, and beer-caramelized onions is a favorite, best enjoyed with a farmhouse-style saison. **Known for:** seating overlooking the river; beer tastings; great pizzas. ⑤ *Average main: $14* ⊠ *18 Mill St.* ☎ *603/444–4800* ⊕ *www.schillingbeer. com.*

★ Tim-Bir Alley

$$$ | **MODERN AMERICAN** | In this terrific contemporary downtown restaurant, you can sample some of the tastiest farm-to-table fare in the White Mountains. The menu changes frequently and uses regional American ingredients in creative ways—try country pâté with venison and pistachio, followed by skin-on salmon with olive oil–poached tomatoes and a black-olive vinaigrette. **Known for:** stylish yet unpretentious; local artisan cheese plates; beautifully plated desserts.

$ *Average main: $28* ⊠ *7 Main St.* ☎ *603/444–6142* ⊕ *www.timbirralleyres-taurant.com* ⊟ *No credit cards* ⊘ *Closed Mon. and Tues. No lunch.*

Coffee and Quick Bites

★ Crumb Bum

$ | CAFÉ | Stop by this cute cake shop to stock up on creative, and utterly delectable, baked goods, such as grapefruit-rosemary-cardamom short bread cookies, maple cinnamon rolls, and macarons in a variety of flavors, and egg-bacon-cheese breakfast sandwiches constructed on ethereal duck-fat biscuits. Fine coffees are available, too. **Known for:** great baked goods; duck fat angel biscuit breakfast sandwich; vegan options. $ *Average main:* ⊠ *97 Main St.* ☎ *603/575–5590* ⊕ *www.crumbbumbak-ery.com* ⊘ *Closed Tues.–Wed.*

The Inkwell

$ | CAFÉ | Drop by this funky old yellow house with indoor and outdoor seating overlooking the Ammonoosuc River for a light bite, to relax with a book, or sip one of the well-crafted fair-trade coffee or organic loose-leaf tea drinks. Several kinds of toast with tasty toppings (ricotta and lemon honey; cheddar, ham, and egg) are available at breakfast, along with myriad scones, cookies, and gluten-free pastries. **Known for:** toasts with creative toppings; endearing riverfront setting; iced and hot coffees with local maple syrup. $ *Average main: $7* ⊠ *42 Mill St.* ☎ *603/324–0942* ⊕ *www.inkwellnh.com* ⊘ *Closed Sun. No dinner.*

🛏 Hotels

Mountain View Grand Resort & Spa

$$ | RESORT | FAMILY | Casual elegance and stunning views of the White Mountains define this stately yellow wedding cake of a hotel that dates to 1865 and sprawls over 1,700 acres that include a working farm and a well-maintained golf course. **Pros:** full-service spa; dozens of activities; babysitting service and summer camp. **Cons:** breakfast not included in rates; not too many dining options nearby; sometimes fills up with corporate meetings and retreats. $ *Rooms from: $189* ⊠ *101 Mountain View Rd., Whitefield* ☎ *855/837–2100* ⊕ *www.mountainview-grand.com* ⇌ *144 rooms* ⦿ *No meals.*

Thayers Inn

$ | HOTEL | This former grande dame with a distinguished roster of past guests—including Ulysses S. Grant, Henry Ford, and P. T. Barnum—offers quirky and fun budget accommodations and a great location in one of the liveliest little downtowns in the White Mountains. **Pros:** some rooms have kitchenettes; fascinating building filled with memorabilia and exhibits; on lively and festival Main Street. **Cons:** no elevator; basic decor; tiny bathrooms. $ *Rooms from: $119* ⊠ *111 Main St.* ☎ *603/444–6469* ⊕ *www. thayersinn.com* ⇌ *34 rooms* ⦿ *Free breakfast.*

Performing Arts

ARTS VENUES

Weathervane Theatre

THEATER | This beloved 250-seat theater near the Mountainview Grand Resort presents seven musicals each summer. ⊠ *389 Lancaster Rd. (U.S. 3), White-field* ☎ *603/837–9322* ⊕ *www.weath-ervanenh.org.*

Shopping

Chutters

FOOD/CANDY | FAMILY | Boasting the world's longest candy counter, at 112 feet, this kid- and adult-approved century-plus-old candy shop with satellite locations in Lincoln, Loon Mountain Resort, and Bretton Woods carries just about every variety of sweet treat you could imagine. ⊠ *43 Main St* ☎ *603/444–5787* ⊕ *www. chutters.com.*

★ Just L Modern Antiques

ANTIQUES/COLLECTIBLES | Fans of mid-century furnishings, from low-slung modern sofas and sleek Danish coffee tables to both fashionable and kitschy housewares, vintage paintings, and kitchen items flock to this enormous two-floor emporium set along Littleton's increasingly hip Main Street. ☒ *35 Main St.* ☎ *603/259–3125.*

Little Village Toy and Book Stop

BOOKS/STATIONERY | **FAMILY** | Maps, history books, unusual children's toys and many adult fiction and nonfiction titles fill this cheerful shop, the lower level of which contains a branch of the venerable League of New Hampshire Craftsmen's gallery. ☒ *81B Main St.* ☎ *603/444–4869* ⊕ *www.littlevillagetoy.com.*

Pentimento

GIFTS/SOUVENIRS | This eclectic shop, packed into a Victorian house a few steps from the historic Opera House, is a great place to find unusual jewelry, candles, fashion eyewear, and handmade cards. ☒ *34 Union St.* ☎ *603/444–7797.*

Franconia

7 miles south of Littleton.

Travelers have long passed through spectacular Franconia Notch, and in the late 18th century this town evolved just to the north. It and the region's jagged rock formations and heavy coat of evergreens stirred the imaginations of Washington Irving, Henry Wadsworth Longfellow, and Nathaniel Hawthorne, who penned a short story about the iconic—though now crumbled—cliff known as the Old Man of the Mountain. There's barely a downtown, just a handful of businesses and the remains of the interesting old 1840s Besaw Iron Furnace. Drive west 4 miles to visit Sugar Hill, a village of about 500 people that's famous for its spectacular sunsets and views of Franconia Ridge, best seen from Sunset Hill, where

a row of grand hotels and mansions once stood.

GETTING HERE AND AROUND

Franconia has few services but is right off Interstate 93, making it a good base for visiting many nearby ski areas and mountain villages.

ESSENTIALS

VISITOR INFORMATION Franconia Notch Chamber of Commerce. ☎ *603/823–5661* ⊕ *www.franconianotch.org.*

Sights

★ Franconia Notch State Park

BEACH—SIGHT | **FAMILY** | Traversed by the Appalachian Trail and a stretch of Interstate 93 that narrows for 8 miles to become Franconia Notch Parkway, this stunning 6,692-acre state park feels as awesome as a national park and offers dozens of diversions, including myriad hiking trails, summer swimming at **Echo Lake Beach,** and winter downhill skiing at **Cannon Mountain,** whose 4,080-foot summit observation deck you can explore on the **Aerial Tramway,** an 80-passenger cable car. One of the top park draws, the dramatic, narrow 800-foot-long **Flume Gorge** is reached from a modern visitor center via a picturesque 2-mile loop hike along wooden boardwalks and stairways. The park was long famous as the site of the **Old Man of the Mountain,** an iconic profile high on a granite cliff that crumbled unexpectedly in 2003. Overlooking Profile Lake, at the small Old Man of the Mountain Park, you can walk the short but pretty paved trail to view the mountain face through steel rods that seem literally to put the beloved visage back on the mountain. You can see related photographs and memorabilia in a small museum, and also visit the **New England Ski Museum** to learn how skiing was popularized as a sport in New England, through artifacts, clothing, and equipment, as well as Bode Miller's five Olympic medals. ☒ *260 Tramway Dr.*

☎ *603/823–8800* ⊕ *www.nhstateparks. org* ◈ *Aerial Tramway $19, Echo Lake parking $4, Flume Gorge $16, museums free.*

The Frost Place Museum

HOUSE | Robert Frost's year-round home from 1915 to 1920, this modest homestead on a peaceful unpaved road is surrounded by well-tended gardens and offers stunning mountain views. The place is imbued with the spirit of his work—two rooms contain memorabilia and signed editions of his books. Out back, you can follow short trails marked with lines from his poetry. Poetry readings are scheduled some summer evenings. ⊠ *158 Ridge Rd.* ☎ *603/823–5510* ⊕ *www.frostplace.org* ◈ *$5* ⊙ *Closed mid-Oct.–Apr.*

 Restaurants

★ Polly's Pancake Parlor

$ | AMERICAN | FAMILY | In the Dexter family for generations, Polly's has been serving up pancakes and waffles (from its own original recipe, with several batter options available, including cornmeal and gingerbread) since the 1930s—the current space dates to 2015 but retains the original country charm. Try the smoked bacon and ham, eggs Benedict, sandwiches on homemade bread, delicious baked beans, and such tempting desserts as raspberry pie. **Known for:** gift shop with maple products; gingerbread pancakes with blueberries and walnuts; pretty hilltop setting. ⑤ *Average main: $11* ⊠ *672 Rte. 117* ☎ *603/823–5575* ⊕ *www.pollyspancakeparlor.com* ⊙ *Closed Wed. No dinner.*

 Hotels

Franconia Inn

$ | RESORT | FAMILY | At this 107-acre family-friendly resort anchored by an affordable three-story inn with unfussy country furnishings, you can play tennis on four clay courts, soak in the outdoor heated pool or hot tub, hop on a mountain bike, or soar in a glider, and cross-country ski on 40 miles of groomed trails. **Pros:** tons of family-oriented activities; outdoor heated pool; peaceful setting with mountain views. **Cons:** a bit remote; historic hotel with some quirks; popularity with families can make it a little noisy. ⑤ *Rooms from: $136* ⊠ *1172 Easton Rd.* ☎ *603/823–5542, 800/473–5299* ⊕ *www. franconiainn.com* ⊙ *Closed Apr.–mid-May* ◈ *34 rooms* ❖ *No meals.*

Sunset Hill House

$ | HOTEL | It's all about the view at this striking Victorian inn set high on a ridge in tiny Sugar Hill, its 70 acres holding lovely gardens, a seasonal outdoor pool, and a great little golf course. **Pros:** mesmerizing views; excellent 9-hole golf course; unusually good restaurant with outdoor dining. **Cons:** slightly remote setting; not a great option for kids; some bathrooms are shower-only. ⑤ *Rooms from: $155* ⊠ *231 Sunset Hill Rd., Sugar Hill* ☎ *603/823–7244* ⊕ *www.thesunsethillhouse.com* ◈ *28 rooms* ❖ *Free breakfast.*

★ Sugar Hill Inn

$$$ | B&B/INN | Although this upscale inn surrounded by neatly manicured gardens dates to 1789, it has a decidedly current vibe, from its sumptuous rooms with such modern perks as whirlpool tubs, gas fireplaces, and Bose sound systems, to the superb prix-fixe restaurant serving sublime contemporary American fare. **Pros:** many rooms have private decks; dining packages available; gorgeous countryside setting. **Cons:** somewhat remote; books up well ahead on weekends; not a good fit for families. ⑤ *Rooms from: $278* ⊠ *116 Sugar Hill Rd. (Rte. 117), Sugar Hill* ☎ *603/869–7543* ⊕ *www.sugarhillinn.com* ◈ *15 rooms* ❖ *Free breakfast.*

Shopping

★ Harman's Cheese & Country Store

FOOD/CANDY | It's worth a slight but pretty detour over the hill from Franconia to visit this rambling old village store and dairy that turns out legendarily rich, sharp aged cheddar, which is also available smoked and in port-and-cognac spreads. The venerable red-clapboard shop carries plenty of other foodie-pleasing products, and on summer Fridays, they hold farm-to-fire pizza nights. ⊠ *1400 Rte. 117, Sugar Hill* ☎ *603/823–8000* ⊕ *www.harmanscheese.com.*

Activities

SKIING

Cannon Mountain

SKIING/SNOWBOARDING | **FAMILY** | Serviced by the first aerial tramway in North America, which was built in 1938, this classic New England ski resort inside Franconia Notch State Park offers terrain that runs the gamut from steep pitches off the peak to gentle blue cruisers. Beginners may want to head over to the separate Tuckerbrook family area, which offers 13 trails and four lifts. Adventurous types will want to try out the Mittersill area, which has 86 acres of lift-accessed "side country" trails and glades where the snow is au naturel. **Facilities:** 97 trails; 285 acres; 2,180-foot vertical drop; 11 lifts. ⊠ *260 Tramway Dr.* ☎ *603/823–8800, 603/823–7771 snow conditions* ⊕ *www.cannonmt.com* 🎟 *Lift ticket: $88.*

Lincoln and North Woodstock

17 miles south of Franconia, 42 miles west of North Conway, 64 miles north of Concord.

These neighboring towns at the White Mountains' southwestern corner are the western gateway to the famed Kancamagus Highway. They form a lively resort base camp, especially for metro Boston families who can make an easy two-hour drive straight up Interstate 93. Although the town itself isn't much of an attraction, myriad festivals and activities keep Lincoln swarming with visitors year-round.

Tiny North Woodstock maintains a more inviting village feel and is close to some easy, scenic, family-friendly hikes, such as Georgiana Falls and the slightly more ambitious Indian Head Trail.

GETTING HERE AND AROUND
Accessed from Interstate 93, Lincoln and North Woodstock are connected by Route 112—it's a short 1-mile drive between the two.

ESSENTIALS
VISITOR INFORMATION Western White Mountains Chamber of Commerce. ☎ *603/745–6621* ⊕ *www.western-whitemtns.com.*

TOURS
Pemi Valley Moose Tours
TOUR—SPORTS | **FAMILY** | If you're eager to see a mighty moose, embark on a moose-watching bus tour into the northernmost White Mountains. The three-hour trips depart at 8:30 pm May to mid-October for the best wildlife-sighting opportunities. ⊠ *136 Main St., Lincoln* ☎ *603/745–2744* ⊕ *www.moosetoursnh.com* 🎟 *$35.*

Sights

Clark's Bears
AMUSEMENT PARK/WATER PARK | **FAMILY** | Chock-full of hokum, this kids-oriented old-time amusement park is famous for its performing live-bear shows. There are also short train trips over a 1904 covered bridge, segway rides, a museum of Americana inside an 1880s firehouse, a restored gas station with antique cars, an Old Man of the Mountain rock-climbing tower, and a huge, kitschy gift shop

with penny-candy. ⊠ *110 Daniel Webster Hwy., Lincoln* ☎ *603/745–8913* ⊕ *www. clarksbears.com* ⌸ *$24* ⊙ *Closed mid-Oct.–mid-May.*

Hobo Railroad
LOCAL INTEREST | FAMILY | Restored vintage train cars take you on 80-minute excursions along the scenic banks of the Pemigewassett River. A Santa Express runs late November–late December. ⊠ *64 Railroad St., Lincoln* ☎ *603/745–2135* ⊕ *www.hoborr.com* ⌸ *$19* ⊙ *Closed Jan.–Apr.*

★ Kancamagus Highway
NATIONAL/STATE PARK | FAMILY | In 1937, two old local roads were connected from Lincoln to Conway to create this remarkable 34.5-mile national designated scenic byway through a breathtaking swath of the White Mountains. This section of Route 112 known as the Kancamagus—often called simply "the Kanc"—contains no businesses or billboards and is punctuated by overlooks, picnic areas, and memorable hiking trailheads. These include **Lincoln Woods,** an easy 6-mile round-trip trek along a railroad bed that departs from the Lincoln Woods Visitor Center, crosses a dramatic suspension bridge over the Pemigewasset River, and ends at a swimming hole formed by dramatic Franconia Falls. There's also **Sabbaday Falls,** a short ½-mile stroll to a multilevel cascade that plunges through two potholes and a flume. For a slightly harder but less crowded trek, take the 3.5-mile **Boulder Loop Trail,** which rises precipitously some 1,000 feet from the banks of the Swift River to a granite-crowned summit with mountain views. The road's highest point, at 2,855 feet, crosses the flank of Mt. Kancamagus, near Lincoln—a great place to view the fiery displays of foliage each autumn. On-site in lots and overlooks costs $5. ☎ *603/536–6100* ⊕ *www.fs.usda.gov/ whitemountain.*

★ Lost River Gorge & Boulder Caves
NATURE SITE | FAMILY | Parents can enjoy the looks of wonder on their kids' faces as they negotiate wooden boardwalks and stairs leading through a granite gorge formed by the roaring waters of the Lost River. One of the 10 caves they can explore is called the Lemon Squeezer (and it's a tight fit). Visitors can also pan for gems and search for fossils and walk through a fascinating giant man-made birdhouse, venture across a suspension bridge, and climb up into a big tree house. The park offers lantern tours on weekend evenings. ⊠ *1712 Lost River Rd., North Woodstock* ☎ *603/745–8720* ⊕ *www.lostrivergorge.com* ⌸ *$20* ⊙ *Closed Nov.–Apr.*

Seven Birches Winery
WINERY/DISTILLERY | With a tasting room at Lincoln's RiverWalk resort and steps away in a bright and modern wine bar with a big patio, this respected winery offers its classic European-varietal dry wines and sweeter fruit wines by the glass or flight, along with a selection of snacks. ⊠ *22 S. Mountain Dr., Lincoln* ☎ *603/745–7550* ⊕ *www.sevenbirches. com.*

Whale's Tale Waterpark
AMUSEMENT PARK/WATER PARK | FAMILY | You can float on an inner tube along a gentle river, plunge down one of five waterslides, hang five on the Akua surf simulator, or bodysurf in the large wave pool at Whale's Tale. There's plenty here for toddlers and small children, too. ⊠ *491 Daniel Webster Hwy. (U.S. 3), Lincoln* ☎ *603/745–8810* ⊕ *www.whalestalewaterpark.net* ⌸ *From $39* ⊙ *Closed early Oct.–Apr.*

 Restaurants

Woodstock Inn Brewery
$$ | AMERICAN | This big and festive brewpub inside a late-1800s train station is decorated with old maps, historic photographs, and other fun curiosities.

The kitchen turns out reliably good pub fare—pizza, burgers, steaks, seafood—and filling breakfasts, and the brewery produces nearly 20 different varieties of exceptionally good beers. **Known for:** game room and kids' menu; brewery tours; inviting indoor and outdoor seating. $ *Average main: $18* ⊠ *135 Main St., North Woodstock* ☎ *603/745–3951* ⊕ *www.woodstockinnnh.com.*

Coffee and Quick Bites

The Moon Bakery & Cafe
$ | CAFÉ | A must for delicious sustenance and potent lattes before hitting the slopes or hiking along the Kancamagus Highway, this homey café offers ample indoor seating in exposed-brick-wall nooks or outside on the sidewalk. Popular items include ham and cheddar sandwiches with maple mustard, avocado-egg breakfast sandwiches, and matcha green tea smoothies. **Known for:** fresh smoothies; hefty sandwiches on house-baked bread; trail mix cookies. $ *Average main: $7* ⊠ *28 S. Mountain Dr., Lincoln* ☎ *603/745–5013* ⊕ *www. themoonnh.com* ⊗ *No dinner.*

🛏 Hotels

Indian Head Resort
$ | RESORT | FAMILY | This early-20th-century resort identified by its 100-foot-tall observation tower and its lovely setting overlooking Shadow Lake, offers inexpensive and spacious rooms, making it a good choice for families on a budget. **Pros:** near kid-friendly attractions; fun, old-school personality; a free ski shuttle to Cannon or Loon Mountain. **Cons:** some rooms overlook parking lot; on busy road 5 miles north of Woodstock; shows wear in places. $ *Rooms from: $131* ⊠ *664 U.S. 3, Lincoln* ☎ *603/745–8000, 800/343–8000* ⊕ *www.indianheadresort. com* ⇦ *148 rooms* ⦿ *Free breakfast.*

Mountain Club on Loon
$$ | RESORT | FAMILY | With a diverse range of accommodations, including large family suites, and many units with full kitchens, this functional if pretty standard condo-style lodge provides convenient ski-in, ski-out accommodations on Loon Mountain. **Pros:** within walking distance of the lifts; full-service spa; easy proximity to hiking in national forest. **Cons:** very busy on winter weekends; decor is a bit dated; not within walking distance of town. $ *Rooms from: $189* ⊠ *90 Loon Mountain Rd., Lincoln* ☎ *603/745–2244, 800/229–7829* ⊕ *www.mtnclub.com* ⇦ *235 rooms* ⦿ *No meals.*

🛍 Shopping

Fadden's General Store
FOOD/CANDY | The Fadden family, who have been making maple syrup since the early 19th century, operates this inviting general store, sugarhouse, and maple museum that dates to 1896. Come in to buy syrup, souvenirs, and gourmet treats, or for a self-guided tour of the operations. ⊠ *109 Main St., North Woodstock* ☎ *603/745–8371* ⊕ *www.nhmaplesyrup. com.*

🏃 Activities

HIKING
Mt. Moosilauke
HIKING/WALKING | One of the most rewarding, though heavily trafficked, summits in the White Mountains, 4,802-foot Mt. Moosilauke soars high to the west of the Pemigewasset Valley and can be approached via a few routes, including the Appalachian Trail and from Route 112 near Lost River Gorge. The most enjoyable trek is via the 7-mile South Peak Loop. It begins near Route 118 at the 1930s Moosilauke Ravine Lodge, which is operated by Dartmouth College and offers basic overnight accommodations.

Continued on page 216

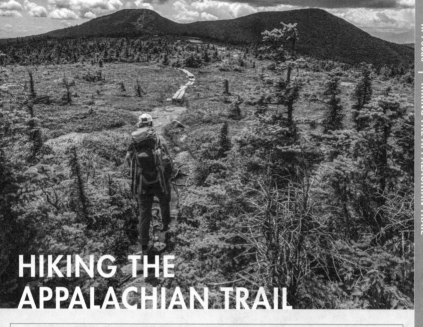

HIKING THE APPALACHIAN TRAIL

Tucked inside the nation's most densely populated corridor, a simple footpath in the wilderness stretches more than 2,200 miles, from Georgia to Maine. The Appalachian Trail passes through some of New England's most spectacular regions, and daytrippers can experience the area's beauty on a multitude of accessible, rewarding hikes. By Melissa Kim

Running along the spine of the Appalachian Mountains, the trail was fully blazed in 1937 and designed to connect anyone and everyone with nature. Within a day's drive of two-thirds of the U.S. population, it draws an estimated three million people every year. Through-hikers complete the whole trail in one daunting six-month season, but all ages and abilities can find renewal and perspective here in just a few hours. One-third of the AT passes through New England, and it's safe to say that the farther north you go, the harder the trail gets. New Hampshire and Maine challenge experienced hikers with windy, cold, and isolated peaks.

Top, hiking in New Hampshire's White Mountains. Above, autumn view of Profile Lake, Pemigewasset, NH.

ON THE TRAIL

New England's prime hiking season is in late summer and early fall, when the blaze of foliage viewed from a high peak is unparalleled. Popular trails see high crowds; if you seek solitude, try hiking at sunrise, a peaceful time that's good for wildlife viewing. You'll have to curb your enthusiasm in spring and early summer to avoid mud season in late April and black flies in May and June.

With the right gear, attitude, and preparation, winter can also offer fine opportunities for hiking, snowshoeing, and cross-country skiing.

FOLLOW THE TRAIL

Most hiking trails are marked with blazes, blocks of colored paint on a tree or rock. The AT, and only the AT, is marked by vertical, rectangular 2- by 6-inch white blazes. Two blazes mark route changes; turn in the direction of the top blaze. At higher elevations, you might also see cairns, small piles of rocks carefully placed by trail rangers to show the way when a blaze might be obscured by snow or fog.

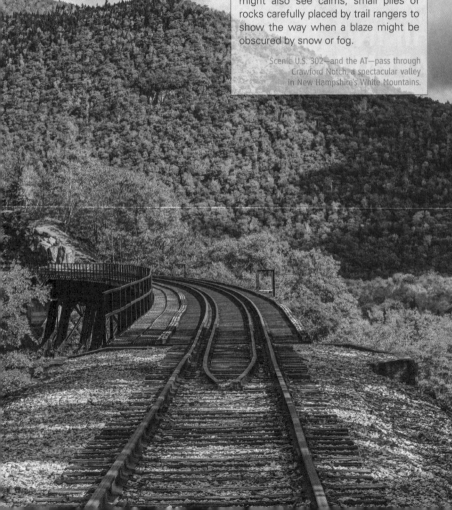

Scenic U.S. 302—and the AT—pass through Crawford Notch, a spectacular valley in New Hampshire's White Mountains.

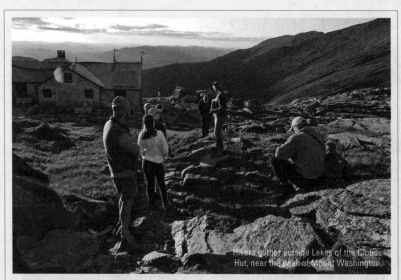

Hikers gather outside Lakes of the Clouds Hut, near the peak of Mount Washington.

TRIP TIPS

WHAT TO WEAR: For clothes, layer with a breathable fabric like polypropylene, starting with a shirt, a fleece, and a wind- or water-resistant shell. Bring gloves, a hat, and a change of socks.

WHAT TO BRING: Carry plenty of water and lightweight high-energy food. Don't forget sunscreen and insect repellent. Bring a map and compass. Just in case: a basic first-aid kit, a flashlight or headlamp, whistle, multi-tool, and matches.

PLAN AHEAD: In your car, leave a change of clothing, especially dry socks and shoes, as well as extra water and food.

PLAY IT SAFE: Tell someone your hiking plan and take a hiking partner. Carry a rescue card with emergency contact information and allergy details.

BE PREPARED: Plan your route and check the weather forecast in advance.

REMEMBER YOUR BEGINNINGS: Look back at the trail especially at the trailhead and at tricky junctions. If you've got a digital camera, photograph trail maps posted at the trailhead or natural landmarks to help you find your way.

WHERE TO STAY

Day hikers looking to extend the adventure can also make the experience as hard or as soft as they choose. Through-hikers combine camping with overnight stays in primitive shelters, mountain huts, comfortable lodges, and resorts just off the trail.

Rustic cabins and lean-tos provide basic shelter in Maine's Baxter State Park. In Maine and New Hampshire, the Appalachian Mountain Club runs four-season lodges as well as a network of mountain huts for backcountry hikers. A hiker code of camaraderie and conviviality prevails in these huts. Experience a night and you might just find yourself dreaming of a through-hike.

FOR MORE INFORMATION

Appalachian Trail Conservancy
(⊕ www.appalachiantrail.org)

Appalachian National Scenic Trail
(⊕ www.nps.gov/appa)

Appalachian Mountain Club
(⊕ www.outdoors.org)

ANIMALS ALONG THE TRAIL

❶ Black bear

Black bears are the most common—and smallest—bear in North America. Clever and adaptable, these adroit mammals will eat whatever they can (though they are primarily vegetarian, favoring berries, grasses, roots, blossoms, and nuts). Not naturally aggressive, black bears usually make themselves scarce when they hear hikers. The largest New England populations are in New Hampshire and Maine.

❷ Moose

Spotting a moose in the wild is unforgettable: their massive size and serene gaze are truly humbling. Treasure the moment, then slowly back away. At more than six feet tall, weighing 750 to 1,200 pounds, a moose is not to be trifled with, particularly during rutting and calving seasons (fall and spring, respectively). Dusk and dawn are the best times to spot the iconic animal; you're most likely to see one in Maine, especially in and around ponds.

⚠ Black flies

Especially fierce in May and June, these pesky flies can upset the tranquility of a hike in the woods as they swarm your face and bite your neck. To ward them off, cover any exposed skin and wear light colors. You'll get some relief on a mountain peak; cold weather and high winds also keep them at bay.

❸ Bald eagles

Countless bird species can be seen and heard along the AT, but what could be more exciting than to catch a glimpse of our national bird as it bounces back from near extinction? Now it's not uncommon to see the majestic bald eagle with its tremendous wing span, white head feathers, and curved yellow beak. The white head and tail distinguish the bald from the golden eagle, a bit less rare but just as thrilling to see. Most of New England's bald eagles are in Maine, but they are now present—albeit in small numbers—in all six states.

WILDFLOWERS ALONG THE TRAIL

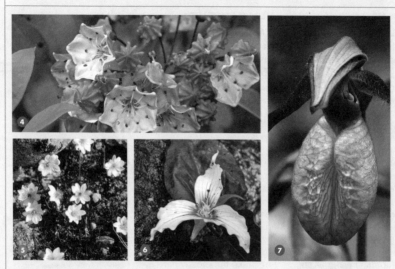

❹ Mountain laurel

The clusters of pink and white blooms of the mountain laurel look like bursts of fireworks. Up close, each one has the delicate detail of a lady's parasol. Blooms vary in color, from pure white to darker pink, and have different amounts of red markings. Connecticut's state flower, mountain laurel flourishes in rocky woods, blooming in May and June. Look for the shrub in southern New England; it's rare along the Appalachian trail in Vermont and Maine.

❺ Mountain avens

A member of the rose family, these showy yellow flowers abound in New Hampshire's White Mountains. You can't miss the large buttercup-like blooms on long green stems when they are in bloom from June through August. So common here, yet extremely rare: the only other place in the whole world where you can find mountain avens is on an island off the coast of Nova Scotia.

❻ Painted trillium

You might smell a trillium before you see it; these flowers have an unpleasant odor that may attract the flies that pollinate it. To identify this impressive flower, look for sets of three: three large pointed blue-green leaves, three sepals (small leaves beneath the petals), and three white petals with a brilliant magenta center. It can take four or five years for a trillium to produce one flower, which blooms in May and June in wet woodlands.

❼ Pink lady slippers

These delicate orchids can grow from 6 to 15 inches high and favor specific wet wooded areas in dappled sunlight. The slender stalk rises from a pair of green leaves, then bends a graceful neck to suspend the paper-thin pale pink closed flower. The slow-growing plant needs help from fungus and bees to survive and can live to be 20 years old. New Hampshire's state wildflower, the pink lady slipper blooms in June throughout New England.

● = Somewhat Common ● = Rare

CHOOSE YOUR DAY HIKE

MAINE

GULF HAGAS, Greenville

Difficult, 8-plus miles round-trip, 6–7 hours

This National Natural Landmark in the North Maine Woods is a spectacular sight for the adventurous day hiker. It involves a long drive on logging roads east from Greenville (see Inland Maine section) to a remote spot and a slippery, sometimes treacherous 8-mile hike around the rim of what's been dubbed Maine's Grand Canyon. Swimming in one of the sparkling pools under a 30-foot-high waterfall and admiring the views of cliffs, cascades, gorges, and chasms in this slate canyon, otherwise unthinkable in New England, will take your breath away.

TABLE ROCK, Bethel

Medium, 2.7 miles round-trip, 2 hours

Maine's Mahoosuc Range is thought to be one of the most difficult stretches of the entire AT, but north of Bethel at Grafton Notch State Park, day hikes range from easy walks in to cascading waterfalls to strenuous climbs up Old Speck's craggy peak. The Table Rock trail offers interesting sights—great views of the notch from the immense slab of granite that gives this trail its name, as well as one of the state's largest system of slab caves—narrow with tall openings unlike underground caves.

NEW HAMPSHIRE

ZEALAND TRAIL, Bretton Woods

Easy, 5.6 miles round-trip, 3.5–4 hours

New Hampshire's Presidential range gets so much attention and traffic that sometimes the equally spectacular Pemigewasset Wilderness, just to its west, gets overlooked. Follow State Route 302 to the trailhead on Zealand Rd. near Bretton Woods. For an easy day hike to one of the Appalachian Mountain Club's excellent overnight huts, take the mostly flat Zealand Trail over bridges and past a beaver swamp to Zealand Pond. The last tenth of a mile is a steep ascent to the mountain retreat, where you might spot an AT through-hiker taking a well-deserved rest. (Most north-bound through-hikers reach this section around July or August.) In winter, you can get here by a lovely cross-country ski trip.

TRAIL NAMES

For through-hikers, doing the AT can be a life-altering experience. One of the trail's most respected traditions is taking an alter ego: a trail name. Lightning Bolt: fast hiker. Pine Knot: tough as one. Bluebearee: because a bear got all her food on her very first night on the trail.

VERMONT

HARMON HILL, Bennington

Medium to difficult, 3.3 miles round-trip, 3–4 hours

This rugged hike in the Green Mountains goes south along the AT where it coincides with the Long Trail, Vermont's century-old "footpath in the wilderness." From the trailhead on Route 9 just east of Bennington, the first half mile or so is strenuous, with some rock and log staircases and hairpins. The payback is the sweeping view from the top; you'll see Mount Anthony, Bennington and its iconic war monument, and the rolling green hills of the Taconics to the west.

STRATTON MOUNTAIN, Stratton

Difficult, 6.6 miles round-trip, 5–6 hours

A steep and steady climb from the trailhead on Stratton Arlington Rd. (west of the village of Stratton) up the 3,936-foot-high Stratton Mountain follows the AT and Long Trail through mixed forests. It's said that this peak is where Benton MacKaye conceived of the idea for the Appalachian Trail in 1921. An observation tower at the summit gives you a great 360-degree view of the Green Mountains. From July to October, you can park at Stratton resort and ride the gondola up (or down) and follow the .75-mile Fire Tower Trail to the southern true peak.

MASSACHUSETTS

MOUNT GREYLOCK, North Adams

Easy to difficult, 2 miles round-trip, less than 1 hour

There are many ways to experience Massachusetts's highest peak. From North Adams, follow Route 2 to the Notch Rd. trailheads. For a warm-up, try the Rounds Rock trail (Easy, 0.7 mi) for some spectacular views. Or drive up the 8-mile-long summit road and hike down the Robinson's Point trail (Difficult, 0.8 miles) for the best view of the Hopper, a glacial cirque that's home to an old-growth red spruce forest. At the summit, the impressive **Bascom Lodge**, built in the 1930s by the Civilian Conservation Corps, provides delicious meals and overnight stays (⊕ www.bascomlodge.net).

CONNECTICUT

LION'S HEAD, Salisbury

Medium, 4.6 miles round-trip, 3.5–4 hours

The AT's 52 miles in Connecticut take hikers up some modest mountains, including Lion's Head in Salisbury. From the trailhead on State Route 41, follow the white blazes of the AT for two easy miles, then take the blue-blazed Lion's Head Trail for a short, steep push over open ledges to the 1,738-foot summit with its commanding views of pastoral southern New England. Try this in summer when the mountain laurels—Connecticut's state flower—are in bloom.

EXPERIENCE MOUNT WASHINGTON

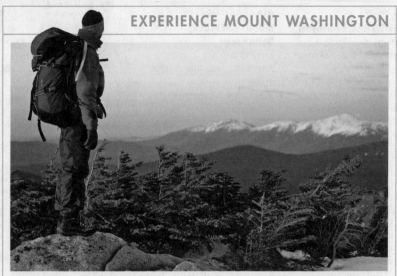

Looking at Mt. Washington from Mt. Bond in the Pemigewasset Wilderness Area, New Hampshire.

Mount Washington is the Northeast's peak of superlatives: worst weather in the world, highest spot in the northeast, windiest place on Earth. It snows in the summer, there are avalanches in winter, and it's foggy 60 percent of the time. Strong 35-mile-per-hour winds are the average, and extreme winds of 100 miles per hour with higher gusts blow year-round. Here, you can literally get blown away.

Explorers, scientists, artists, and botanists have been coming to the mountain for hundreds of years, drawn by its unique geologic features, unusual plants, and exceptional climate.

WHY SO WINDY? The 6,288-foot-high treeless peak is the highest point for miles around, so nothing dampens the force of the wind. Also, the sharp vertical rise causes wind to accelerate. Dramatic changes in air pressure also cause strong, high winds. Add to that the fact that three major storm tracks converge here, and you've got a mountain that has claimed more than 150 lives in the past 175 years.

GOING UP THE MOUNTAIN

An ascent up Mount Washington is for experienced hikers who are prepared for severe, unpredictable weather. Even in summer, cold, wet, foggy, windy conditions prevail. The most popular route to the top is on the eastern face up the Tuckerman Ravine Trail. But countless trails offer plenty of moderate day hikes, like the Alpine Garden Trail, as an alternative to a summit attempt. Start at the Pinkham Notch Visitor Center on Route 16 to review your options.

BACKPACKING ON THE MOUNTAIN

Lakes of the Clouds Hut perches 5,050 feet up the southern shoulder, providing bunkrooms and meals in summer; reservations are required. On the eastern face, the **Hermit Lake Shelter Area** has shelters and tent platforms; to camp here you'll need a first-come, first-served permit from the Visitors Center. Both are operated by the **AMC** (☎ 603/466-2727; ⊕ www.outdoors.org).

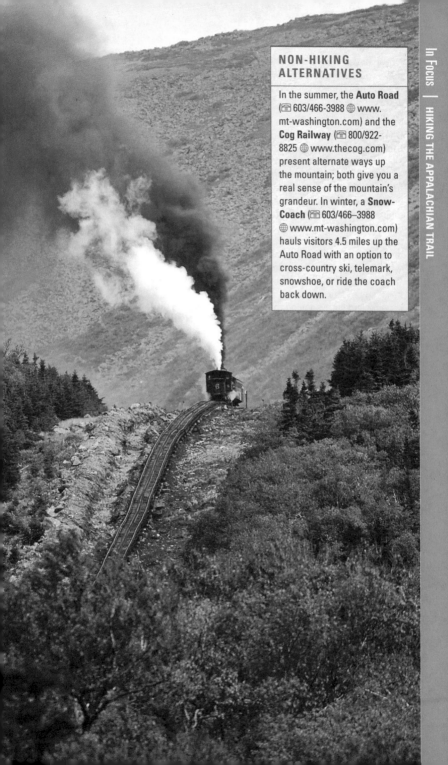

NON-HIKING ALTERNATIVES

In the summer, the **Auto Road** (☎ 603/466-3988 ⊕ www. mt-washington.com) and the **Cog Railway** (☎ 800/922-8825 ⊕ www.thecog.com) present alternate ways up the mountain; both give you a real sense of the mountain's grandeur. In winter, a **Snow-Coach** (☎ 603/466–3988 ⊕ www.mt-washington.com) hauls visitors 4.5 miles up the Auto Road with an option to cross-country ski, telemark, snowshoe, or ride the coach back down.

However you ascend to the treeless peak, you'll enjoy sweeping views of the Presidential Range, Lake Winnipesaukee, and even the Adirondacks. ⊠ *Ravine Rd., North Woodstock.*

SKIING

Loon Mountain

SKIING/SNOWBOARDING | FAMILY | Wide, straight, and consistent intermediate ski trails prevail at this modern resort on the Pemigewasset River. The most advanced runs are grouped on the North Peak, with beginner trails set apart. There's snow tubing on the lower slopes, and eight terrain parks suitable for all ability levels. A base lodge offers dining and lounges. You'll also find 13 miles of cross-country trails, an outdoor ice-skating rink, snow-shoeing and snowshoeing tours, ziplin-ing, and a rock-climbing wall. **Facilities:** 61 trails; 370 acres; 2,100-foot vertical drop; 11 lifts. ⊠ *90 Loon Mountain Rd., Lincoln* ☎ *603/745–8111* ⊕ *www.loonmtn. com* ☟ *Lift ticket: $102.*

Waterville Valley

25 miles southeast of North Lincoln.

Although visitors have been exploring this dramatic southern White Mountains valley since 1835, and the first ski trails were installed on 3,997-foot Mt. Tecum-seh in the 1930s, Watervalley Valley didn't become a major destination until a group of developers led by Olympic skier Tom Corcoran built a full-service ski area here in 1966. That led to a planned resort with several hotels and condominiums, a town square with shops and restaurants, a golf course, and other amenities. Today it's a terrific family-friendly winter-sports destination, but there's also plenty to do in warmer months, including great hiking and mountain-biking. Rates at the resort hotels come with passes that include cross-country ski and bike rentals, access to the well-equipped White Mountain

Athletic Club, and other perks—it's a remarkable value.

GETTING HERE AND AROUND

You get here from Interstate 93 in Camp-ton, via Route 49, which runs alongside the Mad River and dead-ends at the Town Square. Free shuttle buses whisk guests from hotels to the ski area. In summer, you travel here by way of unpaved Tripoli Road, a bumpy but beautiful route through White Mountain National Forest that accesses some amazing camp-grounds and hikes, such as Mt. Osceola and Mt. Tecumseh. It leads out to Inter-state 93 in Woodstock.

Restaurants

Coyote Grill

$$ | AMERICAN | FAMILY | On the second floor of the White Mountain Athletic Club, Waterville Valley's best restaurant is a rambling space with big windows offering up grand views of the White Mountains. The food is hearty and well-prepared, just what you need after a day of hiking or skiing. **Known for:** moun-tain views; lighter fare served downstairs by the pool; Oreo-crusted white-choco-late cheesecake. ⑤ *Average main: $21* ⊠ *98 Valley Rd.* ☎ *603/236–4919* ⊕ *www. wildcoyotegrill.com* ☾ *Closed Mon. and Tues. No lunch.*

Hotels

Golden Eagle Lodge

$$ | HOTEL | FAMILY | Waterville Valley's pre-mier condominium resort, its steep roof punctuated by dozens of gabled dormers, recalls the grand hotels of an earlier era. **Pros:** steps from Town Square; units all have kitchens and lots of elbow room; sweeping mountain views. **Cons:** decor is a little dated; no a/c in many units; lots of kids and families create a sometimes hectic pace. ⑤ *Rooms from: $179* ⊠ *28 Packard's Rd.* ☎ *888/703–2453, 603/236–4600* ⊕ *www.goldeneaglelodge.com* ☟ *139 condos* ❑ *No meals.*

Valley Inn

$ | **HOTEL** | **FAMILY** | One of the town's less expensive options, the Valley Inn offers few frills, but when you factor in the free activities pass and the quiet but convenient location, it's a solid option. **Pros:** good value; largest units have kitchens and can sleep six; peaceful setting. **Cons:** a few minutes' walk to Town Square; cookie-cutter decor; very basic breakfast. ⑤ *Rooms from: $149* ⊠ *17 Tecumseh Rd.* ☎ *603/236–8425* ⊕ *www.valleyinn.com* ⤵ *42 rooms* ⦿ *Free breakfast.*

 ## Activities

BIKING

Adventure Center

BICYCLING | Waterville Valley's one-stop for mountain-bike and cross-country-ski rentals, maps, and trail passes, this well-equipped shop has a helpful staff ready to dispense advice on where to explore. They also offer lessons and clinics. ⊠ *6 Village Rd.* ☎ *603/236–4666* ⊕ *www.waterville.com.*

HIKING

★ Welch-Dickey Trail

HIKING/WALKING | This at times steep but gorgeous 4½-mile loop hike ascends a wooded hillside before climbing above the sheer granite faces of 2,605-foot Welch and 2,734-foot Dickey mountains. There are higher climbs in the White Mountains, but this trail offers incredible views in every direction. Parking costs $5. ⊠ *Orris Rd.*

SKIING

Waterville Valley Resort

SKIING/SNOWBOARDING | **FAMILY** | This family-friendly ski area has hosted many World Cup races, so advanced skiers can look forward to a challenge. About two-thirds of the 50 trails are intermediate: straight down the fall line, wide, and agreeably long. About 20 acres of tree-skiing and six terrain parks add heart-pounding stimulus, and full snowmaking coverage ensures good skiing even when nature doesn't cooperate. The resort also offers 46 miles of groomed cross-country trails. **Facilities:** 50 trails; 220 acres; 2,020-foot vertical drop; 11 lifts. ⊠ *1 Ski Area Rd.* ☎ *603/236–8311, 800/468–2553* ⊕ *www.waterville.com* ⛷ *Lift ticket: $98.*

New London

60 miles southwest of Waterville Valley, 33 miles west of Laconia, 40 miles northwest of Concord.

New London, the home of Colby-Sawyer College (1837), is a good base for exploring the Lake Sunapee region. A campus of stately Colonial-style buildings abuts the picturesque downtown, where you'll find several cafés and boutiques.

GETTING HERE AND AROUND
New London is just off Interstate 89.

 ## Sights

Mt. Kearsarge

NATIONAL/STATE PARK | There are two main ways to access this dramatic 2,937-foot granite peak east of Lake Sunapee. Approach it through **Winslow State Park,** which is closer to New London, by driving to the picnic area and hiking a 1.8-mile loop trail to the top. Or, more popularly, drive the 3½-mile scenic auto route through **Rollins State Park,** which snakes up the mountain's southern slope and leads to a ½-mile summit trail. However you get there, the views from the top are astounding. Rollins State Park is accessed from the cute colonial village of Warner, which is worth a quick stroll through. ⊠ *Rollins State Park, 1066 Kearsarge Mountain Rd., Warner* ☎ *603/456–3808* ⊕ *www.nhstateparks.org* ⛷ *$4.*

Lake Sunapee

Upper Valley · White Mountain Nat'l Forest · Blair · Squam Lake

West Plymouth · Plymouth · Holderness

Goose Pond · 118

Hanover · Newfound Lake · Ashland · Winona · Meredith

Wilder · Enfield · New Hampton

White River Junction · Lebanon · Mascoma Lake · Enfield Shaker Museum · Bristol

VERMONT · 89 · Grafton · 104 · Winnisquam Lake

Plainfield · Meriden · Danbury · Ragged Mountain · Tilton · Belmont

Saint-Gaudens National Historic Site · Grantham

Hartland · Windsor · Cornish-Windsor Bridge · Croydon · Little Sunapee Lake · Andover · Franklin · Northfield

Cornish · South Cornish · Georges Mills · New London · Winslow S.P.

Ascutney · Claremont · Sunapee Harbor · Sunapee · Sunapee Lake · Mt. Kearsarge · North Sutton · Boscawen

Newport · Mt. Sunapee State Park Beach · John Hay Estate at the Fells · Penacook

Springfield · Mt Sunapee · Mount Sunapee · Newbury · Contoocook

Goshen · South Newbury · CONCORD

Charlestown · Bradford

0   6 mi
0   6 km

🍴 Restaurants

★ Oak & Grain

$$$ | MODERN AMERICAN | The refined yet relaxed restaurant in the historic Inn at Pleasant Lake makes a splendid destination for a special occasion dinner, or simply to savor a delicious brunch in the window-lined dining room or out on the patio—both areas have views of the lake in the near distance. The kitchen here turns out artfully plated contemporary fare, such as kebabs of grilled shrimp, pork belly, and veggies with a spicy garlic-chili-lime aioli, and filet mignon with a foie gras–port wine sauce. **Known for:** pretty lake views; knowledgeable, friendly service; locally sourced meats and seafood. ⑤ *Average main: $31* ⊠ *853 Pleasant St.* ☎ *603/873–4833* ⊕ *innatpleasantlake.com* ⊘ *Closed Mon. and Tues. No lunch.*

Peter Christian's Tavern

$$ | MODERN AMERICAN | Exposed beams, wooden tables, a smattering of antiques, and half shutters on the windows make the amiable Peter Christian's a cool summer oasis and a warm winter haven. From shepherd's pie to seafood and grits with lobster butter, the flavorful comfort fare relies heavily on seasonal ingredients. **Known for:** outstanding clam chowder; well-curated craft-beer and wine selection; dog-friendly patio. ⑤ *Average main: $20* ⊠ *195 N. Main St.* ☎ *603/526–2964* ⊕ *www.peterchristiansnh.com.*

☕ Coffee and Quick Bites

Blue Loon Bakery

$ | BAKERY | Have a seat in this cheerful bakery's sunny seating nooks or out on the back patio, while you savor an egg-cheddar sandwich, house-made granola, a Brie-fig-apple baguette, or one of the delectable pastries or cakes. Favorite treats include maple-pumpkin pie, seasonal fruit tarts, raspberry scones, and praline sticky buns. **Known for:** savory artisan breads; fresh-baked pies; picnic supplies for nearby hiking and beach adventures. ⑤ *Average main: $7* ⊠ *12 Lovering La.* ☎ *603/526–2892* ⊕ *www.blueloonbakery.com* ⊘ *No dinner.*

Hotels

Follansbee Inn

$ | **B&B/INN** | Built in 1840, this rambling country inn on the shore of Kezar Lake is the kind of place that almost automatically turns strangers into fast friends. **Pros:** relaxed lakefront setting with 3-mile walking trail; free use of canoes, kayaks, sailboats, rowboats, and bicycles; excellent breakfast. **Cons:** not all rooms have lake views; Wi-Fi can be spotty in places; no restaurants within walking distance. ⑤ *Rooms from: $135* ⊠ *2 Keyser St., North Sutton* ☎ *603/927–4221* ⊕ *www. follansbeeinn.com* ⇨ *17 rooms* ⏻ *Free breakfast.*

★ Inn at Pleasant Lake

$$ | **B&B/INN** | Overlooking the shore of Pleasant Lake, and offering views of majestic Mt. Kearsarge in the distance, and just a short drive from downtown New London, this beautifully appointed 1790s inn has spacious, bright rooms filled with fine country antiques and high-end bedding. **Pros:** adjacent to lakefront and a small beach; tennis courts; rates includes an outstanding full breakfast and afternoon tea. **Cons:** not within walking distance of town; not a good fit for kids; minimum stay at busy times. ⑤ *Rooms from: $219* ⊠ *853 Pleasant St.* ☎ *603/526–6271, 800/626–4907* ⊕ *innat- pleasantlake.com* ⇨ *10 rooms* ⏻ *Free breakfast.*

⏲ Nightlife

Flying Goose Brew Pub

BREWPUBS/BEER GARDENS | Offering a regular menu of about a dozen hand-crafted beers, including a much lauded black IPA and a heady barley wine as well as a few seasonal varieties—made with hops grown on-site—this pub, and solar-powered brewery is a hit with beer connoisseurs. The kitchen serves juicy ribs, paper-thin onion rings, excellent burgers, and other tasty victuals. ⊠ *40 Andover Rd.* ☎ *603/526–6899* ⊕ *www. flyinggoose.com.*

Performing Arts

New London Barn Playhouse

THEATER | **FAMILY** | Broadway-style musicals and children's plays are presented here every summer in New Hampshire's oldest continuously operating theater. ⊠ *84 Main St.* ☎ *603/526–6710* ⊕ *www. nlbarn.org.*

⬤ Shopping

Artisan's

CRAFTS | This downtown boutique gallery carries jewelry, beads, gourmet foods, clothing, and local crafts. ⊠ *11 Pleasant St.* ☎ *603/526–4227* ⊕ *www.artisans- newlondon.com.*

Newbury

8 miles southwest of New London.

Newbury lies at the southern edge of 6-square-mile Lake Sunapee, one of the highest—and one of the cleanest—in the state, and a fine destination for boating, swimming, and fishing. Mt. Sunapee State Park has a picturesque beach on the lake as well as a mountain section that rises to an elevation of nearly 3,000 feet and offers some of the best skiing in southern New Hampshire. The popular League of New Hampshire Craftsmen's

Fair, the oldest crafts fair in the nation, is held here in early August.

GETTING HERE AND AROUND
From Interstate 89, Route 103A leads here via the eastern shore of Lake Sunapee.

Sights

★ John Hay Estate at the Fells

FOREST | The former home of the statesman who served as private secretary to Abraham Lincoln and U.S. Secretary of State to Presidents William McKinley and Theodore Roosevelt, built the 22-room Fells on Lake Sunapee as a summer home in 1890. House tours offer a glimpse of late Victorian life on a New Hampshire estate. The grounds, a gardener's delight, include a 100-foot-long perennial garden and a rock garden with a brook flowing through it. Miles of hiking trails can also be accessed on this 83½-acre estate. ✉ *456 Rte. 103A* ☎ *603/763–4789* ⊕ *www.thefells. org* 🎫 *$10 when house open, $8 when house closed* ⊙ *House closed Mon. and Tues. and mid-Oct.–late May.*

★ Sunapee Harbor

BODY OF WATER | On the west side of Lake Sunapee, this old-fashioned summer resort community has a large marina, a few restaurants and shops on the water, a tidy village green with a gazebo, and a small museum. ✉ *Main St. at Lake Ave., Sunapee.*

Beaches

Mt. Sunapee State Park Beach

BEACH—SIGHT | FAMILY | A great family spot, this beach adjoining a 4,085-acre mountain park has picnic areas, fishing, and a bathhouse, plus access to great hiking trails. You can also rent canoes and kayaks, and there's a campground. **Amenities:** lifeguards; parking (fee); showers; toilets. **Best for:** swimming; walking. ✉ *86 Beach Access Rd.* ☎ *603/763–5561*

⊕ *www.nhstateparks.org* 🎫 *$5 mid-May–mid-Oct.*

Restaurants

Suna

$$ | MODERN AMERICAN | On a wooded country road just up the hill from Lake Sunapee, this lively little bar and bistro is great for a romantic meal or a relaxed bite after a day on the water or the mountain. The eclectic menu features a mix of classic American and Continental dishes with creative touches. **Known for:** excellent craft cocktails; lively après-ski scene; sublime desserts. 💲 *Average main: $22* ✉ *6 Brook Rd., Sunapee* ☎ *603/843–8998* ⊕ *www.magicfoodsrestaurantgroup.com* ⊙ *Closed Mon.*

Wildwood Smokehouse

$ | BARBECUE | The hulking metal smoker outside this Old West–inspired tavern with high pressed-tin ceilings, chandeliers, and red Victorian wallpaper hints at the delicious barbecue served inside. Plates heaped with ribs, beef brisket, pulled chicken, and smoked bratwurst reveal the considerable skill of Wildwood's pit master, and plenty of tasty sides are offered, too, from mac and cheese to dirty rice. **Known for:** pecan pie; "hog wings" (pork shanks in barbecue sauce); popular early evening happy hour. 💲 *Average main: $17* ✉ *45 Main St., Sunapee* ☎ *603/763–1178* ⊕ *www. wildwoodsmokehousesunapee.com* ⊙ *Closed Sun. and Mon. No lunch.*

Hotels

Sunapee Harbor Cottages

$$ | RENTAL | This cozy compound of six charming, eco-friendly cottages—each sleeping five–eight people and with small but well-equipped kitchens—is a stone's throw from Sunapee Harbor and an easy drive from winter skiing at nearby Mt. Sunapee. **Pros:** ideal for families or friends traveling together; free beach passes; pet-friendly. **Cons:** no maid service; limited clothes storage; cottage porches overlook one another. $ *Rooms from: $225* ⊠ *4 Lake Ave., Sunapee Harbor* ☎ *603/763–5052* ⊕ *www.sunapee-harborcottages.com* ⇨ *6 cottages* ⦿ *No meals.*

Shopping

Gibson Pewter
CERAMICS/GLASSWARE | Jon Gibson crafts and sells museum-quality pewter mugs, oil lamps, vases, pitchers, and other stunning works in a barn and workshop overlooking one of the state's prettiest colonial town greens, in the rural hilltop village of Washington—about 15 miles south of Lake Sunapee. ⊠ *26 N. Main St., Washington* ☎ *603/495–1776* ⊕ *www.gibsonpewter.com.*

Wild Goose Country Store
GIFTS/SOUVENIRS | FAMILY | On the harbor in Sunapee, this old-fashioned general store carries teddy bears, penny candy, pottery, and other engaging odds and ends. ⊠ *77 Main St., Sunapee* ☎ *603/763–5516.*

Activities

BOAT TOURS
Sunapee Cruises
TOUR—SPORTS | This company operates narrated afternoon and dinner cruises of Lake Sunapee from June to mid-October. Ninety-minute afternoon cruises on the M/V *Mt. Sunapee* focus on Lake Sunapee's history and the mountain scenery. A buffet dinner is included on the two-hour sunset cruises aboard the M/V *Kearsarge*, a vintage-style steamship. ⊠ *Town Dock, 81 Main St., Sunapee Harbor* ☎ *603/938–6465* ⊕ *www.sunapeecruises.com* 🎟 *From $22.*

HIKING
Monadnock-Sunapee Greenway Trail
HIKING/WALKING | This 50-mile trail starts in Newbury at Mt. Sunapee and snakes through verdant forests and the handsome village greens of Washington and Nelson and over jagged granite peaks south to Mt. Monadnock. One of the most enjoyable ways to access this trail is to hike the 2.3-mile (one-way) Andrew Brook Trail up to the granite ledges above Lake Solitude, where you'll cross with it. ⊠ *Andrew Brook Trailhead, Mountain Rd.* ⊕ *www.msgtc.org.*

SKIING
Mt. Sunapee
SKIING/SNOWBOARDING | FAMILY | This family-friendly resort is one of New England's best-kept secrets. The owners have spent millions upgrading their snow machines and grooming equipment and turning this into a four-season resort. Mt. Sunapee offers 66 trails and slopes for all abilities. There are four terrain parks and nine glade trails. In summer, the adventure park features a canopy zipline tour, an aerial challenge course, an 18-hole disc-golf course, miniature golf, and numerous hiking trails. **Facilities:** 67 trails; 233 acres; 1,510-foot vertical drop; 9 lifts. ⊠ *1398 Rte. 103* ☎ *603/763–3500* ⊕ *www.mountsunapee.com* 🎟 *Lift ticket: $94.*

Hanover

30 miles northwest of New London, 60 miles southwest of Littleton, 20 miles east of Woodstock, Vermont.

Eleazar Wheelock founded Hanover's Dartmouth College in 1769 to educate the Abenaki "and other youth." When he arrived, the town consisted of about 20 families. Over time the college and the town grew symbiotically, with Dartmouth eventually becoming the northernmost Ivy League school. Hanover is still synonymous with Dartmouth, but it's also a respected medical and cultural center. Shops, mostly of the independent variety, fill the town's commercial district, which blends almost imperceptibly with Dartmouth's campus. Hanover and West

Lebanon, with Woodstock, Quechee, Norwich, and White River Junction across the Connecticut River in Vermont, form an appealing two-state vacation destination.

GETTING HERE AND AROUND

Lebanon Municipal Airport is served by Cape Air from Boston and White Plains, New York. By car, Interstates 91 and 89 are both nearby.

ESSENTIALS

AIRPORT Lebanon Municipal Airport. ⊠ 5 Airpark Rd., West Lebanon ☎ 603/298–8878 ⊕ www.flyleb.com.

VISITOR INFORMATION Upper Valley Business Alliance. ☎ 603/448–1203 ⊕ www.uppervalleybusinessalliance.com.

 Sights

Dartmouth College

COLLEGE | The poet Robert Frost spent part of a brooding freshman semester at this Ivy League school before giving up college altogether, but the school counts politician Nelson Rockefeller, actor Mindy Kaling, TV producer Shonda Rhimes, and author Theodor ("Dr.") Seuss Geisel among its many illustrious grads. The buildings clustered around the picturesque green, which is lovely for strolling, include the **Baker Memorial Library,** which houses such literary treasures as 17th-century editions of William Shakespeare's works. The library is also well-known for Mexican artist José Clemente Orozco's 3,000-square-foot murals that depict the story of civilization in the Americas. Free campus tours are available. ⊠ N. Main and Wentworth Sts. ☎ 603/646–1110 ⊕ www.dartmouth.edu.

Enfield Shaker Museum

MUSEUM VILLAGE | In 1782, two Shaker brothers from Mt. Lebanon, New York, arrived on Lake Mascoma's northeastern side, about 12 miles southeast of Hanover. Eventually, they formed Enfield, the ninth of 18 Shaker communities in the United States, and moved it to the lake's southern shore, where they erected more than 200 buildings. The Enfield Shaker Museum preserves the legacy of the Shakers, who numbered 330 members at the village's peak. By 1923, interest in the society had waned, and the last 10 members joined the Canterbury community, south of Laconia. A self-guided walking tour takes you through 13 of the remaining buildings, among them an 1849 stone mill. Demonstrations of Shaker crafts techniques also take place, and overnight accommodations are available in the community's stately six-story Great Stone Dwelling. ⊠ 447 Rte. 4A, Enfield ☎ 603/632–4346 ⊕ www.shakermuseum.org ⊠ $12.

★ Hood Museum of Art

MUSEUM | Dartmouth's excellent art museum owns Picasso's Guitar on a Table, silver by Paul Revere, a set of Assyrian reliefs from the 9th century BC, along with other noteworthy examples of African, Peruvian, Oceanic, Asian, European, and American art. The range of contemporary works—including pieces by John Sloan, William Glackens, Mark Rothko, Fernand Léger, and Joan Miró—is particularly notable. Rivaling the collection is the museum's architecture: a series of austere, copper-roof, redbrick buildings arranged around a courtyard. The museum galleries received an ambitious renovation and expansion in 2019 that added five new galleries and a striking new entrance designed by the husband-and-wife architectural team of Tod Williams and Billie Tsien (known for the Barnes Foundation in Philadelphia and New York's downtown Whitney Museum). ⊠ Wheelock St. ☎ 603/646–2808 ⊕ hoodmuseum.dartmouth.edu ⊘ Closed Mon. and Tues.

Hopkins Center for the Arts

ARTS VENUE | If the towering arcade at the entrance to the center appears familiar, it's probably because it resembles the project that architect Wallace K. Harrison completed just after designing it: New York City's Metropolitan Opera House at Lincoln Center. The complex includes a 900-seat theater for concerts and film screenings, a 480-seat theater for plays, and a black-box theater for new plays. This is the home of the Dartmouth Symphony Orchestra and several other performance groups. ⊠ 2 E. Wheelock St. ☎ 603/646–2422 ⊕ hop.dartmouth.edu.

★ **Upper Valley**

BODY OF WATER | From Hanover, make the beautiful 60-mile drive up Route 10 to Littleton for a stunningly scenic tour of the upper Connecticut River and lower Ammonoosuc river valleys. You'll have views of Vermont's Green Mountains from many points. The road passes through groves of evergreens, over leafy ridges, and through delightful hamlets abundant with fine Georgian- and Feder-al-style mansions. Grab gourmet picnic provisions at the historic general stores in Lyme or Bath, view several covered bridges on nearby side roads, and, stop by pastoral family farms, like Hatchland Farms Dairy Delites, for ice cream and Collins Farm for its corn maze. There are numerous spots for a picnic, including little-visited Bedell Bridge State Park in Haverhill, which overlooks the Connecti-cut River. ⊠ Hanover.

🍴 Restaurants

★ **Ariana's**

$$$ | MODERN AMERICAN | With its stone fireplace, cathedral ceiling, and rustic-ele-gant barnlike interior, this inviting restau-rant in the venerable Lyme Inn turns out farm-fresh modern American fare with international influences. Try the black-ened scallops with an orange-chili-butter sauce or sliced-duck salad with shaved fennel and a ginger dressing, before moving on to herb-crusted swordfish with a saffron-sherry butter sauce. **Known for:** five-course prix-fixe chef dinners; a well-curated wine list; peaceful setting in a historic hamlet. $ Average main: $26

⊠ 1 Market St., Lyme ☎ 603/353-4405 ⊕ www.arianasrestaurant.com ⊘ Closed Mon. and Tues.

Base Camp

$$ | NEPALESE | This inviting restaurant in the lower level of a downtown retail-dining complex serves authentic, prepared-to-order Nepalese cuisine. Start with an order of momos (steamed dumplings) bursting with buffalo, paneer-and-spinach, wild boar, or several other fillings, and then try one of the easily shared tarkari (tomato-based) curries or chilies, offered with an extensive variety of meats and vegetables, from goat and duck to sweet potato and mushroom. **Known for:** everything can be prepared from mild to very spicy; plenty of meatless options; helpful, friendly staff. $ Average main: $20 ⊠ 3 Lebanon St. ☎ 603/643–2007 ⊕ www.basecamp-cafenh.com.

Latham House Tavern

$$ | AMERICAN | This convivial, easygoing gastropub in historic Lyme's rambling Dowd's Country Inn—which also has pleasant guest accommodations—fea-tures an impressive list of New Eng-land craft beers as well as an enticing selection of reasonably priced comfort fare. Favorites include the half-pound house burger topped with bacon and a beer–smoked gouda fondue, and the pulled-pork poutine with a chipotle-cider barbecue sauce. **Known for:** elevated pub fare; interesting list of beers on tap; warmly lighted dining room with beam ceiling. $ Average main: $18 ⊠ 9 Main St., Lyme ☎ 603/795–9995 ⊕ www. lathamhousetavern.com ⊘ Closed Tues.

Lou's Restaurant

$ | AMERICAN | FAMILY | A Hanover tradition since 1948, this diner-cum-café-cum-bak-ery serves possibly the best breakfast in the valley, with favorites that include blueberry-cranberry buttermilk pancakes, and sausage-gravy biscuits with two eggs any style. Or just grab a seat at the old-fashioned soda fountain for a juicy

The Cornish–Windsor Bridge is the second-longest covered bridge in the United States.

burger and an ice-cream sundae. **Known for:** colorful mix of locals and Dartmouth folks; fresh-baked pastries and brownies; breakfast served all day. $ *Average main: $11* ✉ *30 S. Main St.* ☎ *603/643–3321* ⊕ *lousrestaurant.com* ◷ *No dinner.*

Murphy's On the Green

$$ | MODERN AMERICAN | Students, visiting alums, and locals regularly descend on this wildly popular pub, which has walls lined with shelves of old books. The varied menu features burgers and salads as well as meat loaf, lobster mac and cheese, and vegetarian dishes like crispy-tofu pad Thai and house-smoked tofu street tacos. **Known for:** sourcing ingredients from local farms; dinner menu available until late; extensive beer list. $ *Average main: $18* ✉ *5 Main St.* ☎ *603/643–7777* ⊕ *www.murphyson-thegreen.com.*

Hotels

Hanover Inn

$$$ | HOTEL | A sprawling Georgian-style brick structure rising six white-trimmed stories above Hanover's main square contains this chichi boutique hotel and is also home to the acclaimed farm-to-table restaurant, Pine. **Pros:** overlooks campus green in center of town; excellent restaurant and bar; well-equipped fitness center. **Cons:** expensive parking; pricey during busy times; books up way in advance many weekends. $ *Rooms from: $271* ✉ *2 E. Wheelock St.* ☎ *603/643–4300, 800/443–7024* ⊕ *www.hanoverinn.com* ⬢ *108 rooms* ⦿ *No meals.*

★ Lyme Inn

$$ | B&B/INN | With an enchanted setting on the elliptical village common in Colonial Lyme, this four-story inn that began life as a stagecoach stop in the early 1800s offers an elegant, tranquil respite from the crowds of Hanover and offers meals in an esteemed restaurant. **Pros:** quiet setting; rates include a tasty but light breakfast; good base for exploring Hanover as well as Norwich and Woodstock, Vermont. **Cons:** no elevator; a 15-minute drive to Hanover; minimum-night stays during busy times. $ *Rooms from: $229* ⊠ *1 Market St., Lyme* ☎ *603/795-4824* ⊕ *www.thelymeinn.com* ⟿ *14 rooms* ⦿ *Free breakfast.*

Six South St Hotel
$$ | **HOTEL** | With its bold black and red color scheme and angular light fixtures and furnishings, this redbrick boutique hotel just off Hanover's bustling Main Street is a perfect roost for visiting Dartmouth and its museums. **Pros:** hip contemporary design; great little bistro and bar; downtown location steps from campus. **Cons:** expensive parking; breakfast buffet costs extra; busy in-town setting. $ *Rooms from: $209* ⊠ *6 South St.* ☎ *603/643–0600* ⊕ *www.sixsouth. com* ⟿ *63 rooms* ⦿ *No meals.*

Activities

Ledyard Canoe Club
BOATING | On the banks of the Connecticut River, this outfitter rents canoes, kayaks, and standup paddleboards by the hour, as well as rustic cabins. ⊠ *9 Boathouse Rd.* ☎ *603/643–6709* ⊕ *www. ledyardcanoeclub.org.*

Cornish

22 miles south of Hanover.

Today Cornish is best known for its covered bridges and for having been the home of the late reclusive author J. D. Salinger, but at the turn of the 20th century the village was acclaimed as the home of the country's then-most-popular novelist, Winston Churchill (no relation to the British prime minister). His novel *Richard Carvel* sold more than a million copies. Churchill was such a celebrity that he hosted President Theodore Roosevelt in 1902. At that time Cornish was an artistic enclave: painter Maxfield Parrish lived and worked here, and sculptor Augustus Saint-Gaudens set up his studio here, where he created the heroic bronzes for which he is known.

GETTING HERE AND AROUND
About 5 miles west of town off Route 12A, the Cornish–Windsor Bridge crosses the Connecticut River, leading to Interstate 91 in Vermont.

Sights

Cornish-Windsor Bridge
BODY OF WATER | This 460-foot bridge, 1½ miles south of the Saint-Gaudens National Historic Site, connects New Hampshire to Vermont across the Connecticut River. Erected in 1866, it is the longest covered wooden bridge in the United States. The notice on the bridge reads, "Walk your horses or pay two dollar fine." ⊠ *Bridge St.*

★ Saint-Gaudens National Historic Site
GARDEN | On a bluff in rural Cornish with views of Vermont's stately Mt. Ascutney, this pastoral property celebrates the life and artistry of Augustus Saint-Gaudens, a leading 19th-century sculptor with renowned works on Boston Common, Manhattan's Central Park, and Chicago's Lincoln Park. In summer you can tour his house (with original furnishings), studio, and galleries, and year-round it's a pleasure to explore the 150 gorgeous acres of lawns, gardens, and woodlands dotted with casts of his works and laced with 2½ miles of hiking trails. Concerts are held Sunday from late June through August. ⊠ *139 Saint-Gaudens Rd., off Rte. 12A* ☎ *603/675–2175* ⊕ *www.nps. gov/saga* ⟹ *$10* ☉ *Buildings closed Nov.– late May.*

Hotels

Common Man Inn

$ | HOTEL | New Hampshire's distinctive Common Man hotel and restaurant group runs this quirky boutique hotel fashioned out of a striking 19th-century redbrick mill on downtown Claremont's Sugar River; the on-site restaurant serves good pub fare and has great water views. **Pros:** distinct, historic architecture; deck and hot tub overlooking river; good location for exploring both sides of Connecticut River. **Cons:** 12 miles from Cornish; in a slightly downcast but historic small city; not many good dining options in area. ⑤ *Rooms from: $109* ⌧ *21 Water St., Claremont* ☎ *603/542–6171* ⊕ *www.thecmaninnclaremont.com* ⇝ *30 rooms* ⫧ *Free breakfast.*

Walpole

33 miles south of Cornish.

Walpole possesses one of the state's prettiest town greens. Bordered by Elm and Washington streets, it's surrounded by homes dating to the 1790s, when the townsfolk constructed a canal around the Great Falls of the Connecticut River, bringing commerce and wealth to the area. This upscale little town now has 3,900 inhabitants. Walpole is also home to Florentine Films, documentarian Ken Burns's production company.

◼ **TIP➔ Charlestown, which boasts one of the state's largest historic districts, with about 60 homes—all handsome examples of Federal, Greek Revival, and Gothic Revival architecture (and 10 built before 1800), is just down the road from Walpole.**

GETTING HERE AND AROUND

Walpole is a short jaunt off Route 12, north of Keene.

Sights

Fort at No. 4

HISTORIC SITE | FAMILY | In 1747, this timber fort overlooking the Connecticut River, 15 miles north of Walpole, served as an outpost on the periphery of Colonial civilization. That year fewer than 50 militiamen at the fort withstood an attack by 400 French soldiers, ensuring that northern New England remained under British rule. Today, costumed interpreters at this living-history museum cook dinner over an open hearth and demonstrate weaving, gardening, and candle making. The museum also holds reenactments of militia musters and the battles of the French and Indian War. ⌧ *267 Springfield Rd. (Rte. 11), Charlestown* ☎ *603/826–5700* ⊕ *www.fortat4.com* ⫧ *$10* ⊙ *Closed Mon. and Tues. and Nov.–Apr.*

🍴 Restaurants

★ Hungry Diner

$ | MODERN AMERICAN | A departure from the old-school greasy-spoon diners that proliferate in New England, this contemporary space with a white-tile and light-wood interior and a big, inviting outdoor seating area serves delicious, eclectic comfort fare that relies heavily on seasonal, local ingredients, including pasture-raised meats. Think Korean barbecue tacos with house-made kimchi and pickled carrots, or the buttermilk-fried chicken sandwich with a tangy secret sauce and dill pickles. **Known for:** superb craft beer, wine, and cocktail program; mac and cheese with bacon; milk shakes and soft-serve ice cream. ⑤ *Average main: $15* ⌧ *9 Edwards La.* ☎ *603/756–3444* ⊕ *www.hungrydinerwalpole.com* ⊙ *Closed Tues.*

★ The Restaurant at Burdick's

$$ | FRENCH FUSION | Famous artisanal chocolatier and Walpole resident Larry Burdick, who sells his hand-filled, hand-cut chocolates to top restaurants around the country, operates this acclaimed restaurant next door to his shop in Walpole's charming little downtown. With the easygoing sophistication of a Parisian café and incredibly rich desserts, the restaurant features a French-inspired international menu that utilizes fresh, often local, ingredients and changes daily. **Known for:** noteworthy wine list; adjacent gourmet grocery with delicious picnic supplies; decadent desserts featuring house-made chocolates and pastries. $ *Average main: $22* ⊠ *47 Main St.* ☎ *603/756–9058* ⊕ *www.47mainwalpole. com* ⊗ *No dinner Sun. and Mon.*

☕ Coffee and Quick Bites

★ Walpole Creamery

$ | **CAFÉ | FAMILY** | Arguably the state's best purveyor of artisanal, small-batch ice-cream, this modest parlor in Walpole always features a long list of both regular and seasonal flavors, such as Fijan ginger, fresh peach, wild blueberry, and mint dark-chocolate-chip. Thick, rich, and using only all-natural ingredients, this luscious ice cream is also sold in many of the region's restaurants, farmstands, and groceries. **Known for:** using many local, seasonal ingredients; maple cream and maple walnut ice cream; brownie sundaes. $ *Average main: $5* ⊠ *532 Main St.* ☎ *603/445–5700* ⊕ *www.walpolecreamery.com.*

Keene

17 miles southeast of Walpole, 20 miles northeast of Brattleboro, Vermont.

Keene, the largest city in southwestern New Hampshire (population 24,000), has one of the prettiest and widest main streets in the state, with several engaging boutiques and cafés—you can spend a fun few hours strolling along it. Home to Keene State College, the city's atmosphere is youthful and lively, with its funky crafts stores and eclectic entertainment,

like the Monadnock International Film Festival, held in April.

GETTING HERE AND AROUND

Routes 9 and 101 pass through Keene, connecting it with Brattleboro, Vermont and Peterborough.

ESSENTIALS

VISITOR INFORMATION Greater Keene Chamber of Commerce. ☎ *603/352–1303* ⊕ *www.keenechamber.com.*

Sights

Keene State College

ARTS VENUE | The hub of the local arts community is this bustling college. The permanent collection of the Thorne-Sagendorph Art Gallery includes works by Richard Sumner Meryman, Abbott Handerson Thayer, and Robert Mapplethorpe. ⊠ *Thorne-Sagendorph Art Gallery, 229 Main St.* ☎ *603/358–2720* ⊕ *www.keene.edu* ⊗ *Gallery closed June–Aug.*

Madame Sherri Forest

ARCHAEOLOGICAL SITE | FAMILY | The focal point of this rugged 513-acre tract of deciduous forest in West Chesterfield are the stone chimney, grand staircase, and foundation of a chateau-style summer house owned by Parisian-born socialite and theatrical costume designer Madama Antoinette Sherri (the house burned down in 1963, and she died shortly after). A short woodland path from the parking area accesses the fascinating ruins, while two fairly easy but hilly trails offer longer hikes through the surrounding forest, including the 3-mile round-trip trek up Wantastiquet Mountain, which offers clear views up and down the Connecticut River and across to Vermont. Trails also lead into the adjacent Wantastiquet State Forest, and there's more great hiking nearby in Pisgah State Park. ⊠ *Gulf and Egypt Rds., West Chesterfield* ☎ *603/224–9945* ⊕ *www.forestsociety.org.*

Stonewall Farm

FARM/RANCH | FAMILY | At this picturesque nonprofit early 1800s farm and educational center, you can stop by to pick up produce and goods raised on-site (including delicious Frisky Cow Gelato) and procured from other artisanal producers in the area. But be sure to leave time to explore the grounds, dairy and small-animal barns, gardens, and chicken coops—a wide range of education tours are offered, plus seasonal hay and sleigh rides. There's also a maple sugaring house and small farm tool museum, and the property is traversed by hiking trails and accesses the 20-mile Cheshire Rail Trail, which stretches from Walpole through Keene and down to the Massachusetts border. ⊠ *242 Chesterfield Rd.* ☎ *603/357–7278* ⊕ *www.stonewallfarm.org.*

 Restaurants

★ Luca's Mediterranean Café

$$ | MEDITERRANEAN | A deceptively simple storefront bistro with sidewalk tables overlooking Keene's graceful town square, Luca's dazzles with epicurean creations influenced by Italy, France, Greece, Spain, and North Africa. There's always an extensive selection of small plates, such as almond-crusted fried mozzarella and roasted Brussels sprouts with bacon and pomegranate-infused honey, plus handmade pastas and complexly flavored grills and stews. **Known for:** fresh, creative pastas; affable but knowledgeable service; great wine list. ⑤ *Average main: $22* ⊠ *10 Central Sq.* ☎ *603/358–3335* ⊕ *www.lucascafe.com* ⊗ *Closed Sun.*

Machina Kitchen & Art Bar

$$ | ECLECTIC | This farm-to-table restaurant in downtown Keene is a vital force in the community, offering not only stellar, sustainably sourced food and craft cocktails but also an art gallery with rotating exhibits and occasional live music performances. The menu changes often but always features a mix of classics and unexpected adventures like the salt cod croquettes with preserved-lemon remoulade, fried frog legs with mango-habanero salsa, or Korean-spiced-brisket bulgogi bowls with fresh pears and sesame. **Known for:** interesting cocktails and mocktails; friendly, creative-spirited crowd; occasional prix-fixe dinners with cocktail pairings. ⑤ *Average main: $18* ⊠ *9 Court St.* ☎ *603/903–0011* ⊕ *www.machinaarts.org* ⊗ *Closed Sun. No lunch weekdays.*

 Hotels

★ Chesterfield Inn

$$ | B&B/INN | Fine antiques and Colonial-style fabrics adorn the spacious guest quarters in this opulent yet unpretentious country inn nestled on a 10-acre farmstead a couple of miles from the Connecticut River. **Pros:** beautifully tended gardens; kids and pets are welcome; excellent full breakfast included. **Cons:** restaurant closed on Sunday; two-night minimum at busy times; remote town that's a 20-minute drive from Keene. ⑤ *Rooms from: $183* ⊠ *20 Cross Rd., off Rte. 9, West Chesterfield* ☎ *603/256–3211* ⊕ *www.chesterfieldinn.com* ⌁ *15 rooms* ⦿ *Free breakfast.*

Fairfield Inn and Suites Keene Downtown

$ | HOTEL | It's unusual to find a mid-range chain property set in a historic building on a picturesque downtown Main Street, but this property—inside the restored early 1900s Goodnow department store—is a rarity with its reasonably priced rooms, exposed-brick walls, 12-foot ceilings, and sleek modern furnishings. **Pros:** the bilevel loft suites have two bathrooms; good fitness room; steps from great dining and shopping. **Cons:** bustling downtown center can be a little noisy; complimentary breakfast is pretty basic; historic building with quirky layout. ⑤ *Rooms from: $161* ⊠ *30 Main St.* ☎ *603/357–7070* ⊕ *www.fairfieldinnkeene.com* ⌁ *40 rooms* ⦿ *Free breakfast.*

The Inn at East Hill Farm

$$$ | RESORT | FAMILY | For those with kids who like animals, East Hill Farm is heaven: a family resort with daylong children's programs on a 160-acre farm overlooking Mt. Monadnock that include milking cows; collecting eggs; feeding the sheep, donkeys, cows, rabbits, horses, chickens, goats, and ducks; horseback and pony rides; hiking and hay rides in summer; and sledding and sleigh rides in winter. **Pros:** family-friendly; farm fun and activities galore; beautiful setting. **Cons:** very remote location; noisy dining room; not an ideal choice for adults seeking a romantic retreat. $ *Rooms from: $310* ✉ *460 Monadnock St., Troy* ☎ *603/242–6495, 800/242–6495* ⊕ *www.east-hill-farm.com* ⇌ *65 rooms* ⊚ *All-inclusive.*

Riverside Hotel

$ | HOTEL | With a boat dock and dazzling views of the Connecticut River, this simple but nicely kept three-story hotel is perfect for price-conscious travelers exploring the southwestern Monadnocks as well as nearby Brattleboro, Vermont. **Pros:** stunning river views; just a hop across river from Brattleboro, Vermont; reasonable rates. **Cons:** decor is pleasant but not especially distinctive; noise travels between rooms; pretty basic breakfast. $ *Rooms from: $159* ✉ *20 Riverside Dr., West Chesterfield* ☎ *603/256–4200* ⊕ *www.riversidehotelnh.com* ⇌ *34 rooms* ⊚ *Free breakfast.*

Nightlife

Branch and Blade Brewing

BREWPUBS/BEER GARDENS | Don't be put off by the location inside a small industrial park—this convivial taproom offers seating at picnic tables with wooden-keg tables, a big outdoor seating area with a food truck, and, most importantly, great beer, including a tart Gose and potent triple IPA. ✉ *17 Bradco St.* ☎ *603/354–3478* ⊕ *www.babbrewing.com.*

Performing Arts

ARTS VENUES

Colonial Theatre

CONCERTS | This renovated 1924 vaudeville theater shows art-house movies on the largest screen in town, and also hosts comedy, music, and dance performances. ✉ *95 Main St.* ☎ *603/352–2033* ⊕ *www.thecolonial.org.*

Shopping

Hannah Grimes Marketplace

GIFTS/SOUVENIRS | The pottery, kitchenware, soaps, greeting cards, toys, and specialty foods of more than 250 artisans are on display in this colorful downtown gallery. ✉ *42 Main St.* ☎ *603/352–6862* ⊕ *www.hannahgrimesmarketplace.com.*

Peterborough

20 miles east of Keene.

Thornton Wilder's play *Our Town* was based on Peterborough. The nation's first free public library opened here in 1833, and the town is home to the country's oldest continuously operating basket manufacturer—it's been making baskets since 1854. The town, which was the first in the region to be incorporated (1760), is still a commercial and cultural hub, drawing big crowds for its theater and concerts in summer. Downtown's charming Depot Square district abounds with distinctive boutiques, galleries, and restaurants. At Putnam Park on Grove Street, stand on the bridge and watch the roiling waters of the Nubanusit River.

GETTING HERE AND AROUND

It's easy to find street parking downtown, which is easy to reach via Route 101 and U.S. 202.

ESSENTIALS

VISITOR INFORMATION Monadnock Travel Council. ⊕ *www.monadnocktravel.com.*

Charming Peterborough was the inspiration for the fictional Grover's Corners in Thornton Wilder's *Our Town*.

 Sights

Cathedral of the Pines

MUSEUM | This 236-acre outdoor memorial pays tribute to Americans who have sacrificed their lives in service to their country. There's an inspiring view of Mt. Monadnock and Mt. Kearsarge from the Altar of the Nation, which is composed of rock from every U.S. state and territory. All faiths are welcome, and you can hear organ music some afternoons. The Memorial Bell Tower, built in 1967 with a carillon of bells from around the world, is built of native stone. Norman Rockwell designed the bronze tablets over the four arches. Flower gardens, an indoor chapel, and a museum of military memorabilia share the hilltop, and several trails lace the property, leading to tranquil peaceful areas. ⊠ *10 Hale Hill Rd., Rindge* ☎ *603/899–3300* ⊕ *www.cathedralofthepines.org.*

Mariposa Museum

MUSEUM | FAMILY | You can play instruments or try on costumes from around the world and indulge your cultural curiosity at this nonprofit museum dedicated to hands-on exploration of international folk art. The three-floor museum is housed inside a historic Baptist church, across from the Universalist church in the heart of town. The museum hosts workshops and presentations on dance and arts and crafts. ⊠ *26 Main St.* ☎ *603/924–4555* ⊕ *www.mariposamuseum.org* ☜ *$8* ⊘ *Closed Mon.*

Monadnock State Park

NATIONAL/STATE PARK | Said to be America's most-climbed mountain—more than 400 people sometimes crowd its bald peak—Monadnock rises to 3,165 feet, and on clear days you can see the Boston skyline. When the parking lots are full, rangers close the park, so it's prudent to get an early morning start, especially during fall foliage. Five trailheads branch out into more than two dozen trails of varying difficulty (though all rigorous) that wend their way to the top. Allow three–five hours for any round-trip hike. The visitor center has free maps as well as exhibits documenting the mountain's history. In winter, you can cross-country ski along roughly 12 miles of groomed trails on the lower elevations. Pets are not permitted in the park. ⊠ *116 Poole Rd., off Rte. 124, Jaffrey* ☎ *603/532–8862* ⊕ *www. nhstateparks.org* ≋ *$15 parking.*

🍴 Restaurants

Cooper's Hill Public House

$ | IRISH | Choose a sidewalk table overlooking bustling Depot Square or a table inside the conversation-filled dining room at this lively gastropub adjacent to Peterborough's popular independent cinema and steps from Mariposa Museum. The specialty here is rare whiskies, and there's also a nice selection of wines, craft beers, and other drinks, but don't overlook the consistently excellent Irish-influenced pub fare, including Guinness stew, mushroom-and-kale flatbread, bangers and mash, and terrific burgers. **Known for:** superb whiskey selection; ingredients sourced from New England farms; pecan bread pudding. $ *Average main: $14* ⊠ *6 School St.* ☎ *603/371– 9036* ⊕ *www.coopershillpublichouse. com* ☾ *No lunch.*

Pearl Restaurant & Oyster Bar

$$ | ASIAN FUSION | Despite its prosaic setting in a shopping center a little south of Petersborough's historic downtown, this sleek, contemporary Asian bistro and oyster bar is quite welcoming once inside. Several types of fresh oysters are always available, along with such diverse offerings as ahi tuna poke, Hanoi-style pork spring rolls, Korean barbecue pork, and coconut-veggie rice bowls. **Known for:** creative fusion fare; superb wine list; oysters on the half shell. $ *Average main: $22* ⊠ *1 Jaffrey Rd.* ☎ *603/924– 5225* ⊕ *www.pearl-peterborough.com* ☾ *Closed Sun. No lunch.*

 ## Hotels

Benjamin Prescott Inn

$ | B&B/INN | Thanks to the dairy farm surrounding this 1853 Colonial house— with its stenciling and wide pine floors—you'll feel as though you're miles out in the country rather than just 10 minutes from Peterborough and even closer to the cute downtown of Jaffrey. **Pros:** reasonably priced; relaxing, scenic grounds; delicious breakfast included. **Cons:** minimum-night stays at busy times; not within walking distance of town; not suitable for young children. $ *Rooms from: $129* ⊠ *433 Turnpike Rd., Jaffrey Center* ☎ *603/532–6637* ⊕ *www.benjaminprescottinn.com* ➫ *10 rooms* ⦿ *Free breakfast.*

Birchwood Inn

$ | B&B/INN | Overlooking the village green of tiny, quiet Temple, this affordable and friendly B&B built in 1775 once hosted Henry David Thoreau. **Pros:** friendly, old-fashioned tavern; quite affordable; good base for exploring Peterborough and Milford areas. **Cons:** secluded small town; quirky place with just three rooms; not suited for kids. $ *Rooms from: $109* ⊠ *340 Rte. 45, Temple* ☎ *603/878–3285* ⊕ *www.thebirchwoodinn.com* ➫ *3 rooms* ⦿ *Free breakfast.*

★ Hancock Inn

$$ | B&B/INN | This Federal-style 1789 inn in the heart of quaint Hancock, close to the village green, is the real deal—the oldest in the state and the pride of this idyllic town 8 miles north of Peterborough. **Pros:** quintessential Colonial inn and New England village; many rooms have Jacuzzi tubs and gas fireplaces; excellent restaurant. **Cons:** quiet, off-the-beaten-path setting; some rooms have twin beds; a little old-fashioned for some. $ *Rooms from: $179* ⊠ *33 Main St., Hancock* ☎ *603/525–3318, 800/525–1789* ⊕ *www.hancockinn.com* ➫ *13 rooms* ⦿ *Free breakfast.*

Jack Daniels Motor Inn

$ | HOTEL | FAMILY | This clean, bright, and handsomely decorated 17-room motor inn just a half-mile north of downtown Peterborough is a terrific find with large, affordable rooms furnished with attractive reproduction antiques. **Pros:** great value; one of the only lodgings in Peterborough; continental breakfast included. **Cons:** unfancy motel-style rooms; some street noise; a 10-minute walk from downtown. ⑤ *Rooms from: $129* ✉ *80 Concord St. (U.S. 202)* ☎ *603/924–7548* ⊕ *www.jackdanielsmotorinn.com* ⌁ *17 rooms* ⋈ *Free breakfast.*

 Nightlife

Post & Beam Brewing

BREWPUBS/BEER GARDENS | Serving boldly flavored saisons, grisettes, and other fine, mostly old-world-style ales and lagers as well as soft pretzels with hummus, chili, and other tasty edibles, this terrific brewery in downtown Peterborough has a beautiful setting inside the stately 1837 G.A.R. (Grand Army of the Republic) meeting hall. ✉ *40 Grove St.* ☎ *603/784–5361* ⊕ *www.postandbeam-brewery.com.*

 Performing Arts

Monadnock Music

CONCERTS | From early July to late August, Monadnock Music sponsors a series of solo recitals, chamber music concerts, and orchestra and opera performances by renowned musicians. Events take place throughout the area, and some of the offerings are free. ✉ *Peterborough* ☎ *603/852–4345* ⊕ *www.monadnockmusic.org.*

Peterborough Folk Music Society

CONCERTS | The Music Society presents folk concerts by artists such as John Gorka, Red Molly, and Cheryl Wheeler at the Peterborough Players Theatre and Bass Hall at Monadnock Center.

✉ *Peterborough* ☎ *603/827–2905* ⊕ *www.pfmsconcerts.org.*

★ Peterborough Players

THEATER | FAMILY | This first-rate summer (mid-June–mid-September) theater troupe has been performing since 1933, these days presenting seven main-stage productions in a converted 18th-century barn throughout the summer. The Players also present children's shows in July and August. ✉ *55 Hadley Rd.* ☎ *603/924–7585* ⊕ *www.peterboroughplayers.org* ⊗ *Closed mid-Sept.–late June.*

 Shopping

★ Harrisville Designs

CRAFTS | Hand-spun and hand-dyed yarn, as well as looms, felt, knitting yarn, and instruction books, are sold at this famous shop that occupies a striking redbrick, water-powered mill in the heart of a Monadnock village that's been famous for textiles since 1794. The shop also conducts classes in knitting, spinning, and weaving. ■**TIP→ Across the street, the inviting Harrisville General Store—open since 1838—serves tasty salads and sandwiches using locally sourced ingredients.** ✉ *4 Mills Alley, 10 miles northwest of Peterborough, Harrisville* ☎ *800/338–9415* ⊕ *www.harrisville.com.*

★ Mayfair Farm

FOOD/CANDY | FAMILY | From Peterborough, it's a scenic 20-minute drive by way of the historic villages of Dublin and Harrisville to reach this sustainable farm set amid rolling fields and hardwood forest. Pick your own berries, apples, and pears in season, and buy humanely raised pork and lamb products as well as gourmet prepared foods from the farm store. If you're wanting to spend a bit more time strolling the farm fields and mingling with the livestock, book a stay in the stylishly furnished guest cottage. ✉ *31 Clymers Dr., Harrisville* ☎ *603/827–3925* ⊕ *www.mayfairfarmnh.com.*

Peterborough Basket Company

HOUSEHOLD ITEMS/FURNITURE | At this retail shop of the oldest continuously operating basket manufacturer in the country, a fixture in Peterborough since 1854, you'll find sturdy and handsome woven-hardwood baskets, perfect for stowing everything from picnic victuals to laundry. You'll also find lazy Susans, planters, pet beds, and other smart storage solutions. ✉ 130 Grove St. ☎ 603/924–3861 ⊕ www.peterborobasket.com.

 Activities

GOLF

Crotched Mountain Golf Club

GOLF | Donald Ross, one of the earliest stars of golf-course architecture, designed this club's hilly, rolling, 18-hole layout. The course has a nice view of the Monadnocks. In winter you can rent cross-country skis and snowshoes from the on-site Nordic center. ✉ 740 Francestown Rd., Francestown ☎ 603/588–2923 ⊕ www.crotchedmtngolf.com ⛳ From $27 ⛳ 18 holes, 6111 yards, par 71.

Manchester

45 miles west of Portsmouth, 53 miles north of Boston.

With 113,000 residents, New Hampshire's largest city grew up around the Amoskeag Falls on the Merrimack River, which drove small textile mills through the 1700s. By 1828 Boston investors had bought the rights to the Merrimack's water power and built the Amoskeag Mills, which became a testament to New England's manufacturing capabilities. In 1906 the mills employed 17,000 people and churned out more than 4 million yards of cloth weekly. This vast enterprise served as Manchester's entire economic base; when it closed in 1936, the town was devastated. Today Manchester is mainly a banking and business center, but many of the old mill buildings have

been converted into condos, restaurants, museums, and office space, and both the dining and arts scenes have flourished in recent years.

GETTING HERE AND AROUND

The state's largest airport, Manchester-Boston Regional Airport, is a modern, cost-effective, and hassle-free alternative to Boston's Logan Airport, with nonstop service from about a dozen cities. Public transit is impractical for visitors—a car is your best way to get around.

ESSENTIALS

AIRPORT Manchester-Boston Regional Airport. ✉ 1 Airport Rd. ☎ 603/624–6539 ⊕ www.flymanchester.com.

VISITOR INFORMATION Greater Manchester Chamber of Commerce. ☎ 603/792–4100 ⊕ www.manchester-chamber.org.

 Sights

★ Currier Museum of Art

BUILDING | The Currier maintains an astounding permanent collection of works by European and American masters, among them Claude Monet, Edward Hopper, Winslow Homer, John Marin, Andrew Wyeth, and Childe Hassam, and it presents changing exhibits of contemporary art. The museum also arranges guided tours of the nearby Zimmerman House. Completed in 1950, it's New England's only Frank Lloyd Wright–designed residence open to the public. Wright called this sparse, utterly functional living space "Usonian," a term he used to describe several dozen similar homes based on his vision of distinctly American architecture. ✉ 150 Ash St. ☎ 603/669–6144 ⊕ www.currier.org ⛳ $15; $35 for Zimmerman House.

Millyard Museum

LIBRARY | FAMILY | In one of the most architecturally striking Amoskeag Mills buildings, state-of-the-art exhibits depict the region's history from when Native Americans lived here and fished the

Monadnock Region and Central New Hampshire

Merrimack River to when the machines of Amoskeag Mills wove cloth. The museum also offers lectures and walking tours, and has a child-oriented Discovery Gallery. There's a very good book and gift shop, too. ⊠ *200 Bedford St.* ☎ *603/622–7531* ⊕ *www.manchesterhistoric.org* 🎟 *$8* ☉ *Closed Sun. and Mon.*

SEE Science Center
LOCAL INTEREST | FAMILY | The world's largest permanent LEGO installation at minifigure scale, depicting Amoskeag Millyard and Manchester as they looked a century ago, is the star attraction at this hands-on science lab and children's museum. The mind-blowing exhibit, covering 2,000 square feet, is made up of about 3 million LEGO bricks. It conveys the massive size and importance of the mills, which ran a mile on each side of the Merrimack.

The museum also contains touch-friendly interactive exhibits and offers daily science demonstrations. ⊠ *Amoskeag Millyard, 200 Bedford St.* ☎ *603/669–0400* ⊕ *www.see-sciencecenter.org* 🎟 *$9.*

🍴 Restaurants

Cotton
$$ | MODERN AMERICAN | Mod lighting and furnishings lend this restaurant inside an old Amoskeag Mills building a swanky atmosphere, although on warm days you may want to have a seat on the patio, set in an arbor. The farm-to-table-inspired comfort food changes regularly but has featured pan-seared crab cakes, tuna tataki with wasabi aioli, and Delmonico steak with a choice of sauces. **Known for:** entrée-size salads; creative mixed drinks; handsome converted-warehouse setting.

$ *Average main: $23* ✉ *75 Arms St.* ☎ *603/622–5488* ⊕ *www.cottonfood.com* ⊘ *No lunch weekends.*

Red Arrow Diner

$ | AMERICAN | One of New England's most celebrated diners, this bustling downtown greasy spoon has been catering to students, artists, and most famously U.S. Presidential candidates since 1922. **Known for:** filling breakfasts; colorful people-watching; house-brewed root beer and cream soda. $ *Average main: $11* ✉ *61 Lowell St.* ☎ *603/626–1118* ⊕ *www.redarrowdiner.com.*

★ Republic Cafe

$$ | MEDITERRANEAN | A key player in downtown Manchester's steady ascendance into a bona fide dining and nightlife hub, this all-day bistro serves artfully prepared Mediterranean fare, with most ingredients sourced within a 50-mile radius. You can make a meal of several small plates—red-lentil cakes, lamb kefta, fig–and–goat cheese flatbreads—or tuck into one of the larger portions, perhaps steak frites or chickpea ragù. **Known for:** first-rate espresso drinks and desserts; creative Mediterranean small plates; outstanding Italian fare in adjacent Campo Enoteca. $ *Average main: $21* ✉ *1069 Elm St.* ☎ *603/666–3723* ⊕ *www.republiccafe.com* ⊘ *Closed Sun. and Mon.*

Coffee and Quick Bites

Restoration Cafe

$ | CAFÉ | Set on the ground floor of a vintage redbrick apartment building on the east side of downtown, this hip café and gathering spot excels both with drinks—everything from nitro cold brews to creative smoothies—and healthy, well-crafted food. At breakfast, consider the egg-cheddar-chive brioche sandwich, while tandoori bowls and rare-seared tuna sandwiches, along with craft cocktails and beers, are popular late in the day. **Known for:** healthy smoothies;

sleek industrial vibe; cheerful outdoor patio. $ *Average main: $9* ✉ *235 Hanover St.* ☎ *603/518–7260* ⊘ *Closed Mon. No dinner.*

Hotels

★ Ash Street Inn

$$ | B&B/INN | Each of the five rooms in this striking sage-green 1885 B&B near the Currier Museum of Art and a few blocks from Elm Street dining is painted a different color, and all have soft bathrobes, flat-screen satellite TVs, and beds topped with Egyptian cotton linens. **Pros:** stylishly decorated rooms; excellent full breakfast included; free off-street parking. **Cons:** pricey for Manchester; not a great choice for children; in busy city neighborhood. $ *Rooms from: $229* ✉ *118 Ash St.* ☎ *603/668–9908* ⊕ *www.ashstreetinn.com* ⊋ *5 rooms* ⫯⊙⫯ *Free breakfast.*

★ Bedford Village Inn

$$$ | RESORT | A few miles southwest of Manchester, this upscale complex consisting of an 1810 Federal inn and a bigger and new boutique hotel is all about luxury and pampering, with Italian marble bathrooms, whirlpool tubs, sumptuous linens, four-poster beds, and Molton Brown bath products in the rooms. **Pros:** ultraposh accommodations and amenities; gorgeous gardens and grounds; outstanding food and beverage. **Cons:** in a suburb outside Manchester; breakfast not included in rates; often booked with weddings on weekends. $ *Rooms from: $259* ✉ *2 Olde Bedford Way, Bedford* ☎ *603/472–2001, 800/852–1166* ⊕ *www.bedfordvillageinn.com* ⊋ *64 rooms* ⫯⊙⫯ *No meals.*

Doubletree Manchester Downtown

$ | HOTEL | Of Manchester's many chain hotels, this 12-story tower with smartly appointed rooms and great views has the most central location: a short walk from Amoskeag Mills and the growing cluster of dining and nightlife options along Elm Street. **Pros:** steps from lots of great eateries and bars; free airport shuttle; indoor pool and fitness center. **Cons:** fee for parking; unattractive building; tends to draw a lot of meetings and conferences. ⑤ *Rooms from: $151* ✉ *700 Elm St.* ☎ *603/625–1000* ⊕ *www.manchesterdowntownhotel.com* ⤳ *252 rooms* ⊚ *No meals.*

Nightlife

BARS

Crown Tavern
BARS/PUBS | Set in a stunningly restored downtown theater with a huge adjacent outdoor patio, the Crown is a splendid venue for dining, but it's the natty bar—with noteworthy craft-cocktail list, exposed-brick walls, and tile floor—that's especially alluring. If you are hungry, try the thick-cut truffle fries or Nashville hot chicken sandwich. ✉ *99 Hanover St.* ☎ *603/218–3132* ⊕ *www.thecrownonhanover.com.*

815
BARS/PUBS | A scene-y crowd mixes and mingles at this dimly lighted Prohibition Era–inspired, speakeasy-style cocktail bar with plush arm chairs and sofas and Oriental rugs, and an impressive list of both innovative and classic cocktails, plus unusual local and international beers. ✉ *825 Elm St.* ☎ *603/782–8086* ⊕ *www.815nh.com.*

Performing Arts

The Palace Theatre
CONCERTS | This 1914 former vaudeville house presents musicals and plays, comedy, and concerts throughout the year. ✉ *80 Hanover St.* ☎ *603/668–5588* ⊕ *www.palacetheatre.org.*

Concord

20 miles north of Manchester, 47 miles west of Portsmouth.

New Hampshire's capital (population 44,000) is a small and somewhat quiet city that tends to state business and little else. With that said, downtown has lately experienced an influx of restaurants and bars. Stop in town to get a glimpse of New Hampshire's State House, which is crowned by a gleaming, eagle-topped gold dome.

GETTING HERE AND AROUND
Interstate 93 bisects Concord north–south and is intersected by Interstate 89 and U.S. 202, which becomes Interstate 393 near the city line. Main Street near the State House is walkable, but a car is the best way to explore farther afield.

ESSENTIALS
VISITOR INFORMATION Greater Concord Chamber of Commerce. ☎ *603/224–2508* ⊕ *www.concordnhchamber.com.*

Sights

McAuliffe-Shepard Discovery Center
MUSEUM | FAMILY | New England's only air-and-space center offers a full day of activities focused mostly on the heavens. See yourself in infrared light, learn about lunar spacecraft, examine a replica of the Mercury-Redstone rocket, or experience what it's like to travel in space—you can even try your hand at being a television weather announcer. There's also a café. ✉ *2 Institute Dr.* ☎ *603/271–7827* ⊕ *www.starhop.com* ⊠ *$12.*

New Hampshire Historical Society
LIBRARY | Steps from the state capitol, this museum is a great place to learn about the Concord coach, a popular mode of transportation before railroads. The Discovering New Hampshire exhibit delves into a number of facets of the state's heritage, from politics to commerce. Rotating shows might

include locally made quilts or historical portraits of residents. ⊠ *30 Park St.* ☎ *603/228–6688* ⊕ *www.nhhistory.org* ☑ *$7* ⊘ *Closed Sun. and Mon.*

Pierce Manse

HOUSE | Franklin Pierce lived in this Greek Revival home, which overlooks a scenic bend in the Merrimack River at the north edge of downtown. He moved to Washington to become the 14th U.S. president—although in the eyes of many historians, one of the least effective and admired. A guided tour covers his life in mid-19th-century historical context. ■ **TIP**→ **Fans of presidential history might want to make the half-hour drive west to Hillsborough's Franklin Pierce Homestead. Tours of his stately 1804 childhood home are offered late May–mid-October.** ⊠ *14 Horseshoe Pond La.* ☎ *603/225–4555* ⊕ *www.piercemanse.org* ☑ *$8* ⊘ *Closed Sun. and early Oct.–mid-June.*

★ State House

GOVERNMENT BUILDING | The gilded-dome state house, built in 1819, is the nation's oldest capitol building in which the legislature still uses the original chambers. From January through June, you can watch the two branches in action. The Senate has 24 members, and the House house has 400—a ratio of 1 representative per 3,500 residents (a world record). The visitor center coordinates guided and self-guided tours, bookable online or on-site, and displays history exhibits and paraphernalia from presidential primaries. ⊠ *Visitor center, 107 N. Main St.* ☎ *603/271–2154* ⊕ *www.gencourt.state.nh.us* ☑ *Free.*

🍴 Restaurants

★ The Grazing Room

$$$ | **CONTEMPORARY** | Floor-to-ceiling windows add a touch of elegance to this superb—if a bit spendy—farm-to-table restaurant in the colonial Colby Hill Inn, which also offers well-appointed accommodations. Fresh produce takes center stage on the diverse, contemporary menu, which might offer a watermelon-tomato-feta salad or goat cheese–blueberry pierogies to start. **Known for:** outdoor seating beside a barn with friendly goats; pierogies with seasonal fillings; fresh fruit tarts and galettes. ⓢ *Average main: $33* ⊠ *33 The Oaks, Henniker* ☎ *603/428–3281* ⊕ *www.colbyhillinn.com* ⊘ *Closed Mon. and Tues. No lunch.*

★ Revival

$$ | **MODERN AMERICAN** | In this handsome, high-ceilinged redbrick building on a downtown side street, foodies and revelers congregate for some of the most creative and accomplished regional American cuisine in the Merrimack Valley. Highlights, in addition to an impressive selection of whiskies and cognacs, might include an artful platter of charcuterie and New England artisanal cheeses, hearty rabbit stew, and seared salmon with pancetta and olive tapenade, but the menu changes regularly. **Known for:** ingredients sourced from local farms; see-and-be-seen vibe; decadent desserts. ⓢ *Average main: $23* ⊠ *11 Depot St.* ☎ *603/715–5723* ⊕ *www.revivalkitchennh.com* ⊘ *Closed Sun. and Mon. No lunch.*

☕ Coffee and Quick Bites

Granite State Candy Shoppe

$ | **CAFÉ** | **FAMILY** | Since 1927, this festive sweet shop and ice cream parlor with a second location in Manchester has been doling out old-fashioned candies, fudge, and other confections. **Known for:** homemade peanut butter–chocolate fudge; root beer floats; Maple Saurus Sundaes (with maple pecan ice cream and maple syrup). ⓢ *Average main: $4* ⊠ *13 Warren St.* ☎ *603/225–2591* ⊕ *www.granitestatecandyshoppe.com* ▭ *No credit cards.*

Hotels

The Centennial

$$ | HOTEL | Concord's most distinctive and romantic hotel occupies an imposing brick-and-stone building constructed in 1892 for widows of Civil War veterans, but the interior has been given a head-to-toe makeover: boutique furnishings and contemporary art immediately set the tone in the lobby; pillow-top beds sport luxurious linens and down pillows; and bathrooms have stone floors, granite countertops, and stand-alone showers. **Pros:** sleek redesign of historic structure; attractive residential setting; great bar and restaurant. **Cons:** not within walking distance of downtown dining; rooms facing road can get a little road noise; breakfast costs extra. ⑤ *Rooms from: $179* ⊠ *96 Pleasant St.* ☎ *603/227–9000* ⊕ *www.thecentennialhotel.com* ⟋ *32 rooms* ⟟⊘ *No meals.*

★ Hotel Concord

$$ | HOTEL | This sleekly stunning contemporary boutique hotel opened in 2018 within a short stroll of the city's top arts venues and eateries; the airy and light-filled rooms, many with balconies, have hardwood floors, distinctive artwork, big windows, and are outfitted with Amazon Echo devices, huge HD TVs, and spacious marble baths. **Pros:** reasonable rates for this level of luxury; hip, cosmopolitan design; lots to see and do within walking distance. **Cons:** on a busy street; some may find the in-room high-tech gadgets a little challenging; books up when statehouse is in session. ⑤ *Rooms from: $179* ⊠ *11 S. Main St.* ☎ *603/504–3500* ⊕ *www.hotelconcordnh.com* ⟋ *38 rooms* ⟟⊘ *Free breakfast.*

 ## Nightlife

Henniker Brewing

BREWPUBS/BEER GARDENS | It's worth the drive 15 miles west of Concord if you're a fan of craft beer to sample the hoppy IPAs, refreshing Kolsch-style ales, and refreshing sour red ales at this laid-back tap room in the woods of Henniker. Grab a seat on the patio in nice weather. ⊠ *129 Centervale Rd., Henniker* ☎ *603/428–3579* ⊕ *www.hennikerbrewing.com.*

 ## Performing Arts

★ Capitol Center for the Arts

ARTS CENTERS | The Egyptian-motif artwork, part of the original 1927 decor, has been restored in this historic 1,304-seat venue that now hosts touring Broadway shows, dance companies, and musical acts. In 2019, the organization took over a disused movie house a few doors away (at 16 S. Main Street) and after an extensive renovation turned it into the **Bank of NH Stage.** This smaller space presents music, comedy, and other notable shows. ⊠ *44 S. Main St.* ☎ *603/225–1111* ⊕ *www.ccanh.com.*

 ## Activities

Scenic RailRiders

TOUR—SPORTS | This family-owned outfitter offers scenic two-hour tours on custom-made "rail-bikes" on a picturesque stretch of disused rail tracks that extends for several miles north of town alongside the Merrimack River. The rail-bikes are easy to pedal and seat two to four participants. ⊠ *188 Sewalls Falls Rd.* ☎ *603/931–1700* ⊕ *www.scenicrailriders.com.*

Chapter 6

INLAND MAINE

6

Updated by
Mary Ruoff

◉ Sights	🍴 Restaurants	🛏 Hotels	💼 Shopping	🍸 Nightlife
★★★☆☆	★★★☆☆	★★★☆☆	★★☆☆☆	★★☆☆☆

WELCOME TO INLAND MAINE

TOP REASONS TO GO

★ **Baxter State Park:** Mt. Katahdin, the state's highest peak, stands sentry over Baxter's forestland in its "natural wild state."

★ **Moosehead Lake:** Surrounded by mountains, Maine's largest lake—dotted with islands and chiseled with inlets and coves—retains the rugged beauty that so captivated author Henry David Thoreau in the mid-1800s.

★ **Water Sports:** It's easy to get out on the water on scheduled cruises on large inland lakes; guided or self-guided boating, canoeing, and kayaking trips; and white-water rafting excursions on several rivers.

★ **Winter Pastimes:** Downhill skiing, snowmobiling, snowshoeing, cross-country skiing, fat-tire biking, and ice fishing are all popular winter sports. You can even go dogsledding!

★ **Foliage Drives:** Maine's best fall foliage is inland, where hardwoods outnumber spruce, fir, and pine trees in many areas.

1 Sebago Lake Area. Less than 20 miles northwest of Portland, the Sebago Lake area bustles with activity in summer.

2 Bridgton. Bridgton is a classic New England town with many nearby lakes to explore.

3 Bethel. In the valley of the Androscoggin River, Bethel is home to Sunday River, one of Maine's major ski resorts.

4 Rangeley. Rangeley, along its namesake lake, anchors a lake-dotted region with long stretches of pine, beech, spruce, and sky.

5 Kingfield. Just north of Kingfield is Sugarloaf Mountain Resort, Maine's other big ski resort, which has plenty to offer year-round.

6 Greenville. The woodsy town, on Moosehead Lake, Maine's largest, is a great base for day trips.

7 Millinocket. The gateway to the premier wilderness destinations of Baxter State Park and the Allagash Wilderness Waterway.

Unlike the state's higher-profile coastline, inland Maine is a four-season destination. Natural beauty is abundant here, in the form of mountains, lakes, rivers, and there's an ample supply of classic New England villages.

Sebago and Long lakes, north of Portland and the gateway to the Western Lakes and Mountains region, hum with boaters and watercraft in the summer. Mt. Katahdin, Maine's highest peak and the terminus of the Appalachian Trail, rises in 210,000-acre Baxter State Park, outside Millinocket in the North Woods.

Come winter, ski resorts—including Maine's largest, Sugarloaf and Sunday River, both in the state's western section—wait for large snowfalls (and make it themselves in between). Maine often receives snow when the rest of New England doesn't and vice versa, so track the weather if you're coming for winter sports or to bask in the serenity of a good snowfall.

Rangeley, in western Maine, has been a haven for anglers since the 19th century, but these days this lakes-strewn area is also known for hiking and winter sports. Remote forestland lines most of Moosehead Lake, New England's largest lake within a single state. Greenville, at its southern end, is the hub. Visitors come to enjoy the lake, explore nearby wilderness locales, and downhill and cross-country ski.

Wealthy urban "rusticators" began flocking to inland Maine on vacation in the mid-1800s. The legacy of the rusticators and the locals who catered to them lives on at sporting camps still found—albeit in smaller numbers than in days past—on

remote lakes and rivers, in displays at small but impressive regional museums, and through Maine's unique system of licensed outdoor guides. Known as Registered Maine Guides, these well-qualified practitioners lead excursions that might involve kayaking, white-water rafting, hiking, fishing, hunting, canoeing, and moose spotting.

MAJOR REGIONS

The sparsely populated **Western Lakes and Mountains** region stretches north and west, bordered by New Hampshire and Québec. Each season offers different outdoor highlights: you can choose from snow sports, hiking, mountain biking, leaf peeping, fishing, swimming, and paddling. **The Sebago Lake area** bustles with activity in summer. **Bridgton** is a classic New England town, as is **Bethel,** in the valley of the Androscoggin River. Sunday River, a major ski resort nearby, also offers summer activities. The more remote **Rangeley Lakes** region contains long stretches of pine, beech, spruce, and sky, and classic inns. Just north of **Kingfield** is Sugarloaf Mountain Resort, Maine's other big ski resort, which has plenty to offer year-round.

Much of **The North Woods** is best experienced by canoeing or kayaking, fishing, hiking, snowshoeing, cross-country skiing, or snowmobiling. **Millinocket** is the gateway to Baxter State Park, Allagash Wilderness Waterway, and Katahdin

Woods and Waters National Monument, all premier wilderness destinations open for public recreation. The woodsy town of **Greenville,** on Moosehead Lake, is a great base for day trips, including excursions into Maine's 100 Mile Wilderness.

Planning

Visitors to inland Maine often spend their entire vacation in the region. That's certainly true of those who come to ski at a resort, fish at a remote sporting camp, or just relax at a lakeside cabin. Resort towns offer scenic cruises, intriguing small museums, and nearby hiking but are also hubs for exploring further afield. Visitors may head out early for a white-water rafting or renowned outdoor recreation area an hour or two away, or day trip among the lake towns closer to Portland. The farther inland you go, the farther between destinations. Lodgings and rentals often have minimum stays during peak times.

Getting Here and Around

AIR

Two primary airports serve Maine: Portland International (PWM) and Bangor International (BGR). Portland is closer to the Western Lakes and Mountains area; Bangor is more convenient to the North Woods. Regional flying services, operating from regional and municipal airports, provide access to remote lakes and wilderness areas and offer scenic flights.

CAR

Because Maine is large and rural, a car is essential. U.S. 2 is the major east–west thoroughfare in Western Maine, winding from Bangor to New Hampshire. Interstate 95 is a departure point for many visitors to inland Maine, especially the North Woods. The highway heads inland at Brunswick and becomes a toll road (the Maine Turnpike) from the New

Hampshire border to Augusta. Because of the hilly terrain and abundant lakes and rivers, inland Maine can get curvy. Traffic rarely gets heavy, though highways often pass right through instead of around the larger towns, which can slow your trip a bit.

There are few public roads in Maine's North Woods, but private logging roads there are often open to the public (sometimes by permit and fee). When driving these roads, always give lumber-company trucks the right-of-way; loggers must drive in the middle of the road and often can't move over or slow down for cars. Be sure to have a full tank of gas before heading onto private roads in the region.

Activities

People visit inland Maine year-round, coming to hike, bike, camp, fish, canoe, kayak, white-water raft, downhill and cross-country ski, snowshoe, and snowmobile.

BIKING

Bicycle Coalition of Maine

BICYCLING | The coalition provides information about biking in the state. ☎ *207/623–4511* ⊕ *www.bikemaine.org.*

FISHING

Maine Department of Inland Fisheries and Wildlife

FISHING | You can get information about and purchase fishing and hunting licenses by phone and online through this state agency. ☎ *207/287–8000* ⊕ *www.maine.gov/ifw.*

GUIDE SERVICES

Maine Professional Guides Association

TOUR—SPORTS | The association can help you find a state-licensed guide to lead a fishing, hunting, hiking, kayaking, canoeing, white-water rafting, snowshoeing, birding, or wildlife-watching trip. ⊕ *www.maineguides.org.*

HIKING

Maine Appalachian Trail Club

HIKING/WALKING | The club publishes seven Appalachian Trail maps ($8), all of which are bound together in its Maine trail guide ($30; $15 without maps). Its interactive online map has information on everything from side trails to communities along the AT in Maine. ⊕ *www.matc. org.*

Maine Trail Finder

HIKING/WALKING | The website has trail descriptions, photos, user comments, directions, and interactive maps for trails to hike, walk, mountain bike, paddle, snowshoe, and cross-county ski. ⊕ *www. mainetrailfinder.com.*

SKIING

Ski Maine Association

SURFING | For alpine and cross-country skiing information. ☎ *207/773–7669* ⊕ *www.skimaine.com.*

SNOWMOBILING

Maine Snowmobile Association

SNOW SPORTS | The website has contacts and links for about 10,000 miles of local and regional trails, and an excellent statewide map of about 4,000 miles of interconnected trails. ☎ *207/622–6983* ⊕ *www.mesnow.com.*

WHITE-WATER RAFTING

Raft Maine Association

WHITE-WATER RAFTING | An association of four white-water rafting outfitters, the website has information on the companies and Maine's three major white-water rafting rivers—the Kennebec, the Dead, and the West Branch of the Penobscot, which together make Maine New England's premier destination for white-water rafting. The Kennebec and Dead rivers converge at The Forks in Western Maine, while the West Branch of the Penobscot flows near Millinocket in the North Woods. ■TIP➜ **Family-friendly rafting trips are available.** ⊕ *www.raftmaine.com.*

Hotels

Well-run inns, bed-and-breakfasts, and motels can be found throughout inland Maine, including some more sophisticated lodgings. At places near ski resorts, peak-season rates may apply in winter and summer. Both hotel rooms and condo units are among the options at the two largest ski resorts, Sunday River and Sugarloaf. Greenville has the largest selection of lodgings in the North Woods region, with elaborate and homey accommodations alike. Lakeside sporting camps, from the primitive to the upscale, are popular around Rangeley and the North Woods; many have cozy cabins heated with wood stoves and serve three hearty meals a day. Conservation organizations also operate wilderness retreats. In Maine's mountains, as on its coast, many small inns don't have air-conditioning. *Hotel reviews have been shortened. For full reviews visit Fodors.com.*

Maine Campground Owners Association

The association's helpful membership directory is available by mail and on its website, which also has an interactive campground map. Many campgrounds have RV spaces and cabin rentals. ☎ *207/782–5874* ⊕ *www.campmaine. com.*

Maine Sporting Camp Association

Representing 45 camps, the association's goal is to "preserve the sporting camp's uniqueness" in Maine. Visit the website to search for camps by activity, meal plan, season of operation, and even the fish in local waters. ☎ *207/888–3931* ⊕ *www.mainesportingcamps.com.*

Maine State Parks Campground Reservations Service

You can get information about and make reservations for 12 state park campgrounds through this service. Note: reservations for Baxter State Park, which is administered separately, are not handled by the service. ☎ *207/624–9950,*

800/332–1501 in Maine ⊕ www.camp-withme.com.

What It Costs in U.S. Dollars			
$	$$	$$$	$$$$
RESTAURANTS			
under $18	$18–$24	$25–$35	over $35
HOTELS			
under $200	$200–$299	$300–$399	over $399

Restaurants

Fear not, lobster lovers: this succulent, emblematic Maine food is on the menu at many inland restaurants, from fancier establishments to roadside places. Dishes containing lobster are more common than boiled lobster dinners, but look for daily specials. Shrimp, scallops, and other seafood are also menu mainstays, and you may find bison burgers or steaks from a nearby farm. Organic growers and natural foods producers are found throughout the state and often sell their products to nearby restaurants. Pumpkins, blackberries, strawberries, and other seasonal foods make their way into homemade desserts, as do Maine's famed blueberries. Many lakeside resorts and sporting camps have a reputation for good food—some of the latter will even cook the fish you catch. *Restaurant reviews have been shortened. For full reviews visit Fodors.com.*

Visitor Information

The more than 2 million acres overseen by the Maine Bureau of Parks and Lands encompass 33 state parks, 15 historic sites, three scenic waterways, and more than 20,000 miles of ATV, snowmobile, and multiuse trails. Its public lands—nearly 600,000 acres—are wilderness areas managed for recreation, wildlife preservation, and timbering. Most areas are free to visit, but camping is primitive. Many lands are in remote areas accessible only by logging roads; others are relatively close to town centers and have trailheads, outhouses, and other facilities.

CONTACTS Maine Office of Tourism. ☎ *888/624–6345* ⊕ *www.visitmaine. com.* **Maine Tourism Association.** ⊕ *www. mainetourism.com.* **Maine Bureau of Parks and Lands.** ☎ *207/287–3821* ⊕ *www. parksandlands.com.*

When to Go

As a rule, inland Maine's most popular hiking trails and lakeside beaches get busier when the weather gets warmer, but if splendid isolation is what you crave, you can still find it. Summertime is when lodging rates peak and traffic picks up—though rarely jams, outside of a few spots—but the weather makes it a beautiful time of year to visit. Inland Maine gets hotter than the coast in July and August; lakes and higher elevations are naturally cooler. September is a good bet: the weather is more moderate, and the crowds thinner.

Western Maine is the state's premier destination for leaf peepers—hardwoods are more abundant here than on the coast. Peak foliage season runs late September–mid-October.

Maine's largest ski areas can make their own snow—at least one of them opens its doors in mid-November and remains open until May. Inland Maine typically has snow cover by Christmas, so cross-country skiing, snowshoeing, and snowmobiling are in full swing by the end of the year.

Early spring snowmelt ushers in mud season, which leads to black fly season mid-May–mid-June. The flies are especially pesky in the woods but less bothersome in town. Spring is prime time for canoeing and fishing.

Sebago Lake Area

20 miles northwest of Portland.

Seasonal and year-round dwellings, from simple camps to sprawling showplaces, line the shores of sprawling Sebago Lake and fingerlike Long Lake. Both are popular with water-sports enthusiasts, as is Brandy Pond and many other bodies of water in the area. Several rivers flow into Sebago Lake—Maine's second largest—linking nearby lakes and ponds to form a 43-mile waterway. Naples, on the causeway separating Long Lake from Brandy Pond, pulses with activity in the summer, when the area swells with seasonal residents and weekend visitors. Open-air cafés overflow with patrons, boats buzz along the water, and families parade along the sidewalk edging Long Lake. On clear days the view includes snowcapped Mt. Washington. The nonextant Cumberland and Oxford Canal was part of a water route from Long Lake to Portland in the mid-1800s. At Sebago Lake State Park, the one remaining canal lock operates on the Songo River, which connects Brandy Pond and Sebago Lake.

GETTING HERE AND AROUND

Sebago Lake, gateway to Maine's Western Lakes and Mountains, is less than 20 miles from Portland on U.S. 302.

VACATION RENTALS

CONTACTS Krainin Real Estate. ⊠ *1539 Roosevelt Tr., Raymond* ☎ *207/655–3811* ⊕ *www.krainin.com.*

VISITOR INFORMATION

CONTACTS Sebago Lakes Region Chamber of Commerce. ⊠ *909 Roosevelt Tr., Suite A, Windham* ☎ *207/892–8265* ⊕ *www. sebagolakeschamber.com.*

Sights

Sabbathday Lake Shaker Village

MUSEUM VILLAGE | FAMILY | Established in the late 18th century, this is the last active Shaker community in the world. Several buildings with Shaker furniture, folk art, tools, farm implements, and crafts from the 18th to the early 20th century are open for guided hour-long tours. The structures include the 1794 Meetinghouse, the 1839 Ministry's Shop, where the elders and eldresses lived until the early 1900s, and the 1821 Sister's Shop, where household goods and candies were made. The 1850 Boys' Shop has a free exhibit about Shaker childhood. An exhibit in the 1816 Granary is included with the tour, but tickets are also sold separately. The Shaker Store sells community-produced foods and goods as well as handicrafts by area artisans. If you're visiting the village in late August, don't miss the popular and free Maine Native American Summer Market and Demonstration. ⊠ *707 Shaker Rd., New Gloucester* ☎ *207/926–4597* ⊕ *www.maineshakers.com* ⊠ *From $7* ⊘ *Closed mid-Oct.–late May and Sun. late May–mid-Oct.*

Sebago Lake State Park

BODY OF WATER | FAMILY | This 1,400-acre expanse on the north shore of Sebago Lake is a great spot for swimming, boating, and fishing for both salmon and togue (lake trout). Its 250-site campground is the largest at any Maine state park. Bicycling along the park's roads is a popular pastime in warm weather, as is hiking. Come winter, the park offers 4 miles of groomed cross-country trails and 6 miles of ungroomed trails, also used for snowshoeing. On the park's edge, Songo Lock State Historic Site, an operational lock along the twisting, narrow Songo River and a remnant of a 19th century canal system, is a pleasant—and free—picnic area. You can also fish off the handicapped-accessible pier and launch a kayak or canoe. ⊠ *11 Park Access Rd., Casco* ☎ *207/693–6231* ⊕ *www.maine. gov/sebagolake* ⊠ *Nonresident $8, Maine resident $6.*

Restaurants

Black Bear Cafe

$$ | **IRISH** | **FAMILY** | Owned by an Irishman and his wife, this pub offers Emerald Isle brews on tap and stocks nine Irish whiskeys. If you're hungry, the fare includes bangers and mash and fish-and-chips, or an entrée of petite beef tenderloin or seafood. **Known for:** seasonal shepherd's pie; beer balls appetizer; rock album covers on the bathroom walls. $ *Average main: $24* ✉ *215 Roosevelt Tr. (Rte 302), Naples* ☎ *207/693–4770* ⊕ *www.theblackbearcafe.com.*

🛏 Hotels

Lakeview Inn

$ | **B&B/INN** | Built in 1906 as a hotel annex, the four-story inn has 16 rooms and suites—all on the upper floors—and a wide, inviting front porch that overlooks gardens and offers an angled view of Long Lake beyond the town's main thoroughfare. **Pros:** owner will carry up your bags; convenience center has kitchenette (no stove top) with courtesy beverages (nonalcoholic); several deluxe larger rooms and family-friendly suites. **Cons:** no elevator; stairs a bit steep; "comfy" rooms are smallish. $ *Rooms from: $169* ✉ *15 Lake House Rd., Naples* ☎ *207/693–9099* ⊕ *www.lakeviewinn-maine.com* ⊗ *Closed Nov.–Apr.* ⇌ *16 rooms* ⚫ *Free breakfast.*

Activities

Sebago and Long lakes are popular areas for sailing, fishing, and motorboating. As U.S. 302 cuts through the center of Naples, at the Naples causeway you'll find rental craft for fishing or cruising.

TOURS

Songo River Queen II

TOUR—SPORTS | **FAMILY** | Departing from the Naples causeway, the *Songo River Queen II*, a 93-foot stern-wheeler, takes passengers on one- and two-hour cruises on Long Lake. The narration is awash in local history and fun facts about noteworthy dwellings along the shore. ✉ *841 Roosevelt Tr., Naples* ☎ *207/693–6861* ⊕ *www.songoriverqueen.net* ⌚ *From $18.*

WATER SPORTS

Dingley's Wharf

WATER SPORTS | **FAMILY** | Smack in the middle of the Naples causeway on Long Lake, Dingley's offers lots of choices for getting out on the water. Wakeboarding, waterskiing, wake surfing, knee boarding, and tube riding excursions with a certified instructor include lessons. If you have your own boat, you can rent equipment for these activities. Dingley's also rents Jet Skis, aqua tikes, kayaks, canoes, standup paddleboards, runabouts, and pontoon boats. ✉ *851 Roosevelt Tr., Naples* ✛ *On Naples causeway* ☎ *207/693–5253* ⊕ *www.dingleyswharf.com* ⌚ *Rentals from $35.*

Bridgton

8 miles north of Naples, 30 miles south of Bethel.

Picturesque, lakeside Bridgton anchors a region whose many lakes and large ponds are popular for boating, fishing, and swimming. Downtown is a great place to spend the day, with its restaurants, movie theater, a museum, and a great mix of unique shops. Steps from the action, a covered pedestrian bridge leads to 66-acre Pondicherry Park, a nature preserve with a unique covered bridge, wooded trails, and two streams. Highland Beach (one of three town beaches) is just off the north end of Main Street, across from an inviting small park along the thoroughfare. On hot summer days, kids dive off the dock as mountains lounge on the horizon. Come winter, visitors hit the slopes at Shawnee Peak and cross-country ski at the ridgetop golf course. The surrounding countryside

is a good choice for leaf peepers and outdoors lovers. A few miles north, Harrison anchors the northern end of Long Lake. In fall, Fryeburg is home to the Fryeburg Fair (⊕ *www.fryeburgfair.org*), the region's largest agricultural fair. North of here, Center Lovell draws boaters to Kezar Lake (author and Mainer Stephen King summers here) and hikers to Mount Sabbatus.

GETTING HERE AND AROUND

From Portland, U.S. 302 runs northwest to Bridgton along the east side of Sebago Lake and the west side of Long Lake. From there it continues west 15 miles to Fryeburg, where Route 5 continues north to Center Lovell.

VISITOR INFORMATION

CONTACTS Greater Bridgton Lakes Region Chamber of Commerce. ✉ *101 Portland Rd.* ☎ *207/647–3472* ⊕ *www.mainelakeschamber.com*.

Sights

Rufus Porter Museum of Art and Ingenuity
MUSEUM | Local youth Rufus Porter became a leading folk artist in the early 1800s, painting landscape and harbor murals on the walls of New England homes, like this museum's barn red Cape Cod–style house, which bears unsigned murals by Porter (or one of his apprentices). In 2016, the late-18th-century structure was moved to the museum's downtown setting, where a circa-1830s dwelling has exhibits about Porter, also an "ahead of his time" inventor, writer, and founder of *Scientific American* magazine. Early issues are on display, as are models of some of his inventions and his miniature portraits. There's a video about Porter, an excellent gift shop with books about the author, and a large lawn with picnic tables. ✉ *121 Main St.* ☎ *207/647–2828* ⊕ *www.rufusportermuseum.org* 🎟 *$8* ⊘ *Closed mid-Oct.–mid-June and Sun.–Tues. mid-June–mid-Oct.*

Restaurants

Standard Gastropub
$ | AMERICAN | FAMILY | Like the facade, a cooler wall—stocked with hundreds of beers from around Maine and the world—attests to Gastropub's gas station past (it even served gas initially). Craft brews, many hard to find, accompany snazzy, farm-to-table takes on American classic and foreign-inspired comfort foods. **Known for:** smash burgers (local grass-fed beef) topped with house sauce and served with twice-fried fries; chili mayo–smothered smoked street corn (seasonal); loads of daily specials. 💲 *Average main: $15* ✉ *233 Main St.* ☎ *207/647–4100* ⊕ *www.standardgastropub.com*.

Hotels

★ Noble House Inn
$ | B&B/INN | On a quiet road, this 1903 estate above Highland Lake offers a convenient location, plenty of creature comforts, and a relaxing atmosphere. **Pros:** homemade cookies daily; skiing and golfing packages; distinctive suites. **Cons:** limited lake views; only suites have TVs; foldable twin beds only fit in some rooms. 💲 *Rooms from: $170* ✉ *81 Highland Rd.* ☎ *207/647–3733, 888/237–4880* ⊕ *www.noblehouseinn.com* 🛏 *8 rooms* ⊚ *Free breakfast.*

🏃 Activities

SKIING

Shawnee Peak
SKIING/SNOWBOARDING | FAMILY | Just a few miles from Bridgton, Shawnee Peak appeals to families and to those who enjoy nighttime skiing—trails are lighted except most Sundays. Three terrain parks and seven glade areas offer alternatives to trails and downhill runs. The main base lodge has a restaurant with an expansive deck; the smaller East Lodge has a second-floor bunkhouse. Lodging choices

also include Shawnee Peak House and a mountaintop yurt and cabin. Summer visitors can hike and pick blueberries. **Facilities:** 43 trails; 249 acres; 1,300-foot vertical drop; 6 lifts. ✉ *119 Mountain Rd., off U.S. 302* ☎ *207/647–8444* ⊕ *www. shawneepeak.com* 🎟 *Lift ticket: $77.*

Shopping

Whether you are a browser or a shopper, downtown Bridgton beckons. Main Street often looks and feels like a Norman Rockwell painting, and it's here that you'll find mostly year-round shops selling books, antiques, gifts, art, handcrafts, chocolates, souvenirs, T-shirts, and clothing, anchored by a branch of Renys (⊕ *www.fryeburgfair.org*), the state's friendly, spic-and-span outlet department store chain, aka "A Maine Adventure."

Firefly Boutique

CLOTHING | Picture windows line the walls of this corner boutique that sells unique women's attire from the "USA and beyond," including flower prints leggings, "cashmere feel" art print shawls, and chic roll-neck alpaca sweaters. The lively dress selection has options for evenings out as well as running about. In business since 2009, Firefly is also known for fashion jewelry—including three Maine-made lines, one featuring recycled guitar string pieces—handbags, and gifts. Don't miss Sassy & Blue's adorable girlswear, also Maine-made, in the rear corner, and store sale items in the back room. ✉ *103 Main St.* ☎ *207/647–3672* ⊕ *www.fireflyshop-maine.com.*

Gallery 302

ART GALLERIES | Creative shop windows showcase an individual artist on a rotating biweekly basis, inviting passers-by into Bridgton Art Guild's wide-open tin-ceilinged gallery in a former hardware store. Eclectic and fun—definitely not stuffy—the gallery opened in 2003 and represents about 50 local and regional artists working in various media. Artists'

displays have their bio and often their photograph. Don't miss the back-corner gift shop with cards, small prints, and the like. Along with hosting wine and cheese receptions and community events, the guild holds classes and workshops—many for a day or half day, so consider signing up. ✉ *112 Main St.* ☎ *207/647–2787* ⊕ *www.gallery302.com.*

Bethel

27 miles north of Bridgton, 65 miles north of Portland, 66 miles south of Rangeley.

Bethel is pure New England: a town with white clapboard houses, a large green, white-steeple churches, and a mountain vista at the end of every street. Gould Academy, a college prep school founded in 1836, anchors the east side of downtown. On Main Street, the new Maine Mineral & Gem Museum honors the region's storied mining history—and has a moon rock collection that rocks. In winter, Bethel is ski country. Sunday River, one of Maine's big ski resorts, is only a few miles north in Newry, while family-friendly Mt. Abram is east of town. On the third weekend in July, Bethel Area Summerfest includes a parade, fireworks, live music, and a frog-jumping contest. Whatever the season folks hit the trails at Bethel Village Trails on the edge of the village and 978-acre Bethel Community Forest a few miles from the town center. Under the tutelage of nonprofit **Mahoosuc Pathways** (⊕ *www. mahoosucpathways.org*), both locales welcome hikers, mountain bikers, snowshoers, and cross-country skiers.

GETTING HERE AND AROUND

From the south, both Routes 35 and 5 lead to Bethel, overlapping several miles south of town. Route 5 from Bethel to Fryeburg is especially pretty come fall, with long stretches of overhanging trees and glimpses of Kezar Lake as the road passes through tiny Center Lovell. If you're coming to Bethel from the west on U.S. 2, you'll pass White Mountain National Forest.

VACATION RENTALS

CONTACTS Four Seasons Realty & Rentals. ⊠ *32 Parkway Plaza, Suite 1* ☎ *207/824–3776* ⊕ *www.fourseasonsrealtymaine. com.*

VISITOR INFORMATION

CONTACTS Bethel Area Chamber of Commerce. ⊠ *8 Station Pl., off Cross St.* ☎ *207/824–2282, 800/442–5826* ⊕ *www. bethelmaine.com.*

Sights

Artist's Bridge

BRIDGE/TUNNEL | The most painted and photographed of Maine's nine covered bridges can be found on a detour from Newry. Head south on U.S. 2 and then northwest on Sunday River Road (stay to the right at "Y" intersections). Trails flow alongside Sunday River from the pedestrian-only bridge, which is a popular swimming spot. ⊠ *Sunday River Rd., 4 miles northwest of U.S. 2, Newry.*

Grafton Notch State Park

NATIONAL/STATE PARK | **FAMILY** | Grafton Notch Scenic Byway along Route 26 runs through Grafton Notch, a favorite destination for viewing fall foliage that stretches along the Bear River Valley 14 miles north of Bethel. It's an easy walk from roadside parking areas to the distinctive Screw Auger Falls, which drops through a gorge, creating pools; Mother Walker Falls; and Moose Cave. Trailhead parking and the nicely shaded Spruce Meadow picnic area are also right along the road. Table Rock Loop Trail (2.4 miles round-trip) rewards hikers with views of the mountainous terrain. More challenging is the 7.6-mile round-trip trek along the Appalachian Trail to the viewing platform atop 4,180-foot Old Speck Mountain, one of the state's highest peaks. The Appalachian Trail also traverses the 31,764-acre

Mahoosuc Public Land—its two tracts sandwich the park—whose trails offer stunning, if strenuous, backcountry hiking (there are backcountry campsites). In winter, a popular snowmobile trail follows the river through the park. ⊠ *1941 Bear River Rd., Newry* ☎ *207/824–2912 mid-May–mid-Oct. only, 207/624–6080* ⊕ *www.maine.gov/graftonnotch* ⊠ *Non-residents $4, Maine residents $3.*

★ Maine Mineral & Gem Museum

MUSEUM | **FAMILY** | Moon rocks, Maine mineralogy, and western Maine's legacy of mining minerals and gems—its pink and "watermelon" tourmaline are renowned—converge at this interactive 15,000-square-foot museum. Opened downtown in 2019 and founded by philanthropists, there's a garden out front with placarded large rocks, some resembling modern sculpture. The museum links two Main Street buildings, and its ticket area doubles as a gift store specializing in fine jewelry featuring Maine gems, as well as educational toys, books, and so on. A brightly lit gallery beside the shop showcases the state's geologic history and finds from around the world. Throughout the museum, touch screens invite you to dig into an item's provenance and makeup, and you can watch video interviews with those preserving the region's mining legacy. Exhibits about Bethel and environs spotlight gem discoveries and mica and feldspar mining—kids love the simulated blast. Don't miss the mica Christmas "snow" made before mining minerals for industrial purposes declined here. There are prized specimens displayed in a replica of a shuttered Maine mineral store and tourist hot spot. "Hall of Gems" bedazzles: the tourmaline necklace worn by Maine's First Ladies and first female governor is here. "Space Rocks," the large final gallery, has displays that include three of the world's ten largest lunar meteorites—five more are in the collection, as are 6,000 meteorites, 40,000 gems, and 15,000 Maine specimens. A 3D film beams about after the room darkens, launching a meteorite shower that blows up the walls, revealing Bethel. ⊠ *99 Main St.* ☎ *207/824–3036* ⊕ *www.mainemineralmuseum.org* 🖾 *$15* ⊘ *Closed Tues.*

Museums of the Bethel Historical Society

MUSEUM | Start your stroll in Bethel here, across from the Village Common. The center's campus comprises two buildings: the 1821 O'Neil Robinson House and the 1813 Dr. Moses Mason House, both listed on the National Register of Historic Places. The O'Neil Robinson House has changing and permanent exhibits pertaining to the region's history and a Maine Ski and Snowmobile Museum display. One parlor room serves as a gift shop with a nice book selection. The Moses Mason House has nine period rooms, and the front hall and stairway are decorated with Rufus Porter School folk art murals. The barn gallery has changing and traveling exhibits. ■TIP→ **Head out back to check out the Sunday River snow roller, pulled by a team of horses back in the day.** ⊠ *10 Broad St.* ☎ *207/824–2908, 800/824–2910* ⊕ *www.bethelhistorical. org* 🖾 *O'Neil Robinson free, Moses Mason $5* ⊘ *O'Neil Robinson closed late Oct.–late May, and Mon. July and Aug., and Sat.–Mon. June and Sept.; Moses Mason closed Sept.–June and Sun.–Wed. July and Aug.*

White Mountain National Forest

FOREST | FAMILY | This forest straddles New Hampshire and Maine, with the highest peaks on the New Hampshire side. The Maine section, though smaller, has magnificent rugged terrain. Hikers can enjoy everything from hour-long nature loops to a day hike up Speckled Mountain. The mountain is part of the 14,000-acre Caribou-Speckled Mountain Wilderness Area, one of several in the forest, but the only one entirely contained within Maine. The most popular Maine access to the national forest is via Route 113, which runs south from its terminus at U.S. 2 in Gilead, 10 miles

from downtown Bethel. Most of the highway is the Pequawket Trail Maine Scenic Byway, and the section through the forest is spectacular come fall. This stretch is closed in winter but is used by snowmobilers and cross-country skiers. Two of the forest's campgrounds are in Maine; backcountry camping is allowed. ⊠ *Rte. 113, off U.S. 2, Gilead* ☎ *603/466–2713* ⊕ *www.fs.usda.gov/whitemountain* 🖾 *From $5 per car.*

☕ Coffee and Quick Bites

Good Food Store

$ | AMERICAN | FAMILY | A cheery red door welcomes customers to this hip, cozy grocery, opened in 1994 and selling specialty, organic, and Maine-produced foods and goods, from sodas to local poultry. Friendly staff suggest items from the specials-friendly, freshly prepared takeout menu, or for picnics or dinner at your cabin. **Known for:** pumpkin whoopie pies; "heat and eat" soups and meals; beer and wine selection. ⑤ *Average main: $8* ⊠ *212 Mayville Rd.* ☎ *207/824–3754* ⊕ *www.goodfoodbethel.com* ⊘ *Smokin' Good BBQ closed mid-Apr.–mid-May and mid-Oct.–mid-Nov.*

Hotels

Holidae House Bed & Breakfast

$ | B&B/INN | Welcoming hospitality keeps guests returning year after year to this charming, affordable downtown B&B, where innkeepers are at the ready with day-trip tips and eight guest rooms occupy two floors of the antiques-filled home. **Pros:** courtesy cordials in parlor; fresh-baked treats in afternoon; blow-up mattresses available. **Cons:** no lawn; no mountain views; no king beds. ⑤ *Rooms from: $159* ⊠ *85 Main St.* ☎ *207/824–3400* ⊕ *www.holidaehouse.com* 🛏 *8 rooms* ⦿ *Free breakfast.*

One of the Rangeley Lakes, Mooselookmeguntic is said to mean "portage to the moose feeding place" in the Abenaki language.

Activities

CANOEING AND KAYAKING

Bethel Outdoor Adventure and Campground
CANOEING/ROWING/SKULLING | FAMILY | On the Androscoggin River, this outfitter rents canoes, kayaks, tubes, standup paddleboards, and a drift boat; runs river shuttles; sells state fishing licenses; leads guided kayak and canoe trips; and has a campground. There's also an open-air facility where you can sluice for precious and semiprecious gems and minerals (the Bethel region has a long history of mining for them). All Bethel Outdoor Adventure activities get customers a free trek on the Burma Bridge, which leads to a walking trail on the company's private, wild river island. For others it's just a buck. ☒ *121 Mayville Rd.* ☎ *207/824–4224* ⊕ *www.betheloutdoor-adventure.com.*

DOGSLEDDING

Mahoosuc Guide Service
LOCAL SPORTS | This acclaimed guide company leads day and multiday dogsledding and canoeing expeditions in the Umbagog National Wildlife Refuge on the Maine–New Hampshire border. The outfitter also offers overnight excursions elsewhere in Maine and in Canada. One of the multiday canoe trips is an immersion in the ways of the Penobscot Nation, a Maine Native American tribe. Mahoosuc also runs fishing trips and has lodging for customers and groups. ☒ *1513 Bear River Rd., Newry* ☎ *207/824–2073* ⊕ *www.mahoosuc.com* ☒ *From $175.*

SKIING

Carter's Cross-Country Ski Center
SKIING/SNOWBOARDING | FAMILY | Mountain views await at this acclaimed cross-country ski center, which offers 34 miles of trails for all levels of skiers. Skis, snowshoes, and sleds to pull children are all available for rental, as are fat-tire bikes. The place also rents lodge rooms and ski-in cabins, available year-round. ☒ *786 Intervale Rd.* ☎ *207/824–3880 Bethel location* ⊕ *www.cartersxcski.com* ☒ *$18.*

Whoopie Pies 🍴

When a bill aiming to make the whoopie pie Maine's official dessert was debated in state legislature, some lawmakers countered that the blueberry pie (made with Maine wild blueberries, of course) should have the honor. The blueberry pie won out, but what might have erupted into civil war instead ended civilly, with whoopie pies designated the official state "treat." Spend a few days anywhere in Maine and you'll notice just how popular it really is.

The name is misleading: it's a "pie" only in the sense of a having a filling between two "crusts"—namely, a thick layer of sugary frosting sandwiched between two saucers of rich cake, usually chocolate. It may have acquired its distinctive moniker from the jubilant "yelp" farmers emitted after discovering it in their lunchboxes. The whoopie pie is said to have Pennsylvania Dutch roots, but many Mainers insist that it originated here. Typically, the filling is made with butter or shortening; some recipes add Marshmallow Fluff. Many bakers have indulged the temptation to experiment with flavors and ingredients, particularly in the filling but also in the cake, offering pumpkin, raspberry, oatmeal cream, red velvet, peanut butter, and more.

Mt. Abram Ski and Ride

SKIING/SNOWBOARDING | FAMILY | Family-friendly and affordable, Mt. Abram is open Thursday–Sunday during ski season. It allows off-trail "boundary-to-boundary" skiing, has two terrain parks, and welcomes uphill snowshoers and skiers ($15 day pass). Westside, the popular lift-served beginner area, has its own base lodge. The main lodge is home to Loose Boots Lounge, which occasionally features live music. Mountain biking is big here during the warm months: Mt. Abram offers rentals and lessons and trails are lift-served—aside from one for the hearty. **Facilities:** 51 trails; 250 acres; 1,150-foot vertical drop; 4 lifts. ✉ *308 Howe Hill Rd., off Rte. 26, Greenwood* 🕾 *207/875–5000* ⊕ *www.mtabram.com* 🎟 *Lift ticket: $49.*

★ Sunday River

SKIING/SNOWBOARDING | FAMILY | Once-sleepy Sunday River has evolved into a sprawling resort that attracts skiers from around the world. Stretching for 3 miles, it encompasses eight trail-connected peaks and five terrain parks.

Off-trail "boundary-to-boundary" skiing is allowed, and there is night skiing on Friday and Saturday. On some weekends and during holiday weeks, fireworks light the skies at the main South Ridge base lodge, one of three at the resort. Sunday River has several lodging choices, including condos and two slope-side hotels: the family-friendly Grand Summit, at one of the mountain bases, and the more upscale Jordan Grand, near a summit at the resort's western end. (It's really up there, several miles by vehicle from the base areas, but during ski season there's a shuttle, or you can ski over for lunch.)

■ **TIP →** **At both slope-side hotels, the outdoor heated pool and hot tub are open year-round.** From the less costly Snow Cap Inn, it's a short walk to the slopes. Come summer, the resort offers archery, kayaking, and standup paddleboarding lessons and guided kayak tours, and the main South Ridge Base Lodge hosts a bungee trampoline, climbing wall, and chairlift rides to North Peak. Many visitors opt to hike down or hit a trail up top before riding down. You can hike or ride up to play disc golf—or head over to Sunday River

Golf Club, acclaimed for its wide-open mountain and valley views and challenging elevation changes. ■ TIP→ **Don't golf? Grab a drink or a bite at the clubhouse and hit those views—there's a building-length deck and a soaring Palladian window framed by polished wood walls.** Facilities: 135 trails (includes glades); 870 acres; 2,340-foot vertical drop; 18 lifts. ⊠ *15 S. Ridge Rd., Newry* ☏ *207/824–3000, 207/824–5200 for snow conditions, 800/543–2754 for reservations* ⊕ *www. sundayriver.com* ☑ *Lift ticket: $119.*

Rangeley

66 miles north of Bethel.

With 100-plus lakes and ponds linked by rivers and streams, the vastly forested Rangeley region has a rough, wilderness feel and has long attracted winter-sports enthusiasts, hikers, and anglers—it's been hailed for centuries as a "fly-fishing mecca." The four-season resort town of Rangeley stretches along the north side of its namesake lake. Right behind Main Street, Lakeside Park ("Town Park" to locals) has a large swimming area, a playground, picnic shelters, and a boat launch. Come winter, Saddleback Mountain (set to reopen in 2020) lures downhill skiers, many of them families. Other winter activities in these parts include cross-country skiing, snowshoeing, fat-tire biking, snowmobiling, and pond skating. In late January, the Rangeley Snowmobile Snodeo offers thrilling snowmobile acrobatics, fireworks, a parade, and a cook-off for which area restaurants enter their chilies and chowders. Seven miles west on Route 4, tucked at the east end of Rangeley Lake near Mooselookmeguntic Lake, tiny Oquossoc is another hub for outdoor activities and dining. At the main crossroads, the Outdoor Heritage Museum beckons visitors; nearby Bald Mountain is a family-friendly day hike. South of the hamlet on Route 17 is the western gateway to the region,

Height of Land—a must-see overlook with distant views stretching to mountains on the New Hampshire border.

GETTING HERE AND AROUND

To reach Rangeley on a scenic drive through Western Maine, take Route 17 north from U.S. 2 in Mexico past Height of Land to Route 4 in Oquossoc, then head east into town. Much of the drive is the **Rangeley Lakes National Scenic Byway** (⊕ *www.exploremaine.org/byways*). From Rangeley, Route 16 continues east to Sugarloaf ski resort and Kingfield.

VACATION RENTALS

CONTACTS Morton & Furbish Vacation Rentals. ⊠ *2478 Main St.* ☏ *207/864–9065, 888/218–4882* ⊕ *www.rangeleyrentals. com.*

VISITOR INFORMATION

CONTACTS Rangeley Lakes Chamber of Commerce. ⊠ *6 Park Rd.* ☏ *207/864–5364, 800/685–2537* ⊕ *www.rangeleymaine. com.*

⊙ Sights

Height of Land
SCENIC DRIVE | Height of Land is the highlight of Rangeley Lakes National Scenic Byway, with unforgettable views of mountains and lakes. One of Maine's best overlooks, it hugs Route 17 atop Spruce Mountain several miles south of Rangeley's Oquossoc village. On a clear day, you can look west to mountains on the New Hampshire border. There's off-road parking, interpretive panels, stone seating, and a short path to the Appalachian Trail. Rangeley Lake unfolds at a nearby overlook on the opposite side of the road. ⊠ *Rte. 17.*

★ Moose Alley
LOCAL INTEREST | **FAMILY** | Bowling is just one reason families, couples, locals, and visitors head to this happening spot for a night out or a rainy (or sunny!) day in, one of the most popular spots in Rangeley. Open 365 days a year, the moose theme

amps up but doesn't overwhelm the chic, fun modern decor. Don't miss the fish, moose, loon, and Rangeley Lake images on the dance floor—there's live music on weekends and sometimes weeknights. Antler chandeliers light the pool tables and walls with geometric patterns frame the 10 bowling lanes. There's also foosball, air hockey, and near the entrance, a video/game arcade. In the restaurant/bar area, settle onto a curved couch or at the warmly lit curved bar—like the pillars, faced to resemble river stones. Roomy armchairs circle the firepit: like the sign says, it's OK to put your feet on the surround, but not your food! That's ordered at a counter and delivered to your table, bar seat, lane, or game spot. The pub fare is delish (try the chipotle sweet potato fries) and the brunch menu available all day—food is served from 11 am until close. ⊠ 2809 Main St. ☎ 207/864–9955 ⊕ www.moosealley.me.

★ Outdoor Heritage Museum

MUSEUM | FAMILY | Spruce railings and siding on the museum's facade replicate a local taxidermy shop from about 1900. Inside, there's an authentic log sporting camp from the same period, when grand hotels and full-service sporting lodges drew well-to-do rusticators on long stays. One of the big draws is the exhibit on local flytier Carrie Stevens, whose famed streamer flies increased the region's fly-fishing fame in the 1920s. The many diverse exhibits include displays on U.S. presidents Dwight D. Eisenhower and Herbert Hoover fishing in Rangeley; vintage watercraft; Native American birch-bark canoes and artifacts; art of the region; and gleaming fish mounts of world-record-size brook trout. With free exhibits out front, this is a popular stop even when closed—don't miss the 12,000-year-old Native American meat cache. ⊠ 8 Rumford Rd., Oquossoc ☎ 207/864–3091 ⊕ www.rangeleyhistoricalsociety.org ⊠ $7 ⊘ Closed Nov.–Apr. and Mon. and Tues. May, June, Sept., and Oct.

Rangeley Lake State Park

NATIONAL/STATE PARK | FAMILY | On the south shore of Rangeley Lake, this 869-acre park has superb lakeside scenery, swimming, picnic tables, a playground, a boat ramp, a few short trails, and a campground. ⊠ 1 State Park Rd. ⊹ Turn on S. Shore Rd. from Rte. 17 or Rte. 4 ☎ 207/864–3858 May–mid-Oct. only, 207/624–6080 for regional state parks office ⊕ www.maine.gov/rangeleylake ⊠ Nonresident $6, Maine resident $4.

Wilhelm Reich Museum

MEMORIAL | FAMILY | The museum showcases the life and work of Austrian physician, scientist, and writer Wilhelm Reich (1897–1957), who believed that all living matter and the atmosphere contain a force called orgone energy. The hilltop Orgone Energy Observatory exhibits biographical materials, inventions, and equipment used in his experiments, whose results were disputed by the Food and Drug Administration and other government agencies. Stone faces the exterior of the boxy 1949 structure, which is listed on the National Register of Historic Places. A midcentury gem inside and out, Reich's second-floor study, library, and laboratory look as they did in his day, with original sleek modern furniture. The observatory deck has magnificent countryside views. In July and August, the museum presents engaging nature programs; trails lace the largely forested 175-acre property, which has a vacation rental cottage. Reich's tomb sits next to one of his inventions, a cloud accumulator. ⊠ 19 Orgonon Cir., off Rte. 4 ☎ 207/864–3443 ⊕ wilhelmreichmuseum.org ⊠ Museum $8, grounds free ⊘ Museum closed Oct.–June, Sun.–Tues. in July and Aug. and Sun.–Fri. in Sept. Private tours May–Oct. by appt.

🍴 Restaurants

Gingerbread House Restaurant

$ | AMERICAN | FAMILY | With a fieldstone fireplace in the main dining room, tables about the garden-side deck, and an antique marble soda fountain, there are lots of reasons to stop at what really does look like a giant gingerbread house at the edge of the woods. The restaurant serves both breakfast and lunch, with expansive menus for each (but no dinner). **Known for:** baguette French toast and lobster eggs Benedict; crab cakes and pesto linguine lunch entrées; proximity to overlooks, hiking. ⑤ *Average main: $12* ✉ *55 Carry Rd., Oquossoc* ☎ *207/864–3602* ⊕ *www.gingerbreadhouserestaurant.net* ⊘ *Closed Apr. and Nov.; closed Mon. and Tues. Dec.–Mar. and May, June, Sept., and Oct. No lunch Sun. except in July and Aug. No dinner.*

☕ Coffee and Quick Bites

Pine Tree Frosty
$ | **FAST FOOD** | **FAMILY** | A summertime visit to Rangeley isn't complete without a stop at this cash-only snack bar—in business since 1964—for ice cream and simple meals like burgers and fries. Both hard and soft ice cream are served, as are sundaes, milk shakes, flurries, and banana splits. **Known for:** Maine-made Gifford's hard ice cream; lobster rolls; waterside Adirondack chairs and picnic tables. ⑤ *Average main: $6* ✉ *2459 Main St.* ⊕ *facebook.com/pinetreefrosty* ▤ *No credit cards.*

🛏 Hotels

The Rangeley Inn
$ | **HOTEL** | **FAMILY** | Painted eggshell blue, this historic downtown hotel was built around 1900 for wealthy urbanites on vacation—from the covered front porch, you step into a grand lobby with polished pine wainscoting and a brick fireplace; the "lodge" is a motel-style building out back on Hayley Pond. **Pros:** tavern with fireplace and elegant original dining room; nice variety of suites (largest sleeps six); courtesy canoes and kayaks for Hayley Pond; guided kayak

photography trips (fee). **Cons:** no elevator; not on Rangeley Lake; a couple minutes walk from lodge to hotel. ⑤ *Rooms from: $175* ✉ *2443 Main St.* ☎ *207/864–3341* ⊕ *www.therangeleyinn.com* ⇆ *42 rooms* ⦿❚ *No meals.*

Activities

Rangeley and Mooselookmeguntic lakes are good for canoeing, kayaking, sailing, fishing, and motorboating. Lake fishing for landlocked salmon and the region's famed brook trout is at its best in May, June, and September. The area's rivers and streams are especially popular with fly-fishers, who enjoy the sport May–October. Ice fishing shacks dot Rangeley Lake come winter.

BIKING
Mountain bikers head to Rangeley Lakes Trails Center on Saddleback Mountain, where trails are groomed in winter for cross-country skiing, snowshoeing, and fat-tire biking. ■TIP→ **Fat-tire bikes, which you can rent in town, are increasingly popular for summer recreation in Rangeley and elsewhere in Maine because of the rough terrain and many rural backroads.**

AJ's Fat Bikes
BICYCLING | **FAMILY** | Half- and full-day and weekly fat-tire bike rentals are available during the warm months and after the snow flies at this friendly shop, which is at the ready with riding tips and routes (many of which aren't easy to find if you aren't in the know). It also sells and repairs bikes (various kinds) and gear. Rentals start at $35. ✉ *2745 Main St.* ☎ *207/864–2850.*

BOATING
★ River's Edge Sports
BOATING | **FAMILY** | Hugging Route 4 in Oquossoc and resembling a sporting lodge, this is a convenient stop for gear galore and great ways to get out on the water. Paddle at your own pace on the popular, shuttle-served canoe and kayak river trips, or rent a kayak, canoe, or

standup paddleboard—you can put in at the dock out back on Rangeley Lake, near the outflow into Rangeley River. River's Edge sells Maine fishing licenses, and owner Gerry White, a Registered Maine Guide, leads fishing trips on Rangeley and Mooselookmeguntic lakes. Along with camping, fishing, hunting, and hiking gear, the 8,000-some-item store stocks souvenirs, apparel—from jackets to Rangeley and Oqussoc hoodies and tees—and gifts, many Maine-made. Don't miss the bins of colorful flies for fishing and the mounted wildlife: the "indoor zoo" has salmon, bobcats, bears, moose, and more. River's Edge's helpful website has information about the area; Gerry and his wife, Sally, happily share tips in person, too. The store is closed from January through mid-April. ⊠ *38 Carry Rd. (Rte. 4), Oqussoc* ☎ *207/864–5582* ⊕ *www.riversedgesports.com* 🖃 *Rentals from $25, trips from $45.*

GOLF

Mingo Springs Golf Course

GOLF | This popular course is known for its mountain and water views. The course is short but challenging, with very angled drives. The front nine holes are the hilliest; the back nine holes the longest. You can also take in the views and spot wildlife on the Mingo Springs Trail & Bird Walk, an easy 3-mile loop trail through the woods along the course. ⊠ *43 Country Club Rd.* ☎ *207/864–5021* ⊕ *www.mingosprings.com* 🖃 *$32 for 9 holes, $44 for 18 holes* 🏌 *18 holes, 6024 yards, par 71.*

HIKING

Hiking options in the Rangeley Lakes region include 35 miles of trails and access roads on Rangeley Lakes Heritage Trust's 14,000 acres of conserved lands, which also welcome many other types of outdoor recreation. Trail maps and information are available at the organization's website (⊕ *www.fryeburgfair.org*) and its downtown Rangeley office (2424 Main Street).

ICE SKATING

Rangeley Skating Club (⊕ *www.fryeburgfair.org*) clears a section of Haley Pond for ice skating, usually by Christmastime. The lake-size pond is behind Main Street at the east end of downtown. Skates, hockey sticks, and pucks are available at pondside Ecopelagicon, just off Main Street. There is a rink-side warming hut, and the ice is lit until 10 nightly.

MULTISPORT OUTFITTERS

Ecopelagicon

KAYAKING | **FAMILY** | Off Main Street on Hayley Pond, this outfitter and retailer has an easy, affordable way to get you on the water: rent a kayak, canoe, or standup paddleboard by the hour. Or rent one for a half-, full-, or multi days and paddle where you please; shuttle service, guided tours, and lessons are also offered. Come winter, you can rent snowshoes or grab courtesy skates to use on the pond rink. In business since 1993, this welcoming "nature store" sells outdoor recreation gear galore; Maine- and Rangeley-theme books, guides, and maps; a slew of New England-made gifts; and lots of games and arts and crafts for adults and kids. Shoppers linger at the back window to gaze at Saddleback Mountain and ducks and loons on the pond. Rentals start at $10. The store closes late October through mid-November and in April. ⊠ *7 Pond St.* ☎ *207/864–2771* ⊕ *www.ecopelagicon.com.*

SEAPLANES

★ Acadian Seaplanes

TOUR—SPORTS | In addition to 15-, 30- and 75-minute scenic flights high above the mountains by seaplane, this operator offers enticing "fly-in" excursions. You can travel by seaplane to wilderness locales to dine at a sporting camp, spot moose in their natural habitat, fish, or go white-water rafting on the remote Rapid River. Acadian also provides charter service, including between the Rangeley area and Boston, New York, Portland, Bangor, and other places within

Maine. ⊠ *2640 Main St.* ☎ *207/864–5307* ⊕ *www.acadianseaplanes.com* ✈ *From $85.*

SKIING

Rangeley Lakes Trails Center

LOCAL SPORTS | A largely wooded, 34-mile trail network stretches along lower Saddleback Mountain and leads to Saddleback Lake. In winter, trails are groomed (double- and single-track) for cross-country skiing, snowshoeing, and fat-tire biking. A yurt lodge has ski, snowshoe, and fat-tire rentals and a snack bar known for tasty soups. Call ahead for ski, snowshoe, and fat-tire tours and cross-country lessons. In warmer weather, the trails are popular with mountain bikers, hikers, and runners. ⊠ *524 Saddleback Mountain Rd., Dallas* ☎ *207/864–4309 winter only* ⊕ *www.rangeleylakestrailscenter.org* ✈ *From $10.*

Saddleback Mountain

SKIING/SNOWBOARDING | FAMILY | Shuttered in 2015 and sold in January 2020, new owners installed what the previous ones had pined for—a high-speed quad lift. The beginner ski area is one of New England's best, partly because it is *below* the base lodge. At the other end of the spectrum, it's black diamonds all the way down at Kennebago Steeps!, touted as the East's largest steep-skiing area. Saddleback also has extensive glade areas, three terrain parks, and lots of natural snow. A fieldstone fireplace keeps things warm in the post-and-beam base lodge, which has a second-story pub. Recent renovations greatly expanded capacity and views. On-mountain lodging choices include ski-in, ski-out homes and trailside condos. The resort plans to ramp up summertime with activities such as mountain biking, kayaking, maple syruping, and guided hikes. **Facilities:** 66 trails; 220 acres; 2,000-foot vertical drop; 5 lifts. ⊠ *976 Saddleback Mountain Rd., Dallas* ☎ *207/864–5671, 866/918–2225* ⊕ *www. saddlebackmaine.com.*

Kingfield

38 miles east of Rangeley.

In the shadows of Mt. Abraham ("Mt. Abram" to locals) and Sugarloaf Mountain, home to the eponymous ski resort, Kingfield is "real" New England, dotted with white clapboard churches. The pretty Carrabassett River slices the village and flows over a dam downtown, creating a great swimming spot below the Route 16 bridge. Small pullouts mark swimming holes along Route 27 as it flows north along the rock-strewn river through Carrabassett Valley (also the name of the neighboring town) to the resort. On the other side of the waterway, the 6.6.-mile Narrow Gauge Pathway rail-trail wends through the narrow, steep-walled valley. The path was first cleared in the late 1800s for a narrower-than-standard railway that transported timber and tourists. Today it's part of an extensive and growing mountain biking network and one of many activities along the 47-mile State Route 27 Maine Scenic Byway (⊕ *www.exploremaine. org/byways*) from Kingfield to the remote Canadian border crossing at Coburn Gorge. Fantastic backcountry recreation awaits in the northern half of the drive around Eustis and Stratton. Near these small recreation hubs, the state's 36,000-acre **Bigelow Preserve** (⊕ *www.maine. gov/bigelowpreserve*) takes in the entire Bigelow Range and borders 20,000-acre Flagstaff Lake.

GETTING HERE AND AROUND

From Kingfield it is 37 miles to Rangeley, via Route 142 to Phillips, and from there, Route 4 north. Or head to Rangeley following the Route 27 Maine Scenic Byway from Kingfield to Stratton and take Route 16 from there to Rangeley—it's just 5 miles longer. You can link these routes for a scenic loop or fall foliage drive.

CONTACTS Franklin County Chamber of Commerce. ⊠ *615 Wilton Rd., Farmington* ☎ *207/778–4215* ⊕ *www.franklincounty-maine.org.*

Sights

Stanley Museum

MUSEUM | Original Stanley Steamer cars built by twin brothers Francis and Freelan Stanley—Kingfield's most famous natives—are the main draw at this museum inside a 1903 Georgian-style former school. Also well worth the stop here are exhibits about the glass-negative photography business the identical twins sold to Eastman Kodak, and the well-composed photographs, taken by their sister, Chansonetta Stanley Emmons, of everyday country life at the turn of the 20th century. ⊠ *40 School St.* ☎ *207/265–2729* ⊕ *www.stanley-museum.org* ⌂ *$8* ⊙ *Closed Jan. and Feb., Sat.–Mon. Mar.–May, and Mon. June–Oct.*

Coffee and Quick Bites

Orange Cat Cafe

$ | **AMERICAN** | **FAMILY** | Just past downtown en route to Sugarloaf, this café serves breakfast burritos and wraps, flavor-filled lunch fare (wraps, sandwiches, soup, salads, quiche) and scrumptious baked goods. Local and organic ingredients are kitchen staples, and the coffee is great. **Known for:** turmeric-flavored coconut Golden Milk; Vegetarians Revenge wrap with hummus; huge chocolate chip cookies. ⑤ *Average main: $9* ⊠ *329 Main St.* ☎ *207/265–2860* ⊕ *www.orangecatcafe.com.*

Activities

BIKING

Carrabassett Valley and environs has emerged as a prime mountain biking destination, with 80-plus miles of trails for all abilities. Several trailheads with kiosks are along or near Route 27 north of Kingfield. Come winter, some of these trails are used for cross-country skiing and fat-tire biking. The network links with the 6.6-mile Narrow Gauge Pathway (nonmotorized) along Carrabassett River through the valley and extends north to the remote Flagstaff Lake area. Maps, trail conditions and closures, and suggested loops are available at the website for the **Carrabassett Region of the New England Mountain Bike Association** (⊕ *www.carrabassettnemba.org*); area businesses distribute the group's large printed maps. You can rent mountain bikes in-season and get maps and trail advice at a couple of spots in Carrabassett Valley.

Allspeed Cyclery

BICYCLING | **FAMILY** | Portland-based Allspeed Cyclery rents mountain bikes from late May through mid-October at its satellite operation at Sugarloaf's Outdoor Center, where there is a trailhead. Adult rentals are $89 per day, and there are less expensive options for kids. The cost per day drops if you rent for multiple days. ⊠ *3001 Outdoor Center Rd., Carrabassett Valley* ☎ *207/779–3951* ⊕ *www.allspeed.com.*

Carrabassett Valley Bike

BICYCLING | A local mountain biking enthusiast runs this rental, repair, and sales outfit from late spring through early fall at Happy Tunes! Ski Service Center, where he works come winter. Rentals are $50 for a full day and $35 half day. ⊠ *1106 Valley Crossing, Carrabassett Valley* ⊹ *Just off Rte. 27 next to Tufulio's Restaurant* ☎ *207/235–6019* ⊕ *www.carrabassettvalleybike.com.*

SKIING
Sugarloaf

SKIING/SNOWBOARDING | **FAMILY** | An eye-catching setting, abundant natural snow, and the only above-the-tree-line lift-service skiing in the East have made Sugarloaf one of Maine's best-known ski resorts. Glade areas, five terrain parks, and a border-cross track amp up the skiing options, as does ungroomed Side-country on Burnt Mountain and Brackett Basin. Snowshoers and uphill skiers can attack this terrain as well as "the Loaf" ($10 uphill ticket). Along with hundreds of slope-side condos and rental homes with ski-in, ski-out access, the resort has two slope-side hotels: Sugarloaf Mountain Hotel is in the ski village, as are shops and restaurants; smaller, more affordable Sugarloaf Inn is a bit down the mountain. Just off Route 27 below the mountain, the Outdoor Center has an NHL-size ice rink; is the gateway to a 56-mile network of groomed trails for cross-country skiing, snowshoeing, and fat-tire biking; and rents equipment for all these activities.

■TIP→ **After skiing or other winter fun, unwind on-mountain at the Sports & Fitness Center (fee), which includes a pool, sauna, hot tubs, steam rooms, and by-appointment massages (fee).** Once at Sugarloaf, you'll find a car unnecessary—a shuttle connects all operations during the November–May ski season. In summer you can mountain bike, hike, or zipline; take a scenic lift ride or off-road Segway tour; rent a kayak or standup paddleboard; or play golf, either disc golf or a round on what many consider Maine's best golf course. **Facilities:** 162 trails (includes glades); 1,240 acres; 2,820-foot vertical drop; 13 lifts. ⊠ *5092 Sugarloaf Access Rd., Carrabassett Valley* ☎ *207/237–2000, 800/843–5623 for reservations* ⊕ *www.sugarloaf.com* 🎟 *Lift ticket: $119.*

Greenville

155 miles northeast of Portland, 70 miles northwest of Bangor.

Greenville, tucked at the southern end of island-dotted, mostly forest-lined Moose-head Lake—at 75,000 acres, Maine's largest and the largest entirely within New England—is an outdoors lover's paradise. In the mid-1800s, Henry David Thoreau departed from here on two of his three famous trips into Maine's wilderness, led by Penobscot guides Chief Joseph Attean and Joseph Polis. In summer, boating, fishing, kayaking, canoeing, and hiking are popular in Moosehead Lake. Come winter, folks head here for ice fishing, snowmobiling, snowshoeing, and cross-country and downhill skiing—you can enjoy both at Big Squaw Mountain ski area just north of town. Greenville has the best selection of shops, restaurants, and inns in the North Woods region. Restaurants and lodgings are also clustered 20 miles north in Rockwood, where the Moose River flows through the village and—across from Mt. Kineo's majestic cliff face—into the lake. There's also a hip cluster in hiking hub Monson, 14 miles south of Greenville. Maine's 100 Mile Wilderness, home to the most difficult and most northerly stretch of the Appalachian Trail, stretches from here to Mt. Katahdin.

GETTING HERE AND AROUND

To reach Greenville from Interstate 95, get off at Exit 157 in Newport and head north, successively, on Routes 7, 23, and 15.

VACATION RENTALS

VACATION RENTALS Vacasa (Moosehead Lake Cabin Rentals). ☎ *207/695–4300, 855/861–5757* ⊕ *www.vacasa.com/usa/Moosehead-Lake.*

VISITOR INFORMATION

CONTACTS Destination Moosehead Lake. ⊠ *480 Moosehead Lake Rd.* ☎ *207/695–2702* ⊕ *www.destinationmooseheadlake.com.*

Sights

★ **Center for Moosehead History and Moosehead Lake Aviation Museum**
MUSEUM | FAMILY | Overlooking East Cove, a former church is home to the Moosehead Historical Society museums. The center has a fine exhibit of Native American artifacts and items from the Moosehead Lake region, dating from

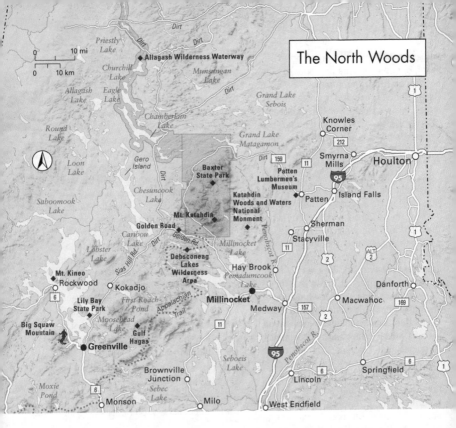

9,000 BC to the present. Displays about Native American families spotlight Henry Perley, a Maliseet guide and author who gained fame as a performer in Wild West shows and silent movies. An interactive exhibit explores life in this logging town in the 1800s. The aviation museum focuses on the impact of aviation—from early bush pilots to Greenville's annual International Seaplane Fly-In on the weekend after Labor Day—in this remote region, in particular the Air Force B-52 crash north of town in January 1963; most of the plane's remnants remain scattered on Elephant Mountain, where seven of nine passengers and crew died. ■TIP→ The museum has handouts if you want to take the popular short hike to the debris-littered site, which is also a memorial. The historical society's Greenville walking tour booklet—available to purchase at the museum gift shop—has

photos of sights past and present. Don't miss the garden with sculptures honoring Henry David Thoreau and his Native American guides, who departed from East Cove for Maine's wilds. ⊠ 6 Lakeview St. ☎ 207/695–2909 Moosehead Historical Society office ⊕ www. mooseheadhistory.org ⊠ $3 (includes both museums) ⊘ Closed mid-Oct.–mid-June and Sun.–Wed. mid-June–mid-Oct.

Gulf Hagas

BODY OF WATER | Called the "Grand Canyon of the East" and part of the Appalachian Trail Corridor, this National Natural Landmark has chasms, cliffs, four major waterfalls, pools, exotic flora, and intriguing rock formations. The West Branch of the Pleasant River flows through the 3-mile, slate-walled gorge east of Greenville in a remote, privately owned commercial forest, KI Jo-Mary, which allows access via gravel logging roads (always yield to trucks). A fee (cash or check only) is charged from late spring to late fall at forest checkpoints, where you can get trail maps and hiking information.

From either parking area you can hike to one of the showcase falls and mostly avoid the difficult rim trail. A good choice for families with young children: start at Head of Gulf parking area for a 3½-mile round-trip hike to Stair Falls on the gorge's western end. From the Gulf Hagas parking area, it's a 3-mile round-trip hike to spectacular Screw Auger Falls on the gulf's eastern end. Gulf hikers who start from this parking area must ford the Pleasant River—usually easily done in summer, but dangerous in high water—and pass through the Hermitage, a stand of old pines and hemlock. A loop route that follows the rim and the less difficult Pleasant River Tote Trail is an 8- to 9-mile trek; there are shorter loops as well. Slippery rocks and rugged terrain make for challenging progress along the rim trail. ⊠ Greenville ✛ From Greenville, travel 11 miles east via Pleasant St., which becomes Katahdin Iron Works Rd., to Hedgehog checkpoint. Follow signs to parking areas: Head of Gulf, 2½ miles; Gulf Hagas, 6½ miles ⊕ www.north-mainewoods.org.

Lily Bay State Park

NATIONAL/STATE PARK | FAMILY | Nine miles northeast of Greenville on Moosehead Lake, this 925-acre park has good lakefront swimming, a 2-mile walking trail with water views, two boat-launching ramps, a playground, and two campgrounds with a total of 90 sites. In winter, the entrance road is plowed to access the groomed cross-country ski trails and the lake for ice fishing and snowmobiling. ⊠ 13 Myrle's Way ✛ Turn onto State Park Rd. from Lily Bay Rd. ☎ 207/695–2700 ⊕ www.maine.gov/lilybay ⊠ Nonresident $6, Maine resident $4.

★ Moosehead Historical Society & Museums

MUSEUM | FAMILY | Guides in period attire lead tours of the Eveleth-Crafts-Sheridan Historical House, a late 19th-century Victorian mansion filled with antiques, most of them original to the home. There's a changing exhibit each year, and cooks will savor the impressive collection of utensils and appliances in the 1880s kitchen. You can even check out the attic. In the lower level of the carriage house, the Moosehead Lumbermen's Museum has exhibits about the region's logging history, anchored by a 30-foot bateau used on log drives until the 1960s. Tools abound, and there are models of steamboats that hauled logs and transported tourists and supplies on Moosehead Lake. Upstairs there's a small gift shop and a popular display about hotels on Mt. Kineo, where wealthy Americans flocked to vacation in the rusticator era. In the barn next door, the Moosehead Outdoor Heritage Museum's wide-ranging displays cover subjects like Maine Warden Service flight rescues; local wildlife (there are bobcat, moose, and caribou mounts); the tradition of Maine Registered Guides; and the region's vast commercial forests. You can enjoy lunch and the architecture of these meticulously maintained buildings from the art-accented sunken garden. ⊠ 444 Pritham Ave., Greenville Junction ☎ 207/695–2909 ⊕ www.mooseheadhistory.org ⊠ Main campus museums including Eveleth-Crafts-Sheridan Historical House $8 ⊗ Closed mid-Oct.–mid-June, except for Lumbermen's Museum (closed Sat.–Mon. off-season); historic home closed Sun.–Wed. mid-June–mid-Oct., other museums closed Sun. and Mon. in-season.

Mt. Kineo

NATIONAL/STATE PARK | FAMILY | Accessible primarily by steamship, Mt. Kineo House was a thriving upscale summer resort that sits below its namesake's 700-foot cliff on an islandlike, 1,200-acre peninsula jutting into Moosehead Lake. The last of three successive hotels with this name was built in 1884 and became America's largest inland waterfront hotel. It was torn down in 1938, but Kineo remains an outstanding day trip. Trails to the summit of the spectacular landmark, now part of Mt. Kineo State Park, lead to a fire tower that rewards with a 360-degree sweep of Maine's largest lake and rugged mountains. Hikers scramble on the challenging Indian Trail, but it also has amazing views. All hikes begin on the Carriage Trail, a flat, shore-hugging remnant of the halcyon hotel days. You can play a round on Mt. Kineo Golf Course, one of New England's oldest. There is no road access, but you can take a 15-minute boat trip from Rockwood on the golf course's seasonal shuttle. Historic summer "cottages" line the greens near the small clubhouse, which has a snack bar and welcomes hikers. ✉ *Kineo Dock, Village Rd., Rockwood* ☎ *207/534–9012 for golf course and shuttle, 207/941–4014 for park regional office* ⊕ *www.maine.gov/mountkineo* 🎫 *Nonresident $3, Maine resident $2.*

☕ Coffee and Quick Bites

Harris Drug Store and Dairy Bar
$ | **AMERICAN** | **FAMILY** | Inside this tidy, well-stocked downtown drug store you can twist on a red stool at the well-kept 1960s-era soda fountain while enjoying a sundae or scoop of ice cream. Hot and cold drinks are also served. **Known for:** soda fountain milk shakes served in traditional glasses; owned by the Harris family since 1896 (not the original locale); soft and hard serve at the Dairy Bar. $ *Average main: $5* ✉ *10 Pritham Ave.* ☎ *207/695–2921* ⊕ *facebook.com/harrisdrugstore* ⊗ *Dairy Bar closed mid-Sept.–mid-May.*

🛏 Hotels

★ Appalachian Mountain Club Maine Wilderness Lodges
$$$ | **RESORT** | **FAMILY** | In Maine's 100-Mile Wilderness, the Appalachian Mountain Club's 75,000 acres includes three historic sporting-camp retreats. **Pros:** courtesy canoes (some on outlying ponds), kayaks, and standup paddleboards (no boards at Little Lyford); Little Lyford and Gorman Chairback are near Gulf Hagas; Medawisla a good choice for beginner cross-country skiers. **Cons:** winter access only by cross-country skis, snowshoes, foot, or snowmobile transport (fee) at Little Lyford and Gorman Chairback; no waterfront cabins at Little Lyford; not many courtesy mountain bikes, none at Little Lyford. $ *Rooms from: $399* ✉ *North Woods outside Greenville* ☎ *207/695–3085 AMC Greenville office, 207/358–5187 reservations* ⊕ *www.outdoors.org/lodging/mainelodges* ⊗ *Closed Apr., Nov., Dec. until after Christmas, and part of Mar. (Little Lyford and Gorman Chairback close early and Medawisla late in month).* 🛏 *Gorman Chairback: 12 cabins, 1 bunkhouse (sleeps 10); Little Lyford: 9 cabins, 1 bunkhouse (sleeps 14); Medawisla, 9 cabins, 2 bunkhouses (each sleeps 16)* 🍽 *Free breakfast.*

★ Blair Hill Inn & Restaurant
$$$$ | **B&B/INN** | Beautiful gardens, high stone walls, and a hilltop location with marvelous views over the lake distinguish this 1891 country estate as one of New England's top inns; enjoy cocktails—and that view—from the veranda or the swank cocktail lounge. **Pros:** free concierge plans outdoor excursions, provides courtesy beach towels, etc.; reservation but no fee to use spa's cozy outdoor hot tub, sauna, and deck; helicopter, Tesla, and electric-car friendly. **Cons:** pricey; no direct lake access; three guestrooms on the third floor. $ *Rooms from: $499* ✉ *351 Lily Bay Rd.* ☎ *207/695–0224* ⊕ *www.blairhill.com* ⊗ *Closed Nov.–mid-May* 🛏 *10 rooms* 🍽 *Free breakfast.*

🏃 Activities

BOATING

Capt. Rogers Pontoon Rental

BOATING | Operated by a captain with decades of experience on local waters, the business rents swim ladder–equipped pontoon boats for full- and half-day excursions (same-day only reservations for the latter) and overnight trips on 40-mile-long Moosehead Lake. In Rockwood on the Moose River a mile from the lake, boaters have plenty of time to head for nearby Mt. Kineo, Moosehead's famed landmark. ⊠ *9 Maynard Rd., Rockwood* ✛ *At Moose River Bridge* ☎ *207/233–3820* ⊕ *www.captrogerspontoonrental.com.*

MULTISPORT OUTFITTERS

Northwoods Outfitters

TOUR—SPORTS | You can rent canoes, kayaks, standup paddleboards, camping and fishing equipment, UTVs and ATVs, comfort and mountain bikes, snowmobiles, snowshoes, cross-country skis, and winter clothing here. Northwoods also guides a host of outdoor trips (some multiday), including open-water and ice fishing, waterfall hikes, photography, snowmobiling, and moose-watching (by land or water); operates a shuttle to remote areas; and offers recreation packages with area lodging establishments. At the base in downtown Greenville, you can pick up sporting goods, souvenirs, and clothing; get trail advice; and kick back in the Hard Drive Café. ⊠ *5 Lily Bay Rd.* ☎ *207/695–3288, 866/223–1380* ⊕ *www.maineoutfitter.com.*

SEAPLANES

Currier's Flying Service

ZIP LINING | You can take sightseeing flights in vintage seaplanes over the Moosehead Lake region from ice-out until mid-October. ⊠ *447 Pritham Ave., Greenville Junction* ☎ *207/695–2778* ⊕ *www.curriersflyingservice.com* ⏴ *From $45.*

SKIING

Big Squaw Mountain

SKIING/SNOWBOARDING | **FAMILY** | A local nonprofit was formed in 2013 to reopen the lower portion of Big Moose Mountain (the resort uses the old name) after it closed for a few years, and the ski area now operates Thursday through Sunday, on holidays, and during school-vacation weeks. The summit chairlift, unused since 2004, and the shuttered hotel loom trailside like something out of a Stephen King novel (he's a Mainer, no less), but the mostly intermediate trails on the lower mountain are plenty high enough to wow skiers with views up and down Moosehead Lake, Maine's largest. On a clear day, Mt. Katahdin, the state's highest peak, accents the mountainous horizon. The terrain, cheap prices, a surface lift for beginners, and the spacious, retro-fun chalet lodge draw families. The resort also has free trails for cross-country skiing, snowshoeing, and fat-tire biking. **Facilities:** 28 trails; 58 acres; 660-foot vertical drop; 2 lifts. ⊠ *447 Ski Resort Rd., Greenville Junction* ☎ *207/695–2400* ⊕ *www.skibigsquaw.com* ⏴ *Lift ticket: $30.*

TOURS

Katahdin Cruises & Moosehead Marine Museum

TOUR—SPORTS | The Moosehead Marine Museum runs 3- and 5-hour afternoon trips on Moosehead Lake aboard the *Katahdin,* a 115-foot 1914 steamship converted to diesel. Cruisers learn about the rich logging and tourism history of Maine's largest lake and environs on the narrated excursions. (The longer one skirts Mt. Kineo's cliffs.) Also called the *Kate,* this ship carried resort guests to Mt. Kineo until 1938; the logging industry then used it until 1975. The boat and the free shoreside museum have displays about the steamships that transported people and cargo on Moosehead Lake for a century starting in the 1830s. ⊠ *12 Lily Bay Rd.* ☎ *207/695–2716* ⊕ *www.katahdincruises.com* ⏴ *From $40.*

Millinocket

67 miles north of Bangor, 88 miles north-west of Greenville.

Millinocket, a former paper-mill town with a population of about 4,000, is the gateway to "forever wild" Baxter State Park and a jumping-off point for Maine's North Woods. The town is the place to stock up on supplies, fill your gas tank, and grab a hot meal or shower before heading into the wilderness. On the east side of Baxter, President Obama created the Katahdin Woods and Waters National Monument in 2016. Numerous rafting and canoeing outfitters and guides are based in the region. **Katahdin Woods & Waters Scenic Byway** (⊕ *www.katahdin-woodsandwaters.com*), much of which flows along Route 11, links the region's conserved lands and scattered towns.

GETTING HERE AND AROUND
From Interstate 95, take Route 157 (Exit 244) west to Millinocket. From here follow signs to Baxter State Park (Millinocket Lake Road becomes Baxter Park State Road), 18 miles from town.

VISITOR INFORMATION
CONTACTS Katahdin Chamber of Commerce. ⊠ *1029 Central St.* ☎ *207/723–4443* ⊕ *www.katahdinmaine.com.*

 Sights

Allagash Wilderness Waterway
BODY OF WATER | A spectacular 92-mile corridor of lakes, ponds, streams, and rivers, the waterway park cuts through vast commercial forests, beginning near the northwestern corner of Baxter State Park and running north to the town of Allagash, 10 miles from the Canadian border. From May to mid-October, the Allagash is prime canoeing and camping country. The Maine Bureau of Parks and Lands has campsites along the waterway, most not accessible by vehicle. The complete 92-mile course, part of the 740-mile Northern Forest Canoe Trail, which runs from New York to Maine, requires 7–10 days to canoe. Novices may want to hire a guide, as there are many areas with strong rapids. A good outfitter can help plan your route and provide equipment and transportation. ⊠ *Millinocket* ☎ *207/941–4014 for regional parks bureau office* ⊕ *www.maine.gov/allagash.*

★ Baxter State Park
NATIONAL/STATE PARK | FAMILY | A gift from Governor Percival Baxter, this is the jewel in the crown of northern Maine: a 210,000-acre wilderness area that surrounds **Mt. Katahdin,** Maine's highest mountain and the terminus of the Appalachian Trail. Every year, the 5,267-foot Katahdin draws thousands of hikers to make the daylong summit, rewarding them with stunning views of forests, mountains, and lakes. There are three parking-lot trailheads for Katahdin. Depart from the Roaring Brook trailhead for a route that includes the hair-raising Knife Edge Trail. ■ **TIP→ Reserve a day-use parking space at the trailheads June 1–October 15.**

The crowds climbing Katahdin can be formidable on clear summer days and fall weekends, so if it's solitude you crave, tackle one of the park's many other mountains. Most are accessible from the extensive trail network, including 11 peaks exceeding an elevation of 3,000 feet. The Brothers and Doubletop Mountain are challenging daylong hikes; the Owl takes about six hours; and South Turner can be climbed in a morning—its summit has a great view across the valley. A trek around Daicey Pond, or from the pond to Big and Little Niagara Falls, are good options for families with young kids. Another option if you only have a couple of hours is renting a canoe at Daicey or Togue Pond (bring cash for this honor system). Park roads are unpaved, narrow, winding, and not plowed in winter; there are no pay phones, gas

There are amazing views from the top of the 5,267-foot-tall Mt. Katahdin.

stations, stores; and cell phone service is unreliable. Camping is primitive and reservations are required; there are 10 campgrounds plus backcountry sites.
■TIP→ **The park has a visitor center at its southern entrance, but you can get information, make parking and camping reservations, and watch a video at park headquarters in Millinocket (64 Balsam Drive).** ⌧ *Baxter State Park Rd.* ✛ *Togue Pond Gate (southern entrance) is 18 miles northwest of Millinocket; follow signs from Rte. 157. Matagamon Gate (northern entrance) is 27 miles west of Patten; follow signs from Rte. 159.* ☎ *207/723–5140* ⊕ *www.baxterstateparkauthority. com* ⌧ *$15 per vehicle; Maine residents free* ⊘ *Mt. Katahdin trails are closed and park access is limited in Nov. and Apr.–mid-May.*

Debsconeag Lakes Wilderness Area

NATURE PRESERVE | Bordering the south side of the Golden Road below Baxter State Park, the Nature Conservancy's 46,271-acre Debsconeag Lakes Wilderness Area is renowned for its rare

ice cave, old forests, abundant pristine ponds, and views of Mt. Katahdin—there are mesmerizing views along the 5-mile Rainbow Loop. The access road for the Ice Cave Trail (2 miles round-trip) and Hurd Pond is 17 miles northwest of Millinocket, just west of the Golden Road's Abol Bridge. The kiosk at this entrance has information about the preserve, including a large map. Nearby the Appalachian Trail exits the conservancy land, crossing the bridge en route to Baxter. Hugging the curving, scenic West Branch of the Penobscot River and revealing Katahdin, the first few miles of the 5-mile dirt access road deserve a drive even if you aren't stopping to recreate. Before hiking, paddling, fishing, or camping in the remote preserve (no fees or reservations required), visit the conservancy's website for directions, maps, and other information. ⌧ *Golden Rd.* ⊕ *www.nature.org/maine.*

Golden Road

SCENIC DRIVE | For a scenic North Woods drive, set off on the roughly 21-mile stretch of this private east–west logging road near Baxter State Park northwest of Millinocket. Have patience with ruts and bumps, and yield to logging trucks (keep right!). From Millinocket follow the signs for Baxter State Park from Route 157. This scenic drive begins 8 miles from the railroad overpass as you exit town, at the crossover from Millinocket Lake Road to the Golden Road, the latter reportedly named for the huge sum a paper company paid to build it.

North Woods Trading Post is at this junction, across from Ambajejus Lake. Stop in not just for takeout, coffee, gas, or North Woods–theme gifts but to pick up a free handout noting stops along the Golden Road, with mileage—a godsend along this remote stretch, where ponds for moose spotting aren't signed and hiking spots that are signed can still be easy to miss. River Pond Nature Trail offers several treks; the access road is on the left about six miles from the trading post. Continuing along the Golden Road, you'll pass the aforementioned ponds (watch for spots to pull over and park); it's 4 miles to one-lane Abol Bridge over the West Branch of the Penobscot River. There are turnouts for parking, or stop before the bridge at Abol Bridge Campground, with a restaurant and store. ■ TIP→ Take photos of Baxter's Mt. Katahdin from the footbridge alongside Abol Bridge: this view is famous. Just beyond the bridge is an access road and kiosk for Debsconeag Lakes Wilderness Area. The 2-mile round-trip Ice Cave trailhead is 5 miles in on a river-hugging dirt road with more Katahdin views. Continuing from Abol Bridge, the Golden Road also flows alongside the waterway.

At the western end of the drive, the river drops 70-plus feet per mile through Ripogenus Gorge, giving white-water rafters a thrilling ride during scheduled releases from Ripogenus Dam. The Crib Works Rapid (Class V) overlook is off the Golden Road about 9 miles from Abol Bridge. (Turn right on Telos Road; parking is on the right after the bridge.) For the best gorge views, return to the Golden Road, and continue west about a mile and turn right into McKay Station, where many rafters put in. Be cautious on the downhill paths and atop the steep cliffs. To drive across the dam on Ripogenus Lake and view the gorge, get back on the Golden Road and head west three-quarters of a mile to Rip Dam Road, which veers right. Returning to the crossover at the North Woods Trading Post, turn left for Baxter or right for Millinocket. ⊠ Golden Rd.

Katahdin Woods and Waters National Monument

NATIONAL/STATE PARK | Two rivers flow and streams and ponds abound at this 87,500-acre North Woods preserve, created east of Baxter State Park in 2016 and home to moose, bald eagles, salmon, and bobcats. Currently there are occasional visitor programs but no visitor center; you can get information at staffed welcome centers in Millinocket (200 Penobscot Avenue; only open Thursday afternoon in winter) and Patten (at Patten Lumbermen's Museum, 61 Shin Pond Road, seasonal). Access and park roads are gravel; sanitary facilities are limited; and there is no water, food, fuel, or reliable cell service. In the monument's southern portion, 16-mile Katahdin Loop Road has scenic views of Baxter's Mt. Katahdin and trailheads to short hikes and Barnard Mountain, a 4-mile round-trip that links with the International Appalachian Trail. There are mountain biking options as a few bike-designated routes link with the loop road (biking is allowed on park roads). In the northern section, visitors hike, mountain bike, cross-country ski (some groomed trails) and snowshoe along and near the water-fall-dotted East Branch of the Penobscot River. Folks paddle and fish on the river and other monument waters. ⊠ Patten ⌖ Southern entrance: From Rte. 11 in Stacyville, head west on gravel Swift

Brook Rd. (use caution when turning; it's about 12 miles to Katahdin Loop Dr.). Northern entrance: from Pattern turn on Rte. 159 (becomes Grand Lake Rd.); it's about 30 miles to entrance (take 2nd left after crossing the East Branch of the Penobscot River). ☎ 207/456–6001 ⊕ www.nps.gov/kaww.

Patten Lumbermen's Museum

MUSEUM | FAMILY | Two reproduction 1800s logging camps are among the 10 buildings filled with exhibits depicting the history of logging in Maine. They include sawmill and towboat models, dioramas of logging scenes, horse-drawn sleds, and a steam-powered log hauler. Exhibits also highlight local artists and history as well as logging-related topics. The museum is a welcome center for nearby Katahdin Woods and Waters National Monument. ⊠ 61 Shin Pond Rd., Patten ☎ 207/528–2650 ⊕ www.lumbermens-museum.org ☞ $10 ☉ Closed mid-Oct.– mid-May and Mon. (except holidays in season); also closed Tues.–Thurs. late May–June.

Penobscot River Trails

TRAIL | FAMILY | A New York philanthropist was so taken with the Mt. Katahdin region he spurred creation of 15.5 miles of free public recreation trails along the East Branch of the Penobscot River, conveniently off Route 11. Opened in 2019, the "crusher dust" paths are akin to the famed carriage trails at coastal Maine's Acadia National Park. The river trails are used for mountain biking and walking and, after the snow flies, groomed for cross-country skiing and fat-tire biking. There are also 9 miles of snowshoe trails. You can chill after a workout or eat your lunch in the woodsy chic visitor center. Come winter, wood stoves heat up two warming huts—one offers an outstanding view of Mt. Katahdin—along the trails. Courtesy bikes, snowshoes, cross-country skis, and reservation-only kayaks are available, or, of course, bring your own. ⊠ 2540 Grindstone Rd.,

Stacyville ☎ 207/746–5807 ⊕ www. penobscotrivertrails.org.

 Restaurants

River Driver's Restaurant

$$$ | AMERICAN | FAMILY | At the deservedly popular restaurant—usually open daily for breakfast, lunch, and dinner—wood for the trim, wainscoting, bar, and floors was milled from old logs salvaged from local waters. Diners enjoy views of Katahdin from behind rows of windows or from the patio, and your dish may feature farm-to-table fare. **Known for:** great view of Katahdin; daily specials; seasonal, local, and fresh ingredients. ⑤ Average main: $25 ⊠ 30 Twin Pines Rd. ☎ 207/723–8475 ⊕ www.neoc.com.

 Coffee and Quick Bites

North Woods Trading Post

$ | AMERICAN | FAMILY | Yummy to-go fare includes breakfast and regular sandwiches, pizza, and baked goods, at this cabin-style "last stop" for gear, supplies, and gas before Baxter State Park. Quality Maine-made gifts and souvenirs; Baxter and Mt. Katahdin art and attire; and Maine- and park-theme books are tastefully arrayed. **Known for:** provides area information, as do placards at rest area next door; co-owned by a former Baxter ranger; across from Ambajejus Lake. ⑤ Average main: $10 ⊠ 1605 Baxter State Park Rd. ☎ 207/723–4326 ⊕ www. northwoodstradingpostme.com ☉ Closed late Oct.–early May.

 Activities

MULTISPORT OUTFITTERS

Katahdin Outfitters

BOATING | This company provides gear and shuttles for overnight canoe and kayak expeditions on the Allagash Wilderness Waterway, the West Branch of the Penobscot River, and the St. John River. You can also rent canoes and kayaks from its location just outside Millinocket on the way to Baxter State Park. ✉ *360 Bates St.* ☎ *207/723–5700* ⊕ *www.katahdinoutfitters.com* ✆ *Call for prices.*

★ **New England Outdoor Center** (*NEOC*) TOUR—SPORTS | FAMILY | With Baxter State Park's Mt. Katahdin rising above the shore opposite both its locations, this business helps visitors enjoy the North Woods. Its year-round home base, NEOC/Twin Pines on Millinocket Lake, 8 miles from the park's southern entrance, has rental cabins and a restaurant (River Driver's Restaurant) and conducts many guided trips, some within the park. Older renovated log cabins (and a few newer ones) sit beneath tall pines on a grassy nub of land that juts into Millinocket Lake; upscale "green" units (spacious lodges and cozy cabins) are tucked among trees on a cove. Amenities include kayaks and canoes for use on the lake and a recreation center with a sauna.

NEOC offers a full slate of guided excursions: whitewater rafting, fishing, canoeing, kayaking, hiking, photography, moose- and wildlife-spotting, snowmobiling, and ice fishing. It also rents canoes, kayaks, standup paddleboards, snowmobiles (attire, too), fat-tire bikes, cross-country skis, and snowshoes and offers cross-country skiing and paddling lessons. Trails for cross-country skiing (15-plus miles, groomed), snowshoeing, and mountain and fat-tire biking are right on the 1,400-acre property and link with adjoining trail networks for longer excursions. About 2 miles from Baxter, the seasonal Penobscot Outdoor Center on Pockwockamus Pond is the base for white-water rafting trips on the West Branch of the Penobscot River and home to a wooded campground. Some sites are near the water, looking toward Katahdin. There are tent sites as well as canvas tents and simple wood-frame cabins with cots or bunks. A circular fireplace anchors the open-plan base lodge with pool tables and, on rafting days, a beer bar. A towering window wall reveals glimpses of water through trees. Outdoors there's a communal fire pit and a sand volleyball court. ◼ TIP→ **Nonguests can use showers for $2 after hiking or camping at Baxter.** ✉ *30 Twin Pines Rd.* ⊹ *From Baxter State Park Rd., take Black Cat Rd. east 1 mile* ☎ *207/723–5438, 800/766–7238* ⊕ *www.neoc.com.*

SEAPLANES
Katahdin Air Service
TOUR—SPORTS | In addition to operating ½- and 1-hour scenic flights over the Katahdin area, this seaplane operator offers fly-in excursions to backcountry locales to picnic at a pond beach, dine at a sporting camp, or moose-watch and bask in nature. It also provides charter service from points throughout Maine to the region's smaller towns and remote areas. ✉ *1888 Golden Rd.* ☎ *207/723–8378* ⊕ *www.katahdinair.com* ✆ *From $125.*

WHITE-WATER RAFTING
North Country Rivers
WHITE-WATER RAFTING | North Country Rivers's base for white-water rafting trips on the West Branch of the Penobscot River is at Big Moose Inn, Cabins & Campground, on Millinocket Lake south of Baxter State Park. The businesses team up on lodging packages. (In Western Maine, the outfitter runs white-water rafting trips on the Dead and Kennebec rivers in The Forks and has a resort south of there in Bingham.) ✉ *102A Baxter State Park Rd.* ☎ *800/348–8871* ⊕ *www.northcountryrivers.com.*

Chapter 7

THE MAINE COAST

Updated by
John Blodgett

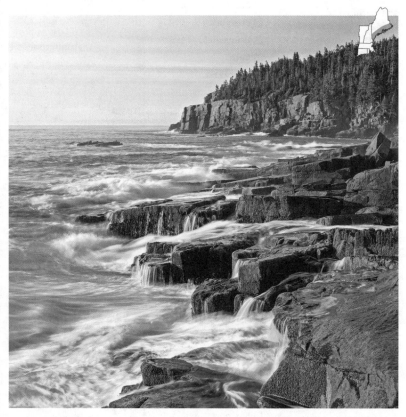

👁 **Sights**
★★★★☆

🍴 **Restaurants**
★★★★☆

🛏 **Hotels**
★★★★★

🛍 **Shopping**
★★★☆☆

🍸 **Nightlife**
★★★☆☆

WELCOME TO THE MAINE COAST

TOP REASONS TO GO

★ **Lobster and Wild Maine Blueberries:** It's not a Maine vacation unless you don a bib and dig into a steamed lobster with drawn butter, and finish with a wild blueberry pie for dessert.

★ **Boating:** The coastline of Maine was made for boaters: whether it's your own boat, a friend's, or a charter, make sure you get out on the water.

★ **Hiking the Bold Coast:** Miles of unspoiled coastal and forest paths Down East make for a hiker's (and a bird-watcher's) dream.

★ **Cadillac Mountain:** Drive a winding 3½ miles to the 1,530-foot summit in Acadia National Park for the sunrise.

★ **Dining in Portland:** With more than 250 restaurants and counting, Forest City is a foodie haven with one of the highest per capita restaurant densities in the United States.

1 **Kittery.**

2 **The Yorks.**

3 **Ogunquit.**

4 **Wells.**

5 **Kennebunk and Kennebunkport.**

6 **Cape Elizabeth and Prout's Neck.**

7 **Portland.**

8 **Casco Bay Islands.**

9 **Freeport.**

10 **Brunswick.**

11 **Bath.**

12 **Wiscasset.**

13 **Boothbay.**

14 **Damariscotta.**

15 **Pemaquid Point.**

16 **Port Clyde.**

17 **Monhegan Island.**

18 **Rockland.**

19 **Rockport.**

20 **Camden.**

21 **Belfast.**

22 **Bucksport.**

23 **Blue Hill.**

24 **Deer Isle.**

25 **Bar Harbor.**

26 **Acadia National Park.**

27 **Bass Harbor.**

28 **Schoodic Peninsula.**

29 **Lubec.**

30 **Campobello Island, Canada.**

31 **Eastport.**

95

191

Old Town

9

Newport

TO LUBEC, EASTPORT, AND
CAMPOBELLO ISLAND, CANADA

29
30
31

Skowhegan

Bangor

179

Machias

9

193

Columbia
Falls

95

Bucksport

22

Cherryfield

Jonesport

Waterville

Ellsworth

182

Hancock

West
Gouldsboro

Beals
Island

Searsport

23

Belfast

Castine

Blue Hill

Bar Harbor

21

3

AUGUSTA

1

Islesboro

Blue Hill
Peninsula

Mt.
Desert
Island

26

25

28

Schoodic Peninsula

Frenchman Bay

17

20

Camden

24

Deer Isle

27

Bass
Harbor

Acadia Nat'l
Park

Northeast Harbor

19

Rockport

Waldoboro

18

Rockland

Stonington

1

Newcastle

Thomaston

12

14

Damariscotta

Penobscot
Bay

Isle
au Haut

11

Wiscasset

Bath

Boothbay

16

Port Clyde

13

15

Pemaquid
Point

eorgetown

17

Monhegan
Island

ds

Atlantic Ocean

0   20 mi

0   20 km

As you drive across the border into Maine, a sign reads, "The way life should be." It's a slogan that's hard to argue with once you've spent some time in the Pine Tree State. Here, time stays in step with you, and Mainers take their play just as seriously as their work.

Romantics thrill at the wind and salt spray in their faces on a historic windjammer. Birders fill their notebooks to the brim with new field notes. Families love the unspoiled beaches and sheltered inlets dotting the shoreline—not to mention the numerous homemade-ice-cream stands. Foodies revel in greater Portland's booming restaurant scene, while artists and art lovers find inspiration both on and off the canvas amid art galleries and museums or along the craggy seaboard. Adventure-seekers find many opportunities to kayak and cycle at the Bold Coast and Acadia National Park, whose trails invigorate hikers with their natural beauty. At night, the sky is dark enough to spot rare constellations and experience the magic of auroras.

The Maine Coast is several places in one. Classic New England townscapes with picturesque downtowns mingle with rocky shorelines punctuated by sandy beaches and secluded coves with sweeping views of lighthouses, forested islands, and the wide-open sea. So, no matter what strikes your fancy—a spontaneous picnic on the beach or a sunset cruise with a bottle of local wine, an afternoon exploring hidden tide pools or a dose of culture followed by shopping and dining in town—there's something to suit every disposition.

Counting all its nooks, crannies, and crags, Maine's coast would stretch thousands of miles if you could pull it straight, which means there's always some new, undiscovered territory awaiting you. Stretching north from Kittery to just outside Portland, the Southern Coast is the most popular area, with many top-notch restaurants, museums, and wineries. Don't let that stop you from heading farther Down East (Maine-speak for "way up the coast"), where you'll be rewarded with the majestic mountains and rugged coastline of Acadia National Park, as well as the unspoiled, dramatic scenery of the Bold Coast.

MAJOR REGIONS

Stretching north from Kittery to just outside Portland, **the Southern Coast** is Maine's most visited region; miles of sandy expanses and shore towns cater to summer visitors. **Kittery, the Yorks, Wells,** and the **Kennebunks** offer low-key getaways, all a stone's throw from **Portland,** Maine's largest city and foodie haven. **Ogunquit** is an artists' colony that's giving Provincetown a run for its money; the very popular Cliff House resort is nearby. The **Casco Bay Islands** lie just off the coast in various sizes, some are easier to access than others. Beautiful **Cape Elizabeth** is home to Portland Head Light; Winslow Homer's Studio is located in nearby Scarborough. About 17 miles north of Portland, **Freeport** is home to the headquarters of L.L. Bean and a lovely harbor.

North of Portland, from Brunswick to Monhegan Island, **the Mid-Coast Region** has a craggy coastline that winds its way around pastoral peninsulas. Its villages boast maritime museums, innovative restaurants, antiques shops, and beautiful architecture. **Brunswick,** while a bigger, more commercial city, has rows of historic brick and clapboard homes and is home to Bowdoin College. **Bath** is known for its maritime heritage. **Wiscasset** has arguably the best antiques shopping in the state. On its waterfront you can choose from a variety of seafood shacks competing for the best lobster rolls. **Damariscotta,** too, is worth a stop for its good seafood restaurants, and you'd be hard-pressed to find better-tasting oysters than those from the Damariscotta River. **Boothbay Harbor** is one of the quaintest towns in the Mid-Coast—and a busy tourist destinations come summer, with lots of little stores that are perfect for window-shopping. It's also one of three towns from which you can take a ferry to **Monhegan Island,** which seems to be inhabited exclusively by painters at their easels, intent on capturing the wind-swept cliffs and weathered homes with colorful gardens. **Pemaquid Point** sits at the tip of the Pemaquid Peninsula, while the sleepy town of **Port Clyde** sits at the end of the St. George Peninsula.

Penobscot Bay covers an estimated 1,070 square miles and is home to more than 1,800 islands. Its dramatic natural scenery highlights its picture-perfect coastal towns, which include **Belfast, Rockport,** and **Camden. Rockland** gets lots of attention thanks to a trio of attractions: the renowned Farnsworth Art Museum, the popular summer Lobster Festival, and the lively North Atlantic Blues Festival. **Bucksport** has the stunning Penobscot Narrows Bridge and the Fort Knox historic site.

The large **Blue Hill Peninsula** juts south into Penobscot Bay. Painters, photographers, sculptors, and other artists are drawn to the peninsula; you can find more than 20 galleries on Deer Isle and at least half as many on the mainland. Not far from the mainland are the islands of Little Deer Isle and **Deer Isle. Blue Hill** and **Castine** are the area's primary business hubs. **Isle Au Haut** is only accessible by mail boat, but worth the effort.

Millions come to enjoy **Acadia National Park and Mount Desert Island's** stunning peaks and vistas. **Bar Harbor** is fun to explore, with its many gift shops and restaurants, while **Bass Harbor** offers quieter retreats.

The "real Maine," as some call the region known as **Down East,** unfurls in thousands of acres of wild blueberry barrens, congestion-free coastlines, vast wilderness preserves, and a tangible sense of rugged endurance. The landscape of **Schoodic Peninsula's** craggy coastline, towering evergreens, and views over Frenchman Bay are breathtaking year-round. Towns on the peninsula include Grindstone Neck, Winter Harbor, and Gouldsboro; the peninsula's southern tip is home to the Schoodic section of Acadia National Park. **Lubec** is a frequent destination for outdoor enthusiasts; a popular excursion is New Brunswick's **Campobello Island,** which has the Roosevelt Campobello International Park. **Eastport** is connected to the mainland by a granite causeway; it was once one of the nation's busiest seaports.

Planning

You could easily spend a lifetime's worth of vacations along the Maine Coast and never truly see it all. But if you are determined to travel the coast end-to-end, allot at least two weeks at a comfortable pace. Count on longer transit time getting from place to place in summer, as traffic along U.S. 1 can be agonizing in high season, especially in the areas around Wiscasset and Acadia National Park.

Getting Here and Around

AIR

Maine has two major international airports, Portland International Jetport and Bangor International Airport, to get you to or close to your coastal destination. Manchester–Boston Regional Airport in New Hampshire is about 45 minutes away from the southern end of the Maine coastline. Boston's Logan Airport is the only truly international airport in the region; it's about 90 minutes south of the Maine border.

BUS

The Shoreline Explorer links seasonal trolleys in southern Maine beach towns from the Yorks to the Kennebunks, allowing you to travel between towns without a car. Concord Coach Lines has express service between Portland and Boston's Logan Airport and South Station. Concord operates out of the Portland Transportation Center (⊠ 100 Thompson's Point Rd.).

CONTACTS Shoreline Explorer. ☎ 207/459–2932 ⊕ www.shorelineexplorer.com.

CAR

Once you are here the best way to experience the winding back roads of the craggy Maine Coast is in a car. There are miles and miles of roads far from the larger towns that have no bus service, and you won't want to miss the chance to discover your own favorite ocean vista while on a scenic drive.

TRAIN

Amtrak offers regional service from Boston to Portland via its Downeaster line, which originates at Boston's North Station and makes six stops in Maine: Wells, Saco, Old Orchard Beach (seasonal), Portland, Freeport, and Brunswick.

Driving in Coastal Maine

	Miles	Time
Boston–Portland	112	2 hours
Kittery–Portland	50	50 minutes
Portland–Freeport	18	20 minutes
Portland–Camden	80	2 hours
Portland–Bar Harbor	175	3 hours 20 minutes

When to Go

Maine's dramatic coastline and pure natural beauty welcome visitors year-round, but note that many smaller museums and attractions are open only in high season (Memorial Day–mid-October), as are many waterside attractions and eateries.

Summer begins in earnest on July 4, and you'll find that many smaller inns, bed-and-breakfasts, and hotels from Kittery on up to Bar Harbor are booked a month or two in advance for dates through August. That's also the case come fall, when the fiery foliage draws leaf peepers. After Halloween, hotel rates drop significantly until ski season begins around Thanksgiving. B&Bs that stay open year-round but are not near ski slopes will often rent rooms at far lower prices than in summer.

In spring, the fourth Sunday in March is designated as Maine Maple Sunday, and farms throughout the state open their doors to visitors not only to watch sap turn into golden syrup but to sample the sweet results.

Activities

No visit to the Maine Coast is complete without some outdoor activity—on two wheels, two feet, holding two paddles, or pulling a bag full of clubs.

If your adventures find you swimming in the ocean or floating close to its surface on a kayak, be on the lookout for sharks. Their populations have rebounded in recent years following conservation and regulatory efforts. In the summer of 2020, off Bailey Island, a swimming woman was killed by a great white shark in Maine's first recorded shark fatality; authorities surmised her wet suit caused her to appear to be a seal, a favored prey of sharks.

BIKING

Both the Bicycle Coalition of Maine and Explore Maine by Bike are excellent resources for trail maps and other riding information.

CONTACTS Bicycle Coalition of Maine. ⊠ *34 Diamond St., Portland* ☎ *207/623–4511* ⊕ *www.bikemaine.org.* **Explore Maine by Bike.** ☎ *207/624–3300* ⊕ *www. exploremaine.org/bike.*

HIKING

Exploring the Maine Coast on foot is a quick way to acclimate yourself to the relaxed pace of life here—and sometimes the only way to access some of the best coastal spots. Many privately owned lands are accessible to hikers, especially Down East. Inquire at a local establishment about hikes that may not appear on a map.

KAYAKING

Nothing gets you literally off the beaten path like plying the saltwaters in a graceful sea kayak.

CONTACTS Maine Association of Sea Kayak Guides and Instructors. ⊕ *maskgi.org.* **Maine Island Trail Association.** ⊠ *100 Kensington St., 2nd fl., Portland* ☎ *207/761–8225* ⊕ *www.mita.org.*

Hotels

Beachfront and roadside motels, historic-home B&Bs and inns, as well as a handful of newer boutique hotels, make up the majority of lodging along the Maine Coast. There are a few larger

luxury resorts, such as the Samoset Resort in Rockport or the Bar Harbor Inn in Bar Harbor, but most accommodations are simple, comfortable, and relatively inexpensive. You will find some chain hotels in larger cities and towns, including major tourist destinations like Portland, Freeport, and Bar Harbor. Many properties close during the off-season (mid-October–mid-May); those that stay open year-round often drop their rates dramatically after high season. (It is often possible to negotiate a nightly rate with smaller establishments during low season.) There is a 9% state hospitality tax on all room rates. *Hotel reviews have been shortened. For full reviews visit Fodors.com.*

What It Costs in U.S. Dollars			
$	$$	$$$	$$$$
RESTAURANTS			
under $18	$18–$24	$25–$35	over $35
HOTELS			
under $200	$200–$299	$300–$399	over $399

Restaurants

Many breakfast spots along the coast open as early as 6 am to serve the working crowd, and as early as 4 am for fishermen. Lunch generally runs 11–2:30; dinner is usually served 5–9. Only in larger cities will you find full dinners offered much later than 9, although in larger towns you can usually find a bar or bistro with a limited menu available late into the evening.

Many restaurants in Maine are closed Monday. Resort areas make an exception to this in high season, but these eateries often shut down altogether in the off-season. *Unless otherwise noted in reviews, restaurants are open daily for lunch and dinner.*

Credit cards are generally accepted at restaurants throughout Maine, even in more modest establishments, but it's still a good idea to have cash on hand wherever you go, just in case.

The one signature meal on the Maine Coast is, of course, the lobster dinner. It typically includes a whole steamed lobster with drawn butter for dipping, a clam or seafood chowder, corn on the cob, coleslaw, and a bib. Lobster prices vary from day to day, but generally a full lobster dinner should cost around $25–$30, or about $18–$20 without all the extras.

Restaurant reviews have been shortened. For full reviews visit Fodors.com.

Visitor Information

CONTACTS Blue Hill Peninsula Chamber of Commerce. ☎ *207/374–3242* ⊕ *www.bluehillpeninsula.org.* **DownEast and Acadia Regional Tourism.** ✉ *7 Ames Way, Machias* ☎ *207/255–0983*, *888/665–3278* ⊕ *www.downeastacadia.com.* **Maine Lobster Marketing Collaborative.** ✉ *2 Union St., Suite 204, Portland* ☎ *207/541–9310* ⊕ *www.lobsterfrommaine.com.* **Southern Midcoast Maine Chamber.** ☎ *207/725–8797* ⊕ *www.midcoastmaine.com.* **State of Maine Visitor Information Center.** ☎ *800/767–8709* ⊕ *www.mainetourism.com.*

Kittery

65 miles north of Boston, 3 miles north of Portsmouth, New Hampshire.

Known as the "Gateway to Maine," Kittery has become primarily a major shopping destination thanks to its massive complex of factory outlets. Flanking both sides of U.S. 1 are more than 120 stores, which attract serious shoppers year-round. But Kittery has more to offer than just retail therapy: head east on Route 103 to the area around **Kittery Point**

to experience the great outdoors. Here you'll find hiking and biking trails, as well as fantastic views of Portsmouth, New Hampshire, Whaleback Ledge Lighthouse, and the nearby Isles of Shoals. The isles and the light, along with two others, can be seen from two forts near this winding stretch of Route 103: Fort McClary State Historic Site and Fort Foster, a town park (both closed to vehicles off-season).

GETTING HERE AND AROUND
Three bridges—on U.S. 1, U.S. 1 Bypass, and Interstate 95—cross the Piscataqua River from Portsmouth, New Hampshire, to Kittery. Interstate 95 has three Kittery exits. Route 103 is a scenic coastal drive through Kittery Point to York.

ESSENTIALS
VISITOR INFORMATION
Kittery Visitor Information Center ✉ *Kittery* ☎ *207/439–1319* ⊕ *www.mainetourism.com.*

 Restaurants

Anju Noodle Bar
$ | ASIAN FUSION | With a cozy, open-plan dining area and a laid-back atmosphere, Anju Noodle Bar serves up reimagined versions of traditional dishes such as house-made slow-roasted pork shoulder buns, spicy miso ramen, and inspired local seafood dishes. This is one of the few places in the Pine Tree State outside Portland where you'll find fresh and innovative Asian-inspired cuisine done really well. **Known for:** sake heaven; free-style dishes; house-made kimchi. ⑤ *Average main: $15* ✉ *7 Wallingford Sq., Unit 102* ☎ *207/703–4298* ⊕ *www.anjunoodlebar.com* ☉ *Closed Mon.*

Chauncey Creek Lobster Pier
$$$ | SEAFOOD | FAMILY | From the road you can barely see the red roof hovering below the trees, but chances are you can see the line of cars parked at this popular outdoor restaurant that has been serving up fresh lobster for more than 70 years.

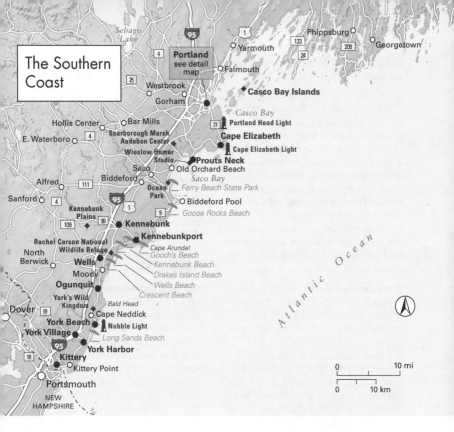

The Southern Coast

Sebago Lake

95

Portland
see detail
map

Yarmouth

Phippsburg

Georgetown

Westbrook

Falmouth

Gorham

Casco Bay Islands

Casco Bay

Portland Head Light

Hollis Center

Bar Mills

Scarborough Marsh
Audubon Center

Cape Elizabeth

E. Waterboro

Winslow Homer
Studio

Cape Elizabeth Light

Saco

Old Orchard Beach

Prouts Neck

Alfred

Biddeford

Saco Bay

Sanford

Ocean
Park

Ferry Beach State Park

Kennebunk
Plains

Biddeford Pool

Goose Rocks Beach

Kennebunk

Kennebunkport

Rachel Carson National
Wildlife Refuge

North
Berwick

Cape Arundel
Gooch's Beach

Wells

Kennebunk Beach

Moody

Drakes Island Beach

Ogunquit

Wells Beach

York's Wild
Kingdom

Crescent Beach

Dover

Bald Head

Cape Neddick

York Beach

Nubble Light

York Village

Long Sands Beach

York Harbor

Kittery

Kittery Point

Portsmouth

NEW
HAMPSHIRE

Atlantic Ocean

0   10 mi

0   10 km

Brightly colored picnic tables fill the deck and enclosed eating areas sit atop the high banks of the tidal river, beside a working pier, which delivers fresh seafood straight to your plate. **Known for:** classic lobster dinners; BYOB; ocean-to-plate. $ *Average main: $25* ⊠ *16 Chauncey Creek Rd.* ☎ *207/439–1030* ⊕ *www.chaunceycreek.com* ⊗ *Closed Columbus Day–mid-May; closed Mon. post-Labor Day–Columbus Day.*

Activities

HIKING AND WALKING
Cutts Island Trail
HIKING/WALKING | For a peek into the Rachel Carson National Wildlife Refuge, this scenic 1.8-mile upland trail leads into the 800-acre Brave Boat Harbor Division and is a prime bird-watching area. There's a restroom and an information kiosk at

the trailhead. The trail is open dawn–dusk year-round; dogs are not allowed. ⊠ *Seapoint Rd.* ☎ *207/646–9226* ⊕ *www.fws. gov/refuge/rachel_carson.*

The Yorks

8 miles north of Kittery via I–95, U.S. 1, and U.S. 1A.

Spending an afternoon in York Village is like going back in time—and you really only need a couple of hours here to roam the historic streets of this pint-size but worthwhile town. One of the first permanent settlements in Maine, the village museums detail its rich history. York is also home to the flagship store of Stonewall Kitchen, one of Maine's signature gourmet-food purveyors; the store has a café and a cooking school. There's also a cluster of vibrant contemporary-art galleries.

A short distance from the village proper, York Harbor opens to the water and offers many places to linger and explore. The harbor itself is busy with boats of all kinds, while the sandy harbor beach is good for swimming. Much quieter and more formal than York Beach to the north, this area has a somewhat exclusive air. Perched along the cliffs on the north side of the harbor are huge "cottages" built by wealthy summer residents in the late 1800s, when the area became a premier seaside resort destination with several grand hotels.

York Beach is a real family destination, devoid of all things staid and stuffy— children are meant to be both seen and heard here. Just beyond the sands of Short Sands Beach are a host of amusements, from bowling to indoor minigolf and the Fun-O-Rama arcade. Nubble Light is at the tip of the peninsula separating Long Sands and Short Sands beaches. The latter is mostly lined with unpretentious seasonal homes, with motels and restaurants mixed in.

GETTING HERE AND AROUND

York is Exit 7 off Interstate 95; follow signs to U.S. 1, the modern commercial strip. From here, U.S. 1A will take you to the village center and on to York Harbor and York Beach before looping back up to U.S. 1 in Cape Neddick.

After passing through York Village to York Harbor (originally called Lower Town), U.S. 1A winds around and heads north to York Beach's village center, a 4-mile trip.

It's a scenic 6 miles to York Beach via the loop road, U.S. 1A, from its southern intersection with U.S. 1. Although 2 miles longer, it's generally faster to continue north on U.S. 1A to Cape Neddick and then U.S 1A south to the village center, home to Short Sands Beach. Here U.S. 1A is known as Ocean Avenue as it heads north from York Harbor along Long

Sands Beach en route to York Beach village and Short Sands Beach.

A trolley along U.S. 1 links the beaches in summer. You can also get from beach to beach on a series of residential streets that wind around Nubble Point between these beaches.

ESSENTIALS

VISITOR INFORMATION

Greater York Region Chamber of Commerce. ☎ 207/363–4422 ⊕ www.gatewayto-maine.org. **York Trolley Co.** ☎ 207/363–9600 ⊕ www.yorktrolley.com.

 Sights

Cliff Walk and Fisherman's Walk

TRAIL | Two walking trails begin near Harbor Beach. Starting in a small nearby park, the Cliff Walk ascends its granite namesake and passes the summer "cottages" at the harbor entrance. There are some steps, but, as signs caution, tread carefully because of erosion. Fisherman's Walk, on the other hand, is an easy stroll. Starting across Stage Neck Road from the beach, it passes waterfront businesses, historic homes, and rocky harbor beaches on the way to York's beloved Wiggly Bridge. This pedestrian suspension bridge alongside Route 103 (there is minimal parking here) leads to Steedman Woods, a public preserve with a shaded loop trail along the York River estuary's ambling waters. You can also enter the preserve near the George Marshall Store in York Village. ✉ Stage Neck Rd., off U.S. 1A, York.

George Marshall Store Gallery

ARTS VENUE | The storefront windows and beadboard trim at the George Marshall Store Gallery (built in 1867) pay homage to its past as a general store, but the focus here is on the present. Changing exhibits, installations, and educational programs focus on prominent and up-and-coming regional artists. ✉ 140 Lindsay Rd. ☎ 207/351–1083 ⊕ www.georgemarshallstoregallery.com.

Museums of Old York

HISTORIC SITE | FAMILY | Nine historic 18th- and 19th-century buildings, clustered on York Street and along Lindsay Road and the York River, highlight York's rich history, which dates back to early Colonial times. The Old York Gaol (1719) was once the King's Prison for the Province of Maine; inside are dungeons, cells, and the jailer's quarters. The many period rooms in the Emerson-Wilcox House, the main part of which was built in 1742, display items from daily life here in centuries past, including furniture from the 1600s and an impressive ceramic dishware collection. The 1731 Elizabeth Perkins House reflects the Victorian style of its last occupants, the prominent Perkins family. Start your visit at the museum's visitor center, located at 3 Lindsay Road in the Remick Barn at the corner of U.S. 1A and Lindsay Road in York. ⊠ *Visitor center, 3 Lindsay Rd.* ☎ *207/363–1756* ⊕ *www.oldyork.org* ⊠ *From $8.*

★ Nubble Light

HISTORIC SITE | On a small island just off the tip of the cape in York Beach jutting dramatically into the Atlantic Ocean between Long Sands Beach and Short Sands Beach, Nubble Light is one of the most photographed lighthouses on the globe. Direct access is prohibited, but the small Sohier Park right across from the light has parking, historical placards, benches, and a seasonal information center that shares the 1879 light's history. ⊠ *End of Nubble Rd., off U.S. 1A, York Beach* ☎ *207/363–1040 (Memorial Day weekend–Labor Day)* ⊕ *www. nubblelight.org.*

Sayward-Wheeler House

HISTORIC SITE | Built in 1718, the waterfront home was remodeled in the 1760s by Jonathan Sayward, a local merchant who had prospered in the West Indies trade. By 1860 his descendants had opened the house to the public to share the story of their Colonial ancestors. Accessible only by guided tour (second and fourth Saturdays June–October 15, 11–4), the house reveals the decor of a prosperous New England family at the outset of the Revolutionary War. The parlor—considered one of the country's best-preserved Colonial interiors, with a tall clock and mahogany Chippendale-style chairs—looks pretty much as it did when Sayward lived here. ⊠ *9 Barrell La. Ext., York Harbor* ☎ *207/384–2454* ⊕ *www.historicnewengland.org* ⊠ *$10* ⊙ *Closed mid-Oct.–May.*

Stonewall Kitchen

STORE/MALL | You've probably seen the kitchen's smartly labeled jars of gourmet chutneys, jams, jellies, salsas, and sauces in specialty stores back home. This complex houses the expansive flagship company store, which has a viewing area of the bottling process and stunning gardens. Sample all the mustards, salsas, and dressings you can stand, or have lunch at the café and take-out restaurant. The campus also houses a cooking school where you can join in evening or daytime courses. Reservations are required; most classes are shorter than two hours and cost $55–$80. ⊠ *2 Stonewall La., off U.S. 1* ☎ *207/351–2712* ⊕ *www.stonewallkitchen.com/yorstore. html.*

York's Wild Kingdom

AMUSEMENT PARK/WATER PARK | FAMILY | Surrounded by forest, this popular zoo has more than 50 species of exotic animals, including lions, kangaroos, ring-tail lemurs, zebras, and numerous monkeys. There's a nostalgic charm to the amusement park, which includes bumper cars, food, and games, and a Ferris wheel with an ocean view, and offers discounts for kids under 10. ⊠ *1 Animal Park Rd., off U.S. 1, York Beach* ☎ *207/363–4911* ⊕ *www.yorkswildkingdom.com* ⊠ *From $12.*

🍴 Restaurants

Dockside Restaurant

$$$ | SEAFOOD | On an islandlike peninsula overlooking York Harbor, this restaurant has plenty of seafood on the menu. Floor-to-ceiling windows in the stepped modern dining space transport diners to the water beyond—every seat has a water view. **Known for:** "drunken" lobster (sautéed lobster, scallops, shallots, and herbs in an Irish-whiskey cream); beef tenderloin; lively, dockside vibe with spectacular views. ⑤ *Average main: $25* ⊠ *22 Harris Island Rd., off Rte. 103, York Harbor* ☎ *207/363–2722* ⊕ *www.dockside-restaurant.com* ☉ *Closed Tues. in summer and late Oct.–mid-May.*

Foster's Downeast Clambake

$$$ | SEAFOOD | FAMILY | Save your appetite for this one. Specializing in the traditional Maine clambake—a feast consisting of rich clam chowder, a pile of mussels and steamers, Maine lobster with drawn butter for dipping, corn on the cob, roasted potatoes and onions, and Maine blueberry crumb cake (phew!)—this massive complex provides musical entertainment to go with its belly-busting meals. **Known for:** finger-licking barbecue; classic Maine fare; gatherings for groups of families and friends. ⑤ *Average main: $28* ⊠ *5 Axholme Rd., at U.S. 1A, York Harbor* ☎ *207/363–3255, 800/552–0242* ⊕ *www.fostersclambake.com* ☉ *Closed early Sept.–late May, and weekdays late May–mid-June.*

The Goldenrod

$ | AMERICAN | FAMILY | People line the windows to watch Goldenrod Kisses being made the same way they have since 1896—and thousands of pounds are made every year at this restaurant that is Maine's oldest. Aside from the famous taffy (there's penny candy, too), this eatery is family oriented, very reasonably priced, and a great place to get homemade ice cream from the old-fashioned soda fountain. **Known for:** laid-back, kid-friendly atmosphere; breakfast served all day; classic American fare, like burgers, hot dogs, and baked dinners. ⑤ *Average main: $10* ⊠ *2 Railroad Ave., York Beach* ☎ *207/363–2621* ⊕ *www.thegoldenrod.com* ☉ *Closed mid-Oct.–mid-May.*

Hotels

Atlantic House Inn

$ | B&B/INN | FAMILY | In a nicely renovated 1888 beauty, this inn's standard guest rooms feel fresh with designer fabrics, gas fireplaces, and large tubs for a relaxing soak. **Pros:** lots of amenities; walk to beach, shops; suites are a good choice for weekly stay; some ocean views. **Cons:** not on beach; lacks public spaces; some rooms have a two-night minimum. ⑤ *Rooms from: $170* ⊠ *2 Beach St., York Beach* ☎ *207/361–6677* ⊕ *www.atlantichouseinn.com* ☉ *Closed Nov.–Apr.* ⟿ *16 rooms* ⦿ *No meals.*

★ Cliff House

$$$$ | HOTEL | FAMILY | This already luxurious hotel overlooking the Atlantic Ocean—you can watch the white crests smash the craggy bluffs below while nestled in your hooded flannel robe on your balcony—refreshed its rooms in a recent renovation. **Pros:** the view, the views, the views; rooms have private terraces; plenty of activities to keep everyone busy. **Cons:** communal coffee station on each floor only (but this is to help reduce waste); meals not included; central location means a drive to the nearest town centers. ⑤ *Rooms from: $600* ⊠ *591 Shore Rd., Cape Neddick* ☎ *207/361–1000* ⊕ *www.cliffhouse-maine.com* ⟿ *226 rooms* ⦿ *No meals.*

Inn at Tanglewood Hall

$$ | B&B/INN | This 1880s shingle-style "cottage" is a haven of antiques, art, and eclectic decor and comfort—artfully painted floors, lush wallpaper, and meticulous attention to detail are the fruits of a former designation as a designers' showcase home. **Pros:** authentic historic lodging; short walk to beaches; fireplaces in all rooms. **Cons:** no water views; dated decor consistent with historic property; no pets or children under 12. ⑤ *Rooms from: $175* ✉ *611 York St., York Harbor* ☎ *207/351–1075* ⊕ *www.tanglewoodhall. com* ⌁ *6 rooms* ⦿❙ *Free breakfast.*

★ Stage Neck Inn

$$$ | **RESORT** | **FAMILY** | A family-run operation that is now in the competent hands of the second generation, this resort hotel takes full advantage of its gorgeous harborside location, with Adirondack chairs, chaise longues and a fire pit on the surrounding lawns, water views from most guest rooms, and floor-to-ceiling windows in the common spaces. **Pros:** elaborate full-breakfast buffet with scrumptious baked goods; poolside service and snack bar in season; rooms have balconies or deck areas and most have water views. **Cons:** spa is on the smaller side; some rooms have only partial water views; rooms with two beds have doubles rather than queens. ⑤ *Rooms from: $300* ✉ *8 Stage Neck Rd., off U.S. 1A, York Harbor* ☎ *800/340–1130, 207/363–3850* ⊕ *www.stageneck.com* ⦿ *Closed 1st 2 wks in Jan.* ⌁ *60 rooms* ⦿❙ *Free breakfast.*

York Harbor Inn

$$ | **B&B/INN** | A mid-17th-century fishing cabin with dark timbers and a fieldstone fireplace forms the heart of this historic inn, which now includes several neighboring buildings. **Pros:** many rooms have harbor views; close to beaches; scenic walking trails; kid-friendly. **Cons:** rooms vary greatly in style, size, and appeal; no ocean views at the Chapman House; some rooms are not pet friendly. ⑤ *Rooms from: $200* ✉ *480 York St., York Harbor* ☎ *207/363–5119* ⊕ *www. yorkharborinn.com* ⌁ *65 rooms* ⦿❙ *Free breakfast.*

 Shopping

Gateway Farmers' Market

OUTDOOR/FLEA/GREEN MARKETS | Bring your own bag for morning shopping at the Gateway Farmers' Market, held in the back lot at the Greater York Region Chamber of Commerce in summer (Saturday June–October, 9 am–1 pm), and inside the building in winter (designated Saturdays November–March, 9 am–1 pm). You'll find fresh local produce, lots of baked goods and artisanal breads, local seafood and meat, fresh flowers, and handcrafted items like soaps and candles. It's a good place to gather the makings for a beach picnic or to stock up on holiday gifts. ✉ *1 Stonewall La., off U.S. 1, York* ☎ *207/363–4422* ⊕ *gateway-tomaine.org.*

Ocean Fire Pottery

CRAFTS | This artist-owned and-operated studio and gallery features unique wheel-thrown stoneware. Live demonstrations are available daily; call ahead to make sure the studio is open during the off-season. ✉ *23 Woodbridge Rd.* ☎ *207/361–3131* ⊕ *www.oceanfirepottery.com.*

 Activities

BIKING

Berger's Bike Shop

BICYCLING | This former auto garage and full-service bike shop rents hybrid bikes for local excursions and sells bikes of all kinds. ✉ *241 York St., York* ☎ *207/363–4070* ⊕ *www.bergersbikeshop.com.*

FISHING

For a list of fishing charters, check the directory on the Maine Fishing Guides website (⊕ *www.maineguides.com/ activity/fishing-guides*).

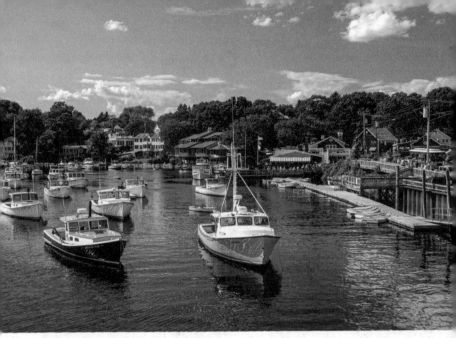

Ogunquit's Perkins Cove is a pleasant place to admire the boats (and wonder at the origin of their names).

Ogunquit

8 miles north of the Yorks via U.S. 1.

A resort village since the late 19th century, Ogunquit made a name for itself as an artists' colony. Today it has become a mini Provincetown, with a gay population that swells in summer, and many inns and small clubs cater to a primarily gay and lesbian clientele. The nightlife in Ogunquit revolves around the precincts of Ogunquit Square and Perkins Cove, where people stroll, often enjoying an after-dinner ice cream cone or espresso. For a scenic drive, take Shore Road from downtown to the 175-foot Bald Head Cliff; you'll be treated to views up and down the coast. On a stormy day the surf can be quite wild here.

GETTING HERE AND AROUND

Parking in the village and at the beach is costly and limited, so leave your car at the hotel or in a public parking space and hop the trolley. It costs $2 per trip and runs Memorial Day weekend–Columbus Day, with weekend-only service during the first few weeks. From Perkins Cove, the trolley runs through town along Shore Road and then down to Ogunquit Beach; it also stops along U.S. 1.

ESSENTIALS

TRANSPORTATION INFORMATION Shoreline Explorer. ☎ *800/965–5762* ⊕ *www. shorelineexplorer.com.*

VISITOR INFORMATION Ogunquit Chamber of Commerce. ☎ *207/646–1279* ⊕ *www. ogunquit.org.*

Sights

Marginal Way

PROMENADE | This mile-long, paved footpath hugs the shore of a rocky promontory known as Israels Head. Thirty-nine benches along the easygoing path allow you to appreciate the open sea vistas. Expect heavy foot traffic, even in the off-season—which is the only time of the year that dogs are allowed. ✉ *Perkins Cove Rd.* ⊕ *www.marginalwayfund.org.*

Perkins Cove

HISTORIC SITE | FAMILY | This neck of land off Shore Road in the lower part of Ogunquit village has a jumble of sea-weathered fish houses and buildings that were part of an art school. These have largely been transformed by the tide of tourism into shops and restaurants. When you've had your fill of browsing, stroll out along the mile-long Marginal Way. ✉ *Perkins Cove Rd., off Shore Rd.*

🍽 Restaurants

Amore Breakfast

$ | AMERICAN | You could hardly find a more satisfying, heartier breakfast than at this smart and busy joint just shy of the entrance to Perkins Cove where a lighthearted mix of retro advertising signs adorn the walls of the bright, open, and bustling dining room. The cornedbeef hash is made with tender pulled brisket with spices and just a bit of diced potatoes and onions—try it topped with hollandaise in the Irish Benedict. **Known for:** innovative, rotating breakfast menus; bustling, laid-back atmosphere; chockfull of locals; community involvement. $ *Average main: $10 ✉ 87 Main St.* ✛ *At blinking light* ☎ *207/646–6667* ⊕ *www.amorebreakfast.com* ⊘ *Closed mid-Dec.–early Apr. No dinner.*

★ **Northern Union**

$$$ | CONTEMPORARY | From the moment you walk into Northern Union you know you're going to be in very good hands. A genuine, welcoming staff and laid-back yet elegant design scheme put you in the mood for a slow, very memorable dinner consisting of seasonally inspired small plates like braised pork belly or duck confit and rotating entrées like seared scallops and lobster fettuccine with spot-on wine pairings that you won't find anywhere else in the area. **Known for:** almost

everything is made in-house; dishes that can easily be shared; a terrific selection of cured meats and cheese boards with a local, seasonal bent. $ *Average main: $27 ✉ 261 Shore Rd.* ☎ *207/216–9639* ⊕ *www.northern-union.me* ⊘ *No lunch.*

☕ Coffee and Quick Bites

Backyard Coffeehouse and Eatery

$ | AMERICAN | This eager-to-please coffee shop is centrally located and a good stop for hot or iced coffee accompanied by a scone or bagel. For something more substantial, choose from a selection of breakfast or lunch sandwiches. **Known for:** locally sourced coffee, tea, and bagels; close to Marginal Way walking path; the North Country bacon, egg, and cheese breakfast sandwich. $ *Average main: $5 ✉ 178 Main St.* ☎ *207/251–4554* ⊕ *www.backyardogunquit.com* ⊘ *Closed mid-Oct.–Apr.*

Wells

5 miles north of Ogunquit via U.S. 1.

Lacking any kind of discernible village center, Wells could be easily overlooked as nothing more than a commercial stretch of U.S. 1 between Ogunquit and the Kennebunks. But look more closely: this is a place where people come to enjoy some of the best beaches on the coast. Until 1980 the town of Wells incorporated Ogunquit, and today this family-oriented beach community has 7 miles of densely populated shoreline, along with nature preserves, where you can explore salt marshes and tidal pools.

GETTING HERE AND AROUND
Just $2 per trip, the seasonal Shoreline Trolley serves Wells Beach and Crescent Beach and has many stops along U.S. 1 at motels, campgrounds, restaurants, and so on. You can also catch it at the Wells Transportation Center when Amtrak's *Downeaster* pulls in.

ESSENTIALS

The Shoreline Trolley is part of the Shoreline Explorer network, which links seasonal trolleys in southern Maine beach towns from York to the Kennebunks, including the Wells area.

VISITOR INFORMATION Wells Chamber of Commerce. ☎ *207/646–2451* ⊕ *www.wellschamber.org.*

Sights

Rachel Carson National Wildlife Refuge

NATURE PRESERVE | FAMILY | At the headquarters of the Rachel Carson National Wildlife Refuge, which has 11 divisions from Kittery to Cape Elizabeth, is the Carson Trail, a 1-mile loop. The trail traverses a salt marsh and a white-pine forest where migrating birds and waterfowl of many varieties are regularly spotted, and it borders Branch Brook and the Merriland River. ⊠ *321 Port Rd.* ☎ *207/646–9226* ⊕ *www.fws.gov/refuge/rachel_carson.*

Beaches

Crescent Beach

BEACH—SIGHT | FAMILY | Lined with summer homes, this sandy strand is busy in the summer, but the beach and the water are surprisingly clean, considering all the traffic. The swimming's good, and beachgoers can also explore tidal pools and look for seals on the sea rocks nearby. **Amenities:** food and drink; lifeguards; parking (fee); toilets. **Best for:** swimming. ⊠ *Webhannet Dr., south of Mile Rd.* ☎ *207/646–5113.*

Drakes Island Beach

BEACH—SIGHT | FAMILY | Smaller and quieter than the other two beaches in Wells, Drakes Island Beach is also a little more natural, with rolling sand dunes and access to salt-marsh walking trails at an adjacent estuary. The ice-cream truck swings by regularly in the

summer. **Amenities:** lifeguards; parking (fee); toilets. **Best for:** walking. ⊠ *Island Beach Rd., 1 mile southwest of U.S. 1* ☎ *207/646–5113.*

Wells Beach

BEACH—SIGHT | FAMILY | The northern end of a 2-mile stretch of golden sand, Wells Beach is popular with families and surfers, who line up in the swells and preen on the boardwalk near the arcade and snack shop. The beach's northern tip is a bit quieter, with a long rock jetty perfect for strolling. **Amenities:** food and drink; lifeguards; parking (fee); toilets. **Best for:** surfing; walking. ⊠ *Atlantic Ave., north of Mile Rd.* ☎ *207/646–5113.*

Wheels and Waves

STORE/MALL | Rent bikes, surfboards, wet suits, boogie boards, kayaks, and all sorts of outdoor gear at Wheels and Waves. ⊠ *365 Post Rd., U.S. 1* ☎ *207/646–5774* ⊕ *www.wheelsnwaves.com.*

🍴 Restaurants

Billy's Chowder House

$ | SEAFOOD | FAMILY | Locals and vacationers head to this roadside seafood restaurant in the midst of a salt marsh en route to Wells Beach. The menu features classic seafood dishes like lobster rolls and chowders, but there are plenty of nonseafood choices, too. **Known for:** views of the Rachel Carson National Wildlife Refuge; generous lobster rolls; one of the oldest waterfront restaurants in Wells. ⑤ *Average main: $19* ⊠ *216 Mile Rd.* ☎ *207/646–7558* ⊕ *www.billyschowderhouse.com* ⊘ *Closed mid-Dec.–mid-Jan.*

★ Bitter End

$$ | SEAFOOD | Pete and Kate Morency, the duo originally behind the ever-popular Pier 77 and the Ramp Bar and Grill in Kennebunkport, are also the masterminds behind this fabulous seafood spot that serves up brilliant, contemporary twists to American and Mediterranean

classics, adding spins on staples such as fish-and-chips (think tempura batter with turmeric breading and tidewater coleslaw). The fabulous decor consists of an unlikely marriage of old-school American sports memorabilia and something that might be described as shabby ballroom chic—crystal chandeliers hang above old leather boxing gloves, and black-and-white photos of sports icons and an array of shiny trophies (including a 1961 Miss Universe cup) line the bar. **Known for:** cuisine fusion and a rotating menu; outdoor seating area with firepit; superbly curated bevy of liquors. $ *Average main: $18 ⊠ 2118 Post Rd. ☎ 207/360–0904 ⊕ www.bitterend.me ⊗ Closed Tues.*

Maine Diner

$ | **DINER** | One look at the 1953 exterior and you'll start craving diner food, but be prepared to get a little more than you bargained for: after all, how many greasy spoons make an award-winning lobster pie? There's plenty of fried seafood in addition to the usual diner fare, and breakfast is served all day. **Known for:** classic Maine diner fare; wild Maine blueberry pie; diner has a vegetable garden, which it uses as much as possible in the creation of its dishes. $ *Average main: $15 ⊠ 2265 Post Rd. ☎ 207/646–4441 ⊕ www.mainediner. com ⊗ Closed at least 1 wk in Jan.*

Spinnakers

$$ | **SEAFOOD** | **FAMILY** | Plenty of seafood shacks dot U.S. 1, but this roadside joint is really worth the stop, even if it's just to grab an ice-cream cone to escape the steady flow of summer traffic. Simple but pleasing contemporary design makes for a cheerful space to enjoy loaded lobster rolls, burgers and sandwiches, and a decidedly unholy lobster poutine consisting of hand-cut fries covered in a delicious mess of local cheese curds and topped with lobster gravy. **Known for:** pick-and-choose seafood basket combos; quick bites that pack a punch and scream Maine; eat in or grab something to go from the take-out window. $ *Average main: $18 ⊠ 139 Post Rd. ☎ 207/216–9291 ⊕ spinnakersmaine.com ⊗ Closed Mon. and Tues.*

Coffee and Quick Bites

Congdon's Doughnuts

$ | **AMERICAN** | **FAMILY** | These superior doughnuts have been made by the same family since 1945 and at the same location since 1955. Congdon's has about 40 different varieties, some seasonal, though the plain variety really gives you an idea of just how good these doughnuts are: it's the biggest seller, along with the honey dipped and black raspberry jelly. $ *Average main: $3 ⊠ 1090 Post Rd. ☎ 207/646–4219 ⊕ www.congdons. com ⊗ Closed Mon.–Wed. No dinner.*

Hotels

Haven by the Sea

$$ | **B&B/INN** | Once the summer mission of St. Martha's Church in Kennebunkport, this exquisite inn has retained many original details from its former life as a seaside church, including cathedral ceilings and stained-glass windows. **Pros:** unusual structure with elegant appointments; beach towels and beach chairs available; rotating breakfasts that cater to dietary restrictions without compromising taste; nightly happy hour with complimentary appetizers and courtesy sherry, port, and brandy in the main parlor. **Cons:** not an in-town location; distant ocean views; $50 cancellation fee no matter how far in advance. $ *Rooms from: $260 ⊠ 59 Church St. ☎ 207/646–4194 ⊕ www. havenbythesea.com ⇨ 9 rooms ⊘ Free breakfast.*

7

The Maine Coast WELLS

Kennebunk and Kennebunkport

5 miles north of Wells via U.S. 1.

The town centers of Kennebunk and Kennebunkport are separated by 5 miles and two rivers, but united by a common history and a laid-back seaside vibe. Perhaps best described as the Hamptons of the Pine Tree State, Kennebunkport has been a resort area since the 19th century. Its most recent residents have made it even more famous: the dynastic Bush family is often in residence on its immense estate here, which sits dramatically out on Walker's Point on Cape Arundel. Newer homes have sprung up alongside the old, and a great way to take them all in is with a slow drive out Ocean Avenue along the cape.

Sometimes bypassed on the way to its sister town, Kennebunk has its own appeal. Once a major shipbuilding center, Kennebunk today retains the feel of a classic New England small town, with an inviting shopping district, steepled churches, and fine examples of 18th- and 19th-century brick and clapboard homes. There are also plenty of natural spaces for walking, swimming, birding, and biking, and the Kennebunks' major beaches are here.

GETTING HERE AND AROUND

Kennebunk's main village sits along U.S. 1, extending west from the Mousam River. The Lower Village is along Routes 9 and 35, 4 miles down Route 35 from the main village, and the drive between the two keeps visitors agog with the splendor of the area's mansions, spread out on both sides of Route 35. To get to the grand and gentle beaches of Kennebunk, continue straight (the road becomes Beach Avenue) at the intersection with Route 9. If you turn left instead, Route 9 will take you across the Kennebunk River, into Kennebunkport's touristy downtown,

called Dock Square (or sometimes just "the Port"), a commercial area with restaurants, shops, boat cruises, and galleries. Here you'll find the most activity (and crowds) in the Kennebunks.

Take the Intown Trolley for narrated 45-minute jaunts that run daily from Memorial Day weekend through Columbus Day. The $18 fare is valid for the day, so you can hop on and off—or start your journey—at any of the stops. The route includes Kennebunk's beaches and Lower Village as well as neighboring Kennebunkport's scenery and sights. The main stop is at 21 Ocean Avenue in Kennebunkport, around the corner from Dock Square.

ESSENTIALS

VISITOR INFORMATION Intown Trolley. ☎ *207/967–3686* ⊕ *www.intowntrolley. com.* **Kennebunk-Kennebunkport Chamber of Commerce.** ☎ *207/967–0857* ⊕ *www. gokennebunks.com.*

WALKING TOURS

To take a little walking tour of Kennebunk's most notable structures, begin at the Federal-style Brick Store Museum at 117 Main Street. Head south on Main Street (turn left out of the museum) to see several extraordinary 18th- and early-19th-century homes, including the **Lexington Elms** at No. 99 (1799), the **Horace Porter House** at No. 92 (1848), and the **Benjamin Brown House** at No. 85 (1788).

When you've had your fill of historic homes, head back up toward the museum, pass the 1773 **First Parish Unitarian Church** (its Asher Benjamin–style steeple contains an original Paul Revere bell), and turn right onto **Summer Street.** This street is an architectural showcase, revealing an array of styles from Colonial to Federal. Walking past these grand beauties will give you a real sense of the economic prowess and glamour of the long-gone shipbuilding industry.

For a guided 90-minute architectural walking tour of Summer Street, contact the museum at ☎ *207/985–4802*. Tours are offered Saturday, May through November, and other days by calling ahead. You can also purchase a $4.95 map that marks historic buildings or a $15.95 guidebook, *Windows on the Past.*

For a dramatic walk along Kennebunkport's rocky coastline and beneath the views of Ocean Avenue's grand mansions, head out on the **Parson's Way Shore Walk,** a paved 4.8-mile round-trip. Begin at Dock Square and follow Ocean Avenue along the river, passing the Colony Hotel and St. Ann's Church, all the way to Walker's Point. Simply turn back from here.

 # Sights

Brick Store Museum

MUSEUM | FAMILY | The cornerstone of this block-long preservation of early-19th-century commercial and residential buildings is William Lord's Brick Store. Built as a dry-goods store in 1825 in the Federal style, the building has an openwork balustrade across the roofline, granite lintels over the windows, and paired chimneys. Exhibits chronicle the Kennebunk area's history and Early American decorative and fine arts. Museum staff lead architectural walking tours of Kennebunk's National Historic District by appointment late May–September. ⊠ *117 Main St., Kennebunk* ☎ *207/985–4802* ⊕ *www. brickstoremuseum.org* ✉ *$7* ⊗ *Closed Mon.*

Dock Square

PLAZA | Clothing boutiques, T-shirt shops, art galleries, and restaurants line this bustling square, spreading out along the nearby streets and alleys. Walk onto the drawbridge to admire the tidal Kennebunk River; cross to the other side and you are in the Lower Village of neighboring Kennebunk. ⊠ *Dock Sq., Kennebunkport.*

First Families Kennebunkport Museum

HOUSE | FAMILY | Also known as White Columns, the imposing Greek Revival mansion with Doric columns is furnished with the belongings of four generations of the Perkins-Nott family. From mid-July through mid-October, the 1853 house is open for guided tours and also serves as a gathering place for village walking tours. It is owned by the Kennebunkport Historical Society, which has several other historical buildings a mile away at 125–135 North Street, including an old jail and schoolhouse. ⊠ *8 Maine St., Kennebunkport* ☎ *207/967–2751* ⊕ *www. kporths.com* ✉ *$10.*

First Parish of Kennebunk Unitarian Universalist Church

RELIGIOUS SITE | FAMILY | Built in 1773, just before the American Revolution, this stunning church is a marvel. The 1804 Asher Benjamin–style steeple stands proudly atop the village, and the sounds of the original Paul Revere bell can be heard for miles. The church holds Sunday service at 9:30 am in the summer (at 10:30 the rest of the year). ⊠ *114 Main St., Kennebunk* ☎ *207/985–3700* ⊕ *www. uukennebunk.org.*

Kennebunk Plains

NATURE PRESERVE | FAMILY | For an unusual experience, visit this 135-acre grasslands habitat that is home to several rare and endangered species. Locals call it Blueberry Plains, and a good portion of the area is abloom with the hues of ripening wild blueberries in late July; after August 1, you are welcome to pick and eat all the berries you can find. The area is maintained by the Nature Conservancy. ⊠ *Webber Hill Rd., Kennebunk* ✛ *4½ miles northwest of town* ☎ *207/729–5181* ⊕ *www.nature.org.*

Seashore Trolley Museum

MUSEUM | FAMILY | Streetcars were built here from 1872 to 1972, including trolleys for major metropolitan areas— from Boston to Budapest, New York to Nagasaki, and San Francisco to Sydney. Many of them are beautifully restored and displayed. Best of all, you can take a nearly 4-mile ride on the tracks of the former Atlantic Shoreline trolley line, with a stop along the way at the museum restoration shop, where trolleys are transformed from junk into gems. The outdoor museum is self-guided. ⊠ 195 Log Cabin Rd., Kennebunkport 🕾 207/967–2800 ⊕ www.trolleymuseum. org 🖻 $12 ⊙ Closed Nov.–Apr. except 1st 2 weekends in Dec.

Beaches

Gooch's Beach
BEACH—SIGHT | FAMILY | Kennebunk has three beaches, one after another, along Beach Avenue, which is lined with cottages and old Victorians. The most northerly, and the closest to downtown Kennebunkport, is Gooch's Beach, the main swimming beach. Next is stony Kennebunk Beach, followed by Mother's Beach, which is popular with families. There's a small playground and tidal puddles for splashing; rock outcroppings lessen the waves. **Amenities:** lifeguards; parking (fee); toilets. **Best for:** walking; swimming. ⊠ Beach Ave., south of Rte. 9, Kennebunk.

Goose Rocks Beach
BEACH—SIGHT | Three-mile-long Goose Rocks, a 10-minute drive north of town, has a good long stretch of smooth sand and plenty of shallow pools for exploring. It's a favorite of families with small children. Pick up a $15 daily parking permit at the Kennebunkport Town Office on Elm Street; the Goose Rocks General Store at 3 Dyke Road; or the Police Department at 101 Main Street. Dogs are allowed (on a leash during the high season), but only before 8 am and after 6 pm. No facilities are available at the beach. **Amenities:** parking (fee). **Best for:** walking. ⊠ Dyke Rd., off Rte. 9, Kennebunkport ⊕ www. visitmaine.com.

🍴 Restaurants

The Boathouse Restaurant
$$$ | SEAFOOD | You can't get more up-close and personal with Kennebunkport's harbor than at this stunning waterside restaurant and bar that serves dressed-up, contemporary takes on classic Maine fare, alongside top-notch cocktails and staples such as perfectly shucked local oysters, lobster tacos, and hearty clam and corn chowder. The inside spaces are warm and welcoming, with a maritime theme that's not too over-the-top; the outdoor wraparound deck is one of the best spots in town to grab a cocktail and watch the sun set over the Kennebunk River. **Known for:** amazing waterside location; cocktails on the outdoor wraparound deck; great seafood. ⑤ Average main: $30 ⊠ 21 Ocean Ave., Kennebunkport 🕾 877/266–1304 ⊕ boathouseme.com.

The Burleigh at the Kennebunkport Inn
$$$ | SEAFOOD | Nautical accents give this trendy restaurant a laid-back vibe that is the perfect transition from a day out on the water (or at the beach) to a relaxed end-of-the-day meal. While fresh seafood plays a central role at the Burleigh, you can't go wrong with one of the excellent burgers or pork chops paired with one of the many rotating local craft-beer choices. **Known for:** the Burleigh burger (prime beef patty, cheddar cheese, smoked bacon, lettuce, tomato, onion, pickles, hand-cut fries); craft cocktails that will knock you off of your feet; excellent happy hour in the inn's Garden Social Club. ⑤ Average main: $30 ⊠ 1 Dock Sq., Kennebunkport 🕾 207/967–2621 ⊕ kennebunkportinn.com/dining.

Duffy's Tavern and Grill
$ | AMERICAN | Every small town needs its own lively and friendly tavern, and this bustling spot is Kennebunk's favorite, housed in a former shoe factory, with exposed brick, soaring ceilings, and hardwood floors; right outside are the

tumbling waters of the Mousam River as it flows from the dam. You'll find lots of comfortable standards, like burgers and pizza; the popular fish-and-chips and the tasty onion rings are hand-dipped. **Known for:** lively vibe that brings locals and visitors together; classic pub fare, such as fried calamari and hearty New England clam chowder; handcrafted pizzas. $ *Average main: $16* ⊠ *4 Main St., Kennebunk* ☎ *207/985–0050* ⊕ *www. duffyskennebunk.com.*

★ Earth at Hidden Pond

$$$$ | FUSION | This splurge-worthy place offers thoughtful attention to flavor and texture, using the freshest locally sourced ingredients—each and every dining experience at Hidden Pond feels like a special occasion. The seasonally inspired menu is always in flux, but you can be sure that even hard-core foodies will be delighted with this culinary experience. **Known for:** wood-fire surf-and-turf dishes; ingredients culled from its own garden; private dining sheds and cabanas for special occasions and groups. $ *Average main: $38* ⊠ *354 Goose Rocks Rd., Kennebunkport* ☎ *207/967–9050* ⊕ *hiddenpondmaine.com/earth.*

Mabel's Lobster Claw

$$$ | SEAFOOD | FAMILY | Since the 1950s, Mabel's has been serving lobsters (baked and in rolls), homemade pies, clam chowder, and lots of seafood for lunch and dinner in this tiny dwelling out on Ocean Avenue. The decor includes paneled walls, wooden booths, and autographed photos of various TV stars (and members of the Bush family), and there's outside seating. **Known for:** blueberry pie; Lobster Savannah: split and filled with scallops and shrimp, and baked in a Newburg sauce; take-out window where you can order ice cream and food. $ *Average main: $25* ⊠ *124 Ocean Ave., Kennebunkport* ☎ *207/967–2562* ⊕ *www. mabelslobster.com* ☉ *Closed Nov.–early Apr.*

★ Ocean Restaurant

$$$$ | SEAFOOD | One of the best seats in town to watch the sun set (or rise) over the Atlantic, the large picture windows at Ocean Restaurant envelope an intimate dining space that features a touch of seaside elegance coupled with captivating, original local art. The menu showcases Maine seafood and other local ingredients and is chock-full of sheer ambrosial delights, with contemporary takes on classic dishes, such as lobster thermidor, foie gras, swordfish, and seafood velouté. **Known for:** equally perfect for a romantic evening or a gathering of friends; gracious, old-world service; ridiculously indulgent desserts that you may want to eat first. $ *Average main: $40* ⊠ *208 Ocean Ave., Kennebunkport* ☎ *855/346–5700* ⊕ *capearundelinn.com.*

Pearl Kennebunk Beach and Spat Oyster Cellar

$$ | SEAFOOD | At this classy but cozy seafood-centric restaurant you'll be treated to stellar seasonal fare using ingredients harvested from the Maine coast. Start with craft cocktails at the large, elegant bar and then move to a table close to the massive stone hearth that is particularly inviting on cooler evenings. **Known for:** excellent daily drink specials from 5–6; rotating selection of specials; crispy panfried chicken dishes. $ *Average main: $22* ⊠ *27 Western Ave., Kennebunk* ☎ *207/204–0860* ⊕ *www.pearlkennebunk.com* ☉ *Closed Mon.–Wed.*

★ Pier 77 Restaurant

$$$ | AMERICAN | The phenomenal seaside view at this restaurant and bar shares center stage with the mouthwatering menu that features sophisticated fare with an emphasis on seafood. Located on the ground level, the restaurant's large windows overlook the harbor, ensuring that every seat has a nice view of the water; the tiny but oh-so-funky-and-fun Ramp Bar & Grill pays homage to a really good burger, fried seafood, and other pub-style classics. **Known for:** live

music in summer; great spot for cocktails on the water while watching boats and sea life pass by; a packed house almost every meal in the summer (reservations highly recommended). [$] *Average main: $25* ✉ *77 Pier Rd., Kennebunkport* ☎ *207/967–8500* ⊕ *www.pier77restaurant.com.*

★ **The Tides Beach Club Restaurant**

$$$ | SEAFOOD | This unfussy, beachside dining spot is decorated in soft maritime accents and a crisp color palette, perfect for a relaxing post-beach meal. The menu features lighter seafood fare and salads alongside heartier options, such as lobster rangoons, crispy fried chicken sandwich, and burgers, which are complemented by a list of delicious craft cocktails. **Known for:** no dress code—think beach-hair-don't-care chic; perfect for a prebeach bite or postbeach sit-down dining experience; exceptional service that isn't cloying. [$] *Average main: $26* ✉ *254 Kings Hwy., Kennebunkport* ☎ *207/967–3757* ⊕ *tidesbeachclubmaine.com/food.*

☕ Coffee and Quick Bites

Dock Square Coffee House

$ | AMERICAN | European-style coffee drinks, tea, pastries, smoothies, and other snacks are on the menu at this bright and cheerful shop in the midst of Dock Square. The coffee is sourced from Portland-based and nationally recognized Coffee By Design, one of the state's best. **Known for:** locally sourced coffee, pastries and breakfast sandwiches; avocado toast; central location. [$] *Average main: $5* ✉ *18 Dock Sq., Kennebunkport* ☎ *207/967–4422* ⊕ *www.docksquarecoffeehouse.biz* ⊗ *Closed Jan.–Mar.*

🛏 Hotels

★ **Cape Arundel Inn and Resort**

$$$ | B&B/INN | This shingle-style 19th-century mansion, originally one of the area's many summer "cottages," commands a magnificent ocean view that takes in the Bush estate at Walker's Point; its location is just far enough from the bustle of town to truly feel like you've gotten away from it all. **Pros:** exceptional staff that are gracious and discreet; luxurious beds and linens that will make you feel like a spring chicken upon waking; champagne welcome. **Cons:** not for the budget-minded; clubhouse amenities are ½ mile away from main house; some rooms without ocean views. [$] *Rooms from: $309* ✉ *208 Ocean Ave., Kennebunkport* ☎ *855/346–5700* ⊕ *www.capearundelinn.com* ⊗ *Closed Jan.* ⏎ *29 rooms* ⏺ *Free breakfast.*

★ **Hidden Pond**

$$$$ | RESORT | This unique resort hideaway, tucked away in a wooded, 60-acre enclave near Goose Rocks Beach, includes hiking trails, two pools, a spa, a phenomenal restaurant, and a working farm. **Pros:** use of beach facilities at the nearby Tides Beach Club, its sister property; complimentary beach shuttle and beach cruiser bikes; guests can cut fresh flowers and harvest vegetables from the property's many gardens; plenty of activities on-site including watercolor painting, children's activities, and fitness classes. **Cons:** steep prices; away from the center of town; no dogs allowed. [$] *Rooms from: $549* ✉ *354 Goose Rocks Rd., Kennebunkport* ☎ *207/967–9050* ⊕ *hiddenpondmaine.com* ⊗ *Closed Nov.–Apr.* ⏎ *46 units* ⏺ *No meals.*

★ **The Inn at English Meadows**

$$$ | B&B/INN | A stone's throw from the bustle of Kennebunkport and just a mile from the beach, this charming boutique B&B is housed in a gorgeously restored, historic 1860s farmhouse. **Pros:** luxurious bathroom amenities including rain showers and toiletries by Malin + Goetz; gas fireplaces in many rooms; home-baked goods available every afternoon. **Cons:** no pool; no water view; not wheelchair accessible. [$] *Rooms from: $339* ✉ *141 Port Rd., Kennebunk* ☎ *207/967–5766*

englishmeadowsinn.com 🛏 *11 rooms* 🍽 *Free breakfast.*

★ Sandy Pines Campground

$$ | RENTAL | The luxe "glamping" (glamorous camping) tents, camp cottages, and A-frame hideaway huts on wheels at Sandy Pines Campground deliver every bit as much comfort and luxury as a fine hotel (with a few caveats, including communal bathing areas), but give you a chance to get up close and personal with nature. **Pros:** the glamping areas of Sandy Pines are quiet zones; nightly bonfires under the stars without roughing it; all tents equipped with generous sitting areas that extend outside the tents. **Cons:** expect all that comes with being in nature; glamping tents are not pet-friendly; three-night minimum stay (seasonal). $ *Rooms from: $266* ✉ *277 Mills Rd., Kennebunkport* ☎ *207/967–2483* ⊕ *sandypinescamping.com* ☉ *Closed mid-Oct.–mid-May* 🛏 *60 units* 🍽 *No meals.*

The Tides Beach Club

$$$ | B&B/INN | The stately building that now houses the Tides Beach Club is a charming grande dame from the heyday of seaside "cure" retreats during the Gilded Age. Just steps from a long, sandy beach—like its sister property, Hidden Pond—this lively inn is the epitome of laid-back, seaside-chic design, which extends into each of the spacious, bungalowlike rooms that are decorated in rich, feel-good ocean blue and coral hues. **Pros:** use of the common spaces (pools, spa, garden) at the very exclusive Hidden Pond; beach service for a relaxed lunch or dinner on the sand; most of the rooms have ocean views and balconies. **Cons:** definitely will lighten your purse; a lot of activity in and around the inn; not pet-friendly. $ *Rooms from: $329* ✉ *254 Kings Hwy., Kennebunkport* ☎ *207/967–3757* ⊕ *tidesbeachclubmaine. com* ☉ *Closed Nov.–Apr.* 🛏 *21 rooms* 🍽 *Free breakfast.*

★ The Yachtsman Hotel and Marina Club

$$$ | HOTEL | These chic new bungalows located smack-dab on the water are a long-overdue addition to Kennebunkport, with their hip beach-vibe design, private lawns that blur the distinction between indoors and outdoors, and harbor views. **Pros:** all rooms have fabulous harbor views; pull-out sofas offer more space in the deluxe harborfront bungalows; large marble showers and luxe toiletries from Malin + Goetz; free shuttle service around town. **Cons:** not on the beach; private lawns aren't exactly private with all the boats passing by; not family-friendly. $ *Rooms from: $309* ✉ *59 Ocean Ave., Kennebunkport* ☎ *207/967–2511* ⊕ *yachtsmanlodge.com* ☉ *Closed Nov.–Apr.* 🛏 *30 bungalows* 🍽 *Free breakfast.*

Activities

FISHING

Cast-Away Fishing Charters

BOATING | FAMILY | Half- and full-day charters are available, as is a two-hour children's charter trip where kids can play lobsterman (or woman) for the day and haul in the traps. ✉ *Performance Marine, 4 Western Ave., Kennebunk* ☎ *207/284–1740* ⊕ *www.castawayfishingcharters. com.*

Rugosa

BOATING | FAMILY | Lobster-trap hauling trips aboard the *Rugosa* in the scenic waters off the Kennebunks run daily, Memorial Day–Columbus Day. ✉ *Nonantum Resort, 95 Ocean Ave., Kennebunkport* ☎ *207/468–4095* ⊕ *www.rugosalobstertours.com.*

WHALE-WATCHING

First Chance

TOUR—SPORTS | FAMILY | This company leads whale-watching cruises on 87-foot *Nick's Chance.* Scenic lobster cruises are also offered aboard 65-foot *Kylie's Chance.* Trips run daily in summer and on weekends in the shoulder season. ✉ *Performance Marine, 4 Western Ave.,*

Kennebunk ☎ 207/967–5507 ⊕ www.
firstchancewhalewatch.com.

★ The Pineapple Ketch
SAILING | FAMILY | Here's a terrific way
to get out on the water and see some
marine life, aboard a classic 38-foot
Down Easter ketch. The captain and crew
are knowledgeable and let the passengers guide the direction of both the boat
and the tour. Bring your own snacks and
beverages, especially for the sunset
cruises. ⊠ 95 Ocean Ave., Kennebunkport ☎ 207/468–7262 ⊕ pineappleketch.
com.

Shopping

Abacus
GIFTS/SOUVENIRS | This shop sells eclectic
crafts, jewelry, and furniture. It's a good
place to pick up gifts. ⊠ 2 Ocean Ave.,
at Dock Sq., Kennebunkport ☎ 207/967–
0111 ⊕ www.abacusgallery.com.

★ Daytrip Society
GIFTS/SOUVENIRS | The impossibly hip and
well-selected array of goods that this
modern-design shop stocks makes it an
excellent place for both window-shopping
and finding gifts for just about anyone on
your list (including yourself). A refreshing
departure from the rest of the somewhat
stodgy gift shops in the village, this boutique is chock-full of eye candy, most of
which is also functional. There are many
locally sourced and decidedly contemporary products, from hats and jewelry to
novelty books, home decor, and scents.
Check out Daytrip Jr., its equally hip children's store around the corner. ⊠ 4 Dock
Sq., Kennebunkport ☎ 207/967–4440
⊕ www.daytripsociety.com.

★ Farm + Table
SPECIALTY STORES | This delightful shop
is housed in a bright-red Maine barn
filled with kitchen items both useful and
pleasing to the eye. ⊠ 8 Langsford Rd.,
Cape Porpoise ☎ 207/604–8029 ⊕ www.
farmtablekennebunkport.com.

Maine Art
ART GALLERIES | Showcasing works by
artists from Maine and New England,
Maine Art has a two-story gallery with
a sculpture garden. ⊠ 14 Western Ave.,
Kennebunk ☎ 207/967–2803 ⊕ www.
maine-art.com.

Cape Elizabeth and Prout's Neck

*Prout's Neck: 7 miles south of Cape
Elizabeth; Cape Elizabeth: 5 miles south
of Portland.*

Follow Route 77 through South Portland
(sometimes called "SoPo") to reach the
affluent bedroom community of Cape
Elizabeth, where a detour along the two-
lane Shore Road shows off the famed
Portland Head Light and quite a few stunning oceanfront homes. A few minutes
farther south is Cape Elizabeth Light, the
subject of a well-known Edward Hopper
painting.

Speaking of famous artists, Winslow
Homer painted many of his famous
oceanscapes from a tiny studio on the
rocky peninsula known as Prout's Neck, a
now exclusive gated community 7 miles
south of Cape Elizabeth. The studio is
open to tours only through the Portland
Museum of Art; otherwise the public
can access Prouts Neck only by parking
outside the gates and walking along a
popular cliff trail.

Sights

★ Cape Elizabeth Light
LIGHTHOUSE | FAMILY | This was the first
twin lighthouses erected on the Maine
coast in 1828—and locals still call it Two
Lights—but one of the lighthouses was
dismantled in 1924 and converted into
a private residence. The other half still
operates, and you can get a great photo
of it from the end of Two Lights Road.

The lighthouse itself is closed to the public, but you can explore the tidal pools at its base for small, edible snails known as periwinkles, or just "wrinkles," as they're sometimes referred to in Maine. Picnic tables are also available. ⊠ *7 Tower Dr.* ⊹ *Off Rte. 77 in Cape Elizabeth. Take Rte. 77 to Two Lights Rd.* ☎ *207/799–5871.*

★ Portland Head Light
LIGHTHOUSE | FAMILY | Familiar to many from photographs and the Edward Hopper painting *Portland Head-Light* (1927), this lighthouse was commissioned by George Washington in 1790. The towering, white-stone structure stands over the keeper's quarters, a white home with a blazing red roof, today the Museum at Portland Head Light. The lighthouse is in 90-acre Fort Williams Park, a sprawling green space with walking paths, picnic facilities, a beach and—you guessed it—a cool old fort. ⊠ *Museum, 1000 Shore Rd.* ☎ *207/799–2661* ⊕ *www. portlandheadlight.com.*

Scarborough Marsh Audubon Center
NATURE PRESERVE | FAMILY | You can explore this Maine Audubon Society–run nature center by foot or canoe, on your own or by signing up for a guided walk or paddle. Canoes and kayaks are available to rent and come with a life jacket and map. The salt marsh is Maine's largest and is an excellent place for bird-watching and peaceful paddling along its winding ways. The center has a discovery room for kids, programs for all ages ranging from basket making to astronomy, and a good gift shop. Tours include birding walks. ⊠ *92 Pine Point Rd., Scarborough* ☎ *207/883–5100* ⊕ *www.maineaudubon. org* ⊠ *Free* ۞ *Closed early Oct.–Apr.*

★ Winslow Homer Studio
HOUSE | FAMILY | The great American landscape painter created many of his best-known works in this seaside home between 1883 until his death in 1910. It's easy to see how this rocky, jagged peninsula might have been inspiring. The only way to get a look is on a tour

with the Portland Museum of Art, which leads 2½-hour strolls through the historic property. ⊠ *5 Winslow Homer Rd., Scarborough* ☎ *207/775–6148* ⊕ *www. portlandmuseum.org* ⊠ *$65* ۞ *Closed Nov.–Apr.*

🍴 Restaurants

★ Bite Into Maine
$$ | SEAFOOD | FAMILY | Hands down Maine's best lobster roll is found at this food truck that overlooks the idyllic Portland Head Light in Cape Elizabeth. Traditional lobster rolls smothered in ungodly amounts of drawn butter are delicious, but you've also got the option to get out of the lobster comfort zone with rolls featuring flavors like wasabi, curry, and chipotle, as well as a toothsome lobster BLT. **Known for:** quick bite; dining with a view over the ocean; always fresh lobster. ⑤ *Average main: $18* ⊠ *1000 Shore Rd.* ☎ *207/289–6142* ⊕ *www.biteinto-maine.com* ۞ *Closed mid-Oct.–mid-Apr.*

The Lobster Shack at Two Lights
$$ | SEAFOOD | FAMILY | A classic spot since the 1920s, you can't beat the location—right on the water, below the lighthouse pair that gives Two Lights State Park its name—and the food's not bad either. Enjoy fresh lobster whole or piled into a hot-dog bun with a dollop of mayo, or opt for the delicious chowder, fried clams, or fish-and-chips. **Known for:** seafood boats; family-friendly environment; mini-homemade blueberry pies. ⑤ *Average main: $18* ⊠ *225 Two Lights Rd.* ☎ *207/799–1677* ⊕ *www.lobstershacktwolights.com* ۞ *Closed late Oct.–late Mar.*

★ Shade Eatery at Higgins Beach
$$ | SEAFOOD | FAMILY | This charming neighborhood restaurant and bar just steps from the beach serves up generous, deeply satisfying dishes filled with locally sourced ingredients. Seafood plays a big role in the menu, with unholy lobster rolls brimming with fresh meat; fish tacos stuffed with cilantro, lime

crema, and coleslaw; a Portuguese seafood stew; and crispy calamari. **Known for:** family-friendly environment; three-season-porch dining; $1 freshly shucked oysters during happy hour. $ *Average main: $20 ⊠ Higgins Beach Inn, 36 Ocean Ave., Scarborough ☎ 207/883–6684 ⊕ www. higginsbeachinn.com/shade.*

Hotels

Black Point Inn

$$$$ | RESORT | FAMILY | Toward the tip of the peninsula that juts into the ocean at Prout's Neck stands this stylish, tastefully updated 1878 resort inn with spectacular views up and down the coast. **Pros:** dramatic setting; geothermally heated pool; discounts in shoulder seasons. **Cons:** non-Atlantic view a little underwhelming with buildings on the horizon; rooms have an older, more stately feel to them; children are asked to only eat in pub area. $ *Rooms from: $490 ⊠ 510 Black Point Rd., Scarborough ☎ 207/883–2500 ⊕ www.blackpointinn. com ۞ Closed late Oct.–early May ⇄ 25 rooms ⋈ Free breakfast.*

★ Higgins Beach Inn

$ | B&B/INN | Decidedly "new Maine," this lovingly renovated inn with a laid-back, beach-hair-don't-care kind of nonchalance is just steps from the surfer's paradise that is Higgins Beach. **Pros:** newly renovated; exceptionally efficient and warm service; small touches that make a difference, such as beach towels and a sparkling water dispenser. **Cons:** no pets allowed; a short walk to the beach; limited common areas. $ *Rooms from: $199 ⊠ 34 Ocean Ave., Scarborough ☎ 207/883–6684 ⊕ www.higginsbeach-inn.com ۞ Closed Oct.–Apr. ⇄ 23 rooms ⋈ Free breakfast.*

★ Inn by the Sea

$$$$ | B&B/INN | With some of the highest-quality, gracious service in the state and a top-notch restaurant that delights at every meal, you'll never want to leave the aptly named Inn by the Sea, which is set on Cape Elizabeth's stunning Crescent Beach. **Pros:** your wish is their command; hands down the most dog-friendly accommodations in Maine; direct access to Crescent Beach with chic beach chairs, towels, and umbrellas at hand; native plants garden; gourmet menu for dogs. **Cons:** a short distance from Portland's food scene; not for the budget-minded; minimum stays in the high season. $ *Rooms from: $580 ⊠ 40 Bowery Beach Rd. ☎ 207/799–3134 ⊕ www.innbythesea.com ⇄ 61 rooms ⋈ No meals.*

Portland

28 miles from Kennebunk via I–95 and I–295.

Maine's largest city may be considered small by national standards—its population is just 66,000—but its character, spirit, and appeal make it feel much larger. It's well worth at least a day or two of exploration, even if all you do is spend the entire time eating and drinking at the many phenomenal restaurants, bakeries and specialty dessert shops, craft cocktail bars, and microbreweries scattered across the city. Work up your appetite roaming the working waterfront and strolling the Eastern Promenade, shopping in the boutiques along the brick streets of the Old Port, or sauntering through the galleries of its top-notch art museum.

A city of many names throughout its history, including Casco and Falmouth, Portland has survived many dramatic transformations, the most recent of which is the massive influx of hipsters and foodies who have opened up artisanal bars and quirky boutiques that are rapidly changing the city's character. Sheltered by the nearby Casco Bay Islands and blessed with a deep port, Portland was a significant settlement right from its start

Portland's busy harbor is full of working boats, pleasure craft, and ferries headed to the Casco Bay Islands.

in the early 17th century. Settlers thrived on fishing and lumbering, repeatedly building up the area while the British, French, and Native Americans continually sacked it. Many considered the region a somewhat dangerous frontier, but its potential for prosperity was so apparent that settlers came anyway to tap its rich natural resources.

In 1632 Portland's first home was built on the Portland Peninsula in the area now known as Munjoy Hill. The British burned the city in 1775, when residents refused to surrender arms, but it was rebuilt and became a major trading center. Much of Portland was destroyed again in the Great Fire on July 4, 1866, when a flicked ash or perhaps a celebratory firecracker started a fire in a boatyard that grew into conflagration; 1,500 buildings burned to the ground.

GETTING HERE AND AROUND
From Interstate 95, take Interstate 295 to get to the Portland Peninsula and downtown. Commercial Street runs along the harbor, Fore Street is one block up in the heart of the Old Port, and the Arts District stretches along diagonal Congress Street. Munjoy Hill is on the eastern end of the peninsula and the West End on the opposite side.

ESSENTIALS
RESTAURANTS
America's "Foodiest Small Town" is how one magazine described Portland, which is practically bursting at the seams with fabulous restaurants to rival those of a major metropolis. It's worth it to splurge and try as many as possible while visiting. Fresh seafood, including the famous Maine lobster, is still popular and prevalent, but it is being served up in unexpected ways that are a far cry from the usual bib and butter. There is a broad spectrum of cuisines to be enjoyed, and many chefs are pushing the envelope in their reinventions of traditional culinary idioms. More and more restaurants are using local meats, seafood, and organic produce as much as possible; changing menus reflect what is available in the region at the moment. Even the many

excellent food trucks that have popped up across the city—several of which remain open in the off-season—reflect this trend. As sophisticated as many of these establishments have become in the way of food and service, the atmosphere is generally laid-back; with a few exceptions, you can leave your jacket and tie at home—just not your appetite.

■TIP➜ **Smoking is banned in all restaurants, taverns, and bars in Maine.**

HOTELS

As Portland's popularity as a vacation destination has increased, so have its options for overnight visitors. Though several large hotels—geared toward high-tech, amenity-obsessed guests—have been built in the Old Port, they have in no way diminished the success of smaller, more intimate lodgings. Inns and B&Bs have taken up residence throughout the West End, often giving new life to the grand mansions of Portland's wealthy 19th-century merchants. For the least expensive accommodations, you'll find chain hotels near the interstate and the airport.

Expect to pay at least $150 or so per night for a pleasant room (often with complimentary breakfast) within walking distance of the Old Port during high season, and more than $400 for the most luxurious of suites. At the height of summer, many places are booked; make reservations well in advance, and ask about off-season specials.

NIGHTLIFE

Portland's nightlife scene is largely centered on the bustling Old Port and a few smaller, artsy spots on Congress Street. There's a great emphasis on live music from local bands and pubs serving award-winning local microbrews. Several hip bars have cropped up, serving appetizers along with a full array of specialty wines and serious craft cocktails. Portland is a fairly sleepy city after midnight, but you can usually find a couple of bars

Cannabis in Vacationland

Though Maine voters approved legalizing the recreational use and sales of marijuana in November 2016, various delays prevented retail shops from opening until October 2020. Many of the initial license applications were from retailers in the Greater Portland area, but availability is expected to expand statewide. Check in with the Maine Office of Marijuana Policy (☎ 207/287–3282 ⊕ www.maine.gov/dafs/omp) for information.

and restaurants open, even after the clock strikes 12.

PERFORMING ARTS

Art galleries and studios have spread throughout the city, infusing many beautiful, old abandoned buildings and shops with new life. Many are concentrated along the Congress Street downtown corridor; others are hidden amid the boutiques and restaurants of the Old Port and the East End. A great way to get acquainted with the city's artists is to participate in the First Friday Art Walk, a free self-guided tour of galleries, museums, and alternative-art venues that happens—you guessed it—on the first Friday of each month.

SHOPPING

Exchange Street is great for arts and crafts and boutique browsing, while Commercial Street caters to the souvenir hound—gift shops are packed with nautical items, and lobster and moose emblems are emblazoned on everything from T-shirts to shot glasses.

ACTIVITIES

When the weather's good, everyone in Portland heads outside, whether for boating on the water, lounging on a beach, or walking and biking the promenades. There are also many green spaces nearby Portland, including Crescent Beach State Park, Two Lights State Park, and Fort Williams Park, home to Portland Head Light. All are on the coast south of the city in suburban Cape Elizabeth and offer walking trails, picnic facilities, and water access.

Various Portland-based skippers offer whale-, dolphin-, and seal-watching cruises; excursions to lighthouses and islands; and fishing and lobstering trips. Board the ferry to see nearby islands. Self-navigators can rent kayaks or canoes.

TOURS
BUS TOURS
Portland Discovery Land and Sea Tours
BUS TOURS | FAMILY | The informative trolley tours of Portland Discovery detail the city's historical and architectural highlights, Memorial Day–October. Options include combining a city tour with a bay or lighthouse cruise. ⊠ *Long Wharf, 170 Commercial St.* ☎ *207/774–0808* ⊕ *www.portlanddiscovery.com* ⊠ *From $23.*

WALKING TOURS
Greater Portland Landmarks
WALKING TOURS | FAMILY | Take 1½-hour walking tours of Portland's historic West End June–October, with Greater Portland Landmarks. Tours past the neighborhood's Greek Revival mansions and grand Federal-style homes begin at the group's headquarters and cost $10. You can also pick up maps for self-guided tours of the Old Port or the Western Promenade. ⊠ *93 High St.* ☎ *207/774–5561* ⊕ *www.portlandlandmarks.org* ⊠ *From $10.*

Maine Foodie Tours
SPECIAL-INTEREST | Learn about Portland's culinary history and sample local delights like lobster hors d'oeuvres, organic cheese, and the famous Maine whoopie pie. The culinary walking tours include stops at fishmongers, bakeries, and cheese shops that provide products to Portland's famed restaurants. From summer into early fall, you can also take a chocolate tour, a bike-and-brewery tour, or a trolley tour with a stop at a microbrewery. Tours begin at various locales in the Old Port. ⊠ *Portland* ☎ *207/233–7485* ⊕ *www.mainefoodietours.com* ⊠ *From $29.*

Portland Freedom Trail
SELF-GUIDED | FAMILY | The Portland Freedom Trail offers a self-guided tour of sites associated with the Underground Railroad and the antislavery movement. ⊠ *Portland* ⊕ *www.mainehistory.org/ PDF/walkingtourmap.pdf* ⊠ *Free.*

VISITOR INFORMATION
CONTACTS Downtown Portland. ☎ *207/772–6828* ⊕ *www.portlandmaine. com.* **Greater Portland Convention and Visitors Bureau.** ☎ *207/772–4994* ⊕ *www. visitportland.com.*

The Old Port and the Waterfront

A major international port and a working harbor since the early 17th century, Portland's Old Port and the Waterfront bridge the gap between the city's historic commercial activities and those of today. It is home to fishing boats docked alongside whale-watching charters, luxury yachts, cruise ships, and oil tankers from around the globe. Commercial Street parallels the water and is lined with brick buildings and warehouses that were built following the Great Fire of 1866. In the 19th century, candle makers and sail stitchers plied their trades here; today specialty shops, art galleries, and restaurants have taken up residence.

As with much of the city, it's best to park your car and explore the Old Port on foot. You can park at the city garage on Fore Street (between Exchange and Union streets) or opposite the U.S. Custom House at the corner of Fore and Pearl

Sights ▼

1 Eastern Promenade..... **I5**
2 Harbor Fish Market **G7**
3 Maine Narrow Gauge Railroad Museum....... **H7**
4 Neal Dow Memorial.... **D6**
5 Portland Fish Exchange................ **E8**
6 Portland Museum of Art **E6**
7 Portland Observatory............. **H6**
8 Victoria Mansion **E7**
9 The Wadsworth-Longfellow House **E6**
10 Western Promenade... **B6**

Restaurants ▼

1 BaoBao Dumpling House **E7**
2 Becky's Diner **E8**
3 Blyth & Burrows **F7**
4 Duckfat.................... **G7**
5 East Ender **G6**
6 Eventide Oyster Co...... **G7**
7 Fore Street.............. **G7**
8 Gilbert's Chowder House **G7**
9 Highroller Lobster Co.... **F6**
10 The Honey Paw **G7**
11 Hugo's................... **G7**
12 Local 188................. **D6**
13 Mami **F7**
14 Rose Foods **D4**
15 The Shop at Island Creek Oysters **H5**
16 Union...................... **F6**

Quick Bites ▼

1 Bard Coffee.............. **F7**
2 Coffee by Design........ **G6**
3 Gelato Fiasco............ **F7**
4 Speckled Ax Wood Roasted Coffee **E6**
5 Standard Baking........ **G7**
6 Two Fat Cats Bakery **F5**

Hotels ▼

1 The Francis.............. **D6**
2 Hilton Garden Inn Portland Downtown Waterfront............... **G7**
3 Morrill Mansion.......... **C6**
4 Portland Harbor Hotel... **F7**
5 The Portland Regency Hotel and Spa **F7**
6 The Press Hotel.......... **F6**
7 West End Inn............. **C6**
8 The Westin Portland Harborview **E6**

streets. A helpful hint: look for the "Park & Shop" sign on garages and parking lots, and get one hour of free parking for each stamp collected at participating shops. Allow a couple of hours to wander at leisure on Market, Exchange, Middle, and Fore streets. The city is very pedestrian-friendly. Maine state law requires vehicles to stop for pedestrians in crosswalks.

Sights

Harbor Fish Market

STORE/MALL | A Portland favorite since 1968, this freshest-of-the-fresh seafood market ships lobsters and other Maine delectables almost anywhere in the country. A bright-red facade on a working wharf opens into a bustling space with bubbling lobster tanks and fish, clams, and other shellfish on ice; employees are as skilled with a fillet knife as sushi chefs. There is also a small retail store. ⊠ *9 Custom House Wharf, The Old Port and the Waterfront* ☎ *207/775–0251* ⊕ *www.harborfish.com* ⊠ *Free.*

Portland Fish Exchange

FISH HATCHERY | You may want to hold your nose as you take a dip into the Old Port's active fish business at the 20,000-square-foot Portland Fish Exchange. Peek inside coolers teeming with cod, flounder, and monkfish, and watch fishermen repairing nets outside. ⊠ *6 Portland Fish Pier, The Old Port and the Waterfront* ☎ *207/773–0017* ⊕ *www. pfex.org* ⊠ *Free.*

Restaurants

Becky's Diner

$ | **DINER** | **FAMILY** | You won't find a more local or unfussy place—or one more abuzz with conversation at 4 am—than this waterfront institution way down on the end of Commercial Street. The food is cheap, generous in proportion, and has that satisfying, old-time-diner quality. **Known for:** classic Maine diner

food featuring many seafood dishes; very lively atmosphere commingling locals and visitors; parking is easy—a rarity in Portland. ⑤ *Average main: $14* ⊠ *390 Commercial St., The Old Port and the Waterfront* ☎ *207/773–7070* ⊕ *www. beckysdiner.com.*

★ Blyth & Burrows

$ | **CONTEMPORARY** | There are craft cocktails and there is Blyth & Burrows, where the alchemy of spirits is taken to the next level with creative concoctions that include the unholy integration of gorgeous (albeit unusual) ingredients such as absinthe foam, house-made black-lime cordial, blackstrap maple-chipotle syrup, and uncommon liqueurs and spirits. Delicious small plates, like lobster rolls, oysters on the half shell, tenderloin and chimichurri, and local meat and cheese boards keep you from falling under the table. **Known for:** knock-you-under-the-table cocktails; nautical-theme atmosphere filled with antique ships and mermaid figureheads; food that goes well with cocktails. ⑤ *Average main: $12* ⊠ *26 Exchange St., The Old Port and the Waterfront* ☎ *207/613–9070* ⊕ *www. blythandburrows.com.*

★ Fore Street

$$$ | **MODERN AMERICAN** | One of Maine's best chefs, Sam Hayward, opened this restaurant in a renovated warehouse on the edge of the Old Port in 1996; today every copper-top table in the main dining room has a view of the enormous brick oven and soapstone hearth that anchor the open kitchen. The menu changes daily to reflect the freshest ingredients from Maine's farms and waters, as well as the tremendous creativity of the staff. **Known for:** Turnspit roasted meats; handmade charcuterie; last-minute planners take heart: a third of the tables are reserved for walk-ins. ⑤ *Average main: $30* ⊠ *288 Fore St., The Old Port and the Waterfront* ☎ *207/775–2717* ⊕ *www.forestreet.biz* ⊙ *No lunch.*

Gilbert's Chowder House

$$ | SEAFOOD | FAMILY | This is the real deal, as quintessential as old-school Maine dining can be. Clam rakes and nautical charts hang from the walls of this unpretentious waterfront diner, and the flavors come from the depths of the North Atlantic, prepared and presented simply: fried scallops, haddock, clams and extraordinary clam cakes, and fish, clam, and seafood chowders (corn, too). **Known for:** family-friendly environment; classic lobster rolls, served on toasted hot-dog buns bursting with claw and tail meat; an ice-cream parlor to round out your meal; chalkboard daily specials. $ *Average main: $19* ⊠ *92 Commercial St., The Old Port and the Waterfront* ☎ *207/871–5636* ⊕ *www.gilbertschowderhouse.com.*

Highroller Lobster Co.

$ | SEAFOOD | Opened in early 2018, this high-energy spot serves lobster numerous ways—in a roll, on a stick, on a burger, over a salad, or even with your Bloody Mary. If you're feeling adventurous, try one of the sauces (lime mayo, lobster ghee) on your roll, and wash it all down with a beer from the ever-changing menu, which depends on availability from local breweries. **Known for:** origins as a food cart; the lobby pop (a lobster tail on a stick); Highroller whoopie pies baked by the owner's mom. $ *Average main: $15* ⊠ *104 Exchange St., The Old Port and the Waterfront* ☎ *207/536–1623* ⊕ *highroller-lobster.com.*

★ Mami

$ | JAPANESE | Japanese street food takes center stage at this cozy locale. The menu rotates regularly, but you're likely to find uncommon takes on burgers and soba noodles as well as some form of *okonomiyaki*—a savory pancake filled with crazy-delicious flavor and texture combinations. **Known for:** ramen; steamed buns; grilled rice balls. $ *Average main: $15* ⊠ *339 Fore St., The Old Port and the Waterfront* ☎ *207/536–4702* ⊕ *mamiportland.com* ☾ *Closed Sun. and Mon.*

★ Union

$$$ | AMERICAN | FAMILY | In the Press Hotel, Union Restaurant has a sophisticated but not stuffy air that is reflected in its menu, which focuses on local ingredients, many of which are foraged and fished, or gathered from its basement greenhouse. Most dishes are modern comfort food; breakfast and brunch are a treat: you'll find maple *pain perdu* served alongside smoked-salmon tartines and classic dishes like eggs Benedict. **Known for:** sustainable ingredients; decadent "chef's table," a multicourse meal with wine pairings and the chef's choice; signature truffle beef pot roast. $ *Average main: $30* ⊠ *Press Hotel, 390 Congress St., The Old Port and the Waterfront* ☎ *207/808–8700* ⊕ *www.unionportland.com.*

☕ Coffee and Quick Bites

Bard Coffee

$ | CAFÉ | The beans sourcing this shop's delicious brew are bought from a handful of small growers—you can read their bios on the website—and roasted in-house. Enjoy your brew hot, cold, or iced with a locally made baked good. **Known for:** close relationships with sources; passionate, knowledgeable baristas; bulk coffee and tea. $ *Average main: $5* ⊠ *185 Middle St., The Old Port and the Waterfront* ☎ *207/899–4788* ⊕ *www.bardcoffee.com.*

★ Gelato Fiasco

$ | CAFÉ | FAMILY | Proper Italian gelato and *sorbetto* here come in traditional flavors as well as more offbeat varieties like torched marshmallow s'more, mascarpone pistachio caramel, and mint brownie cookie. There are new flavors every day, along with espresso and other hot drinks. **Known for:** you can try every single flavor before deciding on what you'll get; long lines out the door in the summer; multigenerational bonding spot. $ *Average main: $5* ⊠ *425 Fore St., The*

Old Port and the Waterfront ☎ 207/699–4314 ⊕ www.gelatofiasco.com.

★ Standard Baking

$ | BAKERY | FAMILY | You'd be hard-pressed to find a more pitch-perfect bakery in the Pine Tree State, but you'll have to pop by early (or put in an order in advance) to get your mitts on these delectable baked goods. The perfectly airy croissants, crusty baguettes, beguiling tarts, dainty Madeleines, and creative breads incorporate locally sourced grains and are nothing short of revelations. **Known for:** good selection of locally roasted coffees; amazing galettes and brioches; creative scones. ⑤ Average main: $3 ⊠ 75 Commercial St., The Old Port and the Waterfront ☎ 207/772–5519 ⊕ www.standardbakingco.com.

 ## Hotels

Hilton Garden Inn Portland Downtown Waterfront

$$$ | HOTEL | This bright, clean, and modern hotel is a perfect base for exploring on foot the adjacent Old Port and nearby East End, and it's only a walk across the street to catch a ferry to the Casco Bay islands. **Pros:** heated saltwater lap pool; central location for exploring; some rooms with harbor view. **Cons:** no pets; no self-parking; some rooms face neighboring businesses. ⑤ Rooms from: $379 ⊠ 65 Commercial St., The Old Port and the Waterfront ☎ 207/780–0780 ⊕ www.hilton.com/en/hilton-garden-inn ⇱ 120 rooms ⦿| No meals.

Portland Harbor Hotel

$$ | HOTEL | Extensively renovated in 2017, this nautically themed hotel is in walking distance of both the waterfront and the Old Port. **Pros:** amid the action of the Old Port; pet-friendly ($50 per pet fee); courtesy car covers 4-mile radius. **Cons:** no pool; rooms facing Union Street pick up lively street noise; no water view. ⑤ Rooms from: $299 ⊠ 468 Fore St., The Old Port and the Waterfront

☎ 207/775–9090, 888/798–9090 ⊕ www.portlandharborhotel.com ⇱ 101 rooms ⦿| No meals.

The Portland Regency Hotel and Spa

$$$ | HOTEL | Not part of a chain despite the "Regency" name, this brick building in the center of the Old Port served as Portland's armory in the late 19th century. **Pros:** easy walk to sites; pet-friendly ($75 nonrefundable cleaning fee); full-service spa with lounges, saunas, steam rooms, hot tub, and an array of luxurious treatments. **Cons:** no pool; busy downtown location; not all rooms have noteworthy views. ⑤ Rooms from: $300 ⊠ 20 Milk St., The Old Port and the Waterfront ☎ 207/774–4200, 800/727–3436 ⊕ www.theregency.com ⇱ 95 rooms ⦿| No meals.

★ The Press Hotel

$$$ | HOTEL | FAMILY | In a former newspaper building, this boutique hotel is part of Marriott's Autograph Collection; the hotel feels both broadly cosmopolitan and distinctly Maine. **Pros:** Frette bed linens and Maine-made Cuddledown comforters and bed throws; sparkling-clean rooms with a modern-design feel; art gallery and excellent public spaces with tasteful furnishings. **Cons:** right next to the fire department; valet parking can be expensive; some rooms have underwhelming views. ⑤ Rooms from: $375 ⊠ 119 Exchange St., The Old Port and the Waterfront ☎ 877/890–5641 ⊕ www.thepresshotel.com ⇱ 110 rooms ⦿| No meals.

 ## Nightlife

Bull Feeney's

BARS/PUBS | For nightly specials, plenty of Guinness, and live entertainment, head to Bull Feeney's, a lively two-story Irish pub and restaurant. ⊠ 375 Fore St., The Old Port and the Waterfront ☎ 207/773–7210 ⊕ bullfeeneys.com.

Gritty McDuff's Portland Brew Pub

BARS/PUBS | Maine's original brewpub serves fine ales, British pub fare, and seafood dishes. There are between six and eight rotating ales on tap, and there's always a seasonal offering. ✉ *396 Fore St., The Old Port and the Waterfront* ☎ *207/772–2739* ⊕ *www.grittys.com.*

★ Novare Res Bier Café

BARS/PUBS | At tucked-away Novare Res Bier Café, choose from some three dozen rotating drafts and about 500 bottled brews. Relax on an expansive deck, munch on antipasti, or share a meat-and-cheese plate. Maine craft beers occupy at least eight of the taps at any given time, and the rest span the globe, with an emphasis on Belgian and Trappist ales. ✉ *4 Canal Plaza, off Exchange St., The Old Port and the Waterfront* ☎ *207/761–2437* ⊕ *www.novareresbiercafe.com.*

★ Portland Hunt and Alpine Club

BARS/PUBS | Scandinavian-inspired dishes and serious craft cocktails drive this hip locale that includes excellent charcuterie and seafood boards in an intimate alpine-style hut. Go for the excellent happy hour, weekdays 1–6. ✉ *75 Market St., The Old Port and the Waterfront* ☎ *207/747–4754* ⊕ *www.huntandalpineclub.com.*

Vena's Fizz House

BARS/PUBS | The old-fashioned soda fountain gets a modern update at Vena's Fizz House, where flavors like cucumber mint, chocolate-cherry cordial, and frothy blood orange go into delicious, fizzy "mocktails," while the cocktails feature artisanal ingredients such as Maine pine bitters, saffron syrup, and ghost pepper extract. ✉ *345 Fore St., The Old Port and the Waterfront* ☎ *207/747–4901* ⊕ *www.venasfizzhouse.com.*

🛍 Shopping

ACCESSORIES
★ Sea Bags

SPECIALTY STORES | At Sea Bags, totes made from recycled sailcloth and decorated with bright, graphic patterns are sewn right in the store. ✉ *25 Custom House Wharf, The Old Port and the Waterfront* ☎ *207/780–0744* ⊕ *www.seabags.com.*

ART AND ANTIQUES
Abacus Gallery

ANTIQUES/COLLECTIBLES | This appealing crafts gallery has gift items in glass, wood, and textiles, as well as fine modern jewelry. ✉ *44 Exchange St., The Old Port and the Waterfront* ☎ *207/772–4880* ⊕ *www.abacusgallery.com.*

Greenhut Galleries

ANTIQUES/COLLECTIBLES | The contemporary art at this gallery changes with the seasons. Artists represented include David Driskell, an artist and leading art scholar. ✉ *146 Middle St., The Old Port and the Waterfront* ☎ *207/772–2693* ⊕ *www.greenhutgalleries.com.*

BOOKS
Longfellow Books

BOOKS/STATIONERY | This shop is known for its good service, author readings, and excellent selection of new and used books and magazines. Even if you go in looking for something specific, you'll almost certainly stumble on something even better you didn't know about before. ✉ *1 Monument Way, The Old Port and the Waterfront* ☎ *207/772–4045* ⊕ *www.longfellowbooks.com.*

★ Sherman's Maine Coast Book Shops

BOOKS/STATIONERY | Open since 1886, Sherman's is Maine's oldest bookstore chain. The Portland store has an impressive stock of well-selected books interspersed with excellent gift choices, such as stationery, candles, and holiday decor, as well as a fun array of toys. It's a good place to spend a cold or rainy day perusing the selection. ✉ *49 Exchange St., The Old Port and the Waterfront* ☎ *207/773–4100* ⊕ *www.shermans.com.*

CLOTHING
★ Aristelle

CLOTHING | For the fanciest knickers in downtown Portland and one of the best bra fittings around head to Aristelle, purveyors of elegant undergarments and lingerie, as well as naughty little numbers that would make Bettie Page blush. ✉ *92 Exchange St., The Old Port and the Waterfront* ☎ *207/842–6000* ⊕ *www. aristelle.com.*

Bliss
CLOTHING | Hip boutique Bliss stocks clothing and accessories by cutting-edge designers, plus jeans by big names like J Brand and Mother. There's also a great selection of Frye boots. ✉ *58 Exchange St., The Old Port and the Waterfront* ☎ *207/879–7125* ⊕ *www.blissboutiques. com.*

Joseph's
CLOTHING | A smart menswear boutique (and mainstay of the Old Port) that will have you looking suave in no time. ✉ *410 Fore St., The Old Port and the Waterfront* ☎ *207/773–1274* ⊕ *www.josephsofport-land.com.*

★ Judith
CLOTHING | Owned and operated by a former fashion designer, this stunning, well-curated concept boutique features women's apparel, shoes, accessories, and contemporary housewares. ✉ *131 Middle St., The Old Port and the Waterfront* ☎ *207/747–4778* ⊕ *www.shopju-dith.com.*

HOME AND GIFTS
Asia West
HOUSEHOLD ITEMS/FURNITURE | For reproduction and antique furnishings with a Far East feel, head to this stylish showroom on the waterfront. ✉ *128 Cassidy Point Dr., The Old Port and the Waterfront* ☎ *207/775–0066* ⊕ *www.asiawest.net.*

Lisa Marie's Made in Maine
GIFTS/SOUVENIRS | Here you'll find an excellent selection of locally sourced items from soaps and candles to dish towels, pottery, and jewelry, all made in the great state of Maine. ✉ *35 Exchange St., The Old Port and the Waterfront* ☎ *207/828–1515* ⊕ *www.lisamariesma-deinmaine.com.*

TOYS
★ Treehouse Toys
TOYS | FAMILY | An instant mood-lifter, this shop is chock-full of offbeat toys and novelty items that are certain to delight children of all ages. ✉ *47 Exchange St., The Old Port and the Waterfront* ☎ *207/775–6133* ⊕ *www.treehousetoys. us.*

Activities

BIKING
Portland Trails
BICYCLING | FAMILY | For local biking and hiking information, contact Portland Trails. The staff can tell you about designated paved and unpaved routes that wind along the water, through parks, and beyond. ✉ *305 Commercial St., The Old Port and the Waterfront* ☎ *207/775–2411* ⊕ *www.trails.org.*

BOATING
Casco Bay Lines
BOATING | FAMILY | Casco Bay Lines operates ferry service to the seven bay islands with year-round populations: Summer offerings include music cruises, lighthouse excursions, and a trip to Bailey Island with a stopover for lunch. ✉ *Maine State Pier, 56 Commercial St., The Old Port and the Waterfront* ☎ *207/774–7871* ⊕ *www.cascobaylines.com.*

Lucky Catch Cruises
BOATING | FAMILY | Set sail in a real lobster boat: this company gives you the genuine experience, which includes hauling traps and the chance to purchase the catch. ✉ *Long Wharf, 170 Commercial St., The Old Port and the Waterfront* ☎ *207/761–0941* ⊕ *www.luckycatch.com.*

Odyssey Whale Watch
BOATING | FAMILY | From mid-May to mid-October, Odyssey Whale Watch leads whale-watching and deep-sea-fishing excursions. ✉ *Long Wharf, 170 Commercial St., The Old Port and the Waterfront* ☎ *207/775–0727* ⊕ *www. odysseywhalewatch.com.*

Portland Discovery Land & Sea Tours

TOUR—SPORTS | FAMILY | For tours of the harbor and Casco Bay in a boat or on a trolley, including an up-close look at several lighthouses, try Portland Discovery Land & Sea Tours. ⊠ *Long Wharf, 170 Commercial St., The Old Port and the Waterfront* ☎ *207/774–0808* ⊕ *www. portlanddiscovery.com.*

★ **Portland Schooner Co.**

TOUR—SPORTS | FAMILY | May through October this company offers daily two-hour windjammer cruises aboard the vintage schooners *Bagheera, Timberwind,* and *Wendameen.* You can also arrange private charters. ⊠ *Maine State Pier, 56 Commercial St., The Old Port and the Waterfront* ☎ *207/766–2500* ⊕ *www. portlandschooner.com.*

The Arts District

This district starts at the top of Exchange Street, near the upper end of the Old Port, and extends west past the Portland Museum of Art. The district's central artery is Congress Street, which is lined with art galleries, specialty stores, and a score of restaurants and cafés. Parking is tricky; two-hour meters dot the sidewalks, but there are several garages nearby.

 Sights

Neal Dow Memorial

HOUSE | The mansion, once a stop on the Underground Railroad, was the home of Civil War general Neal Dow, who became known as the "Father of Prohibition." He was responsible for Maine's adoption of the anti-alcohol bill in 1851, which spurred a nationwide temperance movement. Now a museum, this majestic 1829 Federal-style home is open for guided tours that start on the hour. ⊠ *714 Congress St., Arts District* ☎ *207/773–7773* ⊕ *www.nealdowmemorial.org* ⌨ *$10.*

★ **Portland Museum of Art**

MUSEUM | Maine's largest public art institution's collection includes fine seascapes and landscapes by Winslow Homer, John Marin, Andrew Wyeth, Edward Hopper, Marsden Hartley, and other American painters. Homer's *Weatherbeaten*, a quintessential Maine Coast image, is here, and the museum owns and displays, on a rotating basis, 16 more of his paintings, plus more than 400 of his illustrations (and it offers tours of the Winslow Homer Studio in nearby Prouts Neck). The museum has works by Monet and Picasso, as well as Degas, Renoir, and Chagall. I. M. Pei's colleague Henry Cobb designed the strikingly modern Charles Shipman Payson building. ⊠ *7 Congress Sq., Arts District* ☎ *207/775–6148* ⊕ *www.portlandmuseum.org* ⌨ *$18 (free Fri. 10–8).*

Victoria Mansion

HOUSE | Built between 1858 and 1860, this Italianate mansion is widely regarded as the most sumptuously ornamented dwelling of its period remaining in the country. Architect Henry Austin designed the house for hotelier Ruggles Morse and his wife, Olive. The interior design—everything from the plasterwork to the furniture (much of it original)—is the only surviving commission of New York designer Gustave Herter. Behind the elegant brownstone exterior of this National Historic Landmark are colorful frescoed walls and ceilings, ornate marble mantelpieces, gilded gas chandeliers, a magnificent 6-foot-by-25-foot stained-glass ceiling window, and a freestanding mahogany staircase. A guided tour runs about 45 minutes and covers all the architectural highlights. Victorian era–themed gifts and art are sold in the museum shop, and the museum often has special theme events. ⊠ *109 Danforth St., Arts District* ☎ *207/772–4841* ⊕ *www.victoriamansion.org* ⌨ *$18* ⊙ *Closed mid-Jan.–Apr.*

The Wadsworth–Longfellow House

HOUSE | The boyhood home of the famous American poet was the first brick house in Portland and the oldest building on the peninsula. It's particularly interesting, because most of the furnishings, including the young Longfellow's writing desk, are original. Wallpaper, window coverings, and a vibrant painted carpet are period reproductions. Built in 1785, the large dwelling (a third floor was added in 1815) sits back from the street and has a small portico over its entrance and four chimneys surmounting the roof. It's part of the Maine Historical Society, which includes an adjacent research library and a museum with exhibits about Maine life. After your guided tour, stay for a picnic in the Longfellow Garden; it's open to the public during museum hours. ⊠ *489 Congress St., Arts District* ☎ *207/774–1822* ⊕ *www.mainehistory.org* ⊠ *House and museum $15, gardens free* ⊙ *Closed Nov.–Apr.*

Restaurants

Local 188

$$$ | SPANISH | There's an infectious vibe at this eclectic, Spanish-inspired Arts District hot spot that's accentuated by its 2,000-square-foot space, lofty tin ceilings, worn maple floors, and mismatched chandeliers. Regulars chat with servers about which just-caught seafood will decorate the paella or which organic veggies will star in the tortillas, one of several tapas choices. **Known for:** large bar area; some 150 different wines, mostly from Europe; a lively crowd and warm environment. ⑤ *Average main: $25* ⊠ *685 Congress St., Arts District* ☎ *207/761–7909* ⊕ *www.local188.com* ⊙ *No lunch.*

Coffee and Quick Bites

★ Speckled Ax Wood Roasted Coffee

$ | CAFÉ | The Speckled Ax serves up a seriously delicious coffee, whether cold brewed or piping hot with frothy milk. The secret to the richness of the beans is the painstaking roasting process, using a vintage Italian Petroncini roaster fired with local hardwood—ask to take a peek at that contraption while you wait for your drink. **Known for:** pastries and other baked goods; local gathering space; a hip vibe. ⑤ *Average main: $4* ⊠ *567 Congress St., Arts District* ☎ *207/660–3333* ⊕ *www. speckledax.com.*

Hotels

The Westin Portland Harborview

$$ | HOTEL | This imposing structure was New England's largest hotel, the Eastland, when built in 1927 and is a well-known part of the Portland skyline. **Pros:** the views from the rooftop bar and lounge; pet friendly; on-site laundry. **Cons:** rooms with city views cost more; not all rooms have harbor views; often bustling with event attendees. ⑤ *Rooms from: $254* ⊠ *157 High St., Arts District* ☎ *207/775–5411* ⊕ *www.marriott.com* ⇆ *289 rooms* ⦿ *No meals.*

Performing Arts

Merrill Auditorium

CONCERTS | FAMILY | This soaring concert hall hosts numerous theatrical and musical events, including performances by the Portland Symphony Orchestra and the Portland Opera Repertory Theatre. Ask about organ recitals on the auditorium's huge 1912 Kotzschmar Memorial Organ. ⊠ *20 Myrtle St., Arts District* ☎ *207/842–0800* ⊕ *portlandmaine. gov/574/Merrill-Auditorium.*

Portland Stage

THEATER | FAMILY | This company mounts theatrical productions on its two stages September–May. ⊠ *25-A Forest Ave., Arts District* ☎ *207/774–0465* ⊕ *www. portlandstage.org.*

Space Gallery

ART GALLERIES—ARTS | FAMILY | Space Gallery sparkles as a contemporary art gallery and alternative arts venue, opening its doors to everything from poetry readings and art fairs to live music to documentary films. The gallery is open Wednesday–Saturday. ✉ *538 Congress St., Arts District* ☎ *207/828–5600* ⊕ *www.space538.org.*

Shopping

ART AND ANTIQUES

Portland Flea-for-All

ANTIQUES/COLLECTIBLES | FAMILY | Friday through Sunday, head to the city's Bayside neighborhood for the Portland Flea-for-All, where you'll find all sorts of vintage eye candy from an ever-rotating array of antiques and artisan vendors—a fun excursion, whether or not you actually buy anything. ✉ *585 Congress St., Arts District* ☎ *207/370–7570* ⊕ *www.portlandfleaforall.com.*

Black Dinah Chocolatiers

FOOD/CANDY | Started on the tiny Isle au Haut, artful high-end chocolates and has a small café. ✉ *The Westin Portland Harborview, 157 High St., Arts District.*

Activities

BIKING

Bicycle Coalition of Maine

BICYCLING | FAMILY | For state bike trail maps, club and tour listings, or hints on safety, contact the Bicycle Coalition of Maine. ✉ *38 Diamond St., Arts District* ☎ *207/623–4511* ⊕ *www.bikemaine.org.*

Gorham Bike and Ski

BICYCLING | FAMILY | You can rent several types of bikes, including hybrid and electric models, starting at $35 per day. ✉ *693 Congress St., Arts District* ☎ *207/773–1700* ⊕ *www.gorhambike.com.*

The East End

This neighborhood encompasses Munjoy Hill, the Eastern Promenade, East End Beach, and the Portland Observatory. It's an easy walk to the Old Port, and a great place to watch the harbor goings-on, and see the July 4 fireworks.

Sights

Eastern Promenade

HISTORIC SITE | FAMILY | Between the city's two promenades, this one, often overlooked by tourists, has by far the best view. Gracious Victorian homes, many now converted to condos and apartments, border one side of the street. On the other is 68 acres of hillside parkland that includes Ft. Allen Park and, at the base of the hill, the Eastern Prom Trail and tiny East End Beach and boat launch. On a sunny day the Eastern Prom is a lovely spot for picnicking and people-watching. ✉ *Washington Ave. to Fore St., East End.*

Maine Narrow Gauge Railroad Museum

MUSEUM | FAMILY | Whether you're crazy about old trains or just want to see the sights from a different perspective, the railroad museum has an extensive collection of locomotives and rail coaches, and offers scenic tours on narrow-gauge railcars. The 3-mile jaunts run on the hour and take you along Casco Bay, at the foot of the Eastern Promenade. The operating season caps off with a fall harvest ride (complete with cider), and during the Christmas season there are special Polar Express rides, based on the popular children's book. ✉ *58 Fore St., East End* ☎ *207/828–0814* ⊕ *www.mainenarrowgauge.org* ⬚ *Museum $5, train rides $12* ☺ *Closed Nov.–Apr.*

Portland Observatory

OBSERVATORY | FAMILY | This octagonal observatory on Munjoy Hill was built in 1807 by Captain Lemuel Moody, a retired sea captain, as a maritime signal tower.

Moody used a telescope to identify incoming ships, and flags to signal to merchants where to unload their cargo. Held in place by 122 tons of ballast, it's the last remaining historic maritime signal station in the country. The guided tour leads all the way to the dome, where you can step out on the deck and take in views of Portland, the islands, and inland toward the White Mountains. ✉ *138 Congress St., East End* ☎ *207/774–5561* ⊕ *www.portlandlandmarks.org* 💲 *$10* ◷ *Closed mid-Oct.–late May.*

🍴 Restaurants

Duckfat

$ | **MODERN AMERICAN** | Even in midafternoon, this small, hip panini-and-more shop in the Old Port is packed. The focus here is everyday farm-to-table fare: the signature Belgian fries are made with Maine potatoes cooked, yes, in duck fat and served in paper cones, and standards include meat loaf and the BGT (bacon, goat cheese, tomato). **Known for:** decadent poutine with duck-fat gravy; hopping atmosphere—waits for a table can be long; thick milk shakes prepared with local gelato by Gelato Fiasco. ⑤ *Average main: $12* ✉ *43 Middle St., East End* ☎ *207/774–8080* ⊕ *www.duckfat. com.*

★ East Ender

$$ | **AMERICAN** | **FAMILY** | The emphasis at this cozy neighborhood restaurant is on the superb food rather than the atmosphere, which isn't surprising, given that the owners formerly served their tasty, no-fuss fare from a truck. Lunch and dinner feature locally sourced, sustainable ingredients in dishes that reflect the seasons. **Known for:** mouthwatering house-smoked bacon; crispy, thrice-cooked fries; brunch cocktails that incorporate ingredients from local distilleries and house-made cordials. ⑤ *Average main: $24* ✉ *47 Middle St., East End* ☎ *207/879–7669* ⊕ *www.eastenderportland.com.*

★ Eventide Oyster Co.

$ | **SEAFOOD** | Not only does Eventide have fresh, tasty oysters from all over Maine and New England, artfully prepared with novel accoutrements like kimchi, ginger ices, and cucumber-champagne mignonette, it also serves delicious crudos and ceviches with unique ingredients like blood orange and chili miso. The menu constantly changes, depending on what's in season, so it's best to order a handful of small plates, a glass of bubbly or one of the signature tiki-style cocktails, and, of course, a dozen oysters. **Known for:** brown-butter lobster rolls; a decent selection of alternatives for nonseafood lovers; teaming up with other local restaurants for special cook-offs and menus. ⑤ *Average main: $15* ✉ *86 Middle St., East End* ☎ *207/774–8538* ⊕ *www.eventideoysterco.com.*

The Honey Paw

$ | **ASIAN FUSION** | Come for the salty wontons, piping-hot broths, and wok-fried noodles; stay for the turntable music, the well-stocked cocktail bar, and the soft-serve ice cream that comes in flavors like orange curd, moxie, and charred corn. If you order one thing here, make it the lobster toast, topped with a scallop and lobster mousse, radish, lime, and an amazing tarragon emulsion. **Known for:** sister restaurant to Eventide Oyster Co.; house-made noodles; rotating wines on tap and an excellent selection of sake. ⑤ *Average main: $15* ✉ *7 Middle St., East End* ☎ *207/774–8538* ⊕ *www. thehoneypaw.com* ◷ *Closed Tues.*

Hugo's

$$$ | **ECLECTIC** | Serving the freshest local, organic foods is a priority at Hugo's, and your server is sure to know everything about the various purveyors featured on the menu, which is updated daily and features smartly prepared, seasonally inspired dishes like crispy-skin pork belly and crepe-wrapped arctic char. You can choose five courses with a blind tasting menu for $90 or go à la carte—which

could be dangerous, as you may want to try everything on the creative menu. **Known for:** blind tasting menu; an open kitchen; dangerously delicious craft cocktails. $ *Average main: $28* ⊠ *88 Middle St., East End* ☎ *207/774–8538* ⊕ *www. hugos.net* ☉ *Closed Sun. and Mon. No lunch.*

The Shop at Island Creek Oysters

$ | **SEAFOOD** | This no-fuss counter-service spot, opened by longtime wholesale purveyors of Island Creek Oysters (from Duxbury, MA), serves seriously fresh shellfish and excellent Maine microbrews (and wine) on tap. A clutch of imported, tinned fish and house-made pickled items that pair very well with oysters are also available. **Known for:** laid-back, family-friendly environment; impeccably scrubbed and shucked oysters; housemade mignonettes. $ *Average main: $10* ⊠ *123 Washington Ave., East End* ☎ *207/699–4466* ⊕ *portland.islandcreekoysters.com* ☉ *Closed Mon.*

☕ Coffee and Quick Bites

Coffee By Design

$ | **CAFÉ** | Stop in this hip shop located in a former bakery building for quirky baked goods like vegan poptarts and sturdy coffee brewed from beans that have become a staple in many locals' home kitchens. **Known for:** among Portland's original artisanal coffee roasters; community commitment; three locations citywide. $ *Average main: $6* ⊠ *67 India St., East End* ☎ *207/780–6767* ⊕ *www. coffeebydesign.com.*

🎭 Performing Arts

Mayo Street Arts

ARTS CENTERS | **FAMILY** | An alternative-arts venue for the innovative and up-and-coming, Mayo Street Arts often features intimate concerts, contemporary exhibitions, and offbeat puppet shows in a repurposed church. ⊠ *10 Mayo St., East*

End ☎ *207/879–4629* ⊕ *www.mayostreetarts.org.*

Activities

BIKING
Cycle Mania
BICYCLING | **FAMILY** | Rent hybrid bikes downtown at Cycle Mania. The $30 per day rate includes a helmet and lock. ⊠ *65 Cove St., East End* ☎ *207/774–2933* ⊕ *www.cyclemania1.com.*

BOATING
Portland Paddle
KAYAKING | **FAMILY** | Run by a pair of Registered Maine Guides, Portland Paddle leads introductory sea-kayaking clinics along with guided trips between the Casco Bay islands June through September. Two-hour sunset paddles ($40) are a fave, as are the full-moon standup paddleboard tours ($45). Kayak and SUP rentals are available. ⊠ *Eastern Promenade, East End Beach, off Cutter St., East End* ☎ *207/370–9730* ⊕ *www.portlandpaddle. net* ☉ *Closed Nov.–May.*

The West End

A leisurely walk through Portland's West End, beginning at the top of the Arts District, offers a real treat to historic-architecture buffs. The quiet and stately neighborhood, on the National Register of Historic Places, presents an extraordinary display of architectural splendor, from High Victorian Gothic to lush Italianate, Queen Anne, and Colonial Revival.

Sights

Western Promenade
PROMENADE | A good place to start is at the head of the Western Promenade, which has benches and a nice view. From the Old Port, take Danforth Street all the way up to Vaughn Street; take a right on Vaughn and then an immediate left onto Western Promenade. Pass by

the Western Cemetery, Portland's second official burial ground, laid out in 1829—inside is the ancestral plot of poet Henry Wadsworth Longfellow—and look for street parking. ⊠ *Danforth St. to Bramhall St., West End.*

Restaurants

BaoBao Dumpling House

$ | ASIAN | FAMILY | In a historic town house with traditional Asian decor (a 30-foot copper dragon watches over diners) in Portland's quaint West End, this dumpling house serves deeply satisfying Asian-inspired comfort food in an intimate setting. Start with the house-made Asian slaw, then move to dumplings filled with tried-and-trues such as pork and cabbage or something less traditional, like beef bulgogi or shrimp and bacon. **Known for:** dishes integrating local, seasonal ingredients; tap takeovers by local brewmasters; dishes other than the namesake dumplings. ⑤ *Average main: $12* ⊠ *133 Spring St., at Park St., West End* ☎ *207/772–8400* ⊕ *www. baobaodumplinghouse.com* ⊙ *Closed Mon. and Tues.*

Hotels

★ The Francis

$$$ | HOTEL | In the beautifully restored Mellen E. Bolster House, this charming boutique hotel has a mid-century-modern vibe that seamlessly compliments the building's immaculately preserved historical design elements. **Pros:** bars in rooms; smart spa on second floor; guest rooms feature custom-built furniture. **Cons:** only 15 rooms; some rooms not accessible by elevator; no bathtubs. ⑤ *Rooms from: $300* ⊠ *747 Congress St., West End* ☎ *207/772–7485* ⊕ *www.thefrancis-maine.com* ➲ *15 rooms* ⦿| *No meals.*

Morrill Mansion

$ | B&B/INN | FAMILY | This 19th-century town house has tastefully appointed rooms with well-executed color schemes—blue is a favorite hue here—and abundant thoughtful touches like well-stocked snack areas with fresh whoopie pies baked by the innkeeper. **Pros:** close to Arts District; parlors on each floor for relaxing; tea, coffee, and baked treats available throughout the day. **Cons:** not on a grand block; no children under 14; no elevator. ⑤ *Rooms from: $189* ⊠ *249 Vaughan St., West End* ☎ *207/774–6900, 888/566–7745* ⊕ *www. morrillmansion.com* ➲ *8 rooms* ⦿| *Free breakfast.*

West End Inn

$$ | B&B/INN | Set among the glorious homes of the Western Promenade, this 1871 Georgian displays much of the era's grandeur, with high pressed-tin ceilings, intricate moldings, and ceiling medallions. **Pros:** fireplace library is a cozy place to relax; neighborhood is a historical walking tour; generous breakfast featuring local ingredients. **Cons:** 15- to 20-minute walk downtown; mostly street parking; some rooms without bathtubs. ⑤ *Rooms from: $279* ⊠ *146 Pine St., West End* ☎ *207/772–1374* ⊕ *www.west-endbb.com* ➲ *6 rooms* ⦿| *Free breakfast.*

Back Cove and Bayside

The Back Cove neighborhood is on the north side of 295 near the city's Back Cove basin—you'll hear some locals refer to it colloquially as Back Bay—which has a lovely 3½ mile trail around it. Its borders are Forest Avenue to Washington Avenue, and Canco Road to the Cove.

Bordered by Forest Avenue, Marginal Way, Cumberland Avenue, and Franklin Street, Bayside is home to Whole Foods, Trader Joe's, and the Bayside Trail.

Restaurants

★ Rose Foods

$ | DELI | FAMILY | The co-owner of the fabulous and consistently tasty Palace Diner in Biddeford has filled a long-neglected gap in Portland's food scene with this pitch-perfect bagel shop. Here you'll find spot-on New York-style bagels with both expected and unusual add-ons, including pastrami nova, chopped liver, and whitefish salad. **Known for:** family-friendly, neighborhood environment; house-cured gravlax; general-store-style shop items including books, games, and specialty food items. $ *Average main: $11* ✉ *428 Forest Ave., Back Cove and Bayside* ☎ *207/835–0991* ⊕ *www.rosefoods.me*.

☕ Coffee and Quick Bites

Two Fat Cats Bakery
STORE/MALL | This bakery's whoopie pies rely on light and fluffy, hand-scooped chocolate cake batter and a filling that's based on whipped vanilla buttercream, not the more typical marshmallow. The signature pie is made with wild Maine blueberries sourced from Maine-based and family-owned Wyman's. A second shop is located at 740 Broadway in South Portland. ✉ *195 Lancaster St., West End* ☎ *207/347–5144* ⊕ *www.twofatcatsbakery.com*.

▼ Nightlife

★ **Bayside Bowl**
BOWLING | FAMILY | This 12-lane bowling alley sprang out of a survival technique among a group of friends for getting through Maine's harrowing winters. A community-minded locale that often puts on concerts and other events, Bayside Bowl also serves up some seriously delicious cocktails and local craft beers and snacks like fries and smoked chicken wings; the rooftop, which has a food truck that serves killer tacos, has one of the best views of the city (and the sunset) in town. ✉ *58 Alder St., West End* ☎ *207/791–2695* ⊕ *www.baysidebowl.com*.

Casco Bay Islands

The islands of Casco Bay are also known as the Calendar Islands, because an early explorer mistakenly thought there was one for each day of the year (in reality there are only 140 or so). These islands range from ledges visible only at low tide to populous Peaks Island, a suburb of Portland. Some are uninhabited; others support year-round communities, as well as stores and restaurants. Ft. Gorges commands Hog Island Ledge, and Eagle Island is the site of Arctic explorer Admiral Robert Peary's home. The brightly painted ferries of Casco Bay Lines are the islands' lifeline. There is frequent service to the most populated ones, including Peaks, Long, Little Diamond, and Great Diamond.

There is little in the way of overnight lodging on the islands—the population swells during the warmer months due to summer residents—and there are few restaurants or organized attractions other than the natural beauty of the islands themselves. Meandering about by bike or on foot is a good way to explore on a day trip.

GETTING HERE AND AROUND
Casco Bay Lines provides ferry service from Portland to the islands of Casco Bay.

ESSENTIALS
TRANSPORTATION INFORMATION Casco Bay Lines. ✉ *56 Commercial St., Portland* ☎ *207/774–7871* ⊕ *www.cascobaylines.com*.

Freeport

17 miles north of Portland via I–295.

Those who flock straight to L.L. Bean and see nothing else of Freeport are missing out. The town's charming backstreets are lined with historic buildings and old clapboard houses, and there's

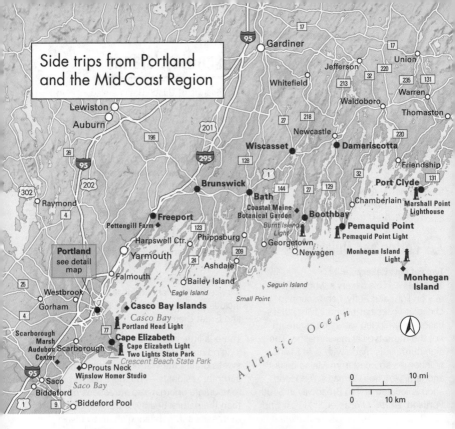

Side trips from Portland and the Mid-Coast Region

a pretty little harbor on the south side of the Harraseeket River. It's true that many who come to the area do so simply to shop: L.L. Bean is the store that put Freeport on the map, and plenty of outlets and some specialty stores have settled here. Still, if you choose, you can stay awhile and experience more than fabulous bargains; beyond the shops are bucolic nature preserves with miles of walking trails and plenty of places for leisurely ambling that don't require the overuse of your credit cards.

GETTING HERE AND AROUND
Interstate 295 has three Freeport exits and passes by on the edge of the downtown area. U.S. 1 is Main Street here.

◉ Sights

Freeport Historical Society
INFO CENTER | FAMILY | Pick up a village walking map and check out the historical exhibits at the Freeport Historical Society, located in Harrington House, a hybrid Federal- and Greek Revival–style home built in the 1830s. Always call ahead when planning a visit. ⊠ 45 Main St. ☎ 207/865–3170 ⊕ www.freeporthistoricalsociety.org.

Pettengill Farm
FARM/RANCH | FAMILY | The grounds of the Freeport Historical Society's saltwater Pettengill Farm—140 beautifully tended acres along an estuary of the Harraseeket River—are open to the public. It's about a 15-minute walk from the parking area down a farm road to the circa-1800 saltbox farmhouse, which is open by

appointment. Little has changed since it was built, and it has rare etchings (called sgraffiti) of ships and sea monsters on three bedroom walls. ✉ *31 Pettengill Rd.* ☎ *207/865–3170* ⊕ *www.freeporthistoricalsociety.org* 🎟 *Free (donations appreciated).*

🍽 Restaurants

Harraseeket Lunch and Lobster Co
$$ | **SEAFOOD** | **FAMILY** | Seafood baskets and lobster dinners are the focus at this popular, bare-bones place beside the town landing in South Freeport. Order at the counter, find a seat inside or out, and expect long lines in summer. **Known for:** great seafood; harbor location; picnic table dining. ⑤ *Average main: $18* ✉ *36 S. Main St., South Freeport* ☎ *207/865–4888* ⊕ *www.harraseeketlunchandlobster.com* 🖃 *No credit cards* 🕙 *Closed mid-Oct.–Apr.*

☕ Coffee and Quick Bites

When Pigs Fly
$ | **AMERICAN** | In addition to upward of two dozen types of classic and artisan breads, this bakery sells cookies and muffin-size cakes to grab and enjoy while walking among nearby outlet stores. Its low-carb option, a whole wheat loaf, is high on flavor and texture. **Known for:** all-natural ingredients with no preservatives; artisan breads like mango, pineapple, and raisin with toasted sesame and ginger; items baked daily. ⑤ *Average main: $4* ✉ *21 Main St.* ☎ *207/865–6006* ⊕ *sendbread.com.*

🛏 Hotels

Harraseeket Inn
$ | **HOTEL** | **FAMILY** | Despite some modern appointments, this large hotel has a country-inn ambience throughout—guest rooms have print fabrics and reproductions of Federal-style quarter-canopy beds. **Pros:** full breakfast; elevators and

other modern touches; walk to shopping district. **Cons:** additions have diminished some authenticity; some rooms without a garden view; fireplaces only in select rooms. ⑤ *Rooms from: $179* ✉ *162 Main St.* ☎ *207/865–9377, 800/342–6423* ⊕ *www.harraseeketinn.com* 🛏 *84 rooms* 🍽 *Free breakfast.*

🎭 Performing Arts

L.L. Bean Summer Concert Series
CONCERTS | **FAMILY** | Throughout the summer, L.L. Bean hosts free activities, including concerts, at the L.L. Bean Discovery Park. It's set back from Main Street, along a side street that runs between the company's flagship and home furnishings stores. ✉ *18 Morse St.* ☎ *877/755–2326* ⊕ *www.llbean.com.*

🛍 Shopping

★ L.L. Bean
CLOTHING | **FAMILY** | Founded in 1912 as a mail-order merchandiser after its namesake invented a hunting boot, L.L. Bean's giant flagship store attracts more than 3 million shoppers annually and is open 365 days a year in the heart of Freeport's outlet shopping district. You can still find the original hunting boots, along with cotton and wool sweaters; outerwear of all kinds; casual clothing, boots, and shoes for men, women, and kids; and camping equipment. Nearby are the company's home furnishings store; bike, boat, and ski store; and outlet. ✉ *95 Main St.* ☎ *877/755–2326* ⊕ *www.llbean.com.*

R. D. Allen Freeport Jewelers
JEWELRY/ACCESSORIES | This shop specializes in brightly colored tourmaline and other gemstones mined in Maine. Most of the pieces are the work of Maine artisans. Watermelon tourmaline is a specialty. ✉ *13 Middle St.* ✛ *2 blocks from L.L. Bean* ☎ *207/865–1818* ⊕ *www.rdallen.com.*

★ **Thos. Moser Cabinetmakers**

HOUSEHOLD ITEMS/FURNITURE | Famed local furniture company Thos. Moser Cabinetmakers sells artful, handmade wood pieces with clean, classic lines. The store has information on tours at the workshop 30 minutes away in Auburn (by appointment only). ⊠ *149 Main St.* ☎ *207/865–4519* ⊕ *www.thosmoser.com.*

 Activities

L.L. Bean Outdoor Discovery Schools

TOUR—SPORTS | **FAMILY** | It shouldn't come as a surprise that one of the world's largest outdoor outfitters also provides its customers with instructional adventures to go with its products. L.L. Bean's year-round Outdoor Discovery Schools offer courses in canoeing, biking, kayaking, fly-fishing, snowshoeing, cross-country skiing, and other outdoor sports. ⊠ *11 Desert Rd.* ☎ *888/552–3261* ⊕ *www.llbean.com/ods.*

Brunswick

10 miles north of Freeport via U.S. 1.

Lovely brick and clapboard buildings are the highlight of Brunswick's Federal Street Historic District, which includes Federal Street and Park Row and the stately campus of Bowdoin College. From the intersection of Pleasant and Maine streets, in the center of town, you can walk in any direction and discover an impressive array of restaurants, as well as bookstores, gift shops, boutiques, and jewelers.

Below Brunswick are Harpswell Neck and the more than 40 islands that make up the town of Harpswell, known collectively as the Harpswells. Route 123 runs down Harpswell Neck, where small coves shelter lobster boats, and summer cottages are tucked away among birch and spruce trees. On your way down from Cook's Corner to Land's End at the

end of Route 24, you cross Sebascodegan Island. Heading east here leads to East Harpswell and Cundy's Harbor. Continuing straight south down Route 24 leads to Orr's Island. Stop at Mackerel Cove to see a real fishing harbor; there are a few parking spaces, where you can stop to picnic and look for beach glass or put in your kayaks. Inhale the salt breeze as you cross the world's only cribstone bridge (designed so that water flows freely through gaps between the granite blocks) on your way to Bailey Island, home to a lobster pound made famous thanks in part to a Visa commercial.

GETTING HERE AND AROUND

From Interstate 295 take the Coastal Connector to U.S. 1 in Brunswick. From here Route 24 runs to Bailey Island and Route 123 down Harpswell Neck.

 Sights

★ **Bowdoin College Museum of Art**

ARTS CENTERS | **FAMILY** | This small museum housed in a stately building on Bowdoin's main quad features one of the oldest permanent collections of art in the United States, comprising paintings, sculpture, decorative arts, and works on paper. The museum often mounts well-curated, rotating exhibitions and has stellar programs for getting children excited about art. ⊠ *245 Maine St.* ☎ *207/725–3275* ⊕ *www.bowdoin.edu/art-museum* ⊠ *Free.*

🍴 **Restaurants**

★ **Cook's Lobster and Ale House**

$$$ | **SEAFOOD** | **FAMILY** | What began as a lobster shack on Bailey's Island in 1955 has grown into a huge, internationally famous family-style restaurant with a small gift shop. The restaurant still catches its own seafood, so you can count on the lobster roll and the haddock sandwich to be delectable. **Known for:** traditional Maine seafood fare prepared simply; terrific selection of local craft beer and spirits; live music and festive atmosphere in the summer. $ *Average main: $26* ✉ *68 Garrison Cove Rd., Bailey Island* ☎ *207/833–2818* ⊕ *www.cookslobster.com* ⊘ *Closed early Jan.–mid-Feb.*

★ Frontier

$ | MEDITERRANEAN | There's nothing typical about Frontier, where indie films roll daily, artists and musicians from all over the world share their art, and a globally inspired menu features locally sourced ingredients in recipes culled from diverse cultures. Come for the inspiring events, stay for the delicious food and dangerously terrific cocktails. **Known for:** poblano and fish tacos and other seafood, as well as Mediterranean and Middle Eastern dishes; acting locally and thinking globally; menu staples such as curried mussels and vegan nachos. $ *Average main: $15* ✉ *14 Maine St., Mill 3 Fort Andross* ☎ *207/725–5222* ⊕ *www.explorefrontier.com* ⊘ *Closed Mon.*

☕ Coffee and Quick Bites

Little Dog Coffee Shop

$ | AMERICAN | Tide yourself over until lunch or dinner with coffee or chai and a muffin at this popular spot. There are also bagel sandwiches and wraps if you're hungrier. **Known for:** exhibiting local art; sidewalk seating; locally sourced goods. $ *Average main: $4* ✉ *87 Maine St., Freeport* ☎ *207/721–9500* ⊕ *www. littledogcoffeeshop.com.*

🏃 Activities

H2Outfitters

KAYAKING | The coast near Brunswick is full of hidden nooks and crannies waiting to be explored by kayak. H2Outfitters, at the southern end of Orr's Island just before the cribstone bridge, is the place in Harpswell to get on the water. It provides top-notch kayaking instruction and also offers half-day, full-day, B&B, and camping trips in the waters off its home base and elsewhere in Maine.

✉ *1894 Harpswell Island Rd., Orrs Island* ☎ *207/833–5257, 800/205–2925* ⊕ *www. h2outfitters.com.*

Bath

11 miles north of Brunswick via U.S. 1.

Bath has been a shipbuilding center since 1607. The result of its prosperity can be seen in its handsome mix of Federal, Greek Revival, and Italianate homes along Front, Centre, and Washington streets. In the heart of Bath's historic district are some charming 19th-century homes, including the 1820 Federal-style home at 360 Front Street; the 1810 Greek Revival mansion at 969 Washington Street, covered with gleaming white clapboards; and the Victorian gem at 1009 Washington Street, painted a distinctive shade of raspberry. All three operate as inns. One easily overlooked site is the town's City Hall; the bell in its tower was cast by Paul Revere in 1805.

The venerable Bath Iron Works completed its first passenger ship in 1890. During World War II, BIW (as it's locally known) launched a new ship every 17 days. Not only is it still in production today, BIW is one of the state's largest employers, with about 6,800 workers, who turn out destroyers for the U.S. Navy. (It's a good idea to avoid U.S. 1 on weekdays 3:15–4:30 pm, when a major shift change takes place.) You can tour BIW through the Maine Maritime Museum.

GETTING HERE AND AROUND

U.S. 1 passes through downtown and across the Kennebec River at Bath. Downtown is on the north side of the highway along the river.

👁 Sights

★ Maine Maritime Museum

MUSEUM | FAMILY | No trip to Bath is complete without a visit to this cluster of buildings that once made up the historic Percy & Small Shipyard. Plan to spend at least half a day here. In fact, admission tickets are good for two days; there's just that much to see at this museum, which examines the world of shipbuilding and which is the only way to tour Bath Iron Works (June–mid-October). From late May through late October, daily nature and lighthouse boat tours cruise the scenic Kennebec River—one takes in 10 lights. The museum's flagship, the 1906 schooner Mary E, offers sails and dockside tours during the same period. Hour-long tours of the shipyard show how these massive wooden ships were built. In the boat shop, you can watch boatbuilders wield their tools, and see blacksmiths at work in the museum's forge. Inside the main museum building, exhibits use ship models, paintings, photographs, and historic artifacts to tell the maritime history of the region. A separate historic building houses a fascinating 6,000-square-foot lobstering exhibit. A gift shop and bookstore are on the premises, and you can grab a bite to eat in the café or bring a picnic to eat on the grounds. ■TIP→ **Kids ages six and younger get in free.** ✉ 243 Washington St. ☎ 207/443–1316 ⊕ www.mainemaritimemuseum.org ⬥ $18, good for 2 days within 7-day period.

🍴 Restaurants

Beale Street Barbecue
$ | **BARBECUE** | Ribs are the thing at one of Maine's oldest barbecue joints, opened in 1996. Hearty eaters should ask for one of the platters piled high with pulled pork, pulled chicken, or shredded beef. **Known for:** three-cheese mac and cheese (American, cheddar, and Pecorino romano); Maine microbrews; Key lime pie. ⑤ Average main: $13 ✉ 215 Water St. ☎ 207/442–9514 ⊕ www.mainebbq.com.

Coffee and Quick Bites

Café Crème
$ | **BAKERY** | Located in the heart of downtown, visitors and locals alike flock to this coffee shop for delicious coffee paired with baked-that-day goods and served with a smile. The cinnamon roll with maple bacon is a savory Maine take on the classic sweet treat. **Known for:** sweet and savory stuffed croissants; on-site bakery; friendly staff. ⑤ Average main: $7 ✉ 56 Front St., at Centre St. ☎ 207/443–6454.

🛏 Hotels

★ Kennebec Inn Bed and Breakfast
$ | **B&B/INN** | Four immaculate, well-appointed rooms tastefully decorated with maritime touches, luxe bedding and towels, and welcoming common spaces await you at this hidden gem in a historic captain's home—you'll feel like you're at an exclusive retreat. **Pros:** calm and quiet atmosphere make for pure relaxation; delicious, multicourse breakfast you can take at your leisure; knowledgeable, warm innkeeper. **Cons:** only four rooms; a short walk into center of town; no pets. ⑤ Rooms from: $180 ✉ 696 High St. ☎ 207/443–5324 ⊕ www.kennebecinn.com ⬥ 4 rooms ⑨ Free breakfast.

Sebasco Harbor Resort
$$ | **RESORT** | **FAMILY** | A family-friendly resort spread over 450 acres on the water near the foot of the Phippsburg Peninsula, this place has a golf course, spa, tennis courts, and a saltwater pool, among a host of other amenities. **Pros:** good choice for families; perfect location; children's activities; wonderful array of lawn games. **Cons:** no sand beach; heavy traffic and large number of rooms can diminish quality and service; golf fee not included in stay. ⑤ Rooms from: $249 ✉ 29 Kenyon Rd., off Sebasco Rd., Phippsburg ☎ 800/225–3819 ⊕ www.

sebasco.com ⊘ *Closed late Oct.–mid-May* ⇌ *110 rooms* ⦿ *No meals.*

Wiscasset

10 miles north of Bath via U.S. 1.

Settled in 1663, Wiscasset sits on the banks of the Sheepscot River. It bills itself "Maine's Prettiest Village," and it's easy to see why: it has graceful churches, old cemeteries, and elegant sea captains' homes (many converted into antiques shops or galleries).

There's also a good wine and specialty foods shop called Treats (stock up here if you're heading north). Pack a picnic and take it down to the dock on Water Street, where you can watch the fishing boats, or grab a lobster roll from Red's Eats or the lobster shack nearby. Wiscasset has expanded its wharf, and this is a great place to catch a breeze on a hot day.

GETTING HERE AND AROUND
U.S. 1 becomes Main Street, and traffic often slows to a crawl come summer. You'll likely have success parking on Water Street rather than Main. It's a good idea to do your driving around Wiscasset very early in the morning and after 7 in the evening when traffic eases a bit. The best way to get around here is on foot.

Restaurants

Red's Eats
$$ | SEAFOOD | FAMILY | It's hard to miss the long line of hungry customers outside this little red shack on the Wiscasset side of the bridge. Red's is a local landmark famous for its hamburgers, hot dogs, lobster and crab rolls, and crispy onion rings and clams fried in house-made batters. **Known for:** more than a whole lobster goes into each lobster roll; the unholy "Puff Dog," a hot dog loaded with bacon and cheese and deep-fried; long

lines in summer. ⑤ *Average main: $20* ✉ *41 Water St.* ☎ *207/882–6128* ⊕ *www.redseatsmaine.com* ⊟ *No credit cards* ⊘ *Closed mid-Oct.–mid-Apr.*

Coffee and Quick Bites

Treats
$ | AMERICAN | What started as a candy shop over 30 years ago has grown into a Wiscasset staple featuring coffee, baked goods, wine, beer, and cheese and more. Order a gourmet picnic basket to go, or stick around and relax with a coffee and scone. **Known for:** scones made from owner's nana's recipe; "bronuts" filled with pastry cream; locally sourced ingredients. ⑤ *Average main: $5* ✉ *80 Main St.* ☎ *207/882–6192* ⊕ *www.treatsofmaine.com.*

⬡ Shopping

Edgecomb Potters
CERAMICS/GLASSWARE | Edgecomb Potters is not to be missed: they make vibrantly colored, exquisitely glazed porcelain known all around the country. The store also carries jewelry, glassware, and glass sculptures. ✉ *727 Boothbay Rd., Edgecomb* ☎ *207/882–9493* ⊕ *www.edgecombpotters.com.*

In the Clover
CLOTHING | There's something charmingly old-school about this pretty boutique with its warm and friendly service and fine displays of women's clothing, accessories, and beauty products. Geared toward elegant but no-fuss women of every age, the shop stocks clothing items such as fine cashmere shawls; pretty but not froufrou lingerie; and sophisticated loungewear as well as a good selection of natural beauty products and fragrances, unique jewelry, and inspiring books. ✉ *85 A. Main St.* ☎ *207/882–9435* ⊕ *inthecloverbeauty.com.* ·

Continued on page 327

MAINE'S LIGHTHOUSES
GUARDIANS OF THE COAST By John Blodgett

Perched high on rocky ledges, on the tips of wayward islands, and sometimes seemingly on the ocean itself are the more than five dozen lighthouses standing watch along Maine's craggy and ship-busting coastline.

Marshall Point Light

LIGHTING THE WAY: A BIT OF HISTORY

Portland Head Light

Most lighthouses were built in the first half of the 19th century to protect vessels from running aground at night or when the shoreline was shrouded in fog. Along with the mournful siren of the foghorn and maritime lore, these practical structures have come to symbolize Maine throughout the world.

SHIPWRECKS AND SAFETY

These alluring sentinels of the eastern seaboard today have more form than function, but that certainly was not always the case. Safety was a strong motivating factor in the erection of the lighthouses. Commerce also played a critical role. For example, in 1791 Portland Head Light was completed, partially as a response to local merchants' concerns about the rocky entrance to Portland Harbor and the varying depths of the shipping channel. In 1789, the federal government created the U.S. Lighthouse Establishment (later the U.S. Lighthouse Service) to manage them. In 1939 the U.S. Coast Guard took on the job.

Maine's lighthouses were built in a much-needed locations, but the points and islands upon which they sat were prone to storm damage. Along with poor construction, this meant that over the years many lighthouses had to be rebuilt or replaced.

LIGHTHOUSES TODAY

In modern times, many of the structures still serve a purpose. Technological advances, such as GPS and radar, are mainly used to navigate through the choppy waters, but a lighthouse or its foghorns are helpful secondary aids, and sometimes the only ones used by recreational boaters. The numerous channel-marking buoys still in existence also are testament to the old tried-and-true methods.

Of the 66 lighthouses along this far northeastern state, 57 are still working, alerting ships (and even small aircraft) of the shoreline's rocky edge. Government agencies, historic preservation organizations, and mostly private individuals own the decommissioned lights.

KEEPERS OF THE LIGHT

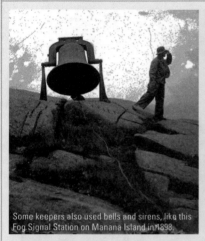

Some keepers also used bells and sirens, like this Fog Signal Station on Manana Island in 1898.

Pemaquid Point's fourth-order Fresnel lens

LIFE OF A LIGHTKEEPER

One thing that has changed with the modern era is the disappearance of the lighthouse keeper. In the early 20th century, lighthouses began the conversion from oil-based lighting to electricity. A few decades later, the U.S. Coast Guard switched to automation, phasing out the need for an on-site keeper.

While the keepers of tradition were no longer needed, the traditions of these stalwart, 24/7 employees live on through museum exhibits and retellings of Maine's maritime history, legends, and lore. The tales of a lighthouse keeper's life are the stuff romance novels are made of: adventure, rugged but lonely men, and a beautiful setting along an unpredictable coastline.

The lighthouse keepers of yesterday probably didn't see their own lives so romantically. Their daily narrative was one of hard work and, in some cases, exceptional solitude. A keeper's primary job was to ensure that the lamp was illuminated all day, every day. This meant that oil (whale or coal oil and later kerosene) had to be

carried about and wicks trimmed on a regular basis. When fog shrouded the coast, they sounded the solemn horn to pierce through the damp darkness that hid their light. Their quarters were generally small and often attached to the light tower itself. The remote locations of the lights added to the isolation a keeper felt, especially before the advent of radio and telephone, let alone the Internet. Though some brought families with them, the keepers tended to be men who lived alone.

THE LIGHTS 101

Over the years, Fresnel (fray-NELL) lenses were developed in different shapes and sizes so that ship captains could distinguish one lighthouse from another. Invented by Frenchman Augustin Fresnel in the early 19th century, the lens design allows for a greater transmission of light perfectly suited for lighthouse use. Knowing which lighthouse they were near helped captains know which danger was present, such as a submerged ledge or shallow channel. Some lights, such as those at Seguin Island Light, are fixed and don't flash. Other lights are colored red.

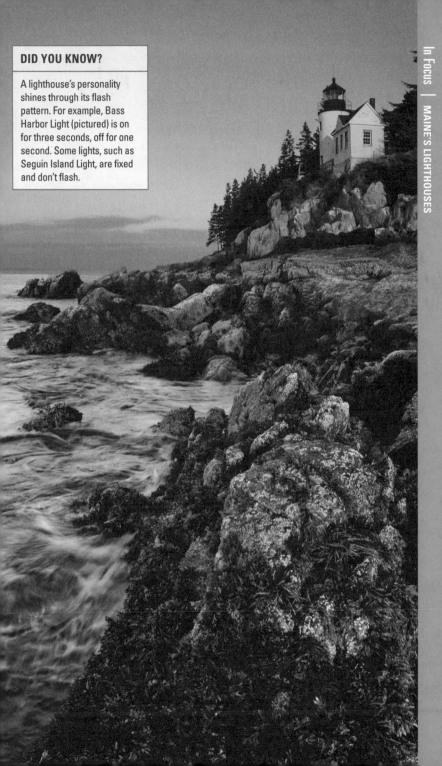

DID YOU KNOW?

A lighthouse's personality shines through its flash pattern. For example, Bass Harbor Light (pictured) is on for three seconds, off for one second. Some lights, such as Seguin Island Light, are fixed and don't flash.

LIGHTHOUSE FINDER

**Map labels:**
Lubec · West Quoddy Head · Machias · Little River Lighthouse · Old Town · Newport · Bangor · Farmington · Jonesport · Narraguagus · Prospect Harbor · Fort Point · Ellsworth · Searsport · Dyces Head · Belfast · Winter Harbor · Bar Harbor · Castine · Mt. Desert Is. · Bass Harbor Head · AUGUSTA · Grindle Point · Camden · Goose Rocks Light · Rockland Breakwater · Burnt Coat Harbor · Auburn · Lewiston · Harrison · Rockland · Owls Head · Browns Head · Isle au Haut · Brunswick · Pemaquid Point · Freeport · Bath · Boothbay · Marshall Point · Matinicus Rock · The Cuckolds · Portland Head · Pond Island · Seguin · Portland · Monhegan Is. · Cape Elizabeth (Two Lights) · Goat Island · Kennebunk · Kennebunkport · Ogunquit · York · Cape Neddick (Nubble Light) · Whaleback · Kittery · Portsmouth

KEY
Top Picks

West Quoddy Head

SEEK OUT STATE PARKS

■ **TIP→ To get the full lighthouse experience your best bet is to visit one that is part of a state or local park.** These are generally well kept and tend to allow up-close approach, though typically only outside. While you're at the parks you can picnic or stroll on the trails. Wildlife is often abundant in and near the water; you might spot sea birds and even whales in certain locations (try West Quoddy Head, Portland Head, or Two Lights).

VISITING MAINE'S LIGHTHOUSES

As you travel along the Maine Coast, you won't see lighthouses by watching your odometer—there were no rules about the spacing of lighthouses. The decision as to where to place a lighthouse was a balance between a region's geography and its commercial prosperity and maritime traffic.

Lighthouses dot the shore from as far south as York to the country's easternmost tip at Lubec. Accessibility varies according to location and other factors. A handful are so remote as to be outright impossible to reach (except perhaps by kayaking and rock climbing). Some don't allow visitors according to Coast Guard policies, though you can enjoy them through the zoom lens of a camera. Others you can walk right up to and, occasionally, even climb to the top. Lighthouse enthusiasts and preservation groups restore and maintain many of them. All told, approximately 30 lighthouses allow some sort of public access.

MUSEUMS, TOURS, AND MORE

Most keeper's quarters are closed to the public, but some of the homes have been converted to museums, full of intriguing exhibits on lighthouses, the famous Fresnel lenses used in them, and artifacts of Maine maritime life in general. Talk to the librarians at the **Maine Maritime Museum** in Bath (⊕ *www.mainemaritimemuseum. org*) or sign up for one of the museum's daily lighthouse cruises to pass by up to ten on the Lighthouse Lovers Cruise. In Rockland, the **Maine Lighthouse Museum** (⊕ *www.mainelighthousemuseum.org*) has the country's largest display of Fresnel lenses. The museum also displays keepers' memorabilia, foghorns, brassware, and more. Maine Open Lighthouse Day is the second Saturday after Labor Day; you can tour and even climb about two dozen lights usually closed to the public.

For more information, check out the lighthouse page at Maine's official tourism site: ⊕ *visitmaine.com*.

SLEEPING LIGHT: STAYING OVERNIGHT

Goose Rocks, where you can play lighthouse keeper for a week.

Want to stay overnight in a lighthouse? There are several options to do so.
■ TIP→ **Book lighthouse lodgings as far in advance as possible, up to one year ahead.**

Our top pick is **Pemaquid Point Light** (*L. Dewey Chase Rentals* ☎ *207/677–2100* ⊕ *newharborrentals.com*) because it has one of the most dramatic settings on the Maine coast. Two miles south of **New Harbor**, the second floor of the lighthouse keeper's house is rented out on a weekly basis early May through mid-November to support upkeep of the grounds. When you aren't enjoying the interior, head outdoors: the covered front porch has a rocking-chair view of the ocean. The one-bedroom, one-bath rental sleeps up to a family of four.

Situated smack dab in the middle of a major maritime thoroughfare between two Penobscot Bay islands, **Goose Rocks Light** (☎ *203/400–9565* ⊕ *www. beaconpreservation.org*) offers lodging for the adventuresome—the 51-foot "spark plug" lighthouse is completely surrounded by water. Getting there requires a ferry ride from Rockland to nearby **North Haven**, a 5- to 10-minute ride by motorboat, and then a climb up an iron-rung ladder from the pitching boat—all based on high tide and winds, of course. There's room for up to six people. It's a bit more cushy experience than it was for the original keepers: there's a flat-screen TV with DVD player and a selection of music and videos for entertainment. In addition, a hammock hangs on the small deck that encircles the operational light; it's a great place from which to watch the majestic windjammers and the fishing fleet pass by.

Little River Lighthouse (☎ *877/276–4682* ⊕ *www.littleriverlight.org*), along the far northeastern reaches of the coast in **Cutler**, has three rooms available for rent from mid-June to September. You're responsible for food and beverages, linens, towels, and other personal items (don't forget the bug spray), but kitchen and other basics are provided. The lighthouse volunteers with Friends of Little River Lighthouse will provide a boat ride to the island upon which the lighthouse sits.

TOP LIGHTHOUSES TO VISIT

BASS HARBOR LIGHT

Familiar to many as the subject of countless photographs is Bass Harbor Light, at the southern end of **Mount Desert Island.** It is within Acadia National Park and 17 miles from the town of Bar Harbor. The station grounds are open year-round.

CAPE ELIZABETH LIGHT

Two Lights State Park is so-named because it's next to two lighthouses. Both of these **Cape Elizabeth** structures were built in 1828. The western light was closed in 1924 and eventually converted into a private residence; the eastern light, Cape Elizabeth Light, still projects its automated cylinder of light. The grounds surrounding the building and the lighthouse itself are closed to the public, but the structure is easily viewed and photographed from nearby at the end of Two Lights Road.

Cape Neddick

CAPE NEDDICK LIGHT

More commonly known as Nubble Light for the smallish offshore expanse of rock it rests upon, Cape Neddick Light sits a few hundred feet off a rock point in **York Beach.** With such a precarious location, its grounds are inaccessible to visitors, but close enough to be exceptionally photogenic, especially during the Christmas season.

MONHEGAN ISLAND LIGHT

Only the adventuresome and the artistic see this light, because **Monhegan Island** is accessible by an approximately one-hour ferry ride. To reach the lighthouse, you have an additional half-mile walk uphill from the ferry dock. The former keeper's quarters is home to the Monhegan Museum, which has exhibits about the island. The tower itself is closed to the public.

Portland Head

PORTLAND HEAD LIGHT

One of Maine's most photographed lighthouses (and its oldest), the famous Portland Head Light was completed in January 1791. At the edge of Fort Williams Park, in **Cape Elizabeth**, the towering white stone lighthouse stands 101 feet above the sea. The Coast Guard operates it and it is not open for tours. However the adjacent keeper's dwelling is now a museum.

WEST QUODDY HEAD LIGHT

Originally built in 1808 by mandate of President Thomas Jefferson, West Quoddy Head Light sits in **Lubec** on the easternmost tip of land in the mainland United States. The 49-foot-high lighthouse with distinctive red and white stripes, is part of Quoddy Head State Park.

West Quoddy Head

★ Rock Paper Scissors

GIFTS/SOUVENIRS | Not your run-of-the-mill gift shop, this well-curated boutique stocks offbeat cards and letterpress stationery, local handcrafted goods such as blankets, purses, and ceramics, and beautiful, one-of-a-kind objects for the home and kitchen. Stocked to the brim with charming goodies for anyone on your list (including yourself), this shop is decidedly contemporary, with a Scandinavian bent, and is well worth a stop, if only to peruse the gorgeously arranged array of products on display. ⊠ *68 Main St.* ☎ *207/882–9930.*

Sheepscot River Pottery

CERAMICS/GLASSWARE | This shop boasts beautifully glazed kitchen tiles, as well as kitchenware and home accessories, including sinks. Jewelry and other items by local artisans are also on sale. ⊠ *34 U.S. 1, Edgecomb* ☎ *207/882–9410* ⊕ *www.sheepscot.com.*

Boothbay

11 miles south of Wiscasset via Rte. 27.

The shoreline of the Boothbay Peninsula is a craggy stretch of inlets, where pleasure craft anchor alongside trawlers and lobster boats. The town of Boothbay comprises the village center, Boothbay Harbor, and East Boothbay. The harbor is like a smaller version of Bar Harbor—touristy, but friendly and fun—with pretty, winding streets and lots to explore. Commercial Street, Wharf Street, Townsend Avenue, and the By-Way are lined with shops and ice-cream parlors. One of the biggest draws here is the stunning Coastal Maine Botanical Gardens, with its beautiful café and gift shop, as well as its famous children's garden.

GETTING HERE AND AROUND

In season, boat trips to Monhegan Island leave from the piers off Commercial Street. Drive out to Ocean Point in East Boothbay for some incredible scenery. Boothbay is 11 miles south of Wiscasset via U.S. 1 and Route 27.

Sights

★ Coastal Maine Botanical Garden

GARDEN | FAMILY | Set aside a couple of hours to stroll among the roses, lupines, and rhododendrons at the 250-acre Coastal Maine Botanical Garden. In the summer, free docent-led tours leave from the visitor center at 11 every day May–October. The "children's garden" is a wonderland of stone sculptures, rope bridges, small teahouselike structures with grass roofs, and even a hedge maze. Children and adults alike adore the separate woodland fairy area. The on-site restaurant and café, as well as the bookshop and resource library, are also delightful. It's easy to spend an entire day here and not see everything—be sure to wear comfortable walking shoes. For those less inclined to go by foot, the gardens offer free shuttle service to most spots on the property. ⊠ *132 Botanical Gardens Dr., off Rte. 27* ☎ *207/633–8000* ⊕ *www.mainegardens.org* ⊠ *$20.*

Restaurants

Boathouse Bistro Tapas Bar and Restaurant

$$ | TAPAS | The multitier rooftop terrace (complete with an outdoor bar) stays crowded all summer at the Boat House Bistro. Austrian-born chef Karin Guerin dishes up tapas-style small plates ranging from mojito ginger wings to Madagascar beef skewers. **Known for:** fried oysters with truffle pearls; Spanish-inspired dishes featuring locally caught seafood; a sizeable array of flatbread grillers featuring different toppings. ⑤ *Average main: $22* ⊠ *12 The By-Way, Boothbay Harbor* ☎ *207/633–0400* ⊕ *www.theboathouse-bistro.com* ⊘ *Closed mid-Oct.–mid-Apr. and Wed. and Thurs.*

Coffee and Quick Bites

Red Cup Coffeehouse

$ | **AMERICAN** | Stop by while walking downtown Boothbay Harbor for a hot or iced espresso drink or cold fruit smoothie. There is also a selection of freshly baked goods to choose from. **Known for:** beans from Portland-based Coffee By Design; cold brew on nitro tap; breakfast sandwiches on fresh bread. ⑤ *Average main: $5* ✉ *29 Commercial St., Boothbay Harbor* ☎ *207/350–4228* ⊕ *www.redcupcoffeehouse.com* ⊘ *Closed Tues. in off-season.*

🛏 Hotels

Spruce Point Inn

$$ | **RESORT** | **FAMILY** | A great base for exploring Boothbay, this lovely seaside inn acts like a resort, while feeling more like you're visiting an old friend's house or a summer home. **Pros:** some pet-friendly lodging; family game room; laundry on-site; shuttle by boat to the town center; private boat launch. **Cons:** some private residences close to premises; no indoor pool; golfing access off-site. ⑤ *Rooms from: $250* ✉ *88 Grandview Ave., Boothbay Harbor* ☎ *207/633–4152* ⊕ *www.sprucepointinn.com* ⊘ *Closed mid-Oct.–mid-May* ⇥ *63 rooms* ❖ *No meals.*

Topside Inn

$$ | **B&B/INN** | The Adirondack chairs on the immense lawn of this historic hilltop B&B have what is probably the best bay view in town. **Pros:** knockout views; plenty of green space for croquet; easy walk downtown. **Cons:** two-person maximum per room; reservations fill quickly in summer; pets only allowed in the cottages. ⑤ *Rooms from: $299* ✉ *60 McKown St., Boothbay Harbor* ☎ *207/633–5404* ⊕ *www.topsideinn.com* ⊘ *Closed Nov.–Apr.* ⇥ *23 rooms* ❖ *Free breakfast.*

Damariscotta

8 miles north of Wiscasset via U.S. 1.

The Damariscotta region comprises several communities along the rocky coast. The town itself sits on the water, a lively place filled with attractive shops and restaurants, as well as some of the best oysters around.

Just across the bridge over the Damariscotta River is the town of Newcastle, between the Sheepscot and Damariscotta rivers. Newcastle was settled in the early 1600s. The earliest inhabitants planted apple trees, but the town later became an industrial center, home to several shipyards and a couple of mills. The oldest Catholic church in New England, St. Patrick's, is here, and it still rings its original Paul Revere bell.

Bremen, which encompasses more than a dozen islands and countless rocky outcrops, has many seasonal homes along the water, and the main industries in the small community are fishing and clamming. Nobleboro, a bit north of here on U.S. 1, was settled in the 1720s by Colonel David Dunbar, sent by the British to rebuild the fort at Pemaquid. Neighboring Waldoboro is situated on the Medomak River and was settled largely by Germans in the mid-1700s. You can still visit the old German Meeting House, built in 1772. The Pemaquid Peninsula stretches south from Damariscotta to include Bristol, South Bristol, Round Pond, New Harbor, and Pemaquid.

GETTING HERE AND AROUND

In Newcastle, U.S. 1B runs from U.S. 1 across the Damariscotta River to Damariscotta. From this road take Route 129 south to South Bristol and Route 130 south to Bristol and New Harbor. From here you can return to U.S. 1 heading north on Route 32 through Round Pond and Bremen. In Waldoboro, turn off U.S. 1 on Jefferson Street to see the historic village center.

Maine is the largest lobster-producing state in the United States.

ESSENTIALS

VISITOR INFORMATION Damariscotta Region Chamber of Commerce. ☎ *207/563–8340* ⊕ *www.damariscottaregion.com.*

🍴 Restaurants

King Eider's Pub and Restaurant

$$$ | **AMERICAN** | **FAMILY** | This cozy, classic pub right downtown bills itself as having the finest crab cakes in New England. Start with the fresh local oysters that the Damariscotta region is known for, then move on to entrées like steak-and-ale pie, sea-scallop Florentine, or sautéed haddock with chips. **Known for:** live music; special gatherings; extensive whiskey collection. ⑤ *Average main: $29* ⊠ *2 Elm St.* ☎ *207/563–6008* ⊕ *www.kingeiderspub.com.*

★ Newcastle Publick House

$$ | **AMERICAN** | **FAMILY** | In a handsomely renovated historic building, Newcastle Publick House serves delicious comfort food, including fresh oysters, house-made pastrami, and local craft beers,

as well as one of the best French onion soups around. There is often live music, making it a great place for a night out on a date or with the entire family. **Known for:** stacked burgers; cozy, old-school atmosphere; desserts and breads made by nearby Oysterhead Pizza Co. ⑤ *Average main: $20* ⊠ *52 Main St., Newcastle* ☎ *207/563–3434* ⊕ *www.newcastlepublickhouse.com* ⊙ *Closed Mon.*

☕ Coffee and Quick Bites

Cupacity

$ | **AMERICAN** | Opened in the heart of downtown in 2019, this bright and friendly women-owned shop offers coffee, tea, wine, hard cider, beer, and small bites like falafel sliders and organic summer salads. **Known for:** locally sourced food and drinks; the "Krunk": part nitro cold brew, part lemonade; outdoor patio seating to watch the world go by. ⑤ *Average main: $10* ⊠ *133 Main St.* ☎ *207/563–6127* ⊕ *www.cupacitycoffee.com* ⊙ *Closed Sun.–Wed.*

Hotels

Newcastle Inn

$$ | B&B/INN | FAMILY | A riverside location, tasteful decor, and lots of common areas (inside and out) make this a relaxing country inn. **Pros:** guests can order beer or wine; suites have sitting areas; water views in many rooms. **Cons:** short walk into the village; not all rooms have water views; some rooms without ample sitting areas. ⑤ *Rooms from: $200* ✉ *60 River Rd., Newcastle* ☎ *207/563–5685* ⊕ *www. newcastleinn.com* ⌁ *14 rooms* ⑩ *Free breakfast.*

Pemaquid Point

10 miles south of Damariscotta via U.S. 1, U.S. 1B, and Rte. 130.

Pemaquid Point is the tip of the Pemaquid Peninsula, bordered by Muscongus and Johns bays. It's home to the famous lighthouse of the same name and its attendant fog bell and tiny museum. Also at the bottom of the peninsula, along the Muscongus Bay, is the Nature Conservancy's Rachel Carson Salt Pond Preserve.

GETTING HERE AND AROUND
From U.S. 1, take U.S. 1B into Damariscotta and head south on Route 130 to Pemaquid Point.

Sights

★ Pemaquid Point Light

LIGHTHOUSE | FAMILY | At the end of Route 130, this lighthouse at the tip of the Pemaquid Peninsula looks as though it sprouted from the ragged, tilted chunk of granite it commands. Most days in the summer you can climb the tower to the light. The former keeper's cottage is now the Fishermen's Museum, which displays historic photographs, scale models, and artifacts that explore commercial fishing in Maine. Also here are the original fog bell and bell house. There are restrooms and picnic tables. ✉ *3115 Bristol Rd., New Harbor* ☎ *207/677–2492* ⊕ *www. bristolmaine.org* ⌁ *$3.*

Restaurants

★ Muscongus Bay Lobster Co.

$$ | SEAFOOD | FAMILY | The food here is practically guaranteed to be fresh: lobsters come in off the boat at one end of the pier, and the restaurant is at the other. Grab a picnic table and be careful not to hit your head on the colorful, dangling wooden buoys. **Known for:** laid-back, BYOB atmosphere; kid-friendly; repeat visitors meet and greet here. ⑤ *Average main: $18* ✉ *28 Landing Rd., Round Pond* ☎ *207/529–5528* ⊕ *www.mainefreshlobster.com* ⊗ *Closed mid-Oct.–mid-May.*

Round Pond Lobster

$$ | SEAFOOD | Sheltered Muscongus Bay is where you'll find this down-home lobster shack, right on the pier with pleasant views of the water. Competition with the neighboring Muscongus Bay Lobster Co. keeps the prices low for fresh-off-the-boat lobster and steamers. **Known for:** BYO drinks and sides; family-friendly; dog-friendly. ⑤ *Average main: $20* ✉ *25 Town Landing Rd., Round Pond* ☎ *207/529–5725* ⊗ *Closed Labor Day–mid-May.*

Activities

Hardy Boat Cruises

BOATING | FAMILY | Mid-May through mid-October, you can take a cruise to Monhegan with Hardy Boat Cruises. The company also offers seal- and puffin-watching trips and lighthouse and fall coastal cruises. Dogs are welcome on the boat for $5. ✉ *Shaw's Wharf, 132 Rte. 32, New Harbor* ☎ *207/677–2026* ⊕ *www.hardyboat.com.*

Port Clyde

5 miles south of Tenants Harbor via Rte. 131.

At the end of the St. George Peninsula, the sleepy fishing village of Port Clyde is a haven for artists, with a number of galleries and a sweeping vista of the ocean that can't be beat. It's also a good spot to spend time nursing a beer or a coffee while waiting for your boat out to Monhegan. Like many places in Maine, lobster fishing is an economic mainstay here. Marshall Point Lighthouse, right in the harbor, has a small museum.

Sights

★ Marshall Point Lighthouse
LOCAL INTEREST | FAMILY | This 31-foot light-house, which has been in operation since it was erected in 1858, is perhaps best known as the spot where Forrest Gump concluded his very long cross-country run in the 1994 film adaptation of the book by the same name. Be prepared for sweeping views of the ocean and a resounding "Run, Forrest, run!" coming from visitors taking full advantage of an exceptional photo op. The site also has a small museum and a gift shop, housed in the old lightkeepers' house. ⊠ *Marshall Point Rd.* ☎ *207/372–6450* ⊕ *www.marshallpoint.org.*

Monhegan Island

East of Pemaquid Peninsula, 10 miles south of Port Clyde.

If you love rocky cliffs, this is your place. And if you happen to be an artist, you might never leave: there are studios and galleries all over the island. The village bustles with activity in summer, when many artists open their studios. Several shops are open for browsing. You can escape the crowds on the island's 17 miles of hiking trails, which lead to the

---

Maine State Prison Showroom

If you're traveling through Thomaston on Route 1, consider popping into the Maine State Prison Showroom. Since 1824, inmates participating in one of the state's skills-building industries programs have been handcrafting goods that are sold to the public. Open year-round, the store contains hundreds of wood items; some are nautical-theme, while many are practical, including cutting boards, bookcases, and coffee and end tables. ⊠ *358 Hwy. 1, Thomaston* ☎ *207/354–9237* ⊕ *www.facebook. com/MSPShowroom*

---

lighthouse and to the cliffs—bring your camera.

GETTING HERE AND AROUND
Three excursion boats dock here. The boat trip out to Monhegan is almost as exhilarating as exploring the island itself. You'll likely pass by the Marshall Point Lighthouse; be on the lookout for porpoises, seals, puffins, and small whales en route to the island.

Monhegan Boat Line
TRANSPORTATION SITE (AIRPORT/BUS/FERRY/TRAIN) | FAMILY | The Port Clyde boat landing is home to the *Elizabeth Ann* and the *Laura B,* the mail boats that serve Monhegan Island, about 10 miles offshore. There are three round-trips daily mid-June–mid-Oct.; one daily in late fall and early spring; and three weekly in the winter. ⊠ *880 Port Clyde Rd., Port Clyde* ☎ *207/372–8848* ⊕ *www.monheganboat. com.*

Sights

Monhegan Island Light

LIGHTHOUSE | FAMILY | Getting a look at this squat stone lighthouse—from land, anyway—requires a slightly steep half-mile walk uphill from the island's ferry dock. The lighthouse was automated in 1959, and the former keeper's quarters became the Monhegan Museum shortly thereafter. Exhibits at the museum have as much to do with life on the island as they do with the lighthouse itself. The tower is open sporadically throughout the summer for short tours. ⊠ *Lighthouse Hill Rd., ½ mile east of dock, Monhegan* ☎ *207/596–7003* ⊕ *monheganmuseum. org.*

 Hotels

The Island Inn

$$ | B&B/INN | Local works of art are displayed throughout this three-story hotel, which dates to 1907; the property has a commanding presence on Monhegan Island's harbor. **Pros:** great food; great view; laid-back atmosphere. **Cons:** a little on the pricey side, but it's on an island after all; no a/c. $ *Rooms from: $200* ⊠ *1 Ocean Ave., Monhegan* ☎ *207/596–0371* ⊕ *www.islandinnmonhegan.com* ⊗ *Closed Columbus Day–Memorial Day* ➡ *32 rooms* ❏ *Free breakfast* ⊟ *No credit cards.*

Rockland

25 miles north of Damariscotta via U.S. 1.

This town is considered the gateway to Penobscot Bay and is the first stop on U.S. 1 offering a glimpse of the often-sparkling and island-dotted blue bay. Though once merely a place to pass through on the way to tonier ports like Camden, Rockland now gets attention on its own, thanks to a trio of attractions: the renowned Farnsworth Art Museum, the increasingly popular summer Lobster Festival, and the lively North Atlantic Blues Festival. Specialty shops and galleries line the main street, yet the town is still a large fishing port and the commercial hub of this coastal area.

Rockland Harbor bests Camden (by one) as home to the largest fleet of Maine windjammers. The best place in Rockland to view these handsome vessels as they sail in and out of the harbor is the mile-long granite breakwater, which bisects the outer portion of Rockland Harbor. To get there, from U.S. 1, head east on Waldo Avenue and then right on Samoset Road; follow this short road to its end.

GETTING HERE AND AROUND

U.S. 1 runs along Main Street here, while U.S. 1A curves through the residential neighborhood west of the business district, offering a faster route if you are passing through.

FESTIVALS

Maine Lobster Festival

FESTIVALS | FAMILY | Rockland's annual Maine Lobster Festival, held in early August, is the region's largest annual event. About 10 tons of lobsters are steamed in a huge lobster cooker—you have to see it to believe it. The festival, held in Harbor Park, includes a parade, live entertainment, food booths, and, of course, the crowning of the Maine Sea Goddess. ⊠ *Harbor Park, Main St., south of U.S. 1* ☎ *800/576–7512* ⊕ *www. mainelobsterfestival.com.*

North Atlantic Blues Festival

FESTIVALS | FAMILY | About a dozen well-known musicians gather for the North Atlantic Blues Festival, a two-day affair held the first or second full weekend after July 4. The show officially takes place at the public landing on Rockland Harbor Park, but it also includes a "club crawl" through downtown Rockland on Saturday night. Admission to the festival is $45 at the gate, $75 for a weekend pass. ⊠ *Public Landing, 275 Main St.*

☎ 207/596–6055 ⊕ www.northatlantic-bluesfestival.com.

VISITOR INFORMATION Penobscot Bay Area Chamber of Commerce. ☎ 207/596–0376, 800/562–2529 ⊕ www.camden-rockland.com.

◉ Sights

★ Center for Maine Contemporary Art

MUSEUM | The newly minted Center for Maine Contemporary Art is a refreshing departure from the many galleries and museums in the state because it features works exclusively on nautical themes. Expect envelope-pushing exhibitions and impressive public programs. ✉ 21 Winter St. ☎ 207/701–5005 ⊕ cmcanow.org ⧉ $8.

★ Farnsworth Art Museum

MUSEUM | **FAMILY** | One of the most important small museums in the country, much of the Farnsworth's collection is devoted to Maine-related works of the famous Wyeth family: N. C. Wyeth, an accomplished illustrator whose works were featured in many turn-of-the-20th-century books; his late son Andrew, one of the country's best-known painters; and Andrew's son James, also an accomplished painter, who like his elders before him summers nearby. Galleries in the main building always display some of Andrew Wyeth's works, such as *The Patriot, Witchcraft,* and *Turkey Pond.* The **Wyeth Center,** a former church, shows art by his father and son. The museum's collection also includes works by Fitz Henry Lane, George Bellows, Winslow Homer, Edward Hopper, Louise Nevelson, and Rockwell Kent. Changing exhibits are shown in the **Jamien Morehouse Wing.** The **Farnsworth Homestead,** a handsome circa-1850 Greek Revival dwelling that's part of the museum, retains its original lavish Victorian furnishings and is open late June–mid-October.

In Cushing, a tiny town about 10 miles south of Thomaston on the St. George River, the museum operates the **Olson House,** which is depicted in Andrew Wyeth's famous painting *Christina's World,* as well as in other works by the artist. It's accessible by guided tour only. ✉ 16 Museum St. ☎ 207/596–6457 ⊕ www.farnsworthmuseum.org ⧉ $15 ☉ Closed Mon. Nov.–May (except Memorial Day); also closed Tues. Jan.–Mar.

Maine Lighthouse Museum

MUSEUM | **FAMILY** | The lighthouse museum has more than 25 Fresnel lighthouse lenses, as well as a collection of lighthouse artifacts and Coast Guard memorabilia. Permanent exhibits spotlight topics like lighthouse heroines—women who manned the lights when the keepers couldn't—and lightships. ✉ 1 Park Dr. ☎ 207/594–3301 ⊕ www.mainelighthousemuseum.org ⧉ $8.

Restaurants

★ In Good Company

$$$ | **MODERN AMERICAN** | As the name suggests, this is an excellent spot to slow down and catch up with good friends over a bottle of wine, while savoring seasonally inspired, locally sourced dishes. The creative blend of textures and flavors that come out of the kitchen will charm your senses, a welcome surprise in this intimate space that was formerly a bank. **Known for:** outside dining in summer; excellent wine pairings; pared-down aesthetic with a focus on the food. ⑤ Average main: $30 ✉ 415 Maine St. ☎ 207/593–9110 ⊕ www.ingoodcompanymaine.com.

☕ Coffee and Quick Bites

Atlantic Baking Company

$ | **AMERICAN** | Classic French and American breads and pastries, made with local and natural ingredients, emanate alongside wonderful smells daily from this bakery's ovens. There's a lunch sandwich menu for those wanting more than a snack. **Known for:** French macarons;

Penobscot Bay and Blue Hill Peninsula

KEY
- - - *Ferry Lines*

0   10 mi

0   10 km

Windjammer Excursions

Nothing defines the Maine coastal experience better than a sailing trip on a windjammer. These vessels were built all along the East Coast in the 19th and early 20th centuries. Designed primarily to carry cargo, these beauties (most are wood hulled) have a rich past: the schooner *Ladona* served in World War II, while others plied the waters in the lumbering, granite, fishing, and oystering trades or served as pilot boats. They vary in size but can be as small as 46 feet, holding six passengers (plus a couple of crew members), or more than 130 feet, holding 40 passengers and 10 crew members. During a windjammer excursion, passengers are usually able to participate in the navigation, be it hoisting a sail or playing captain at the wheel.

During the Camden Windjammer Festival, held Labor Day weekend, crowds gather to watch the region's fleet sail into the harbor, and most boats are open for tours. The schooner-crew talent show later in the weekend is a bit more irreverent than the majestic arrival ceremony.

A windjammer cruise gives you a chance to admire Maine's dramatic coast from the water. They can run anywhere from one to eight days, and day trips usually involve a tour of the harbor and some lighthouse sightseeing. Prices depend on length of trip and include all meals. Trips leave from Camden, Rockland, and Rockport. You can get information on the fleets by contacting one of two windjammer organizations:

Maine Windjammer Association. ☎ 800/807–9463 ⊕ www.sailmaine-coast.com.

Maine Windjammer Cruises. Five handsome vessels offer a variety of cruises. ☎ 207/236–2938, 800/736–7981 ⊕ www.mainewindjammercruises.com.

classic sourdough; apricot pistachio oat cookies. ⑤ *Average main: $5* ⊠ *351 Main St.* ☎ *207/596–0505* ⊕ *atlanticbakingco.com* ☺ *Closed Sun. in mid-Sept.–May.*

🛏 Hotels

Berry Manor Inn

$$ | B&B/INN | Originally the residence of Rockland merchant Charles H. Berry, this 1898 shingle-style B&B sits in Rockland's National Historic District. **Pros:** a guest pantry is stocked with drinks, sweets, and treats—there's always pie; within walking distance of downtown and the harbor; some rooms can be combined to create two-room suites. **Cons:** view limited to the gardens; old-school design consistent with historic property; not pet-friendly. ⑤ *Rooms from: $200* ⊠ *81 Talbot Ave.* ☎ *207/596–7696, 800/774–5692* ⊕ *www.berrymanorinn.com* ⇌ *12 rooms* ⑩ *Free breakfast.*

LimeRock Inn

$ | B&B/INN | Built in 1892 as a private home, the LimeRock is perfectly located in Rockland's National Historic District in the center of town. **Pros:** all rooms have TVs and DVD players; large in-town lot with gazebo; within easy walking distance of the Farnsworth Museum and many restaurants. **Cons:** not on the water; sometimes booked for weddings; not pet-friendly. ⑤ *Rooms from: $180* ⊠ *96 Limerock St.* ☎ *207/594–2257, 800/546–3762* ⊕ *www.limerockinn.com* ⇌ *8 rooms* ⑩ *Free breakfast.*

Walk From Rockport to Camden

For a stunning walk or drive, take the two-lane paved road that winds up and down on its way out of Rockport, with occasional views of the ocean and the village, en route to Camden. Begin at the intersection of U.S. 1 and Pascal Avenue in Rockport. Take a right off U.S. 1 toward Rockport Harbor, then cross the bridge and go up the hill to Central Street. One block later, bear right on Russell Avenue, which becomes Chestnut Street at the Camden town line; take this all the way to downtown Camden.

Lining the way are some of the most beautiful homes in Maine, surrounded by an abundance of flora and fauna. Keep an eye out for views of the sparkling ocean, as well as for Aldermere Farm and its Belted Galloway cows. (These rare cows get their name from the foot-wide white "belt" around their middles.) The walk or drive is beautiful at any time of the year, but in fall it's breathtaking. Like the rest of New England, the coast of Maine gets a large number of fall-foliage "leaf peepers," and the reds and golds of the chestnut, birch, and elm trees along this winding route are especially beautiful.

★ **Samoset Resort**

$$$ | **RESORT** | **FAMILY** | Occupying 230 waterfront acres on the Rockland–Rockport town line, this all-encompassing resort was completely renovated in 2019. **Pros:** full-service spa; children's programs; activities from basketball to croquet; the 18-hole course has been ranked among the best in the region. **Cons:** no beach; pool can be overcrowded in summer; high turnover, so service can be spotty. $ *Rooms from: $350* ✉ *220 Warrenton St., Rockport* ☎ *207/594–2511, 800/341–1650* ⊕ *www.samosetresort.com* 🛏 *254 rooms* ⦿ *Free breakfast.*

★ **250 Main Hotel**

$$$ | **HOTEL** | With gorgeously designed guest rooms that have an inspired, mid-century-modern vibe, 250 Main has brought a forward-thinking lodging choice to Rockland. **Pros:** immaculately maintained; pet-friendly; complimentary wine-and-cheese hour in the evening. **Cons:** no pool; some traffic noise from the harbor in the morning; only guests are allowed on the roof garden. $ *Rooms from: $319* ✉ *250 Main St.* ☎ *207/594–5994* ⊕ *250mainhotel.com* 🛏 *26 rooms* ⦿ *Free breakfast.*

Activities

Schooner *Heritage*

SAILING | **FAMILY** | This striking windjammer offers three- to six-day cruises and caters to individual wishes. Captain Doug Lee is a storyteller and author of nautical histories. ✉ *North End Shipyard, 11 Front St.* ☎ *207/594–8007, 800/648–4544* ⊕ *www.schoonerheritage.com.*

★ Schooner *J. & E. Riggin*

SAILING | **FAMILY** | The family-run schooner *J. & E. Riggin* offers real-deal overnight sailing cruises that thoroughly immerse passengers in life on the water. The experience is distinguished from other local cruises by the culinary delights chef Annie concocts using locally sourced ingredients, including vegetables, eggs, and herbs freshly gathered from her own organic garden. Four-day sleeper cruises, with three freshly prepared, organic meals and snacks each day start at $1,052; it's worth every penny. ⊠ *3 Captain Spear Dr.* ☎ *207/594–1875* ⊕ *www. mainewindjammer.com.*

Schooner *Ladona*

SAILING | A handsome racing yacht built in 1922 (and rebuilt in 1971), recently restored from nose to tail, the schooner *Ladona* leads chartered trips lasting from three to seven nights. All trips include breakfast, lunch and dinner, as well as a selection of wines and beers every evening. ⊠ *Rockland* ☎ *800/999–7352, 207/594–4723* ⊕ *www.schoonerladona. com.*

Rockport

4 miles north of Rockland via U.S. 1.

Heading north on U.S. 1, you come to Rockport before you reach the tourist mecca of Camden. The most interesting part of Rockport—the harbor—is not right on U.S. 1. Originally called Goose River, the town was part of Camden until 1891. The cutting and burning of limestone was once a major industry in this area. The stone was cut in nearby quarries and then burned in hot kilns, and the resulting lime powder was used to create mortar. Some of the massive kilns are still here.

One of the most famous sights in Rockport is the **Rockport Arch,** which crosses Union Street at the town line and says "Camden" on the other side. It was constructed of wood and mortar in 1926, demolished in 1984, then rebuilt by popular demand in 1985. The arch has been displayed in a number of movies, including *Peyton Place* and *In the Bedroom.*

GETTING HERE AND AROUND
Rockport is off U.S. 1 between Rockland and Camden. Turn on Pascal Avenue to get to the village center.

🍴 Restaurants

★ 18 Central Oyster Bar and Grill

$$$ | **SEAFOOD** | The beautiful seaside village of Rockport has come alive with the opening of 18 Central Oyster Bar and Grill, which produces some of the best meals in the Mid-Coast in a cozy spot high above the working harbor. Seasonally inspired, locally harvested seafood with of hint of Southern comfort cooking is the backbone of most of the creative dishes—think fried green tomatoes with crab, chili oil, and microgreens or the crispy fried chicken accompanied by collard greens and heirloom grits. **Known for:** evenly paced, well-balanced dinners transition gracefully from one course to the next; lively atmosphere encouraged by botanically infused cocktails; packed as soon as the door opens for dinner. ⑤ *Average main: $25* ⊠ *18 Central St.* ☎ *207/466–9055* ⊕ *www.18central.com* ⊘ *Closed Tues. and Wed.*

Nina June

$$$ | **MEDITERRANEAN** | **FAMILY** | Serving fresh takes on Mediterranean dishes using seafood harvested from Maine's rocky coast, this lovely trattoria gets just about everything right, from the cheery seaside setting to the family-style meals featuring a constantly changing menu where locally sourced ingredients shine. Everything from the noodles to the pickled veggies are made in-house and the presentation of each dish makes for sheer eye candy. **Known for:** family-style dinners; craft cocktails; harbor views; chef-lead cooking classes. ⑤ *Average main: $26* ⊠ *24 Central St.* ☎ *207/236–8880* ⊕ *www.ninajunerestaurant.com* ⊘ *Closed Sun. and Mon.*

Camden

8 miles north of Rockland.

More than any other town along Penobscot Bay, Camden is the perfect picture-postcard of a Maine coastal village. It is one of the most popular destinations on the Maine Coast, and June–September the town is crowded with visitors—but don't let that scare you away: Camden is worth it. Just come prepared for busy traffic on the town's Main Street, and make reservations for lodging and restaurants well in advance.

Camden is famous not only for its geography, but also for its large fleet of windjammers—relics and replicas from the age of sailing—with their romantic histories and great billowing sails. At just about any hour during warm months you're likely to see at least one windjammer tied up in the harbor. Excursions, whether for an afternoon or a week, are best June–September.

The town's compact size makes it perfect for exploring on foot: shops, restaurants, and galleries line Main Street, as well as the side streets and alleys around the harbor. But be sure to include Camden's residential area on your walking tour. It is quite charming and filled with many fascinating old period houses from the time when Federal, Greek Revival, and Victorian architectural styles were the rage among the wealthy; many of them are now B&Bs. The Chamber of Commerce, at the Public Landing, can provide you with a walking map. Humped on the north side of town are the Camden Hills; drive or hike to the summit at the state park to enjoy mesmerizing views of the town, harbor, and island-dotted bay.

GETTING HERE AND AROUND
U.S. 1 becomes Camden's Main Street. Take Route 90 west from U.S. 1 and rejoin it in Warren to bypass Rockland— this is the quickest route south.

ESSENTIALS
VISITOR INFORMATION Penobscot Bay Regional Chamber of Commerce.
☎ *207/236–4404, 800/562–2529* ⊕ *www. camdenrockland.com.*

FESTIVALS
★ Windjammer Weekend
FESTIVAL | FAMILY | One of the biggest and most colorful events of the year is the Camden Windjammer Festival, which takes place over Labor Day weekend. The harbor is packed with historic vessels, there are lots of good eats, and visitors can tour the magnificent ships. ⊠ *Camden* ☎ *800/807–9463* ⊕ *www.sailmainecoast.com.*

Restaurants

★ Long Grain
$ | ASIAN FUSION | This stylish Asian-fusion eatery places an emphasis on Thai curries and house-made noodles. A very popular restaurant with locals and visitors alike, reservations are essential, though you might be able to squeeze in at the tiny bar without one if you're dining solo and don't mind a little chaos; don't miss the Asian general store in the front of the restaurant, which is stocked with yummy and fun imported items. **Known for:** chef Ravin Nakjaroen is a James Beard–nominated chef; consistently excellent delivery; great take-out options. ⑤ *Average main: $17* ⊠ *20 Washington St.* ☎ *207/236–9001* ⊕ *www.longgraincamden.com* ⊗ *Closed Sun. and Mon.*

★ Natalie's Restaurant
$$$$ | MODERN AMERICAN | Located in the cozy and elegant Camden Harbour Inn, the restaurant is fine dining with a distinctly Maine flair, and seasonal ingredients—including vegetables and herbs from the property's garden—set the tone. One of the most sought-after dining spots in Camden, Natalie's is the creation of Dutch owners Raymond Brunyanszki and Oscar Verest, who brought in creative chefs to create splurge-worthy

dishes in this intimate setting. **Known for:** phenomenal service with true attention to detail; signature five-course lobster tasting menu; an excellent view overlooking the harbor. $ *Average main: $82 ⊠ Camden Harbour Inn, 83 Bay View St. ☎ 866/658–1542, 207/236–7008 ⊕ www.nataliesrestaurant.com �****** Closed Sun. Nov.–May. No lunch.*

☕ Coffee and Quick Bites

★ Owl and Turtle Bookshop and Cafe
$ | CAFÉ | FAMILY | This pint-size but well-stocked independent bookstore with a cozy café has been serving Camden for more than 50 years. The full menu of coffee drinks is based on locally roasted beans and includes a selection of homemade baked goods. **Known for:** triple chocolate chip cookie; author readings; spot-on book recommendations. $ *Average main: ⊠ 33 Bay View St. ☎ 207/230–7335 ⊕ www.owlandturtle.com.*

🛏 Hotels

Camden Hartstone Inn
$ | B&B/INN | This 1835 mansard-roofed Victorian home has been turned into a plush, sophisticated retreat and a fine culinary destination. **Pros:** pet-friendly; extravagant breakfasts; some private entrances. **Cons:** not on water; no wheelchair access; not all rooms have fireplaces. $ *Rooms from: $159 ⊠ 41 Elm St. ☎ 207/236–4259 ⊕ www.hartstoneinn.com ☞ 21 rooms ❢❂❙ Free breakfast.*

Lord Camden Inn
$$ | B&B/INN | FAMILY | If you want to be in the center of town and near the harbor, look for this handsome brick building with the bright blue-and-white awnings. **Pros:** large continental breakfast; all rooms have balconies; mini-refrigerators in rooms. **Cons:** traffic noise in front rooms; no on-site restaurant; no on-site parking. $ *Rooms from: $209 ⊠ 24 Main St. ☎ 207/236–4325, 800/336–4325*

⊕ *www.lordcamdeninn.com ☞ 36 rooms ❢❂❙ Free breakfast.*

★ Norumbega Inn
$$$ | B&B/INN | This welcoming B&B is one of the most photographed pieces of real estate in Maine, and once you get a look at its castlelike facade, you'll understand why. **Pros:** eye-popping architecture; beautiful views of both the ocean and the gorgeously maintained, sloping lawn; champagne welcome toast, baked treats and infused waters throughout the day, and after-dinner port and cheese beside a roaring fire; firepit and lawn games in summer; secret beach within walking distance (ask the innkeepers). **Cons:** stairs to climb; a short distance from the center of town; no pets. $ *Rooms from: $309 ⊠ 63 High St. ☎ 207/236–4646, 877/363–4646 ⊕ www.norumbegainn.com ☞ 11 rooms ❢❂❙ Free breakfast.*

★ Whitehall
$ | B&B/INN | FAMILY | Although the oldest part of the Whitehall is an 1834 white-clapboard sea captain's home, the bright and cheery design is decidedly contemporary with nostalgic touches here and there; the Millay Room pays homage to the poet Edna St. Vincent Millay, who grew up in the area and read her poetry at the Whitehall, where her career was launched. **Pros:** short walk to downtown and harbor; small-plates breakfast choices; beautifully renovated with a design focus. **Cons:** no good water views; walls can be a bit thin; no on-site restaurant. $ *Rooms from: $119 ⊠ 52 High St. ☎ 207/236–3391, 800/789–6565 ⊕ www.whitehallmaine.com �****** Closed mid-Oct.–mid-May ☞ 36 rooms ❢❂❙ Free breakfast.*

🏃 Activities

BOATING
Heron
SAILING | FAMILY | This schooner, which had a cameo in the movie *The Rum Diary,* offers lunchtime sails,

wildlife-watching trips, and sunset cruises. ✉ *Rockport Marine Park, Pascal Ave., Rockport* ☎ *207/236–8605, 800/599–8605* ⊕ *www.sailheron.com.*

★ Mary Day

SAILING | FAMILY | Sailing for more than 50 years, the *Mary Day* is the first schooner in Maine built specifically for vacation excursions. Meals are cooked on an antique wood-fired stove. ✉ *Camden Harbor, Atlantic Ave.* ☎ *800/992–2218* ⊕ *www.schoonermaryday.com.*

Olad

SAILING | Captain Aaron Lincoln runs two-hour trips on both the *Olad* and a smaller sailing vessel, spotting lighthouses, coastal mansions, the occasional seal, and the red-footed puffin cousins known as guillemots. Either boat can also be chartered for longer trips. ✉ *Camden Harbor, Bay View St.* ☎ *207/236–2323* ⊕ *www.maineschooners.com.*

Windjammer *Angelique*

SAILING | FAMILY | Captain Mike and Lynne McHenry have more than three decades' experience on the high seas. Three- to six-day cruise options aboard the *Angelique* include photography workshops and meteor-watching trips, as well as yoga and wellness excursions. ✉ *Camden Harbor* ☎ *800/282–9989* ⊕ *www.sailangelique.com.*

🛍 Shopping

Lily, Lupine and Fern

FLOWERS | This full-service florist offers a wonderful array of gourmet foods, chocolates, wines, imported beers, high-quality olive oils, and cheeses. There's a small deck where you can enjoy harbor views and a cup of coffee. ✉ *11 Main St.* ☎ *207/236–9600* ⊕ *www.lilylupine.com.*

★ Swans Island

HOUSEHOLD ITEMS/FURNITURE | For gorgeous, handmade blankets, throws, and pillows, as well as wraps and scarves, look no further. All products are made in Maine using natural, heirloom-quality yarns—the expert craftsmanship explains the hefty price tag. ✉ *2 Bayview St.* ☎ *207/706–7926* ⊕ *swansislandcompany.com.*

Belfast

13 miles north of Lincolnville via U.S. 1.

Lots of Maine coastal towns like to think of themselves as the prettiest little town in the state, and any judge would be spoiled for choice. Charming Belfast (originally to be named Londonderry) is a strong contender, with a beautiful waterfront; an old and interesting main street rising from the harbor; a delightful array of B&Bs, restaurants, and shops; and friendly townsfolk. The downtown even has old-fashioned street lamps, which set the streets aglow at night.

GETTING HERE AND AROUND

U.S. 1 runs through Belfast as it travels up the coast. From Interstate 95, take U.S. 3 in Augusta to get here. The highways meet in Belfast, heading north. The information center has a large array of magazines, guidebooks, maps, and brochures that cover the entire Mid-Coast. It also can provide you with a free walking-tour brochure that describes the various historic buildings.

ESSENTIALS

VISITOR INFORMATION Belfast Area Chamber of Commerce. ☎ *207/338–5900* ⊕ *www.belfastmaine.org.*

Sights

Belfast is a funky coastal town, where the streets are lined with eclectic boutiques, and a decidedly laissez-faire attitude presides. There is still evidence of the wealth of the mid-1800s, when Belfast was home to a number of business magnates, shipbuilders, ship captains, and so on. Their mansions still stand along High Street and in the residential area above it, offering excellent examples of Greek Revival and Federal-style architecture. In fact, the town has one of the best showcases of Greek Revival homes in the state. Don't miss the "White House," where High and Church streets merge several blocks south of downtown.

🍴 Restaurants

Darby's Restaurant and Pub

$$ | AMERICAN | FAMILY | With pressed-tin ceilings, this charming, old-fashioned restaurant and bar—it's been such since 1865—is very popular with locals. Pad Thai and chicken with chili and cashews are signature dishes, but the menu also has hearty homemade soups and sandwiches and classic fish-and-chips. **Known for:** excellent happy hour; gluten-free menu choices; Buddha bowls. $ *Average main: $18* ⌧ *155 High St.* ☎ *207/338–2339* ⊕ *www.darbysrestaurant.com.*

★ Young's Lobster Pound

$$$ | SEAFOOD | FAMILY | Right on the water's edge, across the harbor from downtown Belfast, this corrugated-steel building looks more like a fish cannery than a restaurant, but it's one of the best places for an authentic Maine lobster dinner. You'll see numerous tanks of live lobsters of varying size when you first walk in. **Known for:** "shore dinner": clam chowder or lobster stew, steamed clams or mussels, a 1½-pound boiled lobster, corn on the cob, and chips; family-friendly environment; BYOB. $ *Average main: $25* ⌧ *2 Fairview St., off U.S. 1* ☎ *207/338–1160* ⊕ *www.youngslobsters.com* ⊙ *Takeout only Jan.–Mar.*

☕ Coffee and Quick Bites

The Only Doughnut

$ | AMERICAN | You can get anything here as long as it's a doughnut (accompanied by hot or iced coffee, if you wish). Made in the traditional cake style, what doughnuts they are; flavors might include salted caramel, buttermilk, and "full-tilt" blueberry with a glorious blueberry glaze. **Known for:** the "citrus" (orange zest in the dough, lemon juice in the glaze); the "sea smoke" (chocolate doughnut, maple glaze, smokey salt); the "chocolate toasted coconut" (chocolate doughnut, coconut milk glaze, toasted coconut). $ *Average main: $3* ⌧ *225 Northport Ave.* ☎ *207/218–1231* ⊕ *theonlydoughnut.com.*

Bucksport

9 miles north of Searsport via U.S. 1.

The stunning Penobscot Narrows Bridge, spanning the Penobscot River, makes Bucksport, a town founded in 1763, well worth a visit, even if you only stop while passing through to points north. Fort Knox, Maine's largest historic fort, overlooks the town from across the river. There are magnificent views of the imposing granite structure from the pleasant riverfront walkway downtown.

GETTING HERE AND AROUND

After you pass over the spectacular Penobscot Narrows Bridge onto Verona Island driving north on U.S. 1, you cross another bridge into Bucksport; turn left for downtown and right to continue on the highway.

Sights

★ Penobscot Narrows Bridge and Observatory Tower/Fort Knox Historic Site

HISTORIC SITE | FAMILY | An "engineering marvel" is how experts describe the

2,120-foot-long Penobscot Narrows Bridge, which opened in 2006 and which is taller than the Statue of Liberty. From the surrounding countryside it pops up on the horizon like the towers of a fairy-tale castle. The bridge's 437-foot observation tower is the tallest in the world; an elevator shoots you to the top. Don't miss it—the panoramic views, which take in the hilly countryside and the river as it widens into Penobscot Bay, are breathtaking. In summer, the observatory often offers moonrise viewings.

Also here is Fort Knox, the largest historic fort in Maine. It was built between 1844 and 1869, when, despite a treaty with Britain settling boundary disputes, invasion was still a concern—after all, the British controlled this region during both the Revolutionary War and the War of 1812. The fort never saw any real action, but it was used for troop training and as a garrison during the Civil War and the Spanish-American War. Visitors are welcome to explore the many rooms and passageways. Guided tours are given daily during the summer and several days a week in the shoulder seasons. ⊠ 711 Ft. Knox Rd., off U.S. 1, Prospect ☎ 207/469–6553 ⊕ www.fortknoxmaine. com ☎ Fort from $7 ☉ Closed Nov.–Apr.

Blue Hill

20 miles east of Castine via Rtes. 166, 175, and 176.

Nestled snugly between 943-foot Blue Hill Mountain and Blue Hill Bay, the village of Blue Hill sits right beside its harbor. About 30 miles from Acadia National Park, Blue Hill makes for a more laid-back base for exploring the Mount Desert Island area, but bear in mind that 30 miles can take at least twice as long to travel with heavy traffic in summertime. Originally known for its granite quarries, copper mines, and shipbuilding, today the town is known for its pottery

and the galleries, bookstores, antiques shops, and studios that line its streets. The Blue Hill Fair (⊕ *www.bluehillfair. com*), held Labor Day weekend, is a tradition in these parts, with agricultural exhibits, food, rides, and entertainment. A charming little park with a great playground is tucked away near the harbor downtown.

GETTING HERE AND AROUND
From U.S. 1 in Orland, Route 15 heads south to Blue Hill. To continue north on the highway, take Route 172 north to Ellsworth.

Restaurants

Arborvine
$$$ | MODERN AMERICAN | Glowing gas fireplaces, period antiques, exposed beams, and hardwood floors covered with Oriental rugs distinguish the four candlelit dining areas in this renovated Cape Cod–style house. The seasonal menu features dishes made with organic ingredients that match well with its own beer, like crispy duck with rhubarb and lime glaze, or roasted rack of lamb with a basil-and-pine-nut crust—fresh fish dishes are also superb. **Known for:** fresh seafood dishes; classic New England fare; its adjacent nautical-themed DeepWater Brew Pub serves dishes made with organic ingredients to go with its own beer. ⑤ *Average main: $31* ⊠ *33 Tenney Hill* ☎ *207/374–2119* ⊕ *www.arborvine. com* ☉ *Closed Mon. No lunch.*

🛏 Hotels

Blue Hill Inn
$ | B&B/INN | One side of this Federal-style inn was built as a home in 1835, but it soon became lodging, adding a wing with a matching facade in the 1850s. **Pros:** plenty of charm; modern suites with kitchens in separate building; 30 miles from Acadia National Park. **Cons:** some narrow stairs and thin walls consistent with historic property; complimentary

appetizers each evening if you order wine or spirits; only some rooms have fireplaces. ⑤ *Rooms from: $195* ✉ *40 Union St.* ☎ *207/374–2844* ⊕ *www.bluehillinn.com* ⊗ *Closed Nov.–mid-May, except for Cape House Suite and Studio* ⇆ *13 rooms* ⑩ *Free breakfast.*

🛍 Shopping

ART GALLERIES
Blue Hill Bay Gallery

ART GALLERIES | This gallery sells oil and watercolor landscapes and seascapes of Maine and New England from the 19th through the 21st century. It also carries the proprietor's own photography. Call ahead in the off-season. ✉ *11 Tenney Hill* ☎ *207/374–5773* ⊕ *www.bluehillbaygallery.com.*

POTTERY
Rackliffe Pottery

CERAMICS/GLASSWARE | A four-generation family business, this shop sells colorful pottery made with lead-free glazes. You can choose between water pitchers, serving platters, tea-and-coffee sets, and sets of canisters, among other lovely items. ✉ *132 Ellsworth Rd.* ☎ *888/631–3321* ⊕ *www.rackliffepottery.com.*

WINE
Blue Hill Wine Shop

WINE/SPIRITS | In a restored barn and cape, one of Blue Hill's earliest houses, the Blue Hill Wine Shop carries more than 3,000 carefully selected wines, cheeses, groceries, local and imported beer and ciders, coffee and teas. ✉ *138 Main St.* ☎ *207/374–2161* ⊕ *www.bluehillwineshop.com.*

Deer Isle

16 miles south of Blue Hill via Rtes. 176 and 15.

Reachable by a bridge, Deer Isle's thick woods give way to tidal coves. Stacks of lobster traps populate the backyards of shingled houses, and dirt roads lead to secluded summer cottages. This region is prized by artists, and studios and galleries are plentiful.

At the southern end of the island, Stonington is a charming seaside town with a lovely Main Street. It's also the gateway to Isle au Haut, which contains a remote section of Acadia National Park.

GETTING HERE AND AROUND
From Sedgwick, Route 15 crosses a 1930s suspension bridge onto Little Deer Isle and continues on to the larger Deer Isle.

Isle au Haut Boat Services provides a daily mail-boat ferry service out of Stonington to Isle au Haut. During the summer season, trips increase from two to five Monday–Saturday and from one to two on Sunday. From mid-June until late September, the boat also stops at Duck Harbor, in the island section of Acadia National Park (it will not unload bicycles, kayaks, or canoes at the Park Landing, but will at the Town Landing). Ferry service is scaled back in the fall, then returns to the regular or "winter" schedule.

VISITOR INFORMATION
CONTACTS Deer Isle–Stonington Chamber of Commerce. ☎ *207/348–6124* ⊕ *www.deerisle.com.* **Isle au Haut Boat Services.** ✉ *37 Seabreeze Ave., Stonington* ☎ *207/367–5193* ⊕ *isleauhaut.com.*

👁 Sights

Edgar M. Tennis Preserve

NATURE PRESERVE | Enjoy several miles of woodland and shore trails at the Edgar M. Tennis Preserve. Look for hawks, eagles, and ospreys and wander among old apple trees, fields of wildflowers, and ocean-polished rocks. ✉ *Tennis Rd., Deer Isle* ☎ *207/348–2455* ⊕ *www.islandheritagetrust.org* ⊠ *Free.*

7

The Maine Coast DEER ISLE

Haystack Mountain School of Crafts

COLLEGE | Want to learn a new craft? This school 6 miles from Deer Isle Village offers one- and two-week courses for people of all skill levels in crafts such as blacksmithing, basketry, printmaking, and weaving. Artisans from around the world present free evening lectures throughout summer. Tours of the school and studios are available on Wednesday. ✉ *89 Haystack School Dr., off Rte. 15, Deer Isle* ☎ *207/348–2306* ⊕ *www.haystack-mtn. org* ⚏ *Tours $5.*

 ## Shopping

Nervous Nellie's Jams and Jellies

FOOD/CANDY | Jams and jellies are made right on the property at Nervous Nellie's. There is a tearoom with homemade goodies, and also a fanciful sculpture garden with everything from knights to witches to a lobster and a flamingo. They are the works of sculptor Peter Beerits, who operates Nervous Nellie's with his wife. ✉ *598 Sunshine Rd., off Rte. 15, Deer Isle* ☎ *207/348–6182* ⊕ *www. nervousnellies.com.*

Bar Harbor

34 miles from Blue Hill via Rte. 172 and U.S. 1.

A resort town since the 19th century, Bar Harbor is the artistic, culinary, and social center of Mount Desert Island, and it serves visitors to Acadia National Park with inns, motels, and restaurants. Around the turn of the last century the island was known as a summer haven for the very rich because of its cool breezes. The wealthy built lavish mansions throughout the island, many of which were destroyed in a huge fire that devastated the island in 1947—a good number of those that survived have been converted into businesses. In Bar Harbor, shops are clustered along Main, Mount Desert, and Cottage streets; take a stroll down West Street, a National Historic District, where you can see some fine old houses.

The island and the surrounding Gulf of Maine are home to a great variety of wildlife: whales, seals, eagles, falcons, ospreys, and puffins (though not right offshore here), and forest dwellers such as deer, foxes, coyotes, and beavers.

GETTING HERE AND AROUND

In Ellsworth, Route 3 leaves U.S. 1 and heads to Bar Harbor. In season, free Island Explorer buses (☎ *207/667–5796* ⊕ *www.exploreacadia.com*) take visitors to Acadia National Park and other island towns. There is also a passenger ferry to Winter Harbor across Frenchman Bay.

ESSENTIALS

VISITOR INFORMATION Bar Harbor Chamber of Commerce. ☎ *207/288–5103* ⊕ *www.visitbarharbor.com.*

 ## Sights

★ Abbe Museum

MUSEUM | FAMILY | This important museum dedicated to Maine's indigenous tribes—collectively known as the Wabanaki—is the state's only Smithsonian-affiliated facility and one of the few places in Maine to experience Native culture as interpreted by Native peoples themselves. The year-round archaeology exhibit displays spear points, bone tools, and other artifacts found around Mount Desert Island and exhibits often feature contemporary Native American art, and there are frequent demonstrations of everything from boatbuilding to basket weaving. Call on rainy days for impromptu children's activities. A second location, inside the park at Sieur de Monts Spring, open only during the summer, features artifacts from the earliest digs around the island. ✉ *26 Mount Desert St.* ☎ *207/288–3519* ⊕ *www.abbemuseum. org* ⚏ *$10.*

🍴 Restaurants

⭐ Burning Tree

$$$ | SEAFOOD | One of the top restaurants in Maine, this easy-to-miss gem with a festive dining room is on Route 3 five miles from Bar Harbor in the village of Otter Creek. The seasonal menu emphasizes freshly caught seafood, and seven species of fish are offered virtually every day—all from the Gulf of Maine. **Known for:** farm to table cuisine; Southeast Asian-inspired flavors; regionally sourced ingredients. ⑤ *Average main: $30* ✉ *69 Otter Creek Dr., Otter Creek ⊹ 5 miles from Bar Harbor, 7 miles from Northeast Harbor* ☎ *207/288–9331* ⊗ *Closed mid-Oct.–mid-June. No lunch.*

⭐ Havana

$$$ | CUBAN | A lively yet intimate spot, Havana serves Latin-inspired dishes paired with robust wines right in the middle of downtown Bar Harbor. In the summer, have a bite on "the Parrilla" (the informal, no-reservations patio); during winter months, dine in a pleasant indoor space with a modern aesthetic, featuring clean lines and cheery colors. **Known for:** Spanish tortillas; a lively atmosphere fueled by craft cocktails; after-dinner affogato made with MDI ice cream. ⑤ *Average main: $34* ✉ *318 Main St.* ☎ *207/288–2822* ⊕ *www.havanamaine. com* ⊗ *No lunch.*

☕ Coffee and Quick Bites

Lompoc Cafe and Books

$ | AMERICAN | This shop is nestled aside a shaded patio just a quick walk from the downtown Bar Harbor bustle. Stop in for a quiet respite for relaxing with a coffee or beer while noshing on a bagel or artisanal pizza and perusing a book. **Known for:** banh mi sandwich in breakfast and lunch versions; eclectic selection of books; located next to public parking lot. ⑤ *Average main: $11* ✉ *36 Rodick St.* ☎ *207/901–0004* ⊕ *www.lompoccafe. com* ⊗ *Closed Mon.*

🛏 Hotels

Bar Harbor Grand Hotel

$$ | HOTEL | Taking one of the well-appointed, modern rooms in this renovated historic building puts you right in the middle of Bar Harbor, just a stone's throw from lively restaurants, cafés, and gift shops. **Pros:** excellent center-of-town location; breakfast included; good value. **Cons:** street noise; decor could use updates; service can be hit or miss. ⑤ *Rooms from: $245* ✉ *269 Main St.* ☎ *207/288–5226* ⊕ *www.barharborgrand. com* ⊗ *Closed mid-Nov.–Mar.* ⇌ *71 rooms* ⦿ *Free breakfast.*

Bar Harbor Inn and Spa

$$$ | HOTEL | Originally established in the late 1800s as a men's social club, this waterfront inn has rooms spread among three buildings on well-landscaped grounds. **Pros:** bay and ocean views; proximity to downtown and Acadia National Park; shore path along the waterfront from the hotel. **Cons:** spotty cell phone service; views often include cruise ships in port; dining reservations recommended. ⑤ *Rooms from: $350* ✉ *1 Newport Dr.* ☎ *207/288–3351, 800/248–3351* ⊕ *www.barharborinn.com* ⊗ *Closed late Nov.–mid-Mar.* ⇌ *153 rooms* ⦿ *Free breakfast.*

Island Place

$ | HOTEL | FAMILY | This motel's clean rooms and central location make it a good base for exploring the Bar Harbor area. **Pros:** centrally located; microwave and refrigerator available for guests in lobby; free parking. **Cons:** two-night minimum in high season; basic rooms; renovated motel-style lodgings are not for everyone. ⑤ *Rooms from: $188* ✉ *51 Holland Ave.* ☎ *207/288–3771* ⊕ *www. islandplacebh.com* ⇌ *10 rooms* ⦿ *No meals.*

⭐ West Street Hotel

$$$$ | RESORT | Maine has some pretty phenomenal resort destinations in the Kennebunks and on the Mid-Coast,

7

The Maine Coast BAR HARBOR

Acadia National Park and Mount Desert Island

Marlboro

Union River Bay

Lamoine State Park

East Lamonie

Trenton

Eastern Bay

Frenchman Bay

Salisbury Cove

Hulls Cove Visitor Center

Western Bay

Town Hill

BAR IS.

Bar Harbor

SEASONAL FERRY TO WINTER HARBOR

Park Loop Road

Somesville

Eagle Lake

Abbe Museum at Sieur de Monts Spring

BARTLETT ISLAND

Somes Sound

Acadia National Park

Cadillac Mountain

Pretty Marsh

Echo Lake

Bubble Pond

Ocean Path Trail

Acadia Mountain Trail

Jordan Pond

Sand Beach

Long Pond

Thunder Hole

Echo Lake Beach

Seal Cove Pond

Otter Point

Seal Cove

Southwest Harbor

Northeast Harbor

Seal Harbor

BEAR ISLAND

Eastern Way

SUTTON ISLAND

Manset

Islesford

LITTLE CRANBERRY ISLAND

West Tremont

Cranberry Isles

BAKER ISLAND

Bernard

Bass Harbor

GREAT CRANBERRY ISLAND

Blue Hill Bay

Bass Harbor Head Light

Atlantic Ocean

Atlantic

SWANS ISLAND

FERRY TO FRENCHBORO

0   2 mi

0   2 km

Page 347

but to enjoy the state's premiere resort experience you'll do best to make the trek Down East to Bar Harbor to stay at the West Street Hotel, where resort culture truly shines. **Pros:** all the expected luxuries of a resort and then some; each floor is equipped with guest pantries filled with snacks and goodies; one of the most tastefully decorated resorts in Maine. **Cons:** it's a trek to get Down East; $25 daily resort fee; dogs allowed, but for an additional $75 per dog per night (two-dog limit). *Rooms from: $479 50 West St. 207/288-0825 www.theweststreethotel.com 85 rooms Free breakfast.*

Shopping

ART

Island Artisans

ART GALLERIES | This shop sells basketry, pottery, fiber work, and jewelry created by over 100 Maine artisans. It's open May–December. *99 Main St. 207/288-4214 www.islandartisans.com.*

Native Arts Gallery

ART GALLERIES | Silver and gold Southwest Indian jewelry is a specialty at Native Arts Gallery, open May–October. *99 Main St. 207/288-4474 www.nativeartsgallery.com.*

★ **The Rock and Art Shop**

BOOKS/STATIONERY | As advertised, there are both "rocks" and "art" for sale at this eclectic family-owned store. There are also taxidermied animals, fossils, home decor and plants, interesting jewelry, and bath products. They're open May–November. *23 Cottage St. 207/288-4800 www.therockandartshop.com.*

SPORTING GOODS

Cadillac Mountain Sports

SPORTING GOODS | One of the best sporting-goods stores in the state, Cadillac Mountain Sports has developed a following of locals and visitors alike. Here you'll find top-quality climbing, hiking, boating, paddling, and camping equipment, and in winter you can rent cross-country skis, ice skates, and snowshoes. *26 Cottage St. 207/288-4532 www.cadillacsports.com.*

Activities

AIR TOURS

★ **Acadia Air Tours**

FLYING/SKYDIVING/SOARING | This outfit runs sightseeing flights over Bar Harbor and Acadia National Park. Most tours run 15 minutes to an hour and range $75–$375 per person. The romantic sunset tour is $50 extra. *1 West St. 207/288-0703 www.acadiaairtours.com.*

BIKING

Acadia Bike

BICYCLING | FAMILY | Rent mountain bikes and hybrids at Acadia Bike, both good models for negotiating the carriage roads in Acadia National Park. *48 Cottage St. 207/288-9605, 800/526-8615 www.acadiabike.com.*

Bar Harbor Bicycle Shop

BICYCLING | Rent bikes for anywhere from four hours to a full week at the Bar Harbor Bicycle Shop. *141 Cottage St. 207/288-3886 www.barharborbike.com.*

BOATING

Coastal Kayaking Tours

KAYAKING | FAMILY | This outfitter has been leading trips in the scenic waters off Mount Desert Island since 1982. Trips are limited to no more than 12 people. The season is mid-May–mid-October. *48 Cottage St. 207/288-9605 www.acadiafun.com.*

Downeast Sailing Adventures

BOATING | FAMILY | Take two-hour sailing trips and sunset cruises for $50 per person with six passengers, or hire a private charter starting at $125 per hour. Boats depart the Upper Town Dock in Southwest Harbor and several other locations.

Long ramps on Maine's many docks make it easier to access boats at either high or low tide.

✉ Eagle Lake Rd. ☎ 207/288–2216 ⊕ www.downeastsail.com.

Margaret Todd

BOATING | FAMILY | The 151-foot four-masted schooner *Margaret Todd* operates 1½- to 2-hour trips three times daily among the islands of Frenchman Bay. The sunset sail has live folk music, and the 2 pm trip is sometimes narrated by an Acadia National Park ranger. Trips are $42–$48 and depart mid-May–mid-October. ✉ *Bar Harbor Inn pier, 7 Newport Dr.* ☎ *207/288–4585* ⊕ *www.downeastwindjammer.com.*

WHALE-WATCHING

Bar Harbor Whale Watch Co.

WHALE-WATCHING | FAMILY | This company has six boats, one of them a 130-foot jet-propelled double-hulled catamaran with spacious decks. The company offers lighthouse, lobstering, sunset, and seal-, puffin- and whale-watching cruises, as well as a trip to Acadia National Park's Baker Island. Most tours run $32–$63 per person; consider spending $199 for a nine-hour tour that passes 18 lighthouses, including seven in Canada. ✉ 1 West St. ☎ 207/288–2386, 800/942–5374 ⊕ www.barharborwhales.com.

Acadia National Park

With about 49,000 acres of protected forests, beaches, mountains, and rocky coastline, Acadia National Park is one of the most visited national parks in America. According to the National Park Service, more than 2 million people visit Acadia each year, and the number is steadily rising. The park holds some of the most spectacular scenery on the Eastern Seaboard: a rugged coastline of surf-pounded granite and an interior graced by sculpted mountains, quiet ponds, and lush, deciduous forests. Cadillac Mountain (named after a Frenchman who explored here in the late 1600s and who later founded Detroit)—the highest point of land on the East Coast—dominates the park. Although rugged, the park also has graceful stone bridges, miles of carriage roads (popular with walkers, runners, and bikers as well as horse-drawn carriages), and the Jordan Pond House restaurant (famous for its popovers).

With some of the most dramatic and varied scenery on the Maine Coast—and home to Maine's only national park—Mount Desert Island (pronounced "dessert" by locals) is Maine's most popular tourist destination, attracting well over 2 million visitors a year. Much of the approximately 12-by-15-mile island belongs to Acadia National Park. You can take a scenic drive along the island's rocky coastline, whose stark cliffs rise from the ocean. A network of old carriage roads lets you explore Acadia's wooded interior, filled with birds and other wildlife, and trails for hikers of all skill levels lead to rounded mountaintops, providing views of Frenchman and Blue Hill bays and beyond. Ponds and lakes beckon you to swim, fish, or boat, and ferries and charter boats provide a different perspective on the island and a chance to explore the outer islands.

Mount Desert Island has four different towns, each with its own personality. The town of Bar Harbor is on the northeastern corner of the island and includes the little villages of Hulls Cove, Salisbury Cove, and Town Hill. Aside from Acadia, Bar Harbor is the major tourist destination here, with plenty of lodging, dining, and shopping. The town of Mount Desert, in the middle of the island, has four main villages: Somesville, Seal Harbor, Otter Creek, and Northeast Harbor, a summer haven for the very wealthy. Southwest Harbor includes the smaller village of Manset south of the village center. Tremont is at the southernmost tip of the island and stretches up the western shore. It includes the villages of Bass Harbor, Bernard, and Seal Cove. Yes, Mount Desert Island is a place with three personalities: the hustling, bustling tourist mecca of Bar Harbor; the "quiet side" on the western half; and the vast natural expanse of Acadia National Park.

The 27-mile Park Loop Road provides an excellent overview, but to truly appreciate the park you must get off the main road and experience it by walking, hiking, biking, sea kayaking, or taking a carriage ride. Get off the beaten path, and you can find places you'll have practically all to yourself. Mount Desert Island was once a preserve of summer homes for the very rich (and still is for some), and, partly because of this, Acadia is the first national park in the United States largely created by donations of private land. There are two smaller parts of the park: on Isle au Haut, 15 miles away out in the ocean, and on the Schoodic Peninsula, on the mainland across Frenchman Bay from Mount Desert.

Acadia National Park Essentials

GETTING HERE AND AROUND
Island Explorer buses, which serve the park and island villages June 23–Columbus Day, offer transportation to and around the park. In addition to regularly scheduled stops, they also pick up and drop off passengers anywhere in the park it is safe to stop.

Route 3 leads to the island and Bar Harbor from Ellsworth and circles the eastern part of the island. Route 102 is the major road on the west side.

CONTACTS Island Explorer. ☎ 207/667–5796 ⊕ www.exploreacadia.com.

ESSENTIALS
A user fee is required May–October. The per-vehicle fee is $30 ($25 for motorcycles) for a seven-consecutive-day pass; you can walk or bike in on a $15 individual pass (also good for seven days); or you can use your National Park America the Beautiful Pass, which allows entrance to any national park in the United States.

There are also a few fee-free days throughout the year.

The park is open 24 hours a day, year-round, but roads are closed December–mid-April, except for the Ocean Drive section of Park Loop Road and a small part of the road with access to Jordan Pond.

Acadia National Park
✉ *Acadia National Park* ☎ *207/288–3338* ⊕ *www.nps.gov/acad.*

Mount Desert Chamber of Commerce
✉ *Northeast Harbor* ☎ *207/276–5040* ⊕ *mtdesertchamber.org.*

Mount Desert Island Information Center at Thompson Island
✉ *Bar Harbor* ☎ *207/288–3338* ⊕ *www. nps.gov/acad/planyourvisit/hours.htm.*

 Sights

TRAILS
★ Acadia Mountain Trail
If you're up for a challenge, this is one of the area's best trails. The 2.5-mile round-trip climb up Acadia Mountain is a steep and strenuous 700-foot climb, but the payoff views of Somes Sound are grand. If you want a guided trip, look into ranger-led hikes for this trail. ✉ *Rte. 102* ☎ *207/288–3338* ⊕ *www.nps.gov/acad.*

★ Ocean Path Trail
This easily accessible 4.4-mile round-trip trail runs parallel to the Ocean Drive section of the Park Loop Road from Sand Beach to Otter Point. It has some of the best scenery in Maine: cliffs and boulders of pink granite at the ocean's edge, twisted branches of dwarf jack pines, and ocean views that stretch to the horizon. Be sure to save time to stop at **Thunder Hole,** named for the sound the waves make as they thrash through a narrow opening in the granite cliffs, into a sea cave, and whoosh up and out. Approximately halfway between Sand Beach and Otter Cliff, steps lead down to the water, where you can watch the

Book a Carriage Ride

Riding down one of the park's scenic carriage roads in a horse-drawn carriage is a truly unique way to experience Acadia. You can book a reservation for a ride, late May–mid-October, with Wildwood Stables, located next to Park Loop Road (☎ 877/276–3622). One of the carriages can accommodate wheelchairs.

wave action close up. Use caution as you descend (access may be limited due to storms), and also if you venture onto the outer cliffs along this walk. ✉ *Ocean Dr. section of Park Loop Rd.*

SCENIC DRIVES
★ Park Loop Road
SCENIC DRIVE | FAMILY | This 27-mile road provides a perfect introduction to the park. You can drive it in an hour, but allow at least half a day, so that you can explore the many sites along the way. The route is also served by the free Island Explorer buses, which also pick up and drop off passengers anywhere it is safe to stop along the route. Traveling south on Park Loop Road toward Sand Beach, you'll reach a small ticket booth, where, if you haven't already, you will need to pay the park entrance fee (May–October). Traffic is one-way from the Route 233 entrance to the Stanley Brook Road entrance south of the Jordan Pond House. The section known as Ocean Drive is open year-round, as is a small section that provides access to Jordan Pond from Seal Harbor. ✉ *Acadia National Park.*

SCENIC STOPS
★ Cadillac Mountain
MOUNTAIN—SIGHT | FAMILY | At 1,530 feet, this is one of the first places in the United States to see the sun's rays at

daybreak. It is the highest mountain on the Eastern Seaboard north of Brazil. Hundreds of visitors make the trek to see the sunrise or—for those less inclined to get up so early—sunset. From the smooth summit you have a stunning 360-degree view of the jagged coastline that runs around the island. The road up the mountain is closed December–mid-May. ⊠ *Cadillac Summit Rd.* ⊕ *www.nps. gov/acad.*

VISITOR CENTER
Hulls Cove Visitor Center

INFO CENTER | FAMILY | This is a great spot to get your bearings. A large 3D relief map of Mount Desert Island gives you the lay of the land, and a free 15-minute video about everything the park has to offer plays every half hour. You can pick up guidebooks, maps of hiking trails and carriage roads, and recordings for drive-it-yourself tours—don't forget to grab a schedule of ranger-led programs, which includes guided hikes and other interpretive events. Junior-ranger programs for kids, nature hikes, photography walks, tide-pool explorations, and evening talks are all popular. The Acadia National Park Headquarters, off Route 233 near the north end of Eagle Lake, serves as the park's visitor center during the off-season. ⊠ *25 Visitor Center Rd., Bar Harbor* ☎ *207/288–3338* ⊕ *www.nps.gov/acad.*

🌀 Beaches

The park has two swimming beaches, Sand Beach and Echo Lake Beach. Sand Beach, along Park Loop Road, has changing rooms, restrooms, and a lifeguard on duty Memorial Day–Labor Day.

Echo Lake Beach

BEACH—SIGHT | A quiet lake surrounded by woods in the shadow of Beech Mountain, Echo Lake draws swimmers to its sandy southern shore. The lake bottom is a bit muckier than the ocean beaches nearby, but the water is considerably warmer. The surrounding trail network

The Early Bird Gets the Sun

During your visit to Mount Desert, pick a day when you are willing to get up very early, around 4:30 or 5 am. Drive with a friend, or a camera with a timer, to the top of Cadillac Mountain in Acadia National Park, and stand on the highest rock you can find and wait for the sun to come up. When it does, have your friend, or your camera, take a photo of you looking at it and label the photo something like, "The first person in the country to see the sun come up today."

skirts the lake and ascends the mountain. The beach is 2 miles north of Southwest Harbor. **Amenities:** lifeguards; toilets. **Best for:** swimming. ⊠ *Echo Lake Beach Rd., off Rte. 102.*

Sand Beach

BEACH—SIGHT | This pocket beach is hugged by two picturesque rocky outcroppings, and the combination of the crashing waves and the chilly water (peaking at around 55°F) keeps most people on the beach. You'll find some swimmers at the height of summer, but the rest of the year this is a place for strolling and snapping photos. In the shoulder season, you'll have the place to yourself. **Amenities:** lifeguards; parking; toilets. **Best for:** solitude; sunrise; walking. ⊠ *Ocean Dr. section of Park Loop Rd., 3 miles south of Rte. 3.*

🏃 Activities

The best way to see Acadia National Park is to get out of your vehicle and explore on foot or by bicycle or boat. There are more than 45 miles of carriage roads that are perfect for walking and biking in the warmer months and for cross-country skiing and snowshoeing in winter. There are 125 miles of trails for hiking, numerous ponds and lakes for canoeing or kayaking, two beaches for swimming, and steep cliffs for rock climbing.

CAMPING

Acadia National Park's two main campgrounds, Seawall and Blackwoods, don't have water views, but the price is right and the ocean is just a 10-minute walk from each. The park added a third campground on the Schoodic Peninsula in 2015.

Blackwoods Campground. Located only 5 miles from Bar Harbor, this is Acadia's most popular campground. It is open year-round and well served by the Island Explorer bus system. ⊠ *Rte. 3, 5 miles south of Bar Harbor* ☎ *877/444–6777 for reservations* ⊕ *www.recreation.gov.*

Schoodic Woods Campground. Opened in September 2015, this campground is in the Schoodic Peninsula section of Acadia, meaning you have to take the ferry from Winter Harbor in order to cross over to Mount Desert Island (or drive). It is open May–Columbus Day. ⊠ *Schoodic Loop Rd., 1 mile south of Rte. 186, Winter Harbor.*

Seawall Campground. On the quiet western side of the island, Seawall is open late May–September. ⊠ *Rte. 102A, 4 miles south of Southwest Harbor* ☎ *877/444–6777 for reservations* ⊕ *www.recreation.gov.*

HIKING

Acadia National Park maintains more than 125 miles of hiking trails, from easy strolls around lakes and ponds to rigorous treks with climbs up rock faces and scrambles along cliffs. Although hiking trails are concentrated on the east side of the island, the west side also has some scenic trails. For those wishing for a longer trek, try the trails leading up Cadillac Mountain or Dorr Mountain; you may also try Parkman, Sargeant, and Penobscot mountains. Most hiking is done

Caution

Every few years, someone falls off one of the park's trails or cliffs and is swept out to sea. There is a lot of loose, rocky gravel along the shoreline, and sea rocks can often be slippery—so watch your step.

mid-May–mid-November; snow falls early in Maine, so from as early as late November to the end of March, cross-country skiing and snowshoeing replace hiking. Volunteers groom most of the carriage roads if there's been 4 inches of snow or more. ■ TIP→ **You can park at one end of any trail and use the free shuttle bus to get back to your starting point.**

Bass Harbor

10 miles south of Somesville via Rtes. 102 and 102A.

Bass Harbor is a tiny lobstering village with a relaxed atmosphere and a few accommodations and restaurants. If you're looking to get away from the crowds, consider using this hardworking community as your base. Although Bass Harbor does not draw as many tourists as other villages, the Bass Harbor Head Light in Acadia National Park is one of the region's most popular attractions and is undoubtedly one of the most photographed lighthouses in Maine. From Bass Harbor, you can hike the Ship Harbor Nature Trail or take a ferry to Frenchboro or Swans Island.

GETTING HERE AND AROUND

From Bass Harbor, the Maine State Ferry Service operates the *Captain Henry Lee*, carrying both passengers and vehicles to Swans Island (40 minutes; $17.50 per adult round-trip, $38.50 per car with driver) and Frenchboro (50 minutes; $17.50

per adult round-trip, $38.50 per car with driver). Round-trip fare for passengers 6–17 is $11.25; children five and under ride free. Round-trip service to Frenchboro on the car ferry is available only on the first and third Wednesday; a round-trip passenger-only service to Frenchboro on a smaller boat is offered Friday April–November with trips departing Bass Harbor at 8 am and 5:15 pm with returns at 9 am and 6 pm.

ESSENTIALS

TRANSPORTATION INFORMATION Maine State Ferry Service. ⊠ 45 Granville Rd. ☎ 207/244-3254 ⊕ www.maine.gov/mdot/ferry.

Sights

★ Bass Harbor Head Light
LIGHTHOUSE | Built in 1858, this lighthouse is one of the most photographed lights in Maine. Now automated, it marks the entrance to Bass Harbor and Blue Hill Bay. You can't actually go inside—the grounds and residence are Coast Guard property—but two trails around the facility have excellent views. It's within Acadia National Park, and there is parking. ■ **TIP→ The best place to take a picture is from the rocks below—but watch your step, as they can be slippery.** ⊠ Lighthouse Rd., off Rte. 102A ☎ 207/244-9753 🖾 Free.

Restaurants

Thurston's Lobster Pound
$$ | SEAFOOD | Right on Bass Harbor, looking across to the village, Thurston's is easy to spot because of its bright yellow awning. You can order everything from a grilled-cheese crab sandwich, haddock chowder, or hamburger to a boiled lobster served with clams or mussels and dine at covered outdoor tables, or you can buy fresh lobsters to go. **Known for:** family-friendly environment; lobster fresh off the boat; good place to watch sunsets. ⑤ Average main: $20 ⊠ Steamboat Wharf, 9 Thurston Rd., Bernard

☎ 207/244-7600 ⊕ www.thurstonforlobster.com ⊗ Closed mid-Oct.–Memorial Day.

Schoodic Peninsula

25 miles east of Ellsworth via U.S. 1 and Rte. 186.

The landscape of Schoodic Peninsula's craggy coastline, towering evergreens, and views over Frenchman Bay are breathtaking year-round. A drive through the well-to-do summer community of Grindstone Neck shows what Bar Harbor might have been like before so many of its mansions were destroyed in the Great Fire of 1947. Artists and artisans have opened galleries in and around Winter Harbor. Anchored at the foot of the peninsula, Winter Harbor was once part of Gouldsboro, which wraps around it. The southern tip of the peninsula is home to the Schoodic section of Acadia National Park.

Within Gouldsboro on the Schoodic Peninsula are several small coastal villages. You drive through Wonsqueak and Birch Harbor after leaving the Schoodic section of Acadia National Park. Near Birch Harbor you can find Prospect Harbor, a small fishing village nearly untouched by tourism. In Corea, there's little to do besides watch fishermen at work, wander along stone beaches, or gaze out at the sea.

GETTING HERE AND AROUND
From U.S. 1, Route 186 loops around the peninsula. Route 195 runs from U.S. 1 to Prospect Harbor and on to its end in Corea.

Island Explorer
The Island Explorer operates on the Schoodic Peninsula, with bus service from Prospect Harbor, Birch Harbor, and Winter Harbor to anywhere in the Schoodic Peninsula section of the park that's safe to stop. The bus also connects with the Winter Harbor ferry terminal,

where you can take a ferry back to Bar Harbor. ⊠ *Winter Harbor* ☎ *207/667–5796* ⊕ *www.exploreacadia.com.*

ESSENTIALS
VISITOR INFORMATION Schoodic Chamber of Commerce. ⊕ *schoodicchamber.com.*

Sights

★ Acadia National Park
NATIONAL/STATE PARK | The only section of Maine's national park that sits on the mainland is at the southern end of the Schoodic Peninsula in the town of Winter Harbor. The park has a scenic 6-mile loop that edges along the coast, yielding views of Grindstone Neck, Winter Harbor, Winter Harbor Lighthouse, and, across the water, Cadillac Mountain. At the tip of the point, huge slabs of pink granite lie jumbled along the shore, thrashed unmercifully by the crashing surf, and jack pines cling to life amid the rocks. Fraser Point, at the beginning of the loop, is an ideal place for a picnic. Work off lunch with a hike up Schoodic Head for the panoramic views up and down the coast. During the summer season you can take a passenger ferry ($14 one-way, $28 round-trip) to Winter Harbor from Bar Harbor. In Winter Harbor catch the free Island Explorer bus, which stops throughout the park, but you'll need to take the ferry to get back to Bar Harbor. ⊠ *End of Moore Rd., off Rte. 186, Winter Harbor* ☎ *207/288–3338* ⊕ *www.nps.gov/acad.*

Schoodic Education and Research Center
COLLEGE | In the Schoodic Peninsula section of Acadia National Park, this center offers lectures, workshops, and kid-friendly events about nature. It's worth a drive-by just to see the Rockefeller Building, a massive 1935 French Eclectic and Renaissance-style structure with a stone-and-half-timber facade that served as naval offices and housing. The building now acts as a visitor center after an extensive renovation. ⊠ *9 Atterbury*

Circle, Winter Harbor ☎ *207/288–1310* ⊕ *www.schoodicinstitute.org.*

Restaurants

Chase's Restaurant
$ | SEAFOOD | FAMILY | This family restaurant has a reputation for serving good, basic fare—and in this region that means a whole lot of fresh fish. There are large and small fried seafood dinners, as well as several more expensive seafood platters. **Known for:** family-friendly dining; classic Maine fare; no-frills atmosphere. ⑤ *Average main: $14* ⊠ *193 Main St., Winter Harbor* ☎ *207/963–7171.*

Hotels

Acadia's Oceanside Meadows Inn
$ | B&B/INN | FAMILY | A must for nature lovers, this lodging sits on a 200-acre preserve dotted with woods, streams, salt marshes, and ponds; it's home to the Oceanside Meadows Innstitute for the Arts and Sciences, which holds lectures, musical performances, art exhibits, and other events in the restored barn. **Pros:** one of the region's few sand beaches; staff share info about the area over tea; most rooms have water views. **Cons:** need to cross road to beach; decor a bit dated. ⑤ *Rooms from: $185* ⊠ *Rte. 195 Prospect Harbor Rd., Prospect Harbor* ☎ *207/963–5557* ⊕ *www.oceaninn.com* ☉ *Closed mid-Oct.–late May* ⇨ *15 rooms* ⑩ *Free breakfast.*

Shopping

ANTIQUES
U.S. Bells
ANTIQUES/COLLECTIBLES | Hand-cast bronze doorbells and wind chimes are among the items sold at U.S. Bells. You can also buy finely crafted quilts and wood-fired pottery made by the owner's family. Ask for a tour of the foundry. ⊠ *56 W. Bay Rd., Prospect Harbor* ☎ *207/963–7184* ⊕ *www.usbells.com* ☉ *Closed Nov.–Mar.*

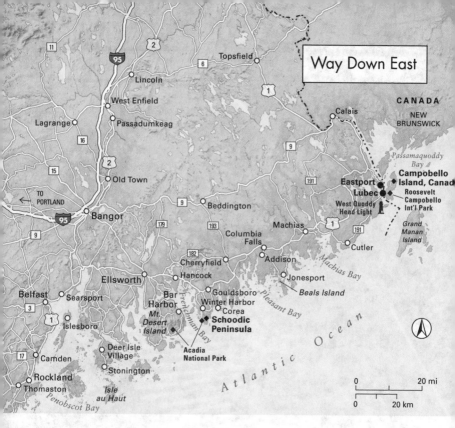

ART GALLERIES

Lee Fusion Art Glass

ART GALLERIES | Window glass is fused in a kiln to create unusual glass dishware. Colorful enamel accents depict birds, lighthouses, flowers, and designs made from doilies. The store is open June–October. ⊠ *679 S. Gouldsboro Rd., Rte. 186, Gouldsboro* ☏ *207/712–2148* ⊕ *www.leefusionartglass.com.*

Lubec

122 miles northeast of Belfast via U.S. 1 and Rte. 189.

Lubec is one of the first places in the United States to see the sunrise. A popular destination for outdoors enthusiasts, it offers plenty of opportunities for hiking and biking, and the birding is renowned.

It's a good base for day trips to New Brunswick's Campobello Island, reached by a bridge—the only one to the island—from downtown Lubec, so don't forget to bring your passport. One of the main attractions there, Roosevelt Campobello International Park, operates a visitor center on the U.S. side of the border, which provides information about the region, generally; it's in a Whiting general store and gas station at the corner of U.S. 1 and Route 189. The village itself is perched at the end of a narrow strip of land at the end of Route 189, so you often see water in three directions in this laid-back, off-the-beaten-path place.

GETTING HERE AND AROUND

From U.S. 1 in Whiting, Route 189 leads to Lubec; it's about 13 miles to the village. You can stock up on groceries in nearby Machias, just before you hit

Whiting, en route to Lubec. In summer you can take a water taxi from here to Eastport—about a mile by boat, but 40 miles by the circuitous northerly land route.

Sights

★ West Quoddy Head Light
LIGHTHOUSE | FAMILY | The easternmost point of land in the United States is marked by candy-stripe West Quoddy Head Light, authorized in 1806 by President Thomas Jefferson. You can't climb the tower, but the former lightkeeper's house has a visitor center with a video with shots of the interior, as well as displays on Lubec's maritime past; a gallery displays works by local artists. The mystical 4-mile round-trip path along the cliffs at Quoddy Head State Park (one of four trails) yields magnificent views of Canada's cliff-clad Grand Manan Island. Whales and seals—as well as the ubiquitous bald eagles—can often be sighted offshore. The 541-acre park has a picnic area with grills, but sometimes the best place to take lunch is perched on a rock overlooking the sea. Don't miss the easy, 1-mile round-trip bog trail that includes a fascinating array of subarctic vegetation, including carnivorous pitcher plants. ⊠ *973 S. Lubec Rd., off Rte. 189* ☎ *207/733–2180* ⊕ *www.westquoddy. com* 🎫 *$4*.

Restaurants

Water Street Tavern and Inn
$$$ | SEAFOOD | FAMILY | Perched right on the water in downtown Lubec, this favorite local restaurant serves some of the sweetest scallops you'll ever eat, Moqueca (a Brazilian seafood stew), and filet mignon for those so inclined. It's also a great place to grab a glass of wine or a cup of coffee while looking out at the water from the deck or through the picture windows. **Known for:** laid-back atmosphere; there's often live music by local performers on Thursday; there are also two cozy suites and three guest rooms, most with good views of the water. ⑤ *Average main: $25* ⊠ *12 Water St.* ☎ *207/733–0122* ⊕ *www.watersttavernandinn.com* ⊗ *Closed late-Oct.–Mar.*

Hotels

★ Peacock House
$ | B&B/INN | Five generations of the Peacock family lived in this 1860 sea captain's home before it was converted to an inn in 1989. **Pros:** piano and fireplace in living room; lovely garden off deck; think-of-everything innkeepers direct guests to area's tucked-away spots. **Cons:** not on the water; nestled in the heart of sleepy Lubec; a short drive to Quoddy Head State Park. ⑤ *Rooms from: $135* ⊠ *27 Summer St.* ☎ *207/733–2403, 888/305–0036* ⊕ *www.peacockhouse.com* ⇆ *7 rooms* ⑩ *Free breakfast*.

Shopping

Monica's Chocolates
FOOD/CANDY | Taking in all the appetizing scents in this shop is almost enough, but sinking your teeth into one of Monica's truffles, bonbons, crèmes, or caramels is pure heaven. ⊠ *100 County Rd.* ☎ *866/952–4500* ⊕ *www.monicaschocolates.com*.

Campobello Island, Canada

4 miles northeast of Lubec.

A popular excursion from Lubec, New Brunswick's Campobello Island has two fishing villages, Welshpool and Wilson's Beach. The only land route is the bridge from Lubec, but in summer a car ferry shuttles passengers from Campobello Island to Deer Island, where you can continue on to the Canadian mainland.

GETTING HERE AND AROUND

After coming across the bridge from Lubec, Route 774 runs from one end of the island to the other, taking you through the two villages and to Roosevelt Campobello International Park.

Sights

★ Roosevelt Campobello International Park

HOUSE | FAMILY | President Franklin Roosevelt and his family spent summers at this estate, which is now an international park with neatly manicured lawns that stretch out to the beach. You can take a self-guided tour of the 34-room Roosevelt Cottage that was presented to Eleanor and Franklin as a wedding gift. The wicker-filled structure looks essentially as it did when the family was in residence. A visitor center has displays about the Roosevelts and Canadian-American relations. Eleanor Roosevelt Teas are held at 11 and 3 daily in the neighboring Wells-Shober Cottage. A joint project of the American and the Canadian governments, this park is crisscrossed with interesting hiking trails. Groomed dirt roads attract bikers. Eagle Hill Bog has a wooden walkway and signs identifying rare plants. ■TIP→ **Note that the Islands are on Atlantic Time, which is an hour later than Eastern Standard Time.** ✉ *459 Rte. 774, Welshpool* ☎ *506/752–2922, 877/851–6663* ⊕ *www.fdr.net* 🎫 *Free.*

Eastport

39 miles northeast of Lubec via Rte. 189, U.S. 1, and Rte. 190; 109 miles north of Ellsworth via U.S. 1 and Rte. 190.

Connected by a granite causeway to the mainland at Pleasant Point Reservation, Eastport has wonderful views of the nearby islands, and because the harbor is so deep, you can sometimes spot whales from the waterfront. Known for its diverse architecture, the island city was one of the nation's busiest seaports in the early 1800s.

If you find yourself in town mid- to late summer, you might catch one of a few notable events. For starters, Maine's largest July 4 parade takes place in Eastport—be sure to get downtown early to secure a viewing spot. Then, on the weekend of the second Sunday in August, locals celebrate Sipayik Indian Days at the Pleasant Point Reservation; this festival of Passamaquoddy culture includes canoe races, dancing, drumming, children's games, fireworks, and traditional dancing. And on the weekend after Labor Day, the Eastport Pirate Festival brings folks out in pirate attire for a ship race, a parade, fireworks, cutlass "battles" by reenactors, and other events, including a children's breakfast and a schooner ride with pirates.

GETTING HERE AND AROUND

From U.S. 1, Route 190 leads to the Island City. Continue on Washington Street to the water. In the summer, you can also take a water taxi from here to Lubec—a mile or so by boat, but about 40 miles by land.

ESSENTIALS

VISITOR INFORMATION Eastport Area Chamber of Commerce. ☎ *207/853–4644* ⊕ *www.eastport.net.*

🍴 Restaurants

Dastardly Dick's Wicked Good Coffee

$ | CAFÉ | FAMILY | The coffee isn't the only thing that's wicked good at this local café; homemade pastries, rich soups, and tasty sandwiches are all prepared daily, and the hot chocolate and chai are worth writing home about. **Known for:** local gathering spot; daily soup specials; wicked good baked goods. ⑤ *Average main: $6* ✉ *62 Water St.* ☎ *207/853–2090* ⊗ *Closed Mon.*

Index

Photo Credits

Front Cover: David Brownell / Alamy [Description: East Andover, New Hampshire USA.]. **Back cover, from left to right:** Sean Pavone/Shutterstock, Boudewijn Sluijk/Shutterstock, Sean Pavone/Shutterstock. **Spine:** cdrin/Shutterstock. **Interior, from left to right:** William Britten/iStockphoto (1). Robert Plotz/iStockphoto (2). Bill Florence/Shutterstock (5). **Chapter 1: Experience Maine, Vermont & New Hampshire:** Doug Lemke/Shutterstock (6-7). James Kirkikis/Shutterstock (8). Nick Cote/Maine Office of Tourism (9). Ann Moore/Shutterstock (9). Courtesy of NH Tourism Board (10). DonLand/Shutterstock (10). Calvin Henderson/Shutterstock (10). QualityHD/Shutterstock (10). Flashbacknyc/Shutterstock (11). jejim/Shutterstock (11). Kelsey Neukum/Shutterstock (12). Cindy Creighton/Shutterstock (12). TJ Muzeni (12). Maine Office of Tourism (12). Jon Bilous/Shutterstock (13). jiawangkun/Shutterstock (13). Jennifer Bakos 2016 (16). Ron Gay/Flickr (16). Mathew Trogner/Allagash Brewing Company (16). Shannonís Unshelled (16). Two Lights Lobster Shack (16). Kelsey Gayle (17). Mia & Steve Mestdagh/Flickr (17). The Highroller Lobster Co (17). DAGphotog.com (17). due_mele/wikimedia.org (17). Punkbarby0/Shutterstock (18). TravnikovStudio/Shutterstock (18). Bogdanhoda/Dreamstime (18). Agnes Kantaruk/Shutterstock (18). Bhofack2 | Dreamstime.com (18). Daniel Rossi Limpi/Shutterstock (19). Alexander Sviridov/Shutterstock (19). Viiviien/Shutterstock (19). E.J.Johnson Photography/Shutterstock (19). Fitr | Dreamstime.com(19). leo w kowal/Shutterstock (20). SNEHIT/Shutterstock (20). Adam Nixon Photography/Shutterstock (20). Kate Sfeir/Shutterstock (21). E.J.Johnson Photography/Shutterstock (21). TonyBaldasaro/Shutterstock (22). due_mele/wikipedia (22). Christine Anuszewski (22). Anthony Dolan/Shutterstock (23). Eric Cote/Shutterstock (23). Maine Maritime Museum (24). Lucky-photographer/Shutterstock (24). jiawangkun/Shutterstock (24). Andy Duback Photography (25). Zack Frank/Shutterstock (25). xiaolin zhang/Shutterstock (26). SamaraHeisz5/Shutterstock (26). Sojourn Bicycling & Active Vacations (26). Ricky Batista/Shutterstock (27). Songquan Deng/Shutterstock (27). **Chapter 3: Best Fall Foliage Drives and Road Trips:** Aivoges | Dreamstime.com (49). rabbit75_ist/iStockphoto (50-51). Lisa Thornberg/iStockphoto (53). magdasmith / iStockphoto (53). Steffen Foerster Photography/Shutterstock (53). Scott Cramer/iStockphoto (53). Michał Krakowiak/iStockphoto (53). Paul Aniszewski/Shutterstock 53. Kevin Davidson/iStockphoto (54). Denis Jr. Tangney/iStockphoto (54). Kindra Clineff (55). DonLand/iStockphoto (56). Donland | Dreamstime.com (57). Sharan Singh/iStockphoto (58). Leesniderphotoimages/Dreamstime (59). Denis Tangney Jr./iStockphoto (60). Jill_InspiredByDesign / iStockphoto (61). DrPospisil/Shutterstock (62). The Wilhelm Reich Infant Trust (63). Shelburne Museum, Shelburne, Vermont, USA (64). **Chapter 4: Vermont:** Sean Pavone/Shutterstock (65). Alizada Studios/Shutterstock (77). Vtphotos/Dreamstime (82). Simon Pearce (97). Dale Halbur/iStockphoto (100). Fraser Hall / age fotostock (112). Dennis Curran / age fotostock (119). Skye Chalmers Photography, inc. (120). Hubert Schriebl (121). Henryk T Kaiser / age fotostock (121). Marcio Silva/iStockphoto (122). Hubert Schriebl (122). SMUGGLERS' NOTCH RESORT/Ski Vermont (123). Okemo Mountain Resort (124). Sean Pavone/Shutterstock (140). Sean Pavone/shutterstock (146). Alan Copson / age fotostock (149). **Chapter 5: New Hampshire:** Sepavo/Dreamstime (153). Edella/Dreamstime (164) Denis Jr. Tangney/iStockphoto (167) Denis Tangney Jr./iStockphoto (176) Zack Frank/Shutterstock (178) Kindra Clineff (180) Appalachianviews | Dreamstime.com (195) BlacklistMauer | Dreamstime.com (207). Liz Van Steenburgh/Shutterstock (207). Jim Lozouski/Shutterstock (208). Mike Kautz, Courtesy of AMC (209). nialat/Shutterstock (210). nialat/Shutterstock (210). RestonImages/Shutterstock (210). J. Carmichael/wikipedia.org (211). rebvt/Shutterstock (211). jadimages/Shutterstock (211). Ansgar Walk/wikipedia.org (211). Matty Symons/Shutterstock (213). Danita Delimont / Alamy (214). Frank Siteman / age fotostock (215). Jet Lowe/Wikimedia Commons (224). John Greim - www.agefotostock.com (230). **Chapter 6: Inland Maine:** E.J.Johnson Photography/Shutterstock (239). mountinez/iStockphoto (253). Kazela/Shutterstock (267). **Chapter 7: The Maine Coast:** Alan Majchrowicz / age fotostock (271). Kirkikisphoto/Dreamstime (284). James Mattil/Shutterstock (297). flashbacknyc/Shutterstock (320). Sean Pavone/Shutterstock (321). Allan Wood Photography/Shutterstock (322). Maine State Museum (322). Paul D. Lemke/iStockphoto (323). Bill Florence/Shutterstock (324). Casey Jordan (325). Robert Campbell (325). Dave Johnston (325). Paul Dionne/iStockphoto (326). Imel9000/iStockphoto (326). Doug Lemke/Shutterstock (326). spwidoff/Shutterstock (329). Kindra Clineff (348). Kindra Clineff (355). **About Our Writers:** All photos are courtesy of the writers.

*Every effort has been made to trace the copyright holders, and we apologize in advance for any accidental errors. We would be happy to apply the corrections in the following edition of this publication.

Notes

Fodor's MAINE, VERMONT & NEW HAMPSHIRE

Publisher: Stephen Horowitz, *General Manager*

Editorial: Douglas Stallings, *Editorial Director*; Jill Fergus, Jacinta O'Halloran, Amanda Sadlowski, *Senior Editors*; Kayla Becker, Alexis Kelly, *Editors*

Design: Tina Malaney, *Director of Design and Production*; Jessica Gonzalez, *Graphic Designer*; Mariana Tabares, *Design and Production Intern*

Production: Jennifer DePrima, *Editorial Production Manager*; Elyse Rozelle, *Senior Production Editor*; Monica White, *Production Editor*

Maps: Rebecca Baer, *Senior Map Editor*; Mark Stroud (Moon Street Cartography), David Lindroth, *Cartographers*

Photography: Viviane Teles, *Senior Photo Editor*; Namrata Aggarwal, Ashok Kumar, Carl Yu, *Photo Editors*; Rebecca Rimmer, *Photo Intern*

Business and Operations: Chuck Hoover, *Chief Marketing Officer*; Robert Ames, *Group General Manager*; Devin Duckworth, *Director of Print Publishing*; Victor Bernal, *Business Analyst*

Public Relations and Marketing: Joe Ewaskiw, *Senior Director Communications and Public Relations*

Fodors.com Jeremy Tarr, *Editorial Director*; Rachael Levitt, *Managing Editor*

Technology: Jon Atkinson, *Director of Technology*; Rudresh Teotia, *Lead Developer*; Jacob Ashpis, *Content Operations Manager*

Writers: John Blodgett, Julia Clancy, Andrew Collins, Mary Ruoff

Editor: Alexis Kelly

Production Editor: Elyse Rozelle

17th Edition

ISBN 978-1-64097-358-9

ISSN 1073–6581

All details in this book are based on information supplied to us at press time. Always confirm information when it matters, especially if you're making a detour to visit a specific place. Fodor's expressly disclaims any liability, loss, or risk, personal or otherwise, that is incurred as a consequence of the use of any of the contents of this book.

SPECIAL SALES
This book is available at special discounts for bulk purchases for sales promotions or premiums. For more information, e-mail SpecialMarkets@fodors.com.

PRINTED IN CANADA

10 9 8 7 6 5 4 3 2 1

About Our Writers

Editor, writer, and photojournalist **John Blodgett** is a "boomerang"—someone, according to *Live and Work in Maine*, who grew up in Maine and moved away only to eventually return; he has contributed to numerous *Fodor's Travel* guides since the early aughts. He considers himself a native Mainiac despite being born, through no fault of his own, in Massachusetts. He lives in Scarborough and is addicted to needhams, a traditional Maine candy made with potatoes. Follow his work at ⊕ *johnmblodgett.com*. He updated the Maine Coast chapter.

Julia Clancy is a nationally published writer, editor, and recipe developer with over a decade of experience as a chef, both privately and in restaurants. She writes about people and place through the lens of food and drink. She was recently the restaurant critic at *Boston Magazine,* and her current work has appeared in *The Boston Globe, The Washington Post, The San Francisco Chronicle, Food 52, Thrillist, Craft Beer* and *Yankee Magazine,* among many others. Follow her on Instagram @ juliaclancy or ⊕ *www.juliarclancy.com*. She updated the Vermont chapter.

Former Fodor's staff editor **Andrew Collins** is based in Mexico City and a small village in New Hampshire's Lake Sunapee region, but he spends much of his time traveling throughout the United States. A long-time contributor to more than 200 Fodor's guidebooks, including Pacific Northwest, Utah, Santa Fe, Inside Mexico City, and National Parks of the West, he's also written for dozens of mainstream and LGBTQ publications —*Travel + Leisure, New Mexico Magazine, AAA Living, The Advocate,* and *Canadian Traveller* among them. Additionally, Collins teaches travel writing and food writing for New York City's Gotham Writers Workshop. You can find more of his work at ⊕ *andrewstraveling. com*, and follow him on Instagram @ TravelAndrew. He updated the New Hampshire chapter.

Based in Belfast, Maine, **Mary Ruoff** has written about travel destinations throughout her adopted state. Many of her travel articles for the *Maine Sunday Telegram/Portland Press Herald* are online at ⊕ *www.mainetoday.com*. Mary is a correspondent for *Shoe Retailing Today* magazine. An award-winning former newspaper reporter, she earned a Bachelor of Journalism degree at the top-ranked School of Journalism at the University of Missouri-Columbia. A proud St. Louis native, her go-to Maine expert is her husband, Michael Hodsdon, a mariner and lifelong Mainer. For this edition Mary updated the Inland Maine chapter.